The WORLD ENCYCLOPEDIA OF CONTEMPORARY THEATRE

THE AMERICAS

The WORLD ENCYCLOPEDIA OF CONTEMPORARY THEATRE

THE AMERICAS

EDITED BY
DON RUBIN AND
CARLOS SOLÓRZANO

LONDON AND NEW YORK

First published in 1996
by Routledge
11 New Fetter Lane, London EC4P 4EE

Simultaneously published in the USA and Canada
by Routledge
29 West 35th Street, New York, NY 10001

as The World Encyclopedia of Contemporary Theatre, Volume 2, Americas

First published in paperback 2000 by Routledge

Routledge is an imprint of the Taylor & Francis Group

© 2001 The World Encyclopedia of Contemporary Theatre Corporation

Typeset in 9/10$\frac{1}{2}$pt Sabon and Optima by MCS Ltd, Wiltshire
Printed in Great Britain by Biddles Ltd, Guildford and King's Lynn
Printed on acid-free paper

This encyclopedia is a project implemented with the support of UNESCO and at the request
of four non-governmental organizations. The opinions expressed in the various articals are
those of the authors themselves and do not necessarily reflect the point of view of the
sponsoring organizations.

British Library Cataloguing in Publication Data
A catalogue record for this book is available from the British Library.

Library of Congress Cataloging-in-Publication Data
A catalog record for this book is available from the Library of Congress.

ISBN 0–415–05929–1 (hbk)
ISBN 0–415–22745–1 (pbk)

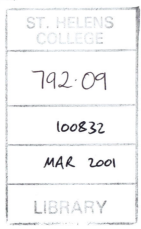

The World Encyclopedia of Contemporary Theatre would like to acknowledge with sincere thanks the financial contributions of the following:

REGIONAL SPONSORS

Department of Canadian Heritage
Ford Foundation
Ontario Ministry of Citizenship and Culture
Rockefeller Foundation
Routledge
Social Sciences and Humanities Research Council of Canada
UNESCO
York University

NATIONAL SPONSORS

Autonomous National University of México
Cameroon National UNESCO Commission
Canadian National UNESCO Commission
Cultural Ministry of France
German Centre of the ITI
Higher Institute of Dramatic Arts, Damascus
Mexican National UNESCO Commission
Joseph S. Stauffer Foundation
University of Bordeaux
University of Dakar
Herman Voaden
Woodlawn Arts Foundation

STATE SPONSORS

Apotex Foundation
Austrian Ministry of Education and the Arts
Samuel and Saidye Bronfman Family Foundation
Floyd S. Chalmers
Faculty of Fine Arts, York University
Finnish Ministry of Education
FIRT
Georgian Ministry of Culture
Greek Ministry of Culture
Calouste Gulbenkian Foundation
International Theatre Institute (Paris) and National Centres in Bangladesh, Belgium, Bulgaria, Canada, Czech Republic, Finland, Hungary, India, Netherlands, Poland, Romania, Slovak Republic, United States, Switzerland and Venezuela
Israeli Ministry of Foreign Affairs, Division of Cultural and Scientific Relations
Japan Foundation Cultural Centre, Bangkok
Henry White Kinnear Foundation
Ministry of the Flemish Community (Cultural Affairs)
Moldovan Theatre Union
Organization of American States
Polish Ministry of Culture
Republic of Macedonia Ministry of Culture
K.M. Sarkissian and the Zoryan Institute
Conn Smythe Foundation
Turkish Embassy in Canada

LOCAL SPONSORS

Marion Andre
Arts Development and Promotions
Australia Council
Mariellen Black
Lyle B. Blair
Canadian Department of Foreign Affairs and International Trade
Canadian Theatre Review
Centre de Recherches et de Formation Théâtrales en Wallonie
Mr and Mrs Max Clarkson
Joy Cohnstaedt
H. Ian Macdonald
Freda's Originals
John H. Moore, FCA
Erminio G. Neglia
Farouk Ohan
Ontario Ministry of Skills Development
Peter Perina
E. Marshall Pollock
Rodolfo A. Ramos
Calvin G. Rand
Lynton Reed Printing
Don Rubin
St Lawrence Centre for the Arts
Storewal International Inc.
Anton Wagner

Special thanks to:

Margrethe Aaby (Norway), Eric Alexander (Netherlands), Ebrahim Alkhazi (India), Ina Andre (Canada), Gaida Barisone (Latvia), Curtis Barlow (Canada), Alison Barr (United Kingdom), Isabelle Barth (France), Alexei Bartoshevitch (Russia), Shaul Baskind (Israel), Jean Benedetti (United Kingdom), Eric Bentley (United States), Don Berkowitz (Canada), Mariellen Black (Canada), Lyle B. Blair (Canada), Gaston Blais (Canada), Monica Brizzi (Italy), Robert Brustein (United States), John Bury (United Kingdom), Judith Cameron (Canada), Richard Cave (United Kingdom), Katarina Ćirić-Petrović (Serbia), Martin Cloutier (United States), Joy Cohnstaedt (Canada), Martha Coigney (United States), Communications Committee (International Theatre Institute), Leonard W. Conolly (Canada), Robert Crew (Canada), Renée L. Czukar (Canada), Michelle Darraugh (United Kingdom), Gautam Dasgupta (United States), Susan Frances Dobie (Canada), Francis Ebejer (Malta), Eldon Elder (United States), Krista Ellis (Canada), John Elsom (United Kingdom), Claes Englund (Sweden), Debebe Eshetu (Ethiopia), Martin Esslin (United Kingdom), Alan Filewod (Canada), Stephen Florian (Malta), Joyce Flynn (United States), Mira Friedlander (Canada), Julia Gabor (Hungary), Bibi Gessner (Switzerland), Madeleine Gobeil (UNESCO), Sevelina Gyorova (Bulgaria), René Hainaux (Belgium), Bartold Halle (Norway), Peter Hay (United States), Ian Herbert (United Kingdom), Nick Herne (United Kingdom), César T. Herrera (Uruguay), Frank Hoff (Canada), Eleanor Hubbard (Canada), Huang Huilin (China), Djuner Ismail (Macedonia), Stephen Johnson (Canada), Sylvia Karsh (Canada), Naïm Kattan (Canada), Ferenc Kerenyi (Hungary), Myles Kesten (Canada), Valery Khasanov (Russia), William Kilbourn (Canada), Pierre Laville (France), George Lengyel (Hungary), Henri Lopes (UNESCO), Paul Lovejoy (Canada), Margaret Majewska (Poland), Lars af Malmborg (Sweden), Georges Manal (France), Suzanne Marko (Sweden), Bonnie Marranca (United States), Vivian Martínez Tabares (Cuba), Ruth R. Mayleas (United States), Giles R. Meikle (Canada), Paul-Louis Mignon (France), Ian Montagnes (Canada), Mavor Moore (Canada), Richard Mortimer (Canada), Judi Most (United States), Julia Moulden (Canada), Irmeli Niemi (Finland), Farouk Ohan (United Arab Emirates), Louis Patenaude (Canada), Oskar Pausch (Austria), André-Louis Perinetti (International Theatre Institute), Donald S. Rickerd (Canada), Roehampton Hotel (Canada), Mr & Mrs Irving Rubin (United States), Marti Russell (Canada), Raimonda Sadauskienė (Lithuania), Suzanne Sato (United States), Willmar Sauter (Sweden), Richard Schechner (United States), Petar Selem (Croatia), Małgorzata Semil (Poland), Mary Ann Shaw (Canada), Neville Shulman (United Kingdom), Mikhail Shvidkoi (Russia), David Silcox (Canada), Phillip Silver (Canada), Singer Travel (United States), Ron Singer (Canada), Mike Smith (Canada), Prince Subhadradis Diskul (Thailand), Anneli Suur-Kujala (Finland), Péter Szaffkó (Hungary), Teatro de la Esperanza (United States), Teatro del Sesenta (Puerto Rico), Jane Thompson (Canada), Carlos Tindemans (Belgium), Indrassen Vencatchellum (UNESCO), Janusz Warminski (Poland), Klaus Wever (Germany), Don B. Wilmeth (American Society for Theatre Research), Claudia Woolgar (United Kingdom), Piet Zeeman (Netherlands), Paul Zeleza (Canada).

DEDICATION

This series is dedicated to the memory of Roman Szydłowski of Poland (1918–83), a former President of the International Association of Theatre Critics. His vision for all international theatre organizations was truly world-wide and his tenacity in the service of that vision was genuinely legendary. It was Dr Szydłowski who first proposed the idea for a *World Encyclopedia of Contemporary Theatre*.

CONTENTS

• THE AMERICAS

Contents · **The Nations and Their Theatres**

GLOSSARY

actos – sketches

areítos – theatrical rituals involving mime, song and dance

astracáns – coarse Spanish farce

autosacramentales – one-act religious plays

batacos – theatrical rituals involving mime, song and dance

besteirol – comic revue composed of short sketches commenting on contemporary life

bufonada – sketch in the form of a satirical joke

bufos – buffoons

carpas – popular entertainments performed in tents

chansonniers – singer-songwriters

Chicanos – Mexican Americans

chigualos – native theatrical dances of the Pacific coast of Colombia

choteo – form of Cuban humour that takes nothing seriously

coloquios – dialogues

comedias de costumbres – comedies of manners

comedias provinciales – provincial plays

corrales – open-air theatres

corrido – ballad

costumbrista – thearte featuring local manners and customs

Creole – person of European ancestry born in the Americas; Caribbean dialect of the French language

criollo – person of Spanish ancestry born in the Americas

diablitos – devil myths

églogas – short pastoral poems in dialogue form

entremeses – one-act farces; interludes

escenoarquitectura – stage architecture

fiestas – festivals

género chico – short comic pieces

grotesco – absurd or grotesque; a Río de la Plata region tragi-comic style

guaranías – native music; native dances

hechicera – sorceress; wise-woman character

loas – short, dramatic panegyrics in verse

mamulengo – Brazilian puppet form exploring a wide range of adventures and emotions using intense comedy and music

mestizo – person of mixed European and native ancestry

Métis – person of mixed aboriginal and French ancestry

montubio – peasant from the coastal region of Ecuador

morcillas – improvised dialogue

nueva canción – new songwriting

Papiamento – local language of the Netherlands Antilles

pastorelas – pastorals

redondel – circus ring

sainetes – one-act farcical sketches

salas de bolsillo – pocket theatres

salitas – pocket theatres

tango – Argentine national urban music or dance form, characterized by long pauses and stylized movements

teatro campesino – country theatre

teatro del grabador – extreme realism

teatro independiente – independent theatre

telenovelas – soap operas

tequino – master

théâtres jeunesses – young companies; new theatre

títere de guante – glove-puppet

veladas – cultural evenings

zarzuelas – Spanish-style musical comedies

THE AMERICAS

AN INTRODUCTION

OF NATIONS AND THEIR THEATRES

The encyclopedia has been with humankind since the ancient Greeks. Aristotle's works are certainly encyclopedic in nature; that is to say, they encircle particular aspects of knowledge, some extremely specialized, some more general. Pliny the Elder (AD 23–79) compiled a thirty-seven-volume encyclopedia of natural science. The largest encyclopedia seems to have been edited by the Emperor of China, Yung Lo, in the fifteenth century. Called the *Yung Lo Ta Tien*, it required 2,169 scholars to write it and ran to 917,480 pages in 11,100 volumes.

The World Encyclopedia of Contemporary Theatre (*WECT*) is a somewhat less exhaustive encyclopedia than Yung Lo's. When complete, we expect it to run to only 3,000 or so pages in a mere six volumes. However, Yung Lo sought to cover a much wider range of subjects than *WECT*. His goal was to examine nothing less than all of Chinese literature from the beginning of time.

WECT makes no such claims about its comprehensiveness. *WECT* is specifically an encyclopedia of nations and their theatres. The starting point is 1945, the end of World War II, a time of change politically, socially and culturally for much of the world. Sketching out a social and political context for each of the countries being studied, *WECT* seeks to explore in a comparative fashion each country's theatrical history since that time. The assumption from the beginning has been that theatre is an art form which grows from its society and which feeds back into it through reflection, analysis and challenge.

No other international theatre encyclopedia has attempted such a comparative, broad-based, cross-cultural study. The fact that virtually all our writers are from the countries being written about adds still another level of authority and uniqueness to this work, which is attempting to present each nation's view of itself, a view not of politicians or propagandists but of each country's theatrical scholars and theatre artists.

It should be made clear here that *WECT* is not intended as a guide to individuals, companies, festivals or forms. One will not find here analyses of Stanislavski, Brecht, Craig, Brook, Grotowski or Artaud. Nor will one find biographies of Soyinka, Fugard or Havel. *WECT* is not the place to look for a history of the Comédie-Française or the Stratford Festival, Venezuela's Rajatabla or Japan's Tenjo Sajiki. Nor will readers find extensive documentation on the Carthage Festival or Edinburgh, on BITEF or Adelaide, on the Cervantes Festival or even Avignon.

The world of theatre is far too large and has become far too specialized for that. Information on the lives of everyone from playwrights to puppeteers, choreographers to composers, directors to designers can be readily found in a wide range of reference works available in every major language. There are book-length analyses and histories – some critical, some just documentation – of all the major companies and festivals that one could ever want to know about. There are dictionaries available that focus on virtually every specialized theatrical subject from semiotics to cultural anthropology. Many fine theatre journals around the world maintain a valuable and continuing dialogue and documentation of current issues.

What has not existed before – and what *WECT* has attempted to create – is a theatrical reference work looking at a wide range of *national* theatrical activity on a country-by-country basis from a specifically *national* standpoint. As we near the end of the twentieth century, as nations in many parts of the world finally shed their colonial pasts, and as new nations emerge in the aftermath of the collapse of the Soviet Union and Yugoslavia, such a gap in our cultural knowledge may seem curious. What, for example, does Romanian theatre look like to a Romanian in this post-modern world? Canadian theatre to a Canadian? What is of import to an Australian about his or her own theatre? To a Senegalese? A Brazilian? A Vietnamese? An Egyptian? And what of all the individual republics that once made up the Soviet Union, Yugoslavia and Czechoslovakia? What is the self-perception of theatre professionals in the new Germany, where two totally different systems were uncomfortably reunited as the 1990s began?

To allow the reader to draw conclusions and to allow comparability, each of WECT's writers was given the challenge of bringing together just such a national impression in a very specifically structured essay which would include not lists of names and dates but rather a context − in some cases, contexts − for international comprehension. That is, each of WECT's extensive national articles − ranging from 3,000 to 30,000 words per country (small books in some instances) − has been written so as to provide theatrical professionals and those concerned with research on the profession with not only the basic material they would need if they were going to work in or visit a particular country for the first time, but also the basic material necessary to identify international trends and movements in the decades since the end of World War II.

Those who already know their own or some other country's theatre very well, no doubt, will find the information contained on those countries useful but probably too basic. Even at 30,000 words, these articles cannot possibly replace the library that would be needed to cover completely the theatre of any one country. In any event, encyclopedias historically have been intended only as introductions. Indeed, it is difficult to imagine them being anything more than that on any given subject. The philosopher and encyclopedist Denis Diderot (1713–84) argued that encyclopedias should be seen as basic libraries in every field but the reader's own. In this case, it is a theatre library for every country but the reader's own. To this end, we have asked writers to think of their ideal reader as a sophisticated professional from abroad.

In this light, we believe that WECT will be most important to readers for the breadth of its coverage; in this case, for the distance from home that each reader can travel through these articles. This is not in any way to suggest a lack of depth but rather to recognize given limitations honestly. WECT is therefore providing extended and extensive articles on every theatre culture in the world, more than 160 countries by the time the project is concluded. Looked at as a whole, they will be more than able to help theatre professionals in every part of the world put plays, companies, policies and productions into a national context, and in our complicated world this seems an important and unique contribution.

WECT material can be accessed in one of two ways: by reading either vertically (from beginning to end in any particular country) or horizontally (focusing on only a single subject such as Puppet Theatre or Dramaturgy across several countries). Having suggested earlier that this is not an encyclopedia of individuals, companies, festivals or forms, the fact is that one *can* identify individuals, companies, festivals and forms by referring to the index at the back of each volume or to the comprehensive multi-volume index planned for the final volume. By going to specific pages, the reader will then be able to follow the influence and development of particular figures or groups within their own countries, within regions and ultimately in the world.

Whichever approach one is using, whether professionally focused or casual, it is probably useful at this point to understand the many section headings in each of the national articles and what each section is intended to include.

How To Use This Volume

Each national article in this volume is divided into twelve sections: History, Structure of the National Theatre Community, Artistic Profile, Music Theatre, Dance Theatre, Theatre for Young Audiences, Puppet Theatre, Design, Theatre Space and Architecture, Training, Criticism-Scholarship-Publishing, and Further Reading. These sections are intended to provide the following information.

History: Each national article opens with basic geographical, historical and/or socio-political material. In the cases of countries whose histories may not be well known outside the immediate region, we have encouraged writers to provide a more extensive background than might normally be found. Included as well is a history of the country's major theatrical movements and events since 1945, treated on a decade-by-decade basis or treated thematically. In each case the intention has been to give the national writer flexibility in interpreting the material being discussed.

Structure of the National Theatre Community: This is essentially a demographic section intended to offer information on the types of theatres (commercial, state-supported, regional or municipal) and the numbers of theatres operating in a particular country, their geographical distribution and relative sizes (both in terms of employees and budgets). One will find in this section information on the various infrastructures that have developed (national associations, national and international linkages), unions, as well as information on the major festivals in the country and national awards.

Artistic Profile: Divided into sub-sections, this examination of the major artistic trends in each national theatre since 1945 begins with **Companies**, goes on to **Dramaturgy** and concludes, where writers have not already dealt with these areas in previous sections, with a discussion of **Directors, Directing and Production Styles**. Because our intention has been to look at the relationship between theatre and society, readers of this section are urged to look as well at the first two sections. Once again, the intention has been to provide the *foreign* theatre professional with an understanding of which groups, writers and directors are the most significant in the country and to put them into a national perspective. The sub-section designated as 'Dramaturgy' was initially called 'Playwriting' but was changed to 'Dramaturgy' to allow WECT to recognize the many companies that have worked collectively during the period being examined and to acknowledge the significant role of the director in script development. In no way is this intended to demean the importance of the playwright, whose work, we believe, still remains central to the process of theatrical creation.

Music Theatre and *Dance Theatre*: We start in both these sections with the assumption that there has long been a relationship between music and theatre, and dance and theatre; we have asked our writers to examine those relationships from a theatrical rather than from a musical or dance standpoint. In suggesting such differentiations we have proposed that the writer take into account the kind of training needed to perform the work (music/dance or

theatrical) and how the work is professionally assessed (by music/dance or theatre critics). In cases where the answers come down firmly on the side of music or dance, we have proposed not including the material in WECT since it might more appropriately be included in a music or dance encyclopedia. In some cases writers have focused exclusively on the line where the forms connect – often in multimedia experiments; in other cases they have written about more traditional opera and important dance or music groups. Those specifically interested in mime will find it discussed – where it has some national artistic significance – in the **Dance Theatre** section.

Theatre for Young Audiences: In many countries – especially in the period since 1945 – theatre for young audiences has developed significantly. By including a separate section in these articles, WECT intends to acknowledge the importance of this very special area of contemporary theatre life. The light thrown on such work seems of significance in the long-term development of theatrical art generally since 1945.

Puppet Theatre: Sometimes linked with the **Theatre for Young Audiences** section but most often recognized on its own, puppet theatre is at once one of the oldest of the popular theatrical arts and, where it has been rediscovered by contemporary theatrical practitioners, one of the most avant-garde. Within this section we have asked writers to trace developments in the form from its theatrical mimetic roots (imitation of actors) to what has come to be known as Object Theatre, in which things take on a dramatic life of their own thanks, very often, to black light techniques that emerged during this period in eastern Europe. We have asked our writers as well to look at experiments involving the interrelationship between live actors and puppets or live actors and objects. This is a fascinating and important area which theatre professionals ignore at their own imaginative risk.

Design: This section examines the work of each theatre community's visual artists. In some cases this has been done thematically; in other cases, on a decade-by-decade basis since 1945. Again, we have asked our writers to avoid lists. Instead of just naming names, we have asked them to choose a small number of representative designers and discuss their individual work.

Theatre Space and Architecture: When we began, this section was simply entitled 'Theatre Architecture'. The words 'Theatre Space' were added as the articles began to arrive. Many of our writers originally interpreted this section as being only about buildings created specifically as theatrical venues. Clearly this would have eliminated many of the experiments relating to theatrical space which began in the 1960s and are still with us today, experiments which seem to have begun in North America out of sheer desperation and which evolved in many parts of the world to the total breakdown of proscenium theatre with its visual accoutrements as an *a priori* requirement for theatrical events.

Training: This section discusses the most important theatre schools and other professional training programmes in each country, their types of curriculum and the traditions they follow.

Criticism, Scholarship and Publishing: The most important theatre research and documentation centres in each country, major performing arts museums and the types of critical approaches being taken by leading critics and theatre scholars are identified in this section. The discussions here range from journalistic reviewing to more analytical philological, anthropological, semiological, and/or other types of structural approaches. In some cases historical context is provided; in others, contemporary developments are emphasized. As well, writers have been asked to identify the most important theatre journals and magazines along with the major theatre publishing houses in their countries.

Further Reading: Each national article concludes with a brief bibliography identifying the major works available in the national language as well as the most important works about the country's theatre that the authors are aware of in other languages. We have tried to follow the bibliographical form recommended by the University of Chicago but in some instances writers followed their own scholarly form leaving us with certain Chicago-style omissions. Though we attempted to fill these gaps it was not always possible. In general, however, enough information has been provided to allow the diligent reader to find the works mentioned.

To some, this structure may seem overly complicated and perhaps even contradictory in terms of allowing each writer or team of writers to identify and define their national theatres. But in every instance, the key was to maintain comparability country-to-country and ultimately region-to-region. It is our belief that interesting and informative as each national article may be, the real value of *WECT* will ultimately lie in its ability to provide comparability

of theatres world-wide, in its ability to allow directors, playwrights, dramaturges, designers, critics, scholars and even those in government to look across a wide range of theatre communities.

Certainly this structure was not arrived at quickly or casually and it continued to be refined almost until publication. When this project was first conceived by the Polish theatre critic Roman Szydłowski (1918–83) in the late 1970s, it was seen simply as an opportunity to provide accurate and up-to-date documentation for theatre critics who were being confronted more regularly than ever before with theatre from all over the world as part of their daily reviewing duties. Visiting groups were no longer rare and exotic events on a critic's schedule. They were appearing with amazing regularity and the best critics simply wanted to do their homework.

But where could a working critic go to find quickly information on Turkish *karagöz*, on Thai *Khon* or South Africa's Market Theatre? Critics just seemed to be expected to know everything and everyone. Even when some information did exist, the sources were too often out-of-date or existed only in a language not widely spoken.

Most scholars would probably point to the nine-volume *Enciclopedia dello spettacolo* as the standard reference in the field. Available, however, only in Italian, the vast majority of the documentation included there was gathered before World War II and was, to say the least, Eurocentric. Published after the war, this encyclopedia of world theatre history was certainly strong the further one went back in time. But despite the fact that non-European theatre generally and the twentieth century specifically were not especially well served, the *Enciclopedia dello spettacolo* did become a standard. Most libraries found it essential for their reference sections. By the 1970s, however, it was clearly out-of-date even in its approaches to some of its early material.

Through the years, less ambitious attempts were made. Along with specialized individual volumes, these were very useful but, because of their specificity or, in some cases, their purely academic approach, they were not always useful to theatre professionals. It was at this point in time that Roman Szydłowski proposed a new type of world theatre reference work to the International Association of Theatre Critics, one of many international theatre communications organizations that had sprung up in the wake of two world wars.

At this organization's Congress in Vienna in 1979, Szydłowski, its president, received wide support for the proposal but no clear directions on how to proceed. Within eighteen months, however, he had convinced the International Theatre Institute's (ITI) Permanent Committee on Theatre Publications – a loose association of editors of theatre magazines and journals – to take up the challenge. The ITI, it was felt, being affiliated with the United Nations Educational, Scientific and Cultural Organization (UNESCO), at a higher level than the other international theatre associations, seemed to be the right agency to bring the idea to fruition on the world stage. At its 1981 Congress, this committee (subsequently to be called the Communications Committee) endorsed the idea and recommended it to the organization as a whole. It was the ITI's new secretary-general, Lars af Malmborg from Sweden, who decided that the project would be a concrete contribution to world theatre communication.

Malmborg, with the support of the ITI Executive Committee, brought the idea forward and in early 1982 called a meeting of interested international theatre organizations and individuals who might be able to help realize the project. It was from this meeting, held under the aegis of the Fine Arts Museum in Copenhagen, that specific plans began to be made. Four organizations – the ITI, the International Association of Theatre Critics (IATC), the International Federation for Theatre Research (FIRT) and the International Society of Libraries and Museums for the Performing Arts (SIBMAS) – agreed to combine efforts towards the realization of what was now being called *The World Encyclopedia of Contemporary Theatre*.

By 1983, with the support of the Faculty of Fine Arts at York University in Toronto and with the initial interest of a major Toronto publishing house, *WECT* was incorporated as an independent not-for-profit project under Canadian law. Initial grants came from York University, UNESCO and, the largest grant to that time, from the US-based Ford Foundation (thanks to a willingness to risk on a project that did not fit neatly into any previously established programme by its Theatre Officer, Ruth Mayleas). During 1984, representatives of the four sponsoring organizations met in Toronto (courtesy of Canadian philanthropist Floyd S. Chalmers) to set up parameters. Without this initial support and all the faith it implied in an unprecedented vision, *WECT* would never have got off the ground.

The year 1945 was established as a starting point though it was agreed that nothing ever really starts or ends neatly in the world of theatre. It was agreed that television and radio would not be dealt with but that music theatre and dance theatre would be included. It was agreed that a socio-cultural approach would be taken and that the relationship between theatres and the nations from which they grew would be explored. It was agreed that comparability would be emphasized and that writers should be chosen from within each country.

During 1984 an outstanding international team of editors was selected to coordinate the work and to advise in such specialty areas as theatre for young audiences (Wolfgang Wöhlert), music theatre (Horst Seeger), dance theatre (Selma Jeanne Cohen) and puppet theatre (Henryk Jurkowski) among others. Over the years the International Editorial Board would expand and contract as needs appeared or as particular individuals found themselves unable to continue the work. But throughout, the notion of self-identification for each national article was maintained and continued to be the primary reason why *WECT* searched for leading writers, critics, scholars and theatre professionals within each country.

The first full International Editorial Board meeting was held in Toronto in 1985 during the twenty-first World Congress of the ITI. There were five people present from North America, another five from Europe (including *WECT*'s two associate editors, Péter Nagy of Budapest and Philippe Rouyer of Bordeaux) and another six from Latin America, Africa, the Arab countries and Asia/Oceania. It was one of our Asian editors who put the first question to the gathering. 'What exactly do we think *we* mean when we use the word theatre?' he asked. 'I'm really not sure there's a definition we can all agree on. And if we can't come to an agreement on this basic question, how can we possibly agree on anything else?'

The apparently simple question led to an enormously involved discussion about the various types of spoken drama that had evolved in Europe and North America. Objections were quickly raised that we were ignoring musical theatre forms and forms involving movement. Others objected that we were locked into text while our puppet theatre editor was concerned that we were leaving out everything from *Wayang Kulang* to Punch and Judy. Our African colleagues suggested that our preliminary definition seemed to be ignoring the social relationships in much African theatre, from wedding ceremonies to circumcision rituals. And what of traditional forms in Asia such as *Kathakali*, *Noh*, *Kabuki*, Chinese opera, or even the Vietnamese *Hat Boi*? What of folk forms in so many parts of the world? What of contemporary experiments?

What had appeared to be a rather innocent question in the beginning quickly turned into a life-or-death debate on the whole future – not even to discuss the international credibility – of the project. During the next few days, we turned to various standard texts on theatre in search of a suitable, internationally acceptable definition. It was a fascinating, though ultimately frustrating, exercise. To our amazement, we couldn't really find such a definition. Examinations of standard dictionaries – including the *Oxford English Dictionary* – were of even less help. Most simply defined 'theatre' as a building.

So we created our own international, intercultural working definition of the word. It is offered here not as a conclusion but rather as a starting point for a continuing consideration of what those of us working in the field mean when 'theatre' is spoken of in a contemporary global context.

Theatre: A created event, usually based on text, executed by live performers and taking place before an audience in a specially defined setting. Theatre uses techniques of voice and/or movement to achieve cognition and/or emotional release through the senses. This event is generally rehearsed and is usually intended for repetition over a period of time.

By the time *WECT's* International Editorial Board next met, it had become clear from discussions with the various international organizations that *WECT* would have to respect various national differences in approaching this work and would have to take, as the US poet Robert Frost once said, 'the road less travelled by' in seeking its writers; that is, it would go to source for its information and interpretation in every instance. Indeed, *WECT* has through the years taken pride in this unique approach, slow and costly though it has been. But it has also been an approach which has led the project to develop close working relationships with theatre people *in* each of the more than 160 countries now involved in what has become the largest international cooperative venture in the history of world theatre, and certainly the largest international publishing venture in world theatre today.

In focusing the work this way, it was obvious that the *WECT* project was taking many risks. The approach was obviously going to make this a much longer project than anyone had ever dreamed of. By the time this work is concluded, it will have taken almost fifteen years. The approach would also force us to find significant international funding at a time when economies were just beginning to go into recession in many parts of the world. As this second volume goes to press, *WECT* is still seeking national and international partners to fund the subsequent volumes in the series: *Africa*, *The Arab World*, *Asia/Oceania*, and the concluding *World Theatre Bibliography/Cumulative Index*.

But we believed when we started – and still believe – that our approach was one which would afford the best opportunity to ensure both the long-term goals and the highest standards of international scholarly excellence and accuracy. This approach was also one of the key reasons why UNESCO decided to support the project and why UNESCO ultimately named *WECT* as an official project of its World Decade for Cultural Development (1988–97). Such recognition is unusual for a scholarly work and we feel with some pride that it is an important model for future intercultural, interdisciplinary arts research.

A few words are needed here about world politics and its effect upon our work. For most people, political change is simply interesting newspaper fodder or the stuff to support opinions – pro or con – on particular subjects. The closer that politics gets to home, however, the more directly it impacts on one's reality and the more it affects how one goes about one's daily business. Political change has constantly impacted on *WECT's* reality and profoundly affected its already complicated work.

To give but one key example, when work began on our European volume, there were only two dozen or so countries to deal with, and those in eastern Europe were guaranteeing they would cover all our writing and translation fees for the region. That was 1985. By 1990, the two Germanys had become one (requiring a significant restructuring of our German material) while the USSR, Yugoslavia and Czechoslovakia went from three separate national entities to twenty-three separate countries (fifteen individual republics from the Soviet Union, six from Yugoslavia and two from Czechoslovakia). Not only did the already completed major articles on the USSR, Yugoslavia and Czechoslovakia have to be completely revised and turned into what we decided to call 'historical overviews' but also new writers needed to be found and new articles had to be commissioned on each of the republics, republics that were, in many instances, in the midst of social, political or armed revolution. With such changes swirling around us, we read the newspapers each day with genuine trepidation. By the time of publication, the volume had expanded to some forty-seven articles. Suffice it to say here that trying to keep up with this ever-changing political landscape continues to be *WECT*'s greatest challenge, a challenge we are trying to meet through computerization and the establishment of *WECT* as an international theatre database.

It was precisely these political changes which Martha Coigney, president of the ITI, was referring to when she said, perhaps optimistically, at the opening of the ITI's 1993 World Congress in Munich that in the future it would no longer be wars between superpowers that people of peace would have to be concerned about, but rather confrontations between cultures. If this is so then we believe that *WECT* may well be able to make a real contribution in at least introducing those cultures to one another. *WECT*'s goal from the beginning has been nothing less than that.

In helping the project to achieve this end, many organizations, many theatre and government agencies, many foundations and individuals have played important roles. A list of the financial sponsors and those who have worked with us appears elsewhere but we would like specifically to acknowledge the ongoing help of UNESCO, the Ford and Rockefeller Foundations (Rockefeller came to *WECT*'s aid at precisely the moment that recession and the enormous political changes in Europe threatened to kill the project), the Faculty of Fine Arts and the Office of Research Administration at York University, the Canadian and Ontario governments, the German Centre of the International Theatre Institute and particularly Rolf Rohmer, who has long served as president of the project's International Executive Board. This project would not have survived without the help of the Canadian Centre of the ITI (especially Curtis Barlow in the early years of the project) and the various members of the Canadian-based Board of Directors who worked to find funds to realize this work. The support of our two recent Board presidents has been particularly appreciated – Calvin G. Rand (founding president of Canada's Shaw Festival) and Professor Leonard W. Conolly, formerly of the University of Guelph and now president of Trent University in Ontario.

This project could also not have survived without the ongoing support of the Faculty of Fine Arts and the department of theatre at York University, its deans and its chairs (including Lionel Lawrence, Joyce Zemans, Joy Cohnstaedt, Seth Feldman, Ron Singer and Phillip Silver) and especially the sponsors of the Walter A. Gordon Fellowship, York University's highest research award, which allowed me the time to bring the first volume to fruition.

This project would not have succeeded had *WECT* not had the active support and understanding of all the members of its International Editorial Board, particularly the wisdom and advice of Péter Nagy, whose diplomacy in the face of *WECT*'s own political struggles was never less than brilliant. Nor would it have succeeded without the stubborn belief in this project of its Managing Editor and Director of Research, Anton Wagner, whose work was long funded by the Canadian Social Science and Humanities Research Council, and the project's indefatigable administrator Donna Dawson. Our editors at Routledge – Alison Barr, Michelle Darraugh, Robert Potts, Mark Barragry and Christine Firth – have been most understanding in working with us on what must have appeared to them a mad dream at times. Without their personal commitment and the corporate support behind them, *WECT* would still be in the planning stages.

If I have personally been seen through the many years of this project as its architect, I can only say that the building would never have stood without the strength, determination and belief of my wife and too rarely recognized co-visionary, Patricia Keeney. Against all her writerly instincts and sometimes against all logic, she bravely sat through meeting after meeting of every one of this project's boards, a duty she took on because she believed in the work. Without her faith and goodwill, *WECT* might well have foundered.

There are far too many people to thank here by name. It would be remiss to try, for too many would be left out. But to all of them, particularly to all our editors, writers, national editorial committees, ITI Centres and translators, to all the sponsoring and other organizations which supported this work, thank you for believing with us and in us. We trust that your patience and support will have proven to be worth all the time, the pain and the effort.

DON RUBIN
Toronto, May 1995

TOWARDS CULTURAL INDEPENDENCE AND DIVERSITY

AN INTRODUCTION TO THEATRE IN THE AMERICAS

Anthropological research tells us that it was the Asian peoples of the Pacific Rim – those who lived in what is now Mongolia, China and as far south as Malaysia – who first populated the Americas some 50,000 years ago. Their descendants created sophisticated and advanced societies through what became South, Central and North America, dazzlingly complex societies such as those of the Aztecs, Mayas and Incas in the southern half of the hemisphere along with equally important groupings in the northern hemisphere ranging from the Navajo and the Iroquois in what is now the United States to such artistically unique peoples in what is now Canada as the Haida, Kwakiutl and the Inuit.

It was these peoples whom European explorers – from the Vikings who sailed the north Atlantic to those who later followed in the south Atlantic and the Caribbean – began to encounter from about the tenth century onwards. Little wonder that subsequent European histories of the Americas – histories that tended to begin only with the landing of Columbus in the Caribbean in 1492 – seemed like so much colonial fantasy by the end of the twentieth century. To anyone with a sensitivity to cultural history, it should have come as no surprise that the five hundredth anniversary celebrations of Columbus's journeys to the so-called New World were greeted with such underwhelming enthusiasm by so many of the hemisphere's indigenous people, many of whose ancestors had been either diseased, enslaved or exterminated by those very same Europeans.

In the southern half of the hemisphere it was the Spanish *conquistadores* who, in the name of church and state, exercised their military might in the fifteenth and sixteenth centuries; further north, sixteenth- and seventeenth-century French and English explorers created colonies in areas they called New France and New England, showing themselves, in the process, to be generally oblivious to the needs and desires of the incredulous natives who tried to stand in their way. Other European powers took part in this mercantile development as well: the Dutch (whose colonial vestiges remain in such US states as New York and Pennsylvania and continue in even more significant forms in the Caribbean) and the Portuguese (whose influence in Brazil remains enormous).

For centuries, the conquerors and even their American-born descendants showed little interest in following the native peoples' lead in such things as living harmoniously with the environment (an interest, in fact, that did not even begin to emerge in any significant form until the late twentieth century). And for some three centuries, most of the newcomers showed themselves to be almost totally insensitive to the holocaust they had caused in black African society by the development of slavery as a major transatlantic industry (a holocaust only now being recognized, documented and evaluated by scholars and cultural commentators).

Throughout the centuries, much from these ancient cultures has been lost as Euro-Americanism first neutralized and eventually bricked over the past. Thanks to modern developments in archaeology and anthropology, however, and thanks to an increasing sensitivity to these early cultures during the twentieth century, the hemisphere's rich history is once again being discovered and understood in new and much more positive ways.

Some of the early contacts were, of course, documented by the early European visitors, especially the fifteenth- and sixteenth-century rituals and public religious festivals that are now seen by performance theorists and other cultural analysts as being not so much theatre as inherently theatrical. The significance of such cultural recording and valorization is again only now beginning to be appreciated.

As for the period under examination in this second volume of *The World Encyclopedia of Contemporary Theatre – The Americas* – it had become clear by the end of World War II that language itself was fast emerging as a measure of the vast changes that had occurred throughout the region. The Americas had early on divided into major linguistic groupings – South and Central America being mostly Spanish speaking (with a strong Portuguese influence) while North America was primarily English speaking (with a growing Hispanic influence in the United States and with significant French-speaking cultures in Québec, New Orleans and several Caribbean islands).

But there were other languages operating as well. For their part, what came to be called in North America 'First Nations' peoples were by the end of the century being encouraged to learn (or in some cases relearn) their own native languages, while immigrants from every part of the globe continued pouring into the hemisphere, often maintaining their mother tongues while adding in their adoptive language.

Yet for all this, English had come to dominate in the north and by the end of the twentieth century was even becoming the standard second language of South and Central America as well. Indeed, it was threatening to become a working language for most of the world as the twenty-first century loomed.

Mexican playwright and scholar Carlos Solórzano, regional editor for this volume, writes in his introduction of the active determi-nation by Latin Americans over this period to sever their colonial links with Spain, Portugal and the rest of Europe, especially through the nineteenth and twentieth centuries. This same revolutionary spirit was, of course, obvious in the United States as well when links between the US and England were officially severed by the Declaration of Independence in 1776.

On the other hand, those English-speaking North Americans who chose to retain their ties to England (known at the time of the American Revolution as Tories in the US but as the more positive-sounding United Empire Loyalists in Canada) headed north, while those already in Canada dug in for their own cultural battle, first against the US revolution, much later against British cultural imperialism, and by the end of the twentieth century against a growing US hegemony in culture and communications generally. Even the most loyal anglophone Canadians came to understand over this period that they too were no longer British though the Crown still adorned their money and postage stamps and though they continued to share the same language, albeit with significantly different accents.

When France sold its interests in Louisiana to the US in 1803, French influence began to fade in significance across the region despite the arrival in Louisiana of many French speakers from Acadia (in present-day eastern Canada). Transferring their lives and culture to the southern US, these so-called 'Cajuns' mixed with other French-speaking peoples of the Caribbean to create yet another type of indigenous French culture.

As for the French-speaking majority in Québec, it has, through much of its history, continued the struggle to retain its own cultural autonomy and linguistic uniqueness in the midst of both Canada's and North America's majority anglophone society. In the mid-1990s, francophone Québec was still trying to determine exactly where its greatest opportunities for linguistic and cultural survival lay – as part of a generally sympathetic Canada or as a small but totally independent nation.

Clearly, such linguistic issues have long been part of debates over cultural independence in the Americas. It is possible, in fact, to read the history of theatre in the Americas over the twentieth century as an extended and ongoing debate over language, language, that is, as political and social metaphor. This has been as true in a South America where productions had to be played in classical Spanish accents at the turn of the century as it has been in ongoing debates over the use of British accents in North American Shakespeare; it has been seen and heard in the work of African-American writers in the 1960s and in the use of *joual* (a specifically Québec French) by Québec dramatists in the 1970s and 1980s.

Linguistic freedom – the right to speak with one's own accent and in one's own language both on and off the stage – often became a flag to be carried aggressively and proudly by the most daring of each nation's theatre artists.

By the last quarter of the twentieth century, linguistic freedom had even expanded its definition to include cultural freedom generally. Once marginalized social groups were suddenly demanding and finding opportunities to express their own voices in the theatre, voices that grew over time into articulate, effective and passionate representatives of their time. Led by black voices and later reflecting the manifold voices of women, these new and diverse theatrical communities in the Americas ultimately came to include other voices as well: First Nations artists, gay and lesbian communities, people of colour generally and artists from a wide range of post-World War II immigrant communities. All could be heard and seen in a brilliant, multicultural mix in theatres right across the Americas, from Broadway to Jamaica, from México City to Rio de Janeiro, from Montréal to Montevideo.

Quite clearly, theatre in the Americas during the half-century from 1945 to 1995 witnessed other significant cultural changes as well. In some it was cultural decentralization while in others it was an acceptance of the notion of government support for the arts. In many countries the cultural base broadened during this period through notions of democratization of audiences, radical changes in the use and nature of theatrical space, the shattering of traditional concepts of dramatic form as well as of the historic relationships between actor and audience.

But few of these changes would have as profound and long term an influence as the change in the sound of the human voice on stages across the hemisphere. In this sense, the human voice had become an effective barometer to read the massive social changes taking place in virtually every country of the Americas in this fifty-year period.

On the other hand, the growth and power of US cultural industries during this same period was threatening to draw the hemisphere back into still another colonial relationship. US styles and US values in popular culture – whether in theatre, film or broadcasting – were creating a new kind of transculturalization, a homogenization, in fact, the evolution of a nationless art under the guise of universality and internationality, art that could be played, but perhaps more importantly for some, sold everywhere.

Few in the arts felt comfortable with such a consummation but given the aggressiveness of US business, especially in the selling of popular culture, it was a real danger. And it was a danger not only for the Americas but also for all countries believing in internationalism as, at root, a process of profoundly human exchange, a process that could be realized only by celebrating a multiplicity of cultures and understanding their significance in humanizing an increasingly dehumanized world.

DON RUBIN
Toronto

The Latin American Experience

As Latin America approached the year 2000 and after four centuries of Spanish and Portuguese cultural domination in which the theatrical models of Spain (and Portugal in Brazil) were imitated by Latin American playwrights, a slow process of cultural independence was forging hesitant new forms of authentically Latin American expression. Strictly speaking, the movement began in Argentina, during the years known as the 'glorious decade' (from about 1902 to 1914), with the appearance of truly popular theatre, born in the ring of a circus, created by an immigrant who had hoped to make a quick fortune in the sale of Argentine land. Later, the José Podestá family incorporated dialogue into their spectacles and in doing so established that events based on easily recognizable local happenings could seriously attract the attention of the public.

But to be able to explain why early plays such as *Juan Moreira*, based on the novel by Eduardo Gutiérrez, enjoyed such success one must first become aware of certain historical realities that have determined the type of cultural endeavours that presently can be found both in Latin America and on the Iberian Peninsula. One must also remember that prior to the conquest, great cultures once flourished in many of these countries – the Maya in Guatemala, the Aztec in México and the Inca in Perú. In these countries, which had vast indigenous populations, there slowly evolved over these four centuries of colonialization a grafting of western culture on to the roots of the indigenous cultures. A significant number of intermarriages also occurred and it was the *mestizos* (people of mixed European and native ancestry) who were most instrumental in the reformation of these countries. It was true that the *mestizo* was looked upon with disdain by the Spanish authorities during the time of the viceroyalties, but it was also true that thanks to the determination of these *mestizos* political independence was achieved beginning in 1821.

Other countries, which had not known great pre-Hispanic cultures and which consequently had not fallen under the power of the viceroyalties, remained instead as *capitanías generales* (captaincy-generals) during colonial times. These territories, such as the so-called provinces of the Río de la Plata (River Plate Region), were vast expanses of territory with very small populations that after political independence from Spain attracted successive waves of immigration from Europe – Italians, Germans and Galicians. This gave these countries a racial and cultural flavour much different from those with large indigenous and *mestizo* populations. Another factor adding to the cultural variety of Latin America was that under the domination of Spain and Portugal a great number of black slaves had been brought from Africa, especially to the regions in and surrounding the coast of the Caribbean. These slaves, upon obtaining their freedom, added yet another element to the racial diversity that characterized the general population.

Generally speaking, Latin American countries can be divided into three main categories: the Indo-Hispanic countries, the countries of the extreme south significantly formed through the influx of mostly European immigrants, and those countries that received their essential cultural inheritance from African cultures. Thus, if I have referred to the work *Juan Moreira* as an example of an authentically Latin American play, it is because I am trying to emphasize that these different migrations created in the countries of the south a totally different reality from the one that had been established during the colonial period. Whereas in the Indo-Hispanic countries the mixing of the indigenous and Spanish populations continued to evolve without the existence of any other significant cultural influence, the countries of the south were faced with the kinds of problems that, at that time, also assailed much of central Europe – political persecutions, the formation of anarchist parties and even decreasing populations.

From 1900 to 1910, more than fifty comedies that dealt with these issues made their débuts in Buenos Aires and Montevideo. The author who best described the trauma of immigration was the Uruguayan-born Florencio Sánchez, who, in comedies such as *M'hijo el doctor* (*My Son the Doctor*), *La gringa* (*The Gringa*) and *Los muertos* (*The Dead*), *El conventillo* (*The Tenement*) and more than a dozen other famous plays, laid a base for what has come to be called *criollo* (people of Spanish ancestry born in the Americas) theatre, theatre dealing with the problems of these times and places.

In Indo-Hispanic countries, the imitation of Spanish culture and lifestyles continued, with the addition of some local colour and distinctive characters. Such was the case of *El Sargento Canuto* (*Sergeant Canuto*) by the Peruvian Manuel Asensio Segura and *La venganza de la Gleba* (*Revenge of the Land*) by the Mexican Federico Gamboa.

In those countries in which independence came still later, echoes of their liberation wars could still be heard. This is clear in the work *El grito de Lares* (*The Scream of Lares*) by the Puerto Rican writer Llorens Torrens, an evocation of the *independistas* (people seeking independence from Spain) prior to actual independence in 1898.

Though political freedom was attained in a relatively short period of time, cultural freedom took much longer. The countries of southern South America used immigration to give life to a new literature while most of the other Latin American countries remained more or less faithful to the dictates of peninsular literature. For too many years, the question of whether or not José Zorrilla had premièred his famous play *Don Juan Tenorio* in México before it premièred in Madrid was hotly and proudly debated. Certainly the upper classes throughout Latin America looked down on certain aspects of *costumbrista* (featuring local manners and customs) theatre and the form took many decades to acquire real cultural standing and to attract a middle-class audience. It was not, in fact, until Spain found itself immersed in civil war that the situation changed.

By the beginning of World War I, the *costumbrista* theatre began to seem anachronistic to the Latin American public. The diversity of behaviour in the different countries quickly became evident. Clearly, the light-heartedness of a comedy such as *Las de Barranco* (*The Barranco Family*) by the Chilean Daniel Barros Grez is a long way from the exalted patriotism of a work such as *Así Pasan* (*So They Go By*) by the Mexican Marcelino Dávalos. Nevertheless, there exists in both works elements that make them instantly recognizable as products of their place and time: Latin America at the beginning of the twentieth century. These forms of *costumbrista* theatre extended over the whole of Latin America, defining local conflicts and forms of language free from the disapproving influence of the upper classes. Later these same elements would appear in the new 'nationalist' theatre in different forms, a theatre that dealt much more directly with Latin America's social and political problems.

But if *costumbrista* theatre enjoyed the success of being a new form it also, by repeating the same types, customs and verbal forms, carried the seeds of its own destruction in that it began to distance Latin American theatre from a more universal vision of political and social problems. It was for this reason that after World War I, in all countries of the region, authors began to reclaim the right to express themselves in any style and in any form including the avant-garde. Movements such as surrealism, dadaism and expressionism all found rapid acceptance among Latin America's writers. This period, which took place between World Wars I and II, I have referred to in other writings as a period of 'universalism' and it opened Latin American theatre up to international currents between about 1914 and 1930.

From the universalist movement sprang many writers of importance. It would be impossible to mention all of them here but among those that will long remain in the history of Latin American theatre are the Argentine Roberto Arlt, who in works such as *La isla desierta* (*The Desert Island*) described the state of asphyxiation in which a rapidly mechanizing humanity found itself; the Mexican Xavier Villaurrutia, who in his short plays toys with simultaneity and converts the stage into a space to observe human intimacy; and the Cuban Carlos Felipe, who in

his work *El travieso Jimmy* (*Naughty Jimmy*) explores the tension between reality and fantasy. There were many others who, following the models of Pirandello, O'Neill and Cocteau, tried to modernize Latin American theatre.

World War II was a turning point for theatre in Latin America. It was the first time that a form of theatre developed that was perfectly in tune with Latin American experience. Affected by the same problems as so many other countries at this time, Latin America quickly assimilated ways of thinking, philosophies and ideologies common to all western culture at the time. Theatre was perhaps *the* literary genre, in the literary panorama of Latin America, most transformed by the war. But it was not only dramatic literature that absorbed the new post-war theatre. Theatre artists experimented with new forms of scenic expression, new techniques of acting and new ideas about scenography. According to the postulates of this new theatre, emphasis was to be placed not so much on the images of reality as on philosophical reflection, deeper and more abstract reflections.

The years after World War II found Latin America with a body of literature – dramatic and otherwise – that tried to pinpoint the determining psychological features that go towards shaping the conduct of each nation's population; trying to identify, within the unity of a common language, the differences that define each country – México and Mexican-ness, Argentina and Argentine-ness, Cuba and Cuban-ness. All of these became central concerns for Ibero-American culture. Such challenges in self-definition were enormous given the disparity in historic experiences during the twentieth century in Latin America. Cuba attained its political independence from Spain in 1898 and in the mid-twentieth century became a socialist republic, while Puerto Rico also gained its independence after the Spanish-American War, but went on to assume only a vague identity as an Associate Free State of the American Union. Even in small and neighbouring countries such as Cuba and Puerto Rico, divergent historical experiences have created undeniable differences. Could there ever be a *Latin American* identity as a whole?

The countries labelled by sociologists as *países cerrados* (closed countries) – those countries that have received little external cultural input other than from Spain – offer an image totally different from the so-called open countries in which various waves of immigration have brought very modern Europeanized or

North Americanized ways of life. The African cultures too have left an indelible mark on the theatre of certain Caribbean countries and Brazil, creating theatres unlike any in the world. Clearly, without these three general divisions, it is not possible properly to respond to the varieties of theatre in this part of the Americas. In this sense, those studies that try to take a generalized, global approach to Latin American theatre are doing a major disservice to the works of these extraordinarily varied artists.

In Indo-Hispanic countries, theatre has frequently been described as being formally conservative because it has not made any violent break with realism. Yet as more is understood about the psychology of these nations and the numerous social problems that constitute the true problematic for their populations, this misunderstanding is gradually fading. Certainly these countries have captured in their theatre in the last quarter of the twentieth century the two major cultural currents that have motivated modern western theatre: the idea of human nature and the world as being essentially immutable, which determines humanity's 'condition', and the approach, which springs from materialist philosophy, describing human nature and the state of the world as being elements conditioned by political changes and historical evolution. From the first approach derived a theatre of existential analysis, preoccupied with the essence of one's being and making no significant reference to historical forces. From this current, which in Europe found its greatest champions in the French writers Jean-Paul Sartre and Albert Camus, modern theatre took its tone of pessimism and despair, approaches stemming from the realities of one of the world's most devastating wars. It was also a tone that found resonance in the Indo-Hispanic countries due in great measure to the region's numerous tyrannical regimes, which so frequently led to a sense of defeat, frustration and abandonment. The *costumbrista* theatre simply added in these elements after World War II.

Four Mexican writers reflect this new direction – Elena Garro, Luisa Josefina Hernández, Emilio Carballido and Sergio Magaña. Carballido, an observer of minute social detail in works such as *Yo también hablo de la rosa* (*I Also Speak of the Rose*), and Magaña, who in his play *Moctezuma II* reveals an emperor both defeated and disenchanted, one unable to face the conquest and who in turn demonstrates to Magaña the inherent passivity of the Mexican people, reflect the philosophical aspects of the

modern European drama transposed to the Americas. Carballido is still true to the tenets of *costumbrista* theatre but his originality is in his ability to convert even the most insignificant aspects of daily life into transcendent acts. In plays such as *Los frutos caídos* (*The Fallen Fruits*), Hernández also succeeds in giving audiences a glimpse at the reasons behind *derrotismo*, the social injustices that so dominate daily life.

The figure who most stands out among the aforementioned authors, however, is Elena Garro. Her works evolve from the magical inventions of childhood, which are transformed into entrancing universal myths. Vision and dream substitute for daily realities, the latter considered by the author as philosophically unimportant. Her short plays are extraordinary adventures and represent some of the most important works to be produced in the Spanish language in the twentieth century. Works such as *Un hogar sólido* (*A Solid Home*), *Andarse por las ramas* (*Beat Around the Bush*), *La señora en su balcón* (*The Lady on Her Balcony*) are all moments captured from dreams that, nevertheless, describe a reality denied, a reality abolished, a rejection of life made impossible by grinding poverty. Perhaps her most important work is *La muerte de Felipe Angeles* (*The Death of Felipe Angeles*), a work built on myths of heroism stemming from the Mexican Revolution of 1910.

In Guatemala, the great novelist Miguel Angel Asturias created plays of the more obviously political type, such as *Torotumbo* and *La audiencia de los confines* (*The Audience of the Confines*), but probably his greatest theatrical achievement was the play *Soluna* (*Sun-Moon*), an extraordinary magical comedy that, using as its point of departure Guatemala's feudalistic social customs, leads us to contemplate, in an almost cosmic vision, sun people doing battle against moon people. In this, his theatre also connects to ancient theories of creation as conceived by the region's indigenous populations.

As for my own work as a playwright, it reflects something of both these approaches. Most of my major plays were written after studying in Paris. Plays of mine such as *Las manos de Dios* (*The Hands of God*), *Los fantoches* (*The Puppets*) and *El crucificado* (*The Crucified One*) have been said (perhaps correctly) to be influenced by Camus and de Ghelderode, two writers whom I admire greatly. In all of my works there exists a certain irreverent tone towards the great religious ideas that govern the spiritual life of the people in this part of the Americas, ideas that have been conveniently harmonized to the tyrannical regimes that, almost without interruption, have gained command of almost all of Latin America at one time or another. As well, I have used the folklore and the myths of the region by trying to see them as symbols and signs so that they may also be comprehensible to audiences from other cultures.

Younger than I, but sadly struck down in the flower of his youth, was Manuel José Arce, who with an Aristophanic energy transported these tyrannical regimes to the animal world in plays such as *Delito, condena y ejecución de una gallina* (*Crime, Punishment and Execution of a Hen*). Hugo Carrillo was another who wrote in this style, with his *El corazón del espantapájaros* (*The Heart of the Scarecrow*) standing out.

The extraordinary importance of pre-Hispanic history is particularly evident in the theatre of Perú. One finds there tales of impossible odds as the people struggle against the invading Spanish armies in the wars of the conquest. In the hands of many Peruvian dramatists, they are converted into tragic heroes. Juan Ríos, in his work *Ayar Manko*, works in this way while Bernardo Roca Rey, in *La muerte de Atahualpa* (*The Death of Atahualpa*), replaces verbal tirades with more theatrical elements aimed not at the rational mind but at the subconscious. This would surely have satisfied even Antonin Artaud, who would have been entranced by the expressive force of Rey's use of the tambour (its fast and slow rhythms) as well as the spiritual crises of the last Incan emperor, a man defeated and sacrificed in a hopeless fight.

Probably the most important of Perú's playwrights since World War II was Sebastián Salazar Bondy. He exploited in his work different philosophical tendencies as a result of his own time studying theatre in Paris in the post-war period. His play *No hay isla feliz* (*There Is No Happy Island*) is reminiscent of Camus. In this play, a family of peasants wait with excitement for the construction of a highway next to their dwelling so they can then set up a business. Their hopes are dashed when they learn that the 'road of salvation' will not pass close to them. The impossibility of penetrating irrationality with reason is a central theme in this touching play, one of the major successes of Latin American theatre in the post-war period.

Another Peruvian writer of note is Alonso Alegría (son of the celebrated novelist Ciro Alegría), who wrote one short but very significant work entitled *El cruce sobre Niágara* (*Crossing Niagara*), a tragi-comedy about the impossibility of undertaking ambitious tasks with people unprepared for the challenge.

Clearly, in the Indo-Hispanic countries, the dominant philosophical current has been that of human alienation. While the Latin American novel earlier presented nature as ferocious and hostile in works such as *Doña Bárbara, Don Segundo Sombra* and *La vorágine* (*The Vortex*), the theatre left such contemplation of nature behind. The characters and situations of post-war Latin American theatre moved in much the same direction as the rest of western theatre. All reveal a sense that the world is not only not theirs but also incomprehensible. Describing the peculiar sensation of feeling like a stranger in one's own land, the plays of this period share Europe and North America's general uncertainty following the war and the philosophical confusion felt in its wake. In the Indo-Hispanic countries, this was exacerbated by the ongoing separation of its two worlds, two cultures that had never been able to unite absolutely. It has been this feeling of alienation combined with a search for identity that has most shaped theatre here. Far removed from the original forms of *costumbrista*, the writers of this theatre, such as Garro and Salazar Bondy, are never simply picturesque but rather transcribe in their plays this orphan-like state felt by people without any existential certainty.

In those Latin American countries that received successive waves of immigration, the themes were westernized even earlier than World War II. Many foreign theatre companies regularly produced seasons in Buenos Aires in their language of origin – Italian or German. Audiences were large for this work as immigrants and their descendants were able to recover and enter into contact with the culture of their ancestors. The companies of Eleonora Duse and Emma Gramática exposed the public fully to the works of Gabriel D'Annunzio and innovative authors such as Pirandello. At the same time, the growing number of independent theatres produced the new Brechtian repertoire starting in the 1950s while at the same time blending in the dramatic forms of existentialism. There was as well an interest in expressionist theatre. A vision of humanity conditioned by history – perhaps the central theme of expressionism – dominates the work of many outstanding authors from Argentina, Uruguay and

Chile. Given the frenetic pace of theatre life in Buenos Aires, the independent groups were also forced to play in non-traditional venues.

Weary of themes connected to family conflicts, works by playwrights such as Agustín Cuzzani – reminiscent of Swiss dramatist Max Frisch – deform reality to the extreme and unite the tragic and the comic in an attempt to reveal the deformities of modern society. Works such as *El centro forward murió al amanecer* (*The Centre Forward Died at Dawn*), *Sempronio* and *Para que se cumplan las escrituras* (*What Is Written Shall Come To Pass*) exploit various well-known myths from Argentine culture or put words from the New Testament into the mouths of the Argentine working classes. Related to those deformed characters that gave so much force to the creations of Dürrenmatt or Kaiser or, somewhat more removed, Georg Büchner, the dramatic focal point of these works is social injustice – slavery in the midst of apparent social liberty and economic limitations for the overwhelming majority of the people who inhabit this planet. Cuzzani, director of the Nuevo Teatro (New Theatre), worked closely with directors Alejandra Boero and Pedro Aschini there and created a group that will long be remembered in the history of Argentine theatre.

Of the same generation as Cuzzani, playwright Osvaldo Dragún also uses expressionist formulations. With a dash of *porteño* (Buenos Aires) humour, he manages to avoid the sentimental in his work. Dragún himself became known to the public after the production of six brief works entitled *Historias para ser contadas* (*Stories To Be Told*) and his prestige has risen steadily. He is without doubt the Argentine playwright best known outside his own borders. Works such as *Tupac Amaru* deal with the notion of freedom through the use of a Peruvian historical figure. At the same time, however, Dragún's plays remain totally contemporary in terms of the conception of submission, dependence and the yearning for independence or self-sufficiency. In his work *Heróica de Buenos Aires* he recreates Brecht's *Mutter Courage und ihre Kinder* (*Mother Courage and Her Children*) but set in a Buenos Aires market-place. Full of local incident, the work's central theme again connects to Brecht's play – economic benefit for some requires a loss of liberty for others.

Historias para ser contadas clearly shows Dragún's variety of themes and interests. From the dramatization of a *tango* (Argentina's national urban music/dance form) to the tale of a man who changes into a dog, from a realism still characterized by sentimental weakness to the cruelty of the expressionist fable, Dragún shows himself a theatrical master, while always maintaining a cautionary tone.

Still another Argentine playwright of wide importance is Carlos Gorostiza, whose plays always begin in the recognizable before turning deeper and full of insight. His best known work is *El pan de la locura* (*The Bread of Madness*), a work set in a bakery in Buenos Aires that evolves into a symbol for the modern business world. When the owner of the bakery learns that the flour in one of his storerooms has developed a poisonous fungus, he insists that it still be used, so as not to lose his investment. An employee, who refuses to commit a crime against public health, tries to convince the others but economic necessity persuades the workers eventually to go along with the boss. Eventually, though, a health inspector arrives and declares the flour to be acceptable and the fungus harmless. All has been a false alarm. The tension between truth and lie, so frequent in Pirandello, is here seen at a domestic level. Life eventually reverts to the way it was before the problem arose. In Mateo, the employee who wanted to sound the alarm, we find an obvious biblical allusion, the pure one in a utilitarian society that places economic interests above all others including human dignity.

Two other dramatists of note from the impressive Argentine theatre scene are Roberto Cossa, who satirizes, in his work *La nona* (*The Granny*), the sentimentality of the Argentine *sainete* (one-act farcical sketch), and Griselda Gambaro, who sees in the modern *sainete* a connection with both the Theatre of the Absurd and the cruelty of Antonin Artaud's theatre. Plays of Gambaro's such as *Decir sí* (*To Say Yes*), *El desatino* (*The Blunder*) and *Sucede lo que pasa* (*Whatever Happens Happens*) show us a humanity resigned to both its immediate and final destinies. Passive characters who cannot even conceive of freedom inhabit these works. There is in them neither struggle nor rebellion, only a sad acceptance of the cruelty that is seen as something inseparable from the lives of the characters.

A large number of Uruguayan authors also became part of the so-called 'glorious decade' in Buenos Aires. Joining writers such as Florencio Sánchez were Ernesto Herrera and José Pedro Bellán. In the years since World War II, Uruguayan theatre has focused on the search for a national identity separate from Argentina. Until

World War II, both countries formed a culturally united block but Uruguayan theatre has established a different tone, a nostalgia rooted in an idealization of the many immigrants' European roots. There is also a diffused sadness, difficult to pinpoint in the actions and characters of Uruguay's novels yet more clearly identifiable in its playwriting.

The principal articulator of this form of expression is Mario Benedetti. Novelist, poet, short-story writer and defender of the rights of the disenfranchised, his theatre illustrates a search for identity by expatriate Europeans living in a poor country of Latin America. His most significant work is *Ida y vuelta* (*The Return Trip*), which presents characters from Uruguay's middle class, a group that has learned its European culture primarily through oral transmission from their parents. Many, in fact, have never seen their country of origin. In Benedetti's plays, the author becomes chronicler, a character in the play, a critic and finally a guide for the spectators, revealing the consequences of this return trip, an exploration of the interior of these characters who end up both culturally and emotionally frustrated. Not only have they not found in Europe the paradise imagined, but they have also been unable to define their own emotions towards any specific cultural framework.

In his play *Pedro y el capitán* (*Pedro and the Captain*), Benedetti attempts a simpler yet, in dramatic terms, equally successful process. It is the tale of a prisoner suffering the consequences of his struggle for the poor, and of a police captain. Typical of all Latin American dictatorships, the play's dialogue is direct, almost without subtext. Yet the power of the play is the truthfulness of the events taking place on stage, the indifference of the governors towards the governed.

Another important Uruguayan dramatist is Carlos Maggi, who has experimented in the realm of Theatre of the Absurd. His is a theatre that flees, artistically speaking, from immediate reality in order to reveal a second reality, perhaps an impossible reality, encountered in the human mind. In his *El apuntador* (*The Prompter*), theatre and reality fuse into a single dimension. A short work, it would have delighted Pirandello.

In Chile, a country that near the end of the nineteenth century received large numbers of German immigrants, expressionism became a visible and robust form. The heart of Chilean theatre has long been the Teatro Universitario (University Theatre), founded by Pedro de la Barra in the 1920s. Most important in its many contributions was its success in accustoming the public to attend works written by national authors. Earlier, in Santiago, a *costumbrista* theatre had emerged though the upper classes preferred the *petipiezas*, works of brief duration allowing more time for people to socialize. It was de la Barra, himself a playwright, who proved that when it is clear that plays will be produced the number of playwrights increases accordingly. Numerous authors appeared under the auspices of the Teatro Universitario – María Asunción Requena, Luis Alberto Heiremans, Alejandro Sieveking and later the two most distinguished figures of modern Chilean theatre, Egon Wolff and Jorge Díaz.

Wolff wrote plays with a powerful expressionist feel, such as *Flores de papel* (*Paper Flowers*) and *Niña-madre* (*Girl-Mother*), in defence of the working classes. The most important of Wolff's works is *Los invasores* (*The Invaders*), which summarizes in both form and content his dominant concerns. The play describes the invasion of a sumptuous Santiago mansion that overlooks a group of shacks inhabited by the poor. Despite an oppressive theatrical climate, the brutal invasion by the poor is nevertheless treated with humour. The ending reveals that the entire violation of the bourgeois aesthetic has been only a terrible dream, but just as the play ends a hand is seen breaking a pane of glass, a foreshadowing of an actual invasion. *Los invasores* is one of the most critically acclaimed works of Latin American theatre. Its speech patterns are recognizably Chilean and its vision allows genuine sympathy with the poor. By creating a scenic universe of exceptional vigour and provocative force, the play also shows kinship with Brecht's ideas of epic drama.

Jorge Díaz, born in Argentina, has lived in both Chile and Spain. His work is also critical of contemporary society, but his theatrical roots are very different from those of Wolff. A sharp irony runs through his plays along with a profound compassion for human failings. More than in history, Díaz is interested in the beings who move through society at history's margins. His best known work, *El cepillo de dientes* (*The Toothbrush*), has been translated into several languages. The story, almost non-existent, describes the difficulties of conjugal coexistence and, by inference, of any form of coexistence. The play shows a married couple living in complete disharmony yet at the same time unable to separate. The opening scene is reminiscent of

Eugène Ionesco's work but the game here is more fiery and desperate, not so distanced. Perhaps Díaz's most successful work is *Amén*, brief, concise and brutally frank in its description of cruelty. Dinner guests turn into ferocious beasts who bite and scratch one another beneath the elegant dinner table, which gradually assumes the shape of a coffin.

Another cultural nucleus is formed by those countries that were influenced by African cultures. Among these, the countries of the Caribbean represent a very significant example, as does Brazil, a country of immense geographical size that is isolated linguistically from the rest of Latin America. Brazil has, nevertheless, had a large number of its plays translated from Portuguese into Spanish and so its theatre has become well known.

Brazilian theatre contains, on the one hand, the assimilated post-war European cultural currents which I have been referring to and, on the other, the presence of African ceremonies, the magic undercurrent, which, similar to Haïtian voodoo rituals, reminds us that all theatre is an act that attempts to isolate spectators from immediate reality so as to help them enter a state of contemplation and leave behind rational awareness. In Caribbean terms, I am speaking especially of Cuba and Puerto Rico, major participants in the theatre of Latin America.

In Cuba, playwrights have long had their creative gaze firmly fixed on the European avant-garde. Similarly, in Puerto Rico the fact of living on an island, physically separated from the continent and prey to the whims of an often violent sea, is demonstrated by an impulse in the literature towards establishing ties with a larger entity. It is a problem described as 'islandism', which implies both a significant territorial individuality and at the same time a segregation imposed by geographic reality. Cuba has paid significant attention to the evolution of its theatre on an international basis although nineteenth-century dramatists such as José Antonio Ramos incorporated much local material, including the inherited caste system of the colonial period. This system, based on the amount of African blood one had in relation to the amount of European blood, was fought against by José Martí.

Cuba's version of the *sainetes* and musical comedies had extraordinarily energetic rhythms, vibrant colours and a defiant sexuality, and reached an impressive level of popularity. The form's most noted author, whose long life took him from *mestizo costumbrista* theatre to forms

of avant-garde theatre, was Virgilio Piñera. His plays, such as *Jesús* – in which a poor barber from Havana is forced to play the character of Jesus – and *Electra Garrigó*, reveal a myth-rooted world that begins in Catholic ritual and ends in allusions to Greek theatre played by black actors. His most important work is probably *Aire frío* (*Cold Air*), which dramatizes, within an asphyxiating environment (an allusion to the heat of Havana), the life of a poor woman whose only ambition is to buy a fan for her tiny bedroom. Allusions to the tyranny of Batista, to moral asphyxiation, and to the prospect of receiving a breath of fresh air to change the static quality of life under the dictatorship run throughout the text of this magnificent realistic work, a work in which everything is at once real and symbolic.

After the Castro revolution, a number of new and important playwrights began to appear such as José Triana, Eduardo Manet, Antón Arrufat and Abelardo Estorino along with some fascinating new groups such as Teatro Escambray. Triana is probably best known internationally for his drama *La noche de los asesinos* (*Night of the Assassins*), which describes the bloody dream of three adolescents who imagine a crime they could never commit – killing their parents. An atmosphere of cruelty is sharpened by the play's ceremonial atmosphere which, like black magic, awakens in the spectator terrors of the subconscious. It is a work of transcendent content that Artaud, along with all those who call for the reappearance of the instinct in theatre, would have loved. The theatre of Triana has found special resonance in Cuba.

Eduardo Manet, the author of several short works, published under the collective title *Scherzo*, reproduced in his play *Ma dea* a kind of black mass. A modern *Medea* transferred to the heart of the Antilles, the play is about an elderly black woman who attempts to kill the children of Jason, which a younger woman is carrying in her womb. Set amidst a group of wailing mourners, the destruction of the children comes to pass through a hypnotic ceremony. The old woman, like an earthly deity, destroys the seed before it has seen the sun.

Antón Arrufat's short plays such as *Del vivo al pollo* (*If You Snooze You Lose*) show us the island's relaxed, sensual and somewhat defiant humour while Abelardo Estorino helped redevelop a realistic theatre after Castro called for an art accessible to the people. Among Estorino's works, which capture Cuban reality, is *El robo del cochino* (*The Theft of a Pig*), a play in which the change that occurred in the peasant classes through the revolution is dramatized.

Collective creation, a form of dramatic social commentary, was given new stimulus in the work of Teatro Escambray. Though collective creation still has not left Latin America with any significant works, it developed as an important alternative technique in the 1970s and 1980s.

In Puerto Rico after World War II there appeared a rich theatre movement sponsored by the Puerto Rican Institute of Culture, which each year also held a festival of new plays. Among the writers to emerge there was René Marqués. From the realism of his play *La carreta* (*The Oxcart*), a study of the exodus of poor families to New York and their desperate return to Puerto Rico, to the symbolism of works of a more profound poetic nature such as *Los soles truncos* (*The Truncated Suns*), a play dealing with the destruction of a rich Puerto Rican family that can remember only the splendour of bygone days, his plays speak powerfully to both the population on the island and those away from it who can identify with dreams. Francisco Arriví, another Puerto Rican, wrote of the social concerns of writers there but with a more magical quality. The most important of his works is *Vejigantes* (*Masquerade*), a carnival of a play in which giant dancing dolls writhe to a wild drum rhythm. A conflict arises here among three women – the grandmother, the mother and the daughter, who are respectively black, mulatto and white – over their varying degrees of Africanness.

Martinique, another Caribbean island with a significant theatrical culture, is French speaking. The most notable event in its theatre life was the première of *La Tragédie du roi Christophe* (*The Tragedy of King Christophe*), from the poem by Martinique writer Aimé Césaire. Not only a dramatic work, this beautiful, exultant poem is an insight into the cruelty of slavery. The ironic quality used to describe this artificially imposed domination has helped to create a genuine sense of black pride and a sense of what Césaire called 'black power'.

As for Brazil, its theatre too has achieved great maturity since 1945. From the revision and resurrection of classic themes in the plays of Guilelhme Figueiredo, author of the great international success *La zorra y las uvas* (*The Fox and the Grapes*), to the development of a theatre of protest focused against the accumulation of national wealth in the hands of the few while the

majority of the Brazilian people remained in poverty, it is in Brazil that the theatre of Brecht has left its mark most clearly and powerfully. Achieved through a fascinating marriage between scripts by some of Brazil's best known authors and music by some of Brazil's most famous musicians, the success of this theatre is largely due to the influence of the country's black population as well as to the magic quality that the Amazon region exercises over the whole national culture.

Perhaps the two most important theatrical names in Brazil are Ariano Suassuna and Oduvaldo Vianna Filho (descendant of a family of playwrights and also known by the pseudonym of Vianninha). Both authors follow in the footsteps of Brecht in their references to social problems but where Brecht recommended that music should explain the text and not idealize it, the works of the Brazilian authors show a direct union between text and music, a direct result of the influence of black African ceremonies on the theatre. The best known play by Suassuna is *O auto da compadecida* (*The Ceremony of the Compassionate*, translated into French as *L'Enterrement du chien/Dog's Funeral*), in which we see an aged millionaire committing all manner of deeds, both legal and illegal, to have her pet dog buried in a cemetery from which blacks are barred. The work is presented as a game of ridicule like those produced during the Middle Ages in Spain and Portugal. An instructive farce, its irreverent tone towards both civil authorities and the church is at once comic and pathetic.

Oduvaldo Vianna Filho's *Cuatro cuadras de tierra* (*Four Acres of Dirt*) has been seen all over Latin America as much for the subject matter as for the tone of this Brechtian-styled chronicle. The work focuses on a serious and frequent conflict experienced in all Latin American countries: a group of peasants is thrown off its land by wealthy landowners. The play is presented as a series of quarrels with background music lamenting the bad luck of the Brazilian people. Vianna Filho's most popular work is *Gota d'agua* (*Drop of Water*), which played for more than a year in Rio de Janeiro. The music of the famous composer Chico Boarque d'Holanda accompanies the dramatic text, an elegy of sorts that weeps for the exploitation suffered by the poor at the hands of the rich. Brecht and Brazilian music create a most interesting combination in the theatre. Instead of the music overpowering the text, it actually supports it while occasionally the contagious force of the music provokes scenes of dance and ceremonial magic. The central story deals with a poor, aged woman, who is scorned by a very successful composer named Jason. Jason would rather marry the daughter of a rich landowner. The play is a potent musical work with an impressive diversity of dramatic expression.

As a general statement, it can be argued that throughout Latin America it has been mainly the universities that have been responsible for the renewal of the region's theatre life. Some of these universities – particularly those in México, Argentina, Uruguay and Brazil – have introduced programmes of study in theatre in general, but, perhaps more significantly, they have supported or created groups that have always been on the cutting edge of theatrical expression. Perhaps Latin America's best known figure is director and theorist Augusto Boal, a Brazilian who created *Teatro para los desheredados* (Theatre of the Oppressed). In his work, he argues that theatre must be a direct part of societal change, it must be an active art form in which viewers and participants do more than seek a passive catharsis. It is an important voice from and for all of Latin America.

Three other Latin American directors who enjoy recognition across the Americas as well as in Europe are the Chilean Víctor García (who died in 1990), the Uruguayan Atahualpa Del Cioppo (who died in 1993) and the Argentine Jorge Lavelli.

It is also important to mention the distinguished Colombian playwright and director, Enrique Buenaventura. One of Latin America's major theatrical innovators, he has written plays in a wide variety of styles, from *costumbrista* (*En la diestra de Dios Padre/In the Right Hand of God the Father*) to the avant-garde (*La orgia/The Orgy*).

The attraction of the theatre has also drawn a number of contemporary writers of prose, such as the Mexican Carlos Fuentes and the Peruvian Mario Vargas Llosa, to write for the theatre. The influence of their novelistic backgrounds is, of course, significant, but they are welcomed by directors who look to the text as only one part of the theatrical experience. The most theatrically interesting work of Fuentes has been *El tuerto es rey* (*The One-Eyed Man Is King*) and from Vargas Llosa, *La chunga* (*The Joke*). In these works, there is an enigmatic spirit that gives directors a very free hand in experimenting and an opportunity to move in many directions.

Carlos Solórzano
México City
Translated by Riley Adams and Montserrat Plá

DANCE THEATRE

In the 1940s the countries of the Americas began seeking their own national dance identities. By the early 1990s most of them had discovered their individual characters, though for some the journey had been slow.

Theatrical dance in the Americas began in the eighteenth century with visits from European ballet companies. Until well into the nineteenth century, there was little respect for native talent: American dancers were most often used only to support performances by foreign stars; choreographers and reputable teachers came from abroad. Starting in the 1930s, tours by various companies calling themselves 'Ballets Russes' created standards for classical techniques and repertoire that Americans tried to emulate. Also in the 1930s, tours by Mary Wigman provided a taste of German modern dance.

Dance activity was spreading throughout the Americas. The Germans Kurt Jooss, Ernst Uthoff and Dore Hoyer started modern dance companies in Argentina and Chile; Nina Verchinina brought her heritage of Russian ballet as well as German modern dance to Argentina and Brazil. Until the 1950s, Russian ballet teachers and choreographers dominated the scene in Canada. Cuba, however, was fortunate in having a native ballerina, Alicia Alonso, who created a distinguished national company.

In the United States, ballet began to flourish after the arrival of the Russian George Balanchine in 1933. His first move was to establish a school for American dancers who would perform in his company, which became the New York City Ballet. In 1940 the group that became American Ballet Theatre was founded, again initially with foreign-born directors and choreographers presiding over American dancers. Jerome Robbins was the first major American to occupy a creative niche in ballet parallel to that of the European establishment.

In the 1930, Hanya Holm had opened a school of German modern dance in New York. But the major move in the modern area came from indigenous dancers Martha Graham and Doris Humphrey, who created their own techniques to train the company members who would perform their works. While not immediately 'popular', the genre of modern dance was eventually recognized as an important twentieth-century innovation.

In time, a number of countries in the Americas began to create works based on native themes and were seeking forms of expression appropriate to them. The Ballet Nacional de México dealt with social and political issues, as did Núcleo Danza of Argentina. Eugene Loring and Agnes de Mille created ballets based on stories of the American west and based their movements on American folk dance motifs. The Dominican Republic, Jamaica, Panamá, Venezuela and others founded companies devoted to their indigenous movement styles and traditions – a development yet to be seen in the United States.

The established classical ballet repertoire remained in favour through much of the Americas. But the range of repertoires was changing, as choreographers became more and more versatile. Notably led by the Joffrey company, ballet groups delved into various styles from classical to modern to 'pop'. Such diversity soon proved appealing to Europe where, in a shift of direction, companies began to borrow choreographers from America. While those from the United States were most in demand, they were not alone. By the 1970s, the Argentine Oscar Araiz had created works for companies in England, Germany and Spain.

Modern dance repertoire travelled less frequently, since it was built deliberately on personal expression. Most often modern dancers taught their individual techniques and then urged students to develop their own movement vocabularies based on the principles they had learned. The styles were expected to grow. In time, each modern dance technique developed differently in different countries which, in theory, was exactly what should have happened.

Although artistic directors of ballet companies in the Americas still came frequently from European countries, some of them tried to encourage American creativity. Thus, the Dane Peter Martins, who succeeded Balanchine as head of the New York City Ballet, inaugurated a biennial spring project to present works by young choreographers. Apart from guest artists, who were frequently featured, ballet company dancers were predominantly of the same nationality as the company.

Ballet dancers, however, were easier to produce than ballet choreographers. Canada, in particular, was slow to begin to cultivate native talent, though this started to change when a major modern group, the Toronto Dance Theatre, was founded in 1969, producing experimental work by Canadians. Ballet companies followed suit. Awakening dance interest in the western part of the country also encouraged the development of new, native companies.

South America, meanwhile, was seeing the creation of new companies in various forms of dance. Visitors from the United States stirred local teachers to evolve their own techniques, based partially on ideas gleaned from the foreigners and partially on their own traditions. Brazil, in particular, found places for its own styles of modern dance in a number of its cities. Venezuela's Carlos Orta, after studying with Pina Bausch in Germany and dancing with José Limón in the United States, founded his own company to explore native folklore in a contemporary manner.

By the 1990s the countries of the Americas were becoming more cohesive in their approach to theatrical dance. Most of them were looking to their own cultures, their own traditions, their own forward-looking artists to shape the repertoires of their futures. While the European classics remained in demand, audiences were willing, sometimes even eager, to give their compatriots a chance.

Selma Jeanne Cohen
New York

THEATRE FOR YOUNG AUDIENCES

Like many theatrical innovations in the western hemisphere, theatre for young audiences as an art form in the Americas – as in the rest of the world – began in the United States, specifically with a production of Shakespeare's *The Tempest* at Alice Minnie Herts's Children's Educational Theatre in New York City in 1903. This company, which inspired similar groups in other US cities, had primarily a socio-pedagogic mission rather than an artistic one. Its aim was to teach English to immigrant children and to encourage them to establish contact with other segments of the population so that they could be absorbed quickly into US society.

In subsequent decades, theatre for young audiences developed into a broad movement, usually sponsored by similar social service programmes and organizations. Teachers and social workers most often wrote the plays and mounted the productions. In school, programmes were developed to encourage the creativity of children through improvisation and creative drama.

By the 1930s, theatre journals oriented in these new directions appeared with play texts, news, descriptions and analyses of productions. In the 1940s, the leaders of several of these still amateur companies united and from these initiatives grew the Children's Theatre Association of America. To this day, there is no other country where such a large number of publications on practical, financial, theoretical and historical aspects of theatre for young audiences exists. Yet despite these efforts, a professional theatre for young audiences – apart from the occasional Broadway show or the rare commercial touring production – did not really develop in the

United States until after World War II. This was not due to a lack of enthusiasm, ideas, artists or programmes but rather to a lack of financing. This pattern held true in the rest of the hemisphere as well.

In every country in the Americas, ticket prices had to be kept low to ensure audiences and state subsidy was all but non-existent until this time. In fact, theatre companies that requested financial subsidy usually received it only if they fulfilled specific educational or social programmes. The result was that talented creative artists all across the Americas tended to flee such a pedagogically driven theatre. Among those who remained, few did so with enthusiasm because their commitment often meant a sacrifice of artistic reputation and financial wellbeing. As well, influential theatre critics rarely covered theatre for young audiences so that even important artistic accomplishments often remained unknown to the public at large.

This began to change – again first in the United States – in 1947 with Monte Meacham and Bette Butterworth's Children's World Theatre. Within two decades, state subsidy began to be made available to such quickly professionalizing companies, the majority of which still had to ensure their existence through touring, educational programming, the conducting of workshops and discussions explaining their work in educational or thematic ways.

In the 1950s and 1960s, other countries in the Americas attempted to establish similar theatres for young audiences or at least to provide performances for children on a more regular basis, usually on weekends. Well-known actors, directors and playwrights, such as the Brazilian Clara Maria Machado and the Colombian Enrique Buenaventura, led the way in Latin America. It might also be noted here that many actors and directors escaped political surveillance and censorship during military dictatorships – particularly in Chile and El Salvador – by engaging in apparently harmless children's theatre. As a result, they strengthened and politicized the form.

In most countries of the region, however, companies still engage in traditional children's theatre or continue to use it only for theatre-in-education or, particularly in the Caribbean, in its puppet theatre form.

In the light of this, the importance achieved by theatre for young audiences in Cuba and Canada appears all the more remarkable. In Cuba the impulse for a broad development of children's and youth theatre evolved after the victory of Castro's revolution in 1959. It established comprehensive literacy and educational campaigns for young people and initiated cultural policies in which theatre for young audiences and puppet theatre played an important role. This development was further encouraged through competitions and prizes for new plays as well as through the training of young artists and invitations to European experts in the field.

In Canada, by contrast, the impetus for the creation of professional companies came from the artists themselves. The creation of Holiday Theatre in Vancouver in 1953 was so successful that it inspired other companies that were resident in their own buildings or that spent their seasons touring. While at first relying extensively on US and European models, Canadian theatre for young audiences since the 1970s has achieved an increasingly national artistic originality in content, themes and artistic forms as well as an increasing international reputation. This maturation has in turn attracted more experienced artists, subsidy and adult audiences to the form so that during the 1980s a quarter of all performances by professional companies were addressed to young audiences. As well, a fully professional Young People's Theatre was in operation in Toronto in its own well-equipped facility, as was the Maison Théâtre pour l'enfance et la jeunesse (Theatre House for Young Audiences) in Montréal.

In many other countries of the Americas, enthusiasts of theatre for young audiences can only dream of the kinds of artistic possibilities now enjoyed in the United States, Canada and Cuba. Unfortunately, the economic situation in most countries suggests that it is unlikely that more positive artistic developments in the form will occur in the very near future.

Wolfgang Wöhlert
Berlin
Translated by Anton Wagner

PUPPET THEATRE

The general truth that ancient native American cultures were destroyed – partly or completely, depending on the region – and replaced by new ones brought by European invaders may be applied to the history of puppets in the region as well.

There is no doubt that the pre-Columbian inhabitants of the Americas knew puppets and used them for both magical and entertainment purposes. The Kwakiutl, Hopi and Pueblo people along with many others in present-day Canada, the United States, México and Colombia are all known for their puppet creations. Europeans, however, brought their own puppets: the first were brought by Cortés and his fellow Spaniards. Later came other immigrant groups with their own forms of puppetry such as Punch and Judy and Pupi Siciliani.

Some scholars argue that African slaves also had influence on the puppet tradition and this may be traced back in several countries including modern-day Brazil and Cuba. Sometimes colonies returned the cultural investment of the European country, giving birth to famous artists who went back to the country of origin, as was the case with Antonio José da Silva, a Brazilian who became one of the greatest Portuguese dramatists, although he wrote plays primarily for Baroque puppet opera.

For many centuries it was difficult to see the development in puppetry in the Americas. Native puppets served primarily tribal needs while imported puppetry was carefully preserved and did not change much until the twentieth century. The only exception, according to certain scholars, was a transformation of Mystery plays using puppets into the folk puppet theatre form *mamulengo* in the north of Brazil. The *mamulengo* has had completely profane functions and characteristics. A similar phenomenon was observed in the nineteenth century in the practice of the well-known Mexican group, Rosete Aranda. It often performed a play about the arrival of the Virgin Mary, which was followed by a series of native songs and scenes from everyday life. Thus *mamulengo* could well have been an earlier result of the natural transformation of Mystery and Miracle plays into profane comic action, a process well known in Europe, especially in folk Nativity plays.

Puppeteers in the Americas started to change the European traditions by the twentieth century due to specific social situations, different in each country. This process started first in the United States at the beginning of the century, later spread to México and overtook the rest of North and South America in the second half of the century.

Many puppeteers visited the United States and some eventually settled there, making it the country most advanced in puppetry in the Americas. These immigrant puppeteers also counted on the immigrant public. Thus German puppeteers performed Kasperle shows; English, Punch and Judy; Italian, Pupi; Greek, the shadow plays of *Karagiozis*. All of them staged marionette variety shows, a form of Italian and/or English origin. Gradually theatre managers put local American colour into variety bills with versions of the Christy Minstrels (black puppets that sang spirituals). Shows were produced as part of circuses, playhouses and even in museums. The biographies of some of these puppet players became part of American history, as happened with the Lano family, who performed during the Civil War for soldiers on both sides of the front lines and in the west, where they performed for cowboys and indigenous peoples with the same success.

The first US steps towards modern and artistic puppetry were made at the beginning of the twentieth century by Tony Sarg, Remo Bufano, and others. Sarg, under European influences, produced plays and adaptations. One of his most popular was his puppet version of Thackeray's *The Rose and the Ring*. Through his touring, he strongly influenced American puppetry. Bufano, for his part, experimented with repertoire as well as with the form and size of puppets. He produced important modern plays by writers such as Schnitzler and Rostand with puppets and also staged American poetic plays by Alfred Kreymborg. He initiated working relationships with symphony orchestras by producing Stravinsky's oratorio *Oedipus Rex* and by performing with the Philadelphia Orchestra using huge puppets more than 3 metres high.

New puppet companies found some support in groups such as the Chicago Little Theatre and at universities such as Yale. The Yale puppeteers later performed at the Teatro Torito in Los Angeles. The majority of puppeteers, however, tried to create theatre studios in their own homes, where only small audiences could be accommodated.

According to new trends in education theory, puppets were accepted in school as both entertainment and instruments of teaching. Thus puppets were used for such things as religious classes and language lessons. Local authorities invited puppeteers to perform in parks, playgrounds and settlement houses. In years of economic crisis, workers on relief rolls performed with puppets as part of government supported make-work projects.

Until the 1990s, puppet theatre did not enjoy subsidy in the United States. Occasionally, small grants were given directly to individual artists. Extra money, however, could be earned by commercials or from shows for national associations as varied as the Animal Rescue League or the American Dental Association.

After World War II the situation did not change much. Puppet theatre in the United States essentially remained a theatre for children with multiple functions of which entertainment held the highest recognition. Puppets nevertheless continued to provoke the interest of social bodies responsible for recreation, for example, the work of the Vagabond Puppet Theatre funded by the Oakland Recreation Department in California in 1953. Puppet theatre also worked well in libraries and museums that ran social programmes. At least it worked well

enough to encourage the organization of courses and puppetry classes in schools, colleges and even universities.

During the war, some puppeteers worked for the armed forces giving entertainment programmes or advertising war bonds. Among them was Burr Tillstrom and his famous puppet, Kukla. When the war ended, puppet artists such as Rufus and Margo Rose and Cora and Bil Baird turned to the new medium of television, staging variety shows or children's stories with puppets. They were, in fact, continuing the kind of puppetry that had been established and fixed in the 1930s in Europe; most of these artists did not perceive their growing isolation from the newer European trends utilizing puppetry in actors' theatre and the fine arts.

A break in this isolation finally came at the beginning of the 1960s, when a new generation of puppeteers appeared. Some of them – such as Peter Schumann, who started his Bread and Puppet Theatre in 1963 in New York – abolished all the classic puppet theatre rules. In his shows, he focused on social problems, reacted violently against many US political positions, especially the Vietnam War, and addressed youthful street audiences. For this purpose he used puppets of different sizes, often giant ones for street parades, and mixed them with other forms of expression such as actors and masks. Soon he started to travel, mainly to Europe, where he received an even more enthusiastic reception.

Robert Anton gave a new impulse to American puppetry in the 1970s and 1980s creating a new form of solo performance, giving to it ritualistic and psychological background. His miniaturized art consisted of the transmutation of inanimate material from one form to another as he explored the darker aspects of subconscious life. The same ritualistic intentions have been acknowledged in the works of his younger colleagues such as Bruce Schwartz, Roman Paska and Eric Bass in the 1980s and 1990s.

Theodora Skipitares represents these new trends in puppetry as she combines elements of performance art and puppet theatre. Julie Taymor is fascinated by multimedia theatre, merging puppets, actors, singers, props and masks that serve to express universal values of myth and legend. Some American puppeteers, such as Paul Zaloom and Stuart Sherman, have turned towards the so-called Object Theatre. Zaloom, especially, delivers contemporary messages as he uses objects from the consumer culture to create a satiric image of the American landscape. Many of these new tendencies are now common as well in European puppetry.

Some of these ideas were used with enormous success by Jim Henson, creator of television's *The Muppet Show*. In his programme, Henson developed in an original way the old ideas of educational children's puppetry as well as creating entertaining programmes for adult audiences. Henson's Muppets became an important model for many puppeteers both in the United States and abroad. While Henson became an important show-business figure, he did not abandon his puppeteer colleagues and before his untimely death founded the Henson Foundation for the promotion of American puppetry.

US puppeteers had tried to found a national puppetry organization as early as 1913 but it was not until 1937, when Paul McPharlin created what would become the Puppeteers of America, that such a group succeeded. By the 1990s, the organization had thousands of members and a large number of local guilds and leagues, all involved in organizing regional and national festivals. The association also produces its own magazines. US puppeteers joined the Union Internationale de la Marionnette (UNIMA, the International Puppeteers' Union) in 1957.

From the beginning of the 1950s puppeteers in the United States also tried to found a school. The result was the establishment of departments of puppet theatre arts at both the University of California at Los Angeles (UCLA) and the University of Connecticut. In the 1980s, the Institute of Professional Puppetry Arts in Waterford, Connecticut, was founded but did not survive, sharing the destiny of UCLA's puppet department. The Center for Puppetry Arts in Atlanta, founded in the 1970s, promoted other aspects of puppetry and initiated many national and international activities. The major support for such initiatives remains the Henson Foundation.

The situation was similar in Canada. Universities and colleges organized courses for teachers and beginners. Novelties tended to come always from abroad, mainly from Europe. Occasionally, though, the Canada Council and local ministries of culture were able to offer puppeteers grants for special projects and sometimes even for permanent activities. Parallel to European and US movements in the 1970s, Canadian puppet theatre modernized, blending such disparate elements as Japanese *bunraku*, the

Japanese puppet form in which lifesize puppets act out dramatic narratives set to music (in the work of Felix Mirbt), the integration of puppets and actors, the use of puppets of varying sizes (the Mermaid Theatre) and even turning to storytelling with puppets. The new puppet repertoire included dramas by Brecht, Wilde, Maeterlinck and García Lorca, along with popular children's stories and sometimes native Indian legends.

In Québec Micheline Legendre started the important Théâtre des Marionnettes in 1948. Dora and Leo Velleman were tireless in their promotion of puppetry in English Canada, founding the Canadian Puppet Festivals in Ontario in 1950 and touring across the country. However, it was Mirbt, an immigrant from Germany, who produced *Woyzeck* (1974) by Büchner and Strindberg's *The Dream Play* (1977), both recognized as being among the most important achievements in the development of Canadian puppetry for adults. Le Théâtre sans Fil also had success with its Ojibwa Indian legends, such as *The Blue Sky Takes a Wife*. Another important group was Québec's Théâtre de l'Oeil.

Canadian puppeteers now have several regional puppet organizations as well as the Canadian Centre of UNIMA. They have organized regional, national and international festivals and they participate in virtually all US enterprises.

It was mainly Spanish puppet groups that visited Latin American countries in the period of their colonization. This did not change much when these countries became independent. Many Italian groups also regularly visited Argentina, Brazil, Colombia and México in the nineteenth and early twentieth centuries. Normally these touring groups used rod- and string-marionettes, traditional for performances of Mystery plays and variety shows. Later in the twentieth century, glove-puppets, originating from Catalonia in Spain, became very popular, especially in México. Some players performed in the streets but starting in 1929 they, as Bernardo Ortiz de Montellano first did, performed in parks and children's playgrounds, under the auspices of the Departamento de Bellas Artes. This enterprise encouraged other artists and writers including Germán Cueto and Roberto Lago, who founded in 1932 a glove-puppet theatre that very soon was sponsored by the Departamento de Bellas Artes of the Education Ministry. This was the first of many strong links in México between puppetry and educational bodies. As far back as the 1930s, the Guignol Group of the Fine Arts Theatre 'El Nahual' took part in literacy, anti-alcoholism and anti-racist programmes.

Puppetry in Argentina was heavily influenced by a circle of artists and writers in Buenos Aires and the ideas of Federico García Lorca. García Lorca visited Argentina in 1932–4 and encouraged puppet activities – among them puppet productions of Aeschylus and Cervantes, and his own *Retablillo de Don Cristobal*. The young poet-puppeteer Javier Villafañe followed this inspiration and started the touring puppet theatre La Andariega. In a simple cart his group visited, in the course of several years, almost every country in South America. In 1940, his work was recognized by the Argentine Comisión Nacional de Cultura, which awarded him a special grant for children's arts education.

In the majority of Latin American countries, puppetry found protection in national educational bodies and at universities, such as Escuela de Bellas Artes at the Universidade Federal de Minas Gerais and the Centro de Educación y Cultura Popular, both in Brazil. In Argentina, educational institutions encouraged the development of special schools that would serve as workshops and centres of puppetry, such as the Escuela Nacional de Títeres de Rosario supported by the Ministry of Education and Culture.

In Colombia, the puppet theatre is less tied to educational functions. The National Puppet School is part of the Escuela Nacional de Arte Dramático (National School of Dramatic Arts). In México it is the National Institute of Fine Arts and the National Fund for Social Activities that support the activities of the puppet theatre, while in Perú universities and the National Institute of Culture fulfil similar functions. In Chile some help is given by Catholic organizations such as the department of music at the Universidad Católica (Catholic University).

In Bolivia, puppeteers are generally left to their own initiatives, which has resulted in a variety of independent puppet enterprises such as the Cooperativa Cultural Taypikala. In Ecuador a similar function is filled by the Instituto del Niño y la Familia (Institute for Children and Families).

Cuban puppetry is organized according to the principle of socialist cultural politics, which means that it is fully supported and controlled by state authorities. Puppeteers in Venezuela also enjoy special protection by the state. Eighty per cent of puppeteers are state employees with regular salaries for their work at universities, boards of education, boards of culture and other state agencies. They have nine playhouses adapted especially for puppets. In 1976 a National Puppet Theatre Research Centre was started in Maracaibo.

In 1956 Argentine puppeteers created the Asociación de Titiriteros de la Argentina (Argentine Puppet Association), a move that was followed by the Brazilians, who founded the Associação de Teatro de Bonecos (Puppet Theatre Association), in 1972. Over the course of the 1970s, the majority of puppeteers in Latin America joined UNIMA. The majority of these organizations produce their own magazines, such as the Brazilian *Mamulengo* and the Argentine *Trujaman*.

Among the most active Latin American puppeteers in the 1980s and 1990s was the Argentine Eduardo de Mauro, who, after long activities in Argentina, began trying to link puppeteers in Latin America. At the end of the 1980s he began a series of travels through Latin America to establish international links and to encourage the general development of puppetry in a spirit similar to that of Javier Villafañe's earlier travels.

Latin American puppetry now tends towards multimedia experiments (masks, actors, puppets and props). This is especially true for theatres such as Del Alma Mágica in Argentina, La Libélula Dorada in Colombia, Teatro de Títeres y Objetos in Venezuela, the Guignol Nacional of Cuba and the Teatro Giramundo in Brazil. Many companies perform a classical repertoire of European, mainly Spanish, tradition (Cervantes, Zorrilla and García Lorca), while plays by Villafañe are also popular, as are dramatizations of tales for children.

In many Latin American countries, puppet theatres base their work on local mythology and folklore, while others deal with contemporary social problems. Moderno Teatro de Muñecos in Costa Rica, for example, produces satirical commentaries on local political realities. Rana Sabia, a group from Quito, Ecuador, tries to provoke social sensibilities, while the Teatro Nacional de Sombras in Puerto Rico works among indigenous peoples. Marionetas Cajamarca in Perú is an example of the creativity of local peasants and craftspeople who present their own problems in their dramatic work. Cooperativa Cultural Taypikala is another group working for peasants and actually belongs to the Quechua-Aymará culture.

Throughout Latin America, puppet theatre is for the most part an instrument for cultural, educational and social activities. As a result, Latin American puppeteers tend to be profoundly involved in their own nation's cultural and social problems.

Henryk Jurkowski
Warsaw

THE NATIONS AND THEIR THEATRES

ANTIGUA AND BARBUDA

(see **COMMONWEALTH CARIBBEAN**)

ARGENTINA

Occupying most of the southern tip of South America, Argentina extends some 3,700 kilometres (2,300 miles) from north to south and varies in width from 1,450 kilometres in the north to less than 16 kilometres on Tierra del Fuego in the south. Second in Latin America only to Brazil in land area (2.77 million square kilometres or 1.07 million square miles), Argentina is bordered by Chile to the west, Uruguay and Brazil to the east and Bolivia and Paraguay to the north. In 1992, the country had a population of 33.1 million.

Juan Díaz de Solís, a Spanish navigator, is said to have been the first European to visit Argentina, exploring the shores of the Río de la Plata in 1516. Other explorers, including Sebastian Cabot ten years later, followed. During the sixteenth and seventeenth centuries, Argentina was part of the Spanish colony of Perú. In 1776, Spain made the country part of the viceroyalty of Río de la Plata with Buenos Aires designated as the viceroyalty's capital. This new colony also included all of Uruguay, Paraguay and the southern part of Bolivia.

Taking advantage of Napoleon's invasion of Spain, the residents of Buenos Aires revolted in 1810 and in 1816 the western provinces joined Buenos Aires and independence was formally declared. During the nineteenth century, Argentina developed many new industries and became one of Latin America's wealthiest countries. In 1868, President Domingo F. Sarmiento (1811–88) made schooling compulsory for all children and actively encouraged European immigration. In later years, as many as 200,000 Europeans immigrated to Argentina annually, including large numbers of Jewish families from eastern Europe, and Italians, two groups that have made significant contributions in the cultural area. Indeed, Argentina's Yiddish-language theatre is one of the largest in Latin America.

In 1946, Juan Perón (1895–1974) took control of the government vowing to make Argentina an industrial power. Marrying María Eva

Duarte (1919–52), known to all as Evita, and establishing her in the Ministry of Labour, Perón raised workers' wages but the country eventually teetered on the edge of bankruptcy dividing the population into pro- and anti-Perón camps.

For the next eighteen years Perón remained a political force despite the fact that he was living in exile. In 1973, he was elected president again but died a year later. He was succeeded by his second wife, María Estela Martínez de Perón (b. 1931), known as Isabelita, who became the first female head of government in the western hemisphere. She was ousted by the military in 1976, and the *junta* held tight control of the country until 1983, outlawing political parties and censoring the press. During this period, thousands of artists, intellectuals and others simply 'disappeared' as Argentina suffered its worst depression since the 1930s and inflation soared to over 400 per cent annually.

Following Argentina's war with Britain in 1982 over control of the Malvinas, an island chain known to the British as the Falklands, the military regime was ousted and Raúl Alfonsín of the Radical Party became president. With civilian rule restored, intellectual and artistic life normalized, though inflation continued to worsen until 1989 and then dropped in the early 1990s.

Given such stormy politics, Argentina's theatre history seems calm by comparison. Yet Argentina was one of the first countries in Latin America to assume a national cultural personality and identity in the modern period.

Before 1900, the activities of Argentina's theatre were predominantly centred in Buenos Aires. Historians trace its origins back to the sixteenth century, to the culture brought over by the Spanish *conquistadores* and the missionary work of the Jesuits. These had a decidedly Spanish character. Yet even at the time of Argentina's liberation in 1810, the country's stage did not display any particularly individual characteristics. Though isolated experiments were made and inexperienced writers put forth their efforts, including the popular *gaucho* (cowboy) romances, sustained creativity was still lacking, as were trained critics, actors and regular audiences.

By 1884, the theatre began to acquire its own character when writers and actors began to gain the support of critics and the public. The José Podestá family of circus performers served as the nucleus of one of these early groups of professionals. After initially experimenting with a

pantomime, *Juan Moreira* (1884), they moved away from circus forms to more dramatic forms. By 1902 they were even breathing new life into the *gaucho* romances.

In 1902, the Podestás moved to a theatre in central Buenos Aires where they began to develop a programme of activities that would lead to the creation of one of Latin America's first genuinely national theatres. The period between 1902 and 1914, therefore, was a golden age in the history of Argentina's theatre, and these years are known as the 'glorious decade'. Many playwrights emerged at this time, including Ezequiel Soria (1873–1936), who wrote comedies of manners such as *Ley suprema* (*Supreme Law*, 1897), *La beata* (*The Pious Woman*, 1902) and *El medallón* (*The Medallion*, 1902); Enrique García Velloso (1880–1938), who produced some 200 titles in a variety of genres including *Eclipse del sol* (*Eclipse of the Sun*, 1904), *El zapato de cristal* (*The Crystal Shoe*), *Gabino el mayoral* (*Gabino the Tram Conductor*, 1898) and *Mamá Culepina*; and Martín Coronado (1850–1919), a romantic poet, whose name is primarily associated with *La piedra de escándalo* (*Cause for Scandal*, 1902), his most popular play.

Other writers from this period are Roberto J. Payró (1867–1928), author of *Sobre ruinas* (*Over the Ruins*, 1904) and *Marco Severi* (1905); Alberto Ghiraldo (1875–1946), who dramatized social themes in *Alma gaucha* (*Cowboy Soul*, 1906) and *La copa de sangre* (*The Cup of Blood*); José León Pagano (1875–1964), who became a master of high comedy in *La ofrenda* (*The Gift*), *Almas que luchan* (*Fighting Souls*) and *Blasón de fuego* (*Burning Blazon*); Vincente Martínez Cuitiño (1887–1964), a prolific Uruguayan contributor to Argentina's theatrical repertoire with such works as *El derrumbe* (*The Collapse*, 1909), *Rayito de sol* (*Little Sunbeam*, 1908), *Diamantes quebrados* (*Broken Diamonds*), *Horizontes* (*Horizons*, 1934) and over 100 others; and Pedro E. Pico (1882–1945), who gave a sensitive rendering of the people and their customs in sentimental dramas such as *Pueblerina* (*Country Girl*, 1927), *La novia de los forasteros* (*The Foreigner's Girl*, 1926) and *Caminos en el mar* (*Tracks in the Sea*, 1930).

The year 1914 marked the first appearance in Argentina of the Spanish-style one-act farcical sketch known as the *sainete*, similar to the *género chico* (short comic piece). Its immediate success, however, inspired over-simplification and distortion, undercutting the public taste for more profound work. It should be pointed out, nevertheless, that the *sainete* produced its own distinguished writers; indeed, this popular genre gave birth to an important and enduring new dramatic form, the *grotesco* (absurd or grotesque). At the same time, the *sainete*'s commercial nature led the Argentine theatre into a period of literary decline.

The period 1925–40 was characterized by experimentation by a small group of playwrights. New independent theatres appeared, the best known being El Teatro del Pueblo (People's Theatre). Authors such as Roberto Arlt (1900–42) experimented with expressionism in plays such as *Saverio el cruel* (*Saverio the Cruel*, 1936) and *La isla desierta* (*The Desert Island*, 1938). A Pirandellian independence of characters is noticeable in his *300 millones* (*300 Million*, 1932) and *El fabricante de fantasmas* (*The Creator of Ghosts*, 1936). Arlt's grotesque world had a strong influence on future generations of authors.

Another influential figure of this period was Armando Discépolo (1887–1971). Working in a more realistic vein, he has been associated with the Río de la Plata tragi-comic style, the *grotesco criollo*. This style was an offshoot of the *sainete*, but was not as superficial: it dealt with the psychology of the immigrant. Discépolo's best plays are *Mateo* (1923) and *Stéfano* (1928), which deal with the problems of immigrants in Argentina.

In the years after 1945 then, three types of theatres existed simultaneously: the private enterprises, which had been growing since the 1920s; the independent theatres, which began in the 1930s; and the official or government-sponsored enterprises, which had begun in 1936 with the creation of the Teatro de la Comedia and which grew in 1943 with the Teatro Municipal de Buenos Aires. Theatre also began to spread beyond Buenos Aires at this time, and as a consequence, dramatic activity and the public's interest in the theatre increased, although spectators remained relatively few in number. Smaller theatre spaces also proliferated. All this was a consequence of the social changes that Argentine society had undergone in the years following 1930, particularly between 1945 and 1955, the first, 'classical', period of the Peronist movement.

After 1955, as theatre gradually grew once again in Buenos Aires, new forms tended to convert the stage into an instrument for proselytizing. Influenced by the theories of Bertolt Brecht, a new school of authors and works emerged, and the tradition of romance and psychological realism was broken.

There was as well a clear increase at this time in the number of actors and private theatre schools; children's theatres began to appear; various provinces developed their own amateur and professional groups; and many people of letters tried writing for the stage. Carlos Gorostiza (b. 1920), for example, made his theatrical début in 1949 with *El puente* (*The Bridge*), the first of some twenty works he wrote for the theatre. A number of writers also emerged whose militant stands for democracy later resulted in their being refused production. Among these were Samuel Eichelbaum (1894–1967), the author of *Un guapo del novecientos* (*A Nineteenth-Century Bully*, 1940), *Un tal Servando Gómez* (*A Man Called Servando Gómez*, 1942) and *Rostro perdido* (*Lost Face*, 1961); and Bernardo Canal Feijóo (1893–1971), author of *Silverio Leguizamón* (1944), *Tungasuka* (1963) and *Los casos de Juan* (*The Tales of Juan*, 1954), a drama with roots in the country's folklore.

The evolution of Argentina's theatre between 1950 and 1965 was shaped by the *teatro independiente* (independent theatre) movement, which gave a home to a remarkable group of young writers, actors and directors. Their early productions were mostly in the European avant-garde tradition, but many new Argentine plays sprang from the social and political uncertainties of the day.

One of the most interesting writers to emerge from this movement was Pablo Palant (b. 1914), whose play *El cerco*, a teenage tragedy, opened in 1950. Aurelio Ferretti (1907–63), a prolific writer for the *teatro independiente*, was recognized early on as a master of farce in such works as *Bonome* and *Farsa del cajero que fue hasta la esquina* (*Farce of the Man who Went to the End of the Block*, 1958). Other writers of note were Juan Carlos Ferrari (b. 1917), author of *Las nueve tías de Apolo* (*The Nine Aunts of Apollo*, 1958); Atilio Betti (b. 1922), author of *Farsa del corazón* (*Farce of the Heart*) and *Fundación del desengaño* (*Foundation of Disappointment*); Carlos Carlino (b. 1910), who attempted to revive a kind of rural theatre with *Biunda* (*Blondie*, 1953) and *Esta vieja serpiente engañadora* (*This Deceiving Snake*, 1959); and Juan Carlos Ghiano (1920–90), who revived (with an absurdist flavour) the *sainete* in *Narcisa Garay, mujer para llorar* (*Narcisa Garay, A Woman to Weep For*, 1959).

In 1956, playwright Osvaldo Dragún (b. 1929) tried to revive classical Greek themes in his play *La peste viene de Melos* (*The Plague of Melos*), an idea he abandoned in favour of a more militant Brechtian style in works such as *Historias para ser contadas* (*Stories To Be Told*, 1957), *Historia de mi esquina* (*Story of my Neighbourhood*, 1957) and *Y nos dijeron que éramos inmortales* (*And They Told Us We Were Immortal*, 1963). A similar attempt was made by Agustín Cuzzani (1924–90) in *Una libra de carne* (*A Pound of Flesh*, 1954), *Sempronio* (1958) and *El centro forward murió al amanecer* (*The Centre Forward Died At Dawn*, 1955). This activity continued to grow through the late 1970s. By the 1980s, the line that had separated the contributions made by professionals and the anti-professional independent theatres became blurred to the point where in the 1990s all these groups regularly exchanged actors, directors, technicians and spaces.

In terms of style, the *teatro independiente* movement encouraged realism in the Stanislavski style. This was further reinforced by the presence of Hedy Crilla, an Austrian actress who had been trained by pupils of the Russian maestro and who first performed in Buenos Aires in 1959.

Right through 1983, theatre increasingly became a platform in the fight against social hypocrisy and censorship, although there was no sustained direction. In fact, disorientation became a form of creation and dramatic experiment reflecting a general confusion felt in Argentine society. Even interdisciplinary experiments proved to be fruitful though they did not always meet with the approval of critics and public. Running the gamut from intellectual gymnastics to physical exercises, from rites to mysticism, some of these works imposed a rigid set of working methods on the performers while others permitted informality and improvisation. Methodological approaches also varied: some advocated ensemble and/or depersonalization of the specific author; some argued in favour of a continuation of the Stanislavski system. Still others extolled the mystic nature of Grotowski's Poor Theatre experiments.

Playwriting prospered only briefly through the 1960s and 1970s and *teatro del grabador* (literally, tape recorder theatre) emerged, a very direct and extreme realism eliminating most imaginative or poetic possibility. A marriage of daily life with socialist-realism, *teatro del grabador* prospered between 1960 and 1965. By the early 1970s, there were also experiments

in 'alienation' taken from Brecht's epic theatre, ventures into the Theatre of the Absurd and Antonin Artaud's Theatre of Cruelty, happenings built on the influences of John Cage, group events inspired by the Living Theatre and collective creations. At the same time, commercial theatre degenerated into an 'industry', becoming dependent on sex, nudity, the spectacular, exhibitionism and crude language.

A special word should be said here about language. In the works of many traditional playwrights, a pseudo-educated language created a wide gap between stage and public. At every important point in the development of Argentina's theatre, this contradiction in linguistic usage was apparent. Only a few realists and the *sainete* writers avoided this tendency. Authors who achieved distinction after 1950, as well as those who came to the forefront in the 1960s, worked hard to mitigate this problem. The many problems at the end of the 1970s – political crisis, the military government, inhumane repression – exacerbated this tendency. Despite this, theatre fell into a sorry state, in both artistic and economic terms.

One highpoint, however, was the creation of the experimental Teatro Abierto (Open Theatre) in 1981, a communal attempt to change direction. Though the quality of its productions was uneven, the integrity and resonance of the undertaking was impressive. Unable to silence the group, the military government eventually burned down the theatre in 1981, obliging it to move to a new location. Burned down again a year later, the company nevertheless persisted and, in total, presented forty-nine plays during its short existence. Of these, fourteen were experimental in nature. A celebration of freedom and democracy, its final productions coincided with the end of the years of repression and the election of a new political regime in 1983. Significantly revitalizing Argentina's theatre, Teatro Abierto – with its emphasis on inexpensive tickets and reaching a broad public – also represented an important chapter of rebellion and democratic intensity.

By the late 1980s, the Argentine stage was almost completely decentralized, though Buenos Aires still remained an important theatre city with some two dozen companies operating in an area about one kilometre square. In the early 1990s, many of these large spaces gradually disappeared, while smaller, more unconventional locales multiplied, both in the centre and scattered throughout various districts of the city and the suburbs. In the provinces, theatre activity intensified to the point where it can now be found across the country almost year round.

Many of the 1990s experiments are still reactions to the strong censorship, attacks, threats and restrictions of every kind and size that Argentine theatre endured during the late 1970s and early 1980s when anything new or controversial was strongly discouraged.

One last hallmark of cultural life in Buenos Aires during the late 1970s and 1980s was the café-concert. Springing out of the economic crisis that had befallen the entire country and which forced many actors without work to survive by appearing in popular one-person shows, these solo performances escaped the rigorous

political and religious censorship that weighed heavily on the frightened artistic milieu at that time. Presented in small 'paratheatrical' settings where members of the audience occupied their own spaces in a climate of complicity, the shows usually began with the actors putting on makeshift costumes in front of the audience. The plays themselves criticized everyone, especially celebrities from the world of theatre, politicians and the wealthy. In many cases, they included monologues made up of insults spoken at top speed. A single artist was usually responsible for the whole performance as author, actor and director. Among those who worked in this specialized form were Carlos Perciavalle, Antonio Gasalla, Edda Díaz, Enrique Pinti (b. 1940) and Cecilia Rossetto.

Structure of the National Theatre Community

In any given week, over 100 performances are given in the capital by national or municipal theatres, commercial theatres, independent theatre or the city's many experimental and children's groups.

Only the national and municipal troupes of Buenos Aires and the *comedias provinciales* (provincial plays) are maintained by the state. The others depend on private sources of support, receiving occasional grants for particular performances from the National Art Fund, an official entity created to support various artistic endeavours.

In 1994, Buenos Aires was home to several state-supported groups – the Teatro Nacional Cervantes, the home of the Comedia Nacional; the Teatro Municipal General San Martín, founded in 1959; the Teatro Presidente Alvear, established under the aegis of the city as the Teatro de las Provincias to house visiting companies and folk troupes; and the Teatro de la Ribera, an offshoot of the Teatro Nacional Cervantes.

Audiences come from different levels of the country's large and diversified middle class (office workers, students, professionals) as well as from upper economic levels of society. In spite of efforts made at various times by independent theatre ensembles and the pioneering Teatro del Pueblo, no theatre has an authentic popular appeal like that seen in the period of *zarzuelas* (Spanish-style musical

comedies) and the Buenos Aires *sainetes* that appeared in the 1880s and throughout the next four decades.

Most theatre spaces in the provinces are owned by provincial governments and are rented out to companies, most of which come from the capital of the province, but sometimes from smaller cities such as Río Cuarto (in Córdoba). After Buenos Aires, Córdoba is the province with the greatest theatrical activity, led by the Teatro Libertador General San Martín, which since 1959 has had a resident company offering regular seasons as well as an annual festival that alternates between national and international seasons.

National festivals are also a common activity in other interior provinces, such as in Tales los de Zapala (province of Neuquén), Mar del Plata (province of Buenos Aires) and Villa Regina (Province of Río Negro).

There are other regularly producing companies in Tucumán, La Plata (capital of the Buenos Aires province), Jujuy and Nogoyá.

Independent theatres tend to operate mostly in Buenos Aires, but a few also work in the provinces. These provincial groups include Teatro Vocacional de Goya (Vocational Theatre Goya) in Corrientes, founded in the 1940s; the Teatro Libre Florencio Sánchez (Florencio Sánchez Free Theatre) in Rojas; and Litoral (Seaside), which presents its performances in various non-traditional venues.

The Asociación Argentina de Actores (Argentine Actors' Association) represents most theatre artists and has the power of a trade union.

Artistic Profile

Companies

In the 1940s and 1950s, the company of Luis Vehil-Esteban Serrador was the most popular in Buenos Aires, performing mostly comedies by foreign authors such as Somerset Maugham, Jean Anouilh and Marcel Achard. All were characterized by elegance and good taste and were models of fine elocution and polished acting. Actresses were costumed in the latest *haute couture* and moved amid stylish furniture and brilliant scenery. Towards the end of the 1950s, Vehil began to add in occasional dramas, such as *The Lark* by Anouilh.

Vehil's major competitor was Narciso Ibáñez Menta and his company, which did comedies as well as dramas such as *Dirty Hands* by Jean-Paul Sartre, *Death of a Salesman* by Arthur Miller, and *On Earth As In Heaven* by Fritz Hochwalder.

At the end of the 1950s, actor and director Francisco Petrone began to stage plays in a circus tent erected in one of the busiest plazas in Buenos Aires. With Teatro Circo Arena and using a circular stage, he produced *Una libra de carne* by Agustín Cuzzani and *La leyenda de Juan Moreira* by Rodolfo Kusch as well as such modern classics as *Cat on a Hot Tin Roof* by Tennessee Williams and *Long Day's Journey into Night* by Eugene O'Neill.

In 1960, several actors and directors from the Teatro Nacional expressed their political differences with the company by organizing themselves into a new group, the Gente de Teatro Asociada. Its performances between 1961 and 1972 included *Man and Superman* by George Bernard Shaw, *Tres sainetes porteños* (*Three Buenos Aires Sainetes*) and plays by Anouilh and Jerome Kilty.

The Spanish exile companies of Margarita Xirgú and Lola Membrives also occasionally performed in Buenos Aires in the 1950s and 1960s. Xirgú's group specialized in the works of Federico García Lorca and Rafael Alberti and its major contribution was offering Argentines a model of a theatre of high artistic quality, as well as a valiant, vibrant image of Spanish theatre in exile.

The Membrives company, at various times during the period between 1957 and 1974, performed a wide repertoire in Buenos Aires that also included plays by García Lorca along with modern Spanish and French authors such as Antonio Gala and Jean Cocteau.

The country's two major official theatres – Teatro Nacional Cervantes and Teatro Municipal General San Martín – have tended to perform seasons dominated by the classics, major works from the foreign modern repertoire and only occasionally plays by contemporary Argentine authors.

Of the independent theatres, the most important have been Teatro del Pueblo, La Máscara, Nuevo Teatro (New Theatre), Los Independientes, Fray Mocho, Instituto de Arte Moderno, the Idisches Folks Theater (IFT; Yiddish People's Theatre), Teatro Estudio, Teatro Abierto and Teatro Libre Florencio Sánchez.

Dramaturgy

One of the great milestones in the evolution of modern Argentine drama as well as in the *teatro independiente* movement was Carlos Gorostiza's 1949 play *El puente*. Produced by Teatro de la Máscara (Mask Theatre) and directed by Gorostiza and Pedro Doril, the play was written using the speech patterns of the working class on the one hand and the middle class on the other. Such a realistic confrontation on a stage surprised the public, which easily identified with the characters. Set in a bar, it reproduced on stage the attitudes and gestures of Buenos Aires's young people.

Almost a decade later (1958), Gorostiza again offered an extraordinary realistic vision – *El pan de la locura* (*The Bread of Madness*). Once more under his own direction, the new Gorostiza work was even performed by the Comedia Nacional in the Teatro Cervantes. The script examined individual responsibility, compromise and choice. These two plays together helped set a new standard for the Argentine theatre. Another work of note by Gorostiza is the more experimental *Los hermanos queridos* (*Dear Brothers*, 1978).

Another important writer in the development of the modern Argentine theatre is Ricardo Halac (b. 1935), author of *Soledad para cuatro* (*Solitude for Four*). First performed in 1961 under the direction of Augusto Fernandes, the play was set in a small apartment where two young couples meet to spy on one another. *Nuestro fin de semana* (*Our Weekend*, 1964) by Roberto Cossa (b. 1934) was a success in the same style, realistic archetypes of frustrated beings shaped around a loose plot allowing the characters to express in everyday language their states of mind and particularly their apprehensions about the future.

Other plays of significance by Cossa include *El viejo criado* (*The Old Servant*, 1980), *La nona* (*The Granny*, 1977) and *Los compadritos* (*The Show-Offs*, 1984). *La nona*, directed by Gorostiza, offered a cast of rather cynical characters. The *nona* does not impart her bitterness to the audience directly, but rather through her constant eating, devouring everything, a symbol of either survival or self-destruction. In *Los compadritos*, an Italian immigrant family, two Nazi sailors, a representative of the country's wealthy landowners and, in the play's title role, a show-off who lives in a Buenos Aires tenement are brought together to anatomize and satirize forty years of Argentine political life. The play maintained the structure and especially the spirit of the traditional *sainete*.

Tragedy as a modern genre was attempted by several authors in the post-war years, including Osvaldo Dragún in 1957, Bernardo Canal Feijóo in 1963 and David Viñas in 1973 using the character Tupac Amaru, the Cacique rebel who confronted the Spanish during the conquest of the Americas. In these plays, the dying hero was the native; fate came in the shape of the invader.

Eduardo Pavlovsky (b. 1933) explored violence in the late 1960s and early 1970s in *La cacería* (*The Hunt*, 1969), *La mueca* (*The Grimace*, 1971), *Telarañas* (*Cobwebs*, 1976) and *El Señor Galíndez* (1973). Focused on the underworld, these were violent plays about victims and power, about innocent children who bear within themselves the seeds that will turn them too into torturers.

Dragún's first success came in 1956 at a festival of *teatro independiente* held in the city of Mar del Plata – *Historias para ser contadas* (*Stories to be Told*). The play, consisting of four independent stories, clearly depicted the author's critical attitude to social and political problems, namely that power politics was destroying the human race. In addition to having a dramatic structure based on a play within a play, Dragún's stories blended together with dialogue interrupted by the narrator. Done without scenery, light was used to structure the space.

Dragún's 1957 drama *Los de la mesa 10* (*Those at Table 10*, 1957) centred on the deteriorating relationship of a young couple and again used uncomplicated design. It became one of the generation's most performed plays. As in the case of *Historias para ser contadas*, many plays were influenced by this script. Another play of note by Dragún is *Al perdedor* (*To the Loser*, 1982), which breathed a romantic element into his work. In this play a circular stage was used along with innovative props, such as a carpet made of plastic strips held above the floor and shaken by the actors to suggest the movement of the sea.

Germán Rozenmacher (1936–70) is another writer of note, one of several from the country's large Jewish community. His *Réquiem para un viernes a la noche* (*Requiem For Friday Night*, 1964) deals with a conflict between two generations of a Jewish family in Buenos Aires. Taking place in the dining room of a cantor's home, the play focuses on a father's rigid expectations for his son, who considers himself to be first and foremost an Argentine. Rozenmacher's *Simón Brumelstein, el caballero de Indias* (*Simon Brumelstein, Knight of the Indes*, 1982), shows another hero doomed to destroy himself in a search for truth.

Oscar Viale's (1933–94) plays, *El grito pelado* (*The Shriek*, 1967), *Chúmbale* (*Go Get 'em!*, 1969) and *La pucha* (1971) are written in a dialect spoken by the inhabitants of the Río de la Plata region. Their structures are also unusual: an uninterrupted series of scenes showing everyday characters (for example, a travelling coffee salesman), their griefs and joys.

Ricardo Talesnik's (b. 1935) *La fiaca* (*Down in the Dumps*, 1967) depicts a dramatic situation to which many people could respond: an office employee decides not to go to work simply out of laziness. Julio Mauricio's (b. 1919) *La valija* (*The Suitcase*, 1968) also presents the shallowness of everyday living, with a husband and wife unable to find their way out of domestic conflict.

Eduardo Pavlovsky's *Potestad* (*Power*).
Photo: courtesy *Conjunto*.

Three writers whose best work reflected extreme and cruel aspects of Argentine society are Guillermo Gentile (b. 1950), author of *Hablemos a calzón quitado* (*Let's Talk Honestly*, 1970); Roma Mahieu (b. 1937), author of *Juguemos a la hora de la siesta* (*Let's Play During Siesta*); and Roberto Perinelli (b. 1940), author of *Miembro del jurado* (*Member of the Jury*, 1979). In Gentile's play, attention is focused on a destitute, lost young man torn between an over-indulgent, homosexual father and an aggressive friend who browbeats him with his ideas, while in Mahieu's play, an adolescent boy subjugates his playmates by threatening to crush a bird he is holding in his hand. In the Perinelli play, a recently released ex-convict – a rapist and murderer – is castrated by his victim's relatives.

Juan Carlos Ghiano is another writer of significance. His *Narcisa Garay, mujer para llorar* takes place on the patio of a typical tenement house but in this play his protagonist is a woman. In his *Corazón de tango* (*Heart of the Tango*, 1968) he suggests poetic links with the *tango*, Argentina's national urban music/dance form, characterized by long pauses and stylized movements.

Modern *sainetes* by Enrique Wernicke represent the only attempts made at bringing this particular genre up to date. As performed by the Nuevo Teatro on an almost bare stage, the characters were more representative of the country's middle class than they were of workers living in tenements.

In 1981, Eduardo Pavlovsky's *Camaralenta* (*Slow Motion*) brought the audience into contact with the idea of destruction using the image of a boxer. As in a kaleidoscope, cut-away sequences of his agonizing consciousness were seen.

Ricardo Monti (b. 1944) created one of the more unusual scripts of the period: *Historia tendenciosa de la clase media argentina, de los extraños sucesos en que se vieron envueltos algunos hombres públicos, su completa dilucidación y otras escandalosas revelaciones* (*Tendentious History of the Argentine Middle Class, an Elucidation of the Strange Successes of Certain Public Figures, and Other Scandalous Revelations*, 1971). The play was a kind of circus suggesting that Argentina's recent history should be revised, and requesting the audience's contribution to the process. The actors represented the working class, the middle class, foreign powers (mostly British and US) and the theatre itself as an institution. Some were even historical figures and accurately presented a critical and biting vision of the country's history.

Each began in reality but eventually grew larger and less articulate, becoming circus clowns in the process.

Monti's 1980 play, *Marathon*, directed by Jaime Kogan, was staged in a dance-hall environment in which a competition is held though the dancers do not know what the first prize is. All the characters here also double as historical figures.

Bernardo Canal Feijóo, author of *Los casos de Juan*, turned to popular tales brought to Argentina by the *conquistadores*, tales that disappeared in the darkness of history and reappeared with the characteristics, rhythm and space of a vast and unknown America. *Los casos de Juan* is a series of allegorical Aesopian fables about the conflict between a cougar and a fox. The stage creates a sense of magic: a little brook, from which Juan the Fox takes a drink, suddenly takes on the capricious form of a blue silk web.

In 1955, *El herrero y el diablo* (*The Blacksmith and the Devil*) by Juan Carlos Gené (b. 1928) first appeared on stage. Taken from the 1926 novel *Don Segundo Sombra* by Ricardo Güiraldes, this adaptation showed a blacksmith, Jesus and St Peter on the great Argentine *pampa* (prairie).

El tango del ángel (*Angel's Tango*, 1968) by Alberto Rodríguez Muñoz and *Subterráneo Buenos Aires* (*Underground Buenos Aires*, 1983) by Jorge Huertas, are two other interesting plays characterized by a melancholy evocation of the *tango*.

Griselda Gambaro (b. 1928) is one of the country's most outstanding playwrights and possibly Latin America's best known woman playwright. Among her psychological/political dramas are *Los siameses* (*The Siamese Twins*, 1967), *El campo* (*The Camp*, 1968), *Decir sí* (*To Say Yes*, 1981) and *La malasangre* (*Bad Blood*, 1982). Politically committed and often controversial, her plays are powerful portraits of contemporary Argentine life. Other playwrights of note since the 1960s have been Aída Bortnik (b. 1938), Sergio De Cecco (b. 1931), Mauricio Kartún (b. 1946), Eduardo Rovner (b. 1942) and Carlos Somigliana (b. 1932).

Directors, Directing and Production Styles

For a discussion of directing, see previous material in **Artistic Profile**, and the opening, historical section.

Music Theatre

Many of the forms of music theatre that Argentina has date back to the end of the nineteenth century and the beginning of the twentieth. These include the *revista porteña* (Buenos Aires revue), the *comedia musical porteña* (Buenos Aires musical comedy), the *espectáculo musical folklórico* (folkloric musical theatre), the *espectáculo dramático con música de escena* (theatre piece with music) and traditional opera.

The *revista porteña* is a piece that combines dramatic scenes and comic interludes with music and dance numbers. Humorous, often satirical, the *revista porteña*, though it may have been influenced by the French revue in terms of costume, lighting and set design, is a genre very much indigenous to Argentina, for it is built around the *tango*, an urban music form that expresses the *porteño* soul. Only occasionally is there any other kind of music or song used in it. So popular has this genre been that several theatres have become venues for it: the Teatro Maipo, Teatro Nacional and Teatro Comedia. A number of stand-up comics, variety stars, dancers, *tango* orchestras and singers are also linked to this popular genre.

The *comedia musical porteña*, an offshoot of the *revista porteña*, is usually structured around a simple storyline that is interrupted by music, dance or orchestral interludes tied to the main plot. Once again, the *tango* dominates. Since the 1980s, the influence of US musical comedies has been seen in this form. Among its major creators has been Francisco Canaro, a musician and composer, who created *La historia del tango* (*The Story of the Tango*), *Sentimiento gaucho* (*Cowboy Sentiment*) and *El tango en París* (*The Tango in Paris*, 1945). Canaro was deeply influenced by the *zarzuela* form.

In 1945 Sixto Pondal Ríos and Carlos Olivari premièred *Luna de miel para tres* (*Honeymoon for Three*), with music by Canaro and Mariano Mores. With Mores began a new era for this form in which lyrics were given the same importance as music. Mores's principal works are *Con la música en el alma* (*With Music in the Soul*), lyrics by Homero Manzi; *Tangolandia* (*Tangoland*), a spectacular comedy with brilliant choreography; *El otro yo de Marcela* (*Marcela's Other Ego*), with lyrics by Pondal Ríos and Olivari; *Bésame, Petronila* (*Kiss Me, Petronila*), lyrics by Alberto de Zavalía; *Buenos Aries de seda y percal* (*Silky, Wealthy Buenos Aires*); *Estrellas en el Teatro Avenida* (*Stars of the Avenida Theatre*), and *Buenos Aires canta al mundo* (*Buenos Aires Sings to the World*).

In the 1960s, a number of similar shows had extended runs – Astor Piazzolla (d. 1993) premièred *María de Buenos Aires* (*Maria of Buenos Aires*), with lyrics by Horacio Ferrer; *El dedo gordo* (*The Thumb*) by Pablo Palant, with music by Víctor Proncet; and a revision of *Locos de verano* (*Crazy for the Summer*) by Gregorio de Laferrère (1867–1913), with music by Víctor Buccino. Buccino would also première some years later *Dulce, dulce vida* (*Sweet, Sweet Life*), a musical version of *Así es la vida* (*That's Life*) by Malfatti and Las Llanderas.

After 1962 other forms of musical comedies arrived in Buenos Aires from abroad, especially from the United States, and most of them were very successful. About 1975, Pepe Cebrián began presenting the works in this style that made him famous: *Aquí no podemos hacerlo* (*We Can't Do It Here*), *Calígula* and *Las invasiones inglesas* (*The English Invasions*), which was closer to jazz and international rock than to traditional musical forms.

The *espectáculo musical folklórico* is still another genre with a unique musical character, sophisticated choreography and only a very few theatrical scenes in each show. One finds this genre mostly outside of Buenos Aires. These folk shows began in the 1950s, the time of Santiago Ayala, known as El Chúcaro, the form's most significant creator. One of his most popular shows was *Malón ranquelino*, in which El Chúcaro presented several new musical/acrobatic numbers using balls. His shows also featured the popular music of artists such as Los Chalchaleros, Atahualpa Yupanqui (d. 1994), Mercedes Sosa and Marta de los Ríos. Other well-known folk shows were *Danzas y cantares de América y España* (*Dances and Songs from the Americas and Spain*), put together by Joaquín Pérez Fernández; and productions organized by the Vélez-Shulko Folkloric Ballet.

As for opera, Argentine composers were deeply influenced by Italian currents and, therefore, it is almost impossible to speak about a specifically national style of opera. This said, a number of Argentine operas written since the 1950s do stand out: *Bodas de sangre* (*Blood Wedding*, 1956) and *La zapatera prodigiosa* (*The Shoemaker's Prodigious Wife*, 1958), both adaptations of García Lorca's work by Juan José

Castro; *Proserpina y el extranjero* (*Proserpina and the Foreigner*, 1960), also by Castro, with lyrics by Alejandro Casona; *Bomarzo* (1972) by Alberto Ginastera, with lyrics by Manuel Mújica Láinez; *El caso Maillard* (*The Maillard Case*, 1978) by Roberto García Morillo, based on a book by Edgar Allan Poe; *Marianita Limeña* (1957) by Valdo Sciammarella, with lyrics by Francisco Javier; *La pendiente* (*The Hill*, 1959) and *La hacienda* (*The Ranch*, 1987), with music and lyrics by Pompeyo Camps; *La voz del silencio* (*The Voice of Silence*, 1969) by Mario Peruso, with lyrics by Leónidas Barrera Oro; *Escurial* (1989), also by Peruso, based on a text by Michel de Ghel-

derode; *Prometeo 45* (*Prometheus 45*, 1965), music and lyrics by Rodolfo Arizaga; *Pedido de mano* (1968) by Jacobo Ficher, based on Chekhov; *Adonías* (1989), music and lyrics by Alejandro Pinto; *Zincalí* (1954) by Felipe Boero, based on a dramatic poem by Arturo Capdevilla; *El oro del inca* (*The Inca's Gold*, 1953), music and lyrics by Héctor Iglesias; *Medea* (1973) by Claudio Guidi Drei; *La otra voz* (*The Other Voice*, 1954) by José María Castro, lyrics by Jorge de Obieta; and *La cuarterona* (1951), music and lyrics by Juan Agustín García Estrada.

Most of these pieces premièred at the Teatro Colón in Buenos Aires.

Dance Theatre

Dance theatre as a specifically Argentine form dates back only to 1970, when particular performances began to be called dance theatre. In the 1960s, this developing form had a home of sorts at the Instituto Di Tella. Basing itself on total freedom in movement, early creations included *Danse Bouquet* by Ana Kamiens, Marilú Marini and Graciela Martínez; *La fiesta hoy* (*The Holiday Today*) by Kamiens and Marini; and *Casta Diva* by Kamiens. In *Juguemos a la bañadera* (*Let's Play In the Bathtub*), Martínez incorporated daily movement into her choreography while in *Crash* Oscar Araiz (b. 1940) built figurative bridges between painting, sculpture and dance. Susana Zimmermann used improvisation and spontaneity in her *Ceremonies* as a specific expression as she did in *Dies irae* (*Day of Wrath*) and *Oye, humanidad* (*Listen, Humanity*).

Through the 1970s the 'German' school of modern dance in Argentina was enriched by ideas and styles coming from the United States, especially those of Martha Graham as seen through the works of Freddy Romero and Ana María Stekelman. In the 1980s newer influences became evident: on the one hand from the German experimenter Pina Bausch, and on the other from more traditional modernists such as José Limón and Jennifer Müller.

When Ana Itelman returned to Argentina in

1970 she dedicated herself to dance theatre with most of her shows based on dramatic texts with rhythm serving as part of the dramatic conflict. Among her best known shows were *Phaedra*, *Alicia en el País de las Maravillas* (*Alice in Wonderland*), *A Soldier's Story*, *El capote* (*The Cloak*) and *Suite de Percal*. A large number of her creations were done with groups such as Danza Contemporánea (Contemporary Dance) and Teatro Municipal General San Martín, one of the bastions of Argentine dance theatre in the 1970s and 1980s.

Oscar Araiz, now known beyond Argentina's borders, created *Escenas* (*Scenes*, 1974), a dance performance whose structure was certainly theatrical. In 1982, his *Fénix* (*Phoenix*) was a kind of theatre of music instead of words. Other artists who followed in this line of work were Mauricio Wainrot, with *Anne Frank*, produced in the Teatro San Martín, a piece in which he added the academic language of dance to the well-known play; Susana Tambutti from the group Núcleo Danza (Nucleus Dance), who in pieces such as *La puñalada* (*The Stab*), *Patagonia trío* and *Jugar con fuego* (*Playing with Fire*) explored in movement the essence of dramatic conflict; Silvia Vladimisky, who explored pantomime in *El campeón* (*The Champion*); and Alejandro Cervera, Diana Machado and Doris Petroni among others.

Theatre for Young Audiences

In the mid-1990s, on any given weekend in Buenos Aires, audiences can choose from more than fifty different performances for children and teenagers.

The actress Angelina Pagano in the 1930s was one of the pioneers of the form in Argentina. Later in the decade, another great actress, Camila Quiroga, followed in Pagano's footsteps. Later, they were joined by a company of actors remembered in Argentina as the group Marilyn. Other companies actually featured young casts, such as Lavardén, sponsored by the Department of Culture of the Buenos Aires municipal government, named for the playwright Manuel José de Lavardén (1754–1801). As independent companies such as Teatro del Pueblo evolved, they too added in theatre for young audiences as part of their regular seasons.

The modern era of theatre for young audiences began with the work of Roberto Aulés, an actor, director and playwright. Aulés developed a theatre for young audiences in Buenos Aires with the same structures, goals and expectations as theatre for adults. His creations were dramatically effective, extremely poetic and avoided didacticism. Some of his important productions were *El monigote de la pared* (*The Drawing On the Wall*) and *Tiempo de negro y farol* (*Old Times*).

María Elena Walsh appeared in the 1960s and revolutionized the form by creating intelligent and poetic texts based on illogical situations. *Doña Disparate y Bambuco* (*Mrs Nonsense and Bambuco*) and *Canciones para mirar* (*Songs to Look At*) are two of her best known productions. Both premièred at Teatro San Martín and toured across the country. Other names of note in the field have been Hugo Midón with *La vuelta manzana* (*Around the Block*), Ariel Bufano with *Mambrundia y Gasparindia*, and Ariel Allende, Hebe Conte and Alpargato (Roberto Vega). At the Nuevo Teatro, Enrique Pinti created several children's plays of note, including *Mi bello dragón* (*My Beautiful Dragon*) and *Corazón de bizcochuelo* (*Heart of Cake*).

Some of the other companies producing regular seasons in the capital are La Galera Encantada (The Enchanted Galley), Catarsis (Catharsis), Los Calandracas, Agrupación Humorística La Tristeza (Sadness Comedy Troupe) and Caleidoscopio (Kaleidoscope), a collective.

Other children's groups operate in Rosario (province of Santa Fé), in Bahía Blanca (province of Buenos Aires), in Mendoza, in Lomas de Zamora (province of Buenos Aires) and in Santa Rosa (province of La Pampa).

Puppet Theatre

The country's pioneer professional puppet theatre was the Piccoli de Podrecca, which toured widely after 1937 with large-cast marionette shows and sophisticated sets. The hand-puppet tradition began with Javier Villafañe, Mane Bernardo and Sara Bianchi, later the directors of the Argentine Museum of Puppetry. Following in Podrecca's footsteps were also Pepe Ruiz, Cándido Moneo Sanz, the brothers Hector and Eduardo Di Mauro, César López Ocón, Roberto Espina, Otto Freitas, Juan Enrique Acuña and many others.

Puppeteers have been organized since the late 1960s through the national branch of the International Puppeteers' Union (UNIMA), which in 1994 had more than 300 Argentine members. The Centro de Investigaciones Titiriteras (Centre for Research on Puppetry) is the major

centre for scholarship and documentation of the country's puppet theatre.

Ariel Bufano and his company have long been resident at the Teatro Municipal General San Martín in Buenos Aires. Its productions have played at various international festivals including the Festival of Nations in Nancy, France (1983) and the Festival of the Americas in Montréal, Canada (1987).

A number of companies, such as the Teatro Negro de Salta (Black Theatre of Salta) and the Teatro Libre de Buenos Aires (Free Theatre of Buenos Aires), have experimented with the form. The latter group, directed by Luis Rivera López, has produced *La tremebunda tragedia de Macbeth* (*The Frightening Tragedy of Macbeth*) and *A Midsummer Night's Dream* while groups such as Diablomundo, in productions like

El fuego (*Fire*) and *El payaso y el pan* (*The Clown and the Bread*), have successfully combined the use of puppets with popular street music. Several groups in Buenos Aires have also experimented with puppet theatre for young adults.

From the 1960s, some of the urban groups have operated out of Cultural Centres as well as from conventional theatres. They all use a language that is direct, a sharp humour and are influenced by rock music and video. One of the pioneer groups in this form was Los Volatineros (The Acrobats), directed by Francisco Javier, founded in 1976 and still operating in the 1990s.

In the late 1980s, groups such as El Clú del Claun (The Clown Club), La Banda de la Risa (The Laughter Troupe) and Los Quelonios experimented with clown techniques while others, such as Los Macocos, Los Vergara and Los Galangrotes, searched for a revalorization of theatrical games. Groups such as Teatro de la Libertad (Theatre of Freedom), Grupo Dorrego and Caleidoscopio tend to work with the language of street theatre and the Organización La Negra has experimented with theatrical violence.

Training in theatre for young audiences is offered, for the most part, by the companies themselves, many of which have very good schools. This is so in Ariel Bufano's case. Some of the biggest names in Argentine puppet theatre have trained with him. It is also the case with the group Los Volatineros, which has young children as both students and audiences.

Design

During the eighteenth and nineteenth centuries, theatre activity in the area of Río de la Plata followed two major currents: a European one, which brought Spanish styles to the colony; and an indigenous one, expressed through dramatic ceremonies and rituals. As time passed, the two currents began to fuse.

The spaces used for performances in the European style tended to be reproductions of Italian theatres and/or Spanish *corrales* (open-air theatres). For the most part, they were proscenium houses with painted drop-curtains. Indigenous theatre was performed outdoors, in squares, patios, church courtyards, or in the spaces of the *criollo* circus (a *criollo* is a person of Spanish ancestry born in the Americas). Towards the end of the nineteenth century, the success of Eduardo Gutiérrez's *Juan Moreira*, a production by the Podestá family, marked the beginning of Argentine popular theatre and confirmed the *redondel* (the circular space of the *criollo* circus) as the most significant area.

As for settings themselves, at the turn of the twentieth century those intended for formal proscenium theatres were mostly designed by foreigners, mainly Italian and French. Using giant drops brought from Europe and simply put together in Argentina by local crews, their designs were in line with the affluence of the theatres hosting them. It was only later that these theatres would turn to national designers and painters, once it was felt they had acquired the necessary knowledge of foreign techniques.

Most of Argentina's best designers in the 1920s were students of visual artist Rodolfo Franco: Saulo Benavente, Mario Vanarelli, Germán Gelpi and Marciano Longarini. Later these designers were teachers in the Escuela Superior de Bellas Artes Ernesto de la Cárcova (Ernesto de la Cárcova Higher School of Fine Arts) where a set design programme had been created by Franco.

Benavente was also responsible for renovations at many theatres in both the capital and the interior. His work had a strict sense of functionality – spaces to serve the actors. He also used intense lights and colours, which gave his designs a poetic touch.

Gastón Breyer was one of Argentina's first important scholars of scenic space and design. He was also the only Argentine designer to publish widely in the field. His own visual sense led him to create minimalist sets. Mario Vanarelli chose to work with potent lights and colours, emphasizing colourfulness and contrast as forms of expression.

To these pioneers of theatre design it is possible to add several others who came from the field of visual arts: Héctor Basaldúa, Horacio Butler, Pío Collivadino, Raúl Soldi, Gregorio López Naguil, Dante Ortolani and Gori Muñoz. These artists often collaborated on designs for opera at the Teatro Colón, using visual art techniques that gave new life to the work.

During the last half of the twentieth century, Luis Diego Pedreira proposed a new concept, *escenoarquitectura* (stage architecture), emphasizing the fact that design must be both three dimensional and functional as architecture within the theatre space. His ideas influenced many of the country's younger designers.

Among the more innovative designers in the 1990s were Pablo Antón; Leandro H. Ragucci, who used natural materials and even garbage; Guillermo de la Torre, who combined architectural constructions and basic scenic elements;

Roberto Oswald, and Hugo de Ana. These last two particularly stand out in opera and their designs have a magnitude and opulence quite obviously right in this genre.

Other Argentine designers of note include Federico Padilla, Claudio Segovia, Carlos Cytrinowski and Rafael Reyeros, who have all worked overseas; and Ponchi Morpurgo, Oscar Lagomarsino, Nydia Dimitriadis, José Rubén Trifiro, Juan Mario Vasta and Graciela Galán, who are all known for their work with innovative materials such as plastic, mirrors and doors.

Theatre Space and Architecture

The Teatro Colón is the country's major opera and dance house. Inaugurated in 1908, the Colón was built following an architectural model of the French Renaissance and is divided into different levels: an orchestra, a balcony, galleries, halls and upper galleries. It also has a library and a museum. The Colón has 2,487 seats, but with standing room it can hold up to 4,000 people. The acoustics are considered near perfect. The stage itself is 35.25 metres wide and 34.5 metres deep with a revolving inner stage more than 20 metres in diameter. At 19.25 metres high, a cyclorama and a metallic curtain facilitate the projection of slides and the production of a variety of lighting effects.

The Teatro Municipal General San Martín is a much newer space, inaugurated in 1960. It has five different theatre spaces – the Coronado, the Casacuberta, the Lugones, the Cabanellas and the Morel.

The Coronado seats 1,070 people. Its stage has a sophisticated system of elevators that can operate simultaneously or independently, as well as two revolves that can rotate at different speeds. The hall is also equipped with sophisticated lighting and sound equipment for music, dance and spoken theatre.

The Casacuberta is an amphitheatre seating 566 people. Its stage area is 35 metres wide and 6 metres deep and the space is equipped with modern lighting and stage facilities. The Sala Lugones, located on the tenth floor, has seating for 233 people. It has a stage as well as a large screen for films. The Sala Cabanellas seats 200 people. It is an open space, generally used by experimental groups. The Sala Morel, the last of

the San Martín spaces, has a surface of approximately 800 square metres and was originally designed to be part of the main hall. It is now used as an informal space for the presentation of intimate interdisciplinary events.

The Teatro Nacional Cervantes (Cervantes National Theatre) was inaugurated in 1921. Built in the Spanish Renaissance style, the theatre's façade is a reproduction of that of the University of Alcalá de Henares near Madrid. The glazed tiles, tapestries and ornaments inside, including the curtain, were all made in Spain. The Cervantes seats 1,700 people and has sophisticated technical facilities.

The stage, which has been renovated, is 16 metres by 28.5 metres, and has a central revolving disk of 12 metres in diameter. It also has a small built-in stage that can be raised. The Cervantes also has workshop spaces for set building, design, lighting, makeup, wardrobe and rehearsal as well as spacious dressing rooms and administration offices. The Comedia Nacional is the resident company at the theatre, but it also houses many visiting companies.

Major commercial theatres of note include the Astral, the Podestá, the Ateneo, the Membrives, the Monumental, the Teatro del Globo, El Liceo, the Teatro Regina, the Teatro Maipo, the Tabarís and the Lorange. All of these spaces are technically well equipped.

Among the medium-sized and small spaces used regularly by smaller groups are the Colonial, the Teatro de la Campana, the Teatro Contemporáneo, the Teatro de la Cortada, the Teatro de la Fábula, the Teatro de la Piedad, the Galpón del Sur, El Vitral, La Gran Aldea, the

Manzana de las Luces, the Payró and the Piccolo Teatro. These are built in a variety of styles, some in basements, others in high-rise buildings.

Some of the spaces outside Buenos Aires, in cities such as Rosario, Córdoba, Mar del Plata, Bahía Blanca, Santa Fé, Tucumán and La Plata are also important architecturally and some are well equipped. In these cities there are also government-funded theatres and independent spaces for experimental groups.

From the 1930s until the 1970s a large number of theatres were created out of non-conventional spaces by many of the independent theatres. Basements, commercial lofts and even rooms in houses were used by Teatro del Pueblo, La Máscara, Nuevo Teatro, Los Independientes, Fray Mocho, Instituto de Arte Moderno, the Idisches Folks Theater, Teatro Estudio and the Teatro Libre Florencio Sánchez.

In many of these spaces, set designers were challenged to create environments using materials in imaginative new ways. The efforts of everyone to work within these spaces have become legendary, with vapour barriers and tin-can spotlights remaining as living symbols of this legend. Since the 1970s, increasingly non-traditional spaces – from church courtyards to the neo-classical peristyle of the Faculty of Law, from an abandoned ship to a swimming pool – have housed theatre performances of both the independent and the commercial companies.

Training

Professional theatre training in Argentina grew significantly from the 1950s, partly through the efforts of several schools officially supported by the government and partly through the work of the many non-official schools created by the country's independent theatres.

Of the official schools, the most important have been the Escuela Nacional de Arte Dramático (National Theatre School), the Escuela Municipal de Arte Dramático (Municipal Theatre School), the Teatro Colón's Escuela Superior de Arte (Higher Art School) for acting and directing for opera, the Escuela Superior Carlos de la Cárcova for scene design, the Instituto de Teatro (Theatre Institute) of the Faculty of Philosophy and Letters of the University of Buenos Aires for scholarship and theory, the Escuela de Teatro de La Plata of the Ministry of Education of the province of Buenos Aires, the Escuela de Escenografía (School of Set Design) of the University of La Plata and the university theatre schools in Mendoza, Córdoba and Tucumán.

The Escuela Nacional de Arte Dramático, the largest and oldest of this group, broke away in 1958 from the Conservatorio Nacional de Música y Arte Escénico (National Conservatory of Music and Dramatic Arts), which itself was founded in 1948. Under the leadership of Antonio Cunill Cabanellas, a Spanish director and teacher who had lived in Argentina since 1915, the school reached high artistic and teaching standards. A master in the Stanislavski method, he invited in a series of well-known professionals to be part of his faculty and helped train an entire generation of actors who came to be leaders on the national stage. Courses were offered in acting (four years), directing (three years) and drama pedagogy (three years).

The Escuela Municipal de Arte Dramático, another official school, was founded in 1965. It grew out of acting classes for young people instituted in the Instituto Vocacional de Arte Infantil (Young People's Vocational Institute for the Arts). From 1984, the activity of the school grew considerably. New classes in acting were added and a new stream in directing as well as playwriting workshops were created. In any given year, students at the Escuela Municipal staged more than 100 performances.

Independent groups also began to establish their own schools in the 1950s and a great number of important actors and directors were soon coming from them as well. Responsible for their group's training programmes were people such as Enrique Agilda (the Juan B. Justo Company, 1933), Ricardo Passano (La Máscara/The Mask, 1939), Pedro Asquini and Alejandra Boero (Nuevo Teatro), Onofre Lovero (Los Independientes), Marcelo Lavalle (Instituto de Arte Moderno), David Licht (IFT) and Oscar Ferrigno (Fray Mocho). Their excellent programmes constituted a real choice in relation to the official schools.

Early on, these groups sought training in the Stanislavski method. La Máscara turned to Hedy Crilla, an Austrian actress and an expert in the Stanislavski method, who joined La

Filippelli, Eugenio. 'El teatro en el interior del país'. [Theatre in the interior of the country]. *Revista de Estudios de Teatro* 3, no. 7 (1963): 55–9.

Gené, Juan Carlos. 'El teatro y las masas'. [Theatre and the masses]. *Revista de la Universidad* 19 (1965): 117–23.

Giella, Miguel Angel. 'Teatro Abierto 82: el comienzo de un sueño'. [Teatro Abierto 82: The beginning of a dream]. *Latin American Theatre Review* 16, no. 1 (fall 1982): 67–9.

——. 'Teatro Abierto: fenómeno socio-teatral argentino'. [Teatro Abierto: An Argentine social and theatrical phenomenon]. *Latin American Theatre Review* 15, no. 1 (fall 1981): 89–93.

Kaiser-Lenoir, Eva Claudia. 'Argentina's Theater of Collective Creation'. *Theater* 12, no. 1 (fall–winter 1980): 30–2.

Layera, Juan Ramón. 'Contemporary Spanish American Drama of Denunciation and Social Protest: The Case of Argentina and Chile'. PhD dissertation, State University of New York, Binghamton, 1977.

Marial, José. *El teatro independiente*. [The independent theatre]. Buenos Aires: Editorial Alpe, 1955.

——. *Teatro y país: desde 1810 a Teatro Abierto 1983*. [Theatre and nation: From 1810 to Teatro Abierto 1983]. Buenos Aires: Ediciones Agon, 1984. 194 pp.

Martínez, Martha. 'Tres nuevas dramaturgas argentinas: Roma Mahieu, Hebe Uhart y Diana Raznovich'. [Three new Argentine playwrights: Roma Mahieu, Hebe Uhart and Diana Raznovich]. *Latin American Theatre Review* 13, no. 2 (spring 1980): 39–46.

Moreno, Norma. 'Reflexiones sobre el teatro cordobés'. [Reflections on theatre in Córdoba]. *Andén para la cultura* 1, no. 1 (September–October 1979): 56–8.

Naios Najchaus, Teresa. *Conversaciones con el teatro argentino de hoy. Vol II: 1981–4*. [Conversations about Argentine theatre today. Vol II: 1981–4]. Buenos Aires: Ediciones Agon, 1984.

Ordaz, Luis. *El teatro en el Río de la Plata*. [Theatre in the River Plate region]. Buenos Aires: Ediciones Leviatán, 1957.

Pellettieri, O. *Cien años de teatro argentino, 1886–1990: del Moreira al Teatro Abierto*. [One hundred years of Argentine theatre, 1886–1990: From Moreira to Teatro Abierto]. Buenos Aires: Editorial Galerna, 1991.

——. *Teatro argentino de los 60: polémica, continuidad y ruptura*. [Argentine theatre of the 1960s: Polemics, continuity and splits]. Buenos Aires: Corregidor, 1989. 241 pp.

Tschudi, Lilian. *Teatro argentino actual 1960–72*. [Current Argentine theatre 1960–72]. Colección Estudios Latino Americanos no. 10. Buenos Aires: Fernando García Cambeino, 1974. 145 pp.

Zayas de Lima, Perla. *Diccionario de autores teatrales argentinos, 1950–90*. [A dictionary of Argentine playwrights, 1950–90]. Buenos Aires: Editorial Galerna, 1991.

ARUBA

(see **NETHERLANDS ANTILLES AND ARUBA**)

BARBADOS

(see **COMMONWEALTH CARIBBEAN**)

BOLIVIA

(Overview)

A landlocked country of 1.1 million square kilometres (424,200 square miles) located in the centre of South America, Bolivia's roots can be traced back through its two indigenous peoples – the Aymará and the Quechua. The Aymará civilization flourished along the banks of Lake Titicaca from about AD 600 to 900. By 1300, the powerful Incas of Perú, ancestors of the Quechua, had conquered the land.

By the sixteenth century, the country had become a Spanish colony. The harshness of Spanish rule, however, led to a series of rebellions during the nineteenth century. In 1824, Antonio José de Sucre (1795–1830), one of Simón Bolívar's lieutenants, led a revolt that broke Spain's domination, and independence was declared in 1825. Originally named Bolívar, the country's name was later changed to its present form.

From 1864, Mariano Melgarejo (1829–71), one of a series of military dictators, began to sell and lease national territory to neighbouring countries and in later years wars over this and other disputed land cost Bolivia access to the Pacific Ocean (primarily in a war against Chile, 1879–83) and much of its original territory (especially in the costly Chaco War against Paraguay, 1932–35).

The first half of the twentieth century was marked by advances in industry and transportation but it was the world demand for tin – Bolivia is the world's third largest tin producer – that shaped the country's economy. World War II, for example, brought a rise in the price of tin but after the war prices dropped again and the national economy suffered.

A revolution, which lasted from 1952 to 1964, brought the Movimenti Nacionalista Revolucionario (National Revolutionary Movement) to power. Mines were nationalized as was the oil industry and part of the railroad system. Land reforms gave property to the Aymará and Quechua peoples, who were allowed to vote for the first time. In 1969, however, the military again took control and the 1970s saw student protests and labour strikes. A return to civilian rule was scheduled for 1978, when elections were held but again the military took power.

At the end of the 1980s, Bolivia had the world's highest inflation rate and a major source of its income was being derived from the production of cocaine. Pressure to cut back and eventually eliminate this production was exerted by the international community – especially the United States.

The presidential elections of 1989 saw Jaime Paz Zamora of the Movimiento de la Izquierda Revolucionaria (Movement of the Revolutionary Left) come to power despite receiving only 19.6 per cent of the popular vote. Though the new government tried to make both social and economic changes, it was itself accused by the United States of supporting narcotics trafficking.

By the 1993 elections, eighteen different political parties were seeking office. Elected this time was Gonzalo Sánchez de Lozada of the Movimiento Nacionalista Revolucionario with 36 per cent of the vote.

Worth noting in this regard is the fact that more than half the population of 7.8 million were of Aymará and Quechua descent, an ethnic grouping with a high degree of illiteracy. Few of them actually participated in elections.

Sánchez de Lozada, who had studied in

the United States and lived there for extended periods, had committed his government to a new war against drug trafficking along with social and economic reforms that were to include increased involvement by the indigenous population in government, and greater decentralization. The new government received quick US support and a cautious optimism was seen by 1994.

La Paz is the country's largest city and seat of the national government though the capital is the city of Sucre, the country's judiciary seat. In addition to politics, life in Bolivia is significantly affected by the Andes Mountains which run through most of the country and are as much as 640 kilometres across at some points.

Spanish dramatic forms were introduced to Bolivia as early as the sixteenth century and Spanish missionaries utilized the *autosacramentales* (one-act religious plays) in their religious work. It is still possible to see a mixing of Christian ritual and Aymará/Quechua forms, especially in the many national and local festivals. The largest is the Alacitas Fair held in La Paz each January, a celebration of the Aymará god of abundance, Ekeko. During carnival time, dancers in the city of Oruro also perform the Diablada (Devil Dance), another throwback to Medieval religious drama. Dedicated to the Virgin of the Mines, it is the miners' way of asking for protection against the devil, whom they fear meeting in the underground darkness.

Aspects of the cult of Pachamama (the Earth Goddess) and the mythological Tío (Uncle), who, according to legend, lives in the mines and is responsible for the yield, have also been integrated into the spectacle. The most impressive mask in this celebration is that of Satan, formed by seven smaller masks representing the seven deadly sins. The mask is adorned with snakes and two large horns. Originally the dance contained dialogue that has since disappeared. Although the origins of the festival are to be found in the Spanish *autosacramentales*, the addition of Aymará/Quechua traits is evident.

More traditional European forms – ultimately including many historical, verse and romantic dramas – dominated Bolivia's urban dramatic literature into the early years of the twentieth century. Fabián Vaca Chávez's (1883–1949) *Carmen Rosa* (1912) showed Bolivian theatre a new realistic direction.

The modern history of Bolivia's theatre dates from 1923, when the Sociedad Boliviana de Autores Teatrales (Bolivian Society of Playwrights) was founded in La Paz. The main objective of the society was to support the many national festivals and to use them as venues for the performance of plays by national dramatists. The nucleus of the society's members were known as the Generation of 21 and their dramatic work revealed a new and more realistic look at the country's social and political problems. New subjects also appeared in their work, including the effects of urbanization on the indigenous population (the so-called *cholo-señorito*) and issues related to the loss of the country's access to the Pacific.

At the same time, an attempt was made to professionalize the theatre through the creation of a theatre school, a professional organization for actors – the Asociación Boliviana de Actores (Bolivian Association of Actors) – national awards, and the production, where possible, of Bolivian plays in major theatres such as El Municipal in La Paz, El Achá in Cochabamba and El Mariscal Sucre in the city of Sucre. Over the next decade, many professional companies emerged following the new ideas, including companies run by Wenceslao Monroy (1893–1954) and Carlos Cervantes (1897–1949), the Festivales Julianos (Julian Festivals) and the Juegos Florales (Floral Games). As well, significant numbers of plays began to be published for the first time.

Special stimulation came in 1925, the nation's centennial, which saw another outburst of national activities and the appearance in La Paz of many visiting troupes, including the Colón Opera troupe from Buenos Aires and the Soler de México, which also offered a series of seminars.

Four Bolivian playwrights of note stand out from this period: Enrique Baldivieso, Humberto Palza Solíz (1901–75), Saturnino Rodrigo (1894–1979) and, perhaps the most interesting writer of the period, Antonio Díaz Villamil (1896–1948).

Baldivieso wrote in a variety of styles, sometimes socially aware, other times with an eye to history. His best works are *Lo que traemos al mundo* (*What We Bring To the World*), *Derecho a matar* (*The Right to Kill*) and the historical drama *El Dios de la Conquista* (*God of the Conquest*). Palza Solíz's major works include *Mi novio el extranjero* (*My Fiancé, the Foreigner*, 1922), *El viajero* (*The Traveller*, 1922) and *Silencio y sexo* (*Silence and Sex*, 1927).

Rodrigo's most successful play was *En la pendiente* (*On the Slope*, 1926), a drama of daily

Tito Landa's La Paz Municipal Theatre production of Alberto Saavedra Pérez's historical drama *Melgarejo*.

life and the conflict between different social and economic classes. The play received First Prize in the Circle of Fine Arts competition in 1926. In another of his works, *Sangre de la tierra* (*Blood of the Land*, 1928), Rodrigo turns Bolivia's eastern jungle into a character.

Díaz Villamil was not only the country's most important writer during this period but also an outstanding teacher. His early work was inspired by folk forms and his drama *La Rosita* (1925) is a classic of the genre. Two other early plays by him, *La hoguera* (*The Bonfire*, 1924) and *Cuando vuelva mi hijo!* (*When My Son Returns*, 1926), both received national playwriting awards.

During the Chaco War, Díaz Villamil wrote three important plays in collaboration with Palza Solíz – *El diluvio nacional* (*The National Flood*, 1931), *Boquerón* (*The Opening*, 1930) and *Canción de acero* (*Song of Steel*, 1930). After the war he turned to writing children's plays.

Díaz Villamil's late work again turned towards social criticism. His play *El hoyo* (*The Mine*, 1941) was a call for nationalization of the mining industry. First presented by the Cervantes Company in La Paz, the play was eventually toured nation-wide.

Bolivia's humiliating defeat in the Chaco War affected many people deeply and a number of writers simply turned away from their art at this point. Revolution also became a way of life and governments began to change regularly as popular dissatisfaction became obvious. With the lack of interest in theatre, theatre buildings began to close down across the country and were quickly turned into cinemas. This was the fate of El Municipal in La Paz, the Princesa and El Achá, among others. The country's leading actors had already left – Monroy for Lima and Cervantes for Buenos Aires.

The rise in the price of Bolivian tin during World War II helped generate new interest in national culture, and Monroy, Cervantes and others returned to La Paz. Playwrights at this time began to reflect the new Bolivian reality and tried to create a theatre for the masses. It was an attempt to make theatre as popular as film and soccer while at the same time being a Theatre of Social Protest.

One notable director of the 1950s was Liber Forti. Working in the small town of Tupiza with his group Nuevos Horizontes (New Horizons), Forti staged a wide range of plays and was also the editor of the theatre magazine *Nuevos Horizontes*.

Perhaps the playwright who most effectively represented this movement was Raúl Salmón (1925–90), whose works were staged during the 1950s and into the 1960s by a group calling itself the Social Theatre. Joining with Salmón in this movement were many other playwrights including Carlos Aramayo, Ernesto Vaca Guzmán and Joaquín Gantier Valda, who between them wrote more than twenty folk-based, socially critical, historic and romantic plays.

At long last, popular audiences saw themselves reflected on the stage and were affected by the situations presented, both comedic and dramatic. At the same time, upper-class audiences rejected the Theatre of Social Protest, classifying it as coarse, degrading and vulgar, and refused even to sit in the same theatre with people who could, in fact, be their servants.

One of Salmón's earliest plays was *La calle del pecado* (*Street of Sin*, 1944), which provoked an enormous controversy about the role of art and the appropriateness of street language on the stage. The play remained in the repertoire of the Teatro Municipal for 1,623 performances, not closing until 1949. The play has been regularly remounted somewhere in the country almost every year since its première. The success of this script also made Salmón one of Bolivia's best known personalities and he eventually became mayor of La Paz.

Other significant plays of Salmón's from this Social Protest period include *El canillita* (*The Newsboy*, 1942), *Mi madre fue una chola* (*My Mother Was a Half-Breed*, 1944) and *Sangre indígena* (*Native Blood*, 1944).

The revolution of 1952 put its mark on Bolivia in a way that none of the other 200 revolutions in the country's 175-year history ever had: the nationalization of the mining and oil industries and agrarian reform were just three of the most significant changes to be seen. But eventually political pressure was also felt in the creation of concentration camps and in the uncontrollable devaluation of the Bolivian currency. Hunger strikes and suicides became daily occurrences. During that year, one US dollar was worth 2.5 million Bolivian *pesos*. Banks stopped counting the money and just weighed bags of currency. Children could even be seen using paper *pesos* for making planes and boats.

The country's theatres quickly became political podiums and when the government disagreed with what was said, it routinely persecuted and prosecuted writers and actors. Many more artists were exiled at this time; others fled the country.

Folk art achieved a renewed popularity and artists – out of reasons of safety or on occasion out of its imaginative possibilities – turned to the country's early history. Folk festivals were even promoted by the government in an effort to encourage tourism and the Diablada in Oruro, the Gran Poder (Great Power Festival) in La Paz and the Carnival of Santa Cruz (which begins in January and does not end until March) all found new audiences at this time. Folk plays were even broadcast in the Aymará and Quechua languages.

A number of writers simply found themselves unproduced during the period. One such was Guillermo Francovich (1901–90), who, despite writing nineteen plays, is better known as an essayist and a philosopher than a playwright. Nevertheless, two volumes of his plays were published by Los Amigos del Libro in 1975 and 1983 under the title *Teatro Completo*. Among the few plays of his that have been staged successfully were *El monje de Potosí* (*The Friar of Potosí*, 1954), undoubtedly the best of his works; *Como los gansos* (*Like Geese*, 1957), a play about the life of Bolívar's teacher; *La sombra* (*The Shadow*, 1952); and *Un puñal en el noche* (*Dagger in the Night*, 1953).

By 1960, groups of young theatre artists were finding homes for their work within the country's universities. Their objective was to break away from traditional Spanish forms such as the *costumbrista* (featuring local manners and customs) and to try and create a modern Bolivian theatre that would follow contemporary theatrical and dramatic trends.

The most important Teatro Experimental Universitario in Bolivia was in Santa Cruz. Directed by Jorge Rozsa and Humberto Parada Caro, it staged national and international plays dealing with poverty, hunger and lack of education.

Two government agencies for the support of

the arts were founded in the 1960s – the Instituto Boliviano de Cultura (Bolivian Institute of Culture) in La Paz and the Instituto Boliviano de Arte Teatral (IBART; Bolivian Institute of Theatrical Art) in the city of Cochabamba. Both sought to encourage new writers. Thanks to these agencies – especially to IBART – many new plays were premièred during the 1970s and 1980s. As well, new awards began to be presented: the Julio Travesí Award for Drama for each season's best staging in Cochabamba, the Franz Tamayo Award for the best new play, the Rose Marie Vélez de Canedo Award for actors and the Casa de la Cultura (House of Culture) Award for Dramatic Literature.

New performing arts magazines began to be published as well, such as *Acto* and *Música y Arte* (*Music and Art*). Unfortunately, neither publication lasted very long because of a constant scarcity of funding.

Also during the 1960s and 1970s, a number of new companies appeared, most not lasting very long but all of them attesting to the changing theatrical situation. The most important of these were Teatro Runa, El Juglar (The Minstrel), La Ronda (The Round), Teatro Canata, Bambalinas (Flies) and, still operating in the mid-1990s, the Casa de la Cultura Theatre in Santa Cruz, run by one of the country's most talented directors, René Hohenstein (b. 1954).

Three new playwrights of significance also appeared – Sergio Suárez Figueroa (1924–66), Gastón Suárez (1928–82) and Guido Calabi Abaroa (b. 1935). Suárez Figueroa reflected the wide restlessness of the 1970s. Writing in both a symbolist and surrealist style, he created nearly a dozen plays before his death at the age of 42. A year later, he was posthumously awarded the Jornadas Julianas (Julian Days) Prize for his dramas *El hombre del sombrero de paja* (*Man With the Straw Hat*, 1967) and *La peste negra* (*The Black Plague*, 1967).

Another winner of the Jornadas Julianas Prize was Gastón Suárez, for his plays *Vértigo o el perro vivo* (*Vertigo, or The Live Dog*, 1968) and *La muchacha de Hamburgo* (*The Girl from Hamburg*, 1968), both existential works. *Vértigo* was later produced in both San Francisco and México City.

The works of Calabi Abaroa, for many years an actor in the Cervantes Company, also had surrealist and existentialist tendencies as revealed in many cases by the titles alone: *La nariz* (*The Nose*, 1968), *El diablo se fue al diablo* (*The Devil Went To Hell*, 1969), *Las nalgas* (*The Buttocks*, 1969), *Las piernas* (*The Legs*,

1969), *El vientre* (*The Womb*, 1972) and *El ombligo* (*The Belly Button*, 1978).

In 1972, Bolivian drama received its first international recognition when playwright, poet and novelist Adolfo Costa du Rels (1895–1980) received the prestigious Gulbenkian Award given by the Academy of the Latin World for his drama *Los estandartes del rey* (*The King's Standards*, 1956). In this play, Costa du Rels, a career diplomat and Bolivia's ambassador to the League of Nations and later the United Nations, looks at the question of rebellion and change from within. Based on an historical incident in which Catholic priests were first urged by the church to lead by example by working alongside peasants and factory employees but were later ordered by the church to return to more traditional religious pursuits, the play follows the consequences faced by those priests who refuse to go back to the old ways. The play, translated into Italian (by Ugo Betti), English, Dutch and Polish was subsequently staged in Paris, Brussels and New York.

Costa du Rels's overall output includes five other plays, four novels and poetry, for which he received international awards. The standard work on Costa du Rels was written by Roberto Querejazu Calvo.

It was in the 1970s as well that the long and colourful career of the great actress Rose Marie Vélez de Canedo (d. 1978) came to an end. One of the country's greatest and most committed actresses, her memory was honoured by the creation of an annual series of events in her name – seminars, workshops, forums, courses and studies.

By the end of the 1970s, it was clear that the structures of a professional theatre had been established in Bolivia and that at least some basic government support could be counted on for the promotion of national festivals, open-air theatre events and even the creation of tent theatres in local parks in the major cities of La Paz, Cochabamba and Santa Cruz. Nevertheless, if a true professional theatre is one in which people make their living entirely by working on the stage, Bolivia still did not have one even in the mid-1990s.

Perhaps the closest anyone came to a fully professional company was that of director René Hohenstein in Santa Cruz. In 1985, Hohenstein took over as director of the Otero Reiche Cultural Centre there and began to put on seasons of plays. Unfortunately, not all of his actors could commit themselves fully to the endeavour, still having to make their living by working as

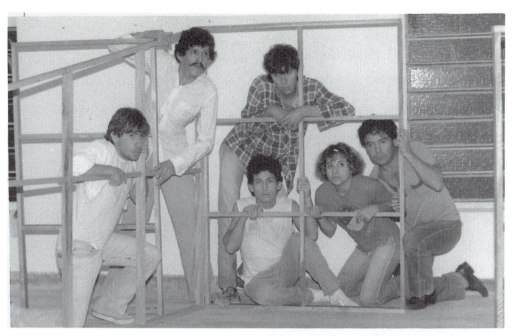

René Hohenstein's 1988 Casateatro production of Oscar Barbery Suárez's *Labyrinths*.

doctors, office clerks, engineers or secretaries. Nevertheless, Hohenstein's work was consistent. Influenced by the ideas of Brecht, many of his productions have focused on concepts of social justice. They have ranged from Dürrenmatt's *The Visit* to Lope de Vega's *Fuenteovejuna* (*The Sheep Well*), from Sartre's version of *Antigone* to García Lorca's *Yerma*.

Hohenstein began as an actor in the city of Cochabamba with La Ronda and Hombres Trabajando (Working Men). Later turning to directing, he staged successful productions of Brecht's *Die Dreigroschenoper* (*The Threepenny Opera*) and *Der gute Mensch von Sezuan* (*The Good Person of Setzuan*). He subsequently committed himself to staging plays by Bolivian writers and achieved particular note with *Laberintos* (*Labyrinths*, 1988) by Oscar Barbery Suárez (b. 1954), which had a sold-out run of some fifty performances and was later seen nation-wide as a television mini-series. His group, known locally as Casateatro, not only is the most active theatre in Santa Cruz but also has been the most active producing company in the country. From 1988 to 1992, Hohenstein also edited seven issues of *Casateatro* (*Theatre House*), the only magazine of its kind in Bolivia.

Several other playwrights of note emerged during the 1980s including Luís Ramiro Beltrán Salmón (b. 1930), a journalist and essayist;

Adolfo Mier Rivas (b. 1939), Raúl Botelho Gosálvez (b. 1917) and Alcira Cardona Torrico (b. 1926). Beltrán Salmón's best known play, *El cofre de selenio* (*The Selenium Chest*), came to public note after winning first prize in a major Ecuadoran playwriting competition in 1987, which Beltrán Salmón entered under the pseudonym Quijote de la Pampa. The play was hailed for its high literary and humanist values and universal themes. Written in an abstract style beyond time and space, the play is a condemnation of dehumanization as created by materialist values as well as a passionate anti-war statement.

Mier Rivas, for his part, has written twenty-two plays. In 1981, his play *Rutuchi* won first prize in the fifteenth National Franz Tamayo Festival. Written in a folkloric style but dealing with existential concerns, the play focuses on drug addiction. Many of his plays tend towards comedy – *El Quijote de la cancha* (*Quixote of the Playing Field*, 1974), *El que mon man* (*He's My Man*, 1977) and *La cigueña* (*The Swan*, 1984) – but he has also written a history play – *La Juana* (1980), which follows the life of the Bolivian heroine of the war of independence, Juana Azurduy de Padilla – and a cabaret, *Santa Cruz* (*Holy Cross*).

Raúl Botelho Gosálvez's first produced play was *Lanza capitana* (1961). Later turning to

René Hohenstein's 1980 production of Adolfo Mier Rivas's *Carrito de Mano*.

Maritza Wilde, born in Perú, began her career as an actress in La Paz and later moved on to study in Lima and Madrid (the Royal Higher School of Drama). A well-known teacher, she has staged more than twenty productions including an award-winning version of García Lorca's *La casa de Bernarda Alba* (*The House of Bernarda Alba*, 1986). She later committed herself to teaching and to theatre administration.

Another director who should be mentioned in this overview is Peter Travesí Canedo (1957–90), creator of the group Tra-La-La in Cochabamba in 1983. By 1989, the company was one of the most active in Bolivia, producing both political satires and folk-rooted dramatic pieces. Travesí's death at the age of 33 cost the Bolivian theatre heavily and the whole nation mourned the loss of this extraordinary artist.

César Brie and his Teatro de los Andes, based in Sucre, incorporate indigenous myths into an authentic Bolivian social theatre. His stagings were seen in 1993 at international theatre festivals in Chile and Brazil.

Mario T. Soria
Translated by Angela Maria Neglia

novels, he moved back to the theatre in 1979 with an adaptation of his novel *Borrachera verde* (*Green Drunkenness*). A powerful drama, it follows the existential struggles of a man determined but unable to control his own destiny.

Cardona Torrico is probably best known as a poet but her verse play *Letanía de las moscas* (*Litany of the Flies*) was a controversial success when it was premièred in 1986. Also influenced by Brechtian concepts, the play is an attack on opportunism and abuse of power.

Two women directors of note emerged in the 1980s – Ninón Dávalos (b. 1948) and Maritza Wilde (b. 1948). Dávalos, trained in Spain and with a successful acting career behind her, returned to her native Bolivia in the 1970s and began teaching acting. She later began staging plays from the modern European and US repertoire which had, for the most part, not been done before in Bolivia. Among these were productions ranging from Ibsen's *Doll's House* to lightweight comedies such as *Cactus Flower*, and even musicals. Her popularity continues into the 1990s.

Further Reading

Alvarez García, Francisco. 'Medio siglo de teatro boliviano'. [Half a century of Bolivian theatre]. *Revista Municipal Khana* 33/34 (July 1959): 327–38.

Díaz Machicago, Porfirio. Foreword to *Antología del teatro boliviano*. [Anthology of Bolivian theatre]. La Paz: Editorial Don Bosco, 1979.

Gómez de Fernández, Dora. 'Notas sobre el teatro boliviano'. [Notes on Bolivian theatre]. *Kollasuyo* 72 (April–June 1970): 97–118.

Muñoz Cadima, Willy Oscar. 'IBART: su historia'. [IBART: Its history]. *Teatro. Revista de Estudios Teatrales* 2 (1992): 157–65.

——. 'Producción dramática boliviana: las dos últimas décadas'. [Bolivian dramatic production: The last two decades]. *Diógenes: Anuario Crítico del Teatro Latinoamericano. 1987*. [Diógenes: Critical annual of Latin American theatre, 1987], vol. 3., ed. Marina Pianca, 31–6. Ottawa: Girol Books, 1988.

——. 'Teatro boliviano: 1990'. [Bolivian theatre: 1990]. *Gestos* 12 (November 1991): 182–9.

——. *Teatro boliviano contemporáneo*. [Contemporary Bolivian theatre]. La Paz: Casa Municipal de la Cultura Franz Tamayo, 1981. 214 pp.

——. 'Teatro boliviano contemporáneo'. [Contemporary Bolivian theatre]. *Revista*

Iberoamericana 52, no. 134 (January–March 1986): 181–94.

——. 'El teatro boliviano en la década de los ochenta'. [Bolivian theatre in the 1980s]. *Latin American Theatre Review* 25, no. 2 (spring 1992): 13–22.

——. 'Teatro boliviano: la última época, 1967–85'. [The last period of Bolivian theatre, 1967–85]. *Bolivia: 1952–86. Los Ensayistas*. Georgia Series on Hispanic Thought, nos. 20–1 (1986): 175–87.

——. 'Teatro de los Andes: en busca de un nuevo teatro boliviano'. [Teatro de los Andes: The search for a new Bolivian theatre]. *Latin American Theatre Review* 27, no. 1 (fall 1993): 23–7.

Soria, Mario T. *Teatro boliviano en el siglo XX*. [Bolivian theatre of the twentieth century]. With a Foreword by Carlos Miguel Suárez Radillo. La Paz: Casa Municipal de la Cultura Franz Tamayo, 1980. 217 pp.

Suárez Radillo, Carlos Miguel. 'El teatro boliviano: de lo histórico a lo humano contemporáneo'. [Bolivian theatre: From historical themes to contemporary human themes]. *Cuadernos Hispanoamericanos*, nos. 263–4 (1972): 339–54.

BRAZIL

The fifth-largest country in the world, Brazil occupies the eastern half of South America and has a common border with every South American country except Ecuador and Chile; it covers an area of 8.5 million square kilometres (3.3 million square miles). The republic also has the largest population base in Latin America with over 156 million inhabitants (1992). The vast Brazilian plateau and the Amazon basin are the country's dominant geographical features. The chief manufacturing industries are centred in São Paulo.

The Portuguese explorer Pedro Alvares Cabral reached Brazil in 1500 and claimed the region for Portugal. With subsequent Portuguese colonization, Brazil became the only country in Latin America where Portuguese became the official language. Brazil's economic expansion was due mainly to the discovery of gold and diamonds and the development of sugar, rubber and coffee industries.

In 1822, Dom Pedro, son of the Portuguese monarch João VI, proclaimed the country's independence and became its first emperor. In 1889, Brazil became a republic.

The most important literary figure of the nineteenth century was Joaquim Maria Machado de Assis (1839–1908), who wrote the acclaimed novel *Dom Casmurro* in 1900. The best known chronicler of Brazilian regional life was Euclydes da Cunha (1868–1909), whose *Os sertões* (*Rebellion in the Backland*, 1902) is still popular in the 1990s.

Brazilian theatre life has always been concentrated in São Paulo and Rio de Janeiro and, though that is slowly changing, it is still so in the 1990s. At the conclusion of each season in São Paulo and Rio, companies will often set off on national tours; audiences are keen on seeing the latest performances by leading actors. In essence, this is a throwback to the nineteenth century when small professional companies led by well-known actor-managers followed seasons in Rio with extended tours to other Brazilian states.

In the nineteenth century, the repertoire was almost exclusively composed of European comedies and, on occasion, docile Brazilian imitations. Plays were produced based on the size of the star role and the degree to which the play served as an escape from daily life. Rehearsals dealt with mechanical rather than creative aspects of performance and actors had to learn roles quickly since productions rarely ran more than a week or two. The modern concept of the director did not exist and designs were generally composed of painted panels or precariously built furniture that changed little from one play to another. This nineteenth- and early twentieth-century Brazilian theatre, intensely conservative and always with an eye on the box office, had room for neither creative anxiety nor discussion of the new concepts that were already beginning to transform both European dramatic literature and staging approaches.

It is significant that when São Paulo held an historic Modern Art Week in 1922 enormous changes quickly began to be felt in the plastic arts, literature and music; the event, however, had virtually no impact in theatre. One of the Modern Art Week's most prominent participants, Oswaldo de Andrade (1890–1954), whose varied literary works included three 'modern' plays, never saw any of his scripts mounted during his lifetime. It was not until 1967, in fact, that attention began to be paid to de Andrade's works following a production that year of his play *O rei da vela* (*The Candle King*), now considered a Brazilian classic.

Musical revues were also extremely popular

in the latter part of the nineteenth century. Supported by complicated backdrops and luxurious costumes, the form had considerable vitality and truly reflected the ostentatious society of its time. Enormous audiences attended the annual *Revista do ano* (*Revue of the Year*), which satirized current events. From an artistic viewpoint, however, the form – created by Artur Azevedo (1855–1908) – was little more than formula writing.

The first stirrings of genuinely modern artistic renewal came from the country's amateurs. One of the pioneers in this regard was the Brazilian diplomat Paschoal Carlos Magno (1906–80), who spent a great deal of his time abroad seeing Europe's 'new' theatre. At the end of the 1930s, he organized a new group called the Teatro do Estudante do Brasil (Brazilian Student Theatre) and began producing seasons of modern and world classics and even a number of Brazilian plays. Subsequently, he organized a series of student theatre festivals in various cities in the country, further strengthening the new national amateur theatre movement.

In São Paulo in 1942, Alfredo Mesquita (1907–86) created the Grupo de Teatro Experimental (Experimental Theatre Group). In 1948, he took a further initiative that led to the creation of the Escola de Arte Dramática (School of Dramatic Art), which turned out many of the country's leading performers in the decades that followed.

It was in 1943 that another Brazilian amateur company, Os Comediantes (The Players), staged the play that is generally agreed to be the starting point for contemporary Brazilian theatre. It was that year that the company, founded in 1939, produced Nelson Rodrigues's (1912–80) classic *Vestido de noiva* (*The Wedding Gown*). The play was notable for its simultaneous use of fragmented narration, setting and action; its parallel levels of understanding (the agonized bride's reality, her memory and her fantasies), the use of stream-of-consciousness for psychological depth and, perhaps most important, the first use on a Brazilian stage of Rio's lower-class slang.

The production was staged by Polish-born director Zbigniew Ziembinski (1908–78) and designed by Tomás Santa Rosa (1909–56). Ziembinski, who had moved to Brazil in 1941, brought an extraordinary range of contemporary European technical and artistic skills with him and ideas of staging far more current than had been seen in Brazil to that time. As one example, Ziembinski and Santa Rosa chose to do scene changes using lighting rather than by creating additional sets. This had never been done before in Brazil. The production as a whole, though seen only three times, had an extraordinary impact on the theatrical imagination and drew enthusiastic critical responses.

Os Comediantes disbanded in 1949 but the artists who created it remained active for many years thereafter. Ziembinski became one of Brazil's leading directors and extended his extraordinary work to Brazilian television. Rodrigues, though perhaps never again finding the magic that made *Vestido de noiva* such a success, wrote an additional sixteen plays before his death and is clearly one of the fathers of contemporary Brazilian dramaturgy.

In 1948, the Teatro Brasileiro de Comédia (TBC; Brazilian Comedy Theatre) was founded in São Paulo. Funded by the Italian-born industrialist Franco Zampari (1898–1966), known primarily for his involvement in the city's social scene, TBC was structured on European models. At the height of its success in the early 1950s, TBC had a company of twenty actors, five directors and a full team of designers and technicians producing a repertoire that included Sophocles, George Bernard Shaw, Arthur Miller, Tennessee Williams and Jean-Paul Sartre. There were lighter works as well but the seriousness of the enterprise and the overall balance were impressive.

Chiefly responsible for the company's depth and solidity was its team of directors – Adolfo Celi (1922–86), Ruggero Jacobbi (1920–81), Luciano Salce (b. 1922), Flaminio Bollini (1924–78) and, later on, Alberto D'Aversa (1920–69) and Gianni Ratto (b. 1916), all of them imported from Italy by Zampari. Ziembinski also joined TBC; some years later, Maurice Vaneau (b. 1926), another key director, arrived from Belgium. Jacobbi and D'Aversa later made additional contributions as theorists, professors and theatre critics. Only Vaneau and Ratto were still working in the Brazilian theatre in the 1990s.

Despite the company's impressive level of production, TBC's concern with European styles and approaches meant that Brazilian dramaturgy and Brazilian issues were being ignored for the most part. It was not until a younger generation of TBC directors came along, most notably Flávio Rangel (1934–88) and José Antunes Filho (b. 1929), that significant and politically aggressive works by Brazilian writers began to be included in TBC's seasons. By that time, however, other groups

61

Flávio Rangel's 1960 Teatro Brasileiro de Comédia production of Dias Gomes's *Payer of Promises*.
Photo: Instituto Brasileiro de Arte e Cultura.

with Brazilian plays higher on their list of priorities had begun to appear. Nevertheless, these early TBC plays were extremely important in developing a national theatrical consciousness. Among key plays in this regard are *A semente* (*The Seed*, 1961) by Gianfrancesco Guarnieri (b. 1934), *O pagador de promessas* (*Payer of Promises*, 1960) by Dias Gomes (b. 1922) and *Vereda da salvação* (*Path to Salvation*, 1964) by Jorge Andrade (1922–84).

If the Teatro Brasileiro de Comédia was not to be known finally for its playwrights, the contributions of its directors as developers of performers particularly made TBC the most fertile artistic company in the history of Brazil's professional theatre. By the time TBC ceased operations in 1964, it had clearly defined a new pattern of professionalism for Brazil's theatre.

In Rio de Janeiro, another TBC-inspired company was begun in 1949, calling itself the Artistas Unidos (United Artists). Headed by the French-born actress and director Henriette Morineau (1907–90), this company had much more modest results than TBC but was equally important in developing professional theatre standards in Rio.

But change was in the air by the mid-1950s and a new national consciousness that impacted tremendously on theatrical life was born. A genuinely Brazilian dramaturgy, rooted in the great social and political national conflicts of the period, was struggling into existence and, along with it, a new generation of Brazilian directors ready to challenge the many European directors who were almost totally controlling the country's theatres.

The first to make war on what was called the 'TBC mentality' was the Teatro de Arena (Arena Theatre) in São Paulo. Created in 1953 by a group of young and politically committed artists, the company quickly became a national centre for resistance, theatrical and otherwise. Relying heavily on the charismatic leadership of its director Augusto Boal (b. 1930) and with the involvement of writers and actors such as Gianfrancesco Guarnieri and Oduvaldo Vianna Filho (1936–74), the Arena quickly established itself as a permanent centre for national dramaturgy, a place where plays using Brazilian behaviour and speech were created and produced. Adding to the theatre's attraction was the arena space itself, which was being explored as an alternative to traditional proscenium staging by Boal and his company.

Writer and director Augusto Boal.
Photo: Instituto Brasileiro de Arte e Cultura.

In 1958, the company produced Guarnieri's *Eles não usam black-tie* (*They Don't Wear Black Tie*), a play that for the first time on a Brazilian stage dealt with the day-to-day problems of workers; in this instance, the issue of strikes. A year later, the Arena staged Vianna Filho's *Chapetuba Futebol Clube* (*Chapetuba Soccer Club*), another workers' play but this time focusing on a small professional soccer team that comes to believe that it has been exploited. Over the next seasons, without abandoning its interest in day-to-day political and economic problems, the Arena also began producing classical plays although always adapting them to Brazilian reality.

The Arena's political and theatrical influence was felt across the country in both large and small cities. The Teatro de Equipe (Theatre Team) from Porto Alegre was but one example of the many groups that quickly picked up the Arena style.

In playwriting too, the Arena was committed to dealing with national political and social issues. Gomes's *O pagador de promessas* dealt with rural mysticism and the inability of rural people to come to grips with crushing external influences. De Andrade's *A moratoria* (*The Moratorium*, 1955) dealt with the collapse of the old coffee plantation aristocracy and the

new consciousness sweeping the country. Ariano Suassuna (b. 1920) was creating in *O auto da compadecida* (*The Ceremony of the Compassionate*, 1956) a new type of regional dramaturgy rooted in the traditions of the northern part of the country blending the mystic and fanciful humour of popular literature with the traditions of Iberian Medieval farce.

During the same period, also in the northeast, Hermilo Borba Filho (1917–76) was experimenting with the possibility of merging the traditions of regional dramaturgy with the alienation effects and epic structure of Bertolt Brecht.

It is probably fair to say that in this period Brazilian dramaturgy experienced more growth than it did in the country's entire previous theatrical history. As well, it managed to attract an enormous new public that gave the new generation of Brazilian-born directors a sense of responsibility to explore national reality in ways that the previous generation of European-born directors simply could not.

As the 1960s began and socio-political conflicts became radicalized, these new theatres moved with them. Groups of actors, some of them members of the Arena company, travelled the country creating a kind of mobile agitprop workers' theatre for the 'exploited'. Two important groups were the Centro Popular de Cultura (Popular Cultural Centre), organized by the Brazilian Communist Party and the National Union of Students with centres in several important cities including Rio de Janeiro, and the Movimento de Cultura Popular (Popular Cultural Movement) in Recife.

Interrupting this extraordinary revolution, however, was a military coup in 1964, which set up a right-wing dictatorship that lasted for the next fifteen years. A repression without precedent in the country's history spread over virtually all cultural activities. Leading theatre people were imprisoned and, in many instances, tortured. Others went into exile. For those who remained active in the country, every attempt to stage a play became a war, the end of which simply could not be guessed at. In some instances, government censors would approve a script in advance and then withdraw the approval just before the play opened. In other instances, plays that had previously been authorized were suddenly closed down. In some cases, approval was simply withheld.

The theatre community reacted to these pressures and provocations in various ways. Often, there were simply individual battles against the

José Renato's 1958 Teatro de Arena production of Gianfrancesco Guarnieri's *They Don't Wear Black Tie*.
Photo: Courtesy of Fernando Peixoto.

Gianni Ratto's 1976 Rio de Janeiro production of Chico Buarque and Paulo Pontes's
Drop of Water.
Photo: Ney Robson.

(b. 1933). Some significant plays followed: *Um grito parado no ar* (*A Cry Suspended in the Air*, 1973) by Guarnieri, staged by Fernando Peixoto (b. 1937); *Gota d'agua* (*Drop of Water*, 1976) by Chico Buarque and Paulo Pontes (1940–76), directed by Gianni Ratto; *Pano de boca* (*Stage Curtain*, 1974) by Fauzi Arap (b. 1938), staged by the author; *Tempo de espera* (*Waiting Period*, 1975), written and directed by Aldo Leite (b. 1941); and *Ponto de partida* (*Point of Departure*, 1976) by Guarnieri, directed by Peixoto. Through these and other works, political protest found its way on to Brazilian stages, trying to overcome censorship and bringing back to the stage a social and political discussion.

In 1974, an ensemble that has lasted into the 1990s began its life in Rio de Janeiro. Calling itself Asdrubal Trouxe o Trombone (Asdrubal Brought the Trumpet), the company began with a corrosively irreverent version of Gogol's *The Government Inspector* that attracted enormous audiences and had particular success with young people. In 1978 in São Paulo, a new company, the Centro de Pesquisa Teatral (Centre for Theatrical Investigation), was organized and launched its international hit *Macunaíma*, a spectacular production staged by José Antunes Filho involving almost every stage technique from athleticism through nudity, dazzling fantasy through sheer visual beauty. The play, based on Mário de Andrade's (1893–1945) famous 1928 novel of the same name, played at festivals across Latin America, the United States and Europe. The play brought both Brazilian dramaturgy and staging on to the international stage and set the tone for continued Brazilian theatre development through the 1980s and in to the 1990s.

Structure of the National Theatre Community

Brazilian theatre organization presents a number of peculiarities that distinguish it both from European and North American models and from models found in other Latin American countries. Many of these differences stem from the sheer size of the country while others are because of the socio-economic and cultural diversity of the various regions of Brazil.

Three basic groupings geographically can be identified. The first is the professionals of Rio de Janeiro and São Paulo. Some 15 per cent of the entire Brazilian population lives in these two cities and the largest portion of the country's gross national product is created there. Theatrically too, most of the country's professional activities can be found there. It might be said that it is only in these two cities that true professional theatre life exists, where artists and technicians can find enough work in theatre, film, television, radio and commercials to create viable careers. As the 1990s began, Rio de Janeiro's Sindicato dos Artistas e Técnicos em Espetáculos de Diversões (Union of Variety Show Artists and Technicians) had about 10,000 members; in São Paulo, the union had roughly the same number.

Around this unionized base in the two cities – a base that spans the profession – there exists another large group of younger professionals who are not yet in the union. These people, many of them very talented, do paid theatre work only part time, and so should probably be called semi-professionals. Generally, they all have to rely on alternative sources of income. Many are recent graduates while others have come from amateur companies, a movement that has become more or less irrelevant in these two major cities.

The second group is made up of semi-professionals in the major regional capitals: Porto Alegre and Curitiba in the south, Belo Horizonte in the centre of the country, and Salvador and Recife in the northeast. In these areas, there are a sizeable number of artists and technicians who work somewhat regularly. Not fully professional, in the sense that they are not able to earn their entire living from theatre, this group is nevertheless active and growing. In the same cities and further into the interior there is also an active amateur movement.

As well, there is a large number of amateurs in those parts of the country where it is rare to find professional or even semi-professional activity. With more than 2,500 amateur companies on record, organization and documentation of their activities is the responsibility of the Ministry of Culture's Fundação Nacional de Artes Cênicas (FUNDACEN; National Foundation of Scenic Arts). This organization is in charge of planning and executing federal policies in the realm of amateur theatre. In 1974, the Confederação Nacional de Teatro Amador (CONFENATA; National Amateur Theatre Confederation) was also formed. It is composed of representatives of twenty-six state amateur theatre federations. The amateur tradition in Brazil is indeed a long one. The oldest continuing theatre organization in the country, in fact, is an amateur group, the Teatro dos Amadores de Pernambuco, founded in 1941.

It is clear from this modest schema that young people interested in careers in theatre have traditionally had to leave the smaller cities to try their theatrical hand in Rio de Janeiro and São Paulo. This has caused continuing problems since there has always been significant general unemployment in the centres. As well, their departure has meant that high-level regional groups often have been unable to maintain even their amateur companies.

To try to help this situation somewhat, a theatrical regulatory law was passed in 1978 requiring all theatre professionals to be graduates of recognized theatrical training institutions. The problem with the law was that the main institutions existed only in Rio and São Paulo and a small number of other regional capitals. So the exodus from local communities continued.

In terms of continuing structures, it is important to note that permanent companies are the exception rather than the rule in Brazil. Privately supported groups did exist in the past, however, and between 1940 and 1960 the federal government actually tried on several occasions to create a national theatre company through subsidization. These attempts included the Comédia Brasileira, the Companhia Dramatica Nacional (National Dramatic Company) and the Teatro Nacional de Comédia (National Comedy Theatre). None, however, was of the hoped-for quality and none survived very long.

Because of these subsidized failures and with a decline in the number of private companies by the 1960s, companies in and of themselves ceased to be the ideal. Independent commercial

mised for the 1980s never really materialized. Dramaturgically, work created in the 1970s was stronger in many ways. Certainly authors working during those years had invented a rich theatrical language and were dealing with powerful themes of survival that never resurfaced to any extent in the 1980s.

The serious economic difficulties that Brazil found itself in during the 1980s also had effects in the theatre. Production costs increased as funds for production investment decreased. The result was greater commercialization and fewer artistic risks.

Perhaps the only new style to emerge during the 1980s was the *besteirol*, a comic revue composed of short sketches commenting on contemporary life. The *besteirol* launched a number of satiric authors including Vicente Pereira (b. 1951) and Mauro Rasi (b. 1949).

A number of playwrights have gained acclaim and popularity since the 1980s, among them Paulo César Coutinho (b. 1947), Mauro Rasi, Luís Alberto Abreu (b. 1952), Maria Adelaide Amaral (b. 1942), Carlos Alberto Sofredini (b. 1939) and particularly Naum Alves de Souza (b. 1942). Through a fascinating trilogy – *No Natal a gente vem te buscar* (*We'll Get You at Christmas*, 1979), *A aurora de minha vida* (*The Dawn of My Life*, 1982) and *Um beijo, um abraço, um aperto de mão* (*A Kiss, a Hug, a Handshake*, 1984) – Alves de Souza challenged his middle-class religious upbringing.

A number of promising writers from the earlier generations died young: Vianna Filho at the age of 38, Paulo Pontes at 36 and Armando Costa at 41.

During this same period, a curious new category of serious author also emerged, that of the 'unproduced, unpublished prizewinner'. Included here are writers such as Wilson Sayão (b. 1949) and Ricardo Meirelles (b. 1947), writers who have lived on prizes from national and regional playwriting contests but whose plays are not considered commercially viable by potential producers. Clearly these are writers of talent but writers who continue virtually unknown to the general public.

Instead of staging original plays during the 1980s, many producing groups turned to adaptations of novels as safer choices; *Macunaíma*, based on de Andrade's 1928 novel, is the most successful example. Also popular were stage adaptations of works by Guimaraes Rosa (1908–67), most notably *A hora e a vez de Augusto Matraga* (*The Time and Turn of Augusto Matraga*, 1986), directed by Antunes Filho.

Directors, Directing and Production Styles

Rather than a theatre of playwrights, the Brazilian theatre through the 1980s and early 1990s has become a director's theatre, with the text itself a catalyst rather than the controlling force in the overall theatrical experience. Performers are often used as elements of a silent, living sculpture. The names most often heard in describing this work are international and include the Pole Tadeusz Kantor, Robert Wilson from the United States, the German Pina Bausch and Kazuo Ono from Japan.

Perhaps the leading Brazilian director of the period is Antunes Filho, director of Centro de Pesquisa Teatral (Centre for Theatrical Investigation), who followed his spectacular *Macunaíma* (1978) with *Nelson no. 2 Rodrigues* (1982), a Jungian interpretation of a number of pieces by Rodrigues; *Romeo and Juliet* (1984); *A hora e a vez de Augusto Matraga* (1986); and *Xica da Silva* (1988) by Luís Alberto Abreu. Later he did a powerful *Macbeth* (1992) and a new version of de Andrade's *Vereda da salvação* (1994). Working predominantly with youthful casts and with music and elaborate choreography, Antunes Filho tends to create a living scenography with his actors, in effect a profound portrait of Brazil's people and their lives. His productions are known for both their extreme visual beauty and their symbolic richness.

Bia Lessa (b. 1952) began her career as an actress working most often with Antunes Filho and she was deeply influenced by his ideas. As a director, she too tends to work with young casts and has made her reputation on the basis of five productions in particular – *O pintor* (*The Painter*, 1985), *Ideias e repetições* (*Ideas and Repetitions*, 1986), *Exercício no. 1* (*Exercise Number One*, 1987), a stage adaptation of Dostoevsky's *The Possessed* (1987), and *Orlando* (1992), inspired by Virginia Woolf.

In Lessa's work, inanimate objects play an obsessive role, abstract ideas parade before us in a kind of free association and traditional narrative disappears. Lessa has also conducted regular workshops, and a number of directors who had studied with her later came to prominence.

Gerald Thomas (b. 1954), a director first trained in Europe and the United States, began his career as a visual artist. His first theatrical creation in Brazil was in 1985, *Four Times Beckett*, a production that suggested a theatre of

Antunes Filho's 1978 Centro de Pesquisa Teatral production of *Macunaíma*.
Photo: Derli Barroso.

pure form, a theatrical equivalent of music or abstract art. Thomas continued developing this style with his subsequent productions: Heiner Müller's *Quartett* (1986), two of his own scripts – *Carmen com filtro* (*Carmen With Filter*, 1986) and *Electra com Creta* (*Electra With Crete*, 1986) – a trilogy of Kafka pieces – *O Processo* (*The Trial*), *A Metamorfose* (*Metamorphosis*) and *Praga* (*Prague*) – in 1988 and his own *Flash and Crash Days* (1992). He has also staged a controversial production of Wagner's *The Flying Dutchman* (1987).

Thomas's work depends heavily on living images. In creating them he is greatly assisted both by his skill as a lighting designer and by the scenographer Daniela Thomas (b. 1959). Most of his productions also have sound scores not directly tied to the texts but with their own significance. Thomas works with formally trained actors, a choice that contributes to the precision and quality of his productions.

Among the younger directors, Cacá Rosset (b. 1954), director of the São Paulo group Teatro do Ornitorrinco, had major successes with his acrobatic productions of Alfred Jarry's *Ubu Roi* (1985), the Spaniard Albert Boadella's *Teledeum* (1987) and Shakespeare's *A Midsummer Night's Dream* (1991). Ulysses Cruz (b. 1952), another who started his career in Antunes Filho's Centro de Pesquisa, created his own group in 1985, O Boi Voador (The Flying Bull). Cruz works on an epic scale and has achieved great success with his productions of *Os velhos marinheiros* (*The Old Sailors*, 1985), Frank Wedekind's *Spring's Awakening* (1986), Mauro Rasi's *A ceremonia de adeus* (*The Farewell Ceremony*, 1988) and *Macbeth* (1992).

Most of the aforementioned directors were working with small but permanent groups as the 1990s began, a privileged position in the Brazilian theatre. Among major freelance directors, one should mention Marco Aurélio (b. 1948), who directed Heiner Müller's *Hamletmaschine* in 1988 and who, in his production *O pássaro do poente* (*Sunset Bird*, 1987) by Carlos Alberto Sofredini with the Grupo Ponkã, combined techniques of traditional Brazilian comedy with approaches taken from Oriental theatre, and *Der zerbrochene Krug* (*The Broken Jug*, 1993) by Heinrich von Kleist. Also important are José Possi Neto (b. 1947), who uses dance as a background against which he juxtaposes traditional scripts; and Luís Antonio Martínez Corrêa (1950–87) who, until his tragic death, was exploring the rich musical history of Brazil's revues, burlesques and operettas of the last century, particularly in his productions *Teatro musical Brasileiro no. 1* and *no. 2* (*Brazilian Music Theatre No. 1*, 1985, and *No. 2*, 1987).

Among those who should be mentioned from the 1960s and 1970s are Celso Nunes (b. 1941), an unorthodox Grotowskian; Hamilton Vaz Pereira (b. 1951), director of the Asdrubal Trouxe o Trombone through the 1970s, who used rock music and video as the base for much of his theatre; and José Renato (b. 1926), first director of the Teatro de Arena in the 1950s and later a successful director of commercial comedies. Still working and directing in the mid-1990s were noted directors Antonio Abujamra (b. 1932), Ivan de Albuquerque, Fernando Peixoto, João das Neves and Gianni Ratto.

Music Theatre

Music, from revues to rock, has long been a part of the Brazilian theatre. But the question of whether a true Brazilian music theatre exists is one that is still being asked.

There is, of course, traditional opera production especially in Rio de Janeiro and São Paulo. There are operas written and created by Brazilian composers, but most are in the Italian tradition even when dealing with Brazilian or indigenous subject matter. The most important Brazilian opera composer, Carlos Gomes (1836–86), presented in 1861 his masterpiece, *A noite de castelo* (*A Night in the Castle*), a powerful dramatic musical work. Carlos Gomes was sent by Emperor Peter II to Milan and it was there that he composed his best works: *O Guaraní* (1868), on an indigenous theme and with music inspired by Verdi; *Tosca* (1873); *Salvator Rosa* (1874) and *María Tudor* (1879). Finally, in 1880, Gomes returned to Brazil, where he presented *Lo schiavo* (*The Slave*, 1889), which reflected the writer's abolitionist sentiments and presented a very national issue, sung in Italian.

Cuban writer Alejo Carpentier has often called attention to the contradictions of having national subject matter presented in foreign musical styles, produced in imitation of Italian opera's vocal and instrumental treatments. One of the few Brazilian composers who consciously attempted to break the European mould in the field was Heitor Villa-Lobos (1887–1959). He led the way in the search for an expressive and rich national musical language for the theatre. It must be added, however, that his incursions into music theatre were few and far between. His most famous experiment was with Federico García Lorca's play *Yerma* in 1956. Unfortunately, it was not staged until 1971, twelve years after Villa-Lobos's death, when a production was finally mounted in the United States.

Other composers who have tried their hand with some success in musical theatre forms include Francisco Mignone (1897–1987) and Camargo Guarnieri (b. 1907).

In the area of opera staging, a number of Brazil's leading directors have experimented successfully. Among them are Celso Nunes, Sergio Britto (b. 1923), Antunes Filho, Adhemar Guerra (1933–93), Silney Siqueira (b. 1934) and Gerald Thomas. Fernando Peixoto is credited with the first staging in Brazil of Alban Berg's *Wozzeck* (1982).

A number of younger composers entered the field in the 1980s and 1990s. Among them are Jorge Antunes, who takes a socio-political approach in rebellious works such as *Qorpo Santo*, staged in Brasilia in 1983; Lívio Tragtenberg (b. 1961), who has connected to the innovative poetry of Souzandrade to compose such works as *O inferno de Wall Street* (*The Wall Street Inferno*, 1982); and Cláudio Santoro (1919–89), who wrote his first opera in 1984 – *Alma*, based on the first part of a trilogy of novels by Oswald de Andrade.

Yan Michalski, Fernando Peixoto

Augusto Boal's 1965 Teatro de Arena production of his and Gianfrancesco Guarnieri's *Arena Tells Zumbi's Story*, music by Edú Lobo.
Photo: Instituto Brasileiro de Artes e Cultura.

Dance Theatre

In Brazil, the history of a theatre of dance as an autonomous art form is quite recent. Only in the 1930s did schools and dance groups begin to spring up, created by ballet dancers and scenographers who had received their training with foreign companies that had staged productions in Rio de Janeiro or São Paulo, often organizing lyrical seasons.

In 1936, from the school of Maria Oleneva (1896–1965) emerged the Balé do Teatro Municipal do Rio de Janeiro (Ballet of the Municipal Theatre of Rio de Janeiro), the first state dance company and the one that would prove most prolific. Since its creation the company has produced outstanding seasons that included choreography by, among others, Eugenia Feodorova (b. 1926), Maryla Gremo (1908–85), Vaslav Veltchek (1896–1947), Igor Chvezov (1904–82), Nina Verchinina (b.

1912), Oscar Araiz (b. 1940), Tatiana Leskova (b. 1922) and Dalal Achcar (b. 1937). The final two, during their stints at the company, also exercised control over artistic direction. Guest performers have included Margot Fonteyn and Rudolf Nureyev.

From the Balé da Teatro Municipal do Rio de Janeiro, until then the only state company, came, in 1944, the Conjunto Coreográfico Brasileiro (Brazilian Choreography Group), which has made the most impressive contributions to dance in Brazil. The group had as choreographer, professor and director Vaslav Veltchek. In 1946 the Balé da Juventude (Youth Ballet) was created and directed by Igor Chvezov and operated under the auspices of the União Nacional dos Estudantes (National Students' Union).

In 1946 Nina Verchinina arrived in Brazil

and, as *maestra* and choreographer of the Balé do Teatro Municipal, introduced modern dance, the techniques of Rudolph Laban and the exercises of *barre-au-sol*. In 1954 Verchinina organized her own academy, the Ballet Nina Verchinina. Still in the 1950s, contributing significantly to the maturation of dance in Brazil, the Balé do IV Centenario was created (1953). The company, financed by a group of business people from São Paulo to celebrate the fourth centenary of the city, was directed by the choreographer Aureliano von Millos (1906–88), known for his work in Hungary and Italy. Also contributing substantially to the area of dance was the creation of the Associado de Balé do Rio de Janeiro in 1954 by Dalal Achcar. The list continues with the emergence of Balé Klauss Vianna, founded in Belo Horizonte by Angel (b. 1928) and Klauss (1928–92) Vianna, who also introduced the work of physical expression for actors to Brazil. The Fundação Brasileira de Balé (Brazilian Ballet Foundation) was founded in 1961 by Eugenia Feodorova. The Cia Nacional de Balé (National Ballet Company) was created under the guidance of Murilo Miranda with funds from the Conselho Nacional de Cultura (National Cultural Council) in 1967. The Cia Brasileira de Balé (Brazilian Ballet Company, 1967–9) was sponsored by the shipbuilder Paulo Ferraz, and the Balé da Aldeia (Village Ballet) was founded by Gerry Maretzi (b. 1934) and Mauro Fonseca (b. 1933) with financial support from the diplomat Paschoal Carlos Magno.

Other state dance companies in Brazil include the Balé Teatro Guaira (1969) in Paraná, which has had as directors Cemi Jambay (b. 1934), Yurek Chabelewski (b. 1911) and Carlos Trincheras (1937–92); the Balé de Cidade de São Paulo (São Paulo City Ballet, 1968), directed by, among others, Johnny Franklin, Antonio Carlos Cardoso (b. 1939) and Luiz Arietta (b. 1952); the Balé da Fundação Clovis Salgado (Clovis Salgado Foundation Ballet) from Minas Gerais, which developed out of the school of Carlos Leite (b. 1917); and the Balé da Fundação Castro Alves (Castro Alves Foundation Ballet, 1972) of Bahia, which has been directed by Carlos Moraes (b. 1936) and Victor Navarro (b. 1944).

The world-wide popularization of dance has also been felt in Brazil. Among the many groups to have sprung up, the most interesting has been the Grupo Corpo (Body Group) created in 1975 in Belo Horizonte under the direction of Emilio Khalil (b. 1931). The personal style of the choreographer Rodrigo Pederneiras (b. 1945) and the quality of the cast have guaranteed the company considerable success both in Brazil and abroad. From their repertoire of almost two dozen ballets, important productions include *Préludios* (1985), using Chopin's *24 Preludes op. 88*; *Canções* (*Songs*, 1982), to the music of Richard Strauss; *Missa do orfanato* (*Orphan Mass*, 1989), based on Mozart's *Mass K 139* – all creations of Rodrigo Pederneiras – and *Mulheres* (*Women*, 1988), with choreography by Suzanne Link. By 1990 Grupo Corpo had achieved a structure and organization previously unheard of in Brazil. The company went on to consolidate a position of singular importance and privilege in the panorama of Brazilian national dance.

Other groups that rose to prominence in the 1970s and 1980s, with repertoires of basically modern dance, occasionally combining classical, contemporary and jazz dance, are Atores Bailarinos do Rio de Janeiro (Actors and Dancers of Rio de Janeiro, 1979), directed by Regina Miranda (b. 1948); Balé do Terceiro Mundo (Ballet of the Third World, 1983), directed by Ciro Barcellos (b. 1953); Ballet Stagium (1971), directed by Marika Gidali (b. 1937) and Décio Otero (b. 1936); Grupo de Dança Cisne Negro (Black Swan Dance Group, 1978), directed by Hulda Bittencourt (b. 1934); Studio Lourdes Bastos (1980); Nós da Dança (We of the Dance), directed by Regina Sauer (b. 1940); Vacilou; and Grupo Coringa, directed by Graciela Figuerosa (b. 1944).

The only school of dance that can be considered of high quality in Brazil belongs to the Universidade da Bahia. The school was created in 1956 under the directorship of Yanka Rudzka (b. 1919), who remained in charge until 1959, when she was succeeded by Rolf Gelewski (1930–88). Most groups possess their own academies where the majority of their members are trained. To complete their education Brazilian dancers try to find schools or traineeships abroad. The profession has been regulated since 1978 but the job market for dancers in Brazil is still very small. Television regularly employs dancers, especially those with modern dance training, but there is still no programme on Brazilian television that is totally dedicated to dance.

Susana Macedo

Theatre for Young Audiences

Brazilian theatre professionals are not able to live from children's theatre alone since it normally plays only two days a week. But it does offer young actors and directors an important opportunity to gain entrance into the profession.

It was in 1948 that Brazil's first children's theatre event took place, the opening of Lúcia Benedetti's *O casaco encantado* (*The Enchanted Coat*). It was produced by the Artistas Unidos, headed at that time by the French-born actress Henrietta Morineau, one of the major stars of the Brazilian theatre. The production was so popular that the group had to pull one of its adult productions from its schedule so the children's show could be seen in the evenings as well. *O casaco encantado* later toured throughout Brazil and was subsequently translated into several other languages.

In the same year, another children's production had almost equal success – *A revolta dos brinquedos* (*Revolt of the Toys*) written by Pernambuco de Oliveira (1922–83), a scenographer who, as dramatist, restricted himself to children's plays.

The Teatro Escola de São Paulo (São Paulo School Theatre) was launched in 1948 and toured in virtually every section of the city. Under local and municipal sponsorship, the group produced consistently and successfully for the next three years. In 1951 the company turned its energies to the newly developing art of children's theatre on television. This too had enormous impact on spreading the form's popularity even more widely; the company's television run lasted thirteen years.

Perhaps Brazil's most famous theatre for young audiences is Maria Clara Machado's (b. 1921) Teatro Tablado. Machado launched the company in 1951 to produce adult theatre. But its major success began in 1953 when the company produced Machado's own play for children *O boi e o burro a caminho de Belém* (*The Bull and the Donkey on the Road to Bethlehem*). Machado, trained in France in puppet theatre, gradually moved the company out of adult theatre and exclusively into children's production, where it remains in the 1990s as a model of excellence in this genre. Machado herself quickly became one of the highest profile theatre personalities in the country and wrote and directed some two dozen other plays for children. These ranged from adaptations of children's classics such as *Little Red Riding Hood* to originals such as *O rapto das cebolinhas* (*The Kidnapping of the Onions*, 1954), *Pluft, a fantasminha* (*Pluft, the Little Phantom*, 1955) and *O cavalinho azul* (*The Little Blue Horse*, 1960). The latter two are now considered national classics in the field and are still among the most performed Brazilian children's plays.

As the 1990s began, Teatro Tablado was still in operation not only producing plays but also offering courses to children. From these courses have come many students who have gone on to professional careers in the theatre as actors, directors, designers, technicians and critics.

In 1974, another major children's group was added to the fold, Grupo Ventoforte (Strong Wind) founded by Argentine-born Ilo Krugli (b. 1936). The company's first major production, *Historias de lenços e ventos* (*Stories of Handkerchiefs and Winds*), was the hit of the 1974 Children's Theatre Festival in Curitiba and, following its success there, the company established itself in Rio de Janeiro and later in São Paulo where the group still performs. This company too has done regular theatre workshops for children and has had a major influence on a whole generation of young theatre people in such areas as music, dance, puppets and animated objects.

Among the offshoots of Grupo Ventoforte were the Grupo Ombu, founded in 1977 and known for its productions involving native legends, collective creations and pieces based on poetry; and the Grupo Navegando (Navigation), directed by Lúcia Coelho (b. 1936), with its spectacular scenic effects, music and the integration of movement, light, sound and live actors with puppets. All of its productions have been under the co-authorship of Coelho and Caique Botkay (b. 1951). One must also mention the unique work in the children's field of Tonio de Carvalho (b. 1944), who bases his approach on Brazilian popular art forms.

Grupo TAPA was launched professionally in 1979 with a play by Eduardo Tolentino (b. 1954), the company's founder. TAPA, which also presents adult performances, is realistic in its work and has been influenced by the German children's company Grips-Theater.

In the 1980s, a number of groups also began offering plays specifically for adolescents. A leader in this field was director Carlos Wilson

Calvo. Calvo's theatrical projects used the talents of the greatest names in Brazilian painting – Candido Portinari (1903–62), Lasar Segall (1891–1957) and Heitor dos Prazeres (1898–1966).

Still in the 1950s, the nationalist movement, initiated by the Teatro de Arena in São Paulo, although intent on exploring the organization of stage space, did not favour set, prop and costume design, perhaps because of the lack of material resources. In the same period, the Teatro Oficina was creating works of powerful visual force and aesthetic refinement, including *In the Jungle of the Cities* by Bertolt Brecht, staged by Lina Bo Bardi (1914–92), and *O rei de vela* by Oswaldo de Andrade, the imagery of which, created by Hélio Eichbauer (b. 1941), was characterized by a tropical aesthetic that would later be reflected and developed in music, the plastic arts and poetry.

Some of the most important and active scenographers of the time worked with the Teatro Oficina: Marcos Flaksman (b. 1944), Napoleão Moniz Freire (1928–71), Anisio Medeiros (b. 1922), Joel de Carvalho (1930–74) and Flávio Império (1935–85).

Beginning in the 1960s and 1970s Italian stage traditions in Brazil began to be challenged through works that proposed alternative forms of stage space or new ways of using traditional space on stage. In Genet's *Le Balcon* (*The Balcony*, 1969), directed by the Argentine Víctor García, there appeared a great metallic tower in the form of a funnel; the action of the play took place in its interior. The audience sat on benches constructed as a spiral on the outer walls of the funnel. *Missa Leiga* (1972) by Chico de Assis (b. 1933) was presented in an old factory with sets designed by Joel de Carvalho. *A viagem* (*The Voyage*, 1972), adapted by Carlos Queiroz Telles (1936–93), from a book by Os Lusiadas, and directed by Celso Nunes, had a set, designed by Hélio Eichbauer, that forced the public to travel throughout the theatre following the action as the actors moved from the basement through the building and finally out on to the street. The action in *Dantons Tod* (*Danton's Death*, 1977) by Georg Büchner, directed by Aderbal Freire Filho (b. 1941), took place in the subterranean space of a subway still under construction.

Other productions of this period caused a considerable impact due, in part, to the interesting sets developed for them, productions such as *O ensaio selvagem* (*The Savage Attempt*, 1974) by José Vicente, with set designs

by Eichbauer, *Os convalescentes* (*The Convalescents*, 1970) by Vicente and *Pano de boca* (*Stage Curtain*) by Fauzi Arap, both with sets by Marcos Flaksman; and *Dorotéia vai á guerra* (*Dorothy Goes to War*, 1972) by Carlos Alberto Ratton (b. 1943) and *Hoje é dia de Rock* (1971) by Vicente, both with sets by Luis Carlos Ripper. Stanisław Witkiewicz's *The Mother* (1971), directed by Claude Régy of France, was particularly fascinating for the magnificent architecture of the sets created by Joel de Carvalho. Also important were *O último carro* (*The Last Carriage*, 1976), written and directed by João das Neves with sets designed by Germano Blum; and Peter Shaffer's *Equus*, directed by Celso Nunes with sets by Flaksman and lighting by Jorginho de Carvalho, who began to give the work of lighting designers a new distinction.

In the 1980s styles became marked by an essentially sculptured vision. In this, one finds the works of, among others, Antunes Filho, Bia Lessa and Gerald Thomas. Having begun to work at the TBC in the 1950s, Antunes Filho premièred his masterpiece, *Macunaíma*, in 1978. Adapted from the novel by Mário de Andrade, the work was staged with the help of the powerfully expressive visual environment of Naum Alves de Souza. In the works that followed *Macunaíma* Antunes Filho developed a line of stage composition of extreme visual beauty and a richness of symbolism in which the actors, through elaborate movements, compose a kind of living scenography in the production.

On shows directed by Bia Lessa the visual environment, the use of objects and the occupation of space were so closely associated with the concept of the script that it became difficult to imagine these plays being mounted by anyone other than Lessa, whose ideas have been implemented with great sensitivity by the scenographer Fernando Mello de Costa (b. 1950).

Television and the annual parades by the *escolas de samba* (schools of *samba*) allow scenographers to make their livings when they are not employed in the theatre. Some designers, such as Fernando Pamplona (b. 1926) and Arlindo Rodrigues (1931–87), became *carnavalescos* (carnivalesque) famous for their creativity in the development of stage props, models and the allegorical floats for carnival parades.

Courses specifically for the training of scenographers do not exist in Brazil; the majority of designers, in fact, come from the fields of architecture or visual art.

Susana Macedo

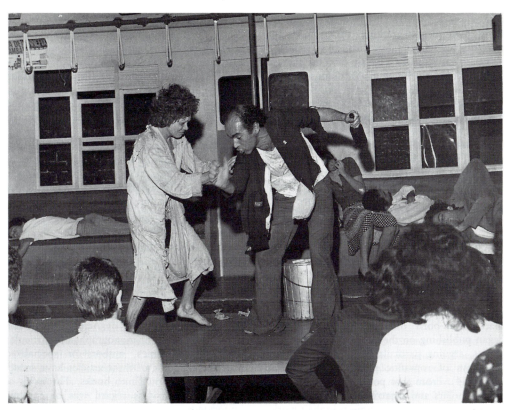

João das Neves's 1976 Grupo Teatro Opinião production of his *The Last Carriage*, designed by Germano Blum.
Photo: Ney Robson.

Training

In 1978, a law regulating the admission of actors and designers into the theatre profession was passed in Brazil; it gave new importance to the country's schools which, to that time, had had a rather chequered history.

The oldest of Brazil's theatre schools is the Escola de Teatro Martins Pena (Martins Pena Theatre School) in Rio de Janeiro, founded in 1911, and supported throughout most of its history by the government and therefore subject to the usual bureaucratic problems of government involvement and lack of sufficient resources. The school essentially focuses on actor training and offers its courses free of charge. The majority of its students come from low-income families living some distance from the school itself.

The Conservatório Nacional de Teatro (National Theatre Conservatory) is an autonomous theatre school based at the University of Rio de Janeiro since 1940. Supported by the federal government, this programme was modelled on the Conservatoire de Paris. In 1978, the Conservatório Nacional became part of the university, its facilities substantially modernized, and its programmes restructured to offer courses in performance, directing, design and theatre theory.

The school that has contributed most to the contemporary Brazilian theatre is the Escola de Arte Dramática de São Paulo (São Paulo School of Dramatic Art). Founded as a private school in 1948 by the writer and critic Alfredo Mesquita, the school was eventually incorporated into the University of São Paulo as a non-degree programme. It has a wide-ranging and complex

São Paulo]. São Paulo: Brasiliense, 1984. 100 pp.

——. *Panorama do teatro brasileiro*. [Overview of Brazilian theatre]. São Paulo: Difusão Européia do Livro, 1962. 276 pp.

Michalski, Yan. *O palco amordaçado*. [A gagged audience]. Rio de Janeiro: Avenir, 1979. 96 pp.

——. *O teatro sob pressão: uma frente de resistência*. [Theatre under oppression: A front of resistance]. Rio de Janeiro: Jorge Hazar, 1985. 96 pp.

——, and Rosyanne Trotta. *Teatro e estado: as companhias oficiais de teatro no Brasil*. [Theatre and state: Brazil's official theatre companies]. São Paulo: Editora Hucitec/IBAC, 1992. 262 pp.

Mostaço, Edelcio. *Teatro e política: Arena, Oficina e Opinião*. [Theatre and politics: Arena, Oficina and Opinião]. São Paulo: Proposta, 1982. 196 pp.

Peixoto, Fernando. *O melhor teatro do CPC da UNE*. [The best of theatre from the CPC (Centre of Popular Culture) of the UNE (National Union of Students)]. São Paulo: Global Editora, 1989. 317 pp.

——. *Teatro em movimento*. [Theatre in movement]. São Paulo: Editora Hucitec, 1985. 244 pp.

——. *Teatro em pedaços*. [Theatre in pieces]. São Paulo: Editora Hucitec, 1980. 362 pp.

——. *Teatro em questão*. [Theatre in question]. São Paulo: Editora Hucitec, 1989. 263 pp.

——. *Teatro Oficina 1958–82: trajetória de uma rebeldia cultural*. [Teatro Oficina 1958–82: A path of cultural rebellion]. São Paulo: Brasiliense, 1982. 126 pp.

Rela, Walter. *El teatro brasileño*. [Brazilian theatre]. Montevideo: Instituto de Cultura Uruguayo-Brasileño, 1980. 142 pp.

Rosenfeld, Anatol. *O mito e o herói no moderno teatro brasileiro*. [On myths and heroes in modern Brazilian theatre]. São Paulo: Perspectiva, 1982. 122 pp.

Roux, Richard. *Le Théâtre Arena, São Paulo, 1953–1977. Du 'théâtre en rond' au 'théâtre populaire'*. [Teatro de Arena, São Paulo, 1953–77. From theatre-in-the-round to popular theatre]. 2 vols. Aix-en-Provence: Université de Provence, 1991.

Schoenbach, Peter Julian. *Modern Brazilian Theatre: Art and Document*. New Jersey, 1973.

'Teatro e realidade brasileira'. [Theatre and reality in Brazil]. *Revista civilição brasileira* 2, special issue (1968). 286 pp.

Vianna Filho, Oduvaldo. *Vianinha: teatro, televisão, política*. [Vianinha: Theatre, television, and politics]. With selection, organization and notes by Fernando Peixoto. São Paulo: Brasiliense, 1983. 224 pp.

Vieira, César. *Em busca de um teatro popular*. [In search of popular theatre]. Santos: Confenata, 1981. 250 pp.

CANADA

The second largest country in the world – only Russia is larger – with a land mass of some 10 million square kilometres (3.9 million square miles), Canada extends from the Atlantic to the Pacific Ocean sharing a 6,400-kilometre (4,000 mile) border with the United States to the south. Despite this great land mass, 89 per cent of which is virtually unsettled, 80 per cent of the country's relatively small population (29.5 million in 1995) live in urban centres within 160 kilometres of the US border.

With only slightly more than one-tenth of the population of the US and with the majority speaking English as well, this close proximity has made it difficult for Canada to resist US economic, cultural and political influences for the past two centuries. A member of the Group of Seven (G-7) industrial nations, 80 per cent of Canada's trade is with the US; it is also the US's largest trading partner. As such, US companies have extensive investments in almost all sectors of the Canadian economy.

Because of its rich resources, Canada, like the Caribbean islands and the American colonies, was fiercely fought over by European colonial powers. During the Seven Years' War (1756–63) between Britain and France, British forces captured Québec City and Montréal in 1759 and 1760. Through the Treaty of Paris in 1763, Canada with its indigenous native peoples was transformed from a French colony of 60,000–70,000 French-speaking inhabitants to a British possession. Political and cultural conflict among these three founding peoples has been part of Canadian life ever since.

As a result of the American Revolution (1775–83), approximately 50,000 Americans who wished to remain loyal to Britain moved to Canada, giving the country a greater British character. Partly in reaction to US expansionist sentiments following the US Civil War (1861–5), the British Parliament passed the British North America Act in 1867, which united Ontario, Québec, Nova Scotia and New Brunswick into the Dominion of Canada. Manitoba joined this confederation in 1870, British Columbia in 1871, Prince Edward Island in 1873, Saskatchewan and Alberta in 1905 and Newfoundland in 1949. Each province elects its own provincial parliament while the country as a whole elects a federal parliament in Ottawa. Several major responsibilities, such as culture, education and employment training, are shared by both levels of government.

Theatrical performances in English and French Canada can be traced to the beginnings of these two European colonies at the end of the 1500s and early 1600s. When the English explorer Sir Humphrey Gilbert claimed Newfoundland for Elizabeth I in 1583, his expedition included musicians, mummers and Morris dancers brought to entertain the North American Indians. In 1606 the Parisian lawyer Marc Lescarbot (1570–1642), then based in Acadia (present-day Nova Scotia), created the first play to be written and performed in the French colony – the nautical masque *Le Théâtre de Neptune en la Nouvelle France* (*The Theatre of Neptune in New France*). It included native Indian characters who humbly submitted to the French colonists.

In fact, Canada's native peoples, both Indian and Inuit, had already developed their own rituals and ceremonies millennia before the arrival of European explorers and colonists. These included Inuit and American Indian death and resurrection spirit plays and paratheatrical rituals and ceremonies. Among these were Micmac marriage and funeral events, the Ojibwa War Dance, the Cree Shaking Tent ceremony, Iroquois healing rituals, the Kwak-iutl potlatch, Coast Salish spirit dances and Tlingit shamanic displays. The theatrically most developed of these rituals occurred among the Pacific Northwest Coast Indians, particularly in the Mystery Cycles of the Nootka and southern Kwakiutl tribes. Most of these rituals and ceremonies and particularly their spirituality were suppressed by the European colonists. Some have been revived by native communities in the last decades of the twentieth century, however, and adapted into modern forms by aboriginal theatre companies.

The French and English European theatrical traditions of the settlers developed along essentially separate linguistic and cultural paths as well. Until the 1930s, even in cities such as Montréal with both French and English populations, only limited contact existed between the two theatre cultures. With the exception of Gratien Gélinas's (b. 1909) dramas in the 1950s and 1960s, it was, in fact, only in the early 1970s that works of Québécois playwrights such as Michel Tremblay (b. 1942) began to be more frequently translated from French and published

and performed in English Canada. Québec theatre companies began on occasion to perform English-Canadian playwrights in French translation only in the 1980s. To explain this historical and cultural divergence, one must examine the French and English traditions separately.

In Québec in the 1600s and 1700s, theatrical presentations were an activity for the elite largely confined to the reciting of didactic religious texts in the Jesuit colleges and Ursuline schools and convents and to *entrées* (welcoming receptions) for French governors and other religious and civil dignitaries in the colonial capital, Québec City. On a few occasions, in 1651, 1652 and the winter of 1693–4, the French gentry produced works by Corneille and Racine for the elite society of the colonial capital. But even the French governor Frontenac had to cancel a planned production of Molière's *Tartuffe* in 1694 because of fierce opposition from the Catholic church to the perceived blasphemy of Molière's text and to live theatre, dancing and other entertainments in general. Molière was not produced in French again in Québec until

The 1972 touring production of 'Ksan, spirit plays and dances by the Tsimshian 'Ksan people near Hazelton, British Columbia.
Photo: Canadian Museum of Civilization.

1774 when officers of the English garrison in Montréal staged two of his comedies.

With the virtual absence of a strong live theatre tradition and an economic basis for theatre production in Québec, there was little encouragement for the development of indigenous theatre artists and playwrights. One of the few who attempted to create cultural activity in the colony was the French immigrant merchant Joseph Quesnel (1746–1809). A poet, composer, actor and dramatist, Quesnel was one of the founders of the short-lived Théâtre de Société (Society Theatre) in Montréal in 1789, which staged his pastoral comedy *Colas et Colinette ou Le Bailli dupé* (*Colas and Colinette or The Bailiff Confounded*) the following year.

The first significant Québec-born dramatist was Antoine Gérin-Lajoie (1824–82), who wrote and acted the title role of his nationalistic drama *Le jeune Latour* (*The Young Latour*) while still a student at the Catholic Collège de Nicolet in 1844.

Patriotism, that is, fighting for the survival of the French language and culture in Québec, is also characteristic of the most popular of the ten dramatic works of the poet and journalist Louis-Honoré Fréchette (1839–1908). Two of his plays, *Félix Poutré* (1862) and *Papineau* (1880), dramatized the heroism of leaders of the 1837 rebellion in which French Canadians attempted to overthrow the British colonial government and win independence. Both plays were immensely popular and were frequently staged by amateur companies well into the twentieth century.

The great increase in touring stars and companies at the end of the nineteenth century also brought notable French artists to Québec. Constant Coquelin, for example, acted in Montréal in 1888, 1889 and 1893, while Sarah Bernhardt arrived in 1880 and had returned to the province seven times by 1917. Professional French-language theatre became established in Montréal in the 1890s with the opening of the 1,500-seat Monument-National (National Monument) in 1894. To counter the perceived decadence and commercialism of dramatic works from the French, US and British stage, the Catholic church in 1898 gave its support to an amateur lay company, Les Soirées de Famille (Family Evenings), whose repertoire was deemed more 'wholesome'. It staged 103 productions at the Monument-National between 1898 and 1901. The great majority of French-language professional actors, directors and repertoire seen in Montréal still came from France, however.

To provide greater professional opportunities for French-Canadian artists, Montréal-born actor, director, manager and playwright Julien Daoust (1866–1943) established a Théâtre National in Montréal in 1900. It helped to launch the professional career of the actor Fred Barry (1887–1964), director in 1927 of the important professional Barry–Duquesne troupe, which toured to France in 1937. The following year, Barry directed the first tour of actor-playwright Gratien Gélinas's popular satirical revue *Fridolinades* and co-directed Gélinas's drama *Tit-Coq* at the Monument-National in 1948, thus helping to lay the foundations for contemporary professional Québécois theatre and drama.

The first recorded production of a play in English Canada occurred during the winter of 1743–4 when the French-born lieutenant-governor of Nova Scotia, Paul Mascarene (1684–1760), translated Molière's *Le Misanthrope* and staged it at Annapolis Royal. Because no language barrier and less church opposition existed in English Canada, theatre in the British colonies was able to establish itself on a professional economic basis by the late 1700s. Audiences in Nova Scotia and New Brunswick were able to attend performances by professional British and American artists touring from the adjoining American colonies beginning with a visit by the American Company of Comedians to Halifax in 1768.

The growth of the performing arts in the colonial period paralleled the flow of settlers inward from the Atlantic coast. Plays were staged in taverns, assembly rooms of hotels, city halls and in playhouses above jails, stores and fire stations. After several decades of makeshift theatres, local audiences increased sufficiently so that theatres such as the 500-seat Grand Theatre (1789–1814) in Halifax, the 800-seat Hopley's Theatre (1828–45) in Saint John, New Brunswick, the 1,000-seat Theatre Royal in Montréal (1825–46) and Québec City (1824–46) and the 750-seat Royal Lyceum Theatre (1848–74) in Toronto provided production facilities for foreign touring artists and Canadian amateurs and professionals.

Productions by the British military garrisons, mostly English comedies and farces, were also an important source of theatre from 1758 to 1870. Military patronage helped to build theatres and provided a cultural link with Great Britain for isolated frontier communities. Garrison theatre also inspired local amateurs and the occasional playwright such as the anonymous 'Sam Scribble', whose political burlesques and farces were staged by garrison amateurs at Montréal's 1,500-seat third Theatre Royal (1852–1913) in 1865.

The first English-language play written and performed in Canada was *Acadius, or Love in a Calm*, staged by amateurs in Halifax in 1774. A romantic comedy with an anti-slavery sentiment, it dramatized the extra-marital activities of a wealthy Boston merchant and the attempts by his black servants to cope with their exploitation. But lacking ongoing indigenous professional companies and sufficiently large audiences interested in Canadian dramatic works, playwrights in English Canada were largely confined to seeing their plays published in newspapers, magazines and by literary presses or staged by amateur societies. Frederick Augustus Dixon's (1843–1919) plays for children and adults, for example, were staged by amateurs for the governor-general's family and entourage at Rideau Hall and at the 1,000-seat Grand Opera House in Ottawa in the 1870s.

A number of nineteenth-century playwrights achieved literary reputations but no stage productions. Among them were Eliza Lanesford Cushing (1794–1886), whose religious and poetic dramas were published in the Montréal *Literary Garland* in the 1840s; Charles Heavysege (1816–76), author of the biblical drama *Saul* (1857); Charles Mair (1838–1927), author of the drama *Tecumseh* (1886) about the Indian leader's struggle against the Americans during the War of 1812; and Sarah Anne Curzon (1833–98), an early feminist and author of *Laura Secord, the Heroine of 1812*, written in 1876 but not published until 1887. The only nineteenth-century Canadian playwright to achieve both publication and a professional Canadian tour was William Henry Fuller. His musical satire of national political life, *HMS Parliament or The Lady Who Loved a Government Clerk* – closely based on Gilbert and Sullivan's *HMS Pinafore* – was toured in 1880 by the E.A. McDowell Comedy Company to thirty cities from Halifax to Winnipeg.

The biggest impetus for the spread of professional theatre in the second half of the nineteenth century was the construction of ever bigger theatre buildings (seating up to 2,000 in the larger urban centres) and improved US and Canadian transcontinental railroad transportation, which by the 1880s allowed companies to tour from one part of the North American continent to the other. These touring companies were almost exclusively US and British, however, and by the turn of the century had come under the control of US monopolies such as the Theatrical Syndicate and the Shubert Brothers in New York.

Most local companies disappeared as these independently packaged shows arrived from New York, Chicago and other US cities. This US cultural influence was exacerbated by the rise of US silent film, burlesque and variety theatre at the beginning of the twentieth century and by radio broadcasting in the 1920s. Canada, which already had been a French and British colony, was now threatened with becoming a US cultural colony as well.

This lack of opportunity for indigenous artistic self-expression helped to propel a nation-wide amateur theatre movement after World War I, influenced in part by European and US art theatres. By the early 1930s the country's rapidly multiplying amateur and little theatres – both French and English – plunged into a unique and gigantic national theatre competition called the Dominion Drama Festival, an annual, co-lingual contest held in Ottawa (1933–7) and then (except during World War II) in a different city every year until 1970. With preliminary run-offs in each province, its fostering of indigenous one-act plays in both languages and its viceregal patronage, the festival became Canada's national theatre during the 1930s and allowed theatre to survive in those economically depressed and unsubsidized times.

However, its imported adjudicators and frequent high-society orientation perpetuated the dying colonial influence of Britain and France before the post-World War II flowering of professionalism. Out of the hundreds of community theatre groups only a few – Montréal's Les Compagnons de Saint Laurent, Calgary's Workshop 14, and the Winnipeg and London Little Theatres – ultimately made the transition to professional status.

In 1949, the government of Prime Minister Louis St Laurent (1882–1973) made a major breakthrough in the understanding of culture as of national importance by establishing a Royal Commission under Vincent Massey (1887–1967) and Georges-Henri Lévesque (b. 1903) on National Development in the Arts, Letters and Sciences. Known popularly as the Massey–Lévesque Commission, this body submitted a series of recommendations to the government in 1951. Those recommendations became the foundation of a national cultural policy some years later.

The Massey–Lévesque Commission deplored

the lack of professional artistic activity in Canada and argued that the development of a national culture was being seriously inhibited by the absence of state subsidy. Its chief recommendation was the establishment of the Canada Council/Conseil des Arts du Canada, which was founded in 1957. Culture came to be recognized as a responsibility shared by all levels of government. The Saskatchewan Arts Board had already been established in 1948 and, following the creation of the Ontario Arts Council in 1963, similar arts councils were founded over the next two decades in most of the country's ten provinces.

The Canada Council itself was mandated to provide grants to professional artists and arts organizations, and in its first year it distributed $250,000 to three theatre companies (two anglophone and one francophone) as well as to the Dominion Drama Festival to enable it to engage a number of theatre professionals. The three theatre companies funded were the Stratford Shakespearean Festival (founded in 1953); its offshoot, the touring Canadian Players; and the Théâtre du Nouveau Monde (Theatre of the New World, 1951) in Montréal. All three companies were dedicated to a classical, essentially European repertoire.

Anton Wagner

English Canada

The evolution of Canadian theatre since the creation of the Canada Council can be seen as responses to government policies, which from the 1960s to the 1980s promoted Canadian nationalism in culture and economics. This evolution can be divided into four general phases: a regional theatre phase, an alternative theatre phase, a consolidation and new wave phase, and new directions.

Phase one – the regional theatre phase – evolved from the Massey–Lévesque Commission conclusion that the underdevelopment of Canadian theatre could be rectified by state funding and the construction of civic theatres in major cities across the country. The Massey–Lévesque Commission had recognized the decentralizing force of regionalism in Canadian culture and therefore proposed that a 'national theatre' in Canada must be considered not as a one-city or one-company entity but as the whole of theatrical effort nation-wide. At the same time, it paid allegiance to the idea of a touring national theatre – an ideal tentatively realized, in form if not in repertoire, by the Canadian Players, which from 1954 to 1966 toured the country with a repertoire of European classics in English.

As a result of these ideas, through the 1950s, 1960s and 1970s there came into being a network of professional regional theatres across the country. The prototype on the English side was the Manitoba Theatre Centre in Winnipeg, founded in 1958 by director John Hirsch (1930–89) and manager-playwright Tom Hendry (b. 1929). It was followed by the Vancouver Playhouse in 1962, Neptune Theatre in Halifax in 1963, the Citadel Theatre, founded by entrepreneur Joe Shoctor in Edmonton in 1965, the Globe Theatre in Regina in 1966, Theatre New Brunswick in Fredericton and Theatre Calgary, both in 1968, Centaur

The Citadel Theatre in Edmonton.
Photo: Ed Ellis.

George Luscombe's 1983 production of his *Hey Rube!* at Toronto Workshop Productions.
Photo: Michael Cooper.

Theatre in Montréal in 1969, CentreStage in Toronto in 1970, Bastion Theatre in Victoria in 1971 and the Grand Theatre in London, Ontario, in 1978. In Québec the French-language regional theatres are the Théâtre du Nouveau Monde in Montréal and Théâtre du Trident, founded in Québec City in 1971.

In each of these cities, many amateur, semi-professional and professional civic companies prepared the way for these 'regional' theatres. In Toronto, for example, the Crest Theatre (1953–66), founded by Donald (b. 1928) and Murray (b. 1924) Davis, was unable to make the economic transition to a genuine community-supported professional civic theatre despite its high production standards and encouragement of Canadian playwrights. Out of the ashes of the Crest and its successor, the short-lived Theatre Toronto (1968–9), a new regional company, CentreStage, was founded in 1970; it subsequently evolved into the Canadian Stage Company, which by 1994 had become one of the country's largest regional theatres.

Most regional theatres appealed to middle-class audiences with a cautious type of programming that relied heavily on a mix of classics with modern European and US hits. Although most theatres expressed interest in Canadian drama, few did much to promote it, and until the early 1970s Canadian plays were rarely seen in the regional theatres.

One notable exception to this model was Toronto Workshop Productions (TWP), which, from 1957 to 1989, was committed to original left-wing drama and ensemble performance. TWP's director, George Luscombe (b. 1926), had travelled to England as a young man, where he worked with director Joan Littlewood; his theatre was in many ways a continuation and refinement of her 'workshop' principles.

By the early 1970s, this national network had proven that Canada would support professional theatres. But with a repertoire that was essentially foreign and increasingly irrelevant to a growing number of Canadians, a new, more nationalistic movement began to develop.

Clearly, the political and cultural turbulence of the 1960s was being felt as keenly in Canada as elsewhere. The period marked the arrival of a young, politicized generation that had been raised in an affluent society and had both the education and the opportunity to pursue careers in the arts. It was this generation that demanded to see *their* reality reflected on the stage, and rejected the international repertoire as an expression of bourgeois colonialism.

The result was the second phase of development. The years between 1968 and 1975 saw the founding of literally hundreds of small theatre companies across Canada, most dedicated to the production of Canadian plays. Commonly known as the 'alternative theatre' movement, this new wave rejected the regional theatre idea as artificial and false: the large theatres might be supported by local or regional sentiment, but their repertoires, largely taken from European or US models, were irrelevant to Canada and virtually indistinguishable from one another. In contrast, the new generation of localist, politically engaged and experimental theatres declared themselves to be Canada's authentic theatrical voice.

This increasingly independent Canadian nationalist theatre was similar in style to much of the new theatre of the 1960s in Europe and the United States with emphasis on collective creation, left-wing populism, a critique of artistic hierarchy, and, in Canada, a strong impulse towards local culture. These theatres repudiated the established model of regional theatre as a product of a colonized, middle-class mentality, and sought to define indigenous culture by returning to historical and local subjects. Historically, the most important example was Toronto's Theatre Passe Muraille (Theatre Beyond Walls), which in 1972 created a prototype documentary play. The actors recorded their conversations with farmers, improvised a performance from the recordings, and the result, *The Farm Show*, became the model for dozens of similar groups across the country and initiated a formal revolution in Canadian theatre. Collective creation, it should be noted, was not simply an ideological preference; it was also a necessity occasioned (with a few exceptions, such as Robertson Davies (b. 1913)), by the initial absence of experienced Canadian playwrights.

Other new anglophone companies of the 1970s gave aspiring playwrights an opportunity to develop their art and many became known for their commitment to Canadian drama. Companies such as Factory Theatre (founded as Factory Theatre Lab, 1970) and Tarragon Theatre (1971) in Toronto, the Great Canadian Theatre Company (1975) in Ottawa, Alberta Theatre Projects (1972) in Calgary, Theatre Network (1975) in Edmonton, the New Play Centre (1970) and Tamahnous Theatre (1971) in Vancouver, Nova Scotia's Mulgrave Road Co-op (1977) and Saskatchewan's 25th Street Theatre (1971) all committed themselves primarily to developing Canadian plays.

In this they were responding to the increasingly vocal demands of the growing community of playwrights who, following a conference organized by the Canada Council in 1971, had formed the Playwrights Co-op (now Playwrights Union of Canada) and called for a quota of 50 per cent Canadian content in all of Canada's subsidized theatres. The newer, smaller and less subsidized alternative theatres saw this demand as quite acceptable and by the 1980s works by Canadian playwrights had become their mainstay.

Paul Thompson's 1972 Theatre Passe Muraille production of the collective creation *The Farm Show*.

But through the early 1970s the more lavishly subsidized regional theatres denounced the demand for such a Canadian content quota as dangerous and radical. Through the 1990s, in fact, most of the large regional theatres were still relying on the same traditional recipe of mixed programming and were often presenting a larger proportion of original plays on 'second' stages than on their main stages. In Canada, therefore, most indigenous plays (even into the 1990s) were being generated by theatres that were receiving the smallest amounts of funding.

A second wave of alternative companies emerged in the late 1970s and 1980s, with even more specialized repertoires. This marked the third phase of Canadian theatre development.

Raoul Trujillo's 1991 Native Earth Performing Arts production of Jim Morris's *Son of Ayash*, designed by Sue LePage and Jim Plaxton.

For these companies, the struggle to legitimize Canadian playwriting already had been won; they were the children of the revolution. The profile of Canadian theatre became more diverse as new theatres emerged, particularly in Toronto, to articulate the experience of different communities. Most significant were feminist companies such as Nightwood Theatre (1979) and Company of Sirens (1985) in Toronto; gay companies, notably Buddies in Bad Times (1978), also in Toronto; and aboriginal theatres, such as Native Earth Performing Arts in Toronto (1982), the De-Ba-Jeh-Mu-Jig (Story Tellers) Theatre Group (1984) on Manitoulin Island, Ontario, Tunooniq Theatre (1986) in the Northwest Territories and Awasikan in Winnipeg, dedicated to native Indian playwrights and performers. Not all major cities have followed this pattern. Vancouver, for example, lacks gay or aboriginal companies and feminist work was emerging only slowly in the 1990s, mostly through its Women in View Festival.

Throughout the 1970s, arts funding from all levels of government continued to increase and for the first time young Canadians could reasonably anticipate professional careers in the theatre. In addition to the fine conservatory training that had been available at the National Theatre School in Montréal since 1960, the profession was aided in this by the rapid growth of university and college theatre departments across the country, graduates of which often helped to found even more theatre companies. In the early 1980s, however, the financial climate took a turn for the worse and support for the arts began to be frozen – largely because of new policies by a succession of federal and provincial governments that placed less importance on arts and cultural autonomy than did the earlier 1970s Liberal government of Pierre Elliott Trudeau (b. 1919). As a result, theatre companies decreased in size and often in vision and the small groups, too, began to rely on season subscription sales and corporate sponsorship, moves that many in the theatre community criticized as regressive and hostile to artistic experimentation.

In the fourth phase of development, the theatres of the 1980s therefore found themselves in constant financial crises that continued into the 1990s, but nevertheless managed to create a number of remarkable innovations. One production – *Tamara* – by a Toronto experimental company, about the Italian nationalist poet Gabriele d'Annunzio, actually became an international industry. Two years after its founding in 1978, Necessary Angel, a small company that tended to explore political themes and non-traditional venues, created *Tamara* by John Krizanc (b. 1956), directed by Richard Rose (b. 1955), in which audience members followed any one of nine characters through various rooms in which the play took place. Picked up by a commercial producer, *Tamara* went on to long runs in Los Angeles, New York and México City.

By the 1980s other important developments had brought renewed energy to theatre in English Canada: popular theatre as a political entity, corporal mime, and improvisational and sketch comedy via theatre-sports and comedy clubs. The use of popular theatre – theatre for social action – itself dates back in Canada to the workers' theatre movement of the 1930s, but a modern approach began in the 1970s when companies such as the Mummers Troupe of Newfoundland (1972–82) began to create collective documentaries to intervene in community and labour struggles. The 1981 founding of the Canadian Popular Theatre Alliance formalized this movement and by the mid-1990s there were dozens of troupes specializing in various forms of political and social action performance, many of them using Brazilian director Augusto Boal's Theatre of the Oppressed methodologies.

Some, like Toronto's Ground Zero Productions (1983), oriented themselves to the labour movement; others addressed environmental issues; and still others, notably Catalyst Theatre (1977) of Edmonton, focused on a variety of social issues such as drug abuse, family violence and housing. Popular theatre troupes were also instrumental in articulating Canada's multicultural reality, as many dealt with the struggles of minority and immigrant communities.

The widespread introduction of the techniques of physical mime and clowning in Canada owes much to the French master Jacques Lecoq and his Paris school, which has trained a large number of Canadian students in the arts of corporal mime and *commedia dell' arte*. The leading figure in Canadian clown theatre, until his untimely death, was Richard Pochinko (1946–89), who fused Lecoq's approach with the native Indian clown traditions of the Trickster. Pochinko taught a generation of clowns at his Theatre Resource Centre in Toronto. In 1994 there were over a dozen Pochinko-inspired 'physical theatre' troupes in Canada, some of which had progressed beyond clowning to a new *commedia* style of playwriting.

By the mid-1990s it had become clear that the traditional dialectic of alternative versus mainstream theatre was inadequate to explain the new forces that were beginning to govern theatrical production in Canada. Since 1984, federal funding for the arts had diminished annually while at the same time production costs had soared. In Toronto in 1990, three large commercial houses, all extensively refurbished touring or vaudeville theatres from early in the century (the Royal Alexandra Theatre, the Elgin/Winter Garden complex and the Pantages Theatre), were selling more seats combined in any one night than all of the other thirty or so subsidized theatres in the city. Local productions of international blockbuster musicals – *Cats* (1985), *Les Misérables* (1989) and *The Phantom of the Opera* (1989) – attracted mass audiences and provided ammunition to politicians hostile to arts funding, who saw in the profitability of these commercial hits evidence that public subsidy of the arts was a waste of money.

This situation intensified in 1993 when Edwin Mirvish (b. 1914) and his son David (b. 1944), owners of the Royal Alexandra Theatre and Canadian franchisees of *Les Misérables*, constructed a new theatre – the opulent $35 million Princess of Wales Theatre – specifically to house their Toronto production of *Miss Saigon*. The same year, Garth Drabinsky (b. 1948), producer of *Phantom* and of the Tony Award-winning *Kiss of the Spider Woman*, took over another newly built theatre, the Ford Centre for the Performing Arts in the Toronto borough of North York, and opened it with a production of *Show Boat*, which went on to a successful, Tony Award-winning Broadway run the following year, with weekly box-office revenues of US$900,000.

Yet what may turn out to be the farthest reaching development of the 1980s also emerged as a response to the changing climate in arts funding. The Canadian 'fringe' phenomenon began in Edmonton in 1980 when the small Chinook Theatre hosted a Fringe Festival that featured over 200 performances by small, new and/or young theatre troupes. That first Fringe Festival set the example for a rapidly expanding movement that by 1994 had reached eight major Canadian cities (Victoria, Vancouver, Edmonton, Saskatoon, Winnipeg, Toronto, Montréal and Halifax) and four smaller towns. The success of the Fringe may have something to do with the tradition of populist activism that is western Canada's most cherished myth. These festivals offer no juries and no prizes. Any group can appear; selection is on a first-come, first-served basis, and shows are assigned venues according to size. The festivals charge a fee ranging from $125 to $400 to the participating groups and set a ceiling on ticket prices, but the performers keep box-office receipts. The unexpected success of these Fringe Festivals was astounding, and even more so when the relatively small size of some of the cities concerned is considered. For example, in Edmonton, a city of 700,000, the Fringe can sell 150,000 tickets to 200 plays in ten days.

While the artistic quality of Fringe productions is often uneven, the success of the Fringe phenomenon in involving local artists and audiences has had a major impact on other English-Canadian theatres. In the early 1970s, novices could take advantage of easily obtained government job-creation financial support to start new theatres; in the 1980s, with those funding programmes discontinued, young artists saw the Fringe as a new type of launching pad to professional careers. The Fringe was, in fact, basically operating as a *laissez-faire* market-place in which young artists could quickly establish a reputation. A principal route into the theatrical profession in the 1990s, the Fringe Festivals, not surprisingly, rely heavily on comedy and parody, although serious experimental work can also be found.

Alan Filewod

Québec

In the 1930s and 1940s, Québec's theatre was inspired by the modernist approaches of the Montréal Repertory Theatre (1930–61), an amateur company that produced in both English and French; the Compagnons de Saint-Laurent (Friends of Saint-Laurent, 1937–52), an amateur company directed by the Catholic priest Émile Legault (1906–83); and L'Équipe (The Team, 1943–7), directed by Pierre Dagenais (1923–90). During the same period, actor-playwright Gratien Gélinas's satirical *Fridolinons* revues (1938–46) established an audience for stage productions with both local sensibilities and self-expression as their primary focuses.

Out of this new generation came companies and artists who would play a key role in the years to come: the Théâtre du Rideau Vert

(Theatre of the Green Curtain), founded in 1948 by Yvette Brind'Amour (1918–92) and later jointly run with Mercedes Palomino (b. 1913); the Théâtre du Nouveau Monde, founded in 1951 and directed successively by Jean Gascon (1921–88), Jean-Louis Roux (b. 1923), Olivier Reichenbach (b. 1942) and Lorraine Pintal (b. 1951); the Théâtre-Club (1953–64), founded by Monique LePage (b. 1930) and Jacques Létourneau (b. 1929); and the Théâtre de Quat'Sous (Threepenny Theatre), established in 1955 by Paul Buissonneau (b. 1926). From its founding, the Théâtre du Nouveau Monde, with its high production standards, particularly in directing and design, was considered as *the* company against which other groups evaluated their own work.

Numerous, generally avant-garde groups, known in Québec as *théâtre jeune* (young companies), often composed of gifted and dynamic amateurs, continued from the middle of the 1950s to take on a variety of creative tasks. This was true of those companies that struggled to produce the works of new European playwrights of that time, particularly from France: Les Apprentis-Sorciers (Sorcerer's Apprentices, 1955–68), L'Égrégore (The Gathering, 1959–68) and Les Saltimbanques (The Entertainers, 1963–8) in Montréal and L'Estoc (The Big Sword, 1957–67) in Québec City.

For audiences particularly interested in new works by Québec writers, Gratien Gélinas founded the Comédie-Canadienne (1958–69), the existence of which predated the desire of the 1970s to accord a more substantial place to national playwrights on major stages. Other companies were also founded, enlarging the institutional base for theatre production. In Montréal new companies included the Théâtre Populaire du Québec (founded in 1963), which toured the province; the Nouvelle Compagnie Théâtrale (New Theatrical Company, 1964), which focused on a student public; and the Compagnie Jean Duceppe (1973), which favoured a wider North American repertoire.

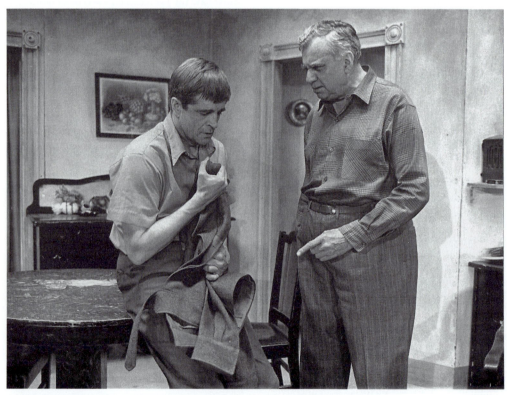

Jacques Létourneau's 1967 Comédie-Canadienne production of Marcel Dubé's *A Simple Soldier.*
Photo: André LeCoz.

Still another group of note, the Théâtre du Trident, was founded in Québec City in 1970. On Montréal's English-language side, Maurice Podbrey (b. 1934) founded the Centaur Theatre in 1969, while director and playwright Marion Andre (b. 1921) founded the Saidye Bronfman Centre in 1967.

Beginning in the 1960s, Paul Buissonneau and the often iconoclastic Jean-Pierre Ronfard (b. 1929) led a new generation of directors who opened the stage to a range of audacious interpretations and the creation of new-style texts. Over the next few years, Roland Laroche (b. 1927), Albert Millaire (b. 1935) and André Brassard (b. 1946), among others, helped to establish a new set of production standards. As a result of these innovators, even basic performance techniques began to be transformed under the need for greater freedom of expression and the experiences of the new US theatre (particularly as represented by the Living Theatre), the theoretical reflections of Antonin Artaud and Bertolt Brecht, and the direct or reflected teaching of such contemporary European practitioners as Etienne Decroux, Lecoq, Grotowski, Eugenio Barba and Alain Knapp.

Perhaps the most profound change in Québec theatre during the 1970s, however, resulted from the massive injection of vernacular language, referred to as *joual*, onto the stage. *Joual* – the name is derived from the local pronunciation of the French word *cheval* (horse) but to a greater extent refers to French as it is spoken in Québec – represented a distancing from the polished language and French-inspired style of performance that reigned supreme on Québec's major stages up until this time. The writers of the so-called 'baby boom' generation put *joual* on stage and kept it there. Preceded by Québec's many *chansonniers* (singer-songwriters), poets and monologists, these new writers celebrated the language spoken by Québec's various social classes. A large number of monologists emerged at this time, ranging from Clémence Desrochers (b. 1933) to Marc (Sol) Favreau (b. 1929) to Yvon Deschamps (b. 1935), and they created a type of solo narrative performance linked directly to the search for Québécois identity and unity.

Running parallel to this development was a series of experiments in stage technique that also left its mark throughout the 1970s. Led by groups such as the Grand Cirque Ordinaire (Great Ordinary Circus, 1969–77), Théâtre Euh! (1970–8), Théâtre de Carton (Cardboard Theatre, 1972–94), Gens d'en Bas (People

Down the River, 1973), Théâtre Parminou (Theatre Among Us, 1973), Théâtre des Cuisines (Theatre of the Kitchens, 1973–81) and the Théâtre de Quartier (District Theatre, 1975), collective creation rapidly became widely used. Immensely popular with young performers, it permitted those who were not necessarily trained in the theatre both to express themselves and to participate in the social, cultural and political crosscurrents of the time: nationalism, class struggles and feminism.

The 'golden age' of Québec collective creation was mainly between 1968 and 1978, when several shows that had been created collectively had a considerable impact and, at the same time, challenged the aesthetic and social orientations of the established theatre. Among the several hundred collective creations performed, mention should be made of *T'es pas tannée, Jeanne d'Arc?* (*Aren't You Fed Up, Joan of Arc?*, 1969) by the Grand Cirque Ordinaire, which blended sketches, mime, songs and giant puppets into a piece about the repression of French Canada using Joan of Arc as a central symbol; and *Môman travaille pas, a trop d'ouvrage* (*Mom's Not Working, She's Got Too Much to Do*, 1975) by the Théâtre des Cuisines, an agitprop spectacle focusing on the domestic alienation of women.

Most of these groups operated under the aegis of the Association Québécoise du Jeune Théâtre (Québec Association of Young Theatre), founded in 1958 under the name Association canadienne du théâtre amateur (Canadian Amateur Theatre Association). Extremely activist and with leftist goals, these groups sought to sensitize the public to an extremely wide range of issues ranging from support for women's issues to the needs of elderly people, from classic power relationships to issues between landlords and tenants, decision makers and average people.

'More good sport', Brecht once demanded for the theatre; Québec echoed this in still another form of theatre activity parodying the national sport of hockey: two teams of improvising actors competing against one another. Called the Ligue Nationale d'Improvisation (National Improvisation League) this popular form was created by Robert Gravel (b. 1941) at the Théâtre Expérimental de Montréal in 1977 and effectively exploited the playful side of collective creation. In English Canada, also in 1977, Keith Johnstone developed the style under the name of theatresports at Calgary's Loose Moose Theatre Company and the form later spread to other

Robert Lepage's 1987 Théâtre Repère production of *The Dragon's Trilogy*.
Photo: Daniel Kieffer.

that could reach all ages. Its productions of *Terre promise/Terra promessa* (*Promised Land*, 1989, a coproduction with the Teatro dell'-Angelo from Italy) and especially its *L'Histoire de l'oie* (*The Tale of Teeka*, 1991) by Michel Marc Bouchard (b. 1958) reflected the new direction and toured extensively both in Canada and internationally.

Théâtre Repère (Landmark Theatre; founded in 1980 in Québec City) was the first important artistic home of the imagistic director Robert Lepage (b. 1957). Here Lepage staged highly evocative performances drawing on contemporary transcultural reality. Among his later productions were *Vinci* (1986), *La Trilogie des dragons* (*The Dragon's Trilogy*, 1986–7), *Polygraphe* (1988), *Plaques tectoniques* (*Tectonic Plates*, 1988–90) and *Les Aiguilles et l'opium* (*Needles and Opium*, 1991), which had enormous success both across the country and abroad.

Whether seen via the imagistic stagings of a Gilles Maheu or a Robert Lepage or through more traditional approaches, theatricality became considerably enriched and more profound in the 1980s, due in part to the work of such major directors as Lorraine Pintal, René Richard Cyr (b. 1958) and Yves Desgagnés (b. 1958). Original approaches based on circus formats resulted in, for example, astonishing productions by Dynamo Théâtre (founded as La Troupe Circus in 1981) and by the Cirque du Soleil (Circus of the Sun; founded in 1984).

The concept of retheatricalization, along with a new window on the world and a general depoliticization, were in the mid-1990s the hallmarks of contemporary theatrical life in Québec.

Gilbert David

Structure of the National Theatre Community

The scale of the theatrical revolution that Canada experienced in the post-war decades can be measured by the increase in professional theatre companies funded by the Canada Council. From three in 1957, the number grew to 197 in 1990 (both French and English). This latter figure does not include the many quasi-professional groups that exist even without federal funding in some of the larger cities. By the early 1990s, Toronto was commonly considered the third most active theatre centre in the English-speaking world, after London and New York.

In 1993, the Canada Council supported 230 theatres, approximately two-thirds of which were anglophone. The annual *Canada on Stage* performance calendar, begun in 1974 by the *Canadian Theatre Review* and now edited by the Professional Association of Canadian Theatres (PACT), lists all professional productions in English and monitored almost 400 theatre troupes in 1990. Of these, only a fraction had their own theatre spaces and guaranteed annual funding. By far the largest concentration of theatres in English Canada was in Toronto, followed by Edmonton, Vancouver and Winnipeg. Virtually all were members of PACT.

Theatres receiving annual operational funding from the Canada Council or provincial arts councils are generally established as not-for-profit corporations; many also have charitable tax status, which permits them to issue tax-deductible receipts for donations. A company so incorporated is legally obliged to have a volunteer (unpaid) board of directors. These boards have the power to approve budgets and staff appointments, and in most cases board members are friends of the theatre. But there are exceptions, and there have been many instances in which artistic directors have been dismissed by the board because of disagreements over policy or poor box-office returns. This issue had escalated into a major controversy by the early 1990s following the dismissal of several high-profile directors from major theatres by boards that appeared to be more concerned with budgets than artistic vision.

In addition to funding from the Canada Council, most theatre companies are eligible for subsidies from provincial and, in a few of the larger cities, municipal arts councils. In the wealthier provinces, such as Ontario and Québec in central Canada and Alberta in the west, theatres often receive more money from provincial arts councils than from the Canada Council, while in poorer provinces, especially in the Atlantic region, the reverse is true. Taken together, public subsidies rarely amount to more than 40 per cent of a theatre's annual revenue; the remainder must be made up from box-office sales and private (including corporate) donations.

In some cases, theatres are funded by sources other than arts councils. Many theatres for young audiences, for example, survive by selling their performances to schools. There are also theatres funded mainly through unions or social welfare agencies. These, however, are the exceptions.

The heavy dependence on box-office revenues even at publicly funded theatres means that most struggle to maintain a balance between artistic integrity and popular appeal in programming. As a consequence, public relations and marketing have grown into major and essential theatrical industries.

Most, but by no means all, of the incorporated English-speaking companies are signatories of the Canadian Theatre Agreement with Canadian Actors' Equity Association, the union that represents actors and stage managers. The theatres negotiate with Actors' Equity annually through PACT, which also maintains a valuable information service and publishes a theatre directory. In 1992, the negotiated minimum weekly salary for a professional Equity actor was CDN$319 per week, significantly less than the average Canadian professional salary.

Although they may belong to a union that sets working conditions and salaries, actors in Canada are considered self-employed, which means that they have no job security and receive no employment benefits. Because most theatres operate at a deficit, they can afford to pay actors only during rehearsals (typically two to three weeks) and the run of a play (up to six weeks). For that reason, long exploratory rehearsal periods are rare in Canada, and there are few ensembles that remain together for more than a season. Most actors may work on stage for only two or three months a year, and generally supplement stage income by appearing on radio, television or doing commercials. Many must also rely on non-theatrical employment to make a living.

work they produce has only a limited direct impact on work produced elsewhere in the country.

The case of the Stratford Festival shows clearly how Canada's largest theatre can be removed from the theatrical culture for which it has historically provided a standard of achievement. Founded in 1953 by a committee of citizens headed by Tom Patterson in Stratford, Ontario, and directed for the first two seasons by Tyrone Guthrie, the Stratford Festival aspired to the leading ranks of classic theatres – an aspiration made possible by Guthrie's visionary leadership, by the corps of talented young Canadian actors that he assembled, and by Tanya Moiseiwitsch's (b. 1914) innovative thrust stage.

As it has grown, Stratford has become the principal showcase of Canadian theatrical ability, but it has also remained essentially a local company. Although it produces a seven-month mixed season of Shakespeare, selected contemporary drama and musicals on three stages (the 2,200-seat Festival Theatre, the 1,000-seat proscenium Avon Theatre and the 493-seat Tom Patterson Theatre), it has never been able to establish a foothold in Toronto, and it has had little direct impact on the development of Canadian playwriting. Stratford draws a great part of its audiences from the United States. This fact has had a defining effect on its programming, and explains in part why the theatre has only intermittently produced Canadian plays.

With a cautiously imaginative approach to classic texts, Stratford has, however, often achieved a distinguished level of production under a succession of skilled artistic directors, most of whom were British or British trained. Following Guthrie (director from 1953 to 1955) and Michael Langham (director from 1956 to 1967), the theatre's board of governors engaged John Hirsch and Jean Gascon to form a partnership that would ideally bring together the two linguistic cultures that defined Canadian theatre. The experiments did not work and Hirsch departed in 1969, leaving Gascon at the helm until 1974.

Gascon was succeeded by Stratford's most controversial appointment, Robin Phillips (b. 1942), who took the job at the height of Canadian nationalist sentiment. Although Phillips was met by fierce and bitter controversy over the question of foreign directors, his work at Stratford became an artistic success story of the period. Not only did he turn Stratford into one of the most exciting theatres in Canada, but his own work with actors – particularly Martha Henry (b. 1938), the English Maggie Smith and William Hutt (b. 1920) – astonished both the public and the theatre profession. Perhaps prodded by the nationalist controversy, Phillips subsequently committed himself to Canada and, after leaving Stratford in 1980, pursued a freelance career. In 1991 he accepted a position as director-general of the Citadel Theatre in Edmonton, one of the largest regional theatres in the country, which he ran until his resignation in 1995.

Phillips's departure from Stratford in 1980 occasioned a controversy even greater than the one that greeted his appointment, when the theatre's board of governors reneged on its contractual commitment to Phillips's Canadian successors in an attempt to hire still another British-born director, John Dexter. After the dust settled, the board of directors appointed John Hirsch, a Canadian who had also achieved an impressive international reputation. Hirsch was succeeded in 1986 by John Neville (b. 1925). Hirsch gave the theatre a much needed sense of purpose but left a painful deficit; Neville in turn brought financial stability and a public presence, but little in the way of artistic excitement.

Neville was succeeded in 1989 by David William (b. 1926), whose performance was competent but less than inspiring. In 1992 the company showed signs of renewed vitality when it appointed Canadian-born Richard Monette (b. 1944) as artistic director. Monette had worked at Stratford as an actor during the Phillips years, and had built an impressive reputation as a director of classics and new work across Canada. His subsequent programming at Stratford demonstrated a commitment to both impeccable classic productions of the Shakespearian canon as well as to new Canadian work. In addition to good critical notices, Monette's first season also succeeded in producing a slight surplus in Stratford's 1994 budget of $23.4 million.

In contrast to the Stratford Festival, the Shaw Festival benefits from its picturesque rural location in the village of Niagara-on-the-Lake. Like Stratford, the Shaw Festival is a large operation devoted to an idiosyncratic purpose. The company's mandate commits it to the works of George Bernard Shaw and 'his contemporaries', which can be, and often is, interpreted to mean modern drama up to 1950 in general. In particular, the company has had notable successes

John Hirsch's 1985 Stratford Festival production of Shakespeare's *King Lear*.
Photo: David Cooper.

with early-twentieth-century British drama-tists, especially (aside from Shaw himself) Noël Coward, J.B. Priestley and Harley Granville-Barker.

Founded in 1962 by lawyer–producer Brian Doherty (1906–74) and educator Calvin G. Rand (b. 1929), the Shaw Festival's first two decades were managed by a succession of artistic directors – Andrew Allan (1963–5), Barry Morse (1966) and Leslie Yeo (1979) – who approached the Shavian canon with reverence and artistic caution. Paxton Whitehead (1967–78), a gifted comic actor, turned the fes-tival in a more popular direction, making Shaw's plays more accessible to a broad public from both Ontario and upstate New York. By the time Christopher Newton (b. 1936) took command in 1980, the festival had expanded to fill three houses: the 847-seat Festival Theatre, designed by Toronto architect Ron Thom; the 240-seat Royal George Theatre, formerly a vaudeville house; and its original home in a 360-seat theatre above the village's Town Hall.

Newton's tenure at Shaw has been marked by three main developments: the expansion of the programming mandate (to the point of including Elmer Rice, Brecht, Gershwin and Piscator), the building of a strong ensemble company that may well be the best in the country, and an imagina-tive reconsideration of Shaw's plays. Newton's work has been marked by lively exploration of style and deep collaboration with innovative designers who bring out the striking visual (and often non-realistic) elements in Shaw's work. As a result, the Shaw Festival is home to some of the most imaginative scenography in Canada, supervised by the company's head of design, Cameron Porteous (b. 1937). As an example of the theatre's scope, in 1994 300,000 people saw 729 performances of ten productions in the Fes-tival's three theatres, generating $8.2 million in box-office revenue.

Like the Stratford Festival, Shaw plays to con-siderable US audiences. However, unlike Strat-ford, the Shaw Festival has been able to build productive links with the Toronto theatre

Robbie O'Neill in his 1981 one-man Mulgrave Road Co-op Theatre show *Tighten the Traces/Haul in the Reins*.
Photo: Chris Reardon.

subjects, ranging from life in western Canada to sexuality (*I Love You, Baby Blue*, 1975). Passe Muraille's approach resulted in the creation of a group of actors who became highly skilled at researching local culture and transforming their research into imagistic theatricality.

Not surprisingly, some of the Passe Muraille actors later became playwrights in their own right. The most successful was Linda Griffiths (b. 1953), whose plays *Maggie and Pierre* (1979), written with Paul Thompson (b. 1940), a one-woman show in which she represented both Pierre Trudeau and his estranged wife Margaret; *O.D. On Paradise* (1982), with Patrick Brymer; *Jessica* (1986), written with Métis writer Maria Campbell (b. 1940); and *The Darling Family* (1991), a searing psychodrama about abortion, made into a film in 1994, are notable for their emotional intensity.

The Passe Muraille approach emphasized colloquial language and physical theatricality and owed much to the genius of Paul Thompson, artistic director through most of the 1970s. Thompson, a student of director Roger Planchon in France, was a passionate advocate of populist culture; he believed strongly that a truly indigenous Canadian theatre was one that could transform the living stories of local people into myth.

No playwright better exemplifies that vision than James Reaney (b. 1926), whose dramatic works of the 1950s and 1960s were followed by several major dramas created with the active assistance of the NDWT (the company is known by the initials only) theatre collective in the early 1970s. A three-time winner of Canada's most prestigious literary prize, the Governor-General's Award, Reaney's theatre delights in children's games, melodrama, puppetry, storytelling and poetry. His epic trilogy of blood feuds among Irish settlers in nineteenth-century Upper Canada, *The Donnellys* – the three plays are *Sticks and Stones* (1973), *The St Nicholas Hotel* (1974) and *Handcuffs* (1975) – must be numbered among the most unusual achievements of Canadian drama. In this trilogy, Reaney's interest in regional culture (the violent fate of the 'Black Donnellys' is part of the folk culture of southwestern Ontario) found its perfect expression in his characteristic theatricality.

Linda Griffiths as Pierre Trudeau in her 1979 Theatre Passe Muraille solo show *Maggie and Pierre*.

The 1975 national tour of the trilogy by NDWT was one of the artistic highlights of Canadian theatre in the 1970s.

Two playwrights who perhaps best typified the theatre of the late 1970s also shared a strong left-wing political commitment. Rick Salutin (b. 1942) began writing for the stage as part of the collective that created Passe Muraille's *1837: The Farmers' Revolt* in 1973. In this examination of a failed revolution by Canadian settlers against the British colonial regime, Salutin drew obvious parallels with Canada's contemporary colonial relationships. In his most popular play, *Les Canadiens*, about the celebrated Montréal hockey team, actors used roller skates to replay the history of Québécois nationalism on simulated ice. Performed in 1978, *Les Canadiens* was one of the first English–Canadian artistic statements to deal with and, in fact, to support Québécois sovereignty.

In contrast, David Fennario's (b. 1947) more naturalistic dramas expressed the anger of alienated working-class youth in an anglophone district of Montréal. His most popular play, *Balconville* (1979), focused on three families, one francophone and two anglophone, that share a tenement balcony as well as the despair of unemployment. Set at the time of the Parti Québécois campaign for separation from

Canada, *Balconville* advanced the unpopular proposition that the politics of nationalism and language conceal the real issues of class struggle. Commonly considered the first bilingual Canadian play, it enjoyed a popular national and international tour, and won the 1979 Chalmers Award for Best Canadian Play.

By the end of the 1970s, Canadian plays were the norm on many stages, and a respectable canon had been legitimized. Critics commonly analysed drama in terms of regionalism, pointing to strong local voices in the Atlantic provinces, notably the collective creations of the Mummers Troupe and the powerful dramas of Michael Cook (1933–94); the Prairies, especially the plays of Rex Deverell (b. 1941) and Ken Mitchell (b. 1940); and in British Columbia, where Beverly Simons's (b. 1938) *Crabdance* (1969), Herschel Hardin's (b. 1936) *Esker Mike and His Wife, Agiluk* (1973), and the satires of Eric Nicol (b. 1919) were proof of what politicians like to call 'unity in diversity'.

If in the 1970s theatre was analysed in terms of nationalism and regional expression, the 1980s introduced a more politicized concept of cultural difference. For the theatres of the 1980s the struggle over nationalism and regionalism had been won, and playwrights began to turn away from the historical dramas of the 1970s to explore new styles and themes.

The first of the new challenges that would characterize the decade came from women. Following on the heels of Simons's powerful works, in the late 1970s and 1980s Sharon Pollock (b. 1936) established herself as one of Canada's most widely produced playwrights. Her *Blood Relations* (1976), based on a famous US axe-murder of the 1890s, won the first-ever Governor-General's Award for Drama in 1981. In her plays, Pollock typically re-examines Canadian history to reveal its hidden racist and patriarchal policies. Joanna McClelland Glass (b. 1936) is still another important dramatist whose works, notably *Artichoke* (1975), have been widely staged.

Many women playwrights went further in repudiating traditional patriarchal approaches. Banuta Rubess, whose plays deconstruct narrative techniques, began as a writer and actor in a collective that produced two important plays in the 1980s: *Smoke Damage* (1982), about the Medieval European witch hunts, and *This Is For You, Anna* (1983), about violence against women. Ann-Marie MacDonald, who collaborated on both plays, won the 1990 Governor-General's Award for her own play *Good Night*

Desdemona, Good Morning Juliet (1988), a feminist deconstruction of Shakespeare.

Not all women playwrights expressed an overtly feminist analysis or rejected traditional methods of theatrical production. In her four major plays, *The Crackwalker* (1981), *White Biting Dog* (Governor-General's Award, 1984), *I Am Yours* (Governor-General's Award, 1989) and *Lion In the Streets* (1991), Judith Thompson (b. 1954) probed the complex internal lives of characters who struggle to maintain their psychic health in a world of brutal emotional violence. Her plays are known for their emotional intensity, honesty of language and the complexity of her narrative structures.

The first contemporary Canadian dramatist to break successfully into the mainstream of commercial theatre was George F. Walker (b. 1947), whose many plays are frequently produced in the United States. Walker's 1990 hit *Love and Anger*, a satirical attack on ruthless urban developers, transferred from the Factory Theatre to a commercial run. Walker's brand of ironic comedy and social conscience has made him one of the most popular playwrights of his generation, and his most celebrated plays, including *Zastrozzi* (1977), *Criminals In Love* (1984), *Better Living* (1986),

George F. Walker's 1981 Factory Theatre Lab production of his *Theatre of the Film Noir*.

Beautiful City (1987) and *Nothing Sacred* (1988), are frequently revived.

Strong dramatic voices have also emerged elsewhere in the country. In Vancouver, Morris Panych (b. 1952) has delighted audiences with his dense post-modern fables (*Last Call: A Post-Nuclear Cabaret*, 1982, and *7 Stories*, 1989). In Edmonton, a group of playwrights has evolved a distinct Prairie dramaturgy that combines realism and lyrical irony; notable examples are Frank Moher's (b. 1955) *Odd Jobs* (1985) and *The Third Ascent* (1988), and Kelly Rebar's (b. 1956) *Checking Out* and *Bordertown Cafe* (1989).

Other Alberta writers of note include John Murrell (b. 1945), for his dramas *Waiting for the Parade* (1977), *Memoir* (1978), *Farther West* (1982) and *Democracy* (1991), and Stuart Lemoine, whose camp genre parodies have found a popular following. Brad Fraser's (b. 1959) gritty play of serial killers, sexual angst and urban alienation *Unidentified Human Remains and the True Nature of Love* (1989) enjoyed a successful commercial run in Toronto, played in New York, London and Edinburgh, was later turned into a film, and in 1991 became one of the few English-Canadian plays to appeal to Montréal audiences in translation. Fraser's later play, *The Ugly Man* (1992), a modern retelling of Middleton and Rowley's *The Changeling*, was also well received in Montréal, confirming Fraser's status as one of the few English-Canadian playwrights respected by Québécois critics and audiences.

Perhaps the most significant challenge to Canadian dramaturgy in the 1990s has come from the country's many ethnic communities (Asian, Hispanic, African and aboriginal), which have traditionally been marginalized from the social mainstream. The importance of multicultural voices was recognized in 1993 when the Governor-General's Award went to Guillermo Verdecchia for his monodrama *Fronteras Americanas* (*American Borders*), which deconstructs social images of Latin American cultures. Probably the most radical challenge has come from the native Indian nations, for whom the theatre has become an effective instrument of cultural recuperation in their struggle to redress historical injustice. By 1990 there were several professional native theatres in Canada committed to aboriginal drama. Two theatres in particular were instrumental in encouraging new dramatists, De-Ba-Jeh-Mu-Jig Theatre and Native Earth Performing Arts. Playwrights whose works have premièred with these companies include Monique Mojica (b. 1954) (*Princess Pocahontas and the Blue Spots*, workshop, 1988; full production, 1990) and Daniel David Moses (b. 1952) (*Coyote City*, 1988).

In the mid-1990s, Canadian theatre's most celebrated native playwright was the Cree writer Tomson Highway (b. 1951), whose rich dramas of life on the Indian reserves, *The Rez Sisters* (1986) and *Dry Lips Oughta Move to Kapuskasing* (1989), written in English with some Cree, combine comic realism with traditional spirituality. Highway was the first native playwright to break into mainstream theatre; *Dry Lips* won several awards, and in 1991 received a major commercial revival at the Royal Alexandra Theatre in Toronto. Highway's success suggests that Canadian theatre is finally prepared to make multiculturalism an artistic reality, although writers, actors and directors from cultural minorities continue to face an uphill struggle for equal representation on Canadian stages.

Alan Filewod

Québec

Modern Québécois playwriting was born with the work of Gratien Gélinas. Beginning between 1938 and 1946 with an annual revue called *Fridolinons*, Gélinas later wrote a number of full-length works in the well-made-play tradition – *Tit-Coq* (1948) and *Bousille et les justes* (*Bousille and the Just*, 1959), his best plays, were acclaimed as syntheses of traditional dramatic form and popular themes. Marcel Dubé's (b. 1930) *Zone* (1953) and *Un Simple Soldat* (*A Simple Soldier*, 1958) showed that this kind of playwriting, with its realistic base, not only was able to reflect mainstream society's marginal elements, but also could begin

Muriel Miguel's 1990 Theatre Passe Muraille/Nightwood Theatre production of Monique Mojica's *Princess Pocahontas and the Blue Spots*, designed by Stephan Droege and Pat Mohan.
Photo: Jim Miller.

to break down traditional assumptions about the family unit.

At the same time, an avant-garde theatre began to appear. Between 1944 and 1946, Claude Gauvreau (1925–71) wrote a series of twenty-six short pieces, *Les Entrailles* (*Entrails*), in a surrealistic style. In 1948 the painter Paul-Émile Borduas (1905–60) created a controversial automatist manifesto, *Refus global* (*Global Refusal*), co-signed by Gauvreau and others, which denounced the stifling conservatism of the time and called for the liberation of the artistic imagination. In *Les Insolites* (*The Odd Ones*, 1956) and *Les Grands Départs* (*The Departure*, 1957), Jacques Languirand (b. 1931) experimented with themes and techniques in an absurdist style while Jacques Ferron (1921–85) adhered to satirical tradition in his one-act plays which emphasized individual liberties. Ferron's play *Les Grands-Soleils* (*The Sunflowers*), written in 1958 but not performed until ten years later, marked the beginning of a neo-nationalist current that significantly transformed traditional colonial interpretations of Québec history.

In the 1960s, one could begin to note in various plays a critique of the elite. As Dubé had done in *Les Beaux Dimanches* (*Oh Day of Rest and Gladness!*, 1960), Françoise Loranger (1913–95) depicted the explosion of the family unit in *Encore cinq minutes* (*Another Five Minutes*, 1965). Later, in *Double Jeu* (*Double Play*, 1969), Loranger presented a psychodrama that questioned familial and social roles, while Robert Gurik's (b. 1932) early plays dissected society's Judaeo-Christian foundation in *Le Pendu* (*The Hanged Man*) and *Api 2967* (1967). The emergence of a true counter-cultural vision could be seen clearly in such multimedia shows as *Équation pour un homme actuel* (*Formula for a Living Man*, 1967) by Pierre Moretti (b. 1931) and *Femme* (*Woman*, 1968) by Maurice Demers (b. 1936), and even in the disjointed writing style of Yves Hébert Sauvageau's (1946–70) *Wouf wouf* (1970).

With the founding of the Centre d'Essai des Auteurs Dramatiques (Playwrights' Development Centre) in 1965, Québec theatre became a vast laboratory. More than anyone else up to that time, Jean-Claude Germain (b. 1939) incarnated the desire for a Québécization of culture and theatre. Eschewing the so-called universal foreign models that he called *ailleurisme* (elsewhere-ism), this multi-talented man of theatre moved from an early career as a theatre critic to become a playwright, pro-

ducer and director of Montréal's Théâtre d'Aujourd'hui.

In the space of a dozen years, starting in 1969, Germain wrote twenty-five plays, of which the most important were *Les Hauts et les bas d'la vie d'une diva: Sarah Ménard par eux-mêmes* (*The Ups and Downs in the Life of a Diva: Sarah Ménard by Themselves*, 1974) and *Un Pays dont la devise est je m'oublie* (*A Country Whose Motto Is I Forget Myself*, 1976). In an admittedly hyperbolic style filled with references and allusions to Québec history, Germain adopted the tone of a pamphleteer, resorting to parody to accentuate the caricaturing and satirical dimension of his writing, which was consistently urbane, current and involved.

Another prolific contributor to the new Québec theatre, with more than thirty plays to his credit, including such noteworthy works as *Ben-Ur* (1971), *Une Brosse* (*The Binge*, 1975) and, later, *Les Gars* (*The Guys*, 1983), was Jean Barbeau (b. 1945). Working in a tragi-comic mode, Barbeau portrayed a series of weak, usually swindled individuals (most often men), victims of illusions and their own short-sighted existence. Barbeau's style quickly made him a speaker for this new populist style of playwriting.

During this period of profound self-questioning by French-Canadian society of inherited moral and political standards and habits, other playwrights focused on identifying the nascent Québécois personality, often with a sense of the absurd presented from a satirically realistic point of view. This is certainly true in the case of the plays of Roch Carrier (b. 1937) such as *La Guerre, Yes Sir!* (*The War, Yes Sir!*, 1970), André Ricard's (b. 1938) *La Gloire des filles à Magloire* (*The Glory of Magloire's Daughters*, 1975), Maryse Pelletier's (b. 1950) *Du Poil aux pattes comme les CWACs* (*When the CWACs Go Marching On*, 1982), and Jean-Raymond Marcoux's (b. 1940) *Bienvenue aux dames, Ladies Welcome!* (1983).

Set in a tavern, *Broue* (*Brew*, 1979), a collectively written series of comic sketches in which three actors portray some twenty eccentric male characters, became the biggest popular success since Gratien Gélinas's revues and continues in performance more than fifteen years after its première.

Other authors tended to probe the collective soul of Québec even more seriously, ranging from the distant past to the burning present, in order to identify signs of alienation evolved from collective social experiences since the British conquest of 1760. Plays such as *Le Procès de Jean-Baptiste M.* (*The Trial of Jean-Baptiste M.*, 1972) by Gurik and *Le Temps d'une vie* (*In a Lifetime*, 1975) by Roland Lepage (b. 1928) offered tragic evidence of what was called *québécitude*, a word formed by the fusion of the words Québec and solitude.

In this politically and socially charged atmosphere, a number of authors as well as collectives began to create an even more politically involved form of theatre. Among these plays were such significant examples as *Hamlet, prince du Québec* (1968) by Gurik and Françoise Loranger's *Medium saignant* (*Medium Rare*, 1970).

Unquestionably, however, the most important dramatist in the country throughout this period was Michel Tremblay. When *Les Belles-Soeurs* (*The Sisters-in-Law*, 1968) appeared on the stage of the Théâtre du Rideau Vert, the theatre which in 1968 represented Parisian-ness in all its glory, the history of French-Canadian theatre made an about-face. Written in *joual*, the Montréal street French, the play united elements of ancient tragedy, burlesque and modern

drama in a powerful dramatic synthesis. Tremblay continued to have an enormous impact in his next plays as he revealed again and again the impasses facing Québécois society: ignorance, cultural alienation, social and religious hypocrisy and lack of communication within the family. The dismantled realism of his polyphonic plays always remained connected, however, to its critical mission of provoking an awareness about the contradictions within the individual and the community itself: *À Toi, pour toujours, ta Marie-Lou* (*Forever Yours, Marie-Lou*, 1971), *Hosanna* (1973), *Bonjour, là, bonjour* (*Hello There, Hello*, 1974), *Sainte Carmen de la Main* (*Saint Carmen of the Main*, 1976), *Albertine, en cinq temps* (*Albertine, in Five Times*, 1984) and *Le Vrai Monde?* (*The Real World?*, 1987). All were dramatically powerful in Québec, across Canada, in the United States, France and in many other countries where his work was played.

During this same period, poet, essayist and playwright Claude Gauvreau denounced a society that he found cruelly asphyxiating in such ferocious but lyrical plays as *La Charge de l'orignal épormyable* (*The Charge of the*

André Brassard's 1968 Théâtre du Rideau Vert production of Michel Tremblay's *Les Belles-Soeurs.*
Photo: Guy Dubois.

As well, following the example of the Italian-born Marco Micone (b. 1945), playwrights from other cultural communities such as the American Indian Yves Sioui Durand (b. 1951) and the Lebanese Abla Farhoud (b. 1945) and Wajdi Mouawad (b. 1968) were beginning to let their voices be heard, demonstrating that Québec society no longer had the homogeneous character it had at the end of World War II.

Mouawad's *Journée de noces chez les Cromagnons* (*Wedding Day at the Cromagnons*, Théâtre d'Aujourd'hui, 1994) is an absurdist portrait of war-torn Beirut. Fahroud's *Jeu de patience* (*Game of Patience*, Théâtre de la Manufacture, 1994), a reflection on war, life and death, looks at war through the eyes of three women.

Outside of Québec, French-language drama had also taken root during this period in francophone centres of Manitoba, Ontario and New Brunswick. Manitoba writers Claude Dorge's (b. 1945) *Le Roitelet* (*The Kinglet*, 1976) and Roger Auger's (b. 1949) *Je m'en vais à Régina* (*I'm Going to Regina*, 1975) had been performed successfully by the Cercle Molière de Saint-Boniface, a theatre founded in 1925. In Ontario, La Vieille 17 (The Old 17) and the Comédie des Deux-Rives in Ottawa, the Théâtre du Nouvel Ontario (New Ontario Theatre) in Sudbury, which premièred *La Vie et les temps de Mérédic Boileau* (*The Life and Times of Mérédic Boileau*) by André Paiement (1950–78) in 1973 and *Le Chien* (*The Dog*, 1988) by Jean-Marc Dalpé (b. 1957), have also striven to maintain and develop a franco-Ontarian repertoire. Dalpé's *In the Ring* was produced as part of the 1994 Stratford Festival season.

In New Brunswick – Canada's only officially bilingual province – several Acadian troupes have been formed since 1974 and found success with playwrights Herménégilde Chiasson (b. 1946), Laval Goupil (b. 1946) and Jules Boudreau (b. 1941).

Unquestionably, however, Acadian theatre owes its revival and its international fame to Antonine Maillet (b. 1923). This prolific playwright, who moved to Montréal at the end of the 1970s, first became known for *La Sagouine* (1971), a play produced across Québec, Canada and France as well as at several European festivals. Other plays of hers – including *Gapi et Sullivan* (1973), *Mariaagélas* (1973) and *Évangéline Deusse* (1976) – have continued her moving, humorous and very human Acadian saga.

Gilbert David

Directors, Directing and Production Styles

Directing is still the most difficult and unstable profession in Canadian theatre. There are few positions available for resident directors, and artistic directors of theatres, working without job security, spend most of their time doing administrative work. In fact, most directors work on a freelance basis, or on limited contracts. This is in large part a consequence of cultural policies, which require that publicly funded theatres be operated under the supervision of a public board of trustees. These boards hire artistic staff; this has had the effect of taking institutional power away from artists.

While this administrative structure has given the theatrical community some degree of financial and institutional stability, it has had serious artistic repercussions. Few directors have the opportunity to work with a stable ensemble over a long period of time, and there are few theatres that develop expressing the guiding vision of the artistic director.

Visionary directors are therefore more often to be found in the small-theatre sector, in which companies subsist on occasional project grants. Perhaps the most successful example is that of George Luscombe, who founded Toronto Workshop Productions in 1959 to pursue his interest in political group theatre. One of the most imaginative and demanding directors in Canada at the time, Luscombe built an impressive canon of experimental and collectivist stagings over three decades, until changing policies required him to turn the theatre over to a board of trustees, which in time fired him because of internal politics.

The late 1960s and early 1970s saw the emergence of distinct schools of Canadian staging in the work of such directors as John Juliani (b. 1940; Savage God), Paul Thompson (Theatre Passe Muraille), Bill Glassco (Tarragon Theatre) and Janet Amos (b. 1945; Blyth Festival). Their work, although diverse, was marked by a common concern for the development of new dramatic forms and performance techniques. Juliani's work in Vancouver included explorations of performance venues (including staging Beckett's *Happy Days* in a tree stump in Stanley Park), pre-Grotowskian experiments in what was later to be called Poor Theatre, and examinations of audience tolerance, while Thompson's early explorations into collective creation (notably *The Farm Show*) played a formative role in the development of new approaches to playwriting in English Canada.

By the 1980s, directorial accomplishment was normally identified in terms of the development of new plays, rather than the reinterpretation of classics. As the theatrical commutniy diversified, new directors came to the fore because of their specialization in particular kinds of work, such as Toronto's Cynthia Grant (b. 1953) and Baṇuta Rubess, who have explored feminist approaches, and Sky Gilbert, artistic director of Buddies in Bad Times since 1978, one of the most successful gay/lesbian theatres in North America. Gilbert has played a critical role in the encouragement of beginning directors, including the controversial and iconoclastic Hillar Liitoja (b. 1954), artistic director of Toronto's experimental DNA Theatre (1982), whose postmodern deconstructions, such as *Poundemonium* (1993), often enrage critics.

Throughout the 1980s, directing was still perceived as a professional enclave of white males, but increasing awareness of cultural diversity has begun to dismantle the ethnic and gender configurations of the theatre. This has brought attention to a new generation of directors, most of whom work in the small-theatre sector on freelance projects. Directors such as Sally Hann and Colin Taylor (b. 1963) have introduced a new awareness of contemporary world drama to Canadian audiences.

Alan Filewod

Québec

Directing, in the modern sense of creating on stage an organic vision of a dramatic work, appeared late in Québec. While its beginnings can be traced to theatrical developments in the 1930s and 1940s, it was with the extensive directorial work of Jean Gascon at the Théâtre du Nouveau Monde from 1951 to 1966 that a directing style combining artistic fidelity to the dramatic text with interpretative reflection began to crystallize.

Gascon's directing at the TNM, of which he was also artistic director, helped to raise the standards of Québécois theatre to the artistic level of the major companies in the West. He staged the great classics of the repertoire from Shakespeare (*Richard II*, 1962) to Brecht (*The Threepenny Opera*, 1961) and achieved particular success with Molière, directing *L'Avare* (*The Miser*) in 1951 and 1963 and *Don Juan* in

1959. Disillusioned by the limited financial support given to the TNM by the Québec government, Gascon directed primarily in English Canada from 1967 on.

From his first productions in the 1950s, Paul Buissonneau, from France, brought to directing a playful imaginative spirit based on the stylization of gesture and carefully regulated movement. An artistic Jack-of-all-trades who ignored fashionable trends, Buissonneau drew on contemporary texts to create a visual poetry that at times became provocative, as in his production of Dario Fo's *Faut jeter la vieille* at the Théâtre du Nouveau Monde in 1969.

Jean-Pierre Ronfard is another first-rate French director who brought a liberating artistic spirit to Québécois theatre. He has staged many controversial works such as Claude Gauvreau's *Les Oranges sont vertes* and Réjean Ducharme's *HA ha!* ... (1978), both at the Théâtre du Nouveau Monde, and has also directed avant-garde foreign playwrights such as Jarry and Ionesco. Since 1977 he has also directed many productions, particularly with the Nouveau Théâtre Expérimental, which have questioned scenic conventions in an often incisive manner. Both in his way of working with (rather than controlling) his actors and of conceiving his playing area between the stage and the auditorium, Ronfard is never satisfied with any one artistic style.

André Brassard, another influential director, imposes less a directorial method (which he mistrusts) than a humanistic and pragmatic vision of the theatrical act in which the actor is considered an essential partner. He has directed the premières and many revivals of Michel Tremblay's works as well as those of other Québécois playwrights such as Michel Marc Bouchard and Normand Chaurette. Brassard has also staged the plays of numerous foreign playwrights (Racine, Chekhov, Beckett and Genet), often echoing local Québécois situations in their works with the aim of creating a subversive shock of recognition in his audience. For Brassard, theatre should address the here and now of spectators and involve an ongoing search for individual and collective authenticity in the face of an alienating society.

During the 1980s a deepening of scenographic conceptions gave directing an even greater role in Québec theatre productions. Directing styles diversified, thanks to the emergence of strong artistic personalities such as Gilles Maheu and Denis Marleau who made directing an art all of its own. This radical attitude contrasted sharply with the approach of other directors such as Guillermo de Andrea (b. 1933) and Olivier Reichenbach who, while drawing on undeniable directing skills, effaced themselves as much as possible in the dramatic texts they were staging.

After gaining experience from working with smaller companies, Lorraine Pintal, René Richard Cyr, Yves Desgagnés, Claude Poissant, Alice Ronfard and Serge Denoncourt have directed numerous productions at the larger theatres since 1985. Thanks to their work, the new repertoire of recent Québécois plays and foreign classics have been remounted and reinterpreted, often with different scenic codes and striking artistic results. Daniel Roussel (b. 1941), Alexandre Hausvater (b. 1949), Brigitte Haentjens (b. 1951), Martine Beaulne (b. 1952)

and Michel Nadeau (b. 1957) have also directed important productions.

Robert Lepage, the first Québécois director to establish a major international reputation, was invited to stage *A Midsummer Night's Dream* at the Royal National Theatre in London in 1992. Soon thereafter, the Festival d'Automne de Paris showcased Lepage's work with the Théâtre Repère by staging his Shakespeare cycle (*Coriolanus*, *Macbeth*, *The Tempest*) as well as Lepage's own *Polygraphe* and *Needles and Opium*. In 1993 Lepage founded his own company, Ex Machina, in Québec City and subsequently applied his multidisciplinary imagistic directing style to productions in Germany, Sweden, Japan and other countries.

Gilbert David

Music Theatre

Because of Canada's proximity to the United States, Canadian music theatre has always had an uneasy relationship with the Broadway musical. Most Canadians are familiar with standard Broadway hits through movies as well as through countless professional and amateur productions, and this has proven to be both a challenge and a hindrance for Canadian artists. In general, Canada's musical theatres have been more successful with small-scale productions, although there have been major exceptions, the most famous being *Anne of Green Gables* – adapted by Don Harron (b. 1924), music by Norman Campbell (b. 1924) – which premièred during the first season of the Charlottetown Festival in 1965. The theatre, founded by Mavor Moore to promote musical theatre, has produced an impressive body of new work, but none has equalled the success of *Anne*. Based on the popular children's book of the same name by Lucy Maude Montgomery (1874–1942), *Anne of Green Gables* has been produced in Charlottetown every year since.

During the 1950s and 1960s numerous Canadian cabarets offered satirical and musical revues and the New Play Society staged the immensely popular *Spring Thaw* series begun by Moore and his mother, Dora Mavor Moore, in 1948. The new theatres that emerged in the 1970s, however, began to introduce a distinct style of populist musical based on local themes. Notable examples are *Cruel Tears* (1975), a country-and-western musical written by Ken

Mitchell (b. 1940) and the country-rock group Humphrey and the Dumptrucks that situates *Othello* on the Canadian prairie; and the plays of composer-playwright John Gray (b. 1946) –

Timothy Bond's 1979 Tarragon Theatre production of John Gray's *Eighteen Wheels*, designed by Debra Hanson.
Photo: Nir Baraket.

Eighteen Wheels (1977), about long-distance truckers; *Billy Bishop Goes to War* (1978), based on the life of the famous Canadian World War I flying ace; *Rock and Roll* (1981), about a small-town band; and *Don Messer's Jubilee* (1985), based on the life of the popular Prince Edward Island fiddler.

The tradition of small-scale musicals also flourished in the 1980s, in part because Canadian theatres usually did not have money for large-scale musicals. Magnus Theatre in Thunder Bay, Ontario, produced two such musicals by Paul Ledoux (b. 1949) and David Young (b. 1946). *Fire* (1986), a rock musical based on the lives of the US singer Jerry Lee Lewis and his cousin, the preacher Jimmy Swaggart, proved to be one of the most popular Canadian musicals of the period. The same team's *Love Is Strange* (1984), exploring a Canadian farmer's obsessive love for the singer Anne Murray, was also well received across the country.

Musical comedies have long been standard fare in summer theatres as well. The Shaw Festival annually produces a 'pocket' musical, normally a revival of a lesser-known Broadway show, such as George Gershwin's *Girl Crazy* (1986). In the late 1970s and early 1980s the Stratford Festival was acclaimed for Brian Macdonald's (b. 1928) stylish revivals of Gilbert and Sullivan, including celebrated productions of *The Mikado* (1982) and *HMS Pinafore*, both of which enjoyed successful tours in the United States.

Many of Canada's most successful small musicals originated with the dramatic theatres. Attempts to replicate the large Broadway-style musical have been less successful, although Cliff Jones, author-composer of *Hey Marilyn* (1980) and *Kronberg: 1582* (1974; also known as *Rock-a-Bye Hamlet*), had short-lived productions on Broadway. Canadian impresarios frequently use US subjects to attract a Broadway production; not surprisingly, these often fail to reach New York.

The production of US and British commercial musicals in Canada has also become a major industry centred on four theatres in Toronto: the Elgin/Winter Garden, which staged *Cats* in 1985; the Pantages, home of *The Phantom of the Opera* (the show opened in 1989); the venerable Royal Alexandra, where Ed and David Mirvish mounted their own production of *Les Misérables* in 1989, which ran for three years; and the Mirvishes' new Princess of Wales Theatre, built to house *Miss Saigon*. The

financial stakes are such that when entrepreneur Garth Drabinsky produced *Phantom of the Opera* through his Live Entertainment Corporation, he invested $22 million to restore the Pantages, a 1920 vaudeville house. Although all four commercial houses claim an interest in Canadian musical theatre, detractors fear that the indigenous musical industry can only suffer from the presence of so many foreign mega-hits. Their fears seemed justified in 1993 when the newly built North York Performing Arts Centre (renamed the Ford Centre for the Performing Arts after a major corporate donor in 1994) opened with Drabinsky's production of the US classic *Show Boat* instead of a new Canadian musical.

The most innovative musical theatre in Canada is probably the least commercial. The works of avant-garde composer R. Murray Schafer (b. 1933), created in close collaboration with designers Diana and Jerrard (b. 1945) Smith and director Thom Sokolowski (b. 1950) of the Autumn Leaf Performance company, were, until the early 1990s, perhaps better known in Europe than in Canada. Schafer's ongoing mythic *Patria* cycle includes *The Princess of the Stars* (1981), performed by masked figures in canoes on a moonlit lake; *Ra* (1983), an overnight environmental descent into the ancient Egyptian underworld; *The Greatest Show* (1988), a metaphysical carnival in which the audience wanders through an actual but bizarre fairground to meet a host of mystical characters; and the ritualistic *Alchemical Theatre of Hermes Trismegistos*, staged at midnight in the great hall of Toronto's railroad station during the 1992 du Maurier World Stage Festival.

While radio broadcasts of operas by the Canadian Broadcasting Corporation (CBC) helped create a national audience for opera in Canada, the seeds for permanent operatic roots can be found in the establishment in 1946 of the Royal Conservatory Opera School (absorbed by the University of Toronto in 1969) and the formation of the CBC Opera Company (1948–55), which provided the first major training and employment facilities for operatic performers. The Canadian Opera Company (COC) grew out of the Opera School and by 1956 it was presenting professional seasons independently of the school. The COC began extensive touring in 1958, sparking the development of opera companies in other major Canadian centres, and quickly became the largest and most productive opera company in the country. The early seasons of the COC concentrated on the most popular of the European standard works in order to attract the largest audiences and minimize the inevitable deficits, but it eventually broadened its repertoire to include twentieth-century works. In 1966, a staging of Healey Willan's (1880–1968) *Deirdre*, with a libretto by John Coulter, marked the company's first foray into home-grown opera. Since then, the COC has been responsible for over a dozen Canadian commissions.

Canada's centennial celebrations in 1967 inspired several operas on national themes. By far the most ambitious was *Louis Riel* by Harry Somers (b. 1925). A full-length opera requiring large-scale production capabilities, it dealt with the Métis insurrections against Canada's westward expansion in the 1880s. The libretto, by Mavor Moore and Jacques Languirand, was written in four languages – English, French, Cree and Latin – in order to reflect the diverse cultures represented, and this diversity was also represented in the eclectic musical styles employed. The opera was commissioned by the Canadian Opera Company with funding from the Floyd S. Chalmers Foundation, a rare instance of private subsidy for a major operatic work. *Louis Riel* was revived twice – in 1968 and 1975, when it played in both Ottawa and Washington, DC. In addition, a CBC-TV telecast of the work was produced in 1969.

The success of *Louis Riel*, both critical and financial, initiated a further burst of operatic activity in Canada, mostly short or medium-length works for relatively small performing forces. For a brief time in the early 1970s, the Stratford Festival's Third Stage became a home for chamber operas and relatively small experimental productions, such as Raymond Pannell's (b. 1935) plotless *Exiles* (1973) with a libretto by Beverley Pannell; Charles Wilson's (b. 1931) church opera *The Summoning of Everyman* (1974), based on the Medieval Morality play; and Harry Somers's *The Fool* (composed in 1953, produced in 1975) with a libretto by Michael Fram, which deals with a court jester who is determined to maintain artistic freedom against his king's will.

Tibor Polgar's (1907–93) one-act comic opera *The Glove*, libretto by George Jonas (b. 1935), represents a minor success in Canadian chamber opera. Written for the touring group Prologue to the Performing Arts in 1973, the work achieved substantial popularity in Ontario schools (over 100 performances by 1980) and in 1975 was telecast by the CBC. One opera

written specifically for television also received wide acclaim: Raymond Pannell's *Aberfan* (libretto by Beverley Pannell), based on the tragic deaths of 116 school children in a Welsh mining village, which won the 1977 Salzburg Prize for the best original television opera and has since been seen in some two dozen countries.

Most opera companies in Canada have remained conservative in their choices of productions, preferring the most popular works in the European repertoire. The Vancouver Opera, for example, founded in 1959, commissioned its first Canadian opera in 1991, David MacIntyre and librettist Tom Cone's (b. 1947) chamber opera *The Architect*, produced in 1994. A few companies have been more adventurous, however. In 1975, the COMUS Music Theatre and the Co-Opera Company were both established in Toronto to develop alternatives to more traditional operatic venues. Co-Opera focused on smaller experimental works, such as Somers's *Death of Enkidu, Part I* (1977) – libretto by Martin Kinch (b. 1943) – which relates part of the ancient Babylonian epic of Gilgamesh.

COMUS Music Theatre was formed by director Michael Bawtree (b. 1937), singer Maureen Forrester (b. 1930) and composer Gabriel Charpentier (b. 1925), with a more commercial approach than Co-Opera. It succeeded in presenting over thirty new Canadian works before financial problems forced it to cease operations in 1987. At the 1984 World Music Days, COMUS was credited with producing more than half of all the premières of contemporary music theatre in North America.

The trend towards small community and specialist opera companies has continued; in the Toronto area alone, Opera Atelier, Opera Ora and the Toronto Operetta Theatre are just three of the companies of this nature. Opera Atelier, a Baroque opera, ballet and theatre company founded by Marshall Pynkoski and Jeannette Zingg in 1986, has begun to earn an international reputation. Its 1994 production of Henry Purcell's *Dido and Aeneas* was remounted at the Houston Grand Opera and in Paris in 1995.

Despite economic obstacles, new large works have also continued to appear from time to time. Charles Wilson's three-act *Héloïse and Abélard*, libretto by Eugene Benson (b. 1928), premièred in 1973 as part of the Canadian Opera Company's twenty-fifth anniversary season. The Guelph Spring Festival has also been responsible for a number of new full-length opera commissions. *Psycho Red*, another Wilson–Benson collaboration, premièred there in 1977. Labelled a 'dramatic mindscape', this unconventional work deals with a psychiatrist, his wife and a female patient, with dancers doubling as the three characters in order to enact their mental states.

That same year, Derek Healey's (b. 1936) *Seabird Island*, libretto by Norman Newton, based on a west-coast native legend, was also premièred at the Guelph Spring Festival. John Beckwith's (b. 1927) *Crazy to Kill*, libretto by James Reaney, appeared at the festival in 1989. This unique operatic murder mystery featured lifesize puppets that at times portrayed various characters. The 1990 Sharon Festival commissioned and premièred Harry Somers's *Serinette* (libretto by Reaney), a 'festival opera' about the small religious sect that set up a commune in the town of Sharon in the 1880s.

The Canadian Opera Company provided a boost to opera composition in 1987 when it established a composer-in-residence programme. By 1993, the programme had resulted in the creation of two full-length and seven one-act operas by Canadian composers. The most notable of these was Somers's three-act *Mario and the Magician* with a libretto by Rod Anderson. This adaptation of Thomas Mann's

1930 novella was staged in 1992 at Toronto's Elgin Theatre and provided a warning about the recurring rise of fascism.

Alan Filewod, Andrew M. Zinck

Québec

Until the 1960s, the production of musical works in Québec usually took place in relatively precarious circumstances. The Opera Guild (1941–69) and the Festival de Montréal (1939–65) produced one opera each year. In 1994 in Québec City the Opéra de Québec (founded in 1984) was continuing the work of the Théâtre Lyrique de Nouvelle-France (Lyric Theatre of New France, 1961–70) and of the Société Lyrique d'Aubigny (founded in 1968) and was making special use of home-grown talent.

The Opéra de Montréal (founded in 1980), following in the footsteps of the Opéra de Québec (1971–5), has long employed mostly foreign singers, directors and set designers. With its seven annual productions, this remains, however, the most important opera company in Québec. In 1989, the company Chants Libres (Free Chants) was founded in Montréal to devote itself to a contemporary repertoire and to indigenous creation.

The Opéra de Montréal production of Puccini's *La Bohème*, designed by Robert Prévost.
Photo: André LeCoz.

longer to register. Canada's oldest surviving modern dance company, Winnipeg's Contemporary Dancers, was founded in 1964 by US-born Rachel Browne (b. 1934), whose early work reflected her own broadly humanist concerns expressed in a style influenced by her choreographic mentors. Her dances include *The Woman I Am* (1977) and *Interiors* (1978), both based on poetry about aspects of womanhood.

The three dancers who founded Toronto Dance Theatre (TDT) in 1968 – David Earle (b. 1939), Peter Randazzo (b. 1943) and Patricia Beatty (b. 1936) – wanted to create a Canadian interpretation of the principles of Martha Graham and her attempt to harness dance's potential to create ecstatic, affirmative theatre of movement on the grand themes of the human condition. Toronto Dance Theatre has contributed a particular and influential aesthetic to the fabric of dance in Canada – dance as philosophical statement, dance as poetic expression, dance as a metaphor for life.

Among the founding TDT choreographers' most important works are Beatty's *Against Sleep* (1968) and *Painters and the Dance* (1983), Earle's *Atlantis* (1973) and *Sacra Conversazione* (1984) and Randazzo's *L'Assassin menacé* (1975). Since 1994, the company has been under the artistic direction of choreographer Christopher House (b. 1955), a company alumnus whose provocative dance explorations of issues such as AIDS (in *Early Departures*) have placed him at the forefront of contemporary Canadian choreography.

Another Canadian choreographer of international reputation is James Kudelka (b. 1955), an alumnus of the National Ballet whose work with all three major Canadian ballet troupes as well as with other North American companies includes issue ballets as well as pure dance ballets. His works include *In Paradisum* (1983) and *Dracula* (1985).

In the 1980s, a highly theatrical school of modern dance emerged in Canada, including a

The 1985 National Ballet of Canada production of Robert Desrosiers's *Blue Snake*, designed by Jerrard Smith.
Photo: Andrew Oxenham.

cluster of young Montréal choreographers who had responded to the loosening of Québec's social bonds in the 1970s with a flood of vivid and provocative theatrical dance works tackling social, sexual and political themes. Their iconoclastic, interdisciplinary vision encouraged young choreographers across the country, among them Robert Desrosiers (b. 1953), who founded the Desrosiers Dance Theatre in Toronto in 1980, Michel Montanaro (b. 1954) in Ottawa and Tedd Robinson (b. 1952) in Winnipeg.

Other Toronto choreographers, such as Danny Grossman (b. 1942) and those involved with Dancemakers and TIDE (Toronto Independent Dance Enterprises), chose to follow other stylistic paths, but all embraced the notion of theatrical dance as a means of emotional and spiritual expression. Grossman's major works, marked by an inventively humorous yet compassionate exploration of the grotesque, include La Valse, about social inequities, Higher (1975) and Endangered Species (1981).

Although Norbert Vesak helped expose Vancouver to modernist trends in the mid-1960s, choreography on Canada's west coast has been less susceptible to outside influences, and until the establishment of Ballet British Columbia in the late 1980s was almost entirely in the area of modern dance. This west-coast choreography includes the raw, emotional dances, such as Coming Together (1975), of Paula Ross (b. 1941), who launched Vancouver's first modern dance company in 1965; the complex theatrical integrations of lights, props, costume, film and movement that characterized the work of Anna Wyman (b. 1928) in such pieces as Here at the Eye of the Hurricane (1972) and Adastra (1982); the myth-making of Karen Jamieson (b. 1946), who has steadily forged for herself a broad-reaching psychosocial vision founded in an expressive dance language that unites elements of native thought and tradition with late-twentieth-century approaches to dance as theatre, for example in Sisyphus and Tales of Descent (1993), based on northwest-coast Indian myths; the experiments of the choreographers at Jumpstart and Special Delivery Moving Theatre, who have explored advanced dance theatre crossovers involving the use of voice and vocal sounds in such productions as Lee Eisler's Four Fridas; and the east–west blends created by Kokoro Dance, with its fascination with Japanese butoh. Headed by Barbara Bourget (b. 1950) and Jay Hirabayashi

(b. 1947), Kokoro's productions have included Rage, which dealt with the treatment of Japanese Canadians during World War II, and Dance of the Dead (1994).

Canada also has a strong tradition of independent solo dance theatre performers dealing with spiritual and emotional issues. Prominent among them are Peggy Baker (b. 1953) and Margie Gillis (b. 1953), whose emotion-charged miniatures and passionate dancing have earned her comparisons with Isadora Duncan. Her major dances include How the Rosehips Quiver (1983) and Torn Roots, Broken Branches (1993).

Professional dance theatre in Canada draws strength from an extensive training infrastructure. All three of the major ballet companies maintain excellent government-funded schools producing well-trained dancers. The most prestigious is the National Ballet School, founded by Betty Oliphant (b. 1918) in 1959 to train dancers for the National Ballet of Canada. Professional-quality schools are also attached to the country's leading modern dance troupes. Training for young, pre-professional students is provided by the School of the Canadian Children's Dance Theatre (CCDT), established in Toronto in 1985. The CCDT itself is a modern troupe of sixteen dancers aged 11–18, founded by Deborah Lundmark (b. 1954) and Michael deConinck Smith (b. 1954) in 1980 to provide young performers and their audiences with a theatre for self-expression and entertainment.

Following the explosion of audience interest in dance in the late 1960s and 1970s, dance also became a focus of concern for Canadian universities. In 1971 Toronto's York University became the first to offer a full degree-granting programme to train dancers, choreographers and teachers, and was the first in the world to offer a graduate degree in dance history and criticism. Degrees in dance are also offered at the Université du Québec à Montréal and Concordia University in Montréal and at Vancouver's Simon Fraser University, where dancers and choreographers work within an interdisciplinary setting. Choreographic activity is intense, and a number of the country's most significant dance theatre companies were created by individuals whose talents were first nurtured in university dance programmes.

An important organizational contact in the 1970s and 1980s between dance groups and individual artists across the country was the Dance in Canada Association (DICA), founded in 1973. Through the publication of its Dance in

Canada magazine, annual national conferences and dance festivals, DICA created a sense of community in the profession and stimulated artistic creation. It also presented dance concerns to funding bodies, particularly the Canada Council, whose touring subsidies had significantly expanded audiences for modern dance in the early 1970s.

In the 1990s, the country's major dance organization is the Canadian Association of Professional Dance Organizations, founded in 1977 to represent the larger, more established and better subsidized ballet and modern dance companies. Dance Ontario and other provincial organizations across the country work primarily on a regional level. The Association for Dance in Universities and Colleges in Canada, founded in 1988, represents dance teachers at the college and university level across the country.

The largest archive on theatrical dance in Canada has been compiled by Dance Collection Danse in Toronto, publisher of *The Encyclopedia of Theatre Dance in Canada* (1990).

Max Wyman

Québec

At the end of World War II, dance was still a very marginal part of artistic activity in Québec despite the efforts of pioneers such as the self-taught Maurice Lacasse-Morenoff (1906–93) and Gérald Crevier (1912–93), who was trained in the Ezzak Ruvenoff method. The latter was the first officially to establish a ballet company in the province, Les Ballets Québec (1948–51).

Elizabeth Leese, a refugee from Nazism, had already brought her dance knowledge, influenced by expressionism, to young dancers in Montréal in 1944. Ludmilla Chiriaeff, born in Latvia in 1924, arrived in Québec in 1952 and helped to bring about a major growth in classical ballet by choreographing for French-language television and by founding Les Grands Ballets Canadiens in 1958. Among leading choreographers for that company were Fernand Nault (b. 1921), whose works include *Carmina Burana* (1967) and *Tommy* (1970); Brian Macdonald, who established a studio for choreographic creation in the mid-1970s; and later, in 1980, James Kudelka, who came from the National Ballet of Canada to instil a new dynamism into the company and helped to win an international reputation for Les Grands Ballets Canadiens, under the artistic direction at that time of Linda Stearns and Danny Jackson. Still the only major ballet company in Québec, Les Grands Ballets has had Lawrence Rhodes (b. 1939) as its artistic director since 1989.

While classical ballet was able to take root and develop relatively rapidly, the same cannot be said for modern dance. Nevertheless, as early as 1948, Françoise Sullivan (b. 1925) and Jeanne Renaud (b. 1928) together mounted their first recital of modern dance, stimulated by the multidisciplinary automatist group centred around the painter Paul-Émile Borduas, which advocated abstraction, spontaneity and an appeal to the unconscious. At the end of the 1950s, Françoise Riopelle (b. 1927) opened a school for modern dance in Montréal that aimed to transcend the artistic gaps between painting, sculpture and movement. As a choreographer, Riopelle favoured an open-ended form, leaving room for a degree of improvisation, and an abstract gestural composition, which she combined with geometric projections that transformed her dancers into living sculptures. She also explored other technologies in order to produce multimedia spectacles.

Paralleling Merce Cunningham in her privileging of dance's autonomy in relation to music, Jeanne Renaud founded the first incorporated modern dance company in Québec, Le Groupe de la Place Royale, in 1966. This company rejected all narrative dimensions in order to concentrate on the purity of form. Renaud's formalist approach meant that her company had difficulty reaching the conservative public of the period. In 1977 Le Groupe de la Place Royale, under the direction of Peter Boneham and Jean-Pierre Perreault (b. 1947), moved to Ottawa.

Le Groupe Nouvelle Aire (New Area Group, 1968–82) was the second modern dance company operating in Montréal. Its principal founder, Martine Époque (b. 1942), an *émigré* from France, understood how to encourage experimentation and innovation in choreographic creation and extended to modern dance a mytho-poetic inclination. Influenced initially by Maurice Béjart, the company emphasized rhythmic complexity that gradually gained in fluidity of movement. The group was a veritable melting pot of talent, which greatly stimulated the choreographic landscape during the 1980s.

Artistic fermentation occurred during the 1970s through the founding of other new companies such as Axis Danse by Iro Tembeck and Christina Coleman in 1977 and Pointépiénu (Point 'n' Bare-feet, 1977–84) but especially through the work of choreographers not associated with a company, such as Linda Rabin

(b. 1946), who created a ritualistic spectacle, *The White Goddess*, in 1977. These companies and independent productions helped to establish the basis for what was soon called the *nouveau bouger montréalais* (new Montréal school of body language).

Parallel to this evolution in modern dance was another phenomenon – a craze for ballet-jazz. Immediately popular with the public, this style of dance derived from a mixture of classic and contemporary jazz dance and the free expressiveness of its physicality, which enabled Les Ballets Jazz de Montréal, founded by Eva Von Gencsy (b. 1924), Geneviève Salbaing and Eddy Toussaint in 1972, quickly to attract an audience. By 1988 the company had performed in over forty countries.

In the 1980s, one of Montréal's leading choreographers was Jean-Pierre Perreault, whose work, while he danced for Le Groupe de la Place Royale, reflected the influence of a formalist dance heritage. He achieved first rank as a creative artist with *Joe* (1983), a work for twenty-four dancers performed internationally. Since then he has drawn extensively on the visual arts to create works with a strong plasticity such as *Nuit* (*Night*, 1986), *Îles*

(*Islands*, 1991) and the cycle *Adieux* (*Farewells*, 1993).

Other choreographers such as Paul-André Fortier (b. 1947), Daniel Léveillé (b. 1952), Édouard Lock (b. 1954) and Ginette Laurin (b. 1955) drew closer to dance theatre, initially characterized by the presence of narration, before creating much more striking works emphasizing a purer physicalization and the natural rhythms of the body in movement. Companies such as La La La Human Steps (founded by Lock in 1982) and O Vertigo (founded by Laurin in 1984) are now recognized internationally.

Marie Chouinard (b. 1955) began a solo career in 1978. Her works, such as *STAB* (*Space Time and Beyond*, 1986) and *Le Faune* (*The Faun*, 1987), convey an intense and savage eroticism. She founded La Compagnie Marie Chouinard in 1991 and undertook to choreograph her first group pieces with an organic strength that confirmed her unusual talent.

In the late 1980s and early 1990s, new companies such as Le Carré des Lombes (founded by Danièle Desnoyers in 1989), Cas Public (founded by Hélène Blackburn in 1989) and Louise Bédard Danse (1990) began to demon-

Jean-Pierre Perreault's 1983 *Joe*.
Photo: Robert Etcheverry.

125

CANADA

strate a renewed artistic effervescence that has maintained Montréal as one of North America's important dance centres. Since 1985 the Festival International de la Nouvelle Danse (International Festival of New Dance), under the direction of Chantal Pontbriand (b. 1950), has contributed to this artistic fermentation. Another important influence has been exerted by the dance department at the Université du Québec à Montréal, which developed a number of contemporary choreographers. In 1984, Le Regroupement des Professionnels de la Danse (Organization of Dance Professionals) was founded to address the many challenges facing the discipline, particularly insufficient government financial support.

Gilbert David,
based on Iro Tembeck's book
Danser à Montréal

Theatre for Young Audiences

Amateur theatre productions for children in English Canada date from the last quarter of the nineteenth century. Some amateur companies, such as the Toronto Children's Theatre, founded in 1931, even managed to stay in existence for several decades and achieved high production standards. The first professional theatre for young audiences in Canada was Holiday Theatre, founded by Joy Coghill (b. 1926) and Myra Benson in Vancouver in 1953. Over its twenty-four-year history, Holiday Theatre strove to win acceptance for the concept of professional theatre for young audiences, toured plays to schools in remote areas and commissioned dozens of new Canadian plays.

In the 1990s, there were approximately thirty professional theatre companies in English Canada whose work was mainly directed at children and adolescents. Few of these companies, however, had their own performance spaces; for the most part, theatre for young audiences was and still is organized through tours to elementary and secondary schools.

The typical 1990s group has, however, adopted the precepts of the theatre-in-education movement, using audience participation techniques to perform socially relevant plays. A key figure in this development has been Brian Way, who pioneered theatre-in-education in Great Britain in the 1960s, and whose work with the Globe Theatre in Regina provided a model for similar Canadian groups in the following decades.

Young audience companies in Canada in the 1990s fall into two general economic categories: independent companies, and troupes that function as subsidiaries of adult regional theatres. For the most part, the companies share common philosophies, although the subsidiary companies can benefit from the larger budgets of their sponsoring theatres. Because of the vast size of the country, touring in schools is still a major endeavour, and at least two groups, sponsored by the Citadel Theatre in Edmonton and the Sudbury Theatre Centre, have made extensive use of air transportation to reach remote areas.

The principle of taking theatre to school audiences has also meant that the typical play is designed for performance in school gymnasiums, classrooms and assembly halls, in which the actors and stage managers have very little time to set the stage. Consequently scenography often consists simply of painted flats and rudimentary lighting.

The most notable exception to this model is Young People's Theatre (YPT) in Toronto, which, since its founding in 1966 by Susan Rubes (b. 1925), has been offering production values that rival any of the adult companies. YPT has been performing in its own theatre facility since 1977. It contains a 468-seat proscenium theatre named after the company's founder and the 150-seat Nathan Cohen Theatre, named after the influential Canadian critic. With an annual operating budget of $2.5 million, the company attracts a wide range of audiences.

YPT's inaugural production in its own theatre was a Czechoslovakian Laterna Magica creation designed by Josef Svoboda, *The Lost Fairy Tale*, adapted by the Czech-born opera singer and actor Jan Rubes (b. 1920). Since its inception, the company has employed leading directors and designers, has invited other groups from Québec and other parts of Canada, and has commissioned dozens of Canadian plays. In 1975, YPT toured its production of Henry Beissel's (b. 1929) poetic Inuit quest-drama *Inook and the Sun* to England. The company has continued to dramatize the challenges facing

Maja Ardal's 1993 Young People's Theatre production of David Holman's *Whale*, designed by Teresa Przybylski, costumes designed by Julia Tribe.

Canada's native peoples, such as David Holman's 1993 Inuit drama *Whale*, about the plundering of the species in the Arctic, and attempts to reflect Toronto's increasingly multicultural composition in its repertoire.

The most significant development since the late 1970s has been the emergence of 'advocacy' theatre for young audiences. Companies such as Green Thumb in Vancouver (1975), Catalyst Theatre in Edmonton (1977), Theatre Direct (1976) and Theatre in the Rough (1985) in Toronto, and Actor's Showcase in Winnipeg focus on social and political issues. The most widely performed plays for young audiences have come out of this movement, many of them written by Dennis Foon (b. 1951), founder of Green Thumb. Foon's *New Canadian Kid* (1981), a gently ironic look at racism and immigrant experience, has been one of the most popular of all Canadian young audience plays. Green Thumb also developed the very successful *Feeling Yes, Feeling No* (1982), a workshop performance used to teach small children how to protect themselves against sexual abuse.

In Toronto, Theatre Direct has also had notable success in performing advocacy plays for teenage audiences, such as *Thin Ice* (1987) by Beverley Cooper and Baṇuta Rubess, which raises awareness of date rape and sexual assault. Other issues commonly addressed include AIDS awareness, domestic violence, drug abuse and alcoholism; often these plays are developed in response to needs expressed by school teachers and administrators. Some of the most effective plays have been written and performed by adolescent actors working with adult facilitators. Such peer productions are often more politically powerful than plays written by adults: two notable examples are *Ntesinan* (*Our Land*), created with aboriginal Innu youth in Labrador by the RCA Theatre (1979) in Newfoundland; and *I.D.* by the Hour Company, a hard-hitting look at police violence against black youth in Toronto.

The increased recognition of theatre for young audiences as a form has brought about professional legitimacy. No longer is it perceived merely as a way into the theatre profession; many playwrights, actors, designers and directors of the first rank regularly work with these companies. Some, especially leading groups such as Green Thumb, Young People's Theatre and Theatre Direct, have even attracted a wide adult following because of their impressive professionalism and innovative theatricality and dramaturgy.

Achievements in playwriting are recognized now by the annual Chalmers Theatre for Young Audiences Canadian Play Awards administered by the Ontario Arts Council. It provides two awards of $10,000 each for original plays produced in the Toronto area.

The Vancouver Children's Festival, established in 1978, and similar festivals across the country, serve as important contact points between some of the best Canadian and international companies and soloists working in the field.

Alan Filewod

Québec

Between 1950 and 1970, Québec's adult companies, out of a desire to experiment with different forms of theatre and out of a growing belief that the 'spectators of tomorrow' could be schooled, introduced a theatre for children section within their structures.

The Compagnons de Saint-Laurent, for example, became home to the Théâtre de l'Arc-en-ciel (Rainbow Theatre), which produced plays for children between 1949 and 1951; the Théâtre-Club was home to the Théâtre des Mirlitons (Reed Pipe Theatre) between 1958 and 1962; and the Théâtre du Rideau Vert operated the Manteau d'Arlequin 5/15 (Harlequin's Cloak) between 1967 and 1978. Productions for the young were offered on the main stages of these adult theatres on weekends, and were mostly adaptations of European traditional stories and folk tales. Episodes from popular television series for the young were also adapted for the theatre and puppets appeared in some productions.

The Manteau d'Arlequin 5/15, under the artistic direction of actor and author André Cailloux (b. 1920), also invited school children to the theatre on weekdays for plays influenced by traditional European tales and infused with lessons of good behaviour, or for the puppet productions of Nicole Lapointe (b. 1932) and Pierre Régimbald (b. 1941). The company also offered quite spectacular productions of *L'Oiseau bleu* (*The Bluebird*, 1967) by Maurice Maeterlinck and *Alice au pays des merveilles* (*Alice in Wonderland*, 1971), adapted by Yvette Brind'Amour in the Place des Arts during Christmas holidays.

An exception to this approach, between 1961 and 1967, was the Apprentis-Sorciers company, which, inspired by their knowledge of Medieval farce, *commedia dell'arte* scenarios and the French *guignol*, improvised performances for children, thus opening the way to original writing. In Québec City, the Théâtre pour Enfants de Québec (Children's Theatre of Québec, 1965–70) – the first autonomous Québec company founded specifically to produce theatre for children – encouraged the writing of new plays by television scriptwriters, novelists and younger authors. At first it produced puppet theatre, then introduced performances created by actors through improvisation. It also initiated school touring, but when it asked for funding to continue its operations, it was left stranded between the ministries of education and culture.

Quite a few municipalities throughout Québec launched touring companies that would travel through parks during the summer. La Roulotte (The Caravan), inaugurated by the parks and recreation department of the city of Montréal under the direction on Paul Buissonneau in 1953, presented visually astonishing shows that borrowed freely from the fantastic, folk tale and science fiction traditions. Along with Le Vagabond, a travelling puppet stage inaugurated in 1957, La Roulotte was also intended as a mobile drama workshop for the children themselves, who could rehearse and present their own sketches, songs and choreography.

Between 1970 and 1980, numerous professional children's theatre companies were founded by young actors who chose the collective approach to writing, directing and designing productions, which would tour extensively in schools and small venues. They wanted theatre to be accessible to all. Proceeding from new options, they emphasized communication with the children, whom they saw as participants in their theatrical endeavours. Their theme-based creative workshops allowed them to get better acquainted with one another. As young adults, they were curious about children, their feelings, thoughts and vision of the world; as artists, they were keen on presenting plays and productions with informative content and a critical outlook on society. They refused the traditional elves, fairies and happy endings and created plays grounded in the observation of social realities, plays akin to child advocacy theatre. Simultaneously, they chose to experiment with staging techniques that included mime, masks, clowns, circus techniques and new performance styles marked by poetic and surrealistic overtones. Stylistically, the realistic

and the poetic gradually merged into what could become a 'lyrical realism', a style that still characterizes Québécois theatre for young audiences.

The Théâtre de la Marmaille (founded in 1973 and renamed Les Deux Mondes in 1993) is one of the longest lived of these groups. Taking a completely playful approach, they led audiences into areas of self-affirmation in such works as Marcel Sabourin's *Pleurer pour rire* (*Crying to Laugh*, 1980) or towards other cultures, for example in the interactive play *L'Umiak* (1982). At the end of the 1980s, the company chose to perform for both adult and child audiences.

The work of Théâtre de Carton (1973) tended to validate young people's emotions while dealing with the creative body in *Je m'imagine* (*I Imagine Myself*, 1980), with topics of sensuality/sexuality in *Les Enfants n'ont pas de sexe?* (*Sex Is Not For Kids*, 1979) and with ecology in *Je regarde le soleil en face* (*I Am Looking Straight at the Sun*, 1982).

The Théâtre de Quartier (1975), for its part, questioned social rules and emphasized behavioural links with studies of domination, racism and intolerance in such plays as *Un Jeu d'enfants* (*Children's Game*, 1979) and *Qui a raison?* (*Who Is Right?*, 1983).

Individual artists contributed to the collective work while also forging their own styles, which became clear in the late 1970s and 1980s. The themes chosen by most writers were resolutely contemporary: what children do on a school holiday other than fight among themselves and with adults in Marie-Francine Hébert's (b. 1943) provocative *Cé tellement 'cute' des enfants* (*Such Cute Children*, 1975), and how to build friendships so as to understand the other in Suzanne Lebeau's (b. 1948) *Une Lune entre deux maisons* (*A Moon Between Two Houses*, 1979), *La Marelle* (*Hopscotch*, 1984) and *Comment vivre avec les hommes quand on est un géant* (*A Giant in the Land of Men*, 1989).

Louis-Dominique Lavigne (b. 1949) deals with individuals who feel rejected and to whom ordinary situations and events of daily life appear as insurmountable obstacles in *On est capable* (*We Can Do It*, 1977), *Où est-ce qu'elle est ma gang?* (*Where's My Gang?*, 1982) and *Le Sous-sol des anges* (*The Angels' Basement*, 1984). Serge Marois (b. 1948) succeeds skilfully in his reappropriation of traditional tales in ways that border on the mythic in *Monsieur Léon* (*Mr Léon*, 1989), while Yves Masson (b. 1954) excelled in writing dialogue and dramatic

Daniel Meilleur's 1980 Théâtre de la Marmaille production of Marcel Sabourin's *Crying to Laugh*, designed by Daniel Castonguay.
Photo: Paul-Émile Rioux.

situations through which teenage characters appeared in all of their fascinating complexity in *Entre parenthèses* (*In Parentheses*, 1989). Jasmine Dubé (b. 1957), for her part, deals in a light and refreshing tone with father–son relationships in *Petit Monstre* (*Little Monster*, 1992).

High-school students were also recognized as potential spectators. The Nouvelle Compagnie Théâtrale was founded in 1964 specifically to introduce them to theatre as an art form. Performing in its own Montréal space (the Gesù; since 1977 the Théâtre Denise-Pelletier), it began by presenting plays from the European repertoire and gradually introduced audiences to US and Québécois authors, accompanying each of its productions with an elaborate programme aimed at informing teachers and students alike. From 1992 to 1995 under the artistic direction of director Brigitte Haentjens, the company resolutely oriented itself towards highly creative theatrical choices.

Other companies have, since 1976, chosen to focus on adolescents as their spectators and have designed shows specifically for them around themes related to the social and cultural experiences of 13–18-year-olds. They use music, rhythm and choreography to appeal to this audi-ence. Claude Poissant, co-founder of Théâtre Petit à Petit (1978), has particularly distinguished himself as an author and director of theatre for teenagers.

The Festival de Théâtre pour Enfants (Festival of Children's Theatre), founded in 1973 under the aegis of the Association Québécoise du Jeune Théâtre, has become an international event. It is now an autonomous corporation known as Coups de Théâtre/Festival International de Théâtre Jeune Public (Theatrical Moments/ International Festival of Theatre for Young Audiences). In 1984, Montréal's Maison Théâtre pour l'Enfance et la Jeunesse (Theatre House for Young Audiences) – founded by the companies as a common performance space and still administered by its members – began presenting full seasons for children and adolescents. At the end of the 1980s, Les Productions Gros Becs (Big Kiss Productions) did the same in Québec City.

Since the mid-1980s, most of the companies mentioned have toured internationally. Most of the plays have been published in French, and translated and produced in English and other languages such as Spanish, Portuguese and German.

Hélène Beauchamp

Puppet Theatre

Puppetry was used in American Indian shamanic rituals of the Kwakiutl, Inuit and Iroquois peoples as an important means of connecting physical reality with the world of the spirit. Puppets representing spirits can still be seen in productions by contemporary native Indian and Inuit companies.

European forms of puppetry were part of the development of the amateur theatre for young audiences in the 1920s and 1930s. But with the exception of a number of professional puppeteers who subsequently pioneered the form in cities across Canada, puppetry has remained a marginalized artistic form both within the theatre community and with the general public. As a result, its history and contributions to Canadian culture have not yet been properly assessed.

Numerous puppet theatres were founded in Canada after 1945 but few enjoyed ongoing success. Those that have survived have done so on the basis of a unique identity or through genuine artistic innovation. An example of the former category is Famous People Players (founded in Toronto in 1974), a company of disabled people who have received international attention for their black light performances featuring puppets using the faces of show business celebrities and other well-known people. Artistic innovation can also be seen in the work of Felix Mirbt (b. 1931), who has adapted the Japanese *bunraku* style (a puppet form in which lifesize puppets act out dramatic narratives to music) to scripts as diverse as Henry Beissel's *Inook and the Sun* (Stratford Festival, 1973), Büchner's *Woyzeck* (National Arts Centre, 1974), Strindberg's *A Dream Play* (Tarragon Theatre, 1977) and Brecht's *Happy End* (Tarragon Theatre, 1981).

Companies such as Lampoon Puppettheatre in Toronto (founded in 1973) and other individual members of the Ontario Puppetry Association (the organization, founded in 1957, has over 200 members) perform in the main for young audiences, often using techniques derived from European puppet theatre. Traditional Punch and Judy shows, although rare, are occasionally revived. The Puppet Centre in Toronto (founded in 1980) is a resource centre and training school that has developed as a focal point for those involved with puppetry; in 1990 it hosted performances by twenty-seven Canadian puppet groups. In 1994 the Centre's

puppetry museum was transferred to the Museum of Civilization in Ottawa.

As for classical marionette theatre, it has been revived with exceptional skill by Ronnie Burkett, a young Calgary puppeteer. His productions of classic texts (such as Bernard Shaw's *Shakes Versus Shav*) and his own risqué and ornate comedies, such as *Tinka's New Dress* (Manitoba Theatre Centre Warehouse, 1994), about puppeteers who staged underground satirical performances in Czechoslovakia during the Nazi occupation, have won him a sophisticated following.

Several companies have explored the use of lifesized and giant puppets. In Nova Scotia the Mermaid Theatre, founded in 1972 by Evelyn Garbary (1911–94), Tom Miller and Sara Lee Lewis, has attained an international reputation for its large-scale puppet renditions of over a dozen traditional native Micmac Indian legends such as *Glooscap's People* (1974) and *The Trickster* (1975). The company presents over 400 performances, blending masks, puppetry, movement and music, for 200,000 young people and their parents each year. One of Mermaid's most popular productions has been *Just So Stories*, first adapted and directed by Graham Whitehead from Kipling in 1983. By 1992 the production had been performed for more than 300,000 spectators in North America and internationally.

In the 1970s, the US Bread and Puppet Theatre influenced several Canadian political troupes. In Newfoundland in 1974, the Mummers Troupe used a giant puppet made of pigs' bladders to represent the United States in *Once a Giant*, a political fable of Canadian resistance to US hegemony; in Vancouver, the Breadbakers' Puppet Theatre (which evolved into the Toronto-based Whole Loaf Theatre) initiated a street-corner agitprop with handpuppets and marionettes.

One of the most original companies was the Manitoba Puppet Theatre, founded by Chris Hurley in 1973, which toured widely with its innovative political plays on topical themes. Hurley's *The Fat Clowns at the Circus and Other Plays for Puppets* was published in 1977. The use of lifesized puppets for political effect was not restricted to puppet theatres: in 1981 the Autumn Angel Repertory Company used grotesque giant puppets to represent the US soldiers who sacked Toronto during the War

Felix Mirbt's 1981 Tarragon Theatre production of Brecht's *Happy End*.
Photo: Nir Baraket.

of 1812 in *Yankees at York*, an outdoor spectacle staged in an historic fort.

One development in puppetry has been inspired by the giant processional figures of the Trinidad Carnival, which has been transplanted to Canada in the annual Caribana Festival parade in Toronto. Theatres such as Shadowland and Kensington Carnival (both in Toronto) have adapted the processional style of the Trinidadian artist Peter Minshall to create outdoor performances on political issues such as urban development and environmental pollution.

Alan Filewod

Québec

Since World War II, marionette theatre in Québec has been carried on professionally on a continuous basis, initially using traditional handling techniques (wires and hand-puppets) to portray classical works and opera libretti. In the 1970s, performers sought new forms in which the objects, materials, handling techniques and dramatic structures formed a closely interrelated block. Thus, the art of the marionette in Québec, once thought minor, has undergone significant changes in a very short period of time.

Modern pioneers, such as Micheline Legendre (b. 1928) and the Marionnettes de Montréal (founded in 1948), contributed to attracting the scenographer Guy Beauregard (1932–92), the creative handlers Nicole Lapointe and Pierre Régimbald and the sculptor Charles Daudelin (b. 1920) to this genre. Edmondo Chiodini (b. 1906), the creator of *Pépinot et Capucine* (1952) for national television, also made an important contribution to popularizing this form.

The next generation of puppeteers progressively abandoned classical texts and broke the bonds of tradition. The Théâtre Sans Fil

André Viens's 1985 Théâtre Sans Fil production of Tolkien's *The Lord of the Rings*.
Photo: Luc Beaulieu.

(Theatre Without Wires, 1972) popularized giant marionettes, particularly in the native Indian love story *Ciel bleu prend femme* (*Blue Sky Takes a Wife*, 1977), and *Bilbo le Hobbitt* (1979) and *Le Seigneur des anneaux* (*The Lord of the Rings*, 1985), both after Tolkien. The Théâtre de l'Oeil (Eye Theatre, 1973) created *Regarde pour voir* (*Look and See*, 1980) and *Les Grandes Vacances* (*The Summer Holidays*, 1981) by Michel Tremblay and the *Chouinard* series (1985), bringing popular Québécois characters based on the *guignol* tradition to the stage.

The Théâtre de l'Avant-Pays (1976) explored new territory where marionettes themselves served as guides and where the themes of the stories were as contemporary as the materials they used: *Une Histoire de marionnettes* (*A Puppet Story*, 1978), *L'École des bouffons* (*The Buffoons School*, 1981) by de Ghelderode and *Impertinence* (1986). Each summer in its region of Upton le Théâtre de la Dame de Coeur (Queen of Hearts Theatre, 1976) offers a major spectacle using giant puppets and special effects.

Founded in 1980, the Association Québécoise des Marionnettistes (Québec Marionette Association) brings together almost 100 members and a dozen companies that perform in a wide range of styles and approaches. In 1986, the organization sponsored an International Marionette Festival in Montréal. Since 1990 a Semaine Mondiale de la Marionnette (World Puppet Week) has been organized every two years in Jonquière.

Gilbert David

Design

Professional stage design in Canada is truly a contemporary phenomenon, for it is only since about 1950 that opportunities have developed for individuals to maintain careers designing theatrical sets, costumes and lighting.

Beginning in the late 1940s, design activity began to increase, generally in central and eastern Canada, in association with such companies as the New Play Society, the Crest Theatre and the Montréal Repertory Theatre. The beginning of television broadcasting also increased design opportunities and designers began careers that covered both stage and television.

In the early 1950s, 'large-scale' companies such as the Stratford Festival, the National Ballet, the Canadian Opera Company and later the Shaw Festival tended to rely on non-Canadian designers. But they presented standards that became goals for many Canadian designers. At Stratford, imported designers such as Tanya Moiseiwitsch, Desmond Heeley (b. 1930), Lesley Hurry (1909–78), Brian Jackson (1926–90), Daphne Dare and Ann Curtis influenced Canadian design through both the example of their productions and their generous teaching of young Canadian designers. Through the realization of designs for these companies, Canadian theatre craftspeople attained a high level of expertise, allowing subsequent designers to anticipate fulfilment of any design challenge.

During the 1960s, the establishment of professional theatres in most major cities in Canada increased the demand for design skills. Many universities and colleges began teaching such courses, with the newly established National Theatre School of Canada offering the most comprehensive professional design programme in the country. Instructors at the National Theatre School have included the noted designers François Barbeau (b. 1935), Robert Prévost (1927–82) and Mark Negin (b. 1932). Under head of design (and graduate of the school) Michael Eagan (b. 1942), the school has continued to provide Canada with many of its most promising design talents.

In 1965, a small group of major designers formed the Associated Designers of Canada. This organization represents the interests of set, costume, lighting and sound designers in dealings with theatre companies and government agencies, as well as serving as a communication forum for designers often separated by great distance. It is of interest that Canadian designers have not maintained the sometimes rigid gender/discipline classifications that exist in many other countries. In 1994 Associated Designers of Canada had a membership of some 130 people, most of whom design in at least two of the disciplines of set, costume and lighting.

Canadian stage design does not have an overt national 'character' or 'look'. Design is practised in theatres, big and small, across a very large country, with a variety of scripts including classics, contemporary works from other countries and contemporary Canadian works dealing with life, urban and rural, in all the regions. In addition, the range of theatre sizes and audiences has an effect on design budgets and design solutions. Hence, a rich diversity of styles can be found across the country.

Many exciting projects have been created by designers working in smaller theatre companies, often with new plays. In this area, designers such as Charlotte Dean (b. 1959), Sue Lepage (b. 1951) and Jim Plaxton (b. 1942) are noted for bold visions using unusual materials in new (and economical) ways, often redefining the actor–audience relationship. Astrid Janson's (b. 1947) set design for *Les Canadiens* (Toronto Workshop Productions, 1978) transformed a small theatre space into a hockey arena, in which the audience looked down on to the actors in bearpit style. Janson and other designers who have worked with similar challenges have subsequently used their talents

to great effect in their work with larger theatre and opera companies, the result often being challenging new approaches that may not have emerged otherwise.

Designers working in larger theatres have explored the manipulation of stage space while maintaining audience focus on the actor. In projects for various companies, Susan Benson (b. 1942) and Debra Hanson (b. 1951), both former heads of design at the Stratford Festival, have produced memorable designs, exploiting the use of subtle colour and texture in both sets and costumes. Benson's *Madame Butterfly* (Canadian Opera Company, 1991) effectively presented the drama on a small, simple rectangular wood floor with a few screens in front of a delicate translucent backdrop.

The set designs of Phillip Silver (b. 1943), resident designer at Edmonton's Citadel Theatre (1967–77), have also focused on the actor's space, whether in the spare simplicity of

Cameron Porteous's set design for the 1983 Shaw Festival production of *Caesar and Cleopatra*.
Photo: David Cooper.

by the Toronto architect Robert Fairfield (1918–94). For the most part, however, theatre architects of the period tended towards versions of the proscenium stage.

The large civic theatres that went up at this time from coast to coast reflected a kind of monumentalism most clearly seen in Ottawa's National Arts Centre, constructed in the nation's capital in 1969 at a cost of over $46 million. Designed by Fred Lebensold (1917–85), this massive concrete structure contains a 2,236-seat opera house, a 969-seat thrust theatre and a flexible 350-seat studio black box theatre. Even larger is the Citadel Theatre in Edmonton, which opened in 1976 and has since expanded to include five stages.

The 1960s and 1970s saw the widespread demolition of old playhouses in small cities and towns in the name of urban renewal. The alternative theatre movement of the 1970s, however, tended to avoid traditional spaces altogether and found its physical plants in whatever inner city spaces its artists could afford. Toronto's Theatre Passe Muraille, one of English Canada's first alternative groups, began in a college basement and later moved into an abandoned church hall. Toronto Free Theatre, another alternative group, worked in an old gasworks, which was later renovated into a sophisticated two-stage playhouse.

The typical Canadian small theatre by 1990 was performing in a converted building, seating an audience of 200 before a modified proscenium. For the most part, Canadian theatre architecture has been more pragmatic than imaginative.

About 100 of Canada's theatre companies operating in 1989 actually had their own facilities. Of those that did have a theatre, many included 'second stages' that could also be rented to other companies. Another solution for companies lacking their own theatre buildings has been the sharing of a single facility. The Theatre Centre, founded in Toronto in 1979, for example, has housed over 300 productions by several dozen small experimental companies and solo artists.

Still another aspect of theatre architecture since the 1970s has been the renovation and reconstruction of old playhouses. The Grand Opera House, home of the Grand Theatre Company in London, Ontario, was originally built in 1881, converted to a cinema in 1924 and remodelled in 1975; it is now one of the most beautiful and well-designed theatres in the country. Other major renovations across the country include the Walker Theatre in Winnipeg, opened as a 1,800-seat touring house in 1907; the Imperial Theatre in Saint John, New Brunswick, opened as a 1,800-seat touring house in 1913 and now housing 930 after a twelve-year, $16 million restoration completed in 1994; and the 2,788-seat Orpheum Theatre in Vancouver, originally a vaudeville house opened in 1927 and now also functioning as a concert hall.

Similar restorations can be found in many small towns, where turn-of-the-century 'opera houses' (usually small proscenium stages located above the town hall) have been rebuilt as community theatres. The Historic Theatres' Trust/Société des Salles Historiques, a federal charitable organization, has compiled and published a 300-page inventory of historic theatres across the country.

That historic theatres can be converted into profitable commercial ventures has been well demonstrated in Toronto where two former vaudeville houses that had been turned into cinemas were restored to their original splendour. The 2,100-seat Elgin Theatre, designed by the New York architect Thomas W. Lamb, was originally built in 1913 and reopened in 1985 with Marlene Smith and Tina VanderHeyden's two-year run of Cats. During the theatre's restoration it was found to contain the world's largest collection of extant vaudeville scenery. A block away, the 2,200-seat Pantages Theatre, also designed by Lamb and built in 1920, was restored in 1989 by Garth Drabinsky's Live Entertainment Corporation at a cost of $22 million to house a commercial production of The Phantom of the Opera. In 1995 the production was still attracting nearly 800,000 spectators and earning a box-office revenue of almost $50 million annually.

In 1993, Ed and David Mirvish opened their 2,000-seat, $35 million Princess of Wales Theatre, designed by Toronto architect Peter Smith (b. 1936), to house the $12 million Toronto production of Miss Saigon. It is the first privately built grand playhouse since the opening in 1907 of the adjoining 1,500-seat Royal Alexandra Theatre, designed by Toronto architect John Lyle (1872–1945) and purchased by Ed Mirvish in 1962 for $215,000. Profits from Royal Alexandra productions enabled the Mirvishes to purchase London's Old Vic in 1982 for $1.3 million.

Audiences in Toronto in 1993 also saw the opening of the $48 million publicly owned North York Performing Arts Centre, designed by Toronto architect Eberhard Zeidler

The interior of the 1993 Princess of Wales Theatre, designed by Peter Smith.

(b. 1926). Renamed the Ford Centre for the Performing Arts the following year, the complex contains a 1,850-seat main stage, a 1,000-seat concert hall and a 250-seat black box studio theatre. The centre's inaugural production of *Show Boat*, managed by Live Entertainment, was scheduled to transfer to Vancouver in late 1995 to inaugurate a $25 million Ford Centre for the Performing Arts in that city.

The technological level of Canadian theatre is similar to that of most western nations: most theatres use computerized lighting systems, but the small theatres have little room for spectacular stage effects. In contrast, innovations in spectacle and technology are expected of the large commercial houses such as the Pantages.

Alan Filewod

Québec

In 1945, when theatre activity was still only modestly developed, Québec companies were forced to work in the few theatres that had not been converted into cinemas. In Montréal the 1,500-seat Monument-National from 1893 provided a proper proscenium stage but with antiquated stage equipment. This theatre was available on a rental basis; it did not house a permanent company. The same was the case at Her Majesty's Theatre, built in 1898; the Théâtre Saint-Denis (1922); and the Gesù (1865), which was owned by the Jesuits, who renovated the theatre in 1942. Only the Théâtre National (1900) was occupied on a year-round basis, by a burlesque company. In Québec City, the Capitol (1903) and the Palais Montcalm (1932) continued to serve as touring houses.

In the 1950s many cinema houses were converted back into theatres and commercial spaces were adapted for pocket theatres seating fewer than 200. In the 1960s new theatres were constructed, particularly as part of Canada's centennial celebrations in 1967. The architecture was hardly innovative and the stages were generally too small, creating many constraints for theatre artists. Noteworthy, nevertheless, was the first modular theatre space, designed by Claude Sabourin (b. 1936) for the Théâtre d'Aujourd'hui in 1968, which, however, could seat only 100 spectators.

Anxious to house (at higher rental fees) prestigious companies and touring productions from abroad, the Québec government constructed new theatre facilities at the Place des Arts in Montréal in 1967 (the 747-seat Port-Royal and the 1,278-seat Maisonneuve) and in Québec City in 1971 (the Louis-Fréchette and Octave-Crémazie). Most companies, however, were left to work in unsuitable spaces.

In the 1980s, the city of Montréal undertook an ambitious programme constructing Maisons de la Culture (Houses of Culture), which included theatre auditoriums seating between 100 and 800 spectators. By the early 1990s, there were over a dozen of these institutions aimed at bringing culture to all corners of the municipality.

From the mid-1980s, one could also note the desire of different levels of government to improve the situation by renovating old buildings or by constructing new ones. The Monument-National, the oldest theatre in Montréal, for example, was renovated at great cost as a production facility for the National Theatre School to celebrate the Monument-National's centenary in 1993 and the same was done for the Palais Montcalm in Québec City. In 1991 the Théâtre d'Aujourd'hui, which focuses on the production of Québec playwrights, was relocated to a new building, as were L'Espace GO and Carbone 14 in 1995. Le Groupe de la Veillée rebuilt on its original location.

By the mid-1990s a number of companies such as Théâtre du Nouveau Monde and the Maison Théâtre pour l'Enfance et la Jeunesse still required major improvements to their physical plants in order to attain their artistic goals. But an even bigger problem was the absence of government policy regarding the subsidy of operating costs for these theatre buildings, which often overwhelmed companies and devoured production budgets.

Gilbert David

Training

Training for the theatre in English Canada is as diversified as the theatre itself. Although there are numerous institutions that offer some form of professional training, there are no regulatory standards to govern the curriculum. Because there is no structural relationship between theatre schools and the profession, graduation from a training programme does not guarantee work in the theatre. In fact, many theatre artists enter the profession with no formal training at all.

Most training programmes are based in universities (which confer degrees) and community colleges (which grant diplomas). The first university programmes were founded in the 1940s, in Saskatchewan and Alberta. In the 1990s most universities were offering some courses in drama and theatre, and approximately twenty were offering specialized degree programmes. Of those, eight were Bachelor of Fine Arts programmes which provided conservatory training in acting, directing, design and playwriting; the remainder were Bachelor of Arts programmes which offered major concentrations in dramatic literature and theatre in the context of a broad-based humanities curriculum.

Six universities were offering Master's programmes, most of which focused on directing, design and playwriting; only one (York) had a Master's programme in acting. Three universities (British Columbia, Victoria and Toronto) were offering academic theatre studies at the PhD level.

Community college programmes tend to be shorter (two or three years, compared to four at universities) and more specialized, focusing on areas such as theatre administration, musical theatre or technology. Taken together, the university and college programmes graduate far more students than the profession can accommodate.

In addition to the universities and colleges, there are a number of autonomous institutions, the most important being the National Theatre School in Montréal. A bilingual school with parallel programmes in English and French, the National Theatre School offers diploma courses in acting, design, directing and technical skills.

In Alberta, the Banff Centre for the Fine Arts has developed a national arts administration programme, a playwrights' colony and master classes in acting. The Banff programme also offers advanced training for young professionals who have already commenced their careers.

In Ontario the Native Theatre School, founded by James Buller (1921–82) in 1974 and renamed the Centre for Indigenous Theatre in 1994, has been training a small number of aboriginal students within their own cultural context of traditional storytelling and non-linear theatre consisting of music, movement, sound, dance, text and oratory; its graduates have been instrumental in the development of an active native theatre community. Several native performers, directors and playwrights such as Tomson Highway have also studied indigenous performance styles with the Tukak Theatre in Denmark.

For the most part, training in English Canada is eclectic, built on the foundations of Stanislavski and British classical methods, but rarely doctrinaire. Many of the existing programmes were founded in the 1960s and 1970s, when there were few Canadian teachers. Consequently, training programmes were greatly influenced by foreign teachers, such as Michel Saint-Denis of France, on whose advice the National Theatre School was founded in 1960. In the 1990s Canadian-trained instructors and professors comprised a majority in most programmes.

Some of the most effective training is offered by the theatres themselves. In Toronto, Tarragon Theatre's Maggie Bassett Studio offers classes in voice, movement and scene study taught by established professionals, as does Equity Showcase in Toronto and Vancouver, sponsored by Canadian Actors' Equity. Numerous private studios also provide specialized courses in various performances techniques.

Alan Filewod

Québec

It was only after World War II that institutionalized teaching of the dramatic arts became established in Québec. Previously, actors were able to acquire a certain amount of training at the Conservatoire Lassalle (founded in 1907) or through private lessons at home or abroad.

The theatre revival of the 1930s led various companies to provide training for their actors; both the Compagnons de Saint-Laurent and the Compagnie du Masque (1946–51) emphasized physical work, while the Théâtre du Nouveau Monde had its own school from 1952 to 1956.

In 1954 the Conservatoire d'Art Dramatique de Montréal was founded, under the direction initially of Jan Doat (1910–88) (trained in France by Copeau and Charles Dullin), who was replaced in 1957 by Jean Valcourt (1906–69) from the Comédie-Française; in 1958, the Conservatoire opened another school in Québec City. In 1970 actor Paul Hébert (b. 1924), a student of Michel Saint-Denis at the Old Vic in London, took over the direction of the two conservatories. The Conservatoire de Québec broke away in 1972, and then Jean Guy (b. 1940), an actor who had himself been a student there, assumed its direction.

The École Nationale de Théâtre (National Theatre School) was founded in Montréal in 1960. The first directors of the French-language section – Jean-Pierre Ronfard (director 1960–4) and André Muller (1964–71) – both came from France. In 1975, under the direction of André Pagé (1931–82), the school established a programme in playwriting headed by the playwright Jean-Claude Germain.

At the end of the 1960s, a teaching reform led to the opening of two new theatre schools integrated into collegiates (junior colleges): one was at the Collège Lionel-Groulx, begun in 1968 under the direction of Jean-Robert Rémillard (b. 1928), and the other at the CÉGEP de Saint-Hyacinthe in 1969, under the direction of Claude Grisé (b. 1939). The foundation of the Université du Québec in 1968 made it possible to create a full theatre department in Montréal, founded by Jean-Guy Sabourin, where both theoretical and practical training opened the way to new perspectives in direction, teaching, research and writing.

Québec's dramatic revival at the beginning of the 1970s led to a new conception of the Québécois actor as a person with a social awareness. This orientation resulted in the creation of companies, brought together by the Association Québécoise du Jeune Théâtre, which favoured ongoing self-training. Important training in physical theatre also began at this time. The École Nationale de Théâtre from 1971, the theatre option at Collège Lionel-Groulx from 1972, the Conservatoire de Québec from 1978, and the Conservatoire de Montréal from 1987, all assumed and developed the concept of the actor-creator in direct relationship to the realities of developing a viable Québécois culture.

In 1989 all the schools joined to create the Conseil Supérieur de la Formation en Art Dramatique (Higher Council for Training in Dramatic Arts).

Gilbert David

Criticism, Scholarship and Publishing

The rapid development of contemporary English-Canadian theatre owes much to the encouragement of a few perceptive critics, some of whom have written for the daily press. The most influential daily reviewers, such as Nathan Cohen (1923–71) in the 1960s and Urjo Kareda in the 1970s, both in the *Toronto Star*, and Herbert Whittaker from the 1950s through the 1970s and Ray Conlogue (b. 1949) in the 1980s in the *Toronto Globe and Mail*, were instrumental in recognizing and advocating Canadian playwriting, new directions in the theatre, and encouraging audience development.

Other significant critics writing in English have included Marianne Ackerman (b. 1952) in the *Montréal Gazette* and David Prosser (b. 1953) in the *Kingston Whig Standard*, both writing during the 1980s. Jamie Portman (b. 1935), writing for the *Calgary Herald* (1959–75) and the Southam News Service (1975–87), was the only reviewer whose mandate was to cover the whole country on a regular basis. Working for the daily press, these writers offered quick, perceptive and often encouraging responses to the emerging new theatre.

The lack of an intellectual weekly press, however, meant that there were fewer critics able to offer more considered reviews, although to some extent this function was assumed by the monthly *Saturday Night*, which, during the 1970s and 1980s, carried insightful reviews by Martin Knelman (b. 1943) and Mark Czarnecki (b. 1945), who also reviewed for the weekly *Maclean's* magazine.

For more reflective criticism the theatre community turned to a handful of specialized periodicals. The quarterly *Canadian Theatre Review* (*CTR*), the country's first national theatre journal, was founded by Don Rubin (b. 1942), Ross Stuart (b. 1945) and Stephen Mezei in 1974. Under Rubin's editorship, *CTR* was an important voice in the nationalist debates of the 1970s both as a journal and as a book publisher; in later years, under the editorial regimes of Robert Wallace (b. 1943) and still later a collective consisting of Alan Filewod (b. 1952), Natalie Rewa (b. 1956) and Ann Wilson (b. 1956), it focused on more scholarly examinations of a wide range of issues. *CTR* was for many years the only journal attempting to straddle the line between scholarship and the theatre profession until the arrival of *Theatrum*

in 1985, a bimonthly oriented more towards experimental theatre, edited by Nigel Hunt (b. 1960), who was succeeded by Sarah Hood (b. 1958) in 1993.

Theoretical and applied scholarship representing many critical schools has thrived in two academic journals, *Canadian Drama/L'Art dramatique canadien* (1975–91), and *Theatre History in Canada/Histoire du théâtre au Canada* (founded in 1980). The latter, known since 1992 as *Theatre Research in Canada/Recherches théâtrales au Canada*, is the official journal of the Association for Canadian Theatre Research (ACTR; founded in 1976 and until 1991 known as the Association for Canadian Theatre History/ACTH). ACTR also publishes a newsletter containing an annual Canadian theatre and drama bibliography of both English and French titles.

Scholarly research accelerated in the 1980s, in part because of support from the Social Sciences and Humanities Research Council of Canada. Also significant were the pioneering efforts of such scholars as Ann Saddlemyer (b. 1932), founding president of ACTH and founding co-editor, with Richard Plant (b. 1942), of *Theatre History in Canada*, and the theatre historians and editors Anton Wagner (b. 1949) and Leonard Conolly (b. 1941). Conolly was the co-editor, with Eugene Benson, of the most comprehensive survey of Canadian theatre and drama published to date, *The Oxford Companion to Canadian Theatre* (1989).

The teaching of Canadian drama in universities has also been made possible by the growth of play publishing as an industry. One of the principal publishers of new scripts in English is Playwrights' Canada Press (formerly Playwrights' Co-op, founded in 1972), the publishing arm of the Playwrights' Union of Canada.

The pioneer in the field and still one of the major publishers is Vancouver-based Talonbooks, whose aggressive Canadian play publishing programme was begun in 1969 under the direction of Hungarian-born Peter Hay (b. 1944). Other notable English-language publishers include Blizzard Press of Winnipeg, NeWest Press of Edmonton and Simon & Pierre of Toronto.

Canadian Theatre Review and *Theatrum* both publish new playscripts in every issue while *CTR* Publications, the book-publishing arm of *CTR* during the 1970s and 1980s, published a wide range of important volumes including the annual performance calendar series *Canada on Stage* and the four-volume *Canada's Lost Plays* anthologies.

There are several regional critics' organizations in the country that are, as well, members of the national Canadian Theatre Critics' Association (CTCA), founded in 1980. The CTCA gives the annual Nathan Cohen Award for excellence in critical writing. The oldest and largest of the regional groups is the Toronto Drama Bench, founded in 1972 and for many years the sole jurors of the prestigious Floyd S. Chalmers Awards for Playwriting.

Though Canada has no theatre library or theatre museum *per se*, a number of important theatre collections and archives exist in various universities and libraries across the country, inventoried in Heather McCallum (b. 1927) and Ruth Pincoe's *Directory of Canadian Theatre Archives* (1992). Among the major collections are those at the University of Guelph (especially strong in the theatres that developed in the 1960s, 1970s and 1980s), York University (CBC-Television archives, the Mavor Moore, Herman Voaden and Herbert Whittaker papers) and the University of Calgary, which holds the papers of many important Canadian playwrights. The Metropolitan Toronto Central Reference Library's theatre collection, for many years under the direction of McCallum, is one of English Canada's largest general theatre reference centres.

Alan Filewod

Québec

With the exception of Jean Béraud (1900–65) and Léopold Houlé (1888–1953), no critic from the period before 1945 has a body of work important enough to be discussed in terms of influence. In the course of the ensuing forty years, however, a progressively Québécois school of criticism did develop. *Tit-Coq*, written by Gratien Gélinas in 1948, sparked a revealing debate between those who called it the long-awaited root work of Québec drama and those who felt that the play was too vulgar.

In the 1950s, Jean Hamelin (1920–70) faithfully and intelligently followed the Québec stage, collecting his major essays in a volume called *Le Renouveau du théâtre au Canada français* (*The Renewal of French-Canadian Theatre*) in 1961. From 1956 until his death,

the Jesuit Georges-Henri D'Auteuil (1900–78) was an attentive observer of Montréal's theatre: his chronicles in *Relations* (1940) cover almost everything to do with the stage of the period, though he sharply criticized any tendency in Québécois plays that he considered '*joualisant*' (tending towards *joual*).

With the development of a true Québécois repertoire and the extraordinary dynamism of French-language theatre activity between 1960 and 1980, more informed critics began to appear in both the French- and English-language Montréal and Québec City dailies: Martial Dassylva (b. 1936) at *La Presse* between 1965 and 1983, Jean Basile (1932–92), Alain Pontaut (1925–91), Michel Bélair (b. 1946) and, from 1980 on, Robert Lévesque at *Le Devoir*.

In 1985 *Voir*, a cultural weekly newspaper distributed free in Montréal, and its counterpart in Québec City (also called *Voir*) at the beginning of the 1990s, expanded the analysis of theatre with its pungent criticism and new perspectives such as those of Luc Boulanger (b. 1963). From the 1980s onwards the growing influence of cultural commentators on radio and television also made itself felt although the distinction between entertainment news and actual critical analysis of performances was not always clear in these media. It was not until 1984 that the Association Québécoise des Critiques de Théâtre (Québec Theatre Critics' Association) was founded and – under the presidency (1987–94) of Michel Vaïs (b. 1946) – began awarding prizes to recognize excellence in various categories of theatre production and playwriting the following year. These critics' prizes frequently provoked controversy within the theatre community, which established an Académie du Théâtre to distribute its own theatre awards in 1993.

In 1964 the *Cahiers de la NCT* (*Notebooks of the NCT*), founded by Gilles Marsolais (b. 1935), started the publication in Québec of important critical and historical dossiers on each of the productions of the Nouvelle Compagnie Théâtrale.

Jeu (*Play*), an important Québec journal that espoused an ideological pluralism, was founded in 1976 and paid particular attention to serious theatre research and creation as well as to the relationship between practice and theory. Under the direction of Gilbert David (b. 1946) and, from 1984, Pierre Lavoie (b. 1950), Lorraine Camerlain (b. 1953) and Michel Vaïs, this quarterly was able to train an important number of younger critics such as Diane Pavlovic

(b. 1961), who attempted, especially in the years after 1980, to develop links between Québécois theatre and international trends.

Since 1970, university research in theatre has also increased. Particularly notable is the research done by Hélène Beauchamp (b. 1943) in the field of theatre for young audiences; the work of Jean Cléo Godin (b. 1936), Laurent Mailhot (b. 1931), Rémi Tourangeau (b. 1938), Jean-Marc Larrue (b. 1952), Lucie Robert (b. 1954) and Chantal Hébert (b. 1950) concerning playwriting and the history of the performing arts in Québec; and the publications of André-G. Bourassa (b. 1936), Gilbert David, Michel Vaïs, Wladimir Krysinski (b. 1935), Louise Vigeant (b. 1951) and Josette Féral (b. 1949) on the topic of theatre aesthetics, sociology and semiotics.

The Société Québécoise d'Études Théâtrales (Québec Society for Theatre Studies) was founded as the Société d'Histoire du Théâtre du Québec (Québec Theatre History Society) in 1976. It has been responsible for the organization of conferences and the publication of the L'Annuaire théâtral (Theatre Annual). This publication's initial volume appeared in 1985, taking its title from a 1908 publication. The society aims at developing theatrical research, an area too often neglected in the past due to restraints in theatre studies programmes at Québec universities and the lack of a government policy concerning the preservation of theatre documents and artifacts.

Theatre publishing itself underwent a noticeable increase during the course of the 1970s: Éditions Leméac alone published more than 150 contemporary plays between 1968 and 1992; other publishing houses (VLB éditeur, Québec/Amérique, La Pleine Lune, L'Hexagone and, more recently, Les Herbes rouges and Boréal) have also done much to foster the publication of Québec plays.

Gilbert David
Québec sections translated by Craig Thomas
and Anton Wagner

Further Reading

Anthony, Geraldine. *Stage Voices: Twelve Canadian Playwrights Talk About Their Lives and Work.* Toronto: Doubleday, 1978. 318 pp.
Ball, John, and Richard Plant, eds. *Bibliography of Theatre History in Canada: The Beginnings Through 1984/Bibliographie d'histoire du théâtre au Canada: des débuts–fin 1984.* Toronto: ECW Press, 1993. 445 pp.
Benson, Eugene, and L.W. Conolly, eds. *English-Canadian Theatre.* Toronto: Oxford University Press, 1987. 134 pp.
——. *The Oxford Companion to Canadian Theatre.* Toronto: Oxford University Press, 1989. 662 pp.
Bessai, Diane. *Playwrights of Collective Creation.* Toronto: Simon & Pierre, 1992. 292 pp.
Brookes, Chris. *A Public Nuisance: A History of the Mummers Troupe.* St John's, NF: Institute for Social and Economic Research, 1988. 249 pp.
Bryden, Ronald, with Boyd Neil, eds. *Whittaker's Theatre: Herbert Whittaker and Theatre in Canada 1944–1975.* Toronto: University of Toronto Press, 1985. 190 pp.
Buller, Edward. *Indigenous Performing and Ceremonial Arts in Canada: An Annotated Bibliography of Canadian Indian Rituals and Ceremonies (up to 1976).* Toronto: Association for Native Development in the Performing and Visual Arts, 1981. 151 pp.
Canadian Plays. Catalogue 1993–94. Toronto: Playwrights' Union of Canada, 1993. 126 pp.
Conolly, L.W. *Canadian Drama and the Critics.* Vancouver: Talonbooks, 1987. 319 pp.
Doolittle, Joyce, and Zina Barnieh. *A Mirror of Our Dreams: Children and the Theatre in Canada.* Vancouver: Talonbooks, 1979. 214 pp.
Edmonstone, Wayne. *Nathan Cohen: The Making of a Critic.* Toronto: Lester & Orpen, 1977. 286 pp.
Filewod, Alan. *Collective Encounters: Documentary Theatre in English Canada.* Toronto: University of Toronto Press, 1987. 214 pp.
Gardner, David, and L. W. Conolly. 'Theatre, English-Language'. *The Canadian Encyclopedia.* 3rd ed. (CD-ROM) Toronto: McClelland & Stewart, 1995.
Glaap, Albert-Rainer, ed. *Das englisch-kanadische Drama.* [English-Canadian drama]. Düsseldorf: Schwann, 1992. 309 pp.
Hendry, Tom. *Cultural Capital: The Care and Feeding of Toronto's Artistic Assets.* Toronto: Toronto Arts Council, 1985. 158 pp.
Johnston, Denis. *Up the Mainstream: The Rise of Toronto's Alternative Theatres.* Toronto: University of Toronto Press, 1991. 337 pp.
Knowles, Richard Paul, ed. *Theatre in Atlantic Canada.* Sackville, NS: Mount Allison University, 1988. 266 pp.
Lane, Harry, ed. *Canada on Stage 1982–8.* 2 vols. Toronto: Professional Association of Canadian Theatres, 1989, 1992.

Lee, Betty. *Love and Whisky: The Story of the Dominion Drama Festival*. Toronto: McClelland & Stewart, 1973 and Toronto: Simon & Pierre, 1982. 335 pp.

McCallum, Heather, and Ruth Pincoe. *Directory of Canadian Theatre Archives*. Halifax, NS: Dalhousie University, 1992. 217 pp.

Officer, Jill. *The Encyclopedia of Theatre Dance in Canada*. Toronto: Dance Collection Danse, 1990. (Electronic publication).

Perkyns, Richard. *The Neptune Story: Twenty-five Years in the Life of a Leading Canadian Theatre*. Hantsport, NS: Lancelot Press, 1989. 266 pp.

Portman, Jamie, and John Pettigrew. *Stratford: The First Thirty Years*. Toronto: McClelland & Stewart, 1989. 512 pp.

Royal Commission on National Development in the Arts, Letters and Sciences 1949–51. *Report*. Ottawa: King's Printer, 1951.

Royal Commission Studies: A Selection of Essays Prepared for the Royal Commission on National Development in the Arts, Letters and Sciences. Ottawa: King's Printer, 1951.

Rubin, Don, ed. *Canada on Stage: Canadian Theatre Review Yearbook*. 8 vols. Toronto: Canadian Theatre Review Publications, 1975–82.

——, and Alison Cranmer-Byng, eds. *Canada's Playwrights: A Biographical Guide*. Toronto: Canadian Theatre Review Publications, 1980. 191 pp.

Rudakoff, Judith, and Rita Much. *Fair Play: Twelve Women Speak. Conversations with Canadian Playwrights*. Toronto: Simon & Pierre, 1990. 220 pp.

Ryan, Toby Gordon. *Stage Left: Canadian Theatre in the Thirties*. Toronto: Simon & Pierre, 1985. 239 pp.

Stuart, E. Ross. *The History of Prairie Theatre*. Toronto: Simon & Pierre, 1984. 292 pp.

Theatre Listing 1994/95. Toronto: Professional Association of Canadian Theatres, 1994. 127 pp.

Usmiani, Renate. *Second Stage: The Alternative Theatre Movement in Canada*. Vancouver: University of British Columbia Press, 1983. 173 pp.

Wagner, Anton, ed. *The Brock Bibliography of Published Canadian Plays in English 1766–1978*. Toronto: Playwrights Press, 1980. 375 pp.

——. *Canada's Lost Plays*. 4 vols. Toronto: Canadian Theatre Review Publications, 1976–82.

——. *Contemporary Canadian Theatre: New World Visions*. Toronto: Simon & Pierre, 1986. 411 pp.

Wallace, Robert. *Producing Marginality*. Saskatoon: Fifth House Press, 1990. 253 pp.

——, and Cynthia Zimmerman. *The Work: Conversations with Canadian Playwrights*. Toronto: Coach House Press, 1982. 377 pp.

Wyman, Max. *Dance Canada: An Illustrated History*. Vancouver: Douglas & McIntyre, 1991. 224 pp.

Québec

Beauchamp, Hélène. *Le Théâtre pour enfants au Québec, 1950–80*. [Children's theatre in Québec, 1950–80]. Cahiers du Québec, Collection Littérature. Montréal: Hurtubise-HMH, 1985. 306 pp.

Bélair, Michel. *Le Nouveau Théâtre québécois*. [The new Québec theatre]. Collection Dossiers. Montréal: Leméac, 1973. 202 pp.

Béraud, Jean. *350 Ans de théâtre au Canada français*. [350 years of theatre in French Canada]. Collection l'Encyclopédie du Canada français, vol. 1. Montréal: Le Cercle du Livre de France, 1958. 316 pp.

Borello, Christine, ed. 'Québec'. *Théâtre/Public* 117 (1994).

Bourassa, André-G., and Jean-Marc Larrue. *Les Nuits de la 'Main': cent ans de spectacles sur le boulevard Saint-Laurent*. [The nights of the 'Main': 100 years of performances on Saint-Laurent Boulevard]. Collection Études québécoises. Montréal: VLB éditeur, 1993. 368 pp.

——. and Gilles Lapointe. *Refus Globale et ses environs 1948–1988*. [Refus Globale and its adherents 1948–1988]. Montréal: l'Hexagone, 1988. 184 pp.

Camerlain, Lorraine, and Diane Pavlovic. *Cent ans de théâtre á Montréal: photographies*. [100 years of theatre in Montréal: photographs]. Montréal: Cahiers de théâtre Jeu, 1988. 160 pp.

Cotnam, Jacques. *Le Théâtre québécois: instrument de contestation sociale et politique*. [Québec theatre: Instrument of social and political protest]. Collection Études littéraires. Montréal: Fides, 1976. 124 pp.

Cusson, Chantale, ed. *Répertoire du Centre d'essai des auteurs dramatiques. Des auteurs, des pièces: portraits de la dramaturgie québécoise*. [Repertoire of the Centre d'essai des auteurs dramatiques. The authors, the plays: Portraits of Québécois playwriting]. 1989 edn edited by Hélène Dumas; 1994 edn edited by Daniel Gauthier. Montréal: Centre des auteurs dramatiques, 1984 and 1994. 307 and 406 pp.

Dassylva, Martial. *Un Théâtre en effervescence: critiques et chroniques 1965–1972*. [An effervescent theatre: Criticism and chronicles

1965–1972]. Collection Échanges. Montréal: La Presse, 1975. 283 pp.

David, Gilbert. *Répertoire théâtral du Québec 1984*. [Theatre repertoire of Québec 1984]. Montréal: Cahiers de théâtre Jeu, 1984. 504 pp.

——, and Pierre Lavoie, eds. *Le Monde de Michel Tremblay: Des 'Belles-Soeurs' à 'Marcel poursuivi par les chiens'*. [The world of Michel Tremblay: From *Les Belles-Soeurs* to *Marcel Pursued by Hounds*]. Montréal/Brussels: Cahiers de théâtre Jeu/Éditions Lansman, 1993. 479 pp.

Dorion, Gilles, ed. *Dictionnaire des oeuvres littéraires du Québec*. [Dictionary of Québec's literary works]. Vol. 6: *1976–1980*. Montréal: Fides, 1994. 1,087 pp.

Féral, Josette. *La Culture contre l'art*. [Culture against art]. Sillery, PQ: Presses de l'Université du Québec, 1990. 341 pp.

Gaboriau, Linda, ed. *Québec Plays in Translation: 1994 Supplement*. Montréal: Centre des auteurs dramatiques, 1994. 28 pp.

Gobin, Pierre. *Le Fou et ses doubles: figures de la dramaturgie québécoise*. [The madman and his doubles: Figures of Québécois playwriting]. Collection Lignes québécoises. Montréal: Presses de l'Université de Montréal, 1978. 263 pp.

Godin, Jean Cléo, and Laurent Mailhot. *Le Théâtre québécois: introduction à dix dramaturges*. [Québécois theatre: Introduction to ten playwrights]. Montréal: Hurtubise-HMH, 1979. 254 pp.

——. *Théâtre québécois II: nouveaux auteurs, autres spectacles*. [Québécois theatre II: New authors, other plays]. Montréal: Hurtubise-HMH, 1980. 248 pp.

Gruslin, Adrien. *Le Théâtre et l'état au Québec*. [Theatre and the state in Québec]. Montréal: VLB éditeur, 1981. 414 pp.

Hamelin, Jean. *Le Renouveau du théâtre au Canada français*. [The renewal of theatre in French Canada]. Montréal: Éditions du Jour, 1962. 160 pp.

Hardy, Gaétan. *La Situation économique des organismes de théâtre subventionnés*. [The economic situation of subsidized theatres]. Québec City: Ministère de la Culture, 1993. 96 pp.

Hébert, Chantal. *Le Burlesque au Québec: un divertissement populaire*. [Burlesque in Québec: A popular entertainment]. Cahiers du Québec, Collection Ethnologie. Montréal: Hurtubise-HMH, 1981. 302 pp.

Lacroix, Jean-Guy. *La Condition d'artiste: une injustice*. [The situation of the artist: An injustice]. Montréal: VLB éditeur, 1990. 249 pp.

Laflamme, Jean, and Rémi Tourangeau. *L'Église et le théâtre au Québec*. [Church and theatre in Québec]. Montréal: Fides, 1979. 356 pp.

Larrue, Jean-Marc. *Le Monument inattendu: Le Monument-National 1893–1993*. [The unexpected monument: The Monument-National 1893–1993]. Collection Cahiers du Québec. Montréal: Hurtubise-HMH, 1993. 322 pp.

Lavoie, Pierre, ed. *Pour suivre le Théâtre au Québec. Les Ressources documentaires*. [Survey of theatre in Québec: Documentary resources]. Collection Documents de recherche. Québec City: Institut Québécois de Recherche sur la Culture, 1985. 522 pp.

Legris, Renée, Jean-Marc Larrue, André-G. Bourassa, and Gilbert David. *Le Théâtre au Québec, 1825–1980*. [Theatre in Québec, 1825–1980]. Montréal: VLB éditeur/SHTQ/BNQ, 1988. 208 pp.

Lemire, Maurice, ed. *Dictionnaire des oeuvres littéraires du Québec*. [Dictionary of Québec literary works]. Vol. 3: *1940–59*; Vol. 4: *1960–69*; Vol. 5: *1970–75*. Montréal: Fides, 1982, 1984, 1988.

McEwen, Barbara. 'Au-delà de l'exotisme: le théâtre québécois devant la critique parisienne 1955–88'. [Beyond exoticism: Québécois theatre as seen by Parisian criticism 1955–88]. *Theatre History in Canada* 7, no. 2 (fall 1986): 134–48.

Nardocchio, Elaine F. *Theatre and Politics in Modern Québec*. Edmonton, AB: University of Alberta Press, 1986. 157 pp.

Pontaut, Alain. *Dictionnaire critique du théâtre québécois*. [A critical dictionary of Québécois theatre]. Montréal: Leméac, 1972. 151 pp.

Rioux, Monique, Diane Bilz and Jean-Marie Boisvert. *L'Enfant et l'expression dramatique*. [Dramatic expression and the child]. Montréal: Editions de l'Aurore, 1976. 185 pp.

Robert, Lucie. 'The New Québec Theatre'. In *Canadian Canons: Essays in Literary Value*, ed. Robert Lecker, 112–23. Toronto: ECW Press, 1982.

Tembeck, Iro. *Danser à Montréal: germination d'une histoire chorégraphique*. [Dance in Montréal: Germination of a choreographic history]. Sillery, PQ: Presses de l'Université du Québec, 1991. 336 pp.

21 Ans de théâtre en français à Vancouver, 1946–1967: histoire de la Troupe Molière. [21 years of French theatre in Vancouver, 1946–1967: A history of the Troupe Molière]. Vancouver: Société historique franco-colombienne, 1982.

Wyczynski, Paul, Julien Bernard, and Hélène
Beauchamp, eds. *Le Théâtre canadien-français:
evolution, temoignages, bibliographie*. [French-
Canadian theatre: Evolution, testimonies,
bibliography]. Archives des lettres canadiennes,
5. Montréal: Fides, 1976. 1,005 pp.

CARIBBEAN

For an overview of the predominantly English-language theatre in Antigua and Barbuda, Barbados, Dominica, Grenada, Guyana, Jamaica, Montserrat, St Kitts and Nevis, St Lucia, and Trinidad and Tobago, see COMMONWEALTH CARIBBEAN. For an overview of the predominantly French-language theatre of French Guyana, Guadeloupe and Martinique, see FRENCH CARIBBEAN. For an overview of the predominantly Dutch-language theatre of Aruba and the Netherlands Antilles (Bonaire, Curaçao, Saba, St Eustatius and St Maarten), see NETHERLANDS ANTILLES AND ARUBA. See also CUBA, DOMINICAN REPUBLIC, HAÏTI and PUERTO RICO.

CHILE

Extending more than 4,100 kilometres (2,600 miles) from north to south and at no point greater than 400 kilometres wide, Chile, a country of 13.6 million people (1992), has a wider range of climate and landscape than any other country in the world. To the east, the Andes Mountains separate Chile from Bolivia and most of Argentina; to the west is the Pacific Ocean. The frontier with Perú lies across the northern desert. Several Pacific islands are also part of Chile, including the Juan Fernández Islands and the Easter Islands; Chile also claims a large part of Antarctica. Its total area is 757,000 square kilometres (292,300 square miles).

Most of the population lives in the centre of the country, particularly around the cities of Santiago, the capital, and Valparaíso. One of the largest cities in South America, Santiago was founded in 1541 by the Spanish *conquistador* Pedro de Valdivia. Valparaíso is one of the largest ports on South America's west coast.

The most important of Chile's indigenous peoples are the Araucanians, the only indigenous group in South America never to be defeated by colonizing Europeans. Many pure-blooded Araucanians still live in the rain forests south of Santiago.

In the sixteenth century, Chile was governed by the Spanish viceroy of Perú. In 1810, two years after Napoleon's conquest of Spain, a new Chilean government was established. War with Spain followed and in 1818 Chile was declared independent. The country grew rapidly in the nineteenth century though government control was mainly in the hands of the landowning families. World War I made Chile even wealthier because of world demand for its copper and nitrates. World War II continued this trend.

In 1964, with the election of Eduardo Montalva Frei (1911–82), a Christian Democrat, Chile began a vast series of social changes including the nationalization of the copper industry. Salvador Allende (1908–73) was elected president in 1970, the first Marxist chosen by popular vote to head the government of a western democracy. But economic problems continued and in 1973 the military overthrew Allende and suspended the constitution. Augusto Pinochet Ugarte (b. 1915) took over as president pledging to return to democratic rule but the military *junta* remained in power until 1990, when Christian Democrat Patricio Aylwin Azócar (b. 1918) replaced Pinochet following national elections. The years of military rule were the longest period of authoritarian dictatorship in the country's republican history.

Under the military, the government annulled all constitutional rights, outlawed political parties and rejected the authority of parliament. This military *junta* maintained legislative power for itself and supervised the creation of special intelligence agencies to guarantee 'national security'. It was these agencies that put down all possible dissidence while dismantling the political parties.

On the excuse that the 'Marxist cancer' had to be eradicated from society – with a definition of Marxism that embraced almost all political attitudes in favour of democratic institutions – thousands of people were persecuted, imprisoned, tortured or assassinated. Eventually most unions and professional associations were dismantled with only the Catholic Church able effectively to challenge the judicial system and protect the families of the persecuted.

The new military government privatized what had previously been nationalized and in 1975 administered a plan of economic 'shock',

149

reducing cash in circulation and lowering government expenditure by reducing public employment. Inflation was reduced, but unemployment rose to 30 per cent at the national level. A new policy favouring an unrestricted free market was implemented, based on private enterprise and free competition in the marketplace. The annulment of protectionist economic measures, however, drove many small businesses into bankruptcy.

The politics of economic liberalization brought new power to more productive forces in the 1980s and, along with modernizations in financial, social and state organization, gave rise to a national economic resurgence, stabilizing many macroeconomic indicators. As a result, a centre-left government coalition came to power bringing with it the return of democratic processes and maintaining an economic balance through 1990 with an accent on a more just distribution of wealth and a general institutional democratization. As well, it seemed important to re-examine the recent past and to speak publicly about the still unsettled issues of human rights. In 1994, Eduardo Frei-Ruiz-Tagle, a Christian Democrat, was elected president of another centre-left coalition. His term was to last until the year 2000.

As for Chile's theatrical history, except for the ceremonial rituals of the indigenous peoples, theatre as such was introduced to the country by Catholic priests who, using Mystery plays and autosacramentales (one-act religious plays), sought to unite the experience of art with that of the transcendental, ethical and sacred. Because of these educational aspects, authorities exercised severe control over theatre, especially over popular secular plays. In the early nineteenth century, leaders of the independence movement used theatre as a way to spread their ideology and to arouse nationalistic feeling among large groups of people. For most of the nineteenth century, theatre was part of the ideological, political and moral debates within Chilean society. It was only during the second half of that century that non-political themes dealing with love and social customs appeared. At this time as well, theatre returned to its roots as a popular public festivity, often taking place outdoors, using the style of the circus, including both acrobats and humorous sketches.

Given such links to popular activities, throughout the nineteenth century Chilean theatre was not considered a profession, nor was it acknowledged as a high cultural activity. Such activity was generally provided in Chile by touring professional companies from Spain and Italy. Their repertoires were composed for the most part of classical and light popular plays. Their styles strongly conditioned the taste and expectations of the country's theatre audiences early in the twentieth century.

When World War I put an end to the flow of European companies to South America, local writers, actors and technicians were suddenly forced to meet the established demand for theatre. Between 1914 and 1930, the development of a national theatre took great leaps forward with most social sectors becoming part of the new theatre audience.

The aesthetic principles and working style of most of these new companies were still greatly influenced by traditional nineteenth-century Spain. Aside from the popular melodramas and social satires, they also performed sainetes (one-act farcical sketches) and costumbristas (featuring local manners and customs). For some artists, however, these styles lacked relevance in the modern world. This sensibility was strengthened when European artists arrived in Chile, exiled by either the Spanish Civil War or World War II. Most were well received with many settling in South America and eventually exercising a strong influence on theatre in the region. The Spaniard Margarita Xirgú's performances of García Lorca, for example, the Ballets Jooss, Louis Jouvet and others brought to Chile a new kind of theatre in which theatrical expression was accomplished not only with dramatic text, but also with visual images.

In the early 1940s, the influences began to bear fruit when Pedro de la Barra (1912–76) and Pedro Mortheiru (1919–94), together with several young teachers from the University of Chile and Universidad Católica (Catholic University), founded the Teatro Experimental and Teatro de Ensayo, respectively. The goals of these theatres were indeed ambitious, and those involved not only were gifted but also had a great deal of passion and energy. Eventually, they were able to accomplish their goals: to experiment theatrically with visual images and language, to follow modern trends in design, to found new professional companies in Chile, to systematically study new performance trends, and to educate theatre professionals at the universities. The first areas to benefit from this kind of work were scholarly research in theatre, teaching and production. Playwriting and theatre criticism followed later, helping not only in the development of 'educated' artists but also in the creation of an 'educated' public for the new theatre.

Play selection was one of the most delicate tasks for the new theatres. The Teatro Experimental of the University of Chile programmed three types of plays: classics, contemporary plays, and plays by national authors. Universidad Católica followed a very similar line, although focusing more on national authors and Catholic writers such as French writers Georges Bernanos and Paul Claudel, as opposed to the Teatro Experimental, which staged writers such as Bertolt Brecht and Luigi Pirandello.

Some of the students from the Teatro Experimental, encouraged by the ideas of Pedro de la Barra, founded similar institutions in the regions. Among them was the theatre group of Concepción University, a company that in the 1960s attempted to develop a national popular theatre inspired by the socio-political youth movements of the period. Other theatre groups emerged in the 1960s at the universities of Valdivia, Antofagasta, Valparaíso and the State Technical University of Santiago.

Theatre practice at this time mostly came out of the universities. Neither pedagogical nor amateur, these were true professional theatres resident at the respective universities. The university environment also gave these groups a financial and material infrastructure that would have been impossible to obtain otherwise since the state gave universities very significant financial support. Most universities became very powerful institutions embracing areas that in other countries were traditionally developed by the private sector, including television channels, hospitals and even sports. At the same time, the universities enjoyed wide freedom of thought and expression, thus giving space to all the political ideologies present in Chilean society. The University of Chile, for instance, expressed a middle-class ideology that nevertheless sympathized with the working classes. Universidad Católica was established under the ideology of the conservatives but later widened its social composition.

From the time the first university theatre was founded in 1941, it was this movement that had the greatest influence on the more traditional Chilean professional theatre, an influence that extended to other Latin American countries through tours, festivals and through the encouragement of Latin American artists to train in Chilean universities. It was the graduates of Chile's university theatre schools who, after 1950, established the country's many 'pocket' theatres and later its independent theatres. In both cases, they drew on the philosophy of the university theatre movement for inspiration.

From 1940 onward, it is possible to identify at least four periods of note in the history of Chilean theatre. The first is 1941–60, which coincides with the development and recognition of theatre as a profession and the creation of many national theatre institutions. The second is 1960–73, distinguished by the maturation of Chilean artistic creation and its growth as part of national reality. A third period can be seen in the years 1973–88, with the articulation of an artistic response to the country's military government. From 1988 onward, a fourth period emerged – a post-modern period with a diversity of strong aesthetic visions.

To look at these periods in detail, from 1941 to 1960, years of foundation work, a firm basis for the development of a national theatrical movement was laid thanks to the creation of core institutions that could provide training for drama teachers, scholars, directors, actors, technicians, designers and choreographers. The study of theorists and practitioners such as Konstantin Stanislavski, Vsevelod Meyerhold, Edward Gordon Craig and Brecht, together with a programme of graduate work in foreign universities, allowed Chilean theatre practitioners for the first time to become aware of modern movements in European theatre.

Among major productions coming from this period were Lope de Vega's *Fuenteovejuna* (*The Sheep's Well*, 1952), directed by Pedro Orthus (1917–74) at the Teatro Experimental, Pirandello's *Six Characters in Search of an Author* (1948), Bernard Shaw's *Pygmalion* (1949) and Brecht's *Die Dreigroschenoper* (*The Threepenny Opera*, 1959). All were landmarks both as dramatic works and for their powerful stagings.

However, those companies that followed the old Spanish styles were still dominant at this time, often staging productions of great quality. Among these were the many satirical comedies and *sainetes* of the Chilean dramatist Lucho Córdoba. Some even tried to synthesize the old and the new, such as actress Ana González (b. 1915). Certainly, the old acting traditions were maintained as a new relationship with the public began to develop. It was not by chance that the greatest success of the university theatres was *La pérgola de las flores* (*The Flower Market*, 1960), a play by Chilean playwright Isidora Aguirre (b. 1919). Written in the *costumbrista*

wide and the prevalence of a Marxist historical dialectic. All contributed to a climate that served as background to the importance of political action in the cultural and social life of Chile.

This environment obviously affected theatre. Until the 1960s, it had been customary for a director or producer to select a repertoire of plays and mount them with the artistic participation of specialists, each exercising his or her own particular field of expertise. During the late 1960s and early 1970s, however, a new ideology of participation and self-expression emerged among actors who were particularly interested in creating a new aesthetic, usually in non-traditional venues. This new art also took to the streets, public spaces, factories and schools, often taking part in real life and acting as an agitational force for new social movements. It was the beginning of collective creation, a genre also explored by playwrights willing to cooperate in script development.

The appearance of collective creation helped break the division between professional and amateur theatre while allowing professional actors to delve into dramatic construction and make contributions to the production as a whole. It also allowed them to get involved in scene design, costuming and lighting. Characterized by its social and theatrical immediacy, collective creation responded quickly to the complicated and changing social scene, thus drawing attention to the relationship between actors and audiences and the role of the latter in the theatre event. Many genres and styles were revivified by these improvisational techniques and by the alteration of texts, actor's self-expression, new themes, new spaces, and the political events of the period. The perishable nature of this new kind of theatre, and its refusal to be classified aesthetically within already existing parameters, were not major concerns for those working within it. Rather, they measured its value in terms of political efficiency and its immediate effect on social behaviour.

Nevertheless, there were casualties. The Teatro de Ensayo de la Universidad Católica, one of the pillars of theatre in Chile, was dismantled in 1968. Some of its members regrouped into a new company called the Taller de Experimentación Teatral (TET; Workshop for Theatrical Experimentation) and mounted an important collective creation called *Peligro a 50 metros* (*Danger at 50 Metres*, 1968) under the direction of actor-director Fernando Colina (d. 1969) and with the collaboration of Enrique Noisvander (1928–90) and playwrights Sieveking and José Pineda (b. 1934). *Peligro a 50 metros* was a play of protest and social criticism denouncing the hypocrisy of people who say they have religious feelings while remaining passive in the face of violence. TET and its later form, Taller de Creación Teatral (Workshop of Theatrical Creation), worked collectively for the next five years. While at the university, the company presented a collective production with a text by Sergio Vodanovic: *Nos tomamos la universidad* (*We Took the University*, 1969), a play criticizing university reforms, which they considered to be biased and unfair. Other creations, such as *Todas las colorinas tienen pecas* (*All Redheads Have Freckles*, 1970), were based on the texts of the anti-poet Nicanor Parra (b. 1914). The group also used Chilean short stories and poems that reflected a sensitivity to popular culture.

Another important collective of this time was Ictus, a group that turned towards collective creation after Jorge Díaz, whose plays they earlier produced, left for Spain. In 1969, Ictus presented *Cuestionemos la cuestion* (*Let's Question the Question*), a socio-political satire of the educational, political and mass communication system and the family. The uninhibited character of the acting, the actors' use of the entire theatre space, the dark comedy (reminiscent of Díaz's style) and the irreverent attitude towards social taboos made this creation a landmark of the period. The actors who helped create this work not only proved their own acting skills, but also managed to become an artistic nucleus that in the future would produce a number of significant plays. This group extended its influence through the television programme *La manivela* (*The Crank*), whose sketches were also created collectively.

Another group of note at the time was Aleph, made up of university students. Working collectively under actor-playwright Oscar Castro (b. 1947), Aleph's themes and style – direct, satirical and sentimental – strongly appealed to young people. In 1969 the company produced *Se sirve usted un cóctel molotov* (*Help Yourself to a Molotov Cocktail*) and in 1970 *Viva Inmundo de Fanta-Cia* (an untranslatable title connected to fantasy, the drink Fanta and the US Central Intelligence Agency), *¿Cuántas ruedas tiene un trineo?* (*How Many Wheels on a Sled?*, 1971) and *Vida, pasión, y muerte de Casimiro Peñafleta* (*The Life, Passion and Death of Casimiro Peñafleta*, 1972).

The use of collective creation also touched amateur, high-school and regional theatre, each adapting the technique to work for its particular modes of expression and reflection about immediate reality. Theatre also began to bring these people together and activated political awareness, often serving as an agitprop weapon. In 1973, the Asociación Nacional de Teatros Aficionados (National Association of Amateur Theatres) listed over 300 members.

The victory of Allende's Socialist Party in 1970 gave strong support to all these organizations and associations, and helped to create an infrastructure for this movement. Likewise, training institutions, social development agencies and cultural committees of large workers' unions openly began to support the movement as well.

Bourgeois and middle-class audiences, however, gradually abandoned the theatre, either because they did not share the radical views promulgated by the new groups or because they were involved in the power struggle provoked by the more revolutionary measures of the new government. Daily life became so influenced by this struggle that live theatre had trouble competing with news broadcasts or street demonstrations. It became, in fact, redundant to go to the theatre for political orientation or interpretation. Plays such as Ictus's *Tres noches de un Sábado* (*Three Nights on a Saturday*, 1972) or Edmundo Villarroel's *Agamos el amor* (*Let's Make Love*, 1971) were nevertheless well received by the public. *Agamos el amor*, which introduced the genre of the café-concert to Chile, dealt with free love and was presented on a circular stage while the audience sat on pillows.

The 1960s were fundamental for Chilean theatre, for they saw the renewal of aesthetic forms and organizational styles, a wider commitment to the profession, a stronger involvement of all social classes in theatre art, the development of spaces and new social organizations, all within a framework of freedom of expression. In 1973, however, the *coup d'état* that overthrew the Allende government established a military regime directed by four members of the armed forces, eventually led by General Pinochet. Freedom of expression was limited, and most of the cultural movements that had been advocates of social change came under severe control. Society again became hierarchical 'in order to recover the true national identity [and] love of order and peace'. The result was the exile of hundreds of Chilean intellectuals, artists and politicians.

It is worth noting here that from 1973 until 1983 the country lived with a permanent curfew that prohibited free movement at night, a curfew that inhibited normal theatrical activity. The year 1983 marked the beginning of political openness but this continued to exclude participation from 'Marxist' sectors. While political parties were allowed to function once again and the alternative media expanded, its practitioners suffered censorship, judicial impositions and even imprisonment.

Nevertheless, state theatres and other groups that received support from the government continued to operate, though the grassroots amateur theatre completely disappeared and the professional theatre lost its greatest support – the universities. All universities in the country were, in fact, taken over by the military, which fired many academics and revised the curriculum. The majority of university theatres across the country were subsequently closed down, thus leaving this area of society with no professional theatre activity whatsoever. This included activities at the department of theatre at the University of Chile in Santiago, the oldest and strongest university theatre in the country.

The theatre at Universidad Católica was the only one that managed to survive. Run by Eugenio Dittborn (1915–79) from 1954, its faculty was allowed to remain. However, its School of Communication Arts – which also included studies in cinema, television and other mass media – was completely dismantled by 1978. From 1973 to 1978, the theatre at Universidad Católica only produced Spanish and French classics (Calderón, Lope de Vega and Molière) which, although departing from its previous philosophy of producing exclusively Chilean and Latin American plays, still aimed at maintaining critical thought and moral values. In 1978 the company again attempted to produce a Chilean play, Marco Antonio de la Parra's (b. 1952) *Lo crudo, lo cocido, lo podrido* (*The Raw, the Cooked, the Rotten*), which was quickly censored politically by university authorities alleging that it was immoral because it contained vulgar words. After this experience, the company returned to the classics for five more years, nevertheless selecting plays that defended freedom and human values.

Given this situation and the subsequent imprisonment of individuals and even entire groups, many theatre people simply left the country. Those who remained created new independent companies, since most of the older ones – with the exception of Ictus and a small number of others – had disappeared. Most independent companies at this time were forced to work without any support whatsoever, depending totally on box-office revenue for survival. The situation worsened when television channels, also under the control of the military government, blacklisted actors, who were then not even allowed to appear on the screen in commercials. Since more than 80 per cent of professional actors had their names on the blacklist at one time or another, economic survival was very difficult indeed.

A small number of professionals worked under the patronage of binational institutes of culture, such as the French or German ones, or of the Catholic Church. This important patronage was not only financial but also political. Because there was no specific law to regulate theatre, the arts were subject to the general rules that in practice covered all of society. Some productions showed the extent of the censorship imposed: every member of the group Aleph and some of their families were imprisoned after the opening of their play *Al principio existía la vida* (*And In the Beginning There Was Life*, 1974), a national allegory; in 1977 the group Teatro La Feria (Theatre of the Fair) was harassed by the government for its production of *Las hojas de Parra* (*Parra's Leaves*), based on texts by Nicanor Parra. The tent in which they performed the play was, in fact, later set on fire.

Another form of censorship, even more direct, was financial. The Law of Protection for National Theatre, which since 1935 had exempted theatre groups from paying taxes, was abolished. Only university and state theatres were now to enjoy this benefit. In order for independent theatres to get tax-exempt status, they had to be sponsored by a university and their work had to be classified as 'cultural' by Ministry of Culture authorities. Otherwise, they would pay taxes of up to 22 per cent of net income, and later on, 18 per cent in Value Added Tax. The ambiguity with which the authorities defined 'cultural' work allowed the ministry to use and abuse this law freely, systematically refusing – with rare exceptions – to exempt independent groups that dared to produce socially critical plays. At one point, even Samuel Beckett's *Waiting for Godot* was considered to be 'non-cultural' by authorities.

Despite the fact that Chile was now a country where theatre artists had to pay the government for their work instead of receiving support from it – perhaps the only such country in the world – independent groups survived because of their deep conviction that they were providing a much-needed social service. The strongest groups during this difficult time were Ictus, directed by Nissim Sharim, Delfina Guzmán and Claudio di Girólamo (b. 1929); Imagen (Image), directed by Gustavo Meza (b. 1938); Taller de Investigación Teatral, directed by Raúl Osorio (b. 1944); and Teatro La Feria, directed by Jaime Vadell and José Manuel Salcedo. Other groups of note to emerge included El Teatro Joven (Youth Theatre), El Teatro de Comediantes (Actors' Theatre), El Teatro de Cámara (Chamber Theatre), and El Télon (The Curtain).

From 1978 through the 1990s many other groups – independent companies mostly but also many university groups – again began to work. The viability of theatre at every level – professional, independent, university, regional and community – was re-established through such non-traditional institutional forms. Among non-professional theatres the most creative and active was the Asociación Cultural Universitaria (University Cultural Association) of the University of Chile.

By 1983, the economic crisis and the bankruptcy of many of the most powerful private businesses led to a political openness that created new political and cultural structures. Even though occasionally states of national emergency were declared and some public liberties cancelled, the new openness included the free printing of books, and the suspension of the curfew that had limited nightlife and entertainment. However, the discriminatory tax was still in force and many theatre artists and their families still lived under constant threat. At the University of Chile in 1987, the arts departments were isolated and in the theatre school the director and most of the teachers were dismissed. But Universidad Católica was again favoured by the openness of the political climate: military intervention gave way to a recovery of the university's faculty and government and the repertoire was expanded with plays by Juan Radrigán (b. 1937) and the exiled Omar Saavedra (b. 1944).

Professional theatre was generally strengthened by the return at this point of hundreds of actors, directors, playwrights and entire companies from exile. As well, recent graduates of the newer theatre schools and artists from other fields had become professionals, thus significantly renewing stage art.

Key among these were El Nuevo Grupo (The New Group), directed by María Elena Duvachelle and Julio Yung; El Teatro de Fin de

Siglo (End of the Century Theatre), directed by Ramón Griffero (b. 1954); and the various theatre activities of Alejandro Sieveking and Bélgica Castro (b. 1921), both in independent theatre and in the Teatro Itinerante (Itinerant Theatre) of the Ministry of Education.

In 1988, a plebiscite was called, asking if Pinochet should continue as head of government. Most theatre people openly backed the 'no' option, and its subsequent triumph meant the calling of free elections during 1989. As politics could again be practised openly, so theatre turned to other themes. A symbol of these new times was the great artistic and public success of La negra Ester (The Black Esther, 1988), directed by Andrés Pérez and created with the new Compañía Gran Circo Teatro (Great Circle Theatre Company). Pérez was returning from exile in Paris, were he worked with the Théâtre du Soleil. Influenced by the aesthetics of Ariane Mnouchkine and also her theatre organization, Pérez created a production with music, masks and an Oriental style of acting. Based on a popular lyric love tragedy, audiences were deeply touched by this play. It was a premonition of the social reconciliation to come, and of the possibility of recreating a national culture through theatre, a culture that could occur in open spaces, with massive audiences and a festival spirit.

In the 1990s, several groups developed theatre in this style using open or non-traditional spaces, linked to street theatre and body expression. Mauricio Celedón (b. 1957), the director of Teatro del Silencio (Theatre of Silence), who had also worked with Mnouchkine and studied with Etienne Decroux and Marcel Marceau in Paris, created aesthetic propositions through his own mimodramas. His Malasangre (Bad Blood, 1991) was a culmination of his work in Chile since 1988, and was defiantly continued in Taca-taca mon amour (1993). Another working in these new ways was Andrés del Bosque, who explored circus techniques and in 1994 created Las siete vidas del Tony Caluga (The Seven Lives of Tony Caluga).

Another trend of post-Pinochet theatre was a return to intimate spaces, where subjective themes were explored using a refined and symbolic language. New generations even began to express themselves in other ways, emphasizing the visual and symbolic, body language, live music and poetic and synthetic texts. Collective theatre continued as the principal form of company organization, implying as well a participatory form of script development.

In the late 1980s, women began to appear as directors. One group, in fact, was run completely by women, a group focusing its work on a feminist perspective. Key in this area have been the playwright Inés Margarita Stranger (b. 1957) and the director Claudia Echenique (b. 1962), directors of Cariño malo (Bad Love, 1990) and Malinche, both produced by the theatre at Universidad Católica.

Teatro de la Memoria (Memory Theatre) is another leading group in the 1990s. Directed by Alfredo Castro (b. 1955), it produced a Trilogía testimonial de Chile (Testimonial Chilean Trilogy), which symbolically revealed different marginal worlds, metaphors of the repressed transgressions of society.

Also in the 1990s, the institutional theatres began to increase their openness to new developments, while in the independent theatre, few groups from the 1970s and 1980s remain. Among the exceptions are Teatro Imagen, which in 1989 staged Cartas de Jenny (Letters from Jenny) and in 1993 continued its experimental work with Murmuraciones acerca de la muerte de un juez (Rumours About a Judge's Death). Both were written and directed by Gustavo Meza.

Although cultural policies are still not clearly defined, freedom of expression and some government funding have lessened the burden of producing theatre. Chile's ability to host the Theatre of Nations Festival in 1993 – a festival that brought thirty-three countries and the participation of sixty Chilean groups – was an important symbol of the country's return to world-theatre, and the willingness of the state to lend support to it once again.

Structure of the National Theatre Community

Professional theatre activity in Chile tends to be concentrated in the capital city, Santiago, since lack of permanent government subsidies still makes it difficult for theatres to operate in the regions. Among the few stable theatres outside the capital are groups at the University of

Antofagasta, El Nations in the city of Concepción, and the Theatre Association in Valparaíso.

In Santiago, there are about twenty regularly producing companies with another fifteen or so operating on a less regular basis in any given year. In total, about fifty productions open each season in Santiago.

Among the regularly producing companies, three are subsidized. One of these three, the Teatro Itinerante, founded in 1977, is, in fact, totally subsidized by the Ministry of Education to tour across the country.

Also partially subsidized is the theatre group from Universidad Católica, which has converted an old movie house into two auditoriums and mounts two or three productions annually. Actors are jobbed in for each show. In general, most artistic decisions are made by a team of actors, directors and designers. Working for the group since the 1970s have been Héctor Noguera (b. 1937), Raúl Osorio, Ramón Núñez (b. 1941), Ramón López (b. 1946), Paz Yrarrázavar (b. 1931), Consuelo Morel (b. 1947) and María de la Luz Hurtado (b. 1950). The group uses its annual subsidy to start the season but it is an amount that must be doubled by its ticket income in order to finance the rest of the season.

The Chilean National Theatre, operating through the University of Chile, leases a downtown space, and receives subsidies for the total cost of two or three shows annually, produced by jobbed-in professionals with the director, actor Serge Aguirre (b. 1935) and the assistant director Fernando González (b. 1939). None of the subsidized theatres pays Value Added Tax.

Other professional theatre companies work within the independent arena, normally leasing or renting the space they occupy. Only a few manage to find corporate sponsorships and only Ictus was able during the 1980s to offer a wider range of activities, such as the creation of an alternative video production company called Ictus-TV, which helps to finance its theatre productions. Box-office revenues, however, are rarely enough to cover production costs.

There are very few individuals willing to invest in theatre on a commercial basis. The most common financing formula, therefore, is producing as an actors' cooperative, in which none of the members receives a working salary but all invest equally in the production and share any profits. The risk of losing everything is always present. In other cases, an actor or director acts as producer. This person either owns or rents a small space and will hire other actors on a salary. In this case, the producer keeps the profits. The budget in the early 1990s for independent productions staged this way was usually anywhere from US$2,000 to US$30,000.

Theatre audiences also vary. A successful production might be seen by 60,000 people, an average one by 25,000 and a neighbourhood or avant-garde production by 3,000. Students and young people are frequent audience members and enjoy specially priced tickets.

Special performances are usually arranged for organizations and businesses. Audiences grew noticeably during the 1970s and 1980s, thanks to the efforts made to take theatre to such groups and organizations. A successful play could be seen this way by more than 80,000 people, with an average of about 30,000.

Newer groups usually either occupy non-traditional venues or use those of international institutes of culture. In the latter case, they must produce playwrights of the institute's nationality.

Finally, amateur theatre has been reborn across the country in the 1980s and 1990s, especially in grassroots organizations trying to cope with the lack of resources of particular social groups while providing recreational, educational and social functions. They normally perform collectively and often experiment with new theatre forms. They are organized into associations and networks that allow them to exchange experiences and work methods. There are about 250 amateur groups, plus a large number of school theatres promoted and directed by primary and secondary school teachers.

SIDARTE, the major theatre union, ceased operation in the 1990s. Some of its international activities were taken over by the Chilean Centre of the International Theatre Institute, CET (the scenographers' union) and the Corporación Nacional de Teatro (National Theatre Corporation).

There are three major national prizes. The most prestigious is the National Arts Award, presented every four years to a distinguished figure in the arts community. The prize carries with it a lifetime pension. The Escuela de Teatro de la Universidad Católica holds a biennial National Playwriting Competition as does the Alcaldia de Santiago.

As for festivals, the Escuela de Teatro de la Universidad Católica is also host to a major national festival each year. Held for the twenty-third time in 1994, this open-air event is held each January – the country's summer. The ten best productions of the preceding year are restaged.

Other important festivals include an annual festival of experimental theatre sponsored by the Instituto Chileno Norteamericano; the Teatro a Mil festival, held in the Centro Cultural Mapocho; the Festival de las Nuevas Tendencias (New Directions), organized by the Escuela de Teatro at the University of Chile; and various popular and community theatre festivals held in and outside of Santiago.

Artistic Profile

Companies

Of Chile's twenty or so regularly producing companies, most offer a standard mix of national and international plays. The stylistic approach or commitment to national authors is usually the major defining factor. This said, the Teatro Itinerante is the only national touring group and it has steadfastly maintained its policy of increasing theatre activity in the regions and training students. Its repertoire is composed of classics along with well-known contemporary plays including plays by Chilean authors.

Since 1983, Universidad Católica's theatre group has begun to produce the works of Chilean playwrights once again – including Egon Wolff's La balsa de la medusa (The Jellyfish's Raft, 1984) and Háblame de Laura (Tell Me About Laura, 1986) and Juan Radrigán's Pueblo de mal amor (Town of Bad Love, 1986) – as well as works by other Latin American authors. Its greatest audience success was the Chilean sainete Su lado flaco (His Weakest Point, 1986) by René Hurtado Borne (b. 1887), which was seen by more than 85,000 people. The group also regularly organizes play-writing contests and workshops in order to encourage new plays. Young directors are also frequently called to stage their plays in this theatre.

Between the military coup d'état of 1973 and 1986, the theatre of the University of Chile abandoned its traditional interest in experimentation and began to produce more conservative shows with an educational aim. After 1986, when the artistic director was again elected by the artists themselves, the group began hiring more innovative directors such as Guillermo Semler, Claudio Pueller (b. 1959), Fernando González, Abel Carrizo and Raúl Osorio.

Among the regularly producing independent theatres, the most consistently innovative and challenging during the late 1970s and the 1980s were Ictus, directed by Nissim Sharim, Delfina Guzmán and Claudio di Girolamo; La Feria, directed by Jaime Valdell and Susana Bomchil; Imagen, directed by Gustavo Meza and Yael Unger; Fin de Siglo, directed by Ramón Griffero; Q, directed by Juan Cuevas and María Cánepa; Teatro del Alma, directed by Carla Cristi; and El Telón, directed by Juan Radrigán and José Herrera.

Leading groups in the 1990s include La Troppa, directed by Juan Carlos Zagal; Teatro La Memoria, directed by Alfredo Castro; Teatro del Silencio, directed by Mauricio Celedón; Gran Circo Teatro, directed by Andrés Pérez; and Teatro Aparte, directed by Rodrigo Bastides (b. 1961). Led by directors, playwrights, actors, designers or independent producers, all these groups have tended towards the experimental in style and have staged almost exclusively original scripts.

A number of other independent groups of significance that generally staged Chilean and Latin American plays critical of the socio-political structures of the continent and which made important contributions during the 1980s have now closed. Among them were El Nuevo Grupo, directed by Julio Yung and María Elena Duvachelle; Los Comediantes, directed by Ana González and Luz María Sotomayor; Teatro de Cámara, later called Abril (April), directed by Ana María Palma; and the group Pedro de la Barra, directed by Fernando Gallardo.

A third category of independent theatre most often produces classics, both traditional and modern. To this category belong the theatre companies of Tomas Vidiella and Alicia Quiroga.

Dramaturgy

Contemporary Chilean dramaturgy had two distinctive stages: between 1974 and 1987, when independent theatres produced some fifty new plays of note; and from 1988 to the present, which connects to post-modernism. Some of these plays were created collectively, but for the most part they were scripted by Chile's playwrights, old and new.

The majority of the plays from the first period were testimonial in style and realistic. Unlike many of the socially critical plays produced before 1973 – which in order to challenge the system and to stress their didactic function used a grotesque style with stereotyped characters and extreme situations – most new plays presented the overwhelming daily life of the dispossessed. It was important to these writers to capture the psychological and social pressures of the authoritarian environment in which they lived, and to describe its context.

The protagonists of these plays were real men and women from real neighbourhoods, families or workplaces whose common lifestyle gave them not only a group identity, but also an ability to survive. Shaken by the nation's economic policy and wide unemployment, these writers discovered that when equilibrium is distorted, life itself is endangered, as is the identity of large institutions, individuals and even the nation itself.

Pedro, Juan y Diego (1976), created by David Benavente (b. 1941) and the Ictus company, is perhaps the best representative of this type of play. Three unemployed men (a former public employee, a one-time peasant and salesman, and an ex-construction worker) are working under a national government employment plan designed to absorb the unemployed. In recalling their pasts, they gradually make connections between their different backgrounds and experiences. The final product of their work – a stone wall – is ultimately destroyed by the authorities but it has now become the symbol of the workers' dignity and their collective efforts. They join together and agree to ignore their differences.

Generally, most of these plays are neither dramas nor tragedies but rather have the popular sense of humour of the traditional *sainete*. But in the modern versions, the dramatic goal is to make the audience aware of the social problems and share in the pain, and deal with reality. This sort of humour is typical of the Chilean personality and it was used as a way to maintain integrity and dignity while dealing with the aggression of those in power.

Other notable plays in this style included *Te llamabas Rosicler* (*Your Name Was Rosicler*,

1976) by Luis Rivano (b. 1933) and the Imagen company, a story of tenants in a rooming house showing Chilean society in a state of decomposition; *Tres Marías y una Rosa* (*Three Marias and a Rose*, 1979), by Benavente and the Taller de Investigacion Teatral, a play that toured widely, presenting the wives of unemployed men trying to keep their families going; *Los payasos de la esperanza* (*The Clowns of Hope*, 1977), a collective by the Taller de Investigacion Teatral, showing five unemployed clowns waiting for a meeting that never takes place while rehearsing circus numbers; and *El último tren* (*The Last Train*, 1978) by Meza and Imagen, showing the destruction of a family that loses everything when the government closes the railway to their town. Other plays in this style include *Testimonios sobre las muertes de Sabina* (*Testimony on the Deaths of Sabina*, 1978) by Juan Radrigán, about a woman who works as a fruit vendor and finds herself involved in a Kafkaesque situation, and *Cuántos años tiene un día* (*How Many Years In a Day*, 1978) by Ictus and Sergio Vodanovic, presenting a group of journalists unable to continue with a television show because of the disappearance of one of their colleagues.

All of these were examples of Theatre of Testimony, a genre so named because the plays were based on true events. Many of these events were investigated by the creators *in situ*, sometimes even with the active participation of those in the situations. Beyond political content or social criticism, the plays realistically presented social groups, language, habitat, social behaviour, customs, and emotional, religious and moral problems. As such, this approach offered a clear sense of social truth to audiences.

A second style of playwriting popular in Chile around 1980 can be called the Theatre of Symbolic Forms, somewhere between the poetic, the grotesque and the ritualistic. Essentially irreverent, it is a kind of theatre that borders on absolute impudence to present themes and characters. Anti-mythic, it also presents common social problems against a ritualistic background. This irreverent theatre is also sensually challenging, visually innovative and is often conceived as a popular festive entertainment. Born in Chile at university festivals, it could also be seen in the plays of the Teatro La Feria, a company whose shows were often done in circus tents.

Teatro La Feria's *Hojas de Parra* (1977) was based on poetic texts by Nicanor Parra. A clear example of this second style, it is a sarcastic and prescient national allegory. Even as his acrobats and jugglers perform, a circus manager is selling his business to the owner of a funeral parlour, who gradually changes the circus into a cemetery as tombs and crosses cover what had been the circus stage. At the same time, an election is held for which Nobody is the main candidate. Nobody's slogan is 'the right and left united will never be defeated'.

Baño a baño (*Bath to Bath*, 1978) by Jorge Vega and Guillermo de la Parra is another grotesque caricature of national politics, this time set in a Turkish bath, involving arbitrary political decisions and sado-masochistic games.

Marco Antonio de la Parra, a psychiatrist, created still another example of this kind of theatre in *Lo crudo, lo cocido, lo podrido*. Using as its central metaphor the lives of restaurant waiters, it is again an allegory of power. Though the restaurant has been closed for years, the waiters still believe that they have some power because they know the secrets and weaknesses of the customers. Those customers who did not meet the waiters' expectations could be destroyed and buried in the building's walls. Eventually produced by Imagen, the play presents an inversion of power in which the fanatic guardians of tradition conspire to stop the course of history.

Historical drama has been another important part of Chilean theatre, both past and present. In its modern incarnation, the heroes are more glorious, the patriotic adventures more daring, and the epic popular struggles are put down more ruthlessly. Rather than confirming a particular moment in history, these plays ask the question: what socio-political phenomena could explain the Chilean reality of the 1970s?

Jaime Vadell and José Manuel Salcedo, actor-playwrights from Teatro La Feria, attempted to ask this question in *Bienaventurados los pobres* (*Blessed Are the Poor*, 1978), which focused on the historical development of ruling class relationships. The same authors wrote *A la Mary se le vio el poppins* (*We Saw Mary's Poppins*, 1981), a work that, through different settings, illustrated in reverse chronological order the principal historical events of the decade and its protagonists. The same self-critical attitude is presented in Benavente's *Tejado de vidrio* (*Glass Ceiling*, 1981), which also focuses on political leaders, in this case those with university educations.

Isidora Aguirre's play *Lautaro* (1981) is another in this style. A native leader taken prisoner by the Spanish conquerors, Lautaro

escapes and successfully leads his people in war. The play explores the ethical and psychological contradiction of war within a people, and also the decisive moment in which one takes up arms to fight against the oppression of those one knows. The poetic and symbolic language of the piece and its historical and psychological exploration of a complex relationship made it a winner of Universidad Católica's Prize for Playwriting. Antonio Skarmeta's *Ardiente paciencia* (1986) is a recreation of the last days of Nobel Prize-winning poet Pablo Neruda (1904–73), in which he becomes involved in his postman's love affair and finally finds his dramatic death interrupted by the repression of the military coup.

Many satirical plays in the 1980s dealt with consumerism and its ethical implications. Some of the plays dealing with this include Meza and Radrigán's *Viva Somoza* (*Long Live Somoza*, 1980), produced by Imagen; *Lindo país esquina con vista al mar* (*Beautiful Country Corner with a Seaside View*, 1979), with episodes written collectively by Ictus, de la Parra, Gajardo and Osses; Meza's *Cero a la izquierda* (*Cero on the Left*, 1981); *El tÿeral* (*The Stork*, 1982), produced by Teatro La Feria; and Julio Bravo's *Renegociación de un préstamo relacionado bajo fuerte lluvia en cancha de tenis mojada* (*Renegotiation of a Loan Made Under Heavy Rain On a Wet Tennis Court*, 1983).

Sueños de mala muerte (*Dreams of a Bad Death*, 1983) by José Donoso (b. 1924), produced by Ictus, also has consumerism as its central metaphor, in this case using people from an impoverished middle-class rooming house. In the play, an old man gets a job in a cemetery and discovers that he is the descendant of a rich family and has the right to a space in the luxurious family mausoleum. He spends his life savings claiming possession of the mausoleum but in the end loses his place when his fiancée chooses to be buried there.

Juan Radrigán is one of the most intense and powerful playwrights in the country. His prolific output – more than eighteen plays since 1978 – focuses on the search for answers to questions of human and divine justice, dealing often with the marginal, his characters connect to the absurd when facing abandonment and violence.

Some of Radrigán's most important works include *El toro por las astas* (*Taking the Bull by the Horns*, 1982), *Las brutas* (*The Brutish*, 1982), *El loco y la triste* (*The Foolish and the Sad*, 1984) and *Hechos consumados* (*Consummations*, 1981). This last play relates the encounter of a man and a woman in a solitary place by a river. She has been thrown in the water; he is looking for a place to live. Despite her negative experiences, she remains optimistic while he is sceptical, always wondering about the ultimate purpose and meaning of things. When a guard comes to drive them away, the man decides not to leave and is finally killed by the guard. Such is the fate of all the characters in Radrigán's plays. A poet of marginality, his works are generally examples of minimalism and work almost exclusively through dialogue. El Telón has produced most of Radrigán's plays both in commercial theatres and in popular venues.

Between 1983 and 1987, Chilean plays tended to deal mainly with reflections of the government's absolute political power and control. Many scripts were written at this time dealing with the psychology of oppression, moral decadence, torture, prison, exile and extermination. This was not a theatre of criticism or education following the style of past decades. Rather, it was a series of experiments in form, fantasy and ambiguity, in which environments and meanings were created through the use of the space and actors' bodies, where the psychoanalytical met the expressionistic, and epic realism met the intimate. A deep understanding of these situations and of personal and historical mechanisms was sought through symbolic games.

Other plays in this style are Marco Antonio de la Parra's La secreta obscenidad de cada día (Each Day's Secret Obscenity, 1984), Enrique Lhin's La Meka (1984); Ramón Griffero's Historia de un galpón abandonado (History of an Abandoned Warehouse, 1984) and Cinema Utopia (1985); Sergio Marras's Macías (1984); and Mario Benedetti's Primavera con una esquina rota (Spring With a Broken Corner, 1984) adapted by Ictus. There were also two important testimonial plays that dealt with this theme: Jaime Miranda's Regreso sin causa (Return Without a Cause, 1984), about exile; and Carlos Cerda's (b. 1942) Lo que está en el aire (What Is in the Air, 1986), a play about repression, also produced by Ictus. Isidora

Aguirre's Retablo de Yumbel (Yumbel's Altar, 1989) and Mauricio Pesutic's Mareago (1989) also explore the theme of people who disappeared during imprisonment.

Internationally, perhaps the best known in this style is La muerte y la doncella (Death and the Maiden) by former journalist Ariel Dorfman (b. 1942). Produced in more than a dozen languages since its première production by Ana Reeves in Santiago in 1991, the play is one of the most powerful indictments of repression and torture to come out of this period.

The late 1980s and 1990s also saw several good examples of Theatre of Images including mime pieces by groups such as the Teatro del Silencio. Among the strongest was the group's Transfusion (1989), about the clash of cultures following the Spanish conquest; Ocho horas (Eight Hours, 1991), about workers' rights; and Malasangre (1991), about Rimbaud. In 1993, Taca-taca mon amour looked at the history of the twentieth century through wooden football-playing puppets of people such as Hitler, Freud, Einstein and Stalin.

The work of Alfredo Castro reveals new directions – a parallel development of text and scenic language. He develops this style in La manzana de Adán (Adam's Apple, 1990); Historia de la sangre (Story of Blood, 1992), a play about crimes of passion; and Los días tuertos (Twisted Days, 1993), a play about disguises. Visually symbolic more than verbal, these works are non-realistic with designs often done by sculptors or in a sculptural style. These works are, in the end, rituals revealing in touching ways the hidden crimes of modern society.

Two important plays by Inés Margarita Stranger – Cariño malo and Malinche – deal with female identity. In the first play, the protagonist is divided into three antagonistic 'shes', while in the second the focus is on an Indian mother and her four daughters. Stranger's plays have found ready audiences both in Chile and abroad along with the plays of Marco Antonio de la Parra, whose works focus much more on violence, sex, love and the obscene.

Music Theatre

Music has always been an integral part of the Chilean theatrical tradition with origins in the rituals of Christian religious theatre and, from the nineteenth century, the Spanish zarzuela as performed by touring companies from Spain. As well, opera is always considered part of each theatrical season. However, with the development of a national theatre at the beginning of the twentieth century, these genres did not retain their popularity, except in musical cabarets.

It was in the university theatres from the 1940s on that music began to reappear on stage, first as an expressive accompaniment to the performance and later as something that could have its own theatrical form. In this latter area, there have been four developments: in folkloric theatre, in Brechtian theatre, in children's and young people's theatre and in pop, rock or post-modern music from the mid-1980s.

The use of traditional musical forms has always been a basic element in popular festivities and theatre with peasant or folkloric roots. The playwright Antonio Acevedo Hernández (1886–1962), popular between 1914 and 1945, built whole scripts around this folk music. During the 1960s, when popular culture was a central element of Chilean art in general, there was a resurgence in this area, and one can see this clearly in the plays of Alejandro Sieveking and Luis Heiremans. Without doubt, however, the two masterpieces in this area – also Chile's two most successful plays in terms of audience appeal – have been *La pérgola de las flores* (1960), a musical comedy by Isidora Aguirre, with music by Francisco Flores del Campo, a type of 'modern *zarzuela*' seen by more than 600,000 people throughout Chile; and *La negra Ester*, a musical tragedy with lyrics written by the popular poet Robert Parra, directed by Andrés Pérez, and with music by Guillermo Aste, Jorge Lobos and Alvaro Henríquez. Jaime Silva (b. 1934) was another who worked in this folk style, a form whose influence is clear in his operas (*El evangelio segrin San Jaime*, 1969).

Aguirre's plays have clear Brechtian roots especially in their use of music, while children's theatre, since the 1960s, made composer Vittorio Cintollesi a well-known figure. By the 1970s, café-concerts and musicals began to be promoted by the actor and impresario Tomás Vidiella, with composer Luis Advis one of the major composers in this area. From the mid-1980s and into the 1990s, music has become a basic component of nearly all stage productions and is usually performed live. Rock, pop and electronic music have continued to theatricalize and have now been integrated into a post-modern vision of total theatre. Clearly, theatrical production and musical composition are growing closer together with composers such as Andreas Bodenhoffer, Patricio Solovera and Miguel Miranda specializing in this area in Chile.

Dance Theatre

One of the major impulses behind the aesthetic renewal of the Chilean theatre in the 1940s was the visit by the German Ballets Jooss during World War II with *The Green Table*. It was the German expressionist aesthetic in this work, more than pure dance, that had the more lasting influence in theatre.

By the 1950s and 1960s, the university theatres required something close to dance choreography to facilitate the movement of their huge casts on stage and foreign choreographers residing in Chile, such as Juana von Laban, Joanne Turner and especially Ernst Uthoff of the Ballets Jooss, made important contributions.

What is now understood as 'dance theatre' has been developed in Chile by modern dancers such as Patricio Bunster, Vicky Larraín and especially Hernán Baldrich. Since about 1970, this last dancer, choreographer and creator of dance theatre has made significant contributions in the field. Usually inspired by the classic tragedies, characters and settings of universal culture, Baldrich makes them into choreographic-dramatic creations, with elements taken from the national aesthetic where visual images created by sculptures, costumes, the use of space in symbolic terms, musical arrangements and audio-visual projections are also important. Among Baldrich's inspirations have been Racine's *Phèdre*, Salvador Dalí, Juana de Arco, biblical psalms and Chopin. All have been used in his free integration of artistic disciplines where ritual, rhythm, masks, emotional movement and poetic text are organized in a dramatic, non-narrative way.

Theatre for Young Audiences
Puppet Theatre

There have been several areas of development in Chilean children's theatre since about 1960. The first phase was linked with the mime theatre of Enrique Noisvander and later continued by young dancers such as Rocío Rovira and Alfonso Unanue, the mimes Oscar Figueroa and Sergio Guzmán, and actors Carla Cristi, Julio Yung and Gonzalo Palta. These artists created shows full of colour, music and visual spectacle.

Later, full plays were written by Mónica Echeverría – *Aventuras de Quiquirico* (*The Adventures of Quiquirico*) and *Chumingo el Pirata de Lata* (*Chumingo, the Tin Pirate*) – by Jorge Díaz (co-author of *Chumingo* and, since then, one of the major children's theatre playwrights in the Spanish language), and by Jaime Silva – *Los grillos sordos* (*The Deaf Crickets*).

Children's theatre also played a social role in the country, being shown in smaller towns to people with few resources, and turning into true popular *fiestas*. In a more classic style, the Theatre of the University of Chile also included children's plays, such as Silva's *La Princesa Panchita* (*Princess Panchita*), in its repertoire.

During the 1970s, as a result of the policies of the military government, many theatrical professionals dedicated themselves to children's theatre simply as a means of survival. By the 1980s, however, a new stage began in which many artists realized that children's theatre allowed them much freer artistic expression. Many joined sculptural elements with body movement and music with colour. Working collectively, they created adaptations where scenery, action and images, together with live music, conveyed the plot. Some of these shows were later performed in streets or in town squares.

Institutionally, the theatre of Universidad Católica has been most consistent in developing a policy of supporting children's theatre groups such as La Troppa with its productions of *Rap del Quijote* (*Quixote Rap*, 1989) and *Pinocchio* (1990). They also create modern versions of classic works that also appeal to adults.

Theatre has also become an important part of school curriculums. Since the 1980s, many schools have included Chilean plays and the study of classical theatre in courses, and theatre as an extra-curricular activity has also meant the creation of hundreds of school groups. As a result, more than 50 per cent of audiences in the 1990s are composed of young people.

The first puppets in Chile were imported from Spain (Don Cristobal). Some influences came from Italy in the twentieth century, particularly the visit of the Picoli de Torino of Rafael Maldini. Javier Villafañe also visited Chile in 1944. Meche Cordova, a famous puppet player, started her own activities for children in 1942. Other important puppeteers included José Fernando Hogado, who started in 1950. In the mid-1990s several companies were operating: the Guiasol of Eugenio Beltrán, Los Encantados of Adolfo and Ilse Schwarzenberg and the Guiñol of Ana María Allende.

Design
Theatre Space and Architecture

In Chile, theatrical architecture is practically non-existent. Most theatre halls are old cinemas or auditoriums that have been adapted. Consequently, stage directors and designers have had to use great imagination and both technical and artistic creativity in order to make up for this deficiency, as well as for the lack of technical resources in lighting and sound.

Even so, stage design and theatrical design have developed progressively in Chile since the 1940s, and now constitute an established tradition with several generations of teachers and their students. The influence in the 1940s of Santiago Otañón, set designer for La Barraca in Spain, and Christian Bérard of the Louis Jouvet company initiated and gave prestige to this occupation in Chile. Architects later developed in this discipline and more recently sculptors, all following general international movements in this area. In the 1990s, set designers, along with designers of costumes, lighting and props, all participate right from the beginning in the planning of most productions.

Among Chile's major designers have been Héctor del Campo (b. 1918) from the University of Chile and Fernando Debesa (b. 1921) from Universidad Católica and, working independently, Oscar Navarro, Bernardo Trumper (b. 1926), Ricardo Moreno, Guillermo Núñez (b. 1930), Amaya Clunes, Claudio de Girólamo (b. 1929), Ramón López (b. 1946), Edith del Campo and Pablo Núñez.

Training

The Schools of Dramatic Arts at the University of Chile and Universidad Católica in Santiago were the first institutions to offer systematic studies in theatre. Working with the participation of many of the country's major theatrical creators, both schools were founded in the early 1940s and have been fundamental in the formation of professional theatre. They have also had an influence on amateur theatre in the country as well as on theatre in other Latin American countries.

At both schools, there are professional companies that put on productions involving the students. Being part of the university also allows these groups to integrate related artistic and humanist disciplines, as well as to participate in university cultural, political and social life.

The national character of the University of Chile allowed it to establish theatre schools in the provinces, especially Valdivia and Antofagasta. It also had great influence in Concepción. By the early 1990s, however, all of these regional schools were closed. The department of dramatic arts of the University of Chile grants degrees in acting as well as in theatrical design. At the end of the 1960s and into the 1970s, it also offered a night course in popular theatre. Universidad Católica offers degrees in acting and, since 1990, grants postgraduate degrees in directing and theatre criticism.

Undergraduate studies at both schools last four-and-a-half years, and include acting, voice and movement, art history, drama and cultural theory. As these are university courses, students can also take related courses in other faculties.

Since 1983, a number of private schools headed by former professors of the University of Chile have opened. Some of the better known ones are the Escuela Teatro Imagen (Image Theatre School) directed by Gustavo Meza, the Club de Teatro (Theatre Club) directed by Fernando González and the Teatro de la Casa (House Theatre) directed by Fernando Cuadra. All offer actor training.

Criticism, Scholarship and Publishing

The most important theatre periodical in the country is the quarterly *Apuntes* (*Notes*), published by Universidad Católica since 1960. It includes sections on theory and current theatre events and each issue includes a complete Chilean play script. There are as well occasional publications coming from the Ministry of Culture and from Teatro Itinerante.

Plays are generally published in these journals as well as by publishing houses such as Nascimento, Pehuén and Zig-Zag. In the late 1980s the Centro de Expresión Cultural y Artística (CENECA; Centre for Cultural and Artistic Expression) began to publish plays as well. Some playwrights, however, have published their work themselves.

National theatre research was encouraged and developed by the University of Chile under the direction of scholars such as Orlando Rodríguez, Agustín Siré and Domingo Piga. Other literary scholars, including Grinor Rojo, Julio Durán Cerda (b. 1914) and Juan Villegas (b. 1934), contributed to theatre scholarship as well. In the 1970s and 1980s, Universidad Católica, in close cooperation with social scientists, has developed an important body of research in the area of theatre history, led by María de la Luz Hurtado and Giselle Munizaga, and theatre and psychology, led by Consuelo Morel (b. 1947), Egon Wolff and Jaime Coloma (b. 1941). CENECA has also carried out important studies on the development of professional and community theatre, especially under the military regime. Among those working in this specialized area have been Hurtado, Carlos Ochsenius (b. 1955) and José Luis Olivarí.

Theatrical reviews of a more journalistic nature are regularly found in daily newspapers and in magazines. During the first half of the century, this type of criticism was written from an impressionistic point of view, whereas since the late 1970s it has become more specialized and professional. Among the reviewers whose work stands out are Hans Ehrman (b. 1924), Juan A. Piña, Luisa Ulibarri, Ana M. Foxley, Yolanda Montecinos, Agustín Letelier, Carlos Oyarzrín and Pedro Labra.

María de la Luz Hurtado
Translated by Mayte Gómez and
Joanne Rotermundt-De la Parra

Further Reading

Alegría, Fernando. 'Chile's Experimental Theatre'. *Interamérica* 4, no. 10. (October 1945): 24–5, 44–55.

Boyle, Catherine M. *Chilean Theatre, 1973–85: Marginality, Power, Selfhood*. London/Toronto: Associated University Presses, 1992. 226 pp.

Brncic, Zlatko. 'El teatro chileno a través de 50 años: 1900–50'. [Chilean theatre over fifty years: 1900–50]. In *Desarrollo de Chile en la primera mitad del siglo XX*. [Chile's development during the first half of the twentieth century]. Santiago: Editorial Universitaria, 1953.

Cánepa Guzmán, Mario. *Historia del teatro chileno*. [History of Chilean theatre]. Santiago: Editorial Universidad Técnica del Estado, 1974. 232 pp.

——. *El teatro en Chile*. [Theatre in Chile]. Santiago: Editorial Arancibia Hermanos, 1966. 135 pp.

——. *El teatro obrero y social en Chile*. [Working-class and social theatre in Chile]. Santiago: Ediciones Culturales y Publicaciones del Ministerio de Educación, 1971.

Castedo-Ellerman, Elena. *El teatro chileno de mediados del siglo XX*. [Chilean theatre in the 1950s]. Santiago: Editorial Andrés Bello, 1982. 240 pp.

Durán Cerda, Julio. Foreword to *Teatro chileno contemporáneo*. [Contemporary Chilean theatre]. México: Editorial Aguilar, 1970. 498 pp.

Fernández, Teodosio. *El teatro chileno contemporáneo, 1941–73*. [Contemporary Chilean theatre, 1941–73]. Colección Nova Scholar. Madrid: Editorial Playor, 1982. 213 pp.

Gomáriz, Enrique. 'Chilenos en el exilio: teatro de resistencia'. [Chileans in exile: A theatre of resistance]. *Conjunto*, 33 (July–September 1977): 56–88.

Hurtado, María de la Luz. *Memorias teatrales: el Teatro de la Universidad Católica en su cincuentenario*. [Theatrical memories: The Catholic University Theatre on its fiftieth anniversary]. Santiago: Revista Apuntes de la Universidad Católica de Chile, 1993. 226 pp.

——. *Sujeto social y proyecto histórico en la dramaturgia chilena actual*. [Social subjects and historical projects in contemporary Chilean drama]. Santiago: CENECA, 1983. 112 pp.

——. 'Teatro y sociedad chilenos: la dramaturgia de renovación universitaria entre 1950 y 1970'. [Theatre and society in Chile: Plays of the university theatres between 1950 and 1970]. Special issue, *Apuntes*, 94 (1986).

——, and María Elena Moreno. *El público del teatro independiente*. [Audiences of the independent theatre]. Santiago: CENECA, 1982. 89 pp.

Hurtado, María de la Luz, and Carlos Ochsenius. *Teatro chileno de la crisis institucional 1973–80*. [Chilean theatre during the institutional crisis 1973–80]. Latin American Series. Minnesota/Santiago: University of Minnesota/Centro de Indagación Cultural y Artística, 1982. 339 pp.

——. *Transformaciones del teatro chileno en la década del '70*. [Transformations of the Chilean theatre during the 1970s]. Buenos Aires: CENECA, 1980. 53 pp.

Hurtado, María de la Luz, and Juan Andrés Piña. 'Los niveles de marginalidad en Radrigán'. [Marginalization in Radrigán]. In *Teatro de Juan Radrigán: once obras*. [Theatre of Juan Radrigán: Eleven plays]. Latin American Series. Minnesota/Santiago: University of Minnesota/Centro de Indagación Cultural y Artística, 1983. 418 pp.

Maldonado, Carlos. 'Brecht in Chile'. *Communications from the International Brecht Society* 13, no. 1 (November 1983): 27–9.

Mayer, Edward Heriberto. 'Chilean Theatre in the Sixties: A Decade of Protest'. PhD dissertation, University of Missouri at Columbia. 144 pp.

Mengod Gimeno, Rosa María. 'Presencias en el teatro chileno del siglo XX'. [What is present in the Chilean theatre of the twentieth century]. *UC/AT* 440, no. 2 (1979): 101–35.

Morgado, Benjamín, ed. *Histórica relación del teatro chileno*. [Historical account of the Chilean theatre]. La Serena: Universidad de La Serena, 1985. 329 pp.

Munizaga, Giselle, and María de la Luz Hurtado. *Testimonios del teatro: treinta y cinco años de teatro en la Universidad Católica de Chile*. [Theatre testimonies: Thirty-five years of theatre at the Catholic University of Chile]. Santiago: Editorial Nueva Universidad, 1980. 186 pp.

Muñoz, Diego, Carlos Ochsenius, José Luis Olivari, and Hernán Vidal. *Poética de la población marginal: teatro poblacional chileno 1978–85. Antología crítica*. [The poetics of the marginalized: Community theatre in Chile 1978–85. A critical anthology]. Minneapolis/Santiago: Prisma Institute/CENECA, 1988. 439 pp.

Obregón, Osvaldo. 'The University Clásico in Chile'. Translated by Jean E. Brody. *Theater Magazine* 15, no. 1 (winter 1983): 18–24.

Ochsenius, Carlos. *Teatro y animación de base en Chile 1973–86*. [Grassroots theatre and theatre of animation in Chile 1973–86]. Buenos Aires: Ediciones Paulinas, 1988. 124 pp.

Piña, Juan Andrés. Teatro chileno en la década de los 80: desarrollo de un movimiento innovador. [Chilean theatre in the 1980s: The development of an innovative movement]. Santiago: Instituto Chileno de Estudios Humanísticos, 1982. 63 pp.

Rela, Walter. *Contribución a la bibliografía del teatro chileno, 1804–1960*. [A contribution to the bibliography of Chilean theatre, 1804–1960]. Montevideo: Universidad de la República, 1960. 51 pp.

Rodríguez, Orlando, and Domingo Piga. *Teatro chileno: su dimensión social*. [The social dimension of Chilean theatre]. Santiago: Editorial Nacional Quimantú, 1973. 95 pp.

Rojo, Grínor. *Muerte y resurección del teatro chileno 1973–83*. [Death and resurrection of theatre in Chile 1973–83]. Madrid: Libros del Meridión, 1985. 198 pp.

Vega, Daniel de la. *Luz de candilejas. El teatro y sus miserias: el teatro 1920–30*. [Footlights. Theatre and its miseries: Theatre 1920–30]. Santiago: Editorial Nascimento, 1930. 272 pp.

Villegas, Juan. 'El discurso teatral y el discurso crítico: el caso de Chile'. [Theatrical and critical discourse: The case of Chile]. *Anuario de la Universidad de Chile* 5 (August 1984): 317–36.

COLOMBIA

Located in northwestern South America, Colombia is crossed from north to south by three ranges of the Andes Mountains. The southeastern region connects to tributaries of the Amazon River while the Magdalena, Colombia's principal river, empties into the Caribbean Sea. Covering an area of 1.14 million square kilometres (439,700 square miles), Colombia had a 1992 population of 34.3 million.

Colonized by the Spanish in the sixteenth century, Colombia later joined with Venezuela and Ecuador in a confederation known as Gran Colombia, which was dissolved in 1830. In 1903 Colombia lost the territory of Panamá when the United States supported Panamá's claims to independence at the time of the building of the Panamá Canal.

Modern Colombia has long been plagued by violence and conflict between its two major political parties, the conservatives and the liberals. In 1957, the two parties agreed to alternate power every four years and this helped calm the turbulence to some extent.

Although a European-style theatre has existed in Colombia since colonial times, a nationally rooted theatre involving playwrights, directors, actors and designers really came into being only in the mid-1950s, more than 150 years after the construction of the first permanent theatre building in the capital, Bogotá. Originally built in the Spanish *corral de comedias* (open-air theatre) style by businessman Tomás Ramírez (d. 1804) and his partner, Joseph Dionisio del Villar, who became the theatre's first director, the new theatre became the epicentre of cultural and even political activity during the nineteenth century. In 1892, under the government of Rafael Núñez (1825–94), it was named the Teatro Colón to commemorate the fourth cen-

tenary of the arrival of Christopher Columbus in the Americas.

For most of this 150-year period, Colombian theatre was dominated by visiting Spanish, Mexican or Argentine companies or by local amateur groups. Some of the amateur companies were quite good – the company of Lorenzo María Lleras (1811–65), for example; Renacimiento, founded by Antonio Álvarez Lleras (1892–1956); and the Compañía Bogotana de Comedias of Luis Enrique Osorio (1896–1966) – but rarely were these groups able to develop. One that did was Osorio's, which trained many actors who continued to work in the theatre as well as in the burgeoning Colombian television industry. After several years' effort, Osorio was even able to realize one of his greatest dreams: the construction of a theatre of his own, the Teatro de la Comedia, which he used to promote the development of a truly Colombian theatre. In the 1980s, the theatre became home to the professional Teatro Libre de Bogotá (Free Theatre of Bogotá), thereby fulfilling one of the desires of its founder.

Even since 1945, the Teatro Colón has tended to host mostly foreign companies though there have been performances there by groups from within the country since the 1980s. Osorio's company, for example, worked at the Teatro Municipal (Municipal Theatre), demolished in 1950, a space that also played an important role in the popularization of a national theatre in the 1930s and 1940s. Osorio's plays, such as *Adentro los de corrosca* (*Inside the Corrosca*, 1965), *Ahí sos, camisón rosao* (*There You Go, Pink Shirt*, 1965), *El doctor Manzanillo* (*Doctor Manzanillo*, 1943) and *El Rajá de Pasturacha* (*The Rajah of Pasturacha*, 1964), were popular among all levels of Colombia's very stratified society. Sometimes plays would be performed for different audiences: on Saturday afternoons, for example, for servants, the police and blue-collar workers, while on Saturday evenings only upper-class society would attend.

The Municipal's repertoire was broad and tended towards the popular – farces, light comedies and revues; the Teatro Colón, however, was reserved for more intellectual 'high comedy', Spanish classics, or productions by touring foreign companies. Even differences in protocol could be seen at the two theatres right into the 1980s. At the Colón there was a dress code, while at the Municipal people could wear whatever they wished.

The distinctions between the theatres were also actively encouraged by theatre management as well as by politicians. Not surprisingly, the more institutional Teatro Colón was supported by the conservatives and, during the first half of the twentieth century, was even the site of speeches and party gatherings. The Teatro Municipal was supported by liberal leaders from the 1930s.

Both Osorio, with his popular comedies, and playwright Emilio Campos (known as Campitos, 1906–84), with his farcical political satires, felt more at home in and preferred the audiences of the Municipal. Although the works of these authors did not strictly represent any political party, many of their works did include direct allusions to current situations and people, especially in the case of Campitos, who used masks, voices and expressions to caricature well-known figures from national political life. In the cases of both writers, their early work tended towards realism and social criticism; their later work, however, began to make concessions to public taste and commercialism. Campitos, although he continued to be politically satirical, eventually found himself moving more into a kind of theatre for social action, foreshadowing the kind of work that would be done in the 1970s and 1980s by university theatre and the so-called 'new theatre'.

The assassination of liberal president Jorge Eliécer Gaitán (b. 1898) on 9 April 1948 had a telling impact on all aspects of the social, cultural and political life of the country. From this date, political violence in Colombia set in; over the next few years, it would leave over 300,000 people dead, the equivalent of any civil war. As well, the old bucolic life of the country and the folkloric and colourful *costumbrista* (featuring local manners and customs) plays with which it was expressed in literature and theatre faded and a new reality emerged, different from that

of those Latin American countries whose urban development took place without such trauma.

This process also saw great migrations from the country to the city, a movement that led to the development of overcrowded slums. From the 1970s this was further aggravated by other forms of violence including various guerrilla movements and drug trafficking.

In the late 1940s and early 1950s Colombian theatre avoided dealing with the new realities, including the demolition of the Teatro Municipal, a political act. In its wake, the government of Laureano Gómez Castro (1889–1965) allowed the founding of an Escuela Nacional de Arte Dramático (National School of Dramatic Art). Much credit for the founding of the school goes to the director of the Teatro Colón at that time, Juan Peñalosa (1905–57).

Peñalosa had lived in Chile from 1942 to 1945, where he had the chance to see the work of one of the great masters of the Latin American stage, Pedro de la Barra. Upon his return to Colombia in 1950, Peñalosa began to argue for the creation of a professional acting school. Through the Ministry of National Education, such a school was created. A small rehearsal hall known as El Palomar (The Dovecote) became the centre of the school's work for the next few years.

Inaugurated in 1951, the school's first director was the Spanish master José María de Mena, formerly the director of the Escuela de Artes Dramático (School of Dramatic Arts) in Madrid. The first play performed by its students was *Una noche de primavera sin sueño* (*A Sleepless Spring Night*) by Enrique Jardiel Poncela. This was followed by two works by Alejandro Casona – *Los árboles mueren de pie* (*Trees Die Standing Up*, 1955) and *La barca sin pescador* (*The Boat Without a Fisherman*, 1955) – and *María Antoineta* (1955) by Joaquín Calvo Sotelo. All were Spanish authors who were in vogue at that time in their homeland.

Soon afterwards, de Mena retired and was replaced by Víctor Mallarino (1909–67). Under his directorship, professors of different nationalities joined the school, such as the Argentine Eduardo Cuitiño, the teacher and director Dina Moscovici from Brazil, the Spaniard Enrique de Hoz, and others. The repertoire changed immediately. Plays such as García Lorca's *Bodas de sangre* (*Blood Wedding*, 1957) were presented, as well as some early experiments in various theatre styles ranging from works by María Clara Machado from Brazil to those of Jean Tardieu from France.

In 1957, a second theatre school was established in the city of Cali – the Escuela Departamental de Teatro (Regional School of Theatre) – which subsequently led to the creation of the Teatro Experimental de Cali (TEC), one of the most important groups in modern Colombian theatre.

For its first year, the school was directed by the Spaniard Cayetano Luca de Tena, whose major production was Shakespeare's *A Midsummer Night's Dream*. After his departure, the Colombian playwright and director Enrique Buenaventura (b. 1925) assumed the directorship. When he arrived at the school, Buenaventura had just returned from a tour of Venezuela, the Antilles, Brazil and Argentina, where he had established relations with these countries' various theatrical communities. Among the foreign teachers who soon began to work at the school were Pedro Martínez and Boris Roth from Argentina, and the Chilean Jaime Errázuris, a member of de la Barra's group.

If the professional theatre at this time tended to be superficial, the repertoires of both the Bogotá and Cali schools were not. Contemporary European and US plays by authors such as Arthur Miller, Eugene O'Neill, Tennessee Williams and Thornton Wilder began to be performed along with plays by Eugène Ionesco, Samuel Beckett, Arthur Adamov and Bertolt Brecht.

A number of Colombian writers soon joined them, writers whose first experience was with radio theatre and television. Among them were Bernardo Romero Lozano (1912–72) and actor-directors Gonzalo Vera Quintana (b. 1920) and Víctor Múñoz Valencia (b. 1938).

Modern methods of acting and stage design also began to appear in Colombia during this time. The ideas of the great Russian teacher Konstantin Stanislavski were taught in Bogotá by the Japanese teacher Seki Sano, who, though he remained in the country for only a short time, gave new perspectives to actor training.

The theatre of Brecht also became known in the late 1950s, first through his plays, then through his theories and methods, especially after such directors as Santiago García (b. 1928) and Jorge Alí Triana (b. 1942) visited Brecht's Berliner Ensemble.

To showcase their work, the Escuela Nacional de Arte Dramático sponsored a local theatre festival for a number of years, which led to the organization of the Primer Festival de

Enrique Buenaventura's 1982 Teatro Experimental de Cali production of his *Ópera Bufa*.
Photo: Juan Camilo Segura.

Teatro Internacional (First International Festival of Theatre) in Bogotá in 1957. University groups also appeared at these festivals, presenting more work by playwrights not seen before in Colombia – Anouilh, Brecht, Pirandello, Labiche and Casona among others. Also appearing at the first festival was the provincial Grupo Escénico de Barranquilla (Barranquilla Stage Group), directed by Alfredo de la Espriella (b. 1926).

At the Second National Festival (1958), held at the Teatro Colón in Bogotá, the Teatro Experimental de Cali appeared for the first time. Made up of advanced students from Buenaventura's school, it was awarded first prize for its staging of *En la diestra de Dios Padre* (*In the Right Hand of God the Father*), Buenaventura's adaptation and production of a short story by Tomás Carrasquilla (1858–1950); it quickly became the signature work of TEC. Six different productions of the play had been staged by the group by the mid-1990s.

A number of other Colombian plays were subsequently presented at this festival – *El camino* (*The Path*, 1962) by Gustavo Andrade Rivera (1921–72), *Hora azul 3:00 a.m.* (*Blue Hour 3:00 a.m.*, 1966) by Oswaldo Díaz Díaz (1910–67), *El asunto diario* (*The Daily Routine*) by Julio J. Fajardo (b. 1926) and *En algún lugar es de noche* (*Somewhere It Is Night*, 1968) by Ignacio Gómez Dávila (1915–63).

Still another group evolved from the training offered by Seki Sano, called La Cueva del Buho (The Owl's Cave), later renamed Teatro Experimental El Buho (The Owl Experimental Theatre). It was begun by Spanish actor-director Fausto Cabrera and became the first independent theatre group in Bogotá. Focusing on theatrical experimentation, Cabrera was awarded the best director's prize at the second Bogotá festival for his production of *Pullman Car Hiawatha* by Thornton Wilder.

Unfortunately, these groups staged very few works outside the festivals. Their main activities took place for the most part in schools. The exception was El Buho, which staged productions in several non-traditional venues. Its main space barely had room for fifty-six spectators but it was usually filled for its performances, from Wednesday to Sunday, of new and experimental pieces. Three years after its founding in 1958, it moved from its tiny basement location in central Bogotá to the abandoned Odeon Theatre, a silent film cinema.

Intense theatrical activity was also developing in Cali, not only in the work of TEC and its

Escuela Departamental de Teatro, but also through the Arts Festivals of Cali, held starting at the beginning of the 1960s and organized through the passion and enthusiasm of the actress Fanny Mickey (b. 1931). During the entire time she was associated with TEC, Mickey did much to organize and promote such events.

During the early period of the Escuela Departamental de Teatro in Cali and of the festivals, Buenaventura wrote *El monumento* (*The Monument*, 1958), a farce about misunderstanding history, and *Réquiem por el Padre Las Casas* (*Requiem for Father Las Casas*, 1963), an historical chronicle presented in one of the last Arts Festivals of Cali.

It was these festivals as much as anything else that managed to rejuvenate the entire national theatre. Several groups were formed for the sole purpose of performing at the festivals, while other groups emerged as well that performed full seasons. From the 1970s, several university theatre groups emerged, turning out actors, directors and playwrights. The university became still another new place for theatre to develop.

The first important productions of Santiago García were at the National University and were testimonies to techniques learned in Europe. His productions included *The Cherry Orchard* by Chekhov and *Man Is Man* by Brecht, the first stage production in Colombia to employ Brechtian distancing techniques.

By the early 1970s, university theatre groups existed not only in Bogotá and Cali but also in Bucaramanga, Barranquilla, Medellín and Manizales. In Bucaramanga, the TEU de Santander (Experimental University Theatre of Santander), under the direction of Carlos José Reyes Posada (b. 1941), staged plays such as *Rashomon* (1963) by Ryunosuke Akutagawa, as well as works by Kafka and Dürrenmatt.

In 1965, a University Theatre Festival was held, mostly involving universities in Bogotá that had stable groups. Little by little, these university festivals transformed the way that theatre festivals were organized, seeking greater participation from the directors of the various groups in the analysis of the works, as well as in the organization of the events themselves. Groups from many different regions of the country became incorporated into the festivals between 1966 and 1970.

From its very first year, the Festival of Manizales caused great controversy. With such important figures as Pablo Neruda, the

Carlos José Reyes Posada's 1982 Teatro Popular de Bogotá production of Valle-Inclán's *Romance de lobos*.
Photo: Víctor Robledo.

Guatemalan Miguel Angel Asturias and the Uruguayan director Atahualpa del Cioppo in attendance, Manizales became an important meeting place for the new Latin American theatre. Augusto Boal, Alfonso Sastre, Jerzy Grotowski and other figures from world theatre would attend the festival through the years. Gradually, participation in the festival ceased to be limited to universities, and it was eventually transformed into an experimental theatre festival.

The political radicalization of the student movement was also reflected in both the new theatre groups and the festivals. Repertoires changed and a new combative attitude evolved including challenges to such people as Boal and Mario Vargas Llosa, especially at the Festival of Manizales.

Unfortunately when López Michelsen (b. 1913) took over as president in 1974, official support for many of these activities was reduced. The political radicalization of the university theatres and their connection to

strikes and work stoppages provoked, in turn, a strong, repressive reaction. Groups found themselves under political attack, directors' contracts were cancelled and the doors of theatres and rehearsal spaces were often found locked.

Groups quickly began to rent alternative spaces. The story behind each of them is different, but from the mid-1960s into the 1990s the formation of new groups and the opening of new spaces did not cease. As well, a national organization was formed to serve as a workers' guild with its own standards and rules – the Corporación Colombiana de Teatro (Colombian Theatre Corporation). The unity of the organization, however, did not last long. The radical student movement and the university theatre movement soon caused confrontations among the various groups, many of which took different positions, especially in the area of politics.

In 1974, the Asociación Nacional de Teatro Universitario (National Association of University Theatre) was created in opposition to the corporation. This association had a very short existence, however, as the main groups that composed it soon broke up (with the exception of the Teatro Libre de Bogotá).

Through the 1980s, new spaces continued to open, including a Teatro Nacional (National Theatre) with a capacity of 280. Soon after, a branch of the Teatro Nacional was opened in Bogotá's Castellana district. Among the important projects undertaken by the Teatro Nacional has been a biennial Festival Iberoamericano in Bogotá, first held in 1988. The festival includes groups not only from Colombia but also from across Latin America, Europe and other parts of the world.

Special events have also been organized in Colombia by the international Centro Latinoamericano de Creación y Investigación Teatral (Latin American Centre for Dramatic Creation and Research). These events, in turn, have contributed greatly to the development of the Colombian theatre.

Among the new buildings to open in Colombia has been the Roberto Arias Pérez Theatre in Bogotá, the Metropolitan Theatre and Auditorium of the University of Medellín and the Jorge Isaacs Theatre in Cali. In Barranquilla, new theatre activity has come from the work of such figures as Alfredo de la Espriella (b. 1926), Gabriel Viloria (b. 1928) and Tomás Urueta (b. 1939), while in Cartagena, the author and director Alberto Sierra (b. 1946) has

Manuel José Álvarez's 1990 Teatro Nacional production of Jorge Amado's *Doña Flor and Her Two Husbands.*
Photo: Juan Camilo Segura.

helped to create new theatre activities, as have Alberto Llerena (b. 1940) and Laura García (b. 1953), the latter as director of the group La Pandorga (Practical Joke).

Structure of the National Theatre Community

Theatre in Colombia is produced almost exclusively through private initiative. There is only occasional government support.

From the 1950s, modest government support came from municipal Ministries of Education or Culture, which themselves had limited budgets. In the mid-1970s, a Colombian Institute of Culture (Colcultura) was created as a decentralized entity connected to the Ministry of Education. From its inception, Colcultura also supported agencies such as the Biblioteca Nacional (National Library), the Escuela Nacional de Arte Dramático (National School of Dramatic Art), the Teatro Colón and the Orquesta Sinfónia Nacional (National Symphony Orchestra). In the late 1980s, attempts were made by the government to institute a stable cultural policy.

Festivals receive some official funding but depend mainly on private support and box-office income. In general, theatre salaries are still far below those of people working in radio or television.

Most theatre groups are established as not-for-profit cultural foundations. In Colombia, this means that they do not have to pay taxes. There are also clear differences in the organizational structures of the various groups. These range from their locations and the type of audience they attract to their facility's maintenance and operating budgets. Some theatres, such as the Candelaria, Teatro La MaMa and the TEC, have their own buildings and permanent companies while others, such as the Teatro Popular de Bogotá (TPB; Popular Theatre of Bogotá) and the Teatro Nacional, bring in artists on a production-by-production basis.

Some productions are simply commercial enterprises. This was the case with several musicals put on in the late 1980s and early 1990s by the Teatro Nacional, such as the Broadway-style *Sugar* (1989), *La mujer del año* (*Woman of the Year*, 1991) and *Doña Flor y sus dos maridos* (*Doña Flor and Her Two Husbands*, 1991), based on the novel by Jorge Amado. This type of theatre is still a novelty in Colombia. Most earlier theatrical initiatives were either experimental, independent or non-commercial.

In Bogotá, with a population of more than 6 million, theatres have begun to move to suburban neighbourhoods. The deterioration of inner-city neighbourhoods, together with fear for personal safety at night, has created a situation in which people prefer to attend theatres closer to their homes and that offer better security.

The violence and terror that Colombia experienced in the 1980s and early 1990s also created a public wanting entertainment and diversion rather than argument or analysis. In such spaces as the Teatro Municipal Jorge Eliécer Gaitán, with a seating capacity of 2,400, more people attend to see light entertainment than any other type of theatrical presentation.

Nevertheless more serious theatres do exist, producing work of an experimental or even an anthropological nature. The groups doing this work generally do not have their own buildings and are constantly attempting to find new spaces to keep their free and independent creative bases operating. Belonging to this category are such groups as the Taller de las Artes (Arts Workshop) in Medellín, directed by Samuel Vásquez, whose *El bar de la Calle Luna* (*The Bar on Moon Street*, 1989) was presented in a bar in which the audience became the bar's patrons.

Many street theatre groups also exist in cities such as Bogotá, Manizales and Pereira. Some of them have studied popular art forms such as carnival and perform at the many regular celebrations that are held in Colombia. Among the most popular are the Carnival of Barranquilla,

Jorge Vargas's 1990 Teatro Taller de Colombia production of *La Cabezo de Gukup*.
Photo: Juan Camilo Segura.

the Carnival of the Devil in Riosucio, and the Black and White Carnival in Pasto. A major influence on the street groups has been the American Peter Schumann and his Bread and Puppet Theatre as well as Eugenio Barba's Odin Teatret of Denmark. In production, one can find a wide range of figures – masked actors on stilts accompanied by mythological creatures mounted on poles, prehistoric birds, ostriches and giants. In general, the musical background includes trumpets and percussion. The Papayeras, a musical group, regularly appear with principal street theatres such as the Teatro Taller de Colombia and P'a lo que sea (For Whatever), a group based in Pereira.

Artistic Profile

Companies

At the end of 1967, a group of Colombian directors who had trained at the Theatre School of Prague – Rosario Montaña (b. 1941), Jaime Santos (b. 1940) and Jorge Alí Triana – jointly founded the Teatro Popular de Bogotá. During its early years, the TPB put on a range of works including plays by Sean O'Casey, Machiavelli and Carlo Goldoni. The group performed in theatres, union halls and public squares in an effort to establish a popular following. As well, TPB toured extensively in the country.

Shortly after the formation of the group, actress Fanny Mickey, who had previously done important work with the Teatro Experimental de Cali and with the Arts Festival of Cali, became its executive director. Her work led to the acquisition of the Odeon Theatre in Bogotá, where El Buho, the Theatre Festival Corporation, and the stage group from the University of America had previously worked.

After this change to a permanent locale, the Teatro Popular de Bogotá became even more solid as a professional group, and has since played an important role both in the training of actors and in the formation of a repertory theatre. Many of the most sought-after cinema and television actors in Colombia have since worked at some point at the Teatro Popular. As for repertoire, TPB has presented both classical and contemporary works from around the world as well as works by Latin American and Colombian authors.

Among its modern productions have been *Die Dreigroschenoper* (*The Threepenny Opera*, 1976) and *Der aufhaltsame Aufstieg des Arturo Ui* (*The Resistible Rise of Arturo Ui*, 1979) by Brecht and *Death of a Salesman* (1972) by Arthur Miller, one of the most constant works in its repertoire.

Its major Latin American productions have included *Delito, condena y ejecución de una gallina* (*The Crime, Sentencing and Execution of a Hen*, 1969) by Manuel José Arce of Guatemala, *El gesticulador* (*The Gesticulator*, 1972) by the Mexican Rodolfo Usigli and *Te juro Juana que tengo ganas* (*I Swear to You I Feel Like It, Juana*, 1966) by the Mexican Emilio Carballido. Outstanding among national works was *I Took Panamá* (1974), written by Luis Alberto García and directed by Jorge Alí Triana, which deals with the separation of Panamá from Colombia in 1903.

Of the university theatre groups that survived after the repressive year of 1970, the Teatro Libre de Bogotá stands out. The group was made up of former members of the experimental group from the University of the Andes and operated under the direction of Jorge Plata (b. 1946) and Ricardo Camacho (b. 1948). The Teatro Libre has staged several important national premières including *El sol subterráneo* (*The Underground Sun*, 1977) and *Los inquilinos de la ira* (*The Tenants of Rage*, 1975), by the playwright, poet, puppeteer, short story writer and novelist Jairo Aníbal Niño (b. 1942). One of the group's most successful plays was *La agonía del difunto* (*The Agony of the Dead Man*, 1976), a black comedy about the struggle of the *campesinos* (farm workers) against the landowners on the Atlantic coast of the country. The play was written by Esteban Navajas Cortés (b. 1947), a member of the group's playwrights' workshop, and directed by Aníbal Niño. Other plays of note coming from this workshop were *Tiempovidrio* (*Glasstime*, 1977) and *La huelga* (*The Strike*, 1977) by Sebastián Ospina (b. 1959), and *El muro en el jardín* (*The Wall in the Garden*, 1985) by Jorge Plata.

The situation of the Candelaria Theatre, directed by Santiago García, changed significantly in 1969 when it acquired a permanent home by building a hall on a vacant lot in central Bogotá. The group's early repertoire was a continuation of García's policy (from the El Buho days) of performing avant-garde plays. With time, however, the need to develop Colombian drama became increasingly evident. Among the early plays performed with this objective was *El menú* (*The Menu*, 1968) by Enrique Buenaventura. In this play, beggars and unemployed people eat the leftovers of the rich. It is a grotesque work reminiscent of the style of Valle-Inclán.

The same year that Candelaria created its own space, the Teatro Experimental de Cali broke off relations with all the official bodies that had supported it to give itself greater independence. In practical terms, this meant that the actors, directors and technicians were without monetary support. Nevertheless, TEC built a new theatre in stages: first, a rustic provisional building; later a transformable hall was added, similar to the one housing Candelaria. The goal of TEC has long been to create a

Santiago García's 1982 La Candelaria
production of his *El dialogo del rebusque*.
Photo: Juan Camilo Segura.

national popular dramatic form and in the
works of Buenaventura it did just that.

Kepa Amuchastegui (b. 1943), an actor at the
University of the Andes, in 1968 founded
Teatro La MaMa in Bogotá with the intention
of creating ties with Ellen Stewart's La MaMa
Experimental Theatre Club in New York. La
MaMa's first productions, directed by
Amuchastegui, Paco Barrero and Germán
Moure (b. 1931), were contemporary plays such
as *Exit the King* (1968) by Ionesco, *Rosencrantz
and Guildenstern Are Dead* (1981) by Tom
Stoppard and *Tom Paine* (1970) by Paul Foster.
As this group developed, it acquired its own per-
sonality, oriented towards the creation of a
specifically national and Latin American style of
drama.

Dramaturgy

Enrique Buenaventura is probably Colombia's
best known man of theatre. As a playwright, his
Los papeles del infierno (*The Papers from Hell*,

1968), a series of one-acts about violence in
Colombia, was one of the models for much of
his later dramatic work. One play from this
text, *La orgía* (*The Orgy*), is itself a complete,
independent play in which the influence of
Valle-Inclán's style is best expressed.

Other works by Buenaventura also deal with
Latin American reality, including the dictatorship of General Ubico in Guatemala, which
inspired *La trampa* (*The Trap*, 1966), and the
events surrounding the killing of workers at the
United Fruit Company in *La denuncia* (*The
Accusation*, 1973). This latter play is seen from
the perspective of the man who actually made
the accusation in Congress, Jorge Eliécer
Gaitán.

In later works, such as *La historia de una bala
de plata* (*The Story of a Silver Bullet*, 1980),
winner of Cuba's prestigious Casa de las
Américas Prize, Buenaventura turned to themes
closely related to conflicts between the small
countries of the region and their larger neighbours to the north.

In 1971, two groups – Candelaria and TEC
– met to discuss theories and experiences with
collective creation. The debate focused on the
use of improvisation, and as a result the two
groups committed themselves to developing a
joint method for collective creation. Buenaventura wrote widely about these discussions and
soon the greater part of the Colombian theatre
community was familiar with them and began to
put them into practice.

As Buenaventura saw it, the director was to
be an organizer, coordinating and motivating
the creativity of the group, embracing all ideas
that might contribute to group unity, and dis-
carding those that moved the poetic discourse in
the wrong direction. The continuing influence
of this method could still be seen in Colombia
the 1990s.

Interpreting the term 'collective' in its own
way, the Candelaria Theatre created such works
as *Nosotros los comunes* (*We the Common
People*, 1972), inspired by the uprising of the
settlers in the New Kingdom of Grenada in
1783; *La ciudad dorada* (*The Golden City*,
1973), about the migration of country people to
the city; and *Guadalupe años cincuenta* (*Guadalupe in the Fifties*, 1975), which evokes the
period of the liberal guerrilla band of Guadalupe
Salcedo in the eastern plains of Colombia during
the 1950s.

Another work of collective creation, but one
with a very different style, was *I Took Panamá*,
composed by Luis Alberto García and directed

Jorge Alí Triana's 1974 Teatro Popular de Bogotá production of *I Took Panamá* by Luis Alberto García.

by Jorge Alí Triana, staged at the Teatro Popular de Bogotá. *I Took Panamá* was based on research done on the events that caused the separation of Panamá from the Republic of Colombia in 1903. Much of the research came from the book *Panamá y su separación de Colombia* (*Panamá and Its Separation From Colombia*, 1972) by Colombian historian Eduardo Lemaitre (b. 1914).

It was the movement to establish theatres on university campuses that allowed dramatists finally to see their plays performed. This was the case with the plays of Antonio Montaña (b. 1933): *Los trotalotodo* (*The Globetrotters*, 1959); *El tiempo de la trompeta* (*The Time of the Trumpet*, 1959), directed by Dina Moscovici; and *Orestes* (1961), directed by Fausto Cabrera; plays by Gustavo Andrade Rivera such as *Remington 22* (1959), a farce with puppets about the struggle between the liberal and conservative parties; *El hombre que vendía talento* (*The Man Who Sold Talent*, 1959); *Historias para quitar el miedo* (*Stories to Stop the Fear*, 1960) and *El camino* (1964); plays by the poet Carlos Castro Saavedra (1924–89) such as *Historias de un jaulero* (*Tales of a Cage-Maker*, 1960) and *El trapecista*

del vestido rojo (*The Trapeze Artist in the Red Dress*, 1961), written in the poetic and literary style of the 'new' groups; the plays of Juan Zapata Olivella (b. 1922) such as *La bruja de Pontezuela* (*The Witch of Pontezuela*, 1972); and those of his brother, the doctor and novelist Manuel Zapata Olivella (b. 1920), such as *Los pasos del indio* (*The Indian's Footsteps*, 1966), *Caronte liberado* (*Caronte Liberated*, 1964), *Mangalonga el liberto* (*Mangalonga the Freedman*, 1966) and *El retorno de Caín* (*The Return of Cain*, 1967), which deals with the problems faced by indigenous peoples and blacks on the Atlantic coast of Colombia.

The Arts Festivals of Cali awarded prizes to such playwrights as Andrade Rivera, Oscar Collazos (b. 1942) and Alberto Dow (b. 1923). Dow is the author of works such as *El amable señor Víveros* (*The Amiable Mr Víveros*, 1965), a satire of the bureaucracy and the vicissitudes of a middle-class worker; *El diablo, el ángel y la mujer* (*The Devil, the Angel and the Woman*, 1951); *Después del veredicto* (*After the Verdict*, 1957); *El duro camino de la noche* (*The Rough Road of Night*, 1964); and *La sangre petrificada* (*Petrified Blood*, 1951).

Another author of note is Guillermo Maldonado (b. 1945), whose works include *A cada historia un sombrero* (*A Hat for Every Story*, 1966), *Historia patria* (*National Story*, 1972), *Crónicas de Pueblo Muerto* (*Chronicles of Dead Town*, 1974) and *Por estos santos latifundios* (*For These Holy Lands*), which won the Casa de las Américas Prize in 1975.

Guillermo Henríquez (b. 1940), a native of Ciénaga, has written *Marta Cibelina* (1982) and *Escarpín de señoras* (*Ladies' Slipper*, 1984), eccentric, surrealist plays that strive to recreate the lush region of the Atlantic coast. Actor, poet and playwright Raúl Gómez Jattin (b. 1945), a native of Cereté, is the author of a strong satire about Latin American dictators entitled *Las nupcias de su Excelencia* (*The Nuptials of His Excellency*, 1972).

Among Gilberto Martínez Arango's (b. 1934) works are plays with much social and political content, some based on historical themes, some documentaries about events that took place in his home city of Medellín. His best known pieces include *Los mofetudos* (*The Chubby-cheeked*, 1968); *El grito de los ahorcados* (*The Cry of the Hanged*, 1965), a play about the 1783 settlers' uprising; as well as works denouncing the violence in Colombia, such as *El interrogatorio* (*The Interrogation*), *Zarpazo* (*The Blow*, 1976) and *Proceso al Señor Gobernador* (*The Trial of the Governor*, 1976), this last piece based on *The Trial of Lucullus* by Brecht.

There is also a more existential theatre that deals mainly with the problems of the individual. Solitary characters with internal and metaphysical conflicts appear on stage in the works of Regina Mejía de Gaviria: *Calle tal, número tal* (*Such-and-such a Street, Such-and-such a Number*), *El gallo cantó tres veces* (*The Cock Crowed Three Times*) and *La pared* (*The Wall*), all published in 1963.

In addition to these, *costumbrista* plays are presented regularly in many towns and municipalities in the Medellín region.

Directors, Directing and Production Styles

For a discussion of directing, see previous material in **Artistic Profile** and the opening, historical section.

Music Theatre

Popular indigenous dramatic manifestations were generally rooted in music and dance, as in the case of the *chigualos* (theatrical dances of the natives of the Pacific coast). These were usually performed at funeral wakes.

In the 1990s, the relationship between music and the theatre again became deeper. Street theatre groups have their own musical groups working with them, and many important productions, such as the collective creation *Guadalupe años cincuenta*, include musical expression as a fundamental part of the show. In the case of *Guadalupe años cincuenta*, the folk music of the eastern plains of Colombia is used.

Ballads, songs and music interpreted by the actors themselves, such as the duet from the play *El paso* (*The Pass*) by the Candelaria Theatre, have also enriched the language of the stage.

Broadway-style musicals and musical revues have become a staple of commercial theatre in Colombia.

The country's most important opera group is Camarín del Carmen (literally Carmen's Dressing Room). Under the administrative direction since 1986 of Gloria Zea de Antei, the company stages annual seasons of mostly major works from the international repertoire – *Rigoletto*, *La Bohème*, *Carmen* and *The Barber of Seville* were all critical successes in the 1980s and 1990s. Among the leading national stars to have sung with Camarín del Carmen are the tenor Alejandro Ramírez (b. 1946) and the sopranos Marta Senn (b. 1955) and Zoraida Salazar (b. 1952).

The Los Hampones project (1961) was a dramatic cantata by Luis Antonio Escobar (1925–93), directed by Santiago García.

Dance Theatre

The Ballet de Colombia, directed by Sonia Osorio, was founded in the early 1960s. Seeking to connect its work to indigenous musical forms, it has created many pieces developed from the music and dance of the country's various regions, many in rather spectacular ways. The group has also brought to the country the latest international dance trends.

The modern dance group Triknia Kábhelioz was started in 1981 by choreographer Carlos Jaramillo. Its most successful production during its first decade was based on the Gabriel García Márquez (b. 1928) novel, *El coronel no tiene quien le escriba* (*The Colonel Has No One to Write to Him*, 1988).

Other dance groups of note in the 1980s and 1990s were Barrio Ballet from Cali, the Peter Palacio dance group from Medellín and Deuxalamori from Bogotá.

From the end of the 1950s, a number of plays began including choreography as part of their construction. This was especially true in productions of classical plays. Since that time, choreographers and dancers have regularly worked as consultants for theatrical productions. This is the case, for example, with Giovanni Brinatti (1928–68), who worked with TEC during its early years, with the Teatro Libre de Bogotá, and with Candelaria on its production of Stravinsky's *L'Histoire du soldat* (*A Soldier's Story*, 1978). The actor and choreographer Alvaro Restrepo (b. 1957) has created works such as *Rebis* (1986), with corporal images and movements that transcend the intentions of dance and become more of a form of theatrical expression.

Alvaro Restrepo's 1991 Anthanor Danza production of *Yo, Arbor, Gonzálo*.
Photo: Juan Camilo Segura.

Theatre for Young Audiences

Many professional groups in Colombia have staged works for children, including the Teatro Experimental de Cali. Many children's adaptations were among the early dramatic works of TEC's playwright-director, Enrique Buenaventura, ranging from *Little Red Riding Hood* (1961) to tales from the popular oral tradition, such as *Uncle Rabbit the Shoemaker* (1958) and *Stone Soup* (1976).

Other authors who have written children's plays include the poet Fanny Sanín (b. 1935) – *Milagro de Navidad* (*The Christmas Miracle*, 1960), presented by the group La Rueda (The Wheel); Fanny Buitrago (b. 1946) – *El angelito Tito* (*The Little Angel Tito*, 1966); and Carlos Castro Saavedra – *Historias de un jaulero* (*Tales of a Cage-Maker*, 1960), a poetic farce. There have also been popular productions of *La espada de madera* (*The Wooden Sword*, 1975) by Jairo Aníbal Niño; *Doña Pánfaga Sabelotodo* (*Miss Panfaga Know-it-all*, 1970) by Gilberto Martínez, based on the poem of the same name by Rafael Pombo (1833–1912); *La comadreja* (*The Weasel*, 1961) and *La auténtica y edificante*

fábula del conejo y los animales poderosos (*The True and Uplifting Fable of the Rabbit and the Powerful Animals*, 1971) by Fernando González Cajiao (b. 1938); and *Dulcita y el burrito* (*Sweetie and the Donkey*, 1964), *La piedra de la felicidad* (*The Stone of Happiness*, 1965) and *La fiesta de los muñecos* (*The Dolls' Party*, 1970) by Carlos José Reyes Posada.

Much of Reyes Posada's work plays with childhood fantasy while placing its audience in the real world. His plays also tend to parody traditional children's stories with their witches, princes and talking animals.

Groups actually involving children and adolescents emerged in the 1980s. The leader among these has been Los Monachos (Stick People), founded in 1988 and directed by María Angélica Mallarino (b. 1952), which has performed such pieces as *Los niños se toman el mundo* (*The Children Take Over the World*, 1989), a comic song and dance revue that suggests that if children ran the world, there would be fewer wars and conflicts.

Puppet Theatre

Colombian puppet theatre – including theatre that uses masks – has developed significantly during the twentieth century. In 1936, a theatre was opened in the National Park in Bogotá, called the Cultural Theatre, dedicated to the presentation of puppet and marionette shows. In 1954, Jaime Manzur (b. 1936) started presenting his own marionette shows, developing a varied repertoire that included classic children's stories, operas, *zarzuelas* (Spanish-style musical comedies) and also classic plays from the world repertoire, performed by puppets.

In 1959, José Antonio Muñoz Rojas (Muñocito; 1893–1976) became director of the Marionettes of the Cultural Theatre. He wrote several plays for the theatre's abundant collection of puppets, including a popular comedy entitled *Un Antioqueño en el Cielo* (*An Antiochan in Heaven*, 1959).

Several puppet theatre groups appeared in the 1970s, many of which were still in existence in the 1990s. The most important of these were La Fanfarria of Medellín and, from Bogotá, El

Biombo Latino, Hilos Mágicos (Magic Threads), La Libélula Dorada (Golden Dragonfly), Paciencia de Guayaba, El Alacrán (The Scorpion; in the early 1990s it merged with the Popular Theatre of Bogotá), Teatrova, Retablo Tiempo Vivo, El Baúl (The Trunk), the marionettes of Jaime Manzur and Ernesto Arona (b. 1936), La Oruga Encantada (Enchanted Caterpillar) and Bucaramanga.

These groups offer a variety of techniques, from the traditional hand-puppet to the Javanese stick-puppet, from the marionette to puppets similar to Japanese *bunraku* (a puppet form in which lifesize puppets act out dramatic narratives to music), from Chinese shadow-puppets to free forms that combine both puppets and actors.

Many plays for puppets have been written and produced since the 1970s, including *El negrito aquel* (*That Little Black Man*, 1985) and *El cuartito azul* (*The Little Blue Room*, 1987) by La Fanfarria of Medellín; *Los héroes que vencieron todo menos el miedo* (*The Heroes*

César E. Iván Álvarez's 1982 La Libélula Dorada production of *Sinfonías inconclusas para desamordazar el silencio*.
Photo: Juan Camilo Segura.

Carlos Parada's Teatrova production of *Las historias del común*.
Photo: Juan Camilo Segura.

Who Conquered Everything But Fear, 1985) and *Ese chivo es puro cuento* (*It's a Lie*, 1990) by La Libélula Dorada; *Globito manual* (*Hand Balloon*, 1973) and *El hombre que escondió el sol y la luna* (*The Man Who Hid the Sun and the Moon*, 1973) by Carlos José Reyes Posada, winner of the Casa de las Américas Prize for Children's and Young People's Literature; *Las historias del común* (*Everyday Stories*, 1988) and *Espreso a Cucaña* (*Cucaña Express*) by Teatrova; and *La gallina de los huevos de oro* (*The Goose That Laid the Golden Egg*, 1977), *Llegaron los marcianos* (*The Martians Are Coming*, 1980), *Las esmereldas del sol* (*Emeralds of the Sun*, 1985) and *El país del arco iris* (*Land of the Rainbow*, 1988), all by Ciro Gómez (b. 1954) with his group Hilos Mágicos, founded in 1975.

Also to be mentioned here is the work of Julia Rodríguez (b. 1930) with the Cocoliche puppets, including *Siriko y la flauta* (*Siriko and the Flute*, 1974) and *El sueño maravilloso* (*The Wonderful Dream*, 1974). The Escuela de Títeres, connected to the Escuela Nacional de Arte Dramático, offers formal training for puppeteers.

Design
Theatre Space and Architecture

Theatres built in Colombia before 1950 tend to be of the Italian style, such as the Teatro Colón, the municipal theatres of Cali, Popayán and Bogotá, and the Heredia Theatre in Cartagena (in ruins by the 1980s).

With the evolution of theatre space in the 1970s, many new venues were created, some by the theatre groups themselves, others by businesses interested in theatre. The most technically well-equipped theatre is the Roberto Arias Pérez Colsubsidio Theatre in Bogotá, where such groups as the Berliner Ensemble have performed.

Leading stage designers early on were often painters and sculptors such as Enrique Grau (b. 1920), who created scenery and costumes for TEC's production of *Oedipus Rex* (1960), for Santiago García's productions of *Mann ist Mann* (*Man Is Man*, 1961) by Brecht and Goldoni's *The Fan*. Grau moved between decorative stage design and periods of abstraction and magic realism. His work also connected to the popular imagination and to the kind of fantasy seen, for example, in the work of García Márquez.

Alejandro Obregón (1920–92) designed the set for *El triciclo* (*The Tricycle*, 1964) by Arrabal, while Santiago Cárdenas (b. 1937) and Juan Antonio Roda (b. 1921) designed many plays presented by the Teatro Libre de Bogotá under the direction of Ricardo Camacho and Germán Moure.

Another painter who has collaborated on many stage productions is David Manzur (b. 1929), who has also worked as an actor. Obregón's designs are characterized by a romantic expressionism while those of Cárdenas are more connected to hyper-realism with, as one would expect from a painter, a meticulous drawing technique that translates effectively to the stage.

Among sculptors, Eduardo Ramírez Villamizar (b. 1923) created a series of stage modules for *Los trotalotodo* (1959) by Antonio Montaña, directed by Dina Moscovici. Architects have also collaborated with the theatre, not only in the construction of theatre buildings, but also in the design of stage sets. One of Colombia's most prestigious architects, Dicken Castro (b. 1922), created the set for Brecht's *Leben des Galilei* (*Life of Galileo*) presented by the Studio Theatre of the National University under the direction of Santiago García.

Since the late 1970s, theatrical groups and directors themselves have tried to be involved in the creation of their own stage settings even when working with a professional designer. That is to say, the designer no longer works autonomously but rather in conjunction with proposals made by other creators.

Training

The most important of the early training schools in Colombia were the Escuela Nacional de Arte Dramático, begun by Juan Peñalosa, and the Escuela Departamental de Teatro (Regional Theatre School) of Cali, founded in 1958 and connected to Enrique Buenaventura's Teatro de Cali.

In 1958 Eduardo Osorio Cañon (1938–76) founded the Teatro de Bogotá. Two other schools began in the 1970s – the theatre department at the University of Antioquia in 1975 under Mario Yepes (b. 1945), and the theatre school at the University of Valle in 1978 under Buenaventura.

As well, the Taller Permanente (Continuing Workshop) of the Corporación Colombiana de Teatro began its operations in 1969 under Santiago García, while a number of private schools emerged in the 1980s, such as the Academia Charlot, begun by Jaime Botero (1928–94) in 1984.

In the mid-1990s, the Academia de Artes of Bogotá, along with the university theatre departments at Antioquia and Valle, was becoming more accessible to those contemplating professional careers while the Escuela de Arte Dramático and the Taller Permanente were beginning to offer training courses divided into semesters and academic years.

Most of these schools follow the Stanislavski system, which was introduced into Colombia by Stanislavski's Japanese student Seki Sano in 1956. Seki Sano, a student at the Moscow Art Theatre, was enormously influential in the development of a Colombian representational school of acting, a style earlier seen in visits by Spanish, Mexican and Argentine groups.

Brecht's influence was seen following a visit to the Berliner Ensemble by several Colombian directors in 1960, among them García. This awareness and direct knowledge of Brechtian aesthetics was also decisive in the career of Buenaventura, Gilberto Martínez and other dramatists.

Collective creation is still another technique being taught at most theatre schools and being used by many groups, such as TEC (under Buenaventura), La Candelaria (under García) and La MaMa (under Eddy Armando, b. 1942).

Criticism, Scholarship and Publishing

The first Colombian to write significant essays about the language and poetics of the theatre was director and playwright Enrique Buenaventura. A few of his many important essays are 'El choque de las culturas' ('Culture Shock', 1975), 'La interpretación de los sueños y la improvisación teatral' ('The Interpretation of Dreams and Theatrical Improvisation', 1975) and 'Apuntes para un método de creación colectiva' ('Notes Towards a Method for Collective Creation', 1973), in which the experiences of the Teatro Experimental de Cali are analysed, and which has been used to develop group theatre work in many other parts of Latin America as well as in Spain.

Another critical writer of note is Gilberto Martínez, who become known for his essays on the theory and practice of the theatre. His works read like a diary of his activities as a playwright and stage director. Among his best are *Hacia un teatro dialéctico* (*Towards a Dialectical Theatre*, 1979) and *Towards an Authentic Collective Creation* (1980).

Among researchers, one must mention the valuable work of Fernando González Cajiao (b. 1938), author of *Historia del teatro en Colombia* (*History of Theatre in Colombia*, 1986), as well as numerous articles, bibliographical notes and commentaries.

The humanist and poet Eduardo Gómez (b. 1932) has also played an important and sometimes controversial role as a critic. Trained in Germany at the Berliner Ensemble, he wrote commentaries that defined the importance of the dramatic text in opposition to bodily expression or collective creation.

Important books on Colombian theatre include *Trabajo teatral* (*Theatrical Work*, 1975) and *Cuadernos de teatro* (*Theatre Notebooks*, 1976–8), put together by the Corporación Colombiana de Teatro; *El teatro colombiano* (*Colombian Theatre*, 1985) by Misael Vargas

Bustamante (b. 1949); *Bibliografía del teatro colombiano* (*Bibliography of Colombian Theatre*, 1974), a publication of the Caro and Cuervo Institute prepared by Héctor H. Orjuela (b. 1930); *La práctica teatral* (*Theatrical Training*, 1983) by Santiago García; and *Nuevo teatro en Colombia* (*New Theatre in Colombia*, 1983) by Gonzálo Arcilla (b. 1942).

Magazines of note include *Teatro* (*Theatre*) in Medellín, edited by Gilberto Martínez, and *Actuemos* (*Let's Act*), published by Dimensión Educativa (Educational Dimension), under the editorship of Jairo Santa (b. 1956).

The interest of several universities and institutions in theatre is reflected in the increasing number of cultural magazines being published, such as those of the University of Antioquia in Medellín, and the National University in Bogotá.

Carlos José Reyes Posada
Translated by Joanne Rotermundt-De la Parra

Further Reading

Arcilla, Gonzálo. *Nuevo teatro en Colombia: actividad creadora, política cultural.* [New theatre in Colombia: Artistic activity and cultural policies]. Bogotá: Ediciones CEIS, 1983. 208 pp.

Duque, Fernando, and Jorge Prada. 'Panorama de la creación colectiva en el nuevo teatro colombiano'. [Overview of collective creation in the new Colombian theatre]. *Communications from the International Brecht Society* 19, no. 1 (winter 1990): 50–63.

García, Santiago. 'Ponencia sobre la creación colectiva como proceso de trabajo en La Candelaria'. [A report on the use of collective creation by La Candelaria]. *Taller de Teatro*, 1 (April–June 1979): 5–22.

González Cajiao, Fernando. *Historia del teatro en Colombia.* [History of theatre in Colombia]. Bogotá: Instituto Colombiano de Cultura, 1986. 444 pp.

González, Patricia. *El nuevo teatro colombiano 1955–80.* [New Colombian theatre 1955–80]. Ann Arbor, MI: University Microfilms International, 1985. 229 pp.

Márceles Daconte, Eduardo. 'El método de creación colectiva en el teatro colombiano'. [Collective creation in Colombian theatre]. *Latin American Theatre Review* 11, no. 1. (Fall 1977): 91–7.

——. 'El nuevo teatro colombiano: diferentes tendencias y un sólo movimiento verdadero'. [The new Colombian theatre: Many tendencies and one true movement]. *El Café Literario* 3, no. 14. (March–April 1980): 38–43.

Martínez, Gilberto. *Hacia un teatro dialéctico.* [Towards a dialectical theatre]. Medellín: Ediciones Revista Teatro, 1979. 95 pp.

Orjuela, Héctor H. *Bibliografía del teatro colombiano.* [Bibliography of Colombian theatre]. Bogotá: Instituto Caro y Cuervo, 1974. 312 pp.

Ortega Ricaurte, José Vicente. *Historia crítica del teatro en Bogotá.* [Critical history of theatre in Bogotá]. Bogotá: Talleres Ediciones Colombia, 1927. 318 pp.

Ovadía Andrade, Renée. 'Teatro social colombiano contemporáneo'. [Contemporary Colombian social theatre]. PhD dissertation, University of California at Irvine, 1978.

Torres Cárdenas, Edgar Guillermo. *Praxis artística y vida política del teatro en Colombia, 1955–80.* [Artistic practice and political life in the Colombian theatre, 1955–80]. Nuevas Lecturas de Historia 11. Tunja: Universidad Pedagógica y Tecnológica de Colombia, 1990. 96 pp.

Vargas Bustamante, Misael, Carlos José Reyes Posada, Giorgio Antei, and Juan Monsalve. *El teatro colombiano.* [Colombian theatre]. Bogotá: Ediciones del Alba, 1985. 122 pp.

Velasco, María Mercedes de. *El nuevo teatro colombiano y la colonización cultural.* [The new Colombian theatre and cultural colonization]. Bogotá: Editorial Memoria, 1987. 207 pp.

Watson Espener, Maida, and Carlos José Reyes Posada, eds. *Materiales para una historia del teatro en Colombia.* [Notes for the history of theatre in Colombia]. Bogotá: Instituto Colombiano de Cultura, 1978. 718 pp.

COMMONWEALTH CARIBBEAN

(Overview)

In 1945, at the end of World War II, what is now known as the Commonwealth Caribbean was a group of British colonies rimming the Caribbean Sea and commonly called the West Indies. The group consisted of some twelve island governments, principal among them being Barbados, Jamaica, and Trinidad and Tobago, as well as the two coastal states of British Honduras (now Belize) in Central America and British Guyana (now Guyana) in South America. The total population at the time was approximately 3 million; the total area is 272,000 square kilometres (105,000 square miles). For several years, these colonies had been agitating for self-government. In response, Britain had set up the Development and Welfare Commission under Sir Frank Stockdale in preparation for handing over the reins of government to a new Federation of the West Indies.

There was, however, no comparable drive at the time to create a national Caribbean theatre. While there had always been an indigenous type of performance as expressed through the street carnivals, the calypso, native comedians such as the Jamaican duo Bim and Bam (Ed Lewis, 1914–76, and Aston Wynter, 1913–78), the Guyanese Sam Chase (1903–69), and Joe Tudor (1922–70) of Barbados, formal live theatre was hardly a regular occurrence. Plays were presented by expatriate groups – resident amateur or travelling professional – and by local amateurs performing works by British or US dramatists. Occasionally there might be a production of a play written by a native playwright. Examples of these in the decade prior to 1945 were *Blue Blood and Black* (1936), a play on the race question by De Wilton Rogers (1910–84) of Trinidad; *Pocomania* (1938), by the Jamaican Una Marson (1905–68), showing the influence of a religious cult on a young middle-class woman; and *Adoniya* (1943), about Moses' Ethiopian wife, who helped him escape from prison in Egypt, written by Norman Cameron (1903–83) of Guyana.

The situation, however, was showing signs of change. In 1941 a Little Theatre Movement was organized in Jamaica by Henry (b. 1915) and Greta (1901–78) Fowler to present an annual pantomime with the specific purpose of raising funds to build a theatre in Kingston. By 1949, with *Bluebeard and Brer 'nancy*, the panto had moved from a traditional British form to incorporate Jamaican folk elements in characters, speech, music, dance and setting. In 1990 the Jamaican pantomine celebrated its fiftieth successive year of performance; it is still going strong. The two outstanding comedians who were associated with the show for many years and helped to make it a national institution are Randolph 'Ranny' Williams (1912–80) and the folk poet Louise Bennett Coverley (b. 1919). They were also featured on the long-running radio serial 'Ranny and Lou'. In 1946 two local drama groups came into existence that would greatly influence the development of the local stage. They were the Caribbean Thespians of Jamaica and the Whitehall Players (later renamed the Company of Players) of Trinidad. Both of these groups would later contribute playwrights, actors and directors to the Caribbean theatre. In 1947 the University College of the West Indies was established in Jamaica and inaugurated its Dramatic Society a year later. Students from the other territories who took part in the society's productions would form an advance guard for inculcating a love of theatre in their communities on their return home. In 1950 a new group formed specifically for the purpose of producing plays written by West Indians, and called the Creative Theatre Workshop, presented *Atalanta In Calydon* by Roger Mais (1905–55) of Jamaica. The director was Noel Vaz (b. 1920). The group, however, dissolved after its first production.

Yet another harbinger of change appeared in the work of Beryl McBurnie (b. *c*.1916) of Trinidad. Trained in New York and with an interest in folk dancing enhanced by visits to rural areas with Andrew Carr (1902–76), Trinidad's leading folklorist, McBurnie presented her first show, *A Trip Through the Tropics* (1940), to a sold-out audience at the Empire Theatre in Port of Spain, Trinidad. In 1945 she became a dance instructor for the Education Department and by 1948 she had opened in Port of Spain the Little Carib Theatre, basically a backyard shed that became a focal point for dance, theatre training and stage productions for many years to come.

Part of the strategy of the British government was to create an understanding and appreciation of British life and culture among those likely to be future leaders of the Caribbean. To achieve this aim, offices of the British Council were opened in Jamaica in 1942 and later in other Caribbean capital cities. The council arranged for visits to the area by notable British personages in the arts and letters. One such was Nugent Monck of the Maddermarket Theatre in Norwich, who came to Jamaica in 1950 to adjudicate the first drama festival of secondary schools, a festival capped by a production of *The Merchant of Venice* directed by Monck with actors drawn from schools. The festival was still being held in the mid-1990s. The British Council also sent native theatre artists and others for training at British institutions, thereby creating a cadre of professionals who would return home and help to develop the native theatre. Among early scholarship holders who made significant contributions to the Caribbean theatre were Noel Vaz, Louise Bennett and Wycliffe Bennett (b. 1922) of Jamaica; Errol Hill (b. 1921), Errol John (1923–88) and

Freddie Kissoon (b. 1930) of Trinidad; and Ken Corsbie (b. 1930) of Guyana.

The 1950s seemed to bring priorities into focus. In 1953 the University College appointed Hill as its first full-time drama tutor. Hill had attended the Royal Academy of Dramatic Art on his scholarship and while in London had produced at the Hans Crescent Students' Centre in 1952 Derek Walcott's (b. 1930) verse drama *Henri Christophe*, about the Haïtian slave who became a king. Later that year Hill accepted an invitation to go to Jamaica and direct the first of the theatre summer schools to be conducted under the aegis of the university extra-mural department (renamed the extra-mural studies unit and now called the School of Continuing Studies). Later appointed to the extra-mural staff, Hill travelled through the islands and mainland territories from British Honduras to Guyana organizing and teaching drama classes and encouraging the writing and staging of Caribbean plays.

To provide scripts for production, Hill began to collect plays and in 1958 published the first volume of Caribbean playscripts. It contained five short plays: *The Sea at Dauphin* by Derek Walcott, *Africa Slingshot* by Cicely Waite-Smith (Cicely Howland, 1910–78), *The Ping Pong* by Errol Hill, *The Harrowing of Benjy* by Roderick Walcott (b. 1930) and *Junction Village* by Rupert Douglas (Jack) Archibald (1919–93). Derek Walcott later emerged as the leading playwright from the Caribbean and a Nobel laureate in literature. Roderick Walcott, his twin brother, also wrote several important plays based on the St Lucia flower festivals. Archibald's plays, covering both folk and middle-class life in Trinidad, would be hailed for their authentic character studies, as were Waite-Smith's of Jamaica. Hill continued to experiment with plays depicting aspects of the carnival experience of Trinidad. He later edited a second collection of Caribbean plays (published in 1965) and the publishing of individual playscripts began in 1966 under the auspices of the extra-mural studies unit in Trinidad.

New theatre groups also began to be formed. The most important at this time was the Arts Guild of St Lucia, founded in 1950 by Maurice Mason (1927–66) and Derek Walcott and led for almost twenty years by Roderick Walcott. While it was not exclusively a drama company, theatre was its principal activity with a growing emphasis on the production of Caribbean plays.

Another new troupe was the Drama Guild, formed in San Fernando, Trinidad, in 1955. It

Errol Hill's 1957 Kingston Federal Theatre Company production of Roderick Walcott's *The Harrowing of Benjy*.

was located in the southern part of the country, where the preponderance of East Indians in the community ensured a significant racial mix in membership. This company's leading playwright was Ralph Maraj (b. 1949), who wrote more than twenty plays including the prize-winning political satire *The Missing File* (1982).

Yet another group was the Theatre Guild of Guyana, founded in 1957. An early advantage was the establishment in 1960 of its own playhouse, quickly making it one of the most vital and active theatre groups in the Caribbean. Among writers whose work has been produced by the Theatre Guild are Sheik Sadeek (b. 1921), whose *Porkknockers* won the Guild's 1958 playwriting competition; and Frank Pilgrim (1926–84), whose farce *Miriamy* (1962) remains a perennial favourite with theatre companies.

An ongoing hope at this time was that the disparate lands of the Caribbean should come to know one another better. It seemed absurd to many that each unit should be more acquainted with the so-called 'mother country' than with its Caribbean neighbours. One way of achieving this, it was hoped, would be through a regional arts festival held periodically in one of the larger territories and to which all neighbouring countries would be invited. The first took place in Puerto Rico in 1952. It did not include scripted plays *per se*. As Ivy Baxter (1923–93) has written:

here, for the first time, with the help of the United States government, the Puerto Rican Tourist Board, and Alcoa Steamship Company, dancers, singers and musicians from about fourteen Caribbean territories met together in a festival. There was an exhibition of art, craft, painting and sculpture from all over the Caribbean (1970).

The newly formed Ivy Baxter Dance Group's contribution to this festival was dance pieces with a Jamaican accent interspersed with folk songs rendered by the all-male Frat's Quintet.

The advent of the West Indies Federation six years later was also greeted with considerable enthusiasm by Caribbean artists. Not only was a much larger festival planned for the new federal capital (Port of Spain) but the centrepiece of the presentations was the commissioned epic drama *Drums and Colours*, written by Derek Walcott and performed on a specially designed open-air thrust stage. Actors were drawn from many of the federated territories. Directing the production was Noel Vaz, another of the university extra-mural drama tutors who had been appointed to the southern Caribbean area. For performing artists, the federation was off to a grand start. Hopes were shattered, however, when, within four years, West Indies politicians decided that the federation would not work and its elaborate structure was dismantled.

Salvaged from the débâcle was the notion of a Caribbean festival of creative arts (known as Carifesta), which has continued to be held periodically in the region despite sinking economies. The first Carifesta was hosted by Guyana for three weeks in 1972. Jamaica held the second in 1976, Cuba the third in 1979, Barbados the fourth in 1981 and Trinidad and Tobago the fifth in 1992. These festivals presented an opportunity for shared experiences among Caribbean artists and audiences; they showcased new work and enabled participating groups to gain government and, in some cases, commercial sponsorship for their work.

For the first festival, the Guyanese playwright Michael Gilkes (b. 1933) was commissioned to write *Couvade*, a dream play about a ritual apparently still practised in his country by Carib Indians at the time of childbirth and which became in the play a symbol for national regeneration. The Barbados festival staged a dramatized reading of George Lamming's (b. 1927) semi-biographical novel, *In the Castle of My Skin*.

For the Jamaica festival a collection of eight Caribbean plays selected and edited by Hill was published under the title . . . *a time and a season* . . . (1976). The collection included entries in English translation from Puerto Rico, Cuba and Colombia as well as four previously unpublished plays from the anglophone Caribbean: *George William Gordon* by Roger Mais of Jamaica; *The Tramping Man* by Trinidad-born Ian McDonald (b. 1933), resident in Guyana; *The Banjo Man* by Roderick Walcott; and *The Black Jacobins* by C.L.R. James (1901–89) of Trinidad.

One singular result of the federal festival was the establishment of the Trinidad Theatre Workshop by Derek Walcott in 1959. With a company of actors recruited partly from the large number who had taken part in his epic drama and partly from others who wished to gain serious training, Walcott began his work without fanfare and with no immediate prospect of rehearsing for a production. Over the next seventeen years, however, the workshop produced a repertoire of his plays and its reputation was firmly established throughout

the Caribbean and in several North American cities.

It should be emphasized that most of the work in theatre at this time was still of a voluntary nature. Local theatres were run on an amateur basis and few if any participants received stipends for their work. It was not surprising therefore that playwrights began to look abroad to have their work produced professionally. This was nothing new. In times past Caribbean playwrights and composers living overseas had their work produced on professional stages with success. One of the earliest was Donald Heywood (1901–67) of Trinidad, who, between 1927 and 1937, had presented on the New York stage *Africana*, a musical comedy; *Ol Man Satan*, a drama; *How Come, Lord*, a folk play; and other works in an attempt to win audiences who had been roused to an interest in black plays and musicals during the so-called Harlem renaissance.

More serious in theme was the 1936 production of *Toussaint Louverture* by C.L.R. James, which received a special showing at the Westminster Theatre by the Stage Society of London. Despite having US actor Paul Robeson in the title role and an impressive supporting cast, this production ultimately failed. Then the 1940s witnessed three original musical productions that hoped to capitalize on the awakened interest in calypso by British and US forces stationed in Trinidad during World War II. The first of these was by William Archibald (1917–70; brother of the Trinidad playwright Jack Archibald), who wrote the book and lyrics for *Carib Song* (1945), which opened in Boston before moving to the Adelphi Theatre in New York. It was judged to be an 'academic and sexy' fable enlivened only by the dancing of Katherine Dunham and the music of Baldwin Bergersen. Next, the calypsonian Sam Manning contributed music and lyrics to *Caribbean Carnival* (1947), a revue-type show featuring the Trinidad-born dancer Pearl Primus (1919–94) and her company, but the production was also poorly reviewed. Faring little better with a script considered not funny and too long was the musical *Calypso* (1948), which opened at the Playhouse Theatre in London with Edric Connor and Evelyn Dove in the cast.

The only consistent writer at this time was William Archibald. As a professional singer, dancer, composer, playwright and screenwriter, he may well have been the most gifted Caribbean theatre artist of the period. With four of his plays (*The Innocents*, 1950, based on Henry

James's *The Turn of the Screw*; *Portrait of a Lady*, 1954; *The Crystal Heart*, 1957; and *The Cantilevered Terrace*, 1957) Archibald eventually won respect on the New York and London stages. He also gained the Best Screenplay award (with Truman Capote) from the Mystery Writers of America for *The Innocents* (1961).

With the exception of James's *Toussaint Louverture*, it is unlikely that any of the above-mentioned plays or musicals would in the 1990s have been considered exemplary material for the Caribbean theatre. Clearly written for commercial stage productions in another country, their depiction of the life, struggles and aspirations of the people of the Caribbean region is apt to be misleading if not wholly inaccurate. For a truer picture it is necessary to turn to the next group of writers, who maintained a link with their home country while seeking a hearing before wider metropolitan audiences.

Barry Reckord (b. 1926) of Jamaica offered his drama *'Della* to Kingston audiences in 1954, then revised it for a 1958 London opening at the Royal Court Theatre under the title *Flesh to a Tiger*. It dealt with the determined attempt by a cult leader to enforce his wishes on a female member of his flock. Reckord, a teacher by profession, has had many other plays produced in London as well as in Jamaica, including *You in Your Small Corner* (1960); *Don't Gas the Blacks* (1969); *A Liberated Woman* (1971); *In the Beautiful Caribbean* (BBC-TV, 1972); *Let It All Hang Out, Daddy* (1973), first produced in London as *X*; *I Man* (1976), first produced in London as *Skyvers*; *The White Witch of Rose Hall* (1978); *Streetwise* (1984); and *Sugar D* (1988). Most of his plays deal with sexual conflict as a means towards women's liberation and have been somewhat controversial. They are often directed by his brother Lloyd Reckord (b. 1929), also a fine actor.

Another Jamaican playwright who settled in London in 1956 to pursue his craft was Evan Jones (b. 1927). Although he has had theatre pieces staged in Jamaica (*Inherit This Land*, 1951, and *Go Tell It on Table Mountain*, 1970) and in Guyana (*In a Backward Country*, 1959), Jones became best known in London for his television and film scripts: *The Widow of Jaffa* (1957), based on his experience at a United Nations-run Arab refugee camp, and *The Fight Against Slavery* (1976), a drama/documentary series which illustrated his interest in social issues. Several of his scripts were directed by the British film director Joseph Losey, including

King and Country (1964) and *Modesty Blaise* (1966).

Errol John, an actor of considerable skill, also went to London from Trinidad on a British Council grant and was catapulted into playwriting fame when he won the London *Observer* Commonwealth Competition with his three-act drama *Moon on a Rainbow Shawl*. A 'yard play' in a communal urban setting, *Moon* was first produced in London in 1958 and in New York in 1962. It has been staged in several other countries, including those of the Caribbean, where it is a deeply respected piece of theatre for the sensitivity of its characterization and the honesty of its writing. In addition to acting on stage, in film and television, John wrote television dramas for the British Broadcasting Corporation and had three screenplays published by Faber & Faber in 1967.

If a federated West Indies was not possible, unitary governments would move expeditiously towards nationhood. Both Jamaica and Trinidad and Tobago gained national independence in 1962, while Barbados became independent in 1964 and Guyana in 1966. Other states followed, from Grenada in 1974 to St Kitts-Nevis in 1983. Other smaller states opted to retain the benefits derived from colonial status or as states associated with Britain. Anniversaries of statehood also provided occasions for festivals, including competitive playwriting, drama and dance productions and other artistic exhibitions. Theatre groups, anticipating the advantages of regionalization, were not discouraged by the turn of events. Some sought to become more professional in order to meet the increasing demands of longer runs and to compensate participants for their roles in productions.

One of the first of these incipient professional groups in the 1960s was the Strolling Players led by Freddie Kissoon of Trinidad. A playwright, actor and school teacher, Kissoon had served his apprenticeship with the Company of Players before forming his own troupe in 1961. Founding members were required to make a small initial investment in the company on the understanding that they would receive compensation from net receipts of each production with a share reserved for the company's future productions. By the end of 1992, the Strolling Players had staged seventy-seven plays, of which Kissoon had written forty-one. In addition, he wrote and produced seventy-eight episodes of the popular radio serial *Calabash Alley* (1970–1) and inaugurated live drama on T&T

Television in 1961 with his one-act play *Zingay*. With over forty teleplays to its credit by 1994, the troupe had also taken live productions to the country district of Trinidad and Tobago, to other Caribbean nations, and further abroad. Kissoon's plays are mostly short farces and melodramas, but he has written a number of serious dramas such as *King Cobo* (1966), on blackmail and prostitution; *God and Uriah Butler* (1967), about the 1937 Trinidad oilfield workers' strike; and *Luisa Calderón* (1992), on the harsh rule of Trinidad's first English governor, Thomas Picton.

Trinidad and Tobago's annual Best Village trophy competition was also established in 1963 by Eric Williams, the country's first prime minister. Intended initially for folk music, in 1989 it began to include folk theatre forms with over 100 groups (some 6,000 people) participating. A non-competitive spin-off is the annual Tobago Heritage Festival, which takes place in July and August and also offers village-based folk theatre and historical re-enactments.

Another attempt to establish a career theatre enterprise in the 1960s was Lloyd Reckord's National Theatre Trust of Jamaica. Reckord had been working as director of (and sometimes actor in) his brother Barry's plays both in London and Jamaica. In 1956 he started the Actors' Theatre in Jamaica as a first attempt to set up a professional theatre but was called to perform in London two years later. Back home in 1968, with support from the local business sector, he started the National Theatre Trust, which has produced a wide variety of plays. Among the most popular were Douglas Archibald's *The Rose Slip*, produced by the Trust in 1971; Barry Reckord's *The White Witch of Rose Hall* (1978); and Sylvia Wynter's *Maskarade* (1988). In 1979 Reckord compiled a dramatized presentation of works from the Caribbean, Africa and black America, which he toured for the next two years to schools, colleges and theatres in the United States, Britain and the French- and English-speaking Caribbean.

The most successful effort at establishing a professional theatre in Jamaica came from the production company known as Theatre 77, founded in 1967 by Yvonne Brewster (b. 1942) and Trevor Rhone (b. 1940), both of whom had studied at Rose Bruford College in England. The company's main purpose was 'to do stage plays relating to local situations, and to encourage people who have never been to a play before to come and see for themselves that drama is not just Shakespeare' (*Jamaica Star*, January 1970). For a stage, they converted Brewster's family garage into an intimate playhouse seating 150 and called it the Barn Theatre. It became the model for several small theatres scattered around Kingston and operating at a professional level.

Rhone had given up teaching to become a full-time playwright. He had successfully written plays and pantomimes for school production and in 1969 his first major play, *The Gadget*, had won the Silver Medal in the Jamaican Arts Festival. A series of remarkable successes at the Barn followed, proving that Jamaica was ready for its own theatre and that it was possible for talented people to make a living on the stage. Rhone's most successful plays included *Smile Orange* (1971), a satire on the tourist trade that ran for 245 performances; *School's Out* (1975), a comedic look inside a teachers' common room; *Old Story Time* (1979), a brilliant use of the conventions of village storytelling, about a single mother's struggles for her son; and the two-hander *Two Can Play* (1982), dealing with a couple's search for love through forgiveness. These and other plays were produced at the Barn, elsewhere in Jamaica, on other Caribbean islands and in metropolitan centres abroad. Rhone collaborated on the script of *The Harder They Come* (1972), a feature-length film about Jamaica; then scripted and directed the film version of *Smile Orange* (1976). *Two Can Play* was produced for television on US public broadcasting.

Yvonne Brewster became a radio announcer and television producer on her return to Jamaica from training in England, though she maintained a residence in London, where she directed plays with African-Caribbean casts primarily for black communities in the city. In 1985 she founded the all-black Talawa Theatre Company in London, and directed plays by Caribbean, Nigerian and English authors, including Wilde's *The Importance of Being Earnest* (co-produced with the Tyne Theatre Company in Newcastle upon Tyne) and *Antony and Cleopatra* (co-produced with Merseyside Everyman Theatre in Liverpool). In 1988 Brewster directed Rhone's *Two Can Play* at the Bristol Old Vic and in 1992 she leased the renovated Cochrane Theatre in Holborn, London, for her company. This was the first black theatre in Britain to have a building of its own. Brewster also published two collections of plays under the titles *Black Plays* (1987) and *Black Plays: Two* (1989). She

Jamaican director and producer Yvonne Brewster.

was made an officer of the Order of the British Empire in 1993.

In Jamaica, after twenty years of consistent effort and struggle, the Little Theatre Movement opened its Little Theatre, seating 615, in 1961. Its fiftieth consecutive pantomime production took place at the Ward Theatre, Kingston, in 1991, playing to audiences in the tens of thousands, a far cry from the five performances with which the pantomime began back in 1941. Meanwhile, in Trinidad the university extra-mural department, under its resident tutor, Esmond Ramesar (b. 1927), recognized the growing need for training in the arts, especially theatre arts, at all levels. Ramesar extended the lead of Jamaica by establishing in 1964 a summer school in the performing arts on the university campus at St Augustine, Trinidad. This school, broadened in scope to include other creative arts such as painting and sculpture and supplemented by classes held during the academic year, has been a regular feature of the extra-mural teaching programme since its inception. On the Jamaica campus a modest new Creative Arts Centre was built in 1967 to focus attention on the arts as an important element of the academic curriculum. Renamed the Philip Sherlock Centre for the Creative Arts, the centre has made its theatre available for plays produced by university students as well as by non-campus groups. In time, courses in creative writing and twentieth-century drama techniques

were offered as electives for a Bachelor of Arts degree. A similar Creative Arts Centre programme was established on the Trinidad campus in 1986 and was expanded to include drama-in-education.

The most ambitious attempt to professionalize the performing arts in the Commonwealth Caribbean was the founding of the Cultural Training Centre (CTC) in Kingston, Jamaica, in 1975. Occupying a ten-acre site, the centre offers training programmes in music, dance, drama and visual art that lead to academic degrees, diplomas or certificates. Its facilities include an amphitheatre and a studio theatre for the School of Drama, the curriculum of which contains an experimental Caribbean laboratory where students may investigate traditional folk forms and consider how to translate them for the dramatic and musical stage. The CTC has also been notable for its 'outreach': students work in drama therapy in prisons, clinics and so on, and its workshops on school syllabus texts tour widely in rural areas. Memorable CTC productions include Stanley French's *Under a Sky of Incense* and Peter Schaffer's *Equus* (1977). In 1982 the Graduate Theatre Company associated with the school was launched and has since dramatized literary texts assigned for secondary school-leaving examinations. The company has also produced James's *The Black Jacobins*, Dario Fo's *Accidental Death of an Anarchist*, two plays by Trinidadian dramatist Victor Questel (1949–82) under the collective title *Sufferer's Song*, and Groundwork Theatre Company and Pat Cumper's *De Fallen Angel and de Devil Concubine*.

One of the biggest events associated with the annual carnival celebrations held in Trinidad and Tobago is the Dimanche Gras (Fat Sunday) show at which, before some 12,500 spectators, final judging takes place of competitions for the best masquerade costumes and the best calypsonian; the best steel orchestra is chosen at the Panorama Competition the week before. To complement these competitions, a variety programme of dancers and other entertainments is usually presented. In the years 1963–5 attempts were made to structure the Dimanche Gras show into a continuous story form with the necessary lacunae to accommodate the contests. These attempts were mostly unsuccessful, except possibly for Errol Hill's spicy political satire *Whistling Charlie and the Monster* (1964), a highpoint in the Dimanche Gras series of presentations.

In 1965 the British government decided to

hold its first Commonwealth Festival of Arts at various locations in the United Kingdom, hosting some 1,500 artists from Commonwealth countries around the world presenting their music, drama, dance, poetry and visual art. Among Caribbean states taking part were Jamaica, represented by its National Dance Theatre Company; Dominica, which also sent a dance troupe; and Trinidad and Tobago, which sent calypso, steel band, folk and Indian dances, and a production of Hill's musical play *Man Better Man* (1960), set in a village at carnival time and featuring stickfighters, an element in Trinidad village festivals from the late nineteenth century. The production later played in London, Croydon and Glasgow.

A new experiment in carnival theatre, under the leadership of Irish-born Helen Camps (b. 1938) and associated with her short-lived Trinidad Tent Theatre, occurred in the 1980s. Her productions were actually first presented at the Little Carib Theatre in Port of Spain in 1980 and moved to a tent in the Botanic Gardens in 1982. In these productions, Camps mounted a series of carnival theatre pieces written by Felix Edinborough (b. 1942) and based entirely on traditional masquerade characters such as Baby Doll, Jab-Jab (Diable-Diable), Jab Molassi, Jamette, King Dragon and his Imps, King Sailor, Midnight Robber, Pierrot Grenade and Wild Indian, among others. Scripts written in the local Creole contained references to contemporary events with well-placed jabs at local figures. Old and familiar calypsos adapted to the occasion were included in the text. At the 1982 Traditional Folk Festival in the UK, Trinidad Tent Theatre staged *J'Ouvert* (*New Dawn*) in several cities including London, Bergerac (France), Rome, Milan, West Berlin, Geneva and others to indicate its hope for an end to the nuclear threat and the emergence of a new era of peace among nations. Among other carnival plays that have been presented by Camps are *Mas' in Yuh Mas'* (1980), *King Jab-Jab* (1981) and *Go to Hell* (1984).

Yet another effort to introduce elements of the Trinidad carnival on the stage took place with three productions of scripts written by Rawle Gibbons (b. 1950), head of the Creative Arts Centre in Trinidad, and presented successively in the carnival seasons of 1991–3. A piece called *De Real Kaiso*, combining highlights of all three, was presented in 1994. The intention was to re-enact the stories of important social and historical events that took place in the 1930s, 1940s and 1950s as revealed in the

calypsos written during the respective time periods. These calypsos were introduced in the scripts and older members of the audience who remembered them could respond by singing the choruses as was customary in the calypso 'tents' of earlier years. Among the shows produced have been *Sing de Chorus* (1991), *Ah Wanna Fall* (1992), *Ten to One* (1993) and *De Real Kaiso*. Gibbons has also written *Shepherd* (1981), a mystical play of revivalism directed by Dennis Scott (1939–91) for the Jamaica School of Drama and taken to Barbados for Carifesta '81, and *I Lawah* (*The King*, 1984), another drama set in the world of the nineteenth-century carnival stickfighters.

Caribbean writers and performing artists continue to be challenged to harness the elements of the carnival – its creative energy, pageantry, mime, dance, song, music and oratory – and convey meaningful statements about the lives of the people engaged in, and those who are simply spectators of, this annual revelry.

Mask-maker, designer, painter and director Peter Minshall (b. 1941) believes that it is possible to produce expressive and significant street theatre through masquerade designs and performances on the open carnival stage. He has achieved considerable success with masquerade creations such as *Paradise Lost* (1976), *Danse Macabre* (1980), *Adoration of Hiroshima* (1985), *Santimanitay* (1989), *Tantana* (1990) and *The Odyssey* (1994). Minshall was one of the designers chosen in 1992 for the Barcelona Olympic Games opening ceremonies, to help stage the pageant of the voyage and arrival of Columbus in the New World.

In the early 1960s, in the interior of Guyana, Canadian-born Joan Dummett Jason (b. 1937) worked with native people, who revealed their history and myths in theatre that involved whole villages. Co-founder and arts editor of *New World Fortnightly*, Dummett Jason later chaired a seminar that asked 'A Guyanese National Theatre?' Under this title, an edited transcript with input from Guyanese from all walks of life and all areas of the country was published and it influenced future trends in Guyanese theatre. Employed by the British Council to conduct speech and drama workshops to promote racial reintegration in communities torn by civil strife, she later directed the 1974 national drama festival, which for the first time brought together the six major ethnic groups of Guyana in one cultural event.

In 1972 Guyanese actor-director Ken Corsbie created a solo show entitled *He-One* and com-

Guyanese actor, director and administrator Ken Corsbie.

prised of Caribbean writings with which he toured the region for six months. This show was succeeded by another called *Dem Two* (1973) involving Corsbie and another Guyanese, Marc Matthews (b. 1937), with a further sequel, *All-Ah-We* (1974), incorporating Henry Muttoo (b. 1948) and two singer-musicians. In total, these shows toured the islands for over 200 performances. Largely as a result of this experience, Corsbie in 1976 organized in St Lucia the first ever Conference of Caribbean Dramatists, from which the Theatre Information Exchange (TIE) was formed with funding from the Inter-American Foundation.

Patricia Charles, then university extra-mural tutor, served as the first TIE coordinator before Corsbie was appointed full time to the position. His mission was to establish a communication system among theatre activities of the English-speaking Caribbean. Data on Caribbean theatre (including taped interviews) were collected, a newsletter started, and new playscripts duplicated and distributed.

A second conference of Caribbean dramatists was held in Barbados in 1978. At this time, a link was made with the Eugene O'Neill Theatre Center in the United States, and a loosely formed association known as CARIBUSTE (Caribbean-United States Theatre Exchange) came into being in 1979, resulting in a third conference of Caribbean dramatists, which was held in the Virgin Islands in 1981. When, by 1984, foundation funds were exhausted, TIE was disbanded. At the time of its demise, it had seventy-nine individual and eight institutional members.

A further attempt to strengthen theatre across the region was the formation in 1986 of the Pan Caribbean Theatre Company, whose members were initially recruited to participate in Caribbean Focus, a series of events held at the Commonwealth Institute, London, and spotlighting the Caribbean region. Plays presented on the occasion were Dennis Scott's *Dog* and Rawle Gibbons's *I Lawah* with casts and crews drawn from many of the territories in the area. The Pan Caribbean Company was quiescent after its return from Caribbean Focus and the regional idea lay dormant until 1988 when, at a playwrights' conference held in Jamaica, it was revived as the Association of Caribbean Theatre Artists. The new organization also published the first few issues of a newsletter and hoped to assume some of the high-minded objectives of earlier regional organizations but foundered for lack of sustaining support.

The drive towards professionalism has been more successful. In Barbados producing companies such as Stage One (1978) and WWB Productions (1987) already operate as independent organizations interested primarily in the efficient management of stage presentations. They choose plays, hire a director such as Earl Warner (b. 1953), who is based in Jamaica, and experienced actors such as Errol Jones (b. 1923) and Errol Sitahal (b. 1941) of Trinidad and Clairmonte Taitt (b. 1932) of Guyana (later resident in Barbados), for the principal characters, and do all that is necessary to facilitate the production, leaving the artistic decisions to the director.

In Guyana, the Theatre Company, directed by Ron Robinson (b. 1946), also operates on a strictly professional basis, as do some small theatres in Jamaica that produce what are locally called 'roots' (grassroots) plays for popular consumption. Among the most important of these small professional theatres are those run by playwright-producers Ginger Knight (b. 1951) and Balfour Anderson (b. 1953). A cadre of skilled designers and technicians is now available in the Caribbean region and can be professionally engaged as required.

Cultural centres or smaller auditoriums where performances are held have also led to the professionalization of managers and technicians.

In Trinidad, professional producers such as the Bagasse Company and Raymond Choo Kong (b. 1949) at the Space Theatre present plays regularly, seldom home-grown but with the occasional localizing of foreign plays.

Dramaturgy

If Trevor Rhone brought professionalism to the Caribbean dramatic theatre, the writer who brought it stature and world regard was Derek Walcott. The St Lucian poet, awarded the 1992 Nobel Prize for Literature, has written some forty plays in verse and prose in native English and French dialects. What distinguishes him from other Caribbean playwrights is his world-view of the Caribbean experience at all levels of society and his ability to express this world-view in incisive language appropriate to character and situation.

Walcott's theatrical career falls generally into three periods. The first runs from his teenage years in St Lucia up to the production of *Drums and Colours*, a period of about twelve years during which he wrote twenty plays, several of which were in verse. Most memorable from this period are *Henri Christophe*, *The Sea at Dauphin* (1954), with its echo of John Millington Synge's *Riders to the Sea*, and one of Walcott's most delightful pieces, *Ti Jean and His Brothers* (1957), based on a folk tale of St Lucia in which three brothers go out to fight the devil. This was first produced as a ballet by the Arts Guild in St Lucia and it became the first Walcott play to have an original score when in 1970 the author revised it with music by Andre Tanker (b. 1941) for a tour of the islands and for performance at Joseph Papp's theatre in New York's Central Park.

The watershed production of Walcott's career was his epic drama *Drums and Colours*. It established him as the foremost Caribbean dramatist if indeed any doubt previously existed as to where he stood. Walcott had earlier held teaching positions in the northern islands. From this point on, he decided to withdraw from teaching and remain in Trinidad, where he would set up his own drama group, eventually to be called the Trinidad Theatre Workshop. In preparation for this, Walcott received a Rockefeller Foundation Fellowship to

The 1974 Westport, Connecticut, White Barn Theatre production of Derek Walcott's *Ti Jean and His Brothers*.
Photo: Howard Moss.

study theatre in New York under José Quintero and Stuart Vaughan, directors of their own Off-Broadway companies. On his return to Trinidad, he arranged for his group to use the Little Carib Theatre. He also began writing occasionally for the *Trinidad Guardian* on art and culture, reviewing plays and art exhibitions.

The second phase of Walcott's theatre career began with the creation of the Workshop in 1959 and ended when he left the company in 1976. During these seventeen years, he wrote ten plays including his finest work, *Dream on Monkey Mountain* (1967), about a poor black charcoal burner named Makak, who is obsessed by his dream of a white goddess; and, on commission from the Royal Shakespeare Company, *The Joker of Seville* (1974), an adaptation of Tirso de Molina's *El Burlador de Sevilla* with a score by the Canadian Galt MacDermot, best known as the composer of the musical *Hair*. To these two should be added *O Babylon!* (1976), about the Rastafari sect of Jamaica, written for the Carifesta festival in that country.

The Trinidad Theatre Workshop began its first overseas tour when it took *Dream on Monkey Mountain* to Canada for Toronto's Caribana Festival. Thereafter the production played in several Caribbean states and at the Eugene O'Neill Center. Supported by the Negro Ensemble Company, it later played in Los Angeles and New York, where in 1971 it won an Obie Award.

The third phase of Walcott's career in theatre, not yet concluded, has found him receiving commissions to write plays and teaching at universities across North America. More than a dozen plays have been written (or rewritten) during this period. *Pantomime* (1978), a two-hander set in a guest house on the island of Tobago, opened in Trinidad and has been popular on stage and radio. Productions have gone as far afield as the United States, the United Kingdom, Germany, the Netherlands and Singapore.

In 1984 Walcott returned to Haïtian history with an ambitious open-air production in St Lucia entitled *Haytian Earth. Steel* (1991), his salute to the birth of the steel band movement in Trinidad, again with a score by MacDermot, premièred at the American Repertory Theatre at Harvard. Meanwhile, another drama, *The Odyssey* (1991), commissioned by the Royal Shakespeare Company (RSC) and based on Homer, opened at The Other Place in Stratford-upon-Avon, England, and later moved to London. A version of this production was performed in 1993 at the Trinidad Theatre Workshop's temporary headquarters in the Old Fire Station in Port of Spain, directed by the RSC's Greg Duran.

In addition to his Nobel Prize for Literature, Walcott has won other honours for his work specifically in theatre. In 1981 he received the prestigious John D. and Catherine MacArthur Foundation Award. In 1983 the University of the West Indies awarded him an honorary Doctor of Letters degree and in 1989 he received a grant from the Massachusetts Fund for the Arts.

Two other poet-dramatists who also deserve mention here are Lennox Brown (b. 1934) of Trinidad and Dennis Scott of Jamaica. Brown attended the University of Western Ontario (BA, 1961) and the University of Toronto (MA, 1969), writing his Master's thesis on Samuel Selvon (1923–94), a major Caribbean novelist of East Indian descent. While working for the Canadian Broadcasting Corporation from 1963 to 1967, he published a number of poems but was drawn to playwriting after winning a prize in a national one-act playwriting contest in Canada. Brown taught for a short time at universities in Connecticut and New York before returning to live in Trinidad.

Of the more than forty plays he has written, Brown has had many produced for radio, television and stage, both in Trinidad and abroad. The Negro Ensemble Company in New York has produced *A Ballet Behind the Bridge* (1972) and *The Twilight Dinner* (1978); the Billie Holiday Theatre in Brooklyn staged *The Winti Train* (1973) and *The Trinity of Four* (1976); and in London, England, the Keskidee Theatre presented *The Crystal Tree* (1979), a quartet of plays (*Fog Drifts in the Spring, Summer Screen, The Thorn in an Autumn Room* and *Wine in Winter*).

Brown has said that he writes about 'injustices. This is my form of protest' (*Black Images*, 1972). Still, it would be naive to consider his work simply as dramas of social realism. His best plays involve supernatural elements; he can invoke ancestral spirits, dancers and music as convincingly as his taut dialogue requires. He appeals to the essential humanity in every individual and shows how fear, inherited customs and institutions can destroy that

Errol Hill's 1987 Hanover, New Hampshire, Dartmouth Players' production of Lennox Brown's *Devil Mas'*.

humanity. In *A Communion in Dark Sun* (1970), a motley group of unhappy people set up a commune in the woods to escape from civilization. A green man who lives in the forest introduces himself to them as a fellow creature but fear of the unknown results in his murder. Many of Brown's plays deal with the Trinidad underclass. In one trilogy, he shows the same characters – but of a different racial type (African, Indian, Chinese) – with white over-lordship set against the background of the Trinidad carnival. His plays on these themes include *Ballet Behind the Bridge*, *Devil Mas'* (1971) and *A Processional from La Basse* (1973).

While Brown has confined himself to playwriting, Dennis Scott was known as a total man of the theatre. Besides being a playwright of growing reputation, Scott was also a skilful director, actor, dancer, drama teacher and critic. In addition, he was a poet whose work had received wide publication and international awards. Born in Jamaica, Scott taught at sec-ondary school for a time before completing studies for an honours degree in English at the University of the West Indies. He also took a post-graduate drama-in-education diploma at the University of Newcastle upon Tyne, England, in 1973.

His early plays, written for school perfor-mance in Trinidad and Jamaica, brought atten-tion, especially when he won gold and bronze medals in the literary category of the Jamaica Arts Festival for *Chariots of Wrath* (1966) and *The Passionate Cabbage* (1969), respectively. In 1970 he turned the Greek drama *Agamemnon* into *The Crime of Anabel Campbell*, thereby shifting the emphasis from the Greek warrior who won the Trojan war to his vengeful wife awaiting his return home. In 1977, on commis-sion for the National Theatre of the Deaf, Scott adapted and dramatized the Medieval poem *Sir Gawain and the Green Knight*, performed at the Kennedy Center for the Performing Arts in Washington.

The two plays on which Scott's reputation mainly rests are *Echo in the Bone* (1974) and *Dog* (1978). In the former, the ritual of spirit possession is invoked at a dead-wake ceremony to explain the death by drowning of a black labourer who has apparently wantonly killed a white estate owner. In the process, episodes from the history of black slavery and its colonial aftermath are revealed to account for the murder. The play was first performed to mark the twenty-fifth anniversary of the founding of the University of the West Indies in Jamaica; it then represented Jamaica at the 1977 Festival of African Arts and Culture in Nigeria, and was an entry at Carifesta '76. It was subsequently produced in Trinidad and Barbados. In *Dog*, Scott presents the underclass of society as wild dogs who have been waiting for their needs to be satisfied while the privileged form vigilante squads to hunt them down. Each group has its own code of ethics that gives credibility to its behaviour, whether human or animal. The work received the Best Experimental Play award at the Jamaica Arts Festival and was revived for showing at the Barbados Carifesta in 1981.

From 1977 to 1983 Scott served as director of the Jamaica School of Drama where he directed a variety of plays including those of Shakespeare and contemporary dramatists. During this period he also offered workshops on other Caribbean islands. At the school he introduced with others a special programme known as the 'Caribbean Lab' to explore the techniques required for presenting the rituals of society on the stage. In 1973 Scott was invited to serve as a director at the National Playwrights' Confer-ence at the Eugene O'Neill Center. He returned there regularly and as a result was asked by Lloyd Richards, head of the conference and later dean of the Yale University Graduate School of Drama, to take a position as visiting professor of directing at Yale. Scott moved to New Haven in 1983, having been awarded the Jamaican Prime Minister's Medal for service to the arts. His untimely death in 1991 at the age of 51 was widely mourned.

One of the most successful Caribbean playwrights to reside abroad is Mustapha Matura (b. 1939) of Trinidad, who moved to England in 1961 and became an important new voice on the British stage. Of East Indian ancestry, Matura succeeded in capturing the speech rhythms and cadences of the different racial groups that comprise his native country. With his first major play, *As Time Goes By* (1971), produced at the Traverse Theatre in Edinburgh and at the Royal Court Theatre in London, Matura won both the George Devine and George Whiting playwriting awards. Since then, he has written some twenty plays, with productions in London, Oxford, Manchester, Edinburgh, Chicago, Washington, New Brun-swick, New Jersey, New Haven, at the Lincoln Center in New York and in Trinidad. As founding director of the Black Theatre Coopera-tive in London in 1978, he toured with his

Trinidad playwright Mustapha Matura.

group to the Netherlands, Denmark and Germany.

In locating the action of his plays either in Trinidad or among Caribbean migrant communities in Britain, Matura dramatizes the effects of colonialism on both the ruler and the ruled. His drama *Play Mas'* (1974) reveals how an unpopular government in Trinidad uses the annual carnival festival to entrap revolutionaries; *Rum and Coca Cola* (1976) exposes the external sycophancy yet deep-seated hostility of calypsonians towards the tourists on whom they rely for their income outside of the carnival season. *Welcome Home Jacko* (1979) looks at unemployed Caribbean youths in Britain who seek identity through their alliances with Rastafarianism, even as they are confronted with the harsh realities of their friend Jacko, newly released from prison. Matura has experimented with some success at adapting well-known western plays to Caribbean locales and language. He rendered Synge's *Playboy of the Western World* into *Playboy of the West Indies* (1984) and Chekhov's *Three Sisters* into *Trinidad Sisters* (1988). In the latter play, the supposed love of the colonial for the mother country is shown to be a hollow sham.

Other playwrights worthy of note from the southern Caribbean are Douglas Archibald of Trinidad and Harold Bascom (b. 1951) of Guyana. A brother of William Archibald, the former was a civil engineer but had other interests, including historical research and writing, especially playwriting. His first play,

Junction Village (1952), staged by Sydney Hill for the New Company in Port of Spain, dealt with the protracted dying of an elderly village woman as neighbours gather to pay their last respects. Its production established Archibald as a penetrating observer of character with a keen ear for the idiosyncrasies of native speech. He went on to write a range of plays such as *Anne Marie* (1958), set on a rural estate and involving a cross-section of characters; *The Rose Slip* (1962), a backyard comedy-drama; and the historical *Defeat with Honour* (1964), on the defeat of the Spanish defence forces by the British navy, which made Trinidad a British colony in 1797. Archibald had several unproduced plays among his works when he died in 1993.

The most popular and productive playwright at work in Guyana in the 1990s was Harold Bascom. He has to his credit more than a dozen full-length plays that have been produced in the 2,000-seat National Cultural Centre in Georgetown, usually to full houses. He writes, he says, for the 'market people', lower-middle-class audiences to whom he offers simple morals sugar-coated with entertaining situations. Thus in *T.V. Alley* (1988) neighbours quarrel over who owns the biggest television set and receiving dish, in *Family Budget* (1989) a wife is forced to enter into a liaison with another man who can help her meet the family expenses and in *The Visa Wedding* (1989) a similar situation arises when a young woman agrees to marry so that she can receive a US passport.

The 1970s also witnessed the emergence of playwrights and theatre companies on the smaller islands of the eastern Caribbean, roused to action by the work of extra-mural tutors and by periodic visits from the University Dramatic Society in Jamaica. The establishment of a branch university campus in Barbados also provided a stimulus to these dramatic efforts. The foremost playwright in Barbados is Anthony Hinkson (b. 1942), a drama teacher at the Garrison Secondary School in Bridgetown. He was a member of the Writers' Workshop, formed in 1969 to provide an outlet for creative writing, and he participated in the authorship of *Unchained* (1972), a dramatization of Caribbean writings that represented Barbados at Guyana's Carifesta. In the absence of staging facilities at his school, Hinkson teamed up with the Pinelands Theatre Workshop, for which he wrote *Teacher Teach 'er* (1976), *Nigger Yard* (1978), *The Candidate* (1986) and other plays. In 1980 he produced *The Genesis*, a cultural extravaganza about the American Indian settlers in Barbados that introduced music, song, dance and drama, and in 1988 his musical *Village Life* incorporated work by Barbadian novelist George Lamming and the Trinidadian story-teller Paul Keens-Douglas (b. 1942).

Whether writing of the working class or the educated middle class, Hinkson, with over thirty plays to his credit, captures the idioms and tonal quality common to most Barbadian speech, giving his plays their wry humour and a ring of authenticity. He is happiest, however, in farce and comedy verging on ridicule, as in *The Candidate* (1986), a satire on political campaigning. His plays have been performed in Guyana and Jamaica as well as in his native Barbados.

Another Barbadian playwright of note is the New York-based Glenville Lovell (b. 1955), who is also a professional dancer. Lovell has had four of his plays produced at festivals in Barbados, where he is held in high esteem. He entered two plays in the 1985 festival; his *Purple Painted Sky* won second prize and his second play, *Echoes of Black Summer*, set among Barbadian emigrants in New York, gained third prize. Two more plays were entered in the 1986 festival: *When the Eagle Screams*, on the US invasion of Grenada, and *A Silver Web*, dealing with the frustrations encountered by Barbadian workers who went to Panamá to help build the canal. Lovell is clearly a serious writer whose work shows great promise.

In Antigua, work in the theatre found a home at the University Centre where an open-air stage seating some 400 patrons had been set up. Several drama groups began operating at this time and new playwrights emerged. Among them was Oliver Flax (b. 1944), whose historical play *The Legend of Prince Klaas*, in a production by the Little Theatre Group, was sent to represent Antigua at the Guyana Carifesta in 1972. The Harambee Open Air Theatre, considered a leading company, produced several plays by its director Dorbrene O'Marde (b. 1950), of which *Fly on the Wall* (1977), succeeded by *Tangled Web* (1979), caused an angry government to legislate against civil servants taking part in plays that were considered critical of the government.

Another Antiguan playwright, Leon Symester (b. 1955), also known as Chaka Waca, wrote two protest plays: *Voices of Protest* (1976) and *Time Bomb* (1977), dealing with the local political situation. Thought to be too libellous for public airing, the latter play was barred from staging at the government-sponsored festival but

played to crowded houses at the University Centre. The Rio Revealers Theatre was organized in 1979 by Eliston Adams (b. 1954), also called Nambulumba. His plays, referred to as slapstick drama, have been taken on tours to the islands of Montserrat, St Martin and St Thomas. This inter-island travel has become one of the distinguishing features of theatre groups in the smaller islands where populations are not large enough to sustain a run of performances sufficient to offset the expenses of production. At the same time, extended runs help to cultivate a more professional approach to theatre organization through regular practice of the craft.

In Dominica, the leading light in the 1970s and early 1980s was Alwin Bully (b. 1948), an actor, director, playwright and designer. On his return from university in Barbados, Bully directed Daniel Cauderon's social commentary *Speak, Brother, Speak* (1972), a play suited to the revolutionary consciousness of the time. Bully then founded the People's Action Theatre, for which he wrote and produced his major plays: *Streak* (1975), on the prevailing attitude towards dreadlock Rastafaris; *The Ruler* (1976), an adaptation of the novel *The Ruler in Hiroona* by G.C.H. Thomas; *The Nite Box* (1977), setting a civil service strike against the background of a murder mystery; the annually produced Christmas play, *Folk Nativity* (1976); and the folk musical *Pio-Pio* (1978). Bully has also produced radio serials and directed a version of Derek Walcott's *Ti Jean and His Brothers* (1981), which he had helped to translate into French Creole. He has won several awards for his work in the arts including the National Sisserou Award from the government of the Commonwealth of Dominica.

The small island of Montserrat (population 15,000) has produced three playwrights whose work has received attention abroad. Vincent Browne (b. 1922), a retired major of the Montserrat Defence Force and past warden of university halls in Jamaica and Barbados, has been writing light farces for many years with productions in Jamaica, Trinidad, Guyana and St Kitts as well as in his home country. Among his plays are *Big Business* (1967) and *Sunquest* (1983), both on the well-worn domestic triangle theme, and *The Meeting*, a satiric comedy chosen for the Barbados Independence Festival of 1978. Browne's most serious work is an historical drama entitled *And on the Seventh Day* (1984), about a slave uprising in Montserrat, written to commemorate the 150th anniversary of slave emancipation. He also directed the play, which was staged at the University Centre in 1985. A collection of his plays was published in 1991 under the title *Big Business and Other Plays*.

The most prolific and well-respected Mont-serratan playwright is Edgar B. White (b. 1946). White was taken to New York at age 5 and grew up in a poor section of the city. He nevertheless retained a close connection with the Caribbean (as with many African diaspora communities in North America and England) through his plays and novels. He received a Bachelor's degree from New York University in 1968 and his first play, written when he was only 16, depicts two black men who complain to an impotent St Peter about the racial injustices they have suffered. Produced by the Public Theater in New York in 1965, the play, as critic Steven Carter points out, introduced several characteristics of White's work: 'an episodic structure, humour based on literary references, whimsical and sym-bolic names, a mixture of farce and seriousness, and themes relating to the plight of the black artist and the indifference of the universe toward men, particularly black men' (*Afro-American Writers After 1955: Dramatists and Prose Writers*, 1985). To this may be added a longing for the memory of a Caribbean home that no longer exists. Between 1969 and 1974 the Public Theater staged six of White's plays, including *The Figures at Chartres* (1969), *The Wonderful Year* (1969), *The Life and Times of J. Walter Smintheus* (1971), *Seigismundo's Tricycle* (1971), *Transformations: A Church Ritual* (1972) and *Les Femmes noires* (*The Black Women*, 1974). During the 1970s White also had additional work produced at the Brooklyn Academy of Music as well as the New Federal Theatre Off-Broadway.

In England, London's Black Theatre Cooper-ative produced White's *Trinity: The Long and Cheerful Road to Slavery* (1982), a series of three one-act plays about blacks seeking to understand how history has affected their rela-tionships, and *The Nine Night* (1983), a comedy-drama of Caribbean *émigrés* in London. Two other plays, *Ritual by Water* (1983) and *Redemption Song* (1984), also had London premières. Among White's more recent plays are *I, Marcus Garvey and the Captivity of Babylon* (1987), *Three Kings Darkly*, seen in Jamaica in 1989 and in Trinidad in 1993, and *Orfeo in a Night World* (1993), a play for dancers that is set on an eastern Caribbean island and was produced at the Henry Street Set-tlement Experimental Theatre in New York.

White has also published several collections of his plays: *Underground: Four Plays* (1970), *Lament for Rastafari and Other Plays* (1983), *The Nine Night and Ritual by Water: Two Plays* (1984) and *Redemption Song and Other Plays* (1985).

A third Montserratan playwright is David Edgecombe (b. 1952), who is also a director and radio and television producer. Edgecombe studied communication arts in Canada, returning to his island home in the summers to work at Radio Antilles. He formed the Mont-serrat Theatre Group with which he produced his first major play, a light domestic comedy entitled *For Better for Worse* (1973). It was later produced at the Black Theatre Workshop in Montréal. Edgecombe's next play, *Sunuvabitch* (1977), first directed in Antigua by the author, also played in St Croix and St Kitts, and later in the Bahamas, the Cayman Islands and St Martin, thus reinforcing the notion that exchanging productions between the islands was advantageous for all concerned. Edgecombe wrote *Strong Currents* (1977), based on two novels by the Barbadian Austin Clarke (b. 1934), on commission for Canada's entry to FESTAC '77 (the Second World Black and African Festival of Arts and Culture) held in Nigeria. His family comedy *Coming Home to Roost* (1979) played at the University of the Virgin Islands in St Thomas and in Cuba for Carifesta '79 while *Kirnon's Kingdom* (1981), a forceful statement on power politics, had a stage life in other islands and was also broadcast by the BBC in 1989. Edgecombe's play *Heaven* (1991) premièred at the University of the Virgin Islands and the opening was followed by a tour to other islands. In 1992, he was appointed director of the Reichhold Center for the Arts at the University of the Virgin Islands.

With increased activity at all levels of society, it was inevitable that the theatre should become an instrument for change in the social conditions of the area. As far back as the 1950s, the Jamaica Social Welfare organization had employed folk poet and storyteller Louise Ben-nett and others to work in rural communities identifying local problems and proposing solu-tions through the playmaking process. Sub-sequently, several approaches were made to deal with the question of what might be called the empowerment of the working class.

In 1974 the Folk Research Centre was estab-lished in St Lucia to encourage the formation of popular theatre groups in villages where the Kweyol (Creole, the Caribbean dialect of French)

Jamaican folk poet and storyteller Louise Bennett.

been represented at overseas festivals, conferences and workshops on popular theatre methods and communications.

Yet another working-class theatre is the Jamaican collective known as Sistren. Started in 1979 with members drawn from a make-work programme for unemployed women, Sistren, led by Honor Ford-Smith (b. 1951), soon became a professional company. With plays built on improvisations around a chosen theme or event and then developed into full-scale dramas, the group has staged a number of major productions on issues that range from teenage pregnancy to the role of women in Caribbean history. Among its presentations have been *Nana Yah* (1980), on the life of the Maroon warrior, Nanny, a national heroine; '*Q.P.H.*' (1981), a memorial to the women who perished in a fire at the Kingston Alms House; and *Domestick* (1982), on the abuse of domestic servants. In 1985 the collective produced a documentary film on women's work in the sugar industry of Jamaica entitled *Sweet Sugar Rage*. Sistren also runs workshops, for example on women's health, and its members are much in demand as tutors. The company has travelled to the rural parts of Jamaica and to other Caribbean countries. It has also appeared in England and in the Netherlands.

Dance

Indigenous dance theatre in the Commonwealth Caribbean began with Beryl McBurnie, who studied the folk forms in her native Trinidad and was formally trained at Columbia University, New York, where she came under the influence of the American Martha Graham and other teachers of modern dance. In 1940 McBurnie presented her first show, *A Trip Through the Tropics*, in Port of Spain. After a short period during which she was engaged in professional theatre in New York, she returned to Trinidad to become a dance instructor in the Department of Education. In 1948 McBurnie opened her show *Talking Drums* in her newly built shed-like Little Carib Theatre in Port of Spain. Thereafter her creative work was centred at the Little Carib, where she produced regular seasons of dance and turned out a number of professional dancers, choreographers and teachers, including Molly Ahye (b. 1933), Percy Borde (1922–79), Jean Coggins-Simmons (b. 1923), Jeff Henry (b. 1926), Boscoe Holder (b. 1920) and Geoffrey Holder (b. 1930).

language is spoken and to help organize drama festivals for them. The centre has also been gathering and publishing Kweyol materials as well as translating plays for production. Associated with the centre is the Eastern Caribbean Popular Theatre Organization (ECPTO). Launched in St Vincent in 1983, the organization is a collaboration of several different groups from St Vincent and the Grenadines, Dominica, St Lucia, Grenada, Antigua and Barbados. Its aims are to help communities overcome problems of daily living through the give and take of argument involved in the process of play construction and performance. Sometimes the plays developed have been so meaningful and entertaining that they have been taken on tour to other locations in the country of origin. As part of an international movement, ECPTO has

Trinidad choreographer and artistic director
Beryl McBurnie.

Ahye and Coggins formed new dance troupes in Trinidad. Borde teamed up in New York with his wife Pearl Primus to form a school of dance and toured extensively in Africa where he performed with indigenous dance groups. Henry moved to Canada and pursued a distinguished teaching career as professor of theatre at the National Theatre School in Montréal and later at York University, Toronto. He also founded the Black Theatre Workshop in Montréal and Theatre Fountainhead in Toronto. Geoffrey Holder works as a choreographer and theatrical designer in the New York theatre; he is also an artist of great repute. In 1989 the government of Trinidad and Tobago paid McBurnie its highest honour by awarding her the Trinity Cross for distinguished and outstanding service in promoting the arts of the country.

The establishment of the Little Carib Theatre in Trinidad inspired the Jamaican dancer and choreographer Ivy Baxter to explore the folk dance and music of her country. In 1949 the first performance of her newly formed company, the Ivy Baxter Dance Group, included a dance entitled *Passing Parade* that reflected a day in the life of a traffic officer at a busy intersection of the city. At the 1958 Arts Festival in Puerto Rico, Baxter presented four indigenous works including *Manuel Road*, a dance of road builders; *Pocomania*, a ritual dance; *Village Scene*, based on an Anancy tale; and *Passing Parade*. In the ensuing decade she not only interpreted Caribbean folk dances but also staged pieces on contemporary life situations, such as the plight of stowaways to England and the dance of other countries in her *South Sea Suite*

(1954). She also created new dances using both classical and contemporary music. After 1962 her company declined and was supplanted by the National Dance Theatre Company (NDTC) of Jamaica led by Rex Nettleford (b. 1933).

Nettleford was in a key position to take the dance of Jamaica to even higher achievements. He had joined the Baxter group on its return from Puerto Rico and took charge of the company when Baxter left Jamaica in 1960 to teach and study in Canada and the United States. A graduate of history at the University College of the West Indies and a Rhodes Scholar at Oxford (1957) where he pursued post-graduate studies in politics, Nettleford became professor and head of the Trade Union Education Institute and director of the extra-mural studies department of the University of the West Indies. He is the author of several books and articles as well as editor of *Caribbean Quarterly*, the university's journal on cultural studies.

As artistic director of the NDTC, Nettleford vigorously recruited and trained dancers for his new company. It was formed in 1962, the year of Jamaica's independence, and it has made remarkable progress. With a membership of

Rex Nettleford, choreographer and artistic director, Jamaica National Dance Theatre Company.

fifty-five, including its own group of singers and musicians, its eclectic repertoire of over 160 dances recognizes the need to define and articulate the identity of Caribbean peoples. The company has performed throughout the region, including in Cuba and Puerto Rico, and abroad in Australia, Bermuda, Canada, England, Germany, México, the former Soviet Union, the United States and Venezuela. Among its most notable Caribbean-oriented works are the ritual dances *Pocomania* (1963), *Kumina* (1971) and *Gerrehbenta* (1983); the celebrative *Plantation Revelry* (1963); the evocative *The Crossing* (1978), a reminder of the slaves' Atlantic passage; and the socially meaningful *Two Drums for Babylon* (1964) and *Court of Jah* (1975), all choreographed by Nettleford. His troupe has established itself as the pre-eminent dance theatre company in the Commonwealth Caribbean.

Other Caribbean dance companies include the Bee Wee Ballet of the 1960s and 1970s, founded in Grenada by Thelma Knight and Alister Bain; and the Barbados Dance Theatre Company, formed in 1968. The latter represented Barbados at Carifesta '72, '76, '79 and '81 and has its own school, the Barbados Dance Centre, with a registration of over 300 students of all ages. Other contemporary groups, by no means a complete list, include Molly Ahye's Oya Kairi Dance Company of Trinidad (Oya is a Yoruba goddess; Kairi the native name for Trinidad), Rajkumar Persad's (b. 1941) Trinidad School of Indian Dance, and the Waitukubuli Dance Theatre Company of Dominica, which has produced full-length dance dramas incorporating Carib motifs.

US-trained Helen Taitt was the founder and director of the School of Guyana Ballet, which trained many of the teachers with the Guyana National School of Dance. Her many productions inspired talented dancers and choreographers to new heights, especially her *Song of Guyana*, based on A.J. Seymour's poem about the American Indian legend *Amalica*. Subsequently, Taitt established the National School of Dance in Dominica. Back in Guyana, she became director of the Taitt Dance Theatre.

The second half of the twentieth century witnessed a remarkable change in the theatre culture of the Commonwealth Caribbean. At first dominated by resident foreigners presenting plays of little consequence to the majority of Caribbean peoples, the Caribbean theatre of the 1990s was largely reflective of Caribbean life without eschewing the works of world-renowned playwrights. In its drive towards cultural identity, it has sought to overcome geographic insularity by attempting to become increasingly more regional and increasingly more professional.

Errol Hill

(See also CUBA, DOMINICAN REPUBLIC, FRENCH CARIBBEAN, HAÏTI, NETHERLANDS ANTILLES AND ARUBA, PUERTO RICO)

Further Reading

Ahye, Molly. *Cradle of Caribbean Dance: Beryl McBurnie and the Little Carib Theatre*. Petit Valley, Trinidad: Heritage Culture, 1983. 166 pp.

——. *Golden Heritage: The Dance in Trinidad and Tobago*. Petit Valley, Trinidad: Heritage Culture, 1978. 176 pp.

Baxter, Ivy. *The Arts of an Island: The Development of the Culture and of the Folk and Creative Arts in Jamaica, 1494–1962 (Independence)*. Metuchen, NJ: Scarecrow Press, 1970. 407 pp.

Bennett, Wycliffe. 'The Jamaican Theatre: A Preliminary Overview'. *Jamaica Journal* 8, nos. 2 and 3 (summer 1974): 3–9.

Carter, Steven R. 'Edgar B. White'. In *Afro-American Writers After 1955: Dramatists and Prose Writers* vol. 38, ed. by Thadious M. Davis and Trudier Harris, 278–83. Detroit, MI: Gale Research, 1985.

Chintoh, Jojo. 'Lennox Brown: A Black Canadian Dramatist'. *Black Images* 1, no. 1 (January 1972): 28–9.

Clark, Vèvè. 'Drama and Disorder'. In *History of Caribbean Literatures in European Languages*, ed. A. James Arnold. Charlottesville, VA: University of Virginia Press, 1992.

Corsbie, Ken. *Theatre in the Caribbean*. With a Foreword by Trevor Rhone. London: Hodder & Stoughton, 1984. 60 pp.

Fido, Elaine. 'Radical Woman: Woman and Theatre in the Anglophone Caribbean'. In *Critical Issues in West Indian Literature*, eds. Erika Sollish Smilowitz and Roberta Quarles Knowles, 33–45. Parkersburg, IA: Caribbean Books, 1984.

Hill, Errol. 'The Emergence of a National Drama in the West Indies'. *Caribbean Quarterly* 18, no. 4 (December 1972): 9–40.

——. 'The First Playwrights of Jamaica'. *Carib* 4 (1986): 16–34.

——. *The Jamaican Stage, 1655–1900: Profile of a Colonial Theatre*. Amherst, MA: University of Massachusetts Press, 1992. 346 pp.

——. 'The Revolutionary Tradition in Black Drama'. *Theatre Journal* 38, no. 4 (December 1986): 408–26.

Institute of Jamaica. *A Guide to Cultural Policy Development in the Caribbean*. Washington, DC: Organization of American States, 1984– .

John, Hans-Rainer. 'Sozialistisches Theater in der Karibik'. [Socialist theatre in the Caribbean]. *Theaterwork* 37, no. 5. (May 1982): 51–7.

Johnston, Robert A. *The Theater of Belize*. North Quincy, MA: Christopher Publishing House, 1973. 96 pp.

Nettleford, Rex. *Caribbean Cultural Identity: The Case of Jamaica. An Essay in Cultural Dynamics*. Los Angeles: University of California Press, 1978. 239 pp.

——. *Dance Jamaica: Cultural Definition and Artistic Discovery. The National Dance Theatre Company of Jamaica, 1962–83*. New York: Grove Press, 1986. 317 pp.

——. *Roots and Rhythms: Jamaica's National Dance Theatre*. Photographs by María La Yacona. London: André Deutsch, 1969. 127 pp.

Nunley, John Wallace, and Judith Bettelheim. *Caribbean Festival Arts: Each and Every Bit of Difference*. Seattle, WA/London: University of Washington Press/St Louis Art Museum, 1988. 218 pp.

Omotoso, Kole. *The Theatrical into Theatre: A Study of Drama and Theatre in the English-Speaking Caribbean*. London: New Beacon Books, 1982. 173 pp.

Pearn, J.C. *Poetry as a Performing Art in the English-Speaking Caribbean*. Sheffield, UK: University of Sheffield, 1986.

Stone, Judy. *Studies in West Indian Literature: Theatre*. London: Macmillan, 1994. 272 pp.

Waters, Harold A. *Théâtre noir: encyclopédie des pièces écrites en français par des auteurs noirs*. [Black theatre: Encyclopedia of plays written in French by black authors]. Washington, DC: Three Continents Press, 1988. 296 pp.

COSTA RICA

Named by Columbus in 1502 for the many gold ornaments worn by the people he encountered there, Costa Rica (rich coast) is a small Central American republic bounded on the north by Nicaragua, on the south by Panamá, on the east by the Caribbean Sea and on the west by the Pacific Ocean; its area is 51,000 square kilometres (20,000 square miles). The majority of the country's 3 million people (1990) lives on the high central plateau; San José is the capital. Just under 50 per cent of the population are of either full or mixed native Indian descent, nearly 48 per cent are of European descent and 3 per cent are black.

One of many early colonies of Spain in the region, Costa Rica was long part of the Spanish Captaincy-General, a territorial subdivision of the Spanish colonial administration, with head-quarters in Guatemala City. After achieving independence in 1821, Costa Rica and the rest of Central America (with the exception of Panamá, which remained part of Colombia) were annexed to México. In 1823, Costa Rica, Guatemala, Honduras, El Salvador and Nicaragua formed the Central American Con-federation. In 1838 the confederation dissolved and Costa Rica became a fully independent state.

Because the country did not experience the phenomenon of large holdings of land by a small number of people, as occurred in many other Latin American countries, a democratic social system was established early on. In the 1990s, for example, Costa Rica boasted the lowest illit-eracy rate in the western hemisphere.

No studies have been done on indigenous the-atrical forms but it is safe to assume that local dances, rituals and events including music existed in Costa Rica from the earliest days. From the eighteenth until the mid-twentieth

century, theatre in Costa Rica was, however, essentially a colonial artifact with visiting com-panies, mainly from Spain and Argentina, dic-tating the theatrical repertoire. The earliest Spanish actors appeared in the country in 1722. Italian-style proscenium playhouses began to be built in 1837.

At the beginning of the twentieth century, when San José was still a village, it nevertheless boasted a 900-seat theatre – the Teatro Nacional, built in 1897 in the Italian rococo style. All foreign companies and national groups performed there. All worked in the same declamatory and highly gestural style. As well, there were other spaces – the 600-seat Variedades, the 1,200-seat Raventós, the 660-seat Adela and the 800-seat América.

Middle- and upper-class audiences tended to frequent the Teatro Nacional most often, and Spanish companies such as the Compañía de Jacinto Benavente staged full seasons of plays there. The same audience, however, did not generally frequent those theatres that staged local farces (several were written between 1900 and 1930).

Until about 1950, most Costa Rican authors tended to write in the Spanish *costumbrista* (featuring local manners and customs) style with its emphasis on local costume and colour, or in the European well-made-play style of the late nineteenth century. By the early 1950s, other styles were added including German expres-sionism, Theatre of the Absurd, documentary and even Artaud-influenced experimentation. Despite such writing and despite a developing theatre public and a relatively large number of theatre groups, what was clearly missing from the mix was a connection to national issues and concerns.

Several important events occurred in the

1950s that marked a genuine transition for Costa Rica's theatre. The first was the emergence of a number of young directors, some of whom – Daniel Gallegos (b. 1930), for example – had recently returned from extended periods of study abroad. Gallegos worked at the Actors Studio in New York in 1961, studying the ideas of the Russian teacher and director Konstantin Stanislavski with Elia Kazan and Lee Strasberg. Along with Alfredo Sancho (b. 1924), Lucio Ranucci (b. 1925) and Lenín Garrido (1925–93), Gallegos began training actors in this style and began staging small productions, which immediately attracted enthusiastic audiences.

Given this interest, the University of Costa Rica and several other small groups opened three new theatres in San José by the mid-1950s, each seating no more than 100. Performances were staged of plays not seen before in Costa Rica, such as the works of Chekhov, García Lorca, Camus, Sartre, Ionesco, Pirandello, Betti, Williams, Miller, Shaw and Priestley, among others. It was not long before local dramatists wanted their own voices to be heard.

Theatre history and theatre appreciation classes at the University of Costa Rica further added to this new interest and drama courses were brought in to the curriculum in high schools. Audiences also increased dramatically from 1950 to 1970 and this encouraged government institutions further to promote professional training for actors, directors, playwrights and technicians, as well as to sponsor the creation of new theatre spaces.

By 1970, the idea of a theatre that connected directly to communities began to develop. The university was again among the first to organize a programme of performances that could be brought into communities and neighbourhoods. Spanish-born Carlos Suárez Radillo (b. 1919) was hired to develop this work and one of his first acts was to call on national playwrights to create pieces that might be appropriate for the programme: plays for a public that might never have seen theatre before, plays that would be easy to stage and tour.

The first one chosen for this new programme was *Las fisgonas de Paso Ancho* (*The Snoopers of Paso Ancho*, 1971) by Samuel Rovinski (b. 1932). Directed by the Argentine Alfredo Catania (b. 1934), the new Teatro Universitario company began touring the play through neighbourhoods in San José and subsequently into the provinces. In less than a year, the production was seen by some 30,000

people. The Teatro Universitario company – semi-professional – soon followed this success with other scripts by both national and foreign authors.

In 1971, the Ministry of Culture created a second major group – the Compañía Nacional de Teatro (National Theatre Company), which performed seasons in San José and toured across the country. Two independent groups formed during this same period were La Carpa (Big Top) in 1978 and Tierranegra (Black Earth) in 1973.

As audiences increased fifteen-fold, subsidy kept the tickets affordable, generally less than the cost of films. Plays were usually topical and most involved post-performance forums, which were well attended. This emergence of a socially based popular theatre was strengthened in the late 1970s by the arrival of a number of other Latin American professional theatre artists, many in exile from Uruguay, Chile, El Salvador and Argentina.

Alejandro Sieveking (b. 1934), Bélgica Castro (b. 1921) and Lucho Barahona (b. 1941) – all Chilean expatriates – founded the Teatro del Ángel (Angel Theatre), named after a company they had worked with in Chile. Salvadoran refugees built the Teatro de la Calle 15 (15th Street Theatre).

Through the 1980s, a number of additional theatrical spaces were created, including a 100-seat studio theatre called the Joaquín Vargas Calvo for the Teatro Nacional and the large Melico Salazar. The Salazar was rebuilt out of a movie house in 1981, seats 900 and is used by various companies on a rental basis.

By the end of the 1980s, economic problems had set in across the country and the government, among other measures, reduced grants for the numerous independent groups that were operating. Only the Compañía Nacional de Teatro and the Taller Nacional de Teatro (National Theatre Workshop) retained sufficient funding to continue.

Across the board, ticket prices rose and audiences decreased. Theatre once again became a privileged activity for the middle and upper classes, the groups that could afford the relatively high prices. The result was greater dependence on private sponsorship and box-office receipts, which translated on stage into the production of mostly light entertainment that would stir little controversy. Artistically, quality also declined and many of the South American artists who had contributed significantly to the general well-being of Costa Rica's

Alfredo Catania's 1975 Compañía Nacional de Teatro production of Joaquín Gutiérrez's *Puerto Limón*, designed by Lenín Garrido.
Photo: Javier Guerrero.

socially rooted theatre simply left. These were often the same actors, directors and writers whose impact had been so enormous in helping to change the perception of Costa Rica's own artists from 'bohemians' into respected theatre workers.

The 1990s began with another large reduc-tion in government support for theatre activity, smaller audiences and disillusionment among many groups. By 1994, theatre was undergoing a serious economic crisis that could be resolved only by further government action in an effort to restore lost audiences.

Structure of the National Theatre Community

Virtually all of Costa Rica's professional theatre activity is concentrated in San José. Theatre activity in the other six provinces has generally been limited to amateur companies (many of which are sustained by government or university funds) and touring professional groups from the capital. Amateur activity blossomed in the early 1970s when some forty-five secondary school theatre groups were formed along with six in factories and sixteen more in various rural communities.

The Ministry of Culture, Youth and Sports has prime responsibility for funding national theatre activity.

Approximately seven professional companies operate in the capital at any given time, ranging from the Compañía Nacional de Teatro on the one hand to an itinerant tent theatre on the other. A number of smaller companies produce shows on a less regular basis.

The Compañía Nacional de Teatro receives a guaranteed grant from the Ministry of Culture each year equal to an annual percentage of the ministry's budget. Between its founding in 1971 and 1986, it had a permanent company; from 1987 onward, artists were hired on a show-by-show basis.

The Asociación Cultural Costarricense de Trabajadores del Teatro (Costa Rican Association of Theatre Workers, founded 1990) has in its ranks directors, actors, playwrights and technicians. Its mandate is to defend their interests although it does not get involved in the hiring process. No theatre company or group ever pays permanent salaries. Normally, they hire actors on a contract basis and pay the standard fee: for a month of rehearsals and thirty performances directors are paid the equivalent of approximately US$2,000 (1992), and actors US$1,200.

Playwrights are paid 10 per cent of box-office receipts as a copyright fee. The average cost for a production with six actors, modest stage design and costumes (based on a month of rehearsal and thirty days of performance) would be equal to approximately US$15,000.

The theatre festival Grano de Oro (Golden Grain) is held every December in the capital, under the auspices of the municipality of San José. Amateur groups present short plays by national and international authors. Prizes are awarded for best production, best director, best actor and best actress. The Festival Internacional de Teatro (International Theatre Festival) was held in 1989; since 1992 a Festival Internacional de las Artes (International Festival of the Arts) has been held.

The Ministry of Culture also awards National Prizes in Theatre – along with literature, visual arts, music, science and journalism – for best play, best company, best director, best actors and best stage designer.

Artistic Profile

Companies

Of the regularly producing theatre companies in Costa Rica, the Compañía Nacional de Teatro is the most highly subsidized. According to the terms of its annual grant from the Ministry of Culture, it must produce at least four plays each season in the capital, one of which must be by a Costa Rican playwright, one by a writer from another Latin American country, one a recognized classic and one a non-Latin American contemporary play. Based at the 350-seat Sala de la Compañía (Theatre of the Company) in San José but using other halls as well, the company tours annually and, between January and April each year, restages successful productions from its previous season.

The oldest continuing theatre company in the country is the Teatro Universitario based at the University of Costa Rica's San José campus. A professional company performing in the university's 150-seat theatre, it is linked to both the university's Social Action Office and the School of Dramatic Arts. The company uses mainly student actors and has a regular administrative and technical staff. Part of its revenue comes directly from the university although it receives dona-

tions from other bodies as well. Its repertoire consists of material from various periods and genres selected by its board of directors.

Operating out of the 120-seat Teatro Arlequín (Harlequin Theatre) in San José, the Teatro Tiempo (Time Theatre) performed contemporary productions, and operated on box-office revenue, private donations and a small subsidy from the Ministry of Culture. It had its major successes with the works of Latin American playwrights such as Dragún, Gorostiza, Gené, Cossa, Cuzzani, Discépolo, Gentile, Cabrujas, Talesnik, Chocrón and Carballido. The company disbanded in 1989.

The Teatro del Ángel, founded in 1975, has its own 200-seat theatre and, like most groups, operates on a combination of box-office revenue, private donations and small government grants. During its early life, the company was able to present world classics, thanks to the financial support of government institutions. In the 1990s the company depended exclusively on box-office revenue and therefore tended towards popular light comedies.

Other regularly producing companies in the capital have included La Carpa, founded in 1978 by Argentine actor and director Alfredo

Catania, a proponent of theatre for social action; Teatro La Colina (Hill Theatre), which produced almost exclusively Latin American plays in its 150-seat theatre; and the Grupo 56, which tended to do plays of social and historic content in the 130-seat Teatro de la Calle 15. At any given time, a number of similar-sized independent theatres also operate in the capital. The Teatro La Comedia (with 200 seats), the Teatro Eugene O'Neill (250 seats) and the Teatro La Máscara (200 seats) all combine serious dramas and commercial comedies. In February 1994 two theatres opened: the FANAL (250 seats) and the 1887 (150 seats), in the Centro Nacional de Cultura. The former is dedicated to theatre and the latter to dance, and both are run by the Ministry of Culture.

Dramaturgy

Costa Rican playwrights have never been able to survive solely on their dramatic activities. Since World War II, three writers stand out, however, for their consistent dramatic output and ongoing work in the theatre – Alberto Cañas (b. 1920), Daniel Gallegos and Samuel Rovinski.

One of Costa Rica's most prolific writers with more than a dozen plays to his credit, Cañas is a novelist and playwright and, from 1970 to 1974, was the country's first Minister of Culture. As minister, he did much to support national indigenous theatre activities. A journalist for a time as well as a storyteller, a number of his outstanding early plays, such as El luto robado (Stolen Mourning, 1962), Uvieta (1970) and La Segua (The Follower, 1971), show a Pirandellian influence, while some of his later plays, such as Ni mi casa es ya mi casa (My House Is No Longer My Home, 1982), deal with social and economic issues. La Segua, for example, is based on a popular myth about a creature with a horse-like face that takes the shape of a beautiful woman who follows men at night. If the man turns to look at her, the grotesque face he sees drives him mad. Using such popular myths, Cañas brought to the Costa Rican stage the everyday language spoken in both the city and the country.

Gallegos, author of six produced plays, is also the founder of the School of Dramatic Arts at the University of Costa Rica and a former director of the Teatro Universitario. As a playwright, Gallegos writes in an urban cosmopolitan style. His play about the death of God, La colina (The Hill, 1968), caused a national scandal when it was produced by the Teatro Arlequín. In addition to La colina, his major works include Los profanos (The Profane, 1960), Ese algo de Dávalos (Something About Dávalos, 1964) and En el séptimo círculo (In the Seventh Circle, 1982), which deals with contemporary violence.

The plays of Samuel Rovinski tend to deal with the problems of individual existence within an alienated society, what he has called 'the dramatization of the immediate'. In his eleven plays, as well as in his novels, short stories, film scripts and essays, he has covered a wide range of social and political issues. His works have been produced most often by the Compañía Nacional de Teatro and tend to be documentary and Brechtian in style. His major plays include Un modelo para Rosaura (A Model for Rosaura, 1975), for which he won an Editorial Costa Rica Award; Las fisgonas de Paso Ancho, a social satire produced by the Teatro Universitario in 1971 and later turned into a television mini-series; Gulliver dormido (Sleeping Gulliver, 1981); and El martirio del pastor (Martyrdom of the Pastor, 1987), a play about the life and assassination of the popular Salvadoran activist Archbishop Oscar Arnulfo Romero.

A number of others have written on a more occasional basis. These include Antonio Yglesias (b. 1943), author of several plays including Las hormigas (The Ants, 1970) and Pinocchio Rey (Pinocchio Rex, 1973), a political allegory; Joaquín Gutiérrez (b. 1918), who has had two novels adapted for the stage – Puerto Limón (Limón Harbour, 1975) and Murámonos Federico (Let's Die, Federico, 1979); and Olga Marta Barrantes (b. 1938), whose play La familia Mora (The Mora Family, 1974) had a successful national tour when it was produced by the Compañía Nacional de Teatro.

Among the dramatists establishing themselves in the 1980s were the actor Víctor Valdelomar (b. 1957), whose play Como semilla de coyol (Like a Coyol Seed, 1982) won a national playwriting prize; Miguel Rojas (b. 1952), author of Los nublados del día (Cloudy Day, 1985), a historical piece about national independence; Jorge Arroyo (b. 1959), also an actor, who wrote in a neo-costumbrista style in such works as El ánima sola de Chico Muñoz (The Lonely Soul of Chico Muñoz, 1985) and La chupeta electrónica (The Electronic Sucker, 1986), a satire on commercial television; Guillermo Arriaga (b. 1960), author of

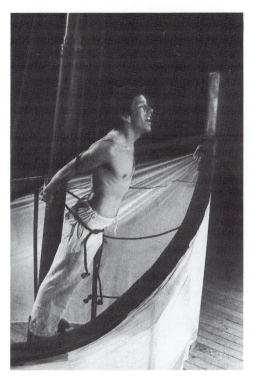

Jean Moulaert's 1990 Compañía Nacional de
Teatro production of Melvin Méndez's *The
Boat Man*, designed by Rafa Hernández.
Photo: Javier Guerrero.

Directors, Directing and Production Styles

From the 1950s on, Costa Rican theatre tended
to follow the Stanislavski system and a
tremendous number of productions were staged
in this style. The key directors working this way
were Daniel Gallegos, Lucio Ranucci, Jean
Moulaert (b. 1930) and Mexican-born Lenín
Garrido. A trained architect, Garrido has staged
all the plays of Alberto Cañas, as well as works
by Lope de Vega, García Lorca, Molière,
Jonson, Frisch, Camus, Hellman, Brecht and
Albee.

By the 1970s, a number of directors from
abroad, particularly the Argentine brothers
Carlos (b. 1932) and Alfredo Catania, and
Chileans Alejandro Sieveking and Lucho Barahona, had consolidated and developed the style
further. Alfredo Catania moved to Costa Rica in
1968. From 1969 to 1972 he worked as an
acting teacher at the School of Dramatic Arts at
the University of Costa Rica. Subsequently, he
became artistic director of Teatro Universitario

Inquilino (*The Tenant*, 1984) and *Última
noticia* (*Last News*, 1984), which also won the
national playwriting prize; Melvin Méndez (b.
1958), author of *Eva, sol y sombra* (*Eva and the
Football*, 1989), *El resucitado* (*The Resur-
rected*, 1987) and *El hombre de la barca* (*The
Boat Man*, 1990); and Juan Fernando Cerdas
(1950), who wrote a new version of the Joan of
Arc story, *Juana de Arco* (1986), and a play
about the Costa Rican filibuster war of the
1850s, *El 56* (1984).

In general terms, Costa Rican playwrights
have experimented with a wide range of theatre
styles, encompassing everything from politics
and realism to documentary. Playwrights normally offer their work to whatever group will
accept it, or present it in playwriting contests.
Only rarely are plays commissioned by either
independent groups or the Compañía Nacional
de Teatro. Normally, once the playwright has
offered the play to a group, the writer does not
have much involvement in the development of
the production.

María Bonilla's 1983 Compañía Nacional de
Teatro production of Ricardo Fernández
Guardia's *Magdalena*, designed by Mario
Alvarez.
Photo: Javier Guerrero.

(1971–2) and of the Compañía Nacional de Teatro as well as general director of the Ministry of Culture (1982–6), where he strongly supported the national popular theatre movement.

From 1975, the most important influence for younger directors became the Brechtian-styled work of the Uruguayan director Atahualpa del Cioppo. A number of Costa Ricans also returned from abroad at this time determined to apply it to the developing national dramaturgy. Among those whose Brecht-influenced productions were important during the late 1970s and 1980s were Alejandra Gutiérrez (b. 1943), who studied in Poland; Virginia Grütter (b. 1934), who trained with the Berliner Ensemble; Jaime Hernández (b. 1955), trained in the United States; Remberto Chaves (b. 1947), trained in the Soviet Union; Luis Carlos Vásquez (b. 1951), who trained in Colombia and tends to emphasize the visual in his work; and María Bonilla (b. 1954), who trained in France.

In the 1990s, three other directors came to prominence – Manuel Ruiz (b. 1957) from the University of Costa Rica, Eugenia Chaverri (b. 1943) and Eduardo Zúñiga (b. 1952).

Foreign influences have long been a part of Costa Rican theatre and directing is no exception. Among the important directors from abroad who have worked in Costa Rica and significantly influenced its theatre, aside from del Cioppo, are Esteban Polls and José Tamayo from Spain; Júver Salcedo, Amanecer Dotta and Héctor Vidal from Uruguay; Oscar Fessler from Argentina; Santiago García from Colombia; William Oliver from the United States and Nicholas Baker from England.

Many important Costa Rican performers have also come from abroad, often as refugees from other Latin American countries. Particularly important here has been the influence from Chile, Argentina and Uruguay.

Music Theatre
Dance Theatre

Music for productions is normally done by young composers who have received their basic training with the Orquesta Sinfónica Juvenil (Youth Symphony Orchestra, founded in 1971) and who have gone abroad for further specialized training. These young composers work closely with theatre directors from the beginning of rehearsals. Some of them also compose for films, concert halls and television commercials.

In the 1990s, the two major centres for music training in the country were the Escuela de Artes Musicales (School of Music Art) at the University of Costa Rica and the Orquesta Sinfónica Juvenil.

The Compañía Lírica Nacional presents one opera per year at either the Teatro Nacional or the Teatro Melico Salazar. In 1992, the Compañía Nacional de Teatro premièred a comic opera, Gobierno de alcoba (Government Bedroom), by the young composer Carlos Castro (b. 1963), with a libretto by Lenín Garrido, who also directed. The work was based on a one-act play of the same name by Samuel Rovinski. The Conservatorio Castella has also presented Joseph and His Amazing Tech-nicolour Dreamcoat (1993) by Andrew Lloyd Webber and Tim Rice.

Several professional modern dance companies were established in Costa Rica in the 1970s. The most important were the Compañía Nacional de Danza (National Dance Company), Danza Universitaria (University Dance) at the University of Costa Rica, Compañía de Cámara Danza UNA at the National University, and the independent group Losdenmédium. The development and practice of modern dance in Costa Rica has been sponsored by the Ministry of Culture, Youth and Sports, the National University and the University of Costa Rica. The Teatro Nacional itself followed in the steps of these organizations by sponsoring foreign dance masters to come to teach in Costa Rica, an activity that is helping develop a new generation of Costa Rican choreographers.

In the early 1990s some of the most successful theatre performances have been those based on narrative tableaux linked through dance.

A new ballet school, organized with the assistance of the Bolshoi Ballet in Moscow, began training dancers in 1994.

The Compañía de Cámara Danza UNA in 1990.

Theatre for Young Audiences
Puppet Theatre

In Costa Rica there is no theatre for young audiences *per se*. Audiences are generally young and many in the 13 to 25 age group regularly attend.

Theatre for children therefore is not a regular activity for professional theatre companies. Most, however, do offer plays for children on weekends. As well, the Ministry of Public Education uses theatre as a didactic tool in its work in the schools and plays are seen regularly.

There is, however, a long tradition of folk puppetry in Costa Rica. In the presentations at outdoor fairs and other public events, one can trace the roots of the form back to Medieval Mystery and Miracle plays and the *commedia dell'arte* through such characters as the Devil, Death and Pantalone (Don Pantaleón).

The major figure in the development of modern Costa Rican puppetry and modern Costa Rican children's theatre was Argentine-born Juan Enrique Acuña (1915–88). In 1968,

Acuña founded the Moderno Teatro de Muñecos (Modern Puppet Theatre), which began to perform a varied repertoire for both children and adults. The activities of this theatre led to the founding of several other groups including one at the University of Costa Rica called the Teatro Universitario de Títeres (University Puppet Theatre).

Acuña's work involved the use of puppets of various types, including Chinese coloured shadow-puppets and Javanese puppets. Productions such as *El lagartijo travieso* (*The Naughty Little Crocodile*, 1968) and *El músico y el león* (*The Musician and the Lion*, 1971) often combined the use of music, song and mime.

Acuña's Moderno Teatro de Muñecos has been the only puppet company in Costa Rica able to provide audiences with regular seasons. The company has offered more than forty seasons in San José and has performed widely across the country.

Acuña later taught at the university and trained an important group of professionals who in the 1980s and 1990s kept up a steady weekend repertoire of children's plays. Besides building and operating their own puppets, these puppeteers write their own plays, sometimes adapted from well-known national plays. Acuña also wrote a major book, *Teatro de títeres y marionetas (Puppet and Marionette Theatre)*, on the history and pedagogy of puppet theatre.

Design
Theatre Space and Architecture

The University of Costa Rica and the National University are the only institutions that offer courses in scene design, theatre architecture and theatre technology as part of the general theatre programme.

With the exception of the outstanding scene designer David Vargas (b. 1943), who has a doctorate in theatre architecture and design from the University of Kansas, all other Costa Rican designers have been trained simply by working in the profession. Two other important Costa Rican designers are Pilar Quirós (b. 1942) and Daniel Torrijano (b. 1954). Quirós has distinguished herself with works of realism and of theatrical reality. Torrijano tends to produce avant-garde designs.

Pilar Quirós's design for the 1987 Compañía Nacional de Teatro production of Samuel Rovinski's *Martyrdom of the Pastor*, directed by Alfredo Catania.
Photo: Javier Guerrero.

The three most important and best equipped theatre spaces are the Teatro Nacional, the Teatro Eugene O'Neill and the Teatro Melico Salazar. Most important productions are mounted at the Compañía Nacional de Teatro's Teatro de la Aduana (Customs House Theatre), and in independent spaces such as the National Museum's Teatro al Aire Libre (Open Air Theatre).

Training

There are three important institutions offering training for the theatre in Costa Rica: the Escuela de Artes Dramáticas (School of Dramatic Arts) at the University of Costa Rica, the independent Taller Nacional de Teatro (National Theatre Workshop) in San José, and the Escuela de Artes Escénicas (School of Stage Arts) at the Universidad Nacional at Heredia. There are also a number of private studios and schools that offer classes in acting and playwriting.

Supported by the Ministry of Culture, the Taller Nacional de Teatro was created with a double function: to educate and to develop a social role for the theatre. It offers programmes for both actors and drama teachers and conducts a series of regular theatre workshops. The Taller Nacional also acts as an advisory body to education authorities on the teaching of drama in primary schools and has been involved in the organization of many new theatre companies, especially outside of the capital. Some 19 per cent of its graduates have become professional actors with another 27 per cent doing theatre work within communities and workplaces. About 9 per cent of the Taller Nacional's graduates are employed by the Ministry of Culture on graduation.

The Escuela de Artes Dramáticas at the University of Costa Rica was created in 1969 as part of the arts and letters programme of the Faculty of Fine Arts. Beginning in 1980, for several years it offered a three-year diploma programme in performance and directing. Two additional years of study lead to the *Bachillerato* (Bachelor's degree) in dramatic arts. Students can obtain a *Licenciatura* (certificate) by taking additional courses in theatre research and passing an oral examination. In 1985, the school began offering short courses in acting, directing, design, costume design and playwriting.

The Escuela de Artes Escénicas at Heredia was founded in 1974 and has a similar programme to that at the University of Costa Rica.

Criticism, Scholarship and Publishing

The leading scholarly theatre publication in Costa Rica is the biannual journal *Escena* (*Stage*), published by the Teatro Universitario at the University of Costa Rica since 1978. It publishes essays on historical and current research, and occasionally scripts. For the most part, plays and books on theatre are published by the national publishing house, Editorial Costa Rica. From time to time, theatre materials are published by the companies themselves, for example the Compañía Nacional de Teatro, by the Ministry of Culture, or by the Editorial Universitaria Centroamericana (University Publishing House of Central America).

The daily newspapers provide basic coverage of theatre openings and significant theatrical events as does the weekly newspaper at the University of Costa Rica. Theatre reviews appear regularly in these same newspapers.

One of the country's most important critics is Alberto Cañas, who has written widely on both theatre and film. A co-founder of the publishing house Editorial Costa Rica (1960), he was involved in the creation of the Escuela de Comunicación Colectiva (School of Mass Communication, 1968) at the University of Costa Rica. Another major critic is Andrés Sáenz, who writes for the country's leading newspaper, *La Nación* (*The Nation*).

Samuel Rovinski
Translated by Mayte Gómez

Further Reading

Acuña, Juan Enrique. 'Teatro de títeres y marionetas'. [Puppet and marionette theatre]. PhD dissertation, Escuela de Artes Dramáticas, Universidad de Costa Rica in San José, 1980. 175 pp.

Barrantes, Olga Marta. 'Antología del teatro costarricense'. [Anthology of Costa Rican theatre]. PhD dissertation, Escuela de Artes Dramáticas, University of Costa Rica in San José, 1978.

Borges, Fernando. *Teatros de Costa Rica*. [Theatres of Costa Rica]. San José: Editorial Costa Rica, 1980. 116 pp.

Cañas, Alberto. 'Teatro costarricense en el teatro costarricense'. [Costa Rican theatre in the Costa Rican theatre scene]. *Escena Costa Rica* 2, no. 4 (1980): 13–14.

Capella Segreda, Yolanda. 'El teatro en Costa Rica'. [Theatre in Costa Rica]. *Memoria de la Academia de Geografía e Historia de Costa Rica* 1, no. 3. (June 1949): 11–17.

Fernández, Guido. *Los caminos del teatro en Costa Rica*. [Paths of the Costa Rican theatre]. San José: Editorial Universitaria Centroamericana, 1977. 183 pp.

Garrido, Lenín. *La imagen teatral*. [The theatrical image]. San José: Editorial Costa Rica, 1973. 173 pp.

Herzfield, Anita, and Teresa Cajiao. *El teatro de hoy en Costa Rica: perspectiva crítica y antológica*. [Theatre in Costa Rica today: Anthology and critical analysis]. San José: Editorial Costa Rica, 1978. 268 pp.

Rovinski, Samuel. *Dramatización de lo inmediato*. [Dramatization of the immediate]. San José: Compañía Nacional de Teatro, 1992.

Sáenz, Andrés. *La comedia es cosa seria*. [Comedy is a serious thing]. San José: Ministerio de Cultura, 1985. 182 pp.

Sandoval de Fonseca, Virginia. *Resumen de literatura costarricense*. [An overview of Costa Rican literature]. San José: Editorial Costa Rica, 1978.

CUBA

The island of Cuba – the largest in the Caribbean archipelago at 114,000 square kilometres (44,000 square miles) – first came to European attention in 1492 when Christopher Columbus stopped there on his first journey to the Americas. Subsequently conquered and settled by Spain in the sixteenth century, Cuba's strategic location helped it become the centre of military expeditions in the region and a crucial point of departure for all shipments sent back to Spain.

As Cuba's indigenous population decreased, the Spanish began to import African slaves to help with the production of sugar cane and Cuba quickly became the largest producer of sugar in the world. The economy of the country expanded further through the production of coffee and tobacco, the raising of cattle and the construction of military vessels.

By the beginning of the nineteenth century, an independence movement began to grow with the rebellion of the *criollos* (people of Spanish ancestry born in the Americas) and *cimarrones* (local slaves). In 1868, Carlos Manuel de Céspedes (1819–73) led Cuba into a full war of independence that ended only in 1878 with the Treaty of Zanjón. Through this treaty, a number of political freedoms were gained including the abolition of slavery.

José Martí (1853–95) was a dominant national figure during the last part of the century both producing extensive literary and political works and reorganizing Cuban forces in exile. With the founding of the Cuban Revolutionary Party under Martí's leadership and inspiration, Cuba resumed its war of independence with Spain in 1895. When the United States intervened to aid Cuba and defeat Spain, it took advantage of the situation to occupy the country itself. This US occupation ensured the neo-colonial character of the new republic, which was proclaimed on 20 May 1902.

Subsequent governments were run by a succession of corrupt leaders and dictatorships, which led to more revolutions and a new occupation by the United States from 1906 to 1909. Once again, the possibility of real Cuban independence and democracy was frustrated.

The new colonial state did not support the development of culture either. It was thanks only to the efforts of a small group of intellectuals that Cuban art and literature were kept alive and in contact with other artists and intellectuals, particularly in the United States and Europe.

With the overthrow of the dictator Gerardo Machado (1871–1939) in 1933, Cuba entered a period of chaos and instability that lasted until 1940, the year of the proclamation of a new constitution. In 1952, Fulgencio Batista (1901–73) led still another military rebellion and became dictator. This resulted in further armed resistance headed by a young lawyer named Fidel Castro (b. 1926) beginning in 1953. The guerrilla war led by Castro culminated in a rebel victory on 1 January 1959.

From this date, the country and its culture were totally transformed. In accordance with Castro's new socialist philosophy, the means of production, both Cuban and US, were nationalized. The economy was taken over by the state, which also began to support recognized forms of cultural activity. Under the new regime, Cuban artists began to find resources to produce their work. With the state now providing generous amounts of money to arts and culture as well as to education, illiteracy was virtually eradicated and free education at all levels began to ensure the basis for a new national and popular culture for Cuba's 11 million people.

In 1961 the Consejo Nacional de Cultura (National Council for Culture) was formed specifically to support artistic and cultural institutions, research centres and art schools, the publication of mass editions of books, and cultural exchanges through festivals and forums.

Cuban theatre itself also sprang from this same slow and complex search for a national identity. In 1492, when the European and Native American cultures met, the Spanish observed *areítos* (theatricalized rituals involving mime, song and dance) as popular artistic expressions of the indigenous culture.

The term *areíto* was first used in a letter to the pope in 1493 and seems to be a variation on the local word *aririn* (to recite). In other areas of the Caribbean the equivalent term is *batocos*. Used as part of fertility or other communal rituals, the *areíto* ceremony was led by a *tequina* (master), who used makeup, wooden drums, trumpets, maracas, flutes and bells in singing, dancing or miming stories from the past. The *areítos* were

forbidden by the Spanish in 1512 and with their banning, Cuban theatre quickly began to follow Spanish dramaturgy.

The first Cuban play in the Spanish style was *El príncipe jardinero y fingido Cloridano* (*The Gardener Prince and Imagined Cloridano*), written by Santiago Pita y Borroto (d. 1755) and published in Seville between 1730 and 1733. More nationalistic concepts were introduced into the theatre by Francisco Covarrubias (1755–1850), a performer and playwright who many still regard as the father of Cuban theatre. An excellent actor, Covarrubias created the popular *negrito* (black boy) role, one of the pillars of Cuban popular theatre, along with the mulatto (of mixed European and black ancestry) and the Galicían (from Galicia, Spain), as early as 1812. The *negrito* was not a specific character but a general type and was always represented by a white man whose face was painted black and who imitated the manners of a black man with a satirical and even dis-

Areítos, the Cuban aboriginal expression of dance, singing and mime.
Photo: Archivo Rine Leal.

criminatory intention. Covarrubias used the *negrito* in a number of *sainetes* (one-act farcical sketches), which featured music, everyday speech and recognizable Cuban characters and dealt with current domestic problems. Though Covarrubias's style and subjects are well known, the scripts themselves have unfortunately all been lost.

The romantic period produced Cuba's first great dramatists: José María Heredia (1803–39), José Jacinto Milanés (1814–63) and Gertrudis Gómez de Avellaneda (1814–73). Gómez's work was also staged and published with great success in Madrid. However, colonial repression and censorship of the theatre impeded the best impulses of the romantics, producing an eclectic product in which individual rebellion was reconciled with Spanish neo-classicism.

Cuban theatrical tradition became firmly established, however, through the plays of Joaquín Lorenzo Luaces (1826–67), a writer largely neglected in his time. His work is a clear expression of a national identity as well as a critique of colonialism and an attack on foreign fashions. It was only in the Castro period that his work began to be appreciated.

Scant months before the onset of the 1868–78 War of Independence, the tradition of the *bufos habaneros* (Havana buffoons) was born, a primary exponent of indigenous popular theatre at a time of tense relations with Madrid. The *bufos habaneros* ridiculed Spanish melodramas and *zarzuelas* (Spanish-style musical comedies) of the time by using recognizable situations from daily Cuban life. The earliest performers in this style were amateur actors and popular musicians who were themselves influenced by the Spanish *bufos* of Francisco Arderíus, who was popular in Spain in the mid-1860s. Less than a year after the first *bufo habaneros* group began, nine such groups were operating in Havana. This was the first time that Cuban actors and musicians found themselves able to earn a living from their work in theatre.

During the War of Independence, *bufos habaneros* were prohibited but returned to the stage as *bufos de Salas*, named after director Miguel Salas (1844–96). They used this name until 1900. Most of their scripts have been lost. The style attained a literary quality in the works of Raimundo Cabrera (1852–1923), and Ignacio Sarachaga (1852–1900), the latter called the Labiche of the buffoon genre.

During the period when the *bufos habaneros* were banned, a repertoire of 'independence plays' began to appear in their place starting with the work of José Martí. Martí modified the treatment of the *negrito* character, moving him from buffoon to dramatic hero and reaffirming his social identity. A new theatrical alternative began to emerge in contradiction to the white, slave-based vision that produced the *negrito*. In processions, ceremonies, liturgical dances, *diablitos* (devil myths) and religious initiations, it offered 'another' theatre in opposition to that of the dominant class.

The *diablitos* were particularly important in this regard as allegorical representations of the different African cultures that the slave system had brought to Cuba. The dances and ceremonies of the *diablitos* were used in celebrations, purification and fertility rites. One of the best known dances – the *írime abakuá* or *ñáñigo* – is part of a very powerful dramatic representation that portrays an ancestral myth of totemic

Diablitos, the magical representation of Afro-Cuban spirits.
Photo: Archivo Rine Leal.

sacrifice and the change from a matriarchal society to a patriarchy. Such *diablitos*, which Fernando Ortiz (1881–1969) has compared in structure and form to Greek tragedy, remained as part of Cuban folklore in carnival and folk performances.

At the time of Cuba's formal independence from Spain in 1902, its theatre ranged from popular culture to high culture, symbolized by the work of the popular Alhambra Theatre (opened in 1900) and by José Antonio Ramos (1885–1946) respectively. On to the stage of the Alhambra came a series of writers, actors and composers, headed by Federico Villoch (1868–1954), author of 412 works, most of which have been lost. Also found at the Alhambra was the composer Jorge Anckermann (1877–1941), with more than 700 theatrical scores to his credit, as well as the actor Regino López (1861–1945), a favourite with audiences for some thirty seasons.

Between 1927 and 1936, this popular Cuban musical tradition continued in the theatre of Ernesto Lecuona (1896–1963), whose work reflects both lyric and *zarzuela* elements. Along with Lecuona, composers such as Gonzalo Roig (1890–1970), Eliseo Grenet (1893–1950), Rodrigo Prats (1909–80) and others created a musical theatre that ranked with the most important in Latin America. The creation of this theatre, supported by the presence of dramatic actors such as Adela Robreño (1840–1920) and Luisa Martínez Casado (1860–1926), as well as by the construction of proscenium theatres in Havana and other principal Cuban cities, produced a rich and varied history.

With the closing of the Alhambra Theatre in 1935, a whole tradition in Cuban theatre ceased, a tradition based on the existence of patrons whose tastes tended towards music-hall burlesque and moralistic melodramas. With the combination of an economic crisis in Cuba, the social failures of the neo-colonial republic, and struggles against the Machado dictatorship, the creation of a national drama that might go beyond the picturesque and anecdotal became all but impossible.

In an attempt to remedy this situation, the Teatro de Arte La Cueva (The Cellar Art Theatre) was formed in 1936 by a group composed of intellectuals and actors. The theatre opened with Luigi Pirandello's *Tonight We Improvise*. This production marked the arrival of a new kind of theatre, one that generally modernized staging and distanced it from 'stars' and nineteenth-century styles. But La Cueva was unable to develop an audience, or to find experienced Cuban playwrights or, alternatively, state support. Within a few months and just five openings, it disappeared.

The seed, however, had been sown, and in 1938 the Teatro Cubano de Selección (Cuban Select Theatre) was born as a vehicle for the production of prize-winning national works selected through official competitions. A new drama finally began to emerge in which experimentation and modern theatrical influences appeared together with a strong social sensibility. The arrival in Cuba of exiled actors from Spain at this time as well as the arrival of refugees from Nazism also began to be felt in the new Cuban theatre.

In 1940, the Academia de Artes Dramáticas de la Escuela Libre de La Habana (ADADEL; Academy of Dramatic Arts of the Free School of Havana) was created, with an approach far removed from the Spanish declamatory tradition. Though it boasted some outstanding professors, it did not survive very long. In 1941, the Teatro Universitario (University Theatre) emerged. It staged open-air productions of world classics, Greek tragedies and contemporary pieces. Credit for its success was due both to the University of Havana for its financial support and to the theatre's director, the Austrian Ludwig Schajowicz, a student of the German director Max Reinhardt. The national struggle against the Batista dictatorship starting in 1952, however, forced the closure of the university. Its theatre did not reopen until after the Castro revolution.

In 1942, the Patronato del Teatro (Theatre Foundation) was established. It would stage 217 productions over the next twenty-five years. The foundation produced the major writers of the day, organized dramatic competitions, awarded prizes to outstanding actors and was vital in the development of Cuban theatre at this time. In 1943, a visit by the French director Louis Jouvet acted as a catalyst for the creation of still another company, Theatralia, but its life was almost as ephemeral as Jouvet's presence.

Finally, in 1945, the Academia de Arte Dramático (ADAD; Academy of Dramatic Art) appeared; it would replace the pioneering ADADEL as the country's major training centre and theatrical company. Organized around the ideas of Modesto Centeno (1912–85), the leading director of the period, the academy offered seventy-four productions in its five years of existence, and produced a valuable contemporary repertoire.

Also in 1944, the Teatro Popular (Popular Theatre) was created, under the direction of Paco Alfonso (1906–89). Closely allied with the growing socialist workers' movement, the Teatro Popular performed widely in factories, public plazas and traditional theatres. In addition, it published magazines and pamphlets, sustaining itself through the voluntary support of workers' unions. The Teatro Popular encouraged the writing of more socially committed drama and staged the work of the first Soviet authors in Cuba: Leonid Leonov and Konstantin Simonov. Political changes in the country, however, accompanied by anti-communist repression, led to the closing of the Teatro Popular in 1945.

In 1947, the Academia Municipal de Artes Dramáticas (Municipal Academy of Dramatic Arts) was organized, with a three-year course of study, which included theatre for children. For the next nineteen years, the academy led an austere and discreet existence, but it trained a generation of actors and offered modest productions. That same year, a magazine, *Prometeo* (*Prometheus*), appeared; one year later it launched its own theatre company with a repertoire based on plays by leading authors of the period. Prometeo was the poorest, most solitary and smallest of Cuban groups, but it was one of the most important contributors to the Cuban stage of the 1950s, thanks to the talent and dedication of its director, Francisco Morín (b. 1918). Still another important group founded at this time was Las Máscaras (The Masks) in 1950. Under the direction of Andrés Castro (b. 1922), it too served as a point of departure for Cuban theatre of the period.

In 1954, the first of a relatively large number of *salitas* (pocket theatres) began offering performances, usually from Thursday to Sunday evenings. Despite their small size, many were immensely popular. Jean-Paul Sartre's *The Respectful Prostitute*, for example, was played over 100 times. By the late 1950s, there were eight *salitas* in Havana ranging in size from 80 to 309 seats.

The first reference to Konstantin Stanislavski's work in Cuba dates back to 1923 when a Cuban journalist interviewed the Russian director during his tour of the United States. In 1952, the Mexican José Gelada offered a practical course on the Stanislavski system. In the late 1950s, the company Nuestro Tiempo (Our Time) began to work with Stanislavski's ideas as its inspiration. In 1958, director Vicente Revuelta (b. 1929) formed his Teatro Estudio (Theatre Studio), which focused on plays by Bertolt Brecht, starting with *Der gute Mensch von Sezuan* (*The Good Person of Setzuan*) in 1959.

With the triumph of the Castro revolution in 1959, socially committed theatre by national writers began to receive strong support from the authorities and quickly became an important expression of national culture. During the seven years of Batista's rule, for example, only forty-one Cuban works were staged and many of those were one-acts; in 1959 alone, however, forty-eight Cuban plays were produced.

Also under Castro, acting became a legitimate profession for the first time with artists suddenly able to dedicate themselves full time to the stage. As well, decentralization became national policy and companies were formed in each provincial capital. Old theatres that had been converted into movie houses were restored to their original function. Among the important ones were the Principal (built in 1850); the Tacón (1838), later called the García Lorca; the Irijoa, later renamed the Martí (1884); the Caridad (1885); and the Milanés (1845).

Within six months of Castro's arrival on the scene, the Teatro Nacional (National Theatre) was created, with five separate sections: theatre, dance, folklore, music and cultural dissemination. The National Council for Culture, founded in 1961, further organized theatrical activity across the country. That same year, Casa de las Américas (House of the Americas) produced its first Festival of Latin American Theatre and instituted an annual prize for playwriting (the Casa de las Américas Prize).

By 1990, Cuban plays represented more than 75 per cent of the country's repertoire. Clearly the Cuban stage had found an audience both in the capital and across the country. From 1959, all these elements – the revolution, the new professionalism of the artist, a positive relationship between actor and spectator, and a new sense of a Cuban cultural identity – transformed Cuban theatre and allowed the creation of ambitious projects and even occasional experiments, although these were limited. Performers also discovered during the 1960s and 1970s a new audience – workers, farmers, professionals, students and even children – both in and out of the cities.

By the 1980s, professional theatrical practice had become an artistic and social fact. Although at times the work was obviously didactic and clearly linked to political agendas, innovative formulas were found by the best and most creative of Cuba's artists and theatre became an important expression of the country's national culture. It was also heavily subsidized. Castro's policy towards the arts, announced in June 1961, was summed up in the phrase 'within the Revolution, everything; against the Revolution, nothing'. Such a cultural policy could not, of course, be exempt from errors, vacillation and subjectivity but, for the most part, the policy stimulated and protected dramatic creation. During the 1970s, however, several theatre groups were forcibly closed, censorship grew, a number of playwrights found themselves ostracized and well-known cultural personalities were silenced by political and moral accusations. The creation of a full Ministry of Culture in 1976, though, brought some change.

Eventually, the ideas of younger actors, playwrights and directors began to dominate more traditional concepts of the stage. Differences between 'high' and 'low' culture gradually disappeared and the very concept of drama itself widened along with the appearance of new approaches to the use of theatrical space and even the aesthetics of communication.

These new approaches, pioneered and perfected by the innovative collective Teatro Escambray, spread across Cuba over the next decade until there were no fewer than ten companies working in this style including one on the Isle of Youth more than 100 kilometres from Havana. The dream of an artistically significant decentralized theatre was becoming a reality.

All the Escambray-inspired groups shared similar theatrical approaches: identification of issues through research within communities, direct contact with audiences, non-traditional venues and methodology and Brechtian aesthetics. Working collectively, these groups, though sharing common artistic ground, each managed to develop and maintain their own style and methods particularly in the use of music and scenic techniques. By 1978, this approach had become a norm of sorts, a Cuban alternative to traditional theatrical practice.

In this sense, the stage of the late 1970s broadened more than ever before in creating theatrical images, revitalizing dramatic techniques and seeking out non-traditional

Carlos Pérez Peña's 1994 Teatro Escambray production of Rafael González's *La paloma negra*.
Photo: Aida Jordão.

audiences. For its leading adherent, director Sergio Corrieri (b. 1938), Escambray's concepts represented 'an enriched continuity'; he became a master of social reality and expressing it in forms quite different from those envisioned by Stanislavski. The new style, which emerged in the early 1980s, made Cuban theatre more direct, more linear and linguistically richer while still utilizing music in various ways. Characteri-

zation was also enriched while time and space were more freely manipulated. Using parables, analogies and elements of what has come to be called Image Theatre, it became more of a synthetic art and began to include as well aspects of ballet, dance and sculpture. Even when dealing with the past, problems were always seen from a contemporary perspective.

Structure of the National Theatre Community

Before 1959, Cuban theatre was really Havana theatre since no permanent artistic activity existed outside the capital. The groups that appeared between 1940 and 1954 were associations that sought to secure members and whose monthly dues assured a financial base. Put simply, the state was indifferent or even hostile to the theatre. Often it was the performers themselves who underwrote, at great personal cost, the modest budget of each production. Costs were limited to the purchase of essential props, the rental of sets and a minimum wage for a few technicians and stagehands. Publicity was provided through the generosity of friendly journalists, who published notes about the productions in the press. Audiences were scarce and fickle, consisting mostly of intellectuals, middle-class professionals, students and a few committed theatregoers.

In spite of their marginalism, however, theatre artists of this period did manage to create a small nucleus of spectators, kept the repertoire reasonably modern, formed a number of professional theatrical troupes, and laid down the foundation for the important steps that followed. The most notable influences during this period were from the United States (some actors travelled there regularly to attend Broadway shows), France (there was great interest in French existentialism and avant-garde forms) and Spain (especially García Lorca, Casona and the golden age classics).

Through the 1950s, there was an increase in the repertoire but still no one could live from the theatre. When the revolution came, there were eight *salitas* in Havana and the number of seats available each night was less than 2,000, a number smaller than that later available at the Sala Avellaneda alone, a theatre facility that opened in 1979 boasting some 2,300 seats.

By 1990, more than fifty groups existed in

Cuba, including companies performing for children and others involved in music and dance. More than seventy-five plays were being produced each season. Clearly, over this period, the Cuban actor had been converted from a part-time hobbyist into a full-time professional with a respectable social status.

By the 1990s as well, all officially recognized professional groups could be subsidized by the state and theatres could be found in every part of the country. At the same time, private theatres were virtually non-existent in Cuba, the last four *salitas* having been nationalized in 1967. Mobility is another factor in the makeup of the Cuban theatre professional; one finds actors moving regularly from one group to another.

Since Castro came to power, the state itself has been deeply involved in the overall planning and organization of the theatre as a whole but each group chooses both its repertoire and its style. There is therefore no 'official' style nor is there an administrative norm for companies. Artistic differences are seen regularly in national festivals, and points of view are debated and analysed in regular meetings and workshops. Freedom of creation is, in fact, guaranteed in the constitution: chapter four establishes free artistic creation and declares that the interest of the state lies in promoting and developing artistic education at no cost to students. Also enshrined is recognition of the state's role in encouraging creative vocations and cultivating art generally, including the appreciation of works of art.

Payments to actors are regulated according to established standards and the frequency of performances. A guaranteed basic wage assures actors economic security but talent and hard work – and connection to a particular company – are what determine the size of an actor's

Víctor Varela's 1983 Teatro El Obstáculo production of his *La cuarta pared*, designed by Varela and David Placeres.
Photo: Archivo revista *Tablas*.

salary. Artists are also protected by retirement laws (these laws also apply to people who worked during the years when theatres could not pay them), which also establish special retirement benefits for those who have made significant contributions to the development of the theatre.

Copyright laws ensure financial compensation for plays and also establish special payments for works destined for children. Legal provisions guarantee the writers' control over their work and protect the works from misinterpretation by directors. In order to ensure income for dramatic authors, the laws also provide guaranteed payments for first performances, with lesser amounts for successive showings.

In this way, playwrights are not dependent on box-office sales. The laws also protect translators and adapters. The country's many dramatic competitions (sponsored by agencies such as Casa de las Américas and other organizations) also guarantee the publication of prize-winning works. In the 1980s, competitions began to be organized by theatre companies, with a guaranteed production as a prize.

Theatre people are included in the Sindicato de Trabajadores de la Cultura (Union of Cultural Workers) and can also join the Unión de Escritores y Artistas de Cuba (Union of Cuban Writers and Artists). The latter was created in 1961 and its Theatrical Arts Association is open to actors and technicians while its Literature Section is open to authors. The Hermanos Saíz Association represents young artists just beginning their careers.

Another important branch of Cuban theatrical activity that emerged in 1961 is the amateur theatre. With some 5,000 groups on the island, these companies generally gave more than 40,000 performances annually in factories, schools, hospitals, cultural centres and farms. The groups utilize the skills of about 500 formally trained theatrical instructors. Regularly scheduled festivals of amateur theatre are also a powerful stimulus to this widespread movement, which guarantees a popular base for professional theatre as well as the development of a massive audience.

From the 1960s on, Havana became an active centre for various festivals, with theatrical groups from more than thirty countries performing in its theatres. At the same time, Cuban companies have taken part in theatrical exchanges and festivals across the Americas, in Europe and in Africa. One can add to this the many international tours by the Ballet Nacional (National Ballet) with its leading dancer, Alicia Alonso (Alicia Martínez, b. 1921), the Danza Contemporánea de Cuba (Contemporary Dance of Cuba), the Conjunto Folklórico Nacional (National Folkloric Company) and the Danza Nacional de Cuba (Cuban National Dance Company) as well as tours by theatre groups for children and individual actors.

Casa de las Américas alone hosted six Festivals of Latin American Theatre in Havana between 1961 and 1966 as well as International Conferences of Theatrical Performers between 1964 and 1987. These festivals brought to Cuba thirty-eight works from twelve Latin American countries, as well as important figures such as Manuel Galich (1913–84), a Guatemalan who lived for many years in Cuba, Argentine playwright Osvaldo Dragún and Colombian directors Enrique Buenaventura and Santiago García.

Another aspect of contemporary Cuban theatrical practice was found at this time in the regular co-production of works with the former Soviet Union, the former East Germany and Bulgaria. Included among them have been productions of *Ten Days that Shook the World* (1977), staged by Soviet director Yuri Lyubimov at the Teatro Estudio; Hannes Fischer's production of Brecht's *Die Tage der Commune* (*Days of the Commune*, 1972), a Cuba–German Democratic Republic co-production; Brecht's *Die Mutter* (*The Mother*, 1975), staged by Ulf Keyn at the Teatro Estudio; *The Dawns Are Silent Here* (1975) and *Bells of the Kremlin* (1977), directed by Yevgeny Radomislenski, both at the Teatro Político Bertolt Brecht; *Humboldt and Bolívar* (1983), staged by Hanns Anselm Perten at the Teatro Político; and Krazimir Spasov's production of *The Suede Jacket* (1980) at the Teatro Estudio.

As well, Cuban theatre artists have collaborated with many Latin American directors such as Julio Babruskinas of Argentina on *Der Brotladen* (*The Bakeshop*, 1980) at the Teatro Político; Santiago García on *Huelga* (*The Strike*, 1980) at the Cubana de Acero; Atahualpa del Cioppo of Uruguay on Pirandello's *Tonight We Improvise* (1983) at the Rita Montaner; Ugo Ulive of Uruguay on Brecht's *Der kaukasische Kreidekreis* (*Caucasian Chalk Circle*, 1961), a Conjunto Dramático Nacional–Teatro Estudio co-production; Néstor Raimondi of Argentina on Brecht's *The Mother* (1961) at the Conjunto Dramático Nacional; and Alberto Panello of Argentina on Shakespeare's *Comedy of Errors* (1966) at the Conjunto Dramático de las Villas. Dozens of Cuban students and professionals have taken specialist training in eastern Europe (especially in the former USSR, the former East Germany, Poland and the former Czechoslovakia), as well as in Colombia, Finland, Sweden and the Netherlands, while Cuba offers training to a great many students from Latin America and Africa, at both the intermediate and advanced levels.

The international Havana Theatre Festivals of 1980, 1982, 1984, 1987, 1991 and 1993 provided important artistic competitions for Cuban artists, but perhaps the most significant aspect of these events (including Carifesta in 1979 and the International Workshop of New Theatre in 1983) has been the growing participation of the public, which, during each event, overflows not only Havana's theatres but also such non-traditional venues as plazas, schools, factories and agricultural cooperatives. The presence of foreign groups, the increase in theatrical companies seeking innovative sites, and the large number of participating national groups, combined with the number of performances and expanded audience, guaranteed the national importance of these events even in the country's difficult economic circumstances during the mid-1990s.

Artistic Profile

Companies

The Teatro Estudio (Studio Theatre) began operation in 1958, making it one of the longest continuing theatre groups in Latin America.

This company defined the theatrical flowering that followed the Castro revolution, especially in its first decade. In 1958, it was the first group in Cuba to stage a play by Brecht, *Der gute Mensch von Sezuan* (*The Good Person*

Reaction (1980) and *We the Undersigned* (1983). These plays, taken together with Teatro Estudio's production of Gelman's *In the Park* (1986), made him the most widely produced Soviet author in Cuba. The Bertolt Brecht group has played in Bulgaria, East Germany and throughout Latin America doing works by both Cuban and internationally known authors. During its tour of the former German Democratic Republic in 1980, the group received a gold medal for its production of Brecht's *Der Brotladen* (*The Bakeshop*).

Still another group, Cubana de Acero, tends to experiment with theatrical space. Housed in a metallurgical factory in Havana, it has been particularly interested in factory-related issues. Likewise, El Teatro de Participación Popular (Theatre of Popular Participation) also works with factory labourers and students, and has even done productions from time to time along the Havana docks.

Of the groups working outside the capital, Cabildo Teatral Santiago (Theatrical Chapter of Santiago) offers original works with a strong accent on music and an approach based on local traditions. Starting from *relaciones* (brief histories), many of Afro-Cuban origin and others with trans-cultural elements, and making full use of songs, dances and changeable spaces, it has created spectacles that, without being folkloric reproductions, establish very clear and direct contacts with the Afro-Cuban working district audiences of Santiago de Cuba, the most 'Caribbean' part of the country. Beginning with expressions often linked to the carnival tradition, the short, everyday stories that serve as the point of departure offer a contemporary vision of reality and express it in a popular, musical sense that transforms these shows into a group party, very close, on occasions, to the Afro-Cuban *conga*. With satire, jeering, musical masquerades, flamboyantly coloured costumes and an effective use of street space, the Cabildo has staged some enormously successful productions. Perhaps the most famous of its shows was done in 1974 – *De cómo Santiago Apóstol puso los pies en la tierra* (*How the Apostle Santiago Came Down to Earth*), written and directed by Raúl Pomares (b. 1934).

Yet another approach is offered by the work of theatre students graduating from the Instituto Superior de Arte (Higher Institute of Art). Centred around Flora Lauten's (b. 1942) collective group Teatro Buendía, these young actors tend towards innovative experiments by using very personal analogies as part of a process of self-discovery. Lauten began her own career as an actress with Teatro Estudio, later moving on to Escambray, the rural group La Yaya and then to Cubana de Acero. Her major works with Teatro Buendía include *La emboscada* (*The Ambush*, 1981), *El pequeño príncipe* (*The Little Prince*, 1983), *Lila la mariposa* (*Lila the Butterfly*, 1985) and *Electra Garrigó* (1984). Her remodelling of literary texts as well as their scenic treatment has widened the traditional concept of the stage for young people by offering alternative readings based on the life experiences of the actors.

Another group of young actors developed on the Isle of Youth, calling themselves Los Pinos Nuevos (The New Pines). Formed by theatre students from the middle and graduate levels, the group's best work sought a union of theory and practice. It came closest to this objective in Francisco Fonseca's (b. 1954) play *El compás de madera* (*The Wooden Compass*, 1981).

Dramaturgy

Between 1947 and 1958, a dramatic movement evolved that would provide its best example in the work of Virgilio Piñera (1912–79), Carlos Felipe (1914–75), Rolando Ferrer (1925–76) and Paco Alfonso. The first of these, Piñera, began his career in 1948 with *Electra Garrigó*, a Cuban adaptation of the Electra myth with a healthy dose of humour and social criticism. Clearly experimental, its 'national' elements included a careful delineation of local customs and many picturesque details. The prolific output of Piñera (more than twenty plays) encompasses a number of styles such as the absurd, existentialism, Artaudian Theatre of Cruelty, farce and 'anti-theatre'. His major plays include *Falsa alarma* (*False Alarm*, 1957), *Jesús* (1950), *Dos viejos pánicos* (*Two Old Terrors*, 1967), *El no* (*The No*, 1965), *La niñita querida* (*The Little Darling*, 1966), *Un arropamiento sartorial en la caverna platómica* (*Sartorial Splendour in Plato's Atomic Cave*, 1971) and *Las escapatorias de Laura y Oscar* (*The Adventures of Laura and Oscar*, 1973). His best known work is *Aire frío* (*Cold Air*, 1959), in which Piñera, across eighteen years of dramatic action and autobiographical background, and with the serenity of an impeccable witness, analyses the frustrations of the Cuban society of his time.

Carlos Felipe's first play appeared in 1947, *El Chino* (*The Chinaman*), a work strongly influenced by Pirandello. This play was followed in rapid succession by *Capricho en rojo* (*Fantasy in Red*, 1948), *El travieso Jimmy* (*Naughty Jimmy*, 1949), *Ladrillos de plata* (*Bars of Silver*, 1957) and *Réquiem por Yarini* (*Requiem for Yarini*, 1960). This last, generally considered to be his best work, is a true tragedy in the classic tradition with a structure that includes everything from choruses to oracles and an epiphany. All of this is set against a Yoruba background that transforms it into one of the best examples of contemporary Cuban drama, free from both folksiness and stereotypes.

Rolando Ferrer began his career with *La hija de Nacho* (*The Daughter of Nacho*, 1951) but enjoyed his first success with *Lila la mariposa* (1954). Influenced by García Lorca as well as by Freudian psychology, Ferrer occupies a major place among pre-revolutionary Cuban playwrights. After the revolution, he wrote *Las de enfrente* (*Women in Front*, 1964), *La taza de café* (*A Cup of Coffee*, 1959) and *Los próceres* (*The Leaders*, 1963). He also worked as a translator and stage director.

Paco Alfonso, founder of the Teatro Popular, has written many plays dealing with social struggle in its many forms, including *Sabanimar* (1943), *Cañaveral* (*The Cane Field*, 1950) and *Yari Yari Mama Olua* (1941).

The works of all these authors were generally unpublished and in many cases unproduced until after 1959 and even then they tended to receive only short runs. Nevertheless, they represent a profound exploration of the Cuban spirit and together form a kind of new repertoire of resistance and social challenge. It is this repertoire that became the foundation upon which contemporary Cuban dramaturgy has been built.

Following the revolution, Abelardo Estorino (b. 1925) emerged as one of the first new playwrights of note. Estorino's work includes such important plays as *El robo del cochino* (*The Theft of the Pig*, 1961), *La casa vieja* (*The Old House*, 1964), *Ni un sí ni un no* (*Neither a Yes Nor a No*, 1980) and *Morir del cuento* (*Death by Short Story*, 1983) as well as adaptations, children's scripts and collages. In 1964, he became one of the artistic directors of Teatro Estudio and created a theatre built on social issues while in his own work he experimented with theatrical time and traditional dramatic structures. Estorino established himself as a major playwright with *La dolorosa historia del amor secreto de Don José Jacinto Milanés* (*The Painful Story of Don José Jacinto Milanés's*

Secret Love, 1974). His work analyses domestic relationships both in the distant past and in socialist society, focusing on the individual's moral responsibility.

Another author working in the early days of the Castro period was José R. Brene (1927–90), whose *Santa Camila de La Habana vieja* (*Saint Camila of Old Havana*, 1962) was the revolution's first popular triumph. Going beyond traditional Cuban formulas, Brene created a theatre stripped of class distinctions, which effectively reflected the new social reality. Brene has written more than forty plays and won the Unión de Escritores y Artistas Prize in 1970 for his play *Fray Sabino* (*Friar Sabino*).

Héctor Quintero (b. 1942) began his career with *Contigo pan y cebolla* (*With You Bread and Onions*, 1964), followed by *El premio flaco* (*Scant Reward*, 1966), which was awarded an International Theatre Institute prize by a jury composed of Eugène Ionesco, Alfonso Sastre, Christopher Fry, Marc Connelly and Diego Fabbri. Quintero's *Los cuentos del Decamerón* (*Tales of the Decameron*, 1969) had a run of over 300 performances at the Teatro Estudio. Other successful works were *Si llueve te mojas como los demás* (*If It Rains You'll Get Wet Like the Others*, 1971), *La última carta de la baraja* (*Last Card in the Deck*, 1978) and *Sábado corto* (*Short Saturday*, 1986). Quintero has also been involved in the development of Cuban musical theatre as both a playwright and a director.

Another writer of note is Eugenio Hernández Espinosa (b. 1936), whose *María Antonia* (1964) is one of the most moving and attractive plays in the Cuban repertoire. Rooted in Afro-Cuban mythology – his work has been called 'Yoruban (Nigerian) *autosacramentales*' (one-act religious plays) – Hernández creates an authentically tragic world in which violence, social discrimination, magic and marginalism all intermingle. In 1977, he won the Casa de las Américas Prize for his play *La Simona*, later exploring *patakines* (ancient Yoruba legends) with a unique dramatic conception that puts him among the ranks of the foremost of Cuban authors.

Perhaps the most unusual figure in Cuban dramatic art is Nicolás Dorr (b. 1946), who, at only 15 years of age, became an applauded playwright with *Las pericas* (*The Parakeets*, 1961), a one-act absurdist/surrealist farce. Dorr continued his work with *La chacota* (*Ridicule*, 1974); *El agitado pleito entre un autor y un ángel* (*Free-For-All Between an Author and an Angel*), which won the Unión de Escritores y Artistas Prize in 1972; *La clave de sol* (*The*

Eugenio Hernández Espinosa's 1982 Conjunto Folklórico Nacional production of his *Odebí el cazador*, choreographed by Manolo Micler.
Photo: Archivo revista *Tablas*.

Treble Clef, 1968); *Una casa colonial (A Colonial House*, 1981); and *Vivir en Santa Fé (Life in Santa Fé*, 1986). Dorr's first plays showed an almost childlike enchantment with a surprising, fantastic and absurd universe, although they always remained popular and accessible in both language and theme. In his later plays, this childlike vision became a more rational attempt to understand behaviour in the chaos of a surrealistic and absurd world.

José Triana (b. 1931) came to national note in 1960 with *Medea en el espejo (Medea in the Mirror*) and followed this with *La noche de los asesinos (Night of the Assassins*, 1965), still considered one of the most important plays in the national repertoire. This play has been performed in more than thirty countries across the Americas and Europe. Breaking from traditional forms, *La noche de los asesinos* explores parent–child relationships in a kind of theatrical ritual, a theatrical culmination of experimental methods that had been evolving for two decades in Cuban dramatic theatre. Triana, a graduate of the Universidad de Oriente in 1953, moved to Spain in 1955 and worked as an actor and director. Returning to

Cuba in 1958, he continued to write for the stage, winning numerous national prizes. He moved to Paris in 1980.

Other significant Cuban authors of the period include Ignacio Gutiérrez (b. 1929), Antón Arrufat (b. 1935), José Milián (b. 1946), Manuel Reguera Saumell (b. 1928), Maité Vera (b. 1939), Raúl González de Cascorro (1922–85), Rómulo Loredo, René Ariza (1940–93), Matías Montes Huidobro (b. 1930) and Fermín Borges (1931–87). Borges began to write short plays in 1955 in a neo-realist style, while Arrufat's poetic plays show conflict through parables – *Seven Against Thebes* and *La tierra permanente* (*A Permanent Land*, 1987). José Milián's *Vade Retro* is an effective example of Theatre of Cruelty. Montes Huidobro, after several productions in Cuba, moved to the United States and became one of the most produced Hispanic playwrights there. Among his plays are *La madre y la guillotina* (*The Mother and the Guillotine*, 1961), *Ojos para no ver* (*Eyes To Be Blind*, 1977) and *Funeral en Teruel* (*Funeral in Teruel*, 1977).

Teatro Escambray must also be given credit for developing two authors: Albio Paz and Roberto Orihuela (b. 1950). Paz, in his plays *La vitrina* (*The Showcase*, 1971), *El rentista* (*The Financier*, 1974) and *El paraíso recobrado* (*Paradise Found*, 1972), radically changed theatrical portrayals of farmers and others living outside of urban environments. Innovative in his use of audience participation and open debate, Paz combined this with more traditional Brechtian devices, elements from Grotowski's Poor Theatre and Theatre of the Absurd. Paz's work offers an image of the rural farmer changing from individual ownership to cooperative ownership and state farms. In his later work, he developed labour themes with *Huelga* (*The Strike*), winner of the Casa de las Américas Prize in 1980.

Orihuela broadened the social perspective with dramatizations of other conflicts – women's issues in *Ramona* (1977), student concerns in *Los novios* (*The Sweethearts*, 1979), familial class struggles in *La emboscada* (*The Ambush*, 1978) and workers in *Accidente* (*Accident*, 1986).

Plays about young people and students, the struggle against imperialism, the conflict between the old social conscience and revolutionary changes, marginalization and the process of collective integration, and biographical plays about historical figures became subjects for Cuban dramatists in the 1990s. Among authors working in these subject areas are Freddy Artiles (b. 1946), Abrahán Rodríguez (b. 1945), Gerardo Fulleda León (b. 1942), Gerardo Fernández (b. 1941), Raúl Macías (b. 1940), Jesús Gregorio (1939–88), Lázaro Rodríguez (b. 1949), Abilio Estévez (b. 1954) and Alberto Pedro (b. 1954).

Directors, Directing and Production Styles

The growth of the Cuban theatre in the 1960s meant that theatrical production was also facing a radical evolution. State support helped accelerate the number of performances and allowed large-scale productions on Cuban stages but it also led to an exploration of integrated approaches, and experimentation in the search for new methods. Brechtian style was dominant for a time and paralleled the emergence of new audiences.

The desire to offer interdisciplinary productions introduced choruses, dancers, photographic slides and complicated scenic effects. Space was used in such a free manner in the 1960s that it was finally defined simply by the presence of the actor in growing proximity to and communication with the spectator, who became an active participant in the performance. The use of flexible space further energized the very concept of staging.

The most important and influential director from the 1960s on was Vicente Revuelta. Revuelta began his career in 1946 and within a few years had become one of the leading actors in the Cuban theatre. Travelling to Paris and Rome, he became involved with Jean Vilar's Théâtre Populaire National and trained with Jean-Louis Barrault. While in Paris, Revuelta also took classes with Etienne Decroux. When he returned to Cuba in 1954, he already possessed a clear sense of theatre. As head of the theatrical section of Nuestro Tiempo, a group that included leading intellectuals of the time, Revuelta developed a theatrical curriculum while at the same time studying Marxism.

In 1958, he created Teatro Estudio and his first clear triumph as a director was with Eugene O'Neill's *Long Day's Journey into Night*. This was followed by stagings of Brecht (*The Good Person of Setzuan*, 1959; *Mother Courage and Her Children*, 1961; and *The Life of Galileo*, 1974) and world classics such as Lope de Vega's *Fuenteovejuna* (1963) and Shakespeare's *Twelfth Night* (1982). He also

Vicente Revuelta in his 1982 Teatro Estudio production of Shakespeare's *Twelfth Night,* designed by José Luis Posada.
Photo: Archivo revista *Tablas.*

successfully staged Cuban plays such as Triana's *La noche de los asesinos* (1966) and Felipe's *El travieso Jimmy* (1980) as well as Latin American scripts such as Lizarraga's *Santa Juana de América* (*Saint Joan of America*, 1978) and plays by writers including Edward Albee (*Zoo Story*, 1964), Tennessee Williams (*The Glass Menagerie*, 1961), Arthur Miller (*The Price*, 1979) and Anton Chekhov (*The Three Sisters*, 1972). A true experimenter, he also introduced the ideas of Polish director Jerzy Grotowski to Cuba.

Another notable director, Berta Martínez (b. 1931), began her career in the 1950s as an actress. Trained at Teatro Estudio, she began her directing career by staging a production of Estorino's *La casa vieja* in 1964. In the early part of her career, she focused on Spanish classics and Shakespeare, which she interpreted in contemporary ways. She had particular success with the plays of García Lorca, especially *La casa de Bernarda Alba* (*The House of Bernarda Alba*, 1981), *Bodas de sangre* (*Blood Wedding*, 1979) and *La zapatera prodigiosa* (*The Shoemaker's Prodigious Wife*, 1986). With the use of choruses to reinforce the central action, lighting as a unifying element, flexibility of physical composition, and an ability to read classic plays from a dialectical perspective, Martínez emerged as one of the major directors of the period.

Roberto Blanco (b. 1936) also began his career in the 1950s and he too was trained at the Teatro Estudio, later studying in Ghana and East Germany. He began his Cuban career by staging Hernández Espinosa's *María Antonia* in 1967, following it with Aimé Césaire's *Lumumba ou une saison au Congo* (*Lumumba, or, A Season in the Congo*, 1969) and Valle-Inclán's *Divinas palabras* (*Divine Words*, 1971). He also staged the musical *Cecilia Valdés* (1981) by Cuban composer Gonzalo Roig. In 1968, he founded the Teatro Ocuje and, in 1982, the theatrical group Irrumpe. At Irrumpe, he presented García Lorca's *Yerma* (1980), Lope de Vega's *Fuenteovejuna* (1983), Estorino's *La dolorosa historia del amor secreto de Don José Jacinto Milanés* (1985), Goldoni's *The Lovers* (1986) and an adaptation of García Lorca's play *Mariana Pineda* under the title *Mariana* (1987). Blanco has regularly integrated dance, folk elements and music into his work.

Raquel Revuelta, director of Teatro Estudio, began her career in the 1940s but remained active well into the 1990s. An actress of great passion, Revuelta worked in theatre, film, television and radio with equal success. With more than fifty leading roles to her credit, she devised ensemble methods at Teatro Estudio. Under her direction, the company assumed an unchallengeable place in the country's theatrical panorama.

Sergio Corrieri, another who began his career as a popular film and television actor, turned to directing at the Teatro Universitario and at Teatro Estudio. He founded Teatro Escambray in 1968 and has since committed the major part of his energy to this innovative collective. Among his major productions with Escambray are *El juicio* (1973), Orihuela's *Ramona* (1977) and *La emboscada* (1978). One of the creators of Cuba's 'new' theatre, Corrieri is credited with recognizing and developing the performance skills of many outstanding actors including his mother, Gilda Hernández, who began acting at Escambray and later collaborated with him in running the group.

Adolfo de Louis (b. 1926), another stage veteran who has contributed much to Cuban theatre, studied in the United States and then travelled to México where he met Japanese director Seki Sano. His work encompassed all areas of the stage – as actor in Camus's *Caligula* (1955), as director in Quintero's *El premio flaco* (1966), as the first Cuban director to work in theatre-in-the-round (1952), and as a theatrical impresario at the Sala Atelier. He also taught acting and became a general activist in the evolution of the modern Cuban theatre.

Armando Suárez del Villar (b. 1936) dedicated his career almost exclusively to the revitalization and reinterpretation of nineteenth-century dramatic works, including early Cuban plays. As such, his work was important in developing the national repertoire. Also worthy of note is the directorial work of Mario Balmaseda (b. 1947), José Antonio Rodríguez (b. 1935), María Elena Ortega (b. 1946), Miriam Lezcano (b. 1943), Pedro Castro (b. 1945), Ramiro Herrero (b. 1938) and, particularly in musical theatre, Nelson Dorr (b. 1939).

Rine Leal

Music Theatre
Dance Theatre

Music and dance theatre in Cuba have grown from popular sources across the island. From the centre of the country have come the songs of Trinidad and the rustic *punto guajiro*: this most representative of peasant artistic forms came originally from the south of Spain and the Canary Islands. In Cuba, the form developed in tobacco-producing areas, where most of the population was of Canarian descent.

The *punto guajiro* has a literary part, or *décima* (ten-line stanza), and a musical part, or *tonada* (tune). The most important kinds of *punto guajiro* are *punto libre* (free), *pinareño*, *vuelta abajo* (upside down), *punto fijo* (fixed), *en clave* (in code) or *camagüeyano* and the *punto espirituano* (spiritual).

From the eighteenth century, the *punto guajiro* was most popular in rural areas and has been used by the peasantry to express musically and poetically a wide range of feelings.

From Havana's port district has come the *guagancó*. From the eastern Cabildo have come the street dances, *conga* and *rumba*, while the Cabildo of Guantánamo is full of sung myths and legends. The Cuban *conga* or *comparsa* is a collective marching dance dating back to the celebrations of Corpus Christi or the Epiphany performed by African slaves. The *cabildos* (ethnic groups) would march towards the Plaza de Armas, competing with one another to show off their costumes and dances.

Although *congas* were outlawed for some time, being considered symbols of barbarism and backwardness, they managed to survive as a true popular form of expression. There are now male, female and mixed groups that deal with themes such as patriotism, social satire and customs. At the end of the nineteenth century some *comparsas* included dramatic passages of ancient totemic content, such as *El pájaro lindo* (*The Beautiful Bird*) and *El alacrán* (*The Scorpion*).

Musical instruments used in the *congas* include drums, cowbells, cornets and even frying pans. The songs and dances of the *comparsas* and *congas* typical of the Carnival of Santiago de Cuba have either kept the soloist–chorus structure of Cuban music and dance of African origin, or use a single sentence repeated many times. In the old style, the soloist was a female singer with a powerful high-pitched voice, called a *clarina*. In modern times her voice has been replaced by trumpets and cornets. Normally the texts are anonymous. Sometimes they are almost unintelligible but very rhythmic and often improvised around a popular tune.

The *rumba*, a Cuban music and dance form that has become a genre on its own, was used as a tool for effecting liberation from slavery and later from republican governments that still discriminated against blacks. It has been used to satirize politicians, comment on a romantic betrayal, exalt a patriotic feeling, or improvise around surrealist speeches.

While some scholars argue that its origin is *gangá*, the *rumba* probably has an eclectic origin, combining *congo*, *lucumíyoruba* and *carabalí* elements in its music and dance, and Hispanic elements in its speech. There are three major forms of *rumba*: *guaguancó*, *yambú* and *columbia*.

Guaguancó, a mainly narrative form often based on improvisation, is of urban origin and narrates anecdotes or ordinary events in a poetic form. In the late twentieth century, the *guaguancó* has dance added to the spoken parts, although purists argue that the original form was spoken only. The dance represents a man courting a woman, and has a profound erotic component.

The *yambú* also has urban origins and is apparently one of the oldest styles of *rumba*. A slow-paced piece, it begins with a *diana*, to which a chorus answers. The soloist and the chorus continue to alternate until the piece reaches a refrain in which a couple dances. This dance represents a woman flirting with a man, and hers is the most spectacular part.

The *columbia* is normally a man's dance, although some women have achieved fame performing it. Of rural origins, its structure is similar to the other *rumbas* (soloist and chorus) with two specific parts: a solo song and a *capetillo*, or danced part. The *llorao*, a series of moans and cries, is typical of the *columbia*. Before the *capetillo*, there are some bragging songs. Its pace is quick but settled.

The musical instruments used for the *rumba* are quite simple: three drums, a pair of metallic *marugas* and two harpsichords. Occasionally musicians have also used wooden boxes, spoons or even banged doors or wooden flats to keep the beat.

Zarzuela, a Spanish-style musical comedy whose text is both spoken and sung, has been especially important in Cuba. Dating back to about 1648, it was introduced to Cuba in 1853 when José Robreño (d. 1879) presented in Havana, with great success, *El duende* (*The Elf*) by the Spaniard Luis Olona. In those days the home of the *zarzuela* was the Albisu Theatre (opened in 1870), where the best Hispanic singers worked, leaving a profound impression and marking the beginning of a national tradition in Cuba.

National productions of *zarzuela* began in 1856, with the works of Robreño and Rafael Otero (1827–76); they were continued by Raimundo Cabrera (1852–1923), author of what is known as *género chico* (short comic pieces), a sort of minor *zarzuela*.

While the interest in *zarzuela* declined during the years of the republic, it was revived again after 1927, when the Teatro Martí (originally founded in 1884 under the name Irijoa) produced Ernesto Lecuona's works *Niña Rita* (*Young Rita*), *María de la O*, and *Lola Cruz*; Gonzalo Roig's *Cecilia Valdés*; Rodrigo Prats's *María Belén Chacón* and *Amalia Batista*; and Eliseo Grenet's *La Vírgen morena* (*The Black Virgin*). These writers began what is now known as the modern expression of musical theatre in Cuba.

In the 1980s and 1990s *zarzuela* was still part of the programme at the Teatro Lírico de la Habana (Havana Musical Theatre), while other groups tended to experiment with more modern musical forms, such as the *opera trova* (troubadour opera) or the musical, in an attempt to modernize the quality of libretto and musical structures.

Cuban dance theatre is an innovative artistic expression that flourished in Cuba during the 1980s. Merging the talents of actors and dancers, the end product is closer to theatre than to dance.

The Cuban troupe Asísomos, founded by the American Lorna Burdsall in 1982 and directed by the Ecuadoran dancer Isabel Bustos, was a precursor of this movement in Cuba. In 1987 the movement gained new impetus with the creation of three new collectives. The Ballet Teatro de La Habana (Havana Ballet Theatre), led by Caridad Martínez (b. 1950), and Danza Abierta (Open Dance), led by Marianela Boan (b. 1954), were both created by former members of the Ballet Nacional, Danza Contemporánea and the Conjunto Folklórico Nacional. The third new collective was Danza Combinatoria (Combining Dance), founded by Rosario Cardenas (b. 1953). In 1990, a series of national tours was initiated.

Teatrova (Troubadour's Theatre) and the Opera Trova (Opera Troubadour), as well as the Conjunto Folklórico and the Teatro Musical, also offer productions that integrate popular forms with traditional dramatic structures.

Teatrova, founded in 1974 in Santiago de Cuba by Argentine-born director Adolfo Gutkin (b. 1935), actress María Eugenia García (b. 1947) and singer Augusto Blanca (b. 1945), was originally created as part of Conjunto Dramático de Oriente (Eastern Dramatic Group). The company remained in Santiago until 1984, when it moved to Havana. Teatrova's productions encourage active communication between performers and audience through the use of storytelling and music. The company has performed regularly in non-traditional venues.

Conjunto Folklórico Nacional is a prestigious group whose aim has been to rescue and revitalize folk dance and music traditions in order to present them in the context of modern theatrical forms while retaining their essence as popular art. Founded in Havana in 1962 by the Cuban folk specialist Rogelio Martínez Furé (b. 1937) and Mexican-born choreographer Rodolfo Reyes Cortés, the Conjunto Folklórico Nacional has developed a style of folk theatre with its own aesthetic reflecting the diverse Cuban traditions, including European (Spanish and French), African (*yorubá*, *congo*, *carabalí* and *arará*) and Caribbean.

The Ballet Nacional de Cuba, founded by prima ballerina Alicia Alonso, has set the standards of professionalism in both its approach to ballet and its technical mastery. Working in a wide range of styles, from classic and romantic to new paths in contemporary forms, the company was founded in 1948 under the name Ballet Alicia Alonso. As early as 1950 its repertoire included classics such as *Giselle*, *Swan Lake* and *Petrushka*, and national works such as *Fiesta negra* (*Black Holiday*) and *Sóngoro Cosongo*.

In 1956, the Batista government withdrew all financial support from the company as an act of political retaliation, and the company disbanded. In 1959, however, it received the support of the newly established revolutionary government. Since then it has expanded its

Gustavo Herrera's 1988 Ballet Nacional de Cuba production of his and Virgilio Piñera's *Electra Garrigó*, designed by Ricardo Rymena.
Photo: Archivo revista *Tablas*.

repertoire, and well into the 1990s was still training and promoting the work of new dancers, teachers, choreographers, designers and musicians. Significant among the different styles it has worked in have been *Sleeping Beauty, Coppélia, La Fille mal gardée, Carmen, Don Quixote, Petrushka, Hamlet* and *Bodas de sangre*.

Alonso, director of both the Ballet Nacional de Cuba and the Gran Teatro de La Habana (Grand Theatre of Havana), is important both as a dancer and as a choreographer. Born in Havana, she began her studies in dance there in 1931 and later studied in the United States with Enrico Zanfretta, Alexandra Feodorova and others from the School of American Ballet. In 1938, she began her professional career, and a year later was among the ranks of the American Ballet Caravan. In 1940 she joined the American Ballet Theatre in New York, where she began an extraordinary career as prima ballerina in the great classic and romantic works. In 1948

Alonso returned to Cuba. Between 1955 and 1959 she was guest dancer for the Ballets Russes de Monte Carlo. In 1957 she also became the first dancer from the western hemisphere to be guest artist at the Bolshoi Ballet in Moscow and the Kirov Ballet in Leningrad. She has also been a guest artist with companies in France and India.

As a choreographer, she has created her own versions of well-known classics for the Paris Opera, the Opera of Vienna, the Teatro San Carlo in Naples, the Opera of Prague and the Teatro alla Scala in Milan.

In Cuba she has been recognized with the title Heroína del trabajo (Workers' Heroine) by the Cuban government.

The development of musical theatre has been of particular interest at the Opera Nacional (National Opera) and at the Teatro Lírico (Lyric Theatre).

Rine Leal, Rogelio Martínez Furé and
Gilda Santana

Theatre for Young Audiences
Puppet Theatre

Developing alongside the many dramatic groups in Cuba since 1959 have been a number of theatres focusing particularly on works for children.

In 1963 Carucha (b. 1927) and José (1929–88) Camejo started their work as puppeteers with an itinerant *retablo* (a religious scene or play presented using wooden puppets). In 1970 they joined José Carril (1931–93) and founded the Guiñol Nacional (National Puppets), forerunner of the Teatro Nacional de Guiñol (National Puppet Theatre). The new group, which has approximately twenty-one performers and four directors, opened its first season with the Brazilian Maria Clara Machado's *Las cebollas mágicas* (*The Magic Onions*), produced in cooperation with visiting Soviet puppeteers.

The Teatro Nacional de Guiñol is known for its use of a wide range of puppetry and acting techniques, as well as for its openness to innovation and experimentation. In several productions, it used live actors not only as manipulators of the puppets but also as active interlocutors with them. Since 1970 the Teatro Nacional de Guiñol has produced more than 115 plays, including works by Aristophanes, García Lorca, Valle-Inclán, Zorrilla, Cervantes, Giraudoux and Molière.

The company has also created shows written by Cuban authors such as Estorino and Brene and others based on Cuban or Afro-Cuban folklore, as well as adaptations of short stories, poems and songs, and short plays for younger audiences.

During the 1970s, other groups emerged and

Eddy Socorro's 1988 Teatro Nacional de Guiñol production of Ulises García's *Tendras estrellas*, based on Saint-Exupéry's *The Little Prince*.
Photo: Archivo Teatro Nacional de Guiñol.

theatre for young audiences expanded, spreading into schools, children's clubs and other locations throughout the country. With the creation in 1970 of the Escuela Nacional de Teatro Infantil, linked to the Ministry of Education, theatre for young audiences expanded to the point of having twenty-three companies across the country. Some of the best were Taller de Teatro Estudio (Studio Theatre Workshop), Frente Infantil de Escambray (Escambray's Children's Front), Los Juglares (The Minstrels), El Anaquillé, El Galpón de la Habana (The Storehouse of Havana) and the experimental group of Parque Lenin (Lenin Park). All these groups work both with pedagogic materials and with plays written by well-known playwrights.

This growth was augmented by a number of festivals. In 1986, for example, one national festival hosted twenty-two groups from eleven provinces, giving fifty-nine performances in fifteen different locales.

Among the major Cuban writers who have created plays for children have been Manuel Galich, Dora Alonso (b. 1910), Freddy Artiles, Bebo Ruiz (b. 1934), Francisco Garzón Céspedes (b. 1947, winner of the Ollantay Prize in 1985), Ignacio Gutiérrez, René Fernández (b. 1944), Gerardo Fulleda León, Rogelio Castillo (b. 1945), Raúl Guerra (b. 1942) and David García (b. 1944), among others. Their work has assured a supply of quality scripts for children's groups everywhere in the country. Ruiz, an expert in this kind of work, has experimented in pieces such as *Fábulas del monte* (*Fables from the Mountains*), in which he explored fairytales and stories of animals and gods, and *El extraño caso de la muñeca que se cayó de un cuento* (*The Strange Case of a Doll Who Fell Into a Story*, 1978). Fernández is the most prolific author, with almost twenty scripts to his credit on many different themes and written in many different styles. Guerra produced *Kolin*, his first original work, in 1972 and continued with *¡Abajo los cocodrilos!* (*Down With Crocodiles!*) in 1975 and *La guerra de los chigüines* (*The Kids' War*), winner of the Prize Edad de Oro (Golden Age) in 1980.

Among the children's theatres that have toured abroad have been the Guiñol Nacional (Perú, Spain, Poland, Romania and the former Czechoslovakia), Papalote (Spain) and the Centro Experimental de Teatro de Santa Clara (Santa Clara Experimental Theatre Centre), which has performed in France. To these should be added the work of Armando Morales (b. 1940), Ulises García (b. 1943) and the one-person performances of Pedro Valdés Piña (b. 1949). These artists combine new theatre techniques generally – not just puppetry techniques – with the tradition of storytelling and establish strong links between performers and audiences.

Rine Leal, Roberto Gacio

Design
Theatre Space and Architecture

The pioneers of theatrical design in Cuba were Rubén Vigon (1917–77) and Luis Márquez (1911–91). The former, a graduate of Yale University Drama School, brought modern concepts of set design and use of space to Cuba. The latter, influenced by his early work in Barcelona, was among the first in Cuba to move away from painted backdrops and false perspective.

However, until the creation of the Talleres Nacionales de Teatro (National Theatre Workshops) in 1960 there was no active base for the study of theatre design. It was the National Workshops that finally allowed designers an opportunity to explore innovative techniques of expression. In 1962, the establishment of the School of Design in Havana marked another decisive step in the evolution of the field, with Czechoslovak professors Ladislav Vychodil and D. Kadrnovzka offering instruction.

From this time on, an integrated concept of design began to emerge that ranged from general scenic arrangements to lighting, costumes, furnishings and even the stage space itself. The inclusion of painters such as René Portocarrero (1912–85), Raúl Martínez (b. 1927), Umberto Peña (b. 1937) and Manuel Mendive (b. 1944) broadened the approaches to design, which were further aided by the use of materials such as jute, natural plant fibres and canvas in an effort to find an economical solution to material shortages while the island nation was under economic blockade.

Among leading contemporary Cuban designers are María Elena Molinet (b. 1919), Salvador Fernández (b. 1937), Raúl Oliva (b. 1935), Julio Castaño (b. 1935), Eduardo Arocha (b. 1934), Jesús Ruiz (b. 1943), Diana Fernández (b. 1949) and Derubín Jácome (b. 1948), many of whom have shown their work at the Prague Quadrennial exhibitions.

Salvador Fernández, Oliva and Arocha have done outstanding work in the area of stage space with a minimum number of on-stage elements, whether in theatre for adults, children's theatre or ballet. Oliva's best work was in *La noche de los asesinos* in 1966, while Fernández has designed many ballets for Alicia Alonso. Arocha's most interesting work was in the children's play *The Little Prince* in 1988. Molinet and Diana Fernández, together with Jácome, have also designed for film. Their experience has been documented in *Metodología para la crítica del diseño teatral* (*Methodology for the Critique of Theatre Design*), written by Fernández and Jácome in 1989.

Economic difficulties in the late 1980s and early 1990s forced artists to focus on open spaces or alternative spaces, avoiding the use of sophisticated technical equipment. Public squares, amphitheatres, churches, warehouses, parks and streets have often become their stages. The more than thirty traditional proscenium theatres across the country have been challenged by this new vision of theatre space, which searches for new ways for performers and audiences to communicate using a minimum of technical elements. Major theatres such as the Teatro Nacional in Havana and Teatro Heredia in Santiago de Cuba often remained empty while there were full houses in the smaller spaces, sometimes seating only fifty people, where much of the new theatre of the 1990s was produced.

Rine Leal

The entrance to the 2,300-seat Sala Avellaneda at Havana's Teatro Nacional, opened in 1979.

Training

Training for the arts in Cuba is a post-1959 phenomenon and, given that relatively short tradition, its achievements have been impressive. The *ad-hoc* quality of training prior to the revolution has been replaced by a national organization of scholarships that assures the possibility of theatrical studies free of charge to any young person with talent. In 1961, the Escuela de Instructores de Arte (School of Art Education) was created, followed a year later by the Escuela Nacional de Arte (National School of Art), housed in the former Havana Country Club. In 1976, the Instituto Superior de Arte (Higher Institute of Art) was founded, with the equivalent of university status for training in the theatre, plastic arts, music, dance, cinema, radio and television.

The Academia Municipal de Artes Dramáticas (Municipal Academy of Dramatic Arts), founded in Havana in 1947, is sponsored by the Dirección de Bellas Artes (Arts Council) of Havana. The school was created by former members of the group ADAD (1945–50), who in turn were graduates of the Academia de Artes Dramáticas de La Escuela Libre (Academy of Dramatic Arts of the Free School, 1940–2). While the Academia Municipal was under the leadership of Julio Martínez Aparicio (1915–88), its director until 1953, it was based in the Conservatorio Municipal de Música (Municipal Conservatory of Music), where the first graduates presented works by Cervantes and Molière.

The first group of 120 students was offered a programme lasting three years that combined theoretical and practical studies. Upper-year subjects included playwriting and dramaturgy, film studies, scene design and radio technology. Advanced students also participated in some of ADAD's professional productions. Modesto Centeno (1912–85), the last director of the school, introduced the study of movement and the Stanislavski method. Under his leadership the academy ran its own theatre, El Corral (The Courtyard), and published a journal with the same name. The Academia de Artes Dramáticas closed in 1966, as a result of the reorganization of the government arts curriculum.

By 1975, forty-seven schools were offering some level of arts training throughout the country to almost 5,000 students. The Escuela de Circo y Variedades (School of Circus and Variety Acts) was created in 1977. Cuba's voice in this field was heard at the First Congress for Schools and Centres of Theatrical Training held in Caracas, Venezuela, in 1977. In 1986, Havana was host to more than 160 specialists at a Latin American convention on arts education.

The Escuela Internacional de Teatro para América Latina y el Caribe (EITALC; International School of Theatre for Latin America and the Caribbean) was founded in 1989, under the auspices of Casa de las Américas. International and itinerant in nature, it attempted to bring together theatre professionals from all across Latin America. Its first director was the Argentine playwright Osvaldo Dragún.

EITALC is an independent, international organization whose main goal is the training of Latin American theatre professionals through the exchange of methods and ideas. EITALC sponsors month-long workshops held several times a year in different countries. They are run by two or three directors, who work with approximately forty young professionals from the region. The development of each workshop is normally recorded on video and documented by a group of international researchers or theorists participating in the experience.

The 1989 workshop, in Cuba, was entitled 'Current Theatre Techniques in Latin America and the Caribbean'; it used as a theme Eduardo Galeano's work *Memorias del fuego* (*Memories of Fire*). The Brazil workshop in 1990 was entitled 'The Actor', and was directed by José Antunes Filho. A 1990 workshop was again in Cuba and was on 'The Kingdom of This World' (based on Alejo Carpentier's work of the same name). In Argentina in 1991, the workshop was entitled 'Cultural Crossing'. A special workshop was held in Germany in 1991, sponsored by the International Theatre Institute and Theater der Welt (World Theatre Festival), with forty participants from Europe, North America and Latin America who worked together on the theme of 'Discovery'.

Technical training is offered through the Talleres Nacionales de Teatro, technical workshops created in Cuba in 1960. They provide technical and material support for the development of theatre in the country. In 1962 these workshops began to expand and decentralize, forming a new structure of production workshops and a number of departments of technical services such as wardrobe, props, stage machinery, lighting and sound. At this time, the workshops found their permanent home, the equipment of most departments was renovated, and classes were created to develop a new generation of apprentices.

In 1970, as a result of an international exchange of experiences, all the workshops became organized as a single entity: the Empresa de Industria Artística (Artistic Industry Company), which was responsible for providing the infrastructure needed for all the theatres in the country. The company has been serving Cuban showbusiness ever since, helping develop not only theatre, but also the circus, musical theatre and dance.

Training in criticism is the responsibility of the Higher Institute of Art, which offers instruction in theatre research, dramaturgy, directing and acting. These are five-year courses of study leading to Bachelor's degrees. The influence of this training can be seen in the ever-increasing number of published essays, books and specialized magazines as well as in the growing number of forums and meetings. Inheriting the rich critical tradition of the 1940s and 1950s of such writers as José Manuel Valdés-Rodríguez (1896–1971), Mirta Aguirre (1912–80), Mario Rodríguez Alemán (1926–86), Luis A. Blanco (1903–75), Rine Leal (b. 1930, winner of the Ollantay Prize in 1987) and Graziella Pogolotti (b. 1932), many of the younger critics have tended to write for the magazine *Tablas* (*Stage*).

Rine Leal, Roberto Gacio,
Derubín Jácome and Magaly Muguercia

Criticism, Scholarship and Publishing

The publication of theatre materials is carried out through the Instituto Cubano del Libro (Cuban Book Institute) which has a publishing house for Cuban works called Letras Cubanas (Cuban Letters) and one for foreign authors called Arte y Literatura (Art and Literature). Between 1959 and 1984, the institute published more than 400 theatrical titles.

Before the revolution, critical studies hardly existed in Cuba. The valuable *Historia de la literatura dramática cubana* (*History of Cuban Dramatic Literature*) by Juan José Arrom had to be published by Yale University and was never printed in Cuba. However, the publication of historical works, criticism, theory, anthologies and bibliographies has continued to build a solid base for a more scientific approach to the study of theatre. Adding to this base have been the publishing activities of Casa de las Américas, the Unión de Escritores y Artistas de Cuba and, specifically for young people, the Editorial Gente Nueva (New People's Press).

Early attempts at publishing theatre magazines in Cuba included, in 1919–20, the magazine *Teatro Cubano* (*Cuban Theatre*), which published eight issues; in 1944, *Arte* (*Art*), three issues; in 1947, *Prometeo* (*Prometheus*), which published twenty-eight issues but folded in 1953; and, in 1961, *Revista de Teatro* (*Theatre Magazine*) appeared, but only for three issues.

Casa de las Américas is the country's major publishing house and cultural institute, founded in April 1959 – only four months after the revolution. It was one of the first cultural institutions in the region to establish networks among writers and artists from across Latin America.

Under the leadership of its founders, first Haydée Santamaría (1925–80) and subsequently the poet and essayist Roberto Fernández Retamar (b. 1930), Casa de las Américas has facilitated and encouraged the production of contemporary Latin American literature, art and culture. The organization has specialized departments for literature, visual arts, music, publishing, libraries, Caribbean studies and theatre. One of its most important activities is the awarding of a series of literary prizes, including one for drama.

Although its department of theatre was not officially founded until 1971 – by theatre historian and critic Manuel Galich – Casa de las Américas had always promoted theatre activities. Since 1961, it has also been a place of encounter for theatre people attending the annual International Theatre Festivals in Havana. In 1964 it began publishing the theatre journal *Conjunto* (*Together*), still the only theatre journal in Spanish that deals with theatre in all of Latin America.

Since 1984, the department of theatre at Casa de las Américas has been directed by Magaly Muguercia (b. 1945), since 1986 also the editor of *Conjunto*. David Fernández (b. 1940) and Rine Leal were the first editors of the journal. In 1972 Galich became editor-in-chief, a position he held until his death in 1984.

Every issue of *Conjunto* includes a script by a Latin American author, several theoretical and critical essays as well as news about theatre in Latin America and the Caribbean. *Conjunto* has published special issues on the theatre of particular countries in Latin America – Nicaragua, Brazil, Perú and Venezuela – and on special topics such as Hispanic theatre in the United States, theatre for young audiences, and theatre and cultural identity. In 1976, *Conjunto* received the Ollantay Prize from the Federation of Theatre Festivals of the Americas, for its contribution to the development of theatre in Latin America.

Tablas is a journal specializing in the performing arts, whose purpose is to reflect the image of contemporary Cuban theatre and serve as a vehicle for orientation and criticism.

Founded in 1982, *Tablas* is published quarterly, and includes opinion pieces, essays, reviews, interviews and reports on national and international theatre. Since 1984, the journal has published a new script in each issue, accompanied by an in-depth subject study. *Tablas* has published works by both new dramatists and established ones. Among them are Virgilio Piñera, Abelardo Estorino and Héctor Quintero.

Under the direction of Rosa Ileana Boudet (b. 1947) between 1982 and 1987 and of Vivian Martínez Tabares (b. 1956) from 1987, *Tablas* has also been awarded the Ollantay Prize for its contribution to contemporary Cuban theatre and drama.

Rine Leal, Vivian Martínez Tabares,
Magaly Muguercia
Translated by Patricia A. Suksi and Mayte Gómez

(See also the **Cuban-American Theatre** subsection in the UNITED STATES OF AMERICA article)

Further Reading

Antuña, María Luisa, and Josefina García-Carranza. 'Bibliografía del teatro cubano'. [Bibliography of Cuban theatre]. *Revista de la Biblioteca Nacional José Martí*, no. 3 (September–December 1971): 87–154.

Arrom, Juan José. *Historia de la literatura dramática cubana*. [History of Cuban dramatic literature]. New Haven, CT: Yale University Press, 1944. 132 pp.

Baliño Cedre, Omar. *La aventura del Escambray: notas sobre teatro y sociedad*. [The Escambray adventure: Notes on theatre and society]. Havana: Editorial José Martí, 1994. 65 pp.

Boudet, Rosa Ileana. *Teatro nuevo: una respuesta*. [New theatre: An answer]. Colección Espiral. Havana: Editorial Letras Cubanas, 1983. 304 pp.

Carrió, Raquel. *Dramaturgia cubana contemporánea: estudios críticos*. [Contemporary Cuban playwriting: Critical essays]. Havana: Pueblo y Educación, 1988. 81 pp.

Espinosa Domínguez, Carlos. 'Una dramaturgia escindida'. [A theatre divided]. In *Teatro cubano contemporáneo: antología*. [Contemporary Cuban theatre: Anthology]: 11–127. Madrid: Instituto Nacional de Artes Escénicas y Músicas del Ministerio de Cultura de España/Fondo de Cultura Económica, 1992.

Garzón Céspedes, Francisco, ed. *El teatro de participación popular y el teatro de comunidad: un teatro de sus protagonistas*. [Participatory and community theatre: A theatre that belongs to its protagonists]. Havana: Unión de Escritores y Artistas de Cuba, 1977. 146 pp.

González, Jorge Antonio. *Historia del teatro en La Habana*. [History of theatre in Havana]. Santa Clara: Dirección de Publicaciones de la Universidad Central de Las Villas, 1961. 163 pp.

——. *La composición operística en Cuba*. [Operatic composition in Cuba]. Havana: Editorial Letras Cubanas, 1986. 587 pp.

González Cruz, Luis F., and Francesca Colecchia. *Cuban Theatre in the United States: A Critical Anthology*. Tempe, AZ: Bilingual Press, 1992.

Graupera Arango, Elena. *Bibliografía sobre teatro cubano: libros y folletos*. [A bibliography of Cuban theatre: Books and pamphlets]. Havana: Biblioteca Nacional José Martí, Departamento de Información y Documentación de la Cultura, 1981. 27 pp.

La investigación como parte de un método de creación teatral. [Research as a form of artistic creation]. Havana: Departamento de Publicaciones y Conservación de la Biblioteca Nacional José Martí/Cuban Centre of the International Theatre Institute, 1981. 101 pp.

Leal, Rine. *Breve historia del teatro cubano*. [A short history of Cuban theatre]. Colección Panorama no. 2. Havana: Editorial Letras Cubanas, 1980. 185 pp.

——. *En primera persona 1954–66*. [In the first person 1954–66]. Colección Teatro y Danza. Havana: Instituto del Libro, 1967. 347 pp.

——. *La dramaturgia del Escambray*. [The playwriting of Escambray]. Mínima Ensayo. Havana: Editorial Letras Cubanas, 1984. 94 pp.

——. *La selva oscura*. [The dark forest]. 2 vols. Colección Teatro y Danza. Havana: Editorial Arte y Literatura, 1975–82.

Montes Huidobro, Matías. *Persona, vida y máscara en el teatro cubano*. [Persona, life and mask in the Cuban theatre]. Miami, FL: Ediciones Universal, 1973. 458 pp.

Muguercia, Magaly. *Teatro: en busca de una expresión socialista*. [Theatre: In search of socialist expression]. Colección Espiral. Havana: Editorial Letras Cubanas, 1981. 148 pp.

La obra de Brecht en Cuba. [Brecht's influence in Cuban theatre]. Havana: Departamento de Publicaciones y Conservación de la Biblioteca Nacional José Martí/Cuban Centre of the International Theatre Institute, 1981. 146 pp.

Ortiz, Fernando. *Los bailes y el teatro de los negros en el folklore de Cuba*. [The dance and theatre of the Negro in Cuban folk traditions]. Havana: Ministerio de Educación, Departamento de Cultura, 1951. 588 pp.

Pogolotti, Graziella. *Oficio de leer*. [The business of reading]. Colección Crítica. Havana: Editorial Letras Cubanas, 1983. 176 pp.

Séjourné, Laurette. *Teatro Escambray: una experiencia*. [The experience of Theatre Escambray]. Havana: Editorial Ciencias Sociales, 1977. 367 pp.

CURAÇAO

(see **NETHERLANDS ANTILLES AND ARUBA**)

DOMINICA

(see **COMMONWEALTH CARIBBEAN**)

DOMINICAN REPUBLIC

Sharing the Caribbean island of Santo Domingo (Hispaniola) with the French-speaking country of Haïti, the Dominican Republic is an independent Spanish-speaking country of 7.5 million people (1992), covering 48,700 square kilometres (18,100 square miles). An appreciation of this geographic situation is important since the unstable history of the country, its location between Puerto Rico and Cuba, and its similarities and differences with Haïti in terms of politics, language and culture are all closely related to the development of its long theatre history.

The Dominican Republic was probably the first country in the New World where theatre was performed in the European style, given that it was the first centre of European culture in the Americas as well as the administrative base for the political and religious conquest of the recently discovered continent. With the establishment of the first religious seminary in 1510 and the founding of the first university in the Americas, Santo Tomás de Aquino in 1538, theatrical activity emerged early on.

According to Willis Knapp Jones's book *Behind the Spanish American Footlights* (1966), when Christopher Columbus's son, Diego, was named governor of Santo Domingo in 1509, his wife, María de Toledo, brought three *églogas* (short, pastoral poems in dialogue form) written in 1492 by the Spanish playwright and poet Juan del Encina (1468–1529). These, along with other Spanish dramatic dialogues, were used as theatrical presentations by students and seminarians, who produced them for entertainment.

Visits to the island by several Spanish playwrights also contributed to theatrical activity. Among these writers were Micael de Carvajal (1490–1545), who visited in 1534, and Tirso de Molina (1538–1648), who may have written two plays while in Santo Domingo. De Molina lived in the Convento de las Mercedes and actually won a national poetry competition in 1616.

Along with other aboriginal people of the Americas, those of Santo Domingo also had their own indigenous form of theatrical expression: the *areíto* (a theatricalized ritual involving mime, song and dance), whose lyrics preserved the history of the native Indians, the Taínos. With some knowledge of the local language, the Spanish missionaries devised theatrical events that served as a bridge between the two cultures. The missionaries produced traditional *autosacramentales* (one-act religious plays) and plays based on the lives of the saints to make Christian instruction more attractive.

The country itself was also clearly attractive to many different colonizers at this time, including the English, who arrived in 1586; the French, who ran the country from 1795 to 1809; and the Spanish, who returned in 1809. Between 1822 and 1844, the Haïtians took control.

Juan Pablo Duarte (1813–76), founder of the state that would be called the Dominican Republic, actually used the theatre as a strategic arm of government, planting seeds for his ideas of liberation and separation of the country from Haïti to create a specific Dominican nationality. To this end, he established the Sociedad Dramática Filantrópica (Philanthropic Dramatic Society) and had works presented that would kindle the flames of independence among the Dominican people. Among the writers whose works were presented were Martínez de la Rosa (1787–1862), Vittorio Alfieri (1749–1803) and Eugenio de Ochoa (1815–72).

Even after the republic's official proclamation of independence and definitive separation from

Haïti on 27 February 1844, it was annexed again by Spain (1861–5) and endured another war before the restoration of the republic in 1865. Later it experienced two US military interventions (1916 and 1965), a harsh, thirty-year dictatorship by Rafael Trujillo (1891–1961) between 1930 and 1961, a *coup d'état* of its first democratically elected government in 1963 and a civil war in 1965–6.

To look at the history of the island from a theatrical standpoint, it probably can be said that the first important playwright in the country was Cristóbal de Llerena (1545–1610), whose famous *Entremés* (*Interlude*) was performed by students of the University of Gorjón in the Cathedral Primada de América on 23 June 1588. It is one of the earliest examples of Latin American theatre.

Records of this work exist thanks to a judicial inquiry that resulted from its 'scandalous' production. Legal proceedings were initiated by the authorities, which resulted in the script being recorded in its entirety in the documents of the judges of the royal court, who considered themselves victims of a 'literary impertinence carried to the extreme of a public performance'.

But despite such a notable exception, dramatic life generally languished during these early years. In 1610, the Synod of the diocese formally allowed theatrical presentations but said that prelates alone could license farces, *autosacramentales*, and plays in churches provided such works were 'pious, Catholic and honest'. The Synod also authorized the inclusion of comic *entr'actes* and even secular elements, so long as they were not 'dishonest or very worldly'.

As a result, by the eighteenth century performances were taking place regularly in private homes. From 1771 to 1778, Governor José Solano y Bote was even allowing performances of both Spanish and Dominican plays in the governor-general's palace.

In 1806 a fleet of English sailors destroyed a French fleet near the island. The French survivors established themselves in Santo Domingo where they ultimately founded the Sociedad Dramática de Santo Domingo (Dramatic Society of Santo Domingo). As dramatic scripts began to be written during the nineteenth century, plays focusing on the relationship between indigenous cultures and colonial and church policies became fashionable across the Americas and Dominican plays reflected this trend. Most dealt with the suffering of the aboriginal peoples at the hands of European conquerors, a theme that evolved through the century into various kinds of statements relating to the notion of independence.

This interest in indigenous themes resulted in such plays as *Iguaniona* (1867), by Javier Angulo Guridi (1816–84); *Ozema o la Virgen Indiana* (*Ozema, or The Virgin Indian*, 1870), by Félix María del Monte (1819–99); and *Anacaona*, by José Joaquin Pérez (1882–1900). Along with this interest in indigenous culture came a fascination with the Spanish folk form known as *costumbrista* (featuring local manners and customs) or, as it was called on the island, *criollismo*. This form, now rarely seen, reflected attitudes towards the native population along with the daily customs of the native-born Spaniards and is best seen in plays such as *Alma Criolla* (*Creole Soul*, 1916) by Rafael Damirón (1882–1946).

Throughout the nineteenth century, Dominican theatre further developed its interest in historic themes as well as in the creation of a national mythology, mostly through the work of amateur companies. Professional theatrical activity – right through 1946 – was limited for the most part to visits by foreign companies (mostly from Spain), to occasional productions by Creole groups (of Spanish ancestry born in the Americas) or to companies formed by foreigners resident in the country.

Quisqueya Players, founded in the early 1940s, was typical. Composed of US, British, Canadian and a few Dominican actors, it performed foreign plays in English. The Alianza Francesa (Alliance Française) occasionally presented works in French. The Unión de Austríacos (Austrian Union) produced German plays. It also introduced the singer Dora Merten to the country; her classes in singing subsequently contributed much to the development of Dominican opera.

During the 1940s there was also the Instituto de Señoritas Salomé Ureña (Salomé Ureña Institute for Young Ladies), founded by Urania Montás. Its members would later be involved in the founding of a new, more professional, experimental theatre centre.

Perhaps the key date in modern Dominican theatre history is 19 May 1946. It was on that date that a government decree created two official, professionally oriented theatrical institutions – the Teatro Escuela de Arte Nacional (National School of Theatrical Art) and the Cuadro Oficial de Comedias de Bellas Artes (State Company of Theatrical Arts) – both of which helped to train a generation of young professionals.

From their founding through to the early 1950s, these two organizations created a group of well-trained theatre professionals who did much to change the amateur and semi-professional nature of early Dominican theatre. By 1952, this young and growing movement got a major boost with the founding of the Cuadro Experimental de Comedias María Martínez (María Martínez Experimental Theatre Company), one of the country's first independent groups. María Martínez was the wife of President Rafael Trujillo.

This new company, founded by Máximo Avilés Blonda (b. 1931), Franklin Domínguez (b. 1931), Niní Germán, Ivelisse Acevedo and José Sanabia, gave further impetus to the growing national theatre and encouraged new approaches by playwrights, actors and directors. As well, the company inspired the creation of other groups such as the Yaqui Club and the Círculo Cultural (Cultural Centre).

From 1930 to 1961, when the country was under the rule of Trujillo, expression in all of the arts began to be controlled both directly and indirectly. The theatre that was produced early in the Trujillo regime is notable only for its occasional daring attempts to document the nation's earlier struggles. In 1944, for example, a group of university students under the direction of the Spaniard Ruddy del Moral commemorated the centenary of national independence with a revival of a play originally presented by Duarte, *La viuda de Padilla* (*The Widow of Padilla*), clearly reinterpreting the text as a new call-to-arms. On 26 April 1960, the group La Comedia del Arte opened the new Bellas Artes (Fine Arts) theatre in the capital with a play called *Espigas maduras* (*Ripe Grain*), written and directed by Franklin Domínguez. Depicting a confrontation between a tyrannical father and his sons, the play was a clear criticism of the Trujillo dictatorship.

From the 1960s to the 1990s, the Dominican theatre continued to professionalize and grow, embracing a multitude of themes and political concerns. Yet escapist plays and musical comedies remained extremely popular, usually being done on a commercial basis by groups of artists formed for single productions.

Structure of the National Theatre Community

In the Dominican Republic, professional theatre exists primarily in the capital city of Santo Domingo. In the provinces one finds mainly student and amateur groups, though in the 1980s a number of new companies emerged and individual theatre artists began working, particularly in theatre for social development.

In Santo Domingo, some fifteen professional and semi-professional groups regularly compete for the use of the two major stages – the 1,585-seat Sala de la República (Hall of the Republic) in the Teatro Nacional (National Theatre) and the 632-seat Auditorium de Bellas Artes (Fine Arts Auditorium). Collectively, the many companies offer a varied repertoire of modern Dominican, Latin American and world drama. It is the exception when any of the groups undertake plays from earlier periods.

Most productions run for just a few nights but particularly popular productions can sell out for fifteen or twenty performances, a far cry from the 1940s when it was difficult to fill a theatre for even a single night. Officially recognized companies are subsidized (the actors being paid directly by the government) and ticket prices are generally kept modest enough so that one can find all economic levels of society represented in the audience.

Among the officially recognized companies in the 1990s were the resident companies of the Teatro de Bellas Artes in Santo Domingo; the Teatro de Bellas Artes en el Interior, which performs in Santiago, San Juan de la Maguana, and San Francisco de Macorís; the Teatro Rodante (Travelling Theatre); and the Teatro Popular del Centro de la Cultura de Santiago (Popular Theatre of the Cultural Centre of Santiago). In general, official salaries are very low so most people working in the theatre seek additional work, often in commercial productions where they can earn the equivalent of a month's official salary in a few days.

Actors are now accepted as legitimate and generally respected artistic workers, a clear result of the professional training programmes created in 1946 and the development of the experimental groups in the 1950s and 1960s. From this period on, most actors, directors and playwrights recognized the importance of a university education. The goal at this time was to

founded in 1974 by Bienvenido Miranda (b. 1946), Michelle Elain and Lillyana Díaz. Giovanni Cruz is the director of two groups: Teatro Independiente Dominicano (Dominican Independent Theatre), an experimental group founded in 1978, and Giovanni Cruz Dirige (Giovanni Cruz Directs), founded in 1983.

In Santiago, the Dominican Republic's second-largest city, are two other important regularly producing groups – Teatro Popular del Centro de la Cultura (Popular Theatre of the Cultural Centre), founded in 1980 by Rafael Villalona, and the Teatro de la Universidad Madre y Maestra, which focuses on productions of classical plays.

There are many other groups operating in the country on an occasional basis. Among the most significant are the English-speaking Santo Domingo Little Theatre, the successor of the Quisqueya Players, which produces mostly US musicals; the musical theatre group Caliope and the Grupo de Expresión Corporal Bambalinas (Bambalinas Corporal Expression Group), both

directed by Servio Uribe; the black theatre group Los Girasoles (The Sunflowers), directed by Juan María Almonte; Producciones Teatrales (Theatrical Productions); Taller de Arte de Onix Báez (Onix Báez Artists' Workshop); Producciones Anamú (Anamú Productions); Productores Anónimos (Anonymous Productions); Los Comediantes (The Players); and the Arroyo Hondo Club (Deep Creek Club).

Since the 1970s, theatre-for-social-action groups have sprung up all across the island, many based on university campuses. Among the most interesting of the non-university-based groups are Teatro Experimental Popular (Popular Experimental Theatre), founded in 1976, Christian Melo's Teatro de la Casa de España (Theatre of the House of Spain), Angel Herrera's Histrión, and the Compañía de Teatro Real (Royal Theatre Company). Popular theatre groups also exist within the Central Bank of the Dominican Republic and at the Dominican Liberation Party.

This movement was very active between 1976

The Teatro Experimental Popular's production of Esteban Navajas Cortés's *La agonía del difunto* (*The Agony of the Dead*).
Photo: courtesy *Conjunto*.

and 1979 following the ideas of Jimmy Sierra, Reynaldo Disla and Basilio Nova. Jornadas de Teatro en la Calle (Street Theatre Days) were held regularly through to the mid-1980s. In the late 1980s, the Street Theatre Days became more structured and turned into Street Theatre Festivals, requiring audiences to go to specific locations to see performances. As well, the festivals no longer included masquerade carnivals, which were a popular feature of the Street Theatre Days and were limited to one or two 'performances' each day. Nevertheless, the Street Theatre Festivals continue to be celebrated each year and are well attended.

One important offshoot of Dominican popular theatre is the work being done in farm areas by the theatrical activist Héctor Jerez, founder and director of the Escuela de Arte Popular Nuevo Teatro (New Theatre School of Popular Art) in Santiago. This is popular theatre for *campesinos* (farm workers), a theatre 'by farm workers' and 'for farm workers'. It has had a significant impact in the hills and mountains of San José de las Matas and is one of the first movements of this kind to emerge in the Caribbean region.

The Dominican theatre does not maintain any kind of artistic relations or cultural exchanges with foreign countries. It therefore operates in virtual isolation, even from its closest neighbours – Puerto Rico, Haïti and Cuba. A certain tentative relationship does exist with the Venezuelan-based Centro Latinoamericano de Creación y Investigación Teatral (CELCIT; Latin American Centre for Theatrical Research) but beyond this there is really no permanent contact with international support groups. As a result, Dominican plays are generally unknown even in the rest of Latin America and other Latin American plays are generally unknown in the Dominican Republic. Only one group, El Nuevo Teatro, has been working actively to change this situation and its efforts constitute a real service to the Dominican theatre community.

Nevertheless, Dominican theatre has never enjoyed a more fruitful period than the late 1980s and 1990s. Audiences were growing, new companies were regularly appearing and interest in theatre was at its height.

Dramaturgy

There are four Dominican playwrights whose extended careers during the period under review give their work special import – Franklin Domínguez, Héctor Inchaustegui Cabral (1912–79), Manuel Rueda (b. 1921) and Máximo Avíles Blonda.

Domínguez has written some sixty theatrical works since 1953 and has won four National Prizes for Theatrical Education for his plays *Omar y los demás* (*Omar and the Rest*, 1975), *Lisístrata odia la política* (*Lysistrata Hates Politics*, 1978), *Los borrachos* (*The Drunkards*, 1983) and *Drogas* (*Drugs*, 1986). His play *La broma del senador* was published by the French theatre magazine *Avant-Scène*. Other works have been translated into various languages (including two into Chinese) and his plays have been performed widely within the Dominican Republic and abroad. In 1962, his play *La silla* (*The Chair*) was made into the first professional full-length Dominican film, and in 1987 *Los borrachos* was produced in New York. In Domínguez's theatre, human sentiments predominate, especially friendship and the solitude of the individual.

Héctor Inchaustegui Cabral is a Dominican poet who has contributed three adaptations of Greek classics – *Philoctetes*, *Hippolytus* and *Prometheus*. The plays were written in verse and have all been performed by the Teatro de Bellas Artes in Santo Domingo. Of the three, *Hippolytus* has the most fluid dialogue. Inchaustegui is an author of great dramatic force and his theatre is often dramatically overwhelming. He was also instrumental in the construction of two theatres at the University of Santiago, where he was vice-rector.

Manuel Rueda began his career as a playwright with *La trinitaria blanca* (*The White Trinitarian*), which won the 1957 National Prize for Literature and which was produced by the Compañia de Bellas Artes that same year. Since then, he has written seventeen plays including *Rey Clinejas* (*King Clinejas*), which won the 1980 National Prize for Theatre. His dramas tend to emphasize the frustrations of women in their daily lives. The plays are intelligent and finely crafted with great power and poetic beauty.

Rueda is equally adept at short stories, essays, novellas and poetry, and won the 1978 National Prize for Poetry. He is also a researcher in Dominican folklore, a cultural editor with the Santiago daily, *Hoy* (*Today*), and an accomplished pianist (a soloist, in fact, with the National Symphonic Orchestra).

Máximo Avíles Blonda is known for his often

religious poetic dramas. Through the 1950s, he worked with a number of experimental groups as an actor and a director. In 1959, he wrote his first play, *Las manos vacías* (*Empty Hands*), which was later performed by the Bellas Artes company. Beginning with his play *Yo, Bertolt Brecht* (*I, Bertolt Brecht*), winner of the Máscara Prize in 1966, his plays have become more political. His drama *Pirámide 179* (*Pyramid 179*, 1969) deals with a pyramid erected on the border between the Dominican Republic and Haïti and carries a clear message of international brotherhood.

In addition to these four, there are other playwrights outside the capital worth noting. Iván García Guerra tends to deal with the responsibility of the individual in relation to society and the necessity of recreating humanity to save humanity. Both themes are connected by a common concern with love in all its manifestations including unselfish love. García won the National Prize for Theatre in 1984 for his play *Andrómaca* (*Andromache*).

Haffe Serulle writes plays that have been compared to erupting volcanoes. His works focus on social issues interpreted from the viewpoint of historic materialism. He employs themes related to economic and political development and historical themes linked to moral disintegration.

Symbols are used in highly concrete ways to express the origins of the fragmentation. His major works include *Prostitucíon en la casa de Dios* (*Prostitution in the House of God*), *La danza de Mingó* (*Mingó's Dance*) and *Duarte*, which won the 1981 National Prize for Theatre.

Also notable is the work of Carlos Acevedo (b. 1932), whose most effective plays have been inspired by the classics and ancient myths. His major works include *Sísifo* (*Sisyphus*), *Gilgamés* (*Gilgamesh*) and *Momo*.

Among the later writers, one of the most promising was Reynaldo Disla (b. 1956). While still in his 30s, he was awarded prizes for his short stories, essays and plays. In 1985, the Casa de las Américas in Cuba gave him a prize for his play *Bolo Francisco*. In 1986, he won the National Prize for Theatre for a collection of four plays written to promote theatre for social action. By the beginning of the 1990s, he had written fifteen plays.

Directors, Directing and Production Styles

For a discussion of directing, see previous material in **Artistic Profile** and the opening, historical section.

Music Theatre
Dance Theatre

The native people of the Dominican Republic were virtually annihilated by the Spaniards at the beginning of the sixteenth century with the result that the nation does not have an indigenous music tradition. The original music of the *areítos* has also been lost. Nevertheless some plays – Jaime Lucero's *Mamasié* for example – have incorporated folk music and used traditional African instruments. But this is still the exception rather than the rule.

Musical theatre in the North American style entered the Dominican theatre in 1979 with the performance of the play *Solano*, with a book by Franklin Domínguez and music by the composer Rafael Solano. Presented at the Teatro Nacional, the production broke all Dominican records for audience attendance, attracting some 15,000 spectators in only eight performances. For the first time, drama, song, dance,

set and action were combined into a single theatrical production.

In 1984, Domínguez premièred another musical comedy, *El vuelo de la paloma* (*Flight of the Dove*), based on his own play of 1952, with music by Claudio Cohén. Also produced at the Teatro Nacional, the show ran for fourteen nights, again establishing attendance records.

Dance has also been slow to appear in the Dominican theatre but in the late 1980s and early 1990s assumed a significant place. Several factors contributed to its importance, including a wave of musical productions, the formation of a number of private academies of dance and ballet, the growing professionalism of Dominican dancers, and the formation of the National Classical Ballet and the National Folkloric Ballet.

The Taller de Danza Moderna (Modern

Dance Workshop) was founded by the dancer Eduardo Villanueva in 1983. It has produced some significant work introducing classical theatre into its dance productions. Villanueva's working philosophy is aimed at elevating dance to an expressionistic art form following the ideas of early German expressionism that were only being felt in the country in the 1980s. He chose to ally his work with drama because of the theatre's vast expressive possibilities. In 1985, he impressed audiences with a work based on García Lorca's *La casa de Bernarda Alba* (*The House of Bernarda Alba*); in 1986, he produced a powerful dance version of *Electra*.

Theatre for Young Audiences

Until the 1980s, there were no theatrical groups dedicated exclusively to productions for young audiences. Rather, the same directors and companies who performed for adults occasionally turned their talents to young people's theatre. The enthusiastic response of children to these performances, however, has led to the formation of theatrical groups specifically interested in works for children, and an increased production of theatre for young people.

Following the inauguration of the Teatro Nacional in 1973, the Puerto Rican children's group Arlequín, founded by Maricusa Ornes, made regular visits to the Dominican Republic and Arlequín now includes Dominican actors in its shows.

Playwright Franklin Domínguez has also worked regularly in this field. His plays *La niña que quería ser princesa* (*The Girl Who Wanted to Be a Princess*, 1957), *Duarte entre los niños* (*Duarte Among the Children*) and *Las aventuras de Chachalaca y Pelón* (*The Adventures of Chachalaca and Pelón*) have drawn large audiences.

In 1982, the Compañia Teatro Chiquito (Little Child's Theatre Company) was created by the actress Flor de Bethania Abreu (b. 1938) but after only one promising production its founder left the country for Spain. In 1985, the children's group Piloncito was founded by Kennedy Holguín-Veras. The group regularly performs for young people and has had great success with an adaptation of *The Little Prince*.

Producciones Teatrales broadened its field of operations in the 1990s and performed plays for children in movie houses in the capital. A number of well-known actors and actresses have also chosen to play from time to time in children's plays, usually with great success.

Under the direction of the Ministry of Education, the Instituto de Cultura (Institute of Culture) has created the Unidad de Teatro (Theatre Department) whose purpose is to train students from Santo Domingo's primary and secondary schools. The department offers instruction in theatre theory and technique and specifically teaches young people how to stage plays for student audiences.

Puppet Theatre

Puppet theatre has always had promoters and followers in the Dominican Republic but until 1978 its history and practice were casual and informal. It was in 1978 that the Ministry of Education's Institute of Culture created the country's first official puppet troupe, the Unidad de Teatro Guiñol (Puppet Theatre Company).

The company's function is to use puppet theatre as a resource for teaching and entertaining young people, especially at the primary school level and in rural regions. It offers regular workshops for both teachers and actors throughout the country and performs in schools and at public events. As well, it acts as an adviser to government agencies that wish to use puppets in their work with children.

In conjunction with the Ministry of Education, the company offers an annual workshop for students at the School of Theatrical Art and provides puppet workshops for teachers and cultural organizations. It also advises in this area within the National Council for Children.

Among the individual puppeteers who have

established reputations, the actress Ana Hilda García is perhaps the best known. Among the groups that deal with puppets regularly, the most significant are the Teatro de Títeres Cúcara-Mácara (Cúcara-Mácara Puppet Theatre) of Basilio Nova; and Chispitín, the children's section of the group Chispa, founded by Angel Mejia.

Two offshoots in the field are the Teatro Dominicano de Pantomima (Dominican Pantomime Theatre), founded in 1985 by the Argentine actor Rodolfo Lozada; and the Teatro Hojalata, a group founded by Margot Santos, based at the Autonomous University of Santo Domingo and which uses both live actors and puppets in its productions. Hojalata's work also crosses the line into the field of dance.

Design

Stage design is a relatively young art in the Dominican Republic. During the 1940s and through to the 1970s, it was unusual to find anyone focusing on the design aspects of productions. The four names one finds during this period – Luis Acevedo, Juan Gil, John García and Gregorio Vásquez – were technicians who either improvised their own scenery or simply copied foreign models.

Nevertheless, a few Dominican professional artists did try their hands at design, with the painters Silvano Lora and Iván García, who created the designs for Domínguez's *Espigas maduras*, achieving some recognition in the field. Also contributing was the Spanish artist Gilberto Hernández Díez.

It was not, however, until the opening of the Teatro Nacional in 1973 that the value and importance of creating sophisticated stage designs was fully appreciated and it is only since that time that Dominican artists have attempted consistently serious work in the field. In the 1980s and 1990s, the most important designers in the country included Bienvenido Miranda, Alejandro Ascuasiati, Lina Hoepelmán, Gerardo Quiróz, Rubén Cordero, Fernando Coste, Federico Arturo Pellerano, José Miura, Salvador Bergés, Bismarck Yermenos, Onix Báez and Ariel Ferrer.

Theatre Space and Architecture

Theatre buildings in the Dominican Republic date back to 1806, when the first permanent theatre space, in the former Santa Regina Church, was constructed. Between that year and 1955, three theatre buildings were built – La Republicana, the Colón and the Independencia.

In 1954, the neo-classical Palacio de Bellas Artes was built; it has a 632-seat proscenium theatre. Originally designed by Bebecito Martínez, the building was remodelled by Mariano Sanz and reopened in 1981.

In addition to the auditorium of the Palacio de Bellas Artes, there are seven other major halls in the country, the largest of these being the Sala de la República of the Teatro Nacional, inaugurated in 1973. Designed by Teófilo Carbonell, the Sala de la República is a proscenium space seating 1,585 (914 in the orchestra; 589 in the balcony). The theatre also has eight boxes. A large stage (31.5 metres high, 25 metres deep and 72 metres wide), it is, in fact, larger than Milan's Teatro alla Scala, Moscow's Bolshoi and Madrid's Teatro Real, whose general measurements served as a reference for its construction.

Within the Teatro Nacional is the Sala Ravelo, which seats 165. Designed by the same architect as the Sala de la República, the Sala Ravelo was conceived as a rehearsal hall but began to be used as a regular performance space in 1979 when a hurricane rendered the main theatre unfit for performances for a time. One of the more popular spaces by the 1990s, the proscenium has a width of about 6 metres.

One of the most intimate spaces in the country is a theatre located in an old home in the colonial district of Santo Domingo, the Casa de Teatro. Designed and built by Danilo Ginebra, it is not so much a theatre as a small, covered space that can be used for performances. Opened in 1974, the Casa de Teatro seats 200 and has its own sound and lighting equipment.

The Dominican-American Institute is a cultural organization with its own 500-seat auditorium that is often lent to theatre groups. The hall is rectangular in shape and has a floor-level stage built on movable platforms.

At the Universidad Católica (Catholic University) in Santiago, there is both a 2,000-seat outdoor amphitheatre and a well-equipped 500-seat indoor theatre. Both were designed by the firm of Mera, Muñoz and Fondeur. The thrust-stage indoor theatre was opened in 1975.

Also in Santiago is the Centro de la Cultura (Cultural Centre), which is a remodelled government building. Its 500-seat theatre was opened in 1980. Though not well equipped, it is a popular venue for theatre groups touring from the capital.

In the Medieval-styled town of La Romana, there is a so-called 'city of artists' and within this section another large outdoor amphitheatre exists, the Anfiteatro de Altos de Chavón, seating up to 5,000. Boasting outstanding natural acoustics, the theatre has been used for large-scale productions. Both the artists' settlement and the amphitheatre were the ideas of the American Charles Bludhorm, president of the Gulf & Western Company. The amphitheatre was designed by Dominican architect José Antonio Caro in collaboration with the Italian designer Roberto Copa.

The last theatre that should be mentioned in this architectural stocktaking is the 600-seat Teatro Vega Real in the town of La Vega. Long used as a cinema, it is regularly used by theatre groups as well. The stage is large enough to accommodate any type of production and discussions have taken place regularly through the years relating to turning the facility into a permanent theatre. A lack of funds has always been the main stumbling block.

Training

Five theatre schools exist in the Dominican Republic. The oldest is the Escuela de Arte Escénico (School of Theatrical Art), founded in 1946. Originally affiliated with the Conservatorio Nacional de Música y Declamacíon (National Conservatory of Music and Oratory), the school is located in the Palacio de Bellas Artes. Until 1987, when Russian-trained actress and director María Castillo became its head, the school could not be said to have a particular style or training philosophy. Under Castillo's direction, many new ideas were introduced and productions have shown her positive influence.

The Escuela de Nuevo Teatro, created in 1983, began as a branch of the Nuevo Teatro group. Perhaps the Dominican Republic's foremost training centre, its philosophy and training methods seek to replace the structures and forms of existing theatre with a new style of work capable of recognizing the country's own cultural roots. Highly resourceful, the school promotes techniques and chooses productions that introduce not only world classics but Latin American and Dominican authors as well.

The Teatro Anamú offers training through participation in productions, often with a 'Creole' flavour. Plays are drawn from the full range of dramatic literature and the mixed student–professional productions offer a very practical approach to theatrical instruction. Its longtime director is Alberto Ruiz.

Two 'popular' theatre training institutions exist in Santiago – the Teatro Popular at the Cultural Centre and the Escuela de Arte Popular connected to the Nuevo Teatro of Santiago. The Teatro Popular is a true theatrical workshop and is one of the country's most serious educational institutions. Founded in 1980, its first director was Rafael Villalona and his teaching methods continue to be used there. The Escuela de Arte Popular was founded by Héctor Jerez and has focused its efforts on developing the theory of agro-theatre in the rural areas of the country. It offers theatrical instruction in various districts of Santiago using both short courses and practical workshops. The school has no fixed location but rather accepts invitations to teach in neighbourhoods and clubs.

Criticism, Scholarship and Publishing

The first important work on Dominican theatre was written by Manuel de Jesús Goico Castro. Published in the annals of the University of Santo Domingo in 1945 and 1946, Goico's useful *Raíz y trayectoria del teatro en la literatura nacional* (*Roots and Evolution of the Theatre in National Literature*) was awarded the university's Fiallo Cabral Prize in 1945. Jaime A. Lockward continued Goico's work, extending the research into the modern period in his 1959 book *Teatro dominicano: pasado y presente* (*Dominican Theatre: Past and Present*).

Américo Cruzado focused on the contribution to Dominican theatre of visiting companies of Creole performers in his 1958 volume *El teatro en Santo Domingo, 1905–1929* (*Theatre in Santo Domingo, 1905–1929*).

In 1984, three major volumes on Dominican theatre history were published. *Panorama del teatro dominicano* (*Panorama of Dominican Theatre*) was put together by the Grupo Teatro El Gratey under the editorial direction of Yanela Hernández, Teófilo Terrero, Juan Félix Arostegui, Danilo Ginebra, Claudio Mir and Máximo Sánchez.

Also published in 1984 were two volumes entitled *Historia crítica del teatro dominicano* (*A Critical History of Dominican Theatre*) edited by José Molinaza. The first volume covered the period 1492 to 1844; the second volume covered 1844 to 1930. Both volumes were published through the Autonomous University of Santo Domingo.

Plays have traditionally been published privately at the writer's expense although in the 1980s a number of small publishing houses

Teatro El Gratey's production of *El proceso* (*The Trial*) at the Third Festival of Popular Theatre in New York in 1982.
Photo: Antonio García, courtesy *Conjunto*.

began to see some value in including plays by Dominican authors on their lists.

As for theatre journals, these have led a precarious life when they have appeared at all. In 1976–7, Frank Disla, Reynaldo Disla and Frank Richardson published six issues of a *Boletín teatro* (*Theatre Bulletin*). In 1984, the publication re-emerged as the bimonthly *Revista teatro* (*Theatre Magazine*), an independent publication directed at the country's theatre-for-social-action movement.

Periódico sobreescena (*On-Stage News*) published six issues in 1979. Distributed without charge, the publication operated exclusively on commercial advertising and provided general information on all theatre groups that were operating as well as reports from abroad.

In 1986, the *Boletín de teatro popular* began publishing under the editorship of Nives Santana. In the mid-1990s, this was the only publication still in operation.

Daily theatrical reviewing did not, for the most part, exist in the Dominican Republic until the 1950s. Even in the 1990s it was rare to find serious writers interested in and knowledgeable about the theatre. It was even rarer to find them working on newspapers. This is not to say, of course, that there were no journalists prior to the 1950s interested in reporting news related to the arts but rather to underscore the notion that these efforts were both sporadic and generally superficial.

Since the 1950s, a fairly large number of individuals have written on theatrical subjects in newspapers and magazines. Among those whose work stood out for its seriousness and professional awareness were Spanish-born Manuel Valledeperes, Pedro René Contín Aybar and Jaime A. Lockward. The critical work of Agustín Martín in the daily paper *Hoy* also stands out for its perceptiveness, responsibility, respect for his subject and concern for informing his readership about new developments in the field. Martín's objectivity distinguishes him from other theatrical commentators, whose ideological or artistic preferences sometimes result in opinions favourable only to certain groups or styles.

However, it can be said with some accuracy that journalistic criticism has very little influence on audience opinion in the Dominican Republic.

Influence on theatre groups themselves is another story, and press opinion genuinely influences the work of companies, actors, directors and producers.

Franklin Domínguez
Translated by Patricia A. Suksi

Further Reading

Aguilera-Malta, Demetrio. 'A propósito del teatro en la República Dominicana'. [Theatre in the Dominican Republic]. *Bulletin of the Pan American Union* 81, no. 12 (December 1947): 679–83.

Bonelly de Díaz, Aida. 'El teatro nacional en Santo Domingo'. [The National Theatre in Santo Domingo]. *Bohío Dominicano* 25 (1973): 2–18.

Goico Castro, Manuel de Jesús. *Raíz y trayectoria del teatro en la literatura nacional.* [Roots and evolution of the theatre in national literature]. Santo Domingo: Anales de la Universidad de Santo Domingo, 1945.

Grupo Teatro El Gratey. *Panorama del teatro dominicano.* [Panorama of Dominican theatre]. Santo Domingo: Editorial Corripio, 1984.

Henríquez Ureña, Max. *Panorama histórico de la literatura dominicana.* [Historical panorama of Dominican literature]. 2nd ed. Santo Domingo: Librería Dominicana, 1966.

Lockward, Jaime A. *Teatro dominicano: pasado y presente.* [Dominican theatre: past and present]. Ciudad Trujillo: Editorial la Nación, 1959.

Molinaza, José. *Historia crítica del teatro dominicano.* [A critical history of Dominican theatre]. 2 vols. Santo Domingo: Editora Universitaria, Universidad Autónoma de Santo Domingo, 1984.

Reynolds, Bonnie Hildebrand. 'La semiótica y la supervivencia en *Cordón umbilical* de Arturo Rodríguez Fernández'. [Semiotics and survival in *Umbilical Cord* by Arturo Rodríguez Fernández]. *Gestos* 12, no. 1 (November 1991): 85–95.

Reyes, Ramón E. 'El tema universal y la libertad en el teatro dominicano actual'. [Freedom and other universal themes in contemporary Dominican theatre]. *Revista Aula* 20 (1972).

Sánchez, Federico. *El teatro dominicano en su historia.* [History of Dominican theatre]. Colección Antológica. Santo Domingo: Nuestra Voz, 1986.

DUTCH CARIBBEAN

(see **NETHERLANDS ANTILLES AND ARUBA**)

ECUADOR

The Republic of Ecuador (equator), with a 1990 population of some 10.3 million, is an Andean country of 283,600 square kilometres (109,500 square miles) situated between Colombia in the north and Perú in the south. The eastern part of the country – the Oriente – is an area of tropical forest crossed by numerous rivers including the Amazón. The capital and major cultural centre since colonial times is Quito, a major Inca settlement even before 1533 when the Spanish first reached the city.

Ecuador became part of the confederation of Gran Colombia along with Colombia and Venezuela in 1822 following the defeat of the Spanish. In 1830, the confederation collapsed and Ecuador became an independent nation.

The country's second most important city is Guayaquil, a lowland port on the Pacific coast. Through the centuries, there has been competition between Guayaquil and Quito leading at times to actual revolutions between the country's conservative elements (centred in Quito) and its liberal elements (centred in Guayaquil). Agriculture has traditionally been the base for the country's economy but petroleum has become increasingly important.

The earliest evidence of theatre in Ecuador may be found in the religious Mystery plays and folk dances that peasants still perform in the towns and countryside. In spite of their colonial Catholic influence, these pieces retain clear links to aboriginal rituals dating back to pre-Columbian times and in them one can recognize traces of lingering native Quechua culture. Unfortunately, no text from the pre-Columbian period survives that can provide a clear image of what this theatre was about.

Father Juan Velasco (1727–92), in his *Historia antigua* (*Ancient History*), referred to some of these early theatrical forms when he wrote about the annual Capac-Rymi Festival:

The celebration took place at the conclusion of the corn harvest as the last festival of the year. Instructional comedies, composed by the wiser members of the royal family, were enacted for the benefit of the people. Once these were over, a variety of popular games took place.

In the 1990s, handed down by oral tradition through many generations, these plays and dances, as enacted in the streets and plazas of numerous villages and towns, represented the vestiges of the country's aboriginal theatre and still managed to maintain something of their original character.

As Ecuador was colonized by the Spanish, theatre forms began to take on a clear sixteenth- and seventeenth-century Spanish style: sketches, dialogues, one-act comedies and short farces. Produced in villages and cities and generally focusing on religious themes, these early colonial plays laid heavy emphasis on morally acceptable outcomes and the dissemination of Catholicism. A propaganda tool for the conquerors, extant examples of this early theatre date from the eighteenth century and provide evidence, mostly through farces, that a theatre of local manners and customs was also manifesting itself despite the emphasis on Spanish styles and forms.

Isaac J. Barrera (1884–1970) noted the existence of two eighteenth-century codices, the first one being entitled *Ramillete de varias y diversas flores compuesto por el D. Diego Molina, Clérigo Presbítero, Colegial que fue de los Reales de S. Fernando y después del de menores de S. Luis, en la ciudad de Quito, año de 1732* (*Anthology of Various and Diverse Flowers Composed by Don Diego Molina, Presbyter, High Scholar of San Fernando and Later of San Luis, in the City of Quito, Year of 1732*). The second codex, *Colección Gangotena*, included two dramatic dialogues, one about Christmas Eve (*Noche Buena*) and the other entitled *Coloquio de las comparaciones de Doña Elena y el casamentero* (*Dialogue Between Doña Elena's Choices and the Matchmaker's*), and a short farce called *Entremés gracioso de Juanillo y Antonio desaciertos* (*Interlude of Juanillo and Antonio the Error-prone*).

An outstanding piece from the first codex is *Bayle o sainete del mercachifle* (*Dance or Farce of the Huckster*). The protagonist is a Spaniard who quickly loses his fortune because of his womanizing. Now a huckster, he is besieged by three women but ultimately avoids their wrath. The farce ends with music and dancing.

Entremés gracioso de Juanillo y Antonio desaciertos, from the second codex, is an original example of the local picaresque in which the author makes fun of the immigrant Spaniard who pretends to be a nobleman.

But apart from these examples of local theatre, the colonial period was poor indeed when it came to producing works of any consequence, mainly because of prevailing socio-economic conditions. Theatre as such was considered dangerous by the ruling classes and a real threat to exposing colonial economic arrangements. At the end of the eighteenth century, as one example, Inspector-General José Antonio de Areche forbade the production of Quechua plays because they were perceived 'to inflame the Indians and to help them start uprisings'.

There was little room for the development and growth of drama in Ecuador during the Wars of Independence culminating in the birth of the republic in 1830. Over the next century, the control of political power in the country by the conservatives did not do much to change the antagonistic attitude of the government towards the theatre.

Paradoxically, out of this rather inhospitable climate three important playwrights emerged by the 1890s: Juan Montalvo (1832–89), Abelardo Moncayo (1847–1917) and Francisco Aguirre Guarderas (1860–1905). In 1872 and 1873, Montalvo wrote five plays under the collective title *El libro de las pasiones* (*The Book of Passions*). Each of the plays is a story of suffering built around a single recognizable type – a dictator, someone who has been excommunicated, a woman with leprosy.

In 1880, the dictator Ignacio De Veintimilla (1828–1908) erected in Quito the Teatro Nacional Sucre (Sucre National Theatre), a Baroque building that became the venue for most of the capital's major theatre productions from that time on.

In 1881, Moncayo made one of the country's first spirited defences of theatre, challenging the church's many attacks on theatrical performances. On 11 June 1892, Aguirre Guarderas's play *Receta para viajar* (*Prescription for Travel*) opened at the Teatro Nacional. It depicted the prejudices of Quito society and of the country at large. One of the landmarks of Ecuador's dramatic art, the play attacks social climbing, the militaristic state's many sinecures and the intelligence of Quito's middle classes. He ridicules marriages of convenience and the continuing importation of foreign styles and tastes. It is an accurate social portrait of the many changes taking place in Ecuador at the time.

By 1925, three theatre companies were in

operation in Quito: the Compañía Dramática Nacional (National Dramatic Company), the Compañía de Comedias y Variedades (Comedy and Variety Company) and the Compañía Lírica (Music Company). Theatre art was being taught formally in Quito for the first time and going to the theatre was becoming popular.

In 1932, Jorge Icaza (1906–78) wrote a play about the oppression of the native Indian population, *Flagelo* (*The Scourge*), the first time this question was addressed in Ecuadoran dramaturgy. Published in 1936, the play was not staged until 1940 when Leónidas Barletta mounted a production of it in Argentina in his Teatro del Pueblo (People's Theatre).

There are two clear trends in Ecuadoran playwriting in the fifty-year period between about 1890 and 1940. The first is a theatre of philosophical, poetic and psychological interest focusing on the eternal problems of individuals – love, loneliness and death. The 1935 play *Paralelogramo* (*Parallelogram*) by Gonzalo Escudero (1903–71) and the plays *El velorio del albañil* (*The Mason's Wake*, 1938) and *La furiosa manzanera* (*The Furious Neighbour's Woman*, 1939) by Augusto Sacotto Arias (1907–79) are good examples of this style – well written, philosophically concerned and better read than seen performed.

The second type of theatre is one that is concerned with social issues, condemns inequality, wants to change reality and supports efforts to effect change in society. *Estampas quiteñas* (*Quito Images*, 1937), first written for the actor Ernesto Albán Mosquera (1912–84) by Alfonso García Muñoz (b. 1900), falls into this category. Albán continued his own brand of social criticism as an actor through the 1930s, both in Quito and across the country, with his performances of a character called Evaristo Corral y Chancleta, a kind of Spanish-American Charlie Chaplin.

From the 1940s on, a number of companies emerged and then disappeared. Among these were the Sociedad de Amigos del Teatro (Friends of Theatre Society), founded in 1947 by playwright Jorge Icaza, and the Marina Moncayo Company, founded in 1947.

Particularly fashionable during this period were comedies of manners but the interest in these works lasted only briefly, perhaps because of the public's new fascination with films. One of the few contemporary genres to attract attention was that of French plays from the immediate post-war period, especially those arriving in the country via literary journals. The few attempts to stage them, however, failed to attract audiences of any size.

In a 1957 study, Francisco Tobar García (b. 1928) drew attention to the state's lack of support for theatre companies and the scarcity of organized theatre groups in Ecuador. Despite this, some cultural institutions, such as the Casa de la Cultura Ecuatoriana (Ecuadoran House of Culture), did lend sporadic support to theatres. Nevertheless, there was no clearly articulated cultural policy to provide economic assistance to theatres. But groups and individuals continued to emerge.

In Guayaquil, the Agora theatre group began to produce in 1960, first under the direction of Paco Villar (b. 1915) and later under the direction of Ramón Arias (b. 1939). For almost a decade, this group created an important repertoire of both Ecuadoran and European plays in the country's main shipping port.

In the early 1960s, the Casa de la Cultura approached the United Nations Educational, Scientific and Cultural Organization (UNESCO), asking them to recommend a theatre teacher who could help the new Ecuadoran theatre develop. Recommended was Italian-born Fabio Paccioni, who arrived in Quito in 1964. Remaining in the country for five years, he convinced the government to implement a major promotional campaign for theatre in general and helped establish both the Teatro Ensayo (Rehearsal Theatre) in 1965, for which he staged eight productions, and the Teatro Popular Ecuatoriano (Popular Ecuadoran Theatre) in 1967. Paccioni also attempted to establish a school of theatre within the Casa de la Cultura, and later founded an independent group, La Barricada (The Barricade).

His productions, including a number of Ecuadoran works such as an adaptation of one of César Dávila Andrade's (1918–67) poems, *Boletín y elegía de las Mitas* (*Indian Forced Labour: Bulletin and Elegy*, 1967), helped establish the significance of theatre in the country. By the late 1960s, Paccioni's ideas of an art theatre in Quito had begun to clash with the idea of some of his younger company members to establish a theatre of social action that could deal directly with contemporary problems. It was at this point that Paccioni formally broke with the Teatro Popular and founded La Barricada. In 1969, he returned to Europe.

In 1968, Eduardo Almeida Naveda (b. 1946) was named director of the Teatro Popular. His early productions set the tone for his years with

Marina Moncayo and Jorge Icaza's 1947 Marina Moncayo Company production of Florence Barclay's *El Rosario*, adapted by André Bisson.

the company. Included were the Argentine Andrés Lizarraga's *¿Quiere usted comprar un pueblo?* (*Do You Want to Buy a Country?*, 1968) and Brecht's *Die Gewehre der Frau Carrar* (*The Rifles of Mother Carrar*, 1969).

In 1970, after being elected president of Ecuador for the fifth time, José María Velasco Ibarra (1893–1978) assumed power as a dictator. Almost immediately, he demanded that the Casa de la Cultura modify the Teatro Popular's repertoire. This demand was rejected by both Almeida and members of the company, many of whom resigned. In 1970 the company was formally disbanded.

In 1971, Almeida founded the Teatro Experimental Ecuatoriano (TEE; Ecuadoran Experimental Theatre). Its first production was an adaptation of Icaza's novel *El chulla Romero y Flores* (*The Young Romero and Flores*), the first of many socially critical Ecuadoran works staged by the company.

Throughout the 1970s, other groups began to follow the lead of Teatro Experimental, working without direct subsidy and without any sort of government approval. Included in this group were Los Guayacanes and Jorge Suárez's (b. 1940) collective El Juglar (The Minstrel), both established in 1970 but the former short-lived; and Teatro Ensayo, under the direction of Antonio Ordóñez (b. 1943), a disciple of Paccioni.

In 1974, the Central University of Quito established the country's first public School of Theatre and in 1979 a theatre workers' association was founded, the Asociación de Trabajadores de Teatro.

During the 1980s, other theatre groups and workshops were established that helped to expand the opportunities for both national dramatists and those interested in working on collective creations. Among the groups in this category were Ollantay, founded in 1968 by Carlos Villareal (b. 1954); Teatro Ensayo de la Universidad Católica, founded in 1971 but which ceased operating in 1986; Taller de Actores Fábulas (TAF), founded in 1978 by Diego Pérez (b. 1948); and Malayerba (Weed), founded in 1981 and composed mostly of non-Ecuadoran nationals. During this same period, a number of street groups began appearing. In this specialized area, the work of actor Carlos Michelena (b. 1954) stands out for its originality.

Despite this increase in theatrical activity between the 1950s and the early 1990s and despite the fact that successes in oil exploration during the 1970s increased the gross national product significantly, there was still virtually no state support for the creation and promotion of new theatre and drama in Ecuador. The only source of support of any size was from the Department of Cultural Dissemination of the Central Bank of Ecuador, which attempted through modest subsidy to promote the work of several theatre groups within the country.

To round out this portrait of theatre in Ecuador, one must underscore the uniqueness of the country's indigenous theatrical forms, whose richness of expression began to be absorbed by theatre professionals only in the 1960s. In almost every mountain village, ritual dances, vocal recitals and even folk-based religious plays take place, attracting large numbers of spectators from every socio-economic background.

Now more structured than in its original forms, this type of performance can be found every September in the town of Latacunga, not far from Quito, during the town's annual religious celebrations. For three days, groups such as Mamá Negra (Black Mama) create performances involving masked dancers, mime artists and musicians on the streets and around the churches. These popular celebrations, involving the entire community, serve as a reaffirmation and reminder of community roots and identity. They are also reminiscent of the enormous theatrical pomp and splendour that was clearly part of these indigenous events from the earliest times.

Among the most important of the still-performed religious plays are *Los caporales* (*The Chiefs*), *Los corazas* (*The Cutlasses*), *La mamá negra*, *Vaca loca* (*Crazy Cow*), *Sanjuanes* and *Aricuchos*.

Structure of the National Theatre Community

Ecuadoran theatre companies, operating without subsidy for the most part, fund themselves primarily through box-office receipts and the occasional public workshop. The companies produce when they have particular productions ready.

There are some twenty groups operating in Quito and another ten in Guayaquil. The companies that produce most regularly are the TEE, Teatro Ensayo, Ollantay, Malayerba and TAF in Quito and El Juglar in Guayaquil. Other Quito groups of note include Teatro CLAM, La Matraca (The Rattle), the Compañía Ecuatoriana de Teatro (Ecuadoran Theatre Company) and Intiñahui.

In the area of children's theatre, three groups stand out: Arlequín (Harlequin), La Rayuela (Hopscotch) and Rana Sabia (Wise Frog).

Among the groups using streets and town squares for their stages are the Teatro de la Calle (Street Theatre), La Vereda (The Footpath), La Oreja (The Ear) and Saltimbanquis (The Jugglers). Groups working in this style appear and disappear with great frequency.

Prizes, including the National Prize for Playwriting, are awarded sporadically. In 1990, for example, the Casa de la Cultura in Quito organized a national playwriting contest and published a volume of the eight winning plays in 1991, called *Teatro ecuatoriano* (*Ecuadoran Theatre*).

The only festival held every year is the one sponsored since 1987 by the Universidad Laica Eloy Alfaro of the city of Manta. Each September and October Latin American groups are invited to submit their projects.

The Asociación de Trabajadores de Teatro (Association of Theatre Workers), founded in 1979, is based in Quito. Its principal objective is to carry out activities related to workers' lives. It has its own office and it organizes seminars and workshops, but does not receive regular government funding.

Theatre tickets usually cost twice as much as film tickets, ranging from 5,000 to 10,000 sucres, the equivalent of US$2–$5.

Artistic Profile

Companies

Since 1945, a large number of theatre companies have operated in Ecuador. Most, however, due to a lack of state support, have had very short lives.

In the 1940s, the Teatro Experimental Universitario (TEU; Experimental University Theatre) began its life under Sixto Salguero (b. 1910). The company performed at the Teatro Nacional Sucre in Quito presenting a repertoire that included works by foreign playwrights. When it closed down in 1963, it had staged some eighteen productions. The TEU did much to encourage theatre activity and was known for its productions of modern European plays.

Two companies were established in 1954 – Intimo (Intimate), by German-born director Carlos Loewemberg (1900–61); and Teatro Independiente (Independent Theatre), by Francisco Tobar García. By 1956, Intimo had been forced to close down due to lack of funds despite Loewemberg's tireless work as both teacher and creator. During the theatre's ten-production existence, he produced a repertoire of mostly major European plays.

Teatro Independiente, on the other hand, was much more committed to the production of scripts by national authors – particularly those of its director-playwright Tobar, the country's most prolific playwright until his retirement and voluntary exile in 1969. Tobar's works – both classically styled tragedies and comedies – satirize the bourgeoisie, Tobar's own social class. His plays consistently dealt with this group's loss of social values and constituted a depiction and condemnation of both its absurdity and its decay. His major plays are the tragedy *En los ojos vacíos de la gente* (*In People's Vacant Eyes*, 1968) and the comedy *Balada para un imbécil* (*Ballad for an Imbecile*, 1968).

Teatro Ensayo, founded in 1965 by Fabio Paccioni and taken over by Antonio Ordóñez in 1969, has included in its repertoire numerous works with a clear social message. Ordóñez's major productions have included Lizarraga's *Santa Juana de América* (*St Joan of America*, 1973), Brazilian-born João Cabral's *Muerte y vida Severina* (*Life and Death, Severina*, 1977) and the stage version of Icaza's famous novel *Huasipungo* in 1970.

Eduardo Almeida's Teatro Experimental Ecuatoriano has attempted to create a popular and activist theatre by including folk customs and music in its works. Among its most typical productions have been *Misterio Barroco* (*Baroque Mystery*, 1980) and *Crónica de la vieja banda* (*Chronicle of the Old Band*, 1981).

Up to 1994, the only Ecuadoran group to receive the Ollantay Continental Prize offered by the Ateneo of Caracas and the Caracas-based Latin American Centre for Theatre Creation and Research has been TEE. The prize was given in 1988 for 'contributing . . . to the evolution and perfection of the modern stage in Quito and the interior of Ecuador'.

The work of Guayaquil's El Juglar is rooted in collective creation and is aimed at a mass audience. The company expresses in direct terms its vision of the psychology of the people of the country's coastal region. Among its major productions have been *Guayaquil Superstar* (1980), *¿Como es la cosa?* (*How Is It?*, 1983) and *Banda de pueblo* (*The Village Band*, 1984).

The work of Ollantay has also focused on collective creations and has been extremely popular with workers' groups, while TAF, sponsored in the beginning by the Alliance Française but now independent, is essentially an actors' workshop. TAF is also involved with developing the work of playwrights. Its director, Diego Pérez, is a playwright himself and won a national prize in 1982 for his children's play *Pródigo Cuscungo* (*Prodigal Cuscungo*). CLAM, under Carlos Villalba (b. 1940), is primarily a company for theatre students.

One other actively working group is Malayerba, founded in 1981 in Quito. It is directed by the Argentine Arístides Vargas (b. 1954). Among its significant productions have been *Robinson Crusoe* (1981), *Francisco de Cariamanga* (1992) and *Jardín de pulpos* (*Octopus's Garden*, 1992), all collective creations. Taller de Teatro (Theatre Workshop), founded in 1977, is directed by Ilonka Vargas (b. 1943), and generally produces an eclectic repertoire.

Dramaturgy

Demetrio Aguilera Malta (1909–81), one of Ecuador's outstanding dramatists, delved into the psychology of his characters with his socially committed dramas. In *Dientes blancos* (*White Teeth*, 1955), he looked at the domination of a

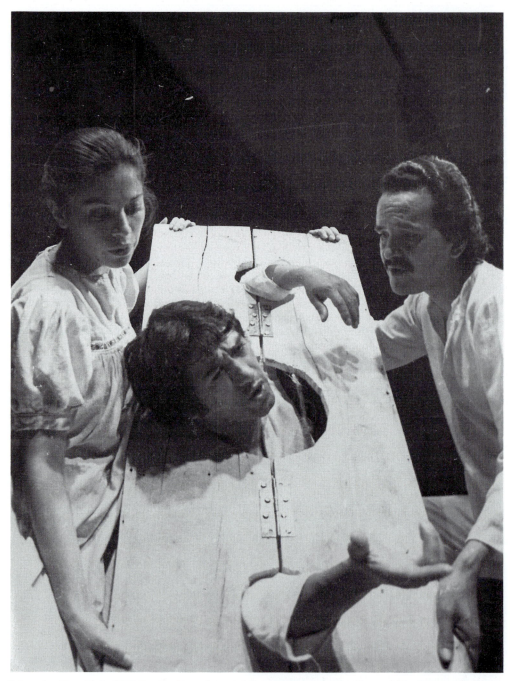

Eduardo Almeida's 1979 Teatro Experimental Ecuatoriano production of his *Dance of the Sad Night*, designed by Almeida.
Photo: Marco Sandoval.

black worker by a white boss. In *El tigre* (*The Tiger*, 1955), Aguilera's best known work, he dramatized episodes in the life of a *montubio* (a peasant from the coastal region) and created a study of fear as a motivating factor in his life. His most accomplished work was probably *Infierno negro* (*Black Hell*, 1967), an exposé of power and capitalism in a theatrically grotesque style.

Ricardo Descalzi (1912–90) wrote *Clamor de sombras* (*Clamour of Shadows*) in 1950. The play, which deals with a brother and sister who are victims of Oedipus and Electra complexes, was written in the well-made-play style, and was awarded the first National Theatre Prize that year. In his next play, *Portovelo* (1951), he attacked both the subhuman working conditions of a small town's gold miners and the US company that owned the mine.

Another playwright with an interest in going beyond folk comedies was Pedro Jorge Vera (b. 1914). Vera's drama *Luto eterno* (*Eternal Mourning*, 1956) was an attack on the false moral values and hypocrisy of a group of people living in the capital in reduced circumstances. Vera's characters tend to be more universal than local: his play *Dios de la selva* (*God of the Jungle*), first produced in 1941, is a good example of this style.

José Martínez Queirolo (b. 1931), a Guayaquil-based author, writes short plays on social themes full of black humour and which vary in tone according to their dramatic form. His most produced work is a dramatic monologue of poetic intensity called *Réquiem por la lluvia* (*Requiem for Rain*, 1963). Other major works by this writer include *La casa del que dirán* (*The House of Gossip*, 1962), *Cuestión de vida o muerte* (*A Matter of Life or Death*, 1962) and the farce-satire *Q.E.P.D.* (*Rest In Peace*), first produced in 1969.

An actor in the 1950s, during the 1960s and 1970s Alvaro San Felix (b. 1931) wrote a number of plays in which he examined Ecuador's history through the lives of various political personalities. Typical of this style are *El caudillo en llamas* (*The Chief in Flames*, 1979), about Eloy Alfaro, and *Espejo alias Chusig* (1979). His play *La herida de Dios* (*God's Wound*, 1978) confronts the different versions historians have of the dictator García Moreno. This last work won the Aurelio Espinosa Polit Prize in 1978 in the prestigious Concurso Nacional de Literatura (National Literature Competition).

In 1991, San Felix's *El ojo de la aguja* (*The Eye of the Needle*) appeared in *Teatro Ecuatoriano*, published by the Casa de la Cultura. In 1968, Hugo Salazar Tamariz (b. 1923) produced three of his most interesting pieces: *La falsa muerte de un ciclista* (*The False Death of a Cyclist*), *Toque de queda* (*Curfew*) and *Por un plato de arroz* (*For a Bowl of Rice*). In these plays, Salazar's social criticism is conveyed by means of a series of lively theatrical games.

Another notable playwright is Jorge Dávila Vásquez (b. 1947), winner of the National Theatre Prize for *El caudillo anochece* (*The Strongman's Twilight*) in 1968. In 1981 the Imprenta Monsalve in Cuenca published his play *Con gusto a muerte* (*With Pleasure to Death*). His *El espejo roto* (*The Broken Mirror*) won the Casa de la Cultura Prize in 1990 and was published in 1991 in *Teatro Ecuatoriano*.

Directors, Directing and Production Styles

For a discussion of directing, see previous material in **Artistic Profile** and the opening, historical section.

Music Theatre
Dance Theatre

The only true music theatre experience in the Ecuadoran theatre is offered by TEE, directed by Eduardo Almeida. The music, usually based on Ecuadoran tradition, is used as inspiration for actors' improvisation; it is also used to give structure to the theatrical language used by the group. TEE combines music with both dance

and mime. It has participated in various festivals in Europe including the Theatre of Nations in 1980 and the Contemporary Musical Theatre Festival in Rennes in 1979 and 1981. The group's performance of *Danza de la noche triste* (*Dance of the Sad Night*, 1970), written and directed by Almeida, is a poetic examination of the lives of Indians of the Andes involving popular melodies, laments, masks, flutes and drums.

Indigenous theatre expression also includes these elements, all structured in a narrative form.

The Compañía Nacional de Danza (National Dance Company) was created in 1976 in Quito. It is directed by Arturo Garrido. Among its important productions have been *Altazor* and *Rite of Spring* by Stravinsky, both with choreography by Garrido and both presented in 1993. Another work, *Siete lunas y siete serpientes* (*Seven Moons and Seven Snakes*), with choreography by Wilson Pico, was performed in 1994, sponsored by the Ministry of Education and Culture.

The Ballet Ecuatoriano de Cámara (Ecuadoran Chamber Ballet), founded in 1980 and directed by Rubén Guardera (b. 1949), depends on the Consejo Provincial de Pichincha (Pichincha Provincial Council) for support. It has a training school for dancers both in classical and modern styles. The group has twenty dancers. Its best known works have been *Tango* (1993) and *Carmen* (1993), both choreographed by Luis Aguilar.

Theatre for Young Audiences
Puppet Theatre

A number of companies in Ecuador now produce theatre for young people. The best known has been Rana Sabia, a puppet company created in 1970 and directed by Fernando Moncayo (b. 1942) and Claudia Monsalve (b. 1950). Rana Sabia's plays tend to re-create, didactically, Ecuador's history.

Another puppet theatre company, Rayuela, founded by Petronio Cáceres (b. 1948) in 1975, specializes in rod-puppets and visual effects. In its production of *Glotito, el lobo que se convirtió en globo* (*Glotito, the Wolf Who Turned Into a Balloon*, 1977), Rayuela used the popular stories of the countryside. The company maintains a year-round weekend repertory.

Teatro Experimental Ecuatoriano is still another group producing plays for young audiences. The company has performed various versions of *The Little Prince* by Saint-Exupéry (adapted for the stage by Eduardo Almeida) since 1973. Other works produced by TEE were *Pluft el fantasmita* (*Pluft, the Little Ghost*, 1984) by the Brazilian Maria Clara Machado, *Pulgarcito* (1984) by the Cuban Francisco Garzón, and *El extraño caso de la muñeca que se cayó en un cuento* (*The Strange Case of the Doll Who Fell Into a Story*, 1985).

In Guayaquil, the Ana Von Buchwald group performs on a more or less regular basis staging a variety of Latin American puppet plays. Ollantay, directed by Carlos Villareal, has been active since 1975 and often combines puppets and clowns. Its plays *Uno es ninguno* (*One is Nobody*, 1988) and *La gata tinta* (*The Black Cat*, 1982) were its most popular successes.

La Pájara Pinta Teatro Estable de Muñecos (Spotted Bird Puppet Theatre), in Cuenca, was founded in 1981 by Felipe Vega de la Cuadra. Its productions have ranged from *Pinocchio* (1982) to *Historia del pájaro feo* (*History of the Ugly Bird*, 1983), based on a Chiapas Indian legend.

Almost all groups, in fact, do some work for children, including collective works that are staged in theatres or, more frequently, in schools and other educational institutions. Many of these shows are taken on tours of the country.

Design
Theatre Space and Architecture

Two notable Ecuadoran designers are Chilean-born José Rosales (b. 1944) and Walberto Quintana (b. 1947). Rosales, a professor of theatre design at the Central University's School of Theatre from 1977 to 1993, worked regularly with dance and theatre troupes. His designs for

José Rosales's design for the 1993 Malayerba production of Ramón del Valle-Inclán's *Lights of Bohemia*, directed by Wilson Pico.
Photo: Eduardo Quintana.

the ballet *La edad de la ira* (*The Age of Wrath*), presented by the Ballet Ecuatoriano de Cámara in 1991, and for *Luces de Bohemia* (*Lights of Bohemia*) by Ramón del Valle-Inclán, staged by

the group Malayerba in 1993, were highlights in his career.

Quintana graduated in design from the Central University in 1980. His major designs include those for *Milagro en el mercado viejo* (*Miracle in the Old Market*) by the Argentine Osvaldo Dragún in 1977 and for *Die Ausnahme und die Regel* (*The Exception and the Rule*) by Bertolt Brecht in 1980. Both works were performed by the Theatre School of the Central University.

There are eight major theatre spaces in Quito, ranging in size from a 5,500-seat amphitheatre (the Agora, owned by the Casa de la Cultura) to the convertible space of TEE, which has a capacity of 120. The oldest of the Quito theatres is the proscenium Teatro Sucre (built in 1880), which holds approximately 1,000. In 1976, the Casa de la Cultura built a 270-seat theatre-in-the-round called the Teatro Prometeo (Prometheus Theatre), which is popular as a rental facility with many small groups.

Other proscenium theatres in Quito range from 300 to 2,500 seats (the largest being the Jaime Roldós Aguilera Theatre); there is also one thrust stage with a capacity of 170 (the Aula Benjamín Carrión).

In Guayaquil, two theatres exist – the 150-seat proscenium Teatro El Juglar and the 500-seat proscenium Humoresque.

Outside of these two cities, auditoriums are usually found within municipal or provincial council buildings or on university campuses.

Teatro Experimental, Ollantay and Malayerba are the only groups that maintain their own rehearsal and performance spaces. Most theatres are used on a rental basis. These groups have adjusted their productions to various available spaces: classrooms, streets, plazas, church atria and esplanades.

Training

The School of Theatre of the Faculty of Arts at the Central University of Ecuador in Quito, founded in 1974, focuses mainly on the techniques of Stanislavski and specializes in acting and theatre design. Since 1980, the Ecuador chapter of the Centro Latinoamericano de Creación e Investigación Teatral (CELCIT; Latin American Centre for Theatrical Creation and Research) has offered acting workshops using a variety of alternative techniques. The Mudanza group, created in the 1980s, bases its work on movement and

dance, and has its headquarters in Quito. Mudanza offers five-semester courses for mime and six-semester courses for instructors of mime.

At the theatre department of the Central University, four years of study are required for actor training, three for design and five to become a director.

Malayerba offers workshops that last one and a half years; students are often invited to continue working with the group on completion of the course.

Criticism, Scholarship and Publishing

The Casa de la Cultura is the country's major publisher of books in the literary and historical fields and publishes plays through its Colección Básica de Escritores Ecuatorianos (Basic Collection of Ecuadoran Writers) and its Colección Letras del Ecuador (Ecuadoran Letters Collection).

The Casa de la Cultura published the standard work in the field, Ricardo Descalzi's *Historia crítica del teatro ecuatoriano* (*A Critical History of Ecuadoran Theatre*, 1968).

The Department of Cultural Dissemination of the Central Bank of Ecuador has published a review, *Cultura*, since 1978, which often includes essays and notes on national theatre activities. There is no specialized source of theatre criticism in the country. Occasional reports and reviews appear in the daily press and in literary reviews.

Eduardo Almeida Naveda
Translated by Rafael Barreto Rivera

Further Reading

Barrera, Isaac J. *Historia de la literatura ecuatoriana*. [History of Ecuadoran literature]. Quito: Libresa, 1979. 1,317 pp.

Barriga López, Franklin, and Leonardo Barriga López. *Diccionario de la literatura ecuatoriana*. [A dictionary of Ecuadoran literature]. Quito: Casa de la Cultura Ecuatoriana, 1973. 780 pp.

Chávez Franco, Modesto. 'El teatro en Guayaquil'. [Theatre in Guayaquil]. In *Guayaquil '70, Metrópolis Dinámica*. [Guayaquil '70: A dynamic metropolis], ed. Demetrio Aguilera Malta. Quito: Imprenta Fray Jadoco Ricke, 1970.

Descalzi, Ricardo. *Historia crítica del teatro ecuatoriano*. [A critical history of Ecuadoran theatre]. 6 vols. Quito: Casa de la Cultura Ecuatoriana, 1968.

Estrella, Ulises. 'El teatro en el Ecuador'. [Theatre in Ecuador]. *Nivel* 10 (October 1963): 5.

——. 'El teatro obrero en el Ecuador'. [Working-class theatre in Ecuador]. *Conjunto* (October 1969): 117–20.

Luzuriaga, Gerardo. *Bibliografía del teatro ecuatoriano, 1900–80*. [Bibliography of Ecuadoran theatre, 1900–80]. Quito: Casa de la Cultura Ecuatoriana, 1984. 131 pp.

——. 'La generación del 60 y el teatro'. [The generation of the 1960s and the theatre]. *UTIEH/C* 34 (1980): 157–70.

EL SALVADOR

Central America's smallest country, El Salvador (The Saviour), has Central America's greatest population density with some 6 million people in 1993 living in an area of just 21,400 square kilometres (8,300 square miles). Inhabited in its pre-Hispanic days by both the Mayas and the Pipils, a branch of the Aztec civilization, El Salvador won its independence from Spain in 1821. In 1823 it joined the Central American Confederation, a union that also included Guatemala, Nicaragua, Honduras and Costa Rica. Three years after the confederation dissolved, El Salvador formally declared its independence.

Civil war and revolution characterized much of the country's history over the next 100 years. In 1944, General Maximiliano Hernández Martínez, a dictator who had ruled since 1931, was driven from office but military dictatorships maintained control until 1960. In 1962 a new constitution was proclaimed. From 1969 until 1976, El Salvador fought a series of wars with neighbouring Honduras over the alleged mistreatment of Salvadoran citizens in Honduras, a dispute eventually settled by the Organization of American States.

When President Carlos Humberto Romero was overthrown in 1979, the leftist Frente Farabundo Martí de Liberación Nacional (Farabundo Martí Front for National Liberation) began a guerrilla war against the government. Well into the 1990s, the activities of the military, aimed at combating the leftist push, resulted in a series of atrocities including the murder of Archbishop Oscar Arnulfo Romero y Galdámez (b. 1917) in 1980, and that of six Jesuits in 1989. The 1990s saw several attempts at national reconciliation.

Theatrically, the nineteenth century saw the arrival in the country of Spanish, Cuban and Mexican touring companies, many including actors of other nationalities, especially Argentines. Their style was essentially the *costumbrista* (featuring local manners and customs) form mixed with low comedy. Many artists who came to El Salvador with these companies stayed in the country. Among these was the Spaniard Valero Locha (1894–1975), a renowned set designer who founded the Academy of Painting that now bears his name. Another was Gerardo de Nieva (d. 1944), founder of the first National School of Dramatic Art in 1928 and its director until 1935. Not surprisingly, the school under de Nieva tended to emphasize the *costumbrista* style.

The period of *costumbrista* theatre in El Salvador was, in fact, a productive one in terms of both dramatic literature and stage productions. Visiting companies would often include performances of plays written by Salvadoran dramatists in their repertoires. Unfortunately, manuscripts of most of these plays have been lost and there are few records. Nevertheless, the titles of some of Roberto Suárez Fiallos's plays are known because they were recorded on programmes and mentioned in newspaper reviews. Also known from public records is that the visiting companies had small box-office receipts because of the large number of complimentary seats that had to be given to official guests.

De Nieva was also one of the first to produce the works of national authors, although the actors he worked with were not always professional. Over time, however, a number of theatre groups emerged from this: La Compañía Oasis (Oasis Company), directed by José Serrano, and Los Amigos del Teatro (Friends of Theatre), among others. These companies did not have regular seasons, but rather gave only occasional performances. Most of the actors worked at other jobs and even put in their own money while seeking additional financial help from both private and government institutions. Salvadoran theatre in the 1990s, to a very great extent, still operated this way.

Theatre activity in El Salvador, as well as cultural activity in general, has been closely tied to political change. However, the dictatorship, which consolidated its power around 1950, also brought to the country important economic growth, political stability and modernization. Under this government, the Dirección General de Bellas Artes (National Directorate for Fine Arts) was created, with a branch to administer theatre. This branch supported de Nieva's school and, eventually, a resident company, the Elenco Estable de Bellas Artes (Fine Arts Permanent Company).

First directed by Darío Cossier (1907–91), originally from Argentina, one of its first productions was Cossier's own *El sueño de la niña pobre* (*The Poor Girl's Dream*, 1951), a play for young audiences that actually included child actors. The play toured hospitals, parks and schools. Cossier later moved on to direct the Teatro Obrero (Workers' Theatre) of the Ministry of Labour and Social Welfare; in 1952 his place was taken by Edmundo Barbero (1899–1985), a Spanish actor and director with a long history of work in Latin America.

Barbero brought to Salvadoran theatre European existentialism. His first production was Jean-Paul Sartre's *No Exit*, which created an extended and heated polemic. Barbero was accused of being immoral and of not being a true artist, a charge that eventually led to more general questions about morality and art, culture and society. But both the Elenco Estable de Bellas Artes and the directorate withstood the charges and even turned them to their advantage as catalysts for activity and discussion in the community.

Barbero also supported the production of the works of national authors and encouraged young artists to write. He produced a wide variety of Spanish and French classics and eventually helped create a national infrastructure, developing actors as well as technicians. Eventually, though, Barbero was accused of attempting to subvert the system, and of being both a communist and a Spanish republican. He was exiled from El Salvador in 1955.

Barbero's replacement was Mexican-born Fernando Torres Laphan but the lack of official financial support to theatres continued. The Elenco Estable soon found itself unable to survive the political, economic and social crises in the country, which were affecting all government operations. Virtually all attempts to make changes were regarded as subversive and there was little room to manoeuvre. Torres Laphan continued as director of the company until 1959 when the Spaniard Alonso de los Ríos replaced him. Subsequent directors included Salvador Salazar Carrión, also a Spaniard; Franco Cerutti, an Italian; Waldo Chávez Velasco (b. 1932), Adelina de Gumero and eventually Margarita de Nieva, Gerardo de Nieva's daughter. Both de Gumero and Margarita de Nieva took the work of the company to the provinces, often for the benefit of charitable institutions. None of these directors, however, left any particular artistic mark on the Elenco Estable de Bellas Artes or on Salvadoran theatre.

The Elenco Estable de Bellas Artes eventually closed, and a new institution took its place – the Centro Nacional de Artes (CENAR; National Arts Centre), launched by Walter Béneke (1930–80), a playwright and, from 1968 to 1972, Minister of Education. As minister, Béneke began educational reforms, attempting to create support for the arts as part of the secondary school curriculum. Hailed initially, the move became bureaucratic and ultimately produced no real change.

When Barbero was fired from Bellas Artes, the Universidad de El Salvador sought to hire him as director of its new Teatro Universitario (University Theatre). Immigration authorities, however, had an order to deport him, and the university hired in his place André Moreau. The desire to found a university theatre was but one of the many struggles that university authorities had to win in order to achieve their final goal: university autonomy. Under Moreau's leadership, the Teatro Universitario helped in this battle, producing in his first season (1956) García Lorca's *Don Perlimplín con Belisa en el jardín* (*Don Perlimplín with Belisa in the Garden*), Molière's *Le Médicin malgré lui* (*The Physician in Spite of Himself*) and Béneke's *El paraíso de los imprudentes* (*The Paradise of the Unwise*).

The Teatro Universitario was a department within the Faculty of Humanities and filled the social gap that Elenco Estable de Bellas Artes had left. The company welcomed students from all university disciplines and individuals from outside the university. Moreau was a creative artist and an organized administrator but eventually he was accused of spending too much money on a production of *Oedipus Rex*, which had been staged for only a single performance. As a result, Moreau quit the Teatro Universitario and left the country with, ironically, Edmundo Barbero returning as the theatre's new leader. Barbero picked up where he had left off at Bellas Artes, but now with a move towards Theatre of the Absurd and other avant-garde forms.

Barbero managed to turn Teatro Universitario into a regularly producing company, first using students, but later adding professionals who had worked with him at Bellas Artes or who were part of his independent company, Grupo Experimental El Colibrí (Hummingbird Experimental Company). Actors were paid a monthly salary whether they performed or not. Public performances were usually free of charge, but were occasional rather than part of regular seasons. Barbero later produced *Waiting for Godot*, which resulted in the same kind of misunderstandings and polemics as had been faced by his earlier *No Exit*.

Teatro Universitario eventually began taking its work to the provinces. Its first touring performance was on the occasion of the inauguration of the Centro Universitarios de Occidente y Oriente (Western and Eastern University Centres) in the cities of Santa Ana and San Miguel. This led to the creation of a new company in Santa Ana by Norman Douglas, who brought together university students from the western region and a few experienced actors from the capital city, San Salvador. Douglas became very involved in linking his theatre to Latin American theatre developments as a whole and later became a leader in Salvadoran collective creation. He also experimented with the ideas of Brazil's Augusto Boal, and the Colombians Enrique Buenaventura, Santiago García, Gilberto Martínez and others. His later work was close in style to Jerzy Grotowski's Poor Theatre.

The university theatre company that began operating in San Miguel was led by David Humberto Trejo, who moved in a much more commercial direction. Playing primarily on the university campus, the company also used the National Theatre and toured to other schools and even played in parks. Trejo experimented with Calderón's *El gran teatro del mundo* (*The Great Theatre of the World*) in the basement of the Metropolitan Cathedral, which at the time was still under construction.

This period of active university theatre ended abruptly on 17 July 1972, the day on which the Salvadoran armed forces occupied the university and suspended all activities.

Educational reform on the secondary school level had begun in El Salvador in 1968 with an attempt to create an arts curriculum involving music, theatre and visual arts. At the same time, several institutions were amalgamated: the Bellas Artes, the Conservatorio Nacional de Música (National Conservatory of Music) and the Escuela Nacional de Artes Plásticas J. Alberto Imery (J. Alberto Imery School of Visual Art). But the attempt to create a true national culture still had not been realized by 1971. The state's five-year plan for 1977–82 acknowledged that 'foreign cultures still dominate El Salvador.... If things remain this way, the Salvadoran of the future will be a European from the last century'.

The new curriculum, however, did bring about some changes. There were scholarships for new students to study art, and prizes given in student cultural festivals that included theatre. The new curriculum continued in operation until 1984, and saw the creation of many student organizations for the promotion of national culture and entertainment, some still functioning in the 1990s.

Barbero also took charge of the Centro Nacional de Artes with the support of his former student Eugenio Acosta Rodríguez and, in 1977–8, with the help of Roberto Salomón (b. 1945). Salomón had studied theatre in the United States from 1967 to 1969 and in 1970 began to work at the Centro Nacional de Artes. Salomón later founded Actoteatro, where he worked until 1981.

This new period was one in which a 'search for the national' took place within the context of the new sense of national liberation, a search also influenced by the beginning of a civil war that the country suffered until 1991.

Although theatre activity in El Salvador continued to increase in the 1990s, it was still an inconsistent activity. The only consistent work was at the commercial level, mostly in the *telenovela* (soap opera) style.

In the subsidized theatre, those who give the money continue to call the tune, making sure that work always stays within certain political lines. Even theatre festivals are limited in their choices, being sponsored by wealthy corporations with specific interests. Only the university theatres have attempted to influence society by taking their work to poorer areas. Yet even here, people are heavily influenced by the values espoused on television.

Structure of the National Theatre Community

Commercial theatre activity dominates Salvadoran theatre life. Such productions can be seen at almost any time and tend to be quite conservative. The country's few subsidized theatres tend for political reasons to be conservative as well in their play choices and only a few exist. Independent theatres and university theatres are the most adventurous in their approaches and the most numerous for occasional work.

In 1994, there were only two theatre companies producing regular seasons – Sol del Río (River Sun) and Hamlet, both independent groups. More than a dozen other companies produce on an occasional basis.

The major artists' union in the country is the Asociación Salvadoreña de Trabajadores de Arte y la Cultura (Salvadoran Association of Art and Cultural Workers).

Artistic Profile

Companies

Until 1950 only the middle class went to the theatre in El Salvador, but the founding by Darío Cossier of the Teatro Obrero in 1952 began a new period in which theatre opened to other social classes. Cossier led Teatro Obrero until 1979 when Herber Escalante took over. Teatro Obrero took theatre to poor neighbourhoods, to outlying areas and to factories. It was founded in the spirit of Peronism and its founder was, in fact, an Argentine who arrived in El Salvador when Peronism was still a populist alternative in the Americas. Members of Teatro Obrero were, for the most part, factory workers themselves and bureaucrats from the Ministry of Labour. For all its ideals, its work never achieved any significant artistic standards. Nevertheless, the fact that it produced the work of important foreign playwrights such as Sean O'Casey was itself of significance.

Two independent companies that came to be more important in the country were Sol del Río and Hamlet. Founded by graduates of the CENAR in 1973, Sol del Río left the country in 1980 because of the civil war. The group worked during this time in México, other parts of Central America and Europe, especially Denmark. It came back to El Salvador in 1988 and since then has produced full seasons and offered theatre training. With an avant-garde global interest, its members have brought to El Salvador many new theatrical ideas.

Hamlet's work and vision, on the other hand, are in direct opposition to those of Sol del Río and its repertoire is more traditional. Because of this, the company enjoys great commercial support, and most of its members have connections with commercial television or advertising agencies, allowing them to have regular seasons along with a sophisticated publicity network.

Hamlet's activity peaked in 1985 when it joined a group of actors graduating from Bellas Artes to create an annual festival, the Gran Teatro Rex. The goal of the festival was primarily to increase audiences. The festival received financial support from the Rex tobacco company for three years but when that support was withdrawn, Hamlet went back to its own regular seasons.

Actors from Hamlet have argued that theatre is only meant to make people laugh and to help them forget the country's conflicts. Their large-scale productions follow these ideas and are extremely costly. Many have argued that such work is inappropriate, however, in such a poor country. Their 1991 production of the farce *Cleopatra metió la pata* (*Cleopatra Put Her Foot In It*) was typical of Hamlet's work: a splendid exhibition of costumes, lights and jewellery.

The university theatres present a true alternative to this kind of theatre but their successes tend to be short-lived and sporadic. As a result, their work does not achieve a high level of quality and often stays within a simple, didactic mode. Among the university groups, however, the Escuela Libre de Teatro (Free Theatre School) of the Universidad de El Salvador, stands out. It presents plays of its own creation with modest financial support from the university. Among the group's original plays are *El crack de Octubre* (*The Crack of October*, 1991), directed by Edwin Pastore, and Alvaro Menén Desleal's (Alvaro Menéndez Leal,

Fernando Umaña's 1993 Sol del Río production of *Tierra de cenizas y esperanzas* by Roberto Salomón, Naara Salomón, Fernando Umaña and Carlos Velis.
Photo: Vera Jursys.

b. 1931) *La bicicleta sobre el muro* (*The Bicycle against the Wall*), which received the University of El Salvador's Anniversary Prize in 1991.

Another important university theatre group is Sueños de Vida (Life Dreams), created by students from the Universidad Centroamericana José Simeón Cañas but operating independently of the university. The group is directed by Edgar Roberto Gustave, who also writes most of the plays produced.

Another group formed by graduates of the CENAR and which has managed to present work of some quality, although in inconsistent seasons, is Bululú (Excitement). Like most independent groups, it also operates in San Salvador.

Dramaturgy

During the early decades of the century, writers favoured a folkloric style and their plays were colourful and energetic. Among the best of these were *Una chica moderna* (*A Modern Girl*) and *Celia en vacaciones* (*Celia On Holiday*) by Alberto Rivas Bonilla (1891–1986); *Candidato* (*Candidate*) by José María Peralta Lagos (1873–1944); *El Padre Eusebio o las píldoras del Dr Naranja* (*Father Eusebio, or Dr Orange's Pills*), *La dulce paz del villorrio* (*The Sweet Peace of a Shantytown*) and *Zacate pal'macho* (*Grass for the Male*) by Ernesto Arrieta Yúdice (b. 1898); *Pájaros sin nido* (*Birds Without Nests*) and *Vientos de Octubre* (*October Winds*) by Pedro R. Quiteño (1899–1962); and *Yo quiero ser diputado* (*I Want To Be a Member of Parliament*) by Cresensio Castellanos Rivas and Antonio Allas.

Among the work of later more realistic writers, plays of note include *La ira del cordero* (*The Lamb's Anger*, 1958) and *Nuevamente Edipo* (*Oedipus Again*, 1968) by Roberto Arturo Menéndez (b. 1930); *Funeral Home* (1958) and *El paraíso de los imprudentes* (*The Paradise of the Unwise*) by Walter Béneke; *Fábrica de sueños* (*Factory of Dreams*) by

271

Waldo Chávez Velasco; and *Júpiter esclavo o Blanca Celis* (*Jupiter Enslaved, or Blanca Celis*, 1895) by Francisco Gavidia (1863–1955).

Alvaro Menén Desleal's *Luz negra* (*Black Light*, 1966) is among El Salvador's most successful plays – some 100 performances in two years – while *Las escenas cumbres* (*The Top Scenes*, 1983) by José Roberto Cea (b. 1939) and *Jugando a la gallina ciega* (*Playing Blind Man's Buff*, 1966) by Roberto Armijo (b. 1937) are other plays premièred by university theatres. *Anastasio Rey* (*King Anastasio*, 1971) by José Napoleón Rodríguez Ruiz, with music by Ezequiel Nunfio (1930–72), was one of the country's few attempts at Brechtian epic theatre.

Among the more nationalistic plays are Sol del Río's *Criaturas* (*Creatures*) by Alberto Adellach, with Fidel Cortez and Fernando Umaña; *El retablo del flautista* (*The Flautist's Altar*), a collective creation based on Jordi Teixidor's work, directed by Umaña; and *Historias con cárcel* (*Stories with Jail*), based on the well-known *Historias para ser contadas* (*Stories To Be Told*) by Argentine playwright Osvaldo Dragún. Among the most important productions after 1988, when the group returned to El Salvador, were *Apócrifos* (*Apocryphal*), based on texts by the Czech writer Karel Čapek,

directed by Umaña; *La segura mano de Dios* (*God's Secure Hand*), based on a poem by Roque Dalton, with stories about the dictatorship of General Maximiliano Hernández Martínez; and *Las Rositas de Lorca* (*Lorca's Rositas*), an adaptation of several texts by García Lorca.

The classical *Historias de Moros y Cristianos* (*Stories of the Moors and Christians*) is still staged in El Salvador as part of religious festivities in many towns. Many of the villagers, in fact, know some of the text by heart because it is part of their local traditions. The earliest playing manuscript is from 1880 with newer versions published in the books *Cuscatlán típico* (*Typical Cuscatlán*) and *Materiales folklóricos de El Salvador* (*Salvadoran Folklore*) by María de Barata and in *Expresión literaria de nuestra vieja raza* (*Literary Expressions of Our Ancestors*) by Adolfo Herrera Vega.

Directors, Directing and Production Styles

For a discussion of directing, see previous material in **Artistic Profile** and the opening, historical section.

Music Theatre
Dance Theatre

Despite the appearance of dance and music in the religiously rooted *Historias de Moros y Christianos*, music and dance have rarely been tied together with drama in Salvadoran productions. It is therefore reasonable to say that except for folk forms in music and the occasional touring dance company, neither music theatre nor dance theatre as such really exist in El Salvador.

This said, there have been some notable exceptions. In 1971 the play *Anastasio Rey* by José Napoleón Rodríguez Ruiz was presented at the Festival Centroamericano de Teatro (Festival of Central American Theatre) by the Teatro Universitario in association with the University Choir and Dance Companies, under the overall direction of Edmundo Barbero. José

Santamaría directed the music and Gilda Hernández the dance, which was part of the overall work and which also acted as liaisons between scenes.

Another of the rare attempts to incorporate music into a theatre piece was in the play *Memoria en carne propia* (*Memory of My Own Skin*, 1990) by José Roberto Cea, using a single actor and music and movement to link the various scenes. The play itself – performed by an actor-dancer – focuses on a man from the countryside who moves to the city.

Both *Anastasio Rey* and *Memoria en carne propia* received literary prizes in Central American Theatre Festivals.

There is, for the record, one school of dance in San Salvador.

Theatre for Young Audiences
Puppet Theatre

Like most forms of theatre in El Salvador, children's theatre and puppet theatre both operate within and against political boundaries. In 1987, Narciso de la Cruz, a member of Teatro Chanchavalancha, one of the few regularly producing children's groups in the country, said at the Prímera Jornada Cultural por la Paz (First Cultural Celebration for Peace) that children's theatre brings together many different kinds of marginalized people who otherwise would never be exposed to artistic work. De la Cruz argued that

> in the context of the historical process that El Salvador is living, this kind of theatre helps immensely to raise consciousness, allowing people to have a clearer perspective of the reality they live. It also contributes to a holistic human development, encouraging people to develop artistic consciousness.

The oldest theatre for children in the country is the Teatro Escolar (School Theatre), founded in 1933. Many of El Salvador's classic children's scripts came from this company, including *Ensueño y realidad* (*Dreams and Reality*), *Regeneración* (*Regeneration*) and *Así se triunfa* (*The Way to Win*) by Antonia Portillo; a dramatization of *Don Quijote de la Mancha* by Concepción Monterrosa; *Entre periodistas* (*Among Journalists*) and *Soldados de la patria* (*Soldiers of the Homeland*) by Ana María de Solís; *La independencia* (*Independence*) by Sara Cosme; *La mecanografista del siglo* (*The Century's Typist*) by Laura Guerrero Ramos, and *Personitas grandes* (*Big Little People*) and *Desengaños* (*Disillusions*) by Adela Salcedo.

The group Hamlet, directed by Nelson Portillo, has also regularly staged a children's season each year, doing mostly adaptations of classic fairy-tales such as *Little Red Riding Hood*, *Sleeping Beauty*, *The Wizard of Oz* and *Snow White*. Perhaps the country's greatest success in this field was a production by Sol del Río in 1969, *Criaturas*. El Unicornio is another group of note.

Puppet theatre, however, has a much older tradition in El Salvador. Anthropologist Stanley Boggs has argued that ancient figurines called *balinas* from the western part of the country – thought to represent girls and women, and probably symbols used for healing and fertility rituals – might also have been puppets used to

Fernando Umaña's 1992 El Unicornio production of *Zili*.
Photo: Luis Galdámez.

represent the gods or other characters in the telling of religious stories.

Using folk puppets in the service of popular theatre, Roberto Franco founded a group called Pequebú. It later changed its name to Teatro de la Ranita (Theatre of the Small Frog). Franco also gave workshops and took puppet theatre to marginal areas and schools. He even worked with Catholic priests committed to his theology of liberation. Out of the classes he taught came new groups: Cipitín, Los Ruiseñores (The Nightingales), Chanchavalancha, Já Já! (Ha Ha!), Bululú and Calabaza (Pumpkin), all using puppets and/or mime techniques. Franco was, sadly, kidnapped – allegedly by the military – and was never seen again.

From 1974 to 1980, Paco Campos was director of Pícolo Teatro, which operated directly under the Secretariat of University Relations at the University of El Salvador. Campos organized a Teatro Guiñol Universitario

(University Puppet Theatre), which toured schools and other institutions. The university, however, was taken over by the army in 1979 and the theatre was closed down, not reopening until 1984. In the 1990s, Campos directed the group Galatea.

Design
Theatre Space and Architecture

Given the minimal subsidy to Salvadoran theatre and the lack of significant physical resources, design *per se* has been an activity almost without importance in the country. Basic designs that can be pulled together inexpensively and easily tend to be used.

As for buildings, there have been only three major theatres in the country's history. The largest was the Teatro Nacional in San Salvador, designed by architect Daniel Beylard and opened in 1917. Used for only a short time exclusively as a theatre space, it was later a cinema and still later municipal offices. In 1961 ownership of the building was transferred to the Dirección General de Bellas Artes, and in 1978 it was remodelled. Since then, it again has been used solely as a theatre. The Teatro Nacional is eclectic in style, a combination of romantic, neo-classical and Baroque, with a surrealist mural in its dome painted in 1976–7 by Salvadoran artist Carlos Gonzalo Cañas.

The Teatro de San Miguel, inaugurated in 1909, has had the same type of history as the Teatro Nacional in San Salvador. The difference is that right from the beginning it was used for nearly everything. It later served as a movie theatre and then as a telecommunications centre for the region. In 1972, a group of university students, under the leadership of David Humberto Trejos, took over the building and began to renovate it to house a theatre festival, but the renovations were never finished and the theatre reverted to its multi-use format.

The Teatro de Santa Ana also began a modern process of renovation that was never finished. Designed and decorated by a group of Italian architects following the *art nouveau* style, the theatre was officially finished in 1910. Its style is also eclectic, combining Doric, Ionic and French forms with Baroque sculptures.

For the most part, theatre productions are held outside these buildings in non-traditional venues ranging from community auditoriums to lecture halls and school rooms.

Training
Criticism, Scholarship and Publishing

The only theatre school operating in the 1990s was connected to the Centro Nacional de Artes (CENAR), although even this was not operating regularly. Despite proposals to create a new curriculum, the school did not have control of its own finances and was therefore unable to maintain a coherent programme of classes and productions. Instead, it was limited to occasional workshops and public performances.

Other training institutions have also lacked clear and consistent policies. This was the case even for the theatre school within the Bellas Artes, directed by Edmundo Barbero, where spontaneity and Barbero's own philosophy were the only consistency.

Neither journalistic criticism nor theatre scholarship operate at a particularly high level in El Salvador. One of the few people who comment consistently on the theatre is Oscar Manuel Doñas, who has long had a permanent arts column, 'Entre bambalinas' ('Behind the Scenes') in the newspaper *La prensa gráfica* (*The Graphic Press*).

As for scholarship, Alvaro Menén Desleal attempted to put together a history of theatre in El Salvador, which was partially published in the magazine *Cultura* in 1965, while Roberto Armijo contributed an important essay to the study *Escenarios de dos mundos* (*Theatre of Two Worlds*), published in Madrid in 1988. José

Roberto Cea's short essays from his unpublished manuscript *Del teatro en El Salvador: panorama histórico crítico* (*On Theatre in El Salvador: A Historical and Critical View*) look at theatre in the country from pre-Hispanic times to the 1990s.

Two publishing houses that pay attention to theatre (usually only as educational material) are Canoa Editores and Clásicos Rocxil. The Dirección de Publicaciones of the Ministry of Education publishes the magazine *Cultura* on an occasional basis.

Darío Cossier published a volume of children's plays, *Teatro infantil* (1984), that contains *El lobo feroz . . . era buenito* (*The Big Bad Wolf . . . Was Nice*), a children's comedy in two acts; *El sueño de la niña pobre* (*The Poor Girl's Dream*); *El escaparate encantado* (*The Magic Storewindow*); and *Muñecos de colores* (*Colourful Puppets*).

Mercedes Maiti de Luarca (1900–74) also published a collection of plays under the title *Teatro para niños* (*Theatre for Children*) in 1954, while Adolfo de J. Márquez (b. 1917) has published some of his pieces for children in the Ministry of Education magazine *Educación* (*Education*).

José Roberto Cea
Translated by Mayte Gómez

Further Reading

Armijo, Roberto. 'El teatro y la lucha de liberación nacional en El Salvador'. [Theatre and the struggle for national liberation in El Salvador]. *Conjunto* 52 (April–June 1982): 129–32.

Barbero, Edmundo. 'Breve historia del teatro universitario'. [A short history of university theatre]. *Caracol* 1, no. 1 (August 1974): 23–4.

——, ed. *Panorama del teatro en El Salvador*. [An overview of theatre in El Salvador]. 5 vols. San Salvador: Editorial Universitaria, 1972. 564 pp.

Campos Menjívar, Juan Francisco. *La dominación cultural y su influencia en el teatro salvadoreño*. [Cultural domination and its influence in Salvadoran theatre]. Colección Tesario. San Salvador: Departamento de Letras, Universidad de El Salvador, 1984.

Cea, José Roberto. 'Del teatro en El Salvador: panorama histórico crítico'. [On theatre in El Salvador: A historical and critical view]. *Cuadernos de Investigación Teatral* 6 (1979): 1–14.

Gallegos Valdés, Luis. *El teatro en El Salvador*. [Theatre in El Salvador]. San Salvador: Ediciones Bellas Artes, 1961.

Lindo, Hugo. 'Jóvenes dramaturgos de El Salvador'. [Young Salvadoran playwrights]. *Estudios Centro Americanos* 15, no. 154 (November 1960): 584–91.

——. 'Literatura dramática en El Salvador'. [Dramatic literature in El Salvador]. *Cultura Hispánica* 1, no. 3 (July–September 1967): 3–50.

Menén Desleal, Alvaro. 'Historia del teatro en El Salvador: José Emilio Aragón y Luigi Pirandello, posibilidad de un paralelismo imposible'. [History of theatre in El Salvador: José Emilio Aragón and Luigi Pirandello, the possibility of an impossible similarity]. *Cultura* 35 (January–March 1965): 31–4.

Ministerio de Cultura. *El Teatro. Historia informal del mismo a través de lo anecdótico y pintoresco*. [An unofficial history of theatre through anecdotes and the picturesque]. San Salvador: Departamento Editorial del Ministerio de Cultura, 1956. 586 pp.

Moisés Calderón, Alfonso Arturo. 'El teatro popular: una alternativa para enfrentar la dominación cultural. Análisis de una experiencia'. [Popular theatre: An alternative for confronting cultural domination. Analysis of an experience]. PhD dissertation, Universidad Centroamericana José Simeón Cañas, 1978.

Salomón, Roberto. 'Theatre in El Salvador During the Eighties'. *Latin American Theatre Review* 25, no. 2 (spring 1992): 173–80.

FRENCH CARIBBEAN

(Overview)

The French Caribbean territories – the islands of Martinique and Guadeloupe, with Guyane (French Guyana) on the South American mainland – share a number of common features. Like Haïti, they are old colonies of French settlement dating back to the early seventeenth century. They began as plantation societies, uneasily divided between a dominant white minority and the mass of uprooted Africans who worked the spice and sugar estates as slaves. After the abolition of slavery in 1848, substitute labourers, including immigrants from India and China, traders from the Middle East and, from the mid-twentieth century, migrants from poorer parts of the Caribbean basin all added to the ethnic mix. In contrast to their independent neighbours, these territories – some 1,300 miles southeast of Florida – voted in 1946 to become overseas *départements* of France, and as such have benefited from an artificially high standard of living as well as from French citizenship.

The intimate connection with France also makes funds available for cultural activities and promotes high levels of general education. However, it also perpetuates a dependent relationship. The old opposition between master and slave, between Europe and Africa, between a dominant written culture in French and an oral culture of resistance in Creole (the Caribbean dialect of the French language) has been overlaid by newer ideologies of *métissage* (racial mixing) and *créolité* (Creoleness). Many underlying tensions remain, but cultural identity is asserted in terms of proud difference from France, a desire to value what is specifically Caribbean, and reflects local creativity rather than what is imposed from outside.

These lands are also small-scale, tropical societies, still rural in temperament despite the encroaching concrete of urban development and tourist resorts. Everyday life slips easily into dramatic form when all shades of the population enjoy virtuosity with words, expressive body language, telling stories and jokes. The various traditions mingling over the years have provided rich resources for the theatre: the wake for the dead, an occasion for mourning, commemoration, storytelling and riddling; and carnival, when the social order is joyously subverted, genders bend, and the mighty are mocked in song and effigy.

Historically a general evolution can be outlined. During the earlier colonial period, the slaves took what comfort they could from surviving African sources, retelling in Creole the animal tales of Br'er Rabbit and Turtle, fashioning drums and other instruments, keeping up dances and religious rites. The visible, official culture was French. Saint-Pierre, before its destruction in the 1902 eruption of Montagne Pelée, boasted an elegant reduced-scale version (*c.*1786) of the neo-classical Grand Théâtre de Bordeaux, used not only for touring opera and theatre, but also for local amateur productions, carnival balls and political meetings. Audiences were racially segregated, as the abolitionist Victor Schoelcher complained when he attended a performance of *Antony*, the romantic drama by Alexandre Dumas, in about 1840 in Pointe-à-Pitre, and there are reports of white Martinicans displaying a scandalous tendency to defect to the middle tier reserved for the mulatto (of mixed black and European ancestry) beauties. A theatre in Guadeloupe, rebuilt in 1862 after one of several fires, was decorated with portraits of Corneille, Molière,

FRENCH CARIBBEAN

Racine, Talma and Rachel, choices symptomatic of an elitist culture, positioned as a distant, rather more disaster-prone but earnestly refined outpost of Paris.

The last theatrical avatar of this assimilationist approach was a touring company run by the French actor-director Jean Gosselin which, from a modest beginning in 1952 until 1989, undertook an annual circuit of the French-speaking Caribbean and other neighbouring territories with an active interest in promoting French language and culture. The repertoire was based on a combination of lightweight successes from the Paris boulevards and classical matinées for schoolchildren. Sometimes Gosselin would bring substantial contemporary works and, at best, some high-quality work in acting and production.

However, resentment grew in some quarters that local theatrical efforts did not enjoy the subsidies of this 'civilizing mission' out of Paris. Particularly in the decade following 1968, a protest theatre of students and militants agitating for independence gained strength. The names of the groups are eloquent enough: Anbajouk (Under the Yoke); Neg Mawon (named after the runaway slaves who chose freedom); Théâtre du Cyclone, du Volcan, Poulbois (Termites), Fer de lance (a poisonous snake), all calling down destruction on the colonial oppressor; and Troupe Angela Davis, positioned in relation not to France but to international black liberation. Most of this agitprop drama used the Creole language, and for many participants it was an idealistic moment, taking art to the people and raising consciousness.

The development of an infrastructure got underway in the 1970s, especially in Martinique. This too, like local politics, generated intense and often personal rivalries. In most instances there is an Office Municipal de Culture organizing workshops, clubs and shows. These offices are usually politically connected and have more than half an eye on winning votes. The Conseil Général for each of these *départements* votes a budget for cultural activity, gives support to festivals and funds a permanent office to handle cultural development. Since François Mitterand's Socialist Party came to power and implemented a decentralizing policy in 1982, the overseas *départements* are also simultaneously '*régions*', with a separate set of regional councillors and a budget disbursed through a Direction Régionale des Affaires Culturelles (DRAC; Regional Cultural Affairs Directorate). As a result of this complex structure, many proposals are delayed while budgets are negotiated and voted through the different assemblies; in addition, many also languish at the ministries in Paris.

Theatre buildings and facilities vary greatly: the best include a charming municipal theatre in central Fort-de-France, Martinique, and, in Guadeloupe, modern stages in the Pointe-à-Pitre Arts Centre (1,100 seats in the main theatre, a smaller area seating 350) and a small auditorium in Basse-Terre. Apart from stages in various municipal centres, used more often for concerts than plays, large cinemas often substitute for theatres. An ambitiously conceived Scène Nationale (National Stage) was under construction on the slopes of Basse-Terre in 1995, and is expected to stimulate more training of skilled technicians in such areas as lighting and scene design.

Taking seriously its destiny as a crossroads of culture at the meeting-place of both halves of the Americas, Europe and Africa, the French Caribbean is developing its own dramatic traditions: historical drama to reappropriate the sites and times of a chequered past, street theatre and storytelling forms from popular tradition, as well as a Creole comedy with genuine mass appeal.

Martinique

When each overseas *département* is taken individually, Martinique – with a 1990 population of 359,000 and an area of 1,100 square kilometres (425 square miles) – claims pride of place in the French Caribbean. Since the destruction of the old city of Saint-Pierre, the capital city of Fort-de-France has developed a concentration of population and has become a sophisticated cultural centre. Moreover, the influence of Martinique writer Aimé Césaire (b. 1913), a proponent of the concept of Negritude (black power), poet, teacher, local and international political leader, patriarch of a gifted family as well as a patron of the arts, has proved crucial. Disciples, imitators and opponents alike bear witness to his stature. In particular, as a successful product of the French educational system who is equally proud of his African roots, Césaire has implemented programmes for the cultural development of the black majority without cutting Martinique off from world culture. Both a *député* in the French parliament and mayor of Fort-de-France from 1945 to 1993, he committed resources to promoting the arts, initially by annual festivals, then in 1976 by setting

277

up the Service Municipal d'Action Culturelle (SERMAC; Municipal Service for Cultural Activity), with his son Jean-Paul (b. 1938) as director. Occupying a large central site, SERMAC offers courses (for many years free of charge) in dance, drumming, mask-making and pottery among other things. Martinique's July festival has also created a vital showcase for smaller companies from the region, as well as encounters with invited major artists and productions. Visits by the French director Jean-Marie Serreau, Ariane Mnouchkine's Paris-based Théâtre du Soleil and the Nigerian playwright Wole Soyinka were particularly influential.

A second complementary cultural organization also exists in Martinique, the Centre Martiniquais d'Action Culturelle (CMAC; Martinique Centre for Cultural Activity), funded predominantly by the Conseil Général and the French Ministry of Culture, and run by Fanny Auguiac. CMAC tends to be more active outside the capital in training activities and sponsors a wide range of international cultural exchanges; since 1981 it has organized an annual spring festival of Caribbean theatre.

A Regional Centre for Drama, headed since 1990 by Elie Pennont (b. 1961), acts as co-producer to consolidate a now professional level of theatre activity. The Théâtre de la Soif Nouvelle (New Thirst Theatre), directed for many years by Annick Justin-Joseph (b. 1949), and the Téat Lari (Street Theatre), directed by José Alpha, are the major groups. But a range of others produce work at a less intense rhythm, annually or occasionally, often using periods of leave from employment in education. Among these are the Théâtre Populaire Martiniquais (Martinique Popular Theatre), directed by Henri Melon (b. 1935), Racines (Roots), directed by Michèle Césaire (b. 1953), and Lomstrom, directed by Serge Lof.

In terms of written drama, Aimé Césaire's works laid the Caribbean foundation for serious plays in French, beginning with an early ritual work, *Et les Chiens se taisaient* (*And the Dogs Were Silent*, 1946), which celebrate in sumptuous verse the last hours of a rebel slave who had slain his blue-eyed master. This character established a prototype for Césaire's visionary heroes, sacrificial figures who grow estranged from kin and from the group they strive to liberate. His *La Tragédie du roi Christophe* (*The Tragedy of King Christophe*, 1963), based on Haïtian oral history, was first mounted by Jean-Marie Serreau and was more successful

than his earlier play in creating a rich dramatic texture, in this case the rise and fall of the self-made king who ruled northern Haïti from 1811 to 1820. Christophe's lasting monument was a mighty stone citadel, witness to the achievements of a people newly freed from slavery. Grandiose and grotesque by turns, weaving together folk song and Alexandrine sonnet, voodoo chant and surrealist rhetoric, this ambitious play can best be seen as a Brechtian structure, provoking its audience into critical awareness by presenting contradictory views of the black leader. The Comédie-Française produced it in 1991, directed by Idrissa Ouedraogo from Burkina Faso.

Césaire continued his exploration of post-colonial nation-building in *Une Saison au Congo* (*A Season in the Congo*, 1967), a factually based and rather didactic play in which Patrice Lumumba is presented as a visionary African leader whose rhetoric can mobilize a crowd but falters when in conflict with unscrupulous interests avid for the country's mineral wealth. *Une Tempête* (1969) attempts a more colloquial tone, rewriting Shakespeare's *The Tempest* as a play within a play, with a sardonic focus on Prospero as a colonial tyrant. Césaire's drama, without doubt, has impressive scope but it is more widely studied than staged. Nevertheless, its poetic power is undeniable.

Edouard Glissant (b. 1928) has also composed a historical tragedy based on Haïtian history, *Monsieur Toussaint* (published in 1961, broadcast in 1971), set in the icy Fort de Joux where Toussaint Louverture, betrayed and imprisoned by Napoleon, met his death. In a form similar to the Caribbean wake for the dead, Toussaint's life and times are re-enacted through a blend of real and imagined characters. All of Glissant's prose fiction springs to life when read aloud, and the study of drama is encouraged at his Institut Martiniquais d'Études (Martinican Institute of Education). Students at the institute toured a poetic montage of Glissant's *Histoire de Nègre* (*Black History*) in 1972.

Gifted with an acute mind and a versatile pen, Vincent Placoly (1946–92) composed more than a dozen plays, some using historical figures to articulate issues of political independence. Among these are *La Fin douloureuse et tragique d'André Aliker* (*The Sad and Tragic End of André Aliker*, 1969), about an investigative journalist/union militant who was assassinated in 1934; and *Dessalines, ou La Passion de l'indépendance* (*Dessalines, or Passion For*

Vincent Placoly's *Dessalines, or Passion For Independence* at the 1994 Fort-de-France Festival.
Photo: Philippe Bourgade.

Independence), published in Cuba in 1983 and produced in 1994, which portrays a heroic freedom-fighter in place of the usual tyrant of tradition. Several adaptations, notably an engaging Creole version of Molière's *Don Juan* (1984), and of Goldoni, enlarge the repertoire for José Alpha's Téat Lari and were commissioned by RFO television. Placoly has also composed material to commemorate significant anniversaries such as Columbus's landing or to enhance an historical site (Joséphine's Domaine de la Pagerie).

As a student in Paris, Placoly also directed a play by Martinique's Georges Mauvois (b. 1922), *Agénor Cacoul* (1966), in which dramatic tension is wonderfully achieved by the deployment of a linguistic code-switching, second nature to Creole speakers. It is seen clearly in scenes where both Creole and French are used, such as a scene about a strike of cane-cutters, or where a secretary drops her mask of refinement to berate callers or to put down a rival. Mauvois writes with insider knowledge of municipal political behaviour. Indignant at abuses, he is an excellent observer. His work has

also attracted the attention of intellectual Creolists for its use of language, but the social satire in plays such as *Misyé Molina* (1987) and *Man Chomil* (1989) is enjoyed by a broad audience.

Mauvois's *Agénor Cacoul* dealt with a very typical subject for the politicized theatre of the 1970s – a strike among agricultural workers against exploitation. Its careful crafting was not so typical, however, as many works of this period were hastily contrived collective creations. A number of the plays were historical in focus, looking at specific moments of resistance to French power such as 1802 in Guadeloupe or the slave revolts on the eve of abolition. A frequent target for attack is the office promoting migration to France, Bureau pour le Développement des Migrations Intéressant les Départements d'Outre-Mer (BUMIDOM; Office for the Development of Migration Involving the Overseas Départements), which is felt to be draining the region of vital energies.

Les Négriers (*Looking Backwards*, 1971) by Daniel Boukman (b. 1936) manages to bring all three topics into a sequence of sarcastic sketches

GUADELOUPE

(see **FRENCH CARIBBEAN**)

GUATEMALA

A small Central American nation bordering on México, El Salvador, Honduras and Belize, Guatemala has a central highland separating its narrow Pacific coast and its lowlands on the Caribbean Sea. It covers an area of 108,900 square kilometres (42,000 square miles). A land of numerous volcanoes, some still active, Guatemala had a 1992 population of 9.7 million.

Independence in 1921 led to a series of dictatorships, ending with a revolution in 1944 when Jorge Ubico was overthrown. In 1954, a more social-minded president, Jacobo Arbenz, was ousted by a United States-supported force of mercenaries and the country was ruled by the military until 1986 when civilian government returned.

More than 50 per cent of the population is of indigenous stock; the rest is mostly *mestizo* (of mixed European and native ancestry). Old centres such as Tikal and El Ceibal are examples of the Maya civilization that flourished in Guatemala and surrounding countries. Miguel

Angel Asturias (1899–1974), winner of the Nobel Prize for Literature in 1967 and the Lenin Prize for Peace in 1966, captured the mythical mind of the Guatemalan natives in novels such as *Hombres de maiz* (*Men of Corn*). He translated the sacred book of the Maya-Quichés people – the *Popol Vuh* – into French in 1926. His best known work was *El Señor Presidente*, which deals with the dictatorship of Estrada Cabrera, who was overthrown in 1920, although his name and that of the country are never mentioned in the book. Asturias also wrote a number of plays in which the influence of the indigenous people appears.

Historically, Guatemala has had a rich theatrical tradition despite profound social, ethnic and economic divisions created by its continuous dictatorships. The oldest theatre forms in Guatemala date from the Maya and Maya-Quichés cultures, of which we have knowledge through the ballet-drama *Rabinal Achí* or *Baile del tún* (*Dance of the Tun*). At the time of the Spanish conquest, Dominican and Franciscan monks brought with them religious plays that they felt would serve as a folk theatre for the country. These plays were added to pre-Hispanic theatrical forms that had survived the power of the colonial inquisition. Beyond these, there were only occasional representations of a European moralistic theatre with religious character and Baroque style.

The first attempts to create a theatre outside the church were made around the time of independence in 1821. By the end of the nineteenth century – the golden period of the Teatro Colón, opened in 1859 – Guatemala was being frequently visited by opera, operetta and *zarzuela* (Spanish-style musical comedy) companies from Spain, Italy and México. It was thanks to these companies that the urban upper classes – mostly composed of foreigners, *criollos* (people of Spanish ancestry born in the Americas) and *ladinos* (*mestizos*) – developed a taste for theatre, especially for the neo-classical and romantic European repertoire.

Modern Guatemalan theatre began to take shape following the revolution of October 1944. It was this revolution that made possible a new kind of theatre, a socially relevant and socially critical *mestizo* theatre.

The earthquakes of 1917 and 1918 had abruptly ended the visits of foreign companies, which usually visited on their way to México. The Teatro Colón was perhaps the greatest victim of the quakes since it was there that these groups usually played. In the 1920s, local groups sprang up imitating the style and repertoire of the European visitors. Official support was eventually granted to some of them.

Along with new groups came occasional visiting companies from Spain: Jacinto Benevente and his company, Ricardo Calvo, Fernando Soler, Enrique Serrano and Sánchez Navarro, to name just a few. With their repertoire of melodramas, comedies, historical and religious plays and *sainetes* (one-act farcical sketches), they created a new public and provided some artistic orientation for local groups.

These companies also had influence on national playwrights such as Alberto de la Riva (1886–1940), author of the comedy *La Rafaila*); Adolfo Drago-Bracco (1894–1965), who wrote a *costumbrista* (featuring local manners and customs) comedy, *El viejo solar* (*The Old Lot*); and María Luisa Aragón (1910–74), author of the *sainete*, *Un loteriazo en plena crisis*. Other playwrights of note during these years were the poet Rafael Arévalo

Martínez (1884–1970), with his plays *El hijo prodigo* (*The Prodigal Son*) and *Los duques de Endor* (*The Duke and Duchess of Endor*), and Daniel Armas (1897–1972), author of the comedy *Como los muérdagos* (*Like the Mistletoe*). Among the later playwrights also influenced by this generation were Carlos Girón Cerna (1904–71), Miguel Marsicovétere y Durán (1910–86), Luis Herrera (1909–73), Carlos Enrique Alvarez (b. 1909) and Miguel Angel Asturias.

Alberto de la Riva founded his Grupo Artístico Nacional (National Artistic Group) in 1912. After the earthquakes, the company was renamed the Grupo Renacimiento (Renaissance Group). During its years of operation, it included the country's most important actors and directors. Other early groups of note were the Agrupación Teatral (Theatre Company) of Alfredo Paralea and Adriana Saravia; and Talia, directed by Alberto Paniagua.

In the mid-1930s, actor-director Alberto Martínez began his career. Martínez, like most artists, had neither financial subsidies nor official support yet kept his company alive against all odds. His group, the Sociedad Dramática Nacional (National Dramatic Society) presented the most popular plays from Spain by writers such as Benavente, Arniches, Echegaray, the Alvarez Quintero brothers and Dicenta. Martínez also kept alive the tradition of staging Zorrilla's *Don Juan Tenorio* each All Saints' Day. From the same period is the actor-director Armando Ortiz, famous for performing the role of Christ in Holy Week celebrations.

The precarious situation of theatre through this period worsened in the fifteen years before the 1944 revolution. The number of productions decreased and performances were rarely seen more than once or twice and then only by very small audiences. It was virtually impossible to earn back production costs. In 1931 General Jorge Ubico took power. For the next fourteen years, Ubico made both national and visiting theatrical activity all but impossible. As a result, most actors and dramatists sought refuge in radio. On stage, one was simply not allowed to produce historical, social or political plays, anything reflecting national reality. The only exception was student Easter festivities on Good Friday, when plays were staged in the style of the *astracán* (coarse Spanish farce), the *sainete*, or the *bufonada* (a sketch in the form of a satirical joke). In each case, the plays would be given a political or social context. Two of the most famous student plays of this time were *Tina de Jarque* and *We Have No Bananas*. Under Ubico's harsh rule, however, even this celebration disappeared. Always looking for a suspicious event or celebration, the government had Alberto Martínez arrested at his theatre and later imprisoned for tampering with dramatic texts, texts that had not yet even been seen by the state censor.

It was in this closed and difficult environment that a new artist appeared: Manuel Galich (1913–84), a young, high-spirited man with only modest education, the child of a family of artists. Influenced by the style of the South American Florencio Sánchez, Galich wrote a play in which the social problems of a *mestizo* family were tackled for the first time. This play, *Papa-Natas* (*The Gullible*), opened at the Palace Theatre in 1938, and its opening is generally agreed to mark the birth of modern Guatemalan theatre.

Ubico's overthrow in 1944 was a direct consequence of World War II, since it was after the war that most Latin American countries formally attempted to break the social structures that had existed since colonial times. Ideas of ethnic superiority (backed up by the army and the church) remained very openly in vogue, however. In 1944 these feudal ideas began to be exposed to profound criticism from the middle and lower classes. This led to a general cry for freedom, dignity and social justice, resulting in both the collapse of Ubico's dictatorship and the restructuring of the upper class. In this way the old colonial, political, social and economic model was slowly dismantled. During the next decade, Guatemalan theatre opened to currents of international influence, which sowed the seeds for the birth of several Guatemalan playwrights.

The democratic governments of Juan José Arevalo (from 1945 to 1951) and Jacob Arbenz (from 1951 to 1954) helped establish social reforms in the country. In the political sphere, political parties and unions were legalized and suffrage was widened. In the economic sphere, traditional roles and privileges were rethought, a plan for agrarian reform drawn up and new measures against foreign monopolies taken. At the centre of this were grievances against the vast United Fruit Company, which had made Central America into an isthmus of 'banana republics'.

In the cultural and educational fields, too, the border was opened to new pedagogical, cultural and artistic ideas. Guatemala welcomed at this time many new immigrants from Europe and North America, people willing to participate in the process of transforming of the country into a free and democratic republic. Among the new cultural institutions created were the Fine Arts Ministry, the Institute for Indigenous Studies, the Museum of Anthropology, the National Symphonic Orchestra and the National Ballet. The country's only university, the University of San Carlos, was also granted autonomy and was allowed to establish a new Faculty of Humanities. Other educational institutions were also created: the Popular University, the School of Visual Arts, the Pineda Ibarra Publishing House, along with a federal network of state schools. These new winds were the perfect climate for the development of the theatre.

In 1945, an illustrious teacher, María de Sellarés, arrived from Spain and immediately became the director of the Belén National Teachers' Institute, a state organization of great tradition and prestige. She quickly began theatre activity there, presenting scenes and short plays of the classic French and Spanish theatres (especially Molière and Cervantes) and plays by Federico García Lorca.

Perhaps the most interesting piece she presented was done by students under the direction of playwright Carlos Girón Cerna, who had just returned from Cuba where he had been working with the University Theatre of Havana. Though the project was presented only to other students of the institute, out of this endeavour came an even more ambitious one: the indigenous drama *Quiche Achí* by Girón Cerna, inspired by the traditional ballet-drama *Rabinal Achí*.

De Sellarés invited Jesús Castillo, a composer trained in Paris who was especially concerned with rescuing indigenous music to work on the new production. *Quiche Achí* opened on 19 August 1945; it was an historic event that would determine the path followed by many subsequent Guatemalan productions.

The orientation that de Sellarés gave to the new theatre movement born at the Belén Institute – educational and socially rooted – would also be seen in the work of subsequent generations, who would later establish theatre schools, children's theatres, school theatres, puppet theatres, indigenous theatre research, university theatres and regional and national theatre festivals.

In 1948 the Teatro de Arte Universitario (TAU; University Art Theatre), directed by

Carlos Menko-Deká, was created as part of the Faculty of Humanities of the University of San Carlos. Two years later, during Manuel Galich's term as Minister of Public Education, the state-supported Teatro de Arte de Guatemala (TAG; Art Theatre of Guatemala), directed by Carlos Girón Cerna, began operation. Both theatre groups functioned until 1954 with the same core of people that de Sellarés had brought together at the Belén Institute. From among them stand out Norma Padilla, who would become involved in the creation of regional theatre festivals; René Molina, who would be influential in the field of children's theatre; Ligia Bernal (b. 1930) in the field of theatre-in-education and playwriting; Matilde Montoya in folklore research; Carmen Antillón in puppet theatre; Consuelo Miranda in the teaching of acting; Samara de Córdova as a performer and writer; Carlos Mencos as a playwright and teacher; Rufino Amezquita as a performer and founder of the Municipal Theatre; and Hugo Carrillo (1928–94) as a playwright.

TAG inaugurated its activities with a season of plays by national authors presented in conjunction with the Central American and Caribbean Olympic Games of 1950. Its early productions included the aforementioned *Quiche Achí*, *La mujer y el robot* (*The Woman and the Robot*) by Miguel Marsicovétere y Durán, a Pirandellian-styled play, and *Ida y Vuelta* (*Going and Coming*) by Galich. Only the Galich play attracted popular and critical attention.

TAG, however, had a very short life. Its directors failed to create a structure that would allow it to survive without state support. Instead of planning ongoing activities, they presented only occasional productions; audiences remained small. As well, the cinemas where they performed were not well adapted for the theatre. All this led to the group's disappearance in 1954.

The TAU, however, directed by Carlos Menko-Deká, continued for more than two decades, embracing all areas of theatre: the establishment of a school of theatre art, the creation of the country's first arena stage, the encouragement of other groups through technical and artistic advice, participation in national festivals, and the successful productions of both classical and modern plays.

There was, to be sure, competition and conflict between those artists who worked after the revolution and those who had come before. The latter remained dependent on the classic Spanish repertoire and the traditional formulas of staging. The former sought to experiment with new forms of contemporary theatre.

At this same time, the Fine Arts Ministry subsidized an itinerant theatre group to travel across the country performing plays by Cervantes, Lope de Vega and Alejandro Casona, while TAU organized its own tours as well. Foreign directors came to Guatemala and opened new horizons with their innovative stagings. In 1953, thirty-two new plays by contemporary European and US authors were presented by Guatemala's twelve regularly producing groups, mostly in the capital. Some were subsidized by the state, others by the university.

Despite this activity, all the shows had to be produced in cinemas. Directors only – and not all of them – received modest salaries for their work. And no production was ever seen by more than 1,000 people. Nevertheless, the playwrights produced by TAG – Galich, Girón Cerna and Marsicovétere y Durán – continued to discuss national problems of identity and direction.

This situation changed somewhat in 1952, when TAU produced the beautiful and innovative play *Doña Beatriz, la sin ventura* (*Doña Beatriz, the Unfortunate*) by Carlos Solórzano (b. 1922), a Guatemalan-born playwright who, after moving to México, had quickly become a prominent figure in its intellectual and artistic world. With this historical play, considered by many to be the most significant of his extensive dramatic productions, Solórzano dealt with the conflict between two cultures, two bloods and two epochs in an ongoing existential clash.

It was in 1954 that a group of mercenaries and exiles attempted a *coup d'état* against the nationalistic economic policy of Jacobo Arbenz's democratic government. As a result of the coup, most reforms were annulled and many of the most important personalities in politics, unions, education and culture left the country. It was this coup and its results that marked the end of this short but intense and vital period in the development of Guatemala's theatre.

The new government of Carlos Castillo Armas (from 1954 to 1957) openly supported artistic activities across the country, although not with the same democratic spirit of the revolutionary years. The city of Antigua hosted the first Festival of Art and Culture, with a series of sophisticated shows exclusively directed at a rather small elite, yet it was because of those shows that Chilean director Domingo Tessier came to Guatemala and carried on important work teaching and directing for many years. He was also fundamental in the creation in 1957 of the first state school dedicated to actor's training. This new school, the National Conservatory, and that of TAU, were the only ones in the country exclusively dedicated to the creation of a new generation of national artists. Both schools taught the Stanislavski system, with courses in stage design, makeup, fencing, art history, scene design and directing.

In the next two decades theatre activity grew and managed to reach the interior of the country. A play could now be seen by 3,000 or 4,000 people. The state encouraged and even subsidized activities, including university theatre. The new Popular University started its own theatre school and company under the leadership of Rubén Morales Monroy with Domingo Tessier as an adviser. Large and expensive Festivals of Art and Culture also came into vogue once again during the Carlos Arana regime (1970–4), though funding was tight and technical resources meagre.

Although no one at this time was able to survive solely on income from the theatre, there were important advances. A number of small auditoriums were created exclusively for the presentation of plays: the theatre of the Popular University; the Gadem Theatre of the Grupo Artístico de Escenificación Moderna (Artistic Group of Modern Performance), who were directed by Luis Herrera, an outstanding director and author of several plays; the Arena Theatre of TAU; the Municipal Theatre; and the auditorium of the National Conservatory. The Teatro del Puente (Theatre of the Bridge) and the Instituto Guatemalteco Americano (Guatemalan American Institute) were also used for the presentation of plays, mostly in English.

In 1960 Rufino Amezquita founded the Municipal Theatre, later directed by Otto René Castillo, Marco Antonio Flores and playwright Víctor Hugo Cruz, author of several plays among which Dos y dos son cinco (Two and Two Is Five) stands out. The Fine Arts Ministry, in those years run by theatre director and producer Luis Domingo, established the Popular Theatre Company, which functioned for two years, and in 1964 the first fully professional company in Guatemala, the Teatro Nacional (National Theatre), which presented seasons of both contemporary and classical plays in Guatemala City. During this same time, numerous directors from other Latin American countries began to be invited regularly to direct and give classes in the country.

Things were relatively quiet through the 1970s and relations between the arts and the government were more or less stable. In 1981, however, police violently broke into the auditoriums of the University Cultural Centre and into La Galera (The Gallery), a gathering place for young theatre artists. The auditorium at the Popular University was mysteriously set on fire one night in 1983.

Facing a daily life full of fear, suspicion and doubt, theatre artists began to impose censorship once again on their own work, which quickly ceased to be the voice of popular social concern. The most important theatre groups in the country began to produce only traditional plays, comedies of the most superficial 'boulevard' style from France, Spain and Italy, musical comedies from the United States, or adaptations of classical Latin American novels. Even student protests disappeared once more. The need to survive drove people into absolute silence and until 1986 there was a cultural 'curfew' throughout the country.

With the arrival of a civilian government in 1986, however, there were hopeful signs of a new democratic opening for national theatre voices. In that year, the country paid homage posthumously to Manuel José Arce (1933–85) in the Teatro de Cámara (Chamber Theatre) of the Cultural Centre, with a staging of his play Sebastián sale de compras (Sebastian Goes Shopping). Also in 1986 the Popular University successfully presented several of Manuel Galich's plays in its improvised tent theatre. In 1986 as well, the Cultural Centre was renamed for Miguel Angel Asturias.

In Guatemala in the 1990s there were theatre audiences, theatre spaces and theatre resources, both human and physical. Though theatre practice was still not completely professionalized there was commitment, enthusiasm and seriousness. But what was still missing most of all was the kind of theatre that could speak to all Guatemalans, without distinction on ethnic, social or economic grounds.

Structure of the National Theatre Community

The majority of theatre activity in Guatemala takes place in the capital, Guatemala City. With a population of just under 1 million, the capital is home to about a dozen theatre groups.

Since 1962, the most important annual event has been the Festival of Guatemalan Theatre, which has regularly produced the major Guatemalan playwrights – Manuel Galich, Carlos Solórzano, Manuel José Arce and Hugo Carrillo. The festival has also regularly shown the work of novelist Miguel Angel Asturias: *El Señor Presidente* (*Mr President*), *Torotumbo* and *Viernes de Dolores* (*Good Friday*) – the theatrical version of which was called *La chalana*, after a student war song – adapted for the stage by Arce and Carrillo. In 1964 the festival became one of the permanent activities of the Popular University.

Norma Padilla, long-time head of the Fine Arts Ministry, in 1975 initiated a series of annual regional theatre festivals that have become showcases for socially rooted creations and outlets for new artistic voices.

The Festival of Guatemalan Theatre has also been the home of newer authors such as Manuel Corleto with *El animal vertical* (*The Vertical Animal*), Augusto Medina with *El retrete* (*The Toilet Seat*), María del Carmen Escobar with *La gente del Palomar* (*The People of the Dovecote*), Alfonso Enrique Barrientos with *El señor Embajador* (*Mr Ambassador*), Edwin Cifuentes with *Fiesta de enterradores* (*The Gravediggers' Party*), Abel Lam with *El conspirator* (*The Conspirator*) and the already mentioned Víctor Hugo Cruz. Antonio García Urea was always present in the festivals with his musicals and *zarzuela* plays; there were also occasional plays by Carlos Alberto Castaneda, Ernestine Porras, Carlos Enrique Alvarez and Ricardo Estrada.

From the regional theatre festivals, and despite the serious problems that theatre encountered at that time, emerged the new voices of Fran Leppe with *Basura* (*Garbage*), Alberto Anleu with *Marranautas*, Mario Barrientos with *La Chana*, Antonio Guitrón with *Candelario* (*The Oil Lamp*), Vicente Cumes Pop with *Acum or Brujo* (*Warlock*) and *Vekol Vak or Curandero* (*Healer*) – an attempt to do theatre in the Cakchiquel language – Victor

Rosal with *La rebelión de los objetos y las cosas* (*The Rebellion of Objects and Things*), Ricardo Búcaro with his adaptation of Asturias's *El espejo de Lida Salt* (*The Mirror of Lida Salt*) and Ingleberto Robles with several monologues. These authors, together with Oswaldo Ortega, Felipe Valenzuela and William Lemus – the most highly awarded author of those years – were the most outstanding writers of this generation.

In 1974, the twelfth Festival of Guatemalan Theatre presented Carrillo's adaptation of Asturias's *El Señor Presidente*. Until then plays generally would be shown on weekends for about two months. This play sold out for ten consecutive months at the theatre of the Popular University and attracted audiences from across the various social sectors. It later toured to other regions and even to major cities in other parts of Central America. More than 50,000 people saw it in total. As a result, other theatre groups began to plan long runs, trying to keep their shows on for a minimum of four to six months.

Unfortunately, the spectacular success of the Asturias play awakened government officials to the potential of theatre as an instrument for raising social consciousness. The use of military symbols on stage, for example, was quickly prohibited. After the earthquake of 1976, the climate of terror that the country had been experiencing once again expanded to other artistic activities and theatre – like other art forms – started to suffer the horrible consequences of this new political and social crisis. Many great theatre artists were threatened with death at this time. Many theatre groups were forced to cease operation because of threats and 'mortuary' gifts – small coffins, wreaths, tombstones and so on. Important theatre artists were kidnapped or assassinated. Actors, directors, technicians and playwrights went into exile. Though afraid of retaliation, artists nevertheless held the 1979 festival and dedicated it to the work of Manuel José Arce, one of the most representative Guatemalan authors. But not a single one of his plays was staged. Arce learned of this honour while in exile in France, where he had been living for a year and where he died in 1985.

Hugo Carrillo's *El corazón del espantapájaros* (*The Scarecrow's Heart*, 1962).
Photo: courtesy *Conjunto*.

Companies

Dramaturgy

Directors, Directing and Production Styles

In the mid-1990s, the most stable theatre groups in Guatemala were Grupo Diez (Group Ten), Grupo Teatro Centro, Grupo Teatro Club, the Academy of Dramatic Arts and Theatre Company UP, the group 9–79, Grupo Maíz (Maize Group) and Jade y Cia (Jade and Co). All were presenting a range of productions, mostly in the capital.

Two early playwrights still dominate Guatemalan dramaturgy: Manuel Galich and Carlos Solórzano. Galich's first important work was *Papa-Natas*, a play that dealt with national social problems for the first time. Galich followed this play with others in an urban folk style, one that exposed the deficiencies of Guatemalan society. To this basically realistic, socially rooted theatre Galich added a number of shorter historical plays and a dramatic comedy, *Ida y Vuelta*, about the life of José Batres Montufar, the most famous Guatemalan romantic poet. After the 1944 revolution, in which Galich played an important role of public leadership, he produced some of his most dramatic and political plays: *Pascual Abaj*, *La mugre* (*The Filth*) and *El pescado indigesto* (*The Indigestible Fish*, 1960). Galich eventually left Guatemala and lived in exile in Cuba until his death in 1984.

Solórzano, formally trained in Paris, was the only dramatic author of his generation whose work was presented as part of the feverish theatre activity during the revolutionary period. His *Doña Beatriz* defined a constant that would

later be taken up by other authors: the *mestizo* culture, symbolized by Doña Leonor, daughter of Pedro de Alvarado, the cruel and bloody *conquistador*, and Xicotencatl, princess of Tlaxcala. This was also the first Guatemalan play to use as a dramatic device one of the most common natural phenomena of the country: earthquakes.

In 1959, the National Conservatory organized a season of plays by young authors. Among those represented were Ligia Bernal, Hugo Carrillo and Manuel José Arce. Bernal and Carrillo had both studied and worked in Paris, the latter establishing himself as an outstanding poet as well. The conservatory presented Bernal's *La piedra en el pozo* (*The Stone in the Well*), Carrillo's *La calle de sexo verde* (*Green Sex Street*) and two one-act plays by Arce, *El Apostol* (*The Apostle*) and *Orestes*. Galich, Solórzano and René García Mejía – a researcher of folk theatre who opened his play *Golpe a las dos a.m.* (*Coup at 2 a.m.*) at an amateur festival – defined the way for Guatemalan theatre in the 1960s and 1970s: plays of political and social criticism, a mixture of realistic elements with magical symbols, absurd, grotesque and poetic styles in the treatment of fables and myths, and especially the use of the *mestizo* and popular cultures in the permanent search for a national identity.

It is worth mentioning that the most outstanding authors in Guatemalan theatre still tend to live, are exiled, or die outside the country. Two of those who lived outside Guatemala are Solórzano and Arturo Girón. Among those exiled were Galich, Arce and Asturias. Also living outside the country were the well-known mime and director Mario Gonzáles and the entire group Teatro Vivo (Theatre Alive).

Music Theatre
Dance Theatre

National folk theatre, performed by indigenous groups across the country, is connected to both dance and music forms. Its roots are, on the one hand, pre-Hispanic and, on the other, colonial, from religious beliefs imposed by the Spaniards.

The Maya culture had its first great permanent establishments in Guatemalan territory. After them remained the kingdoms of their descendants, the Maya-Quichés, and rival cultures such as the Cakchiquel, with whom the

Maya were at war at the time of the conquest. Both the Quichés and the Cakchiquel cultures had a rich religious, literary and theatrical tradition. The *Popol Vuh*, the Cakchiquel archive, and the *Rabinal Achí* (*Dance of the Tun*) are obvious proof of their spiritual and cultural achievements.

It is certain that other Meso-american cultures also had some ceremonies of a theatrical character, but the *Rabinal Achí* is the only complete and assuredly genuine work of the pre-Hispanic theatre found in the Americas to date. The *Rabinal Achí* is dance theatre with a profoundly dramatic plot. It is, according to George Reynaud, one of its original translators, 'the only piece of known Amerindian theatre that does not have a word, an idea or an event – either in form or content – that can be said to be of European style'. He adds that the piece 'entirely belongs to pre-Hispanic times'.

The piece was rescued by the priest Charles Étienne Brasseur of Bourbourg, who discovered it while he was working in San Pablo de Rabinal in the Guatemalan high plateau. He saw it performed in 1856, and with the help of some servants he transcribed all the details of the performance, then translated the Latin version of the Quiché text into French. It was later translated into Spanish by Miguel Angel Asturias and Luis Cardona y Aragón. It is still occasionally performed at its original location on 25 January for the festivities of Saint Paul.

Franciscan and Dominican monks brought another dance piece – the *Dance of Moors and Christians* – from Spain. An adaptation of still another Spanish dance done in Guatemala was the *Danza de la conquista* (*Dance of the Conquest*), of which there are many versions. All these pieces were meant to impose a new spirituality on the defeated indigenous peoples, who, converted to Christianity, became the labour force of society, a status that has remained essentially unchanged throughout the centuries.

The ceremonies and traditions found in works such as the *Dance of the Moors and Christians* and the *Dance of the Conquest*, and pre-Hispanic forms such as the *Dance of the Monkey*, the *Dance of the Serpent* and the *Dance of the Deer* are clear reminders of Guatemala's rich theatrical past. Other such works of note include the ceremonies of Maximon – a saint who was half pagan and half Christian – done beside Lake Atitlán; the ceremonies of Pascual Abaj in Chicastenango; the elaborate processions and marches during Holy Week in the streets of Guatemala City, including the performance of the Passion of Christ, in which the streets are laid with coloured sawdust and the crowds kneel and pray while Jesus is whipped by spear-carrying Roman soldiers; the recitations and songs for the Virgin Mary and other saints; and the noisy, rebellious and critical student festivities on Good Friday.

Working in a more contemporary way is Ballet Guatemala, founded in 1948 by Jean Devaux and his wife, Marcelle Bonge. Since 1962 it has been directed by Antonio Cresop. The company maintains a traditional, classical repertoire and has attracted such guest artists as Erik Bruhn and Violette Verdy.

Theatre for Young Audiences
Puppet Theatre

In 1962 René Molina founded the first children's theatre company in Guatemala. Among the most stable ones operating in the 1990s were the Compañía de Teatro para Niños (Children's Theatre Company), the group UPcito (Little UP), the groups Jasaju, Pierrots, Ditirambo and Teatro Club para Niños (Children's Theatre Club.

The puppet and marionette theatre of Marilena López, founded in the 1950s, was still functioning in the 1990s thanks to the energies of Carmen Antillon.

Design
Theatre Space and Architecture

Many of Guatemala's leading theatre designers come from the realm of visual art, specifically painting. Among these, the most important are Ramón Banús, Arnoldo Ramírez, and Amaya and Max Saravia Gual.

In lighting design the most influential figure for many years was Carlos Obregón, who was exiled and now lives in France. Javier Pacheco is the country's most important costume designer as well as an excellent actor.

The architect and painter Efraín Recinos designed the Cultural Centre of Guatemala City, one of the major theatres in the country. It contains three separate spaces, one of which is used almost exclusively for musical theatre. The second, the Teatro de Cámara, is used for dramatic plays. The third is an outdoor theatre for large-scale spectacles.

Other spaces of note in Guatemala City are the Teatro de Bellas Artes, the auditorium of the Instituto Guatemalteco Americano, and the Abril (April).

Training
Criticism, Scholarship and Publishing

There are two Dramatic Arts Schools in Guatemala, one sponsored by the state and the other by the Popular University.

Theatre critics of note include Luz Mendez de la Vega, Mario Alberto Carrera, Antonio García Urrea and Alberto Mencos. Matilde Montoya is one of the few scholars to carry out important studies and research on indigenous dance.

Hugo Carrillo
Translated by Mayte Gómez

Further Reading

Acuña, René. *Introducción al estudio del Rabinal Achí*. [Introduction to the study of *Rabinal Achí*]. México City: Universidad Nacional Autónoma de México, Centro de Estudios Mayas, 1975.

——. 'Una década de teatro guatemalteco 1962–1973'. [A decade of Guatemalan theatre, 1962–1973]. *Latin American Theatre Review* 8, no. 2 (September 1975): 59–74.

Albizurez, Palma, Francisco Barrios y Barrios, and Catalina Barrios y Barrios. 'Literatura dramática guatemalteca'. [Guatemalan dramatic literature]. Chap. in *Historia de la literatura guatemalteca*. [History of Guatemalan literature]. Guatemala City: Universidad de San Carlos, 1987.

Batres Jáuregui, Antonio. *Memorias de antaño, con una historia del teatro en Guatemala*. [Old memories, and a history of the Guatemalan theatre]. Oakland, CA: Pacific Press, 1986.

Bravo-Elizondo, Pedro. 'Guatemala: VII temporada de teatro departamental, Mayo 19–21, 1989'. [Guatemala: The Seventh Season of Departmental Theatre, May 19–21, 1989]. *Latin American Theatre Review* 23, no. 2 (spring 1990): 111–14.

Carrera, Mario Alberto. 'Ideas políticas en el teatro de Manuel Galich'. [Political ideas in the theatre of Manuel Galich]. Guatemala City: Facultad de Humanidades, Universidad de San Carlos, 1966.

Carrillo, Hugo. 'Orígenes y desarrollo del teatro guatemalteco'. [Origins and development of Guatemalan theatre]. *Conjunto*, 20 (April–June 1974): 72–80.

Fernández Molina, Manuel. *Dos estudios históricos sobre el teatro en Guatemala: el teatro en la ciudad de Guatemala en la época de la independencia y la incidencia de los terremotos en el teatro guatemalteco*. [Two historical studies on Guatemalan theatre: Theatre in Guatemala City during independence and the influence of earthquakes in Guatemalan theatre]. Guatemala City: Dirección General de Bellas Artes, 1982.

García Mejía, René. *Raíces del teatro guatemalteco*. [Roots of Guatemalan theatre]. Guatemala City: Tipografía Nacional, 1972.

Herrera, Ubico, and Ana Sivia. *El teatro en Guatemala en el siglo XX: contribución de Luis Herrera al surgimiento de un quehacer teatral.* [Theatre in Guatemala in the twentieth century: Luis Herrera's contribution to the theatre profession]. Guatemala City: Serviprensa Centroamericana, 1980.

——. 'La escenificación teatral en Guatemala en la segunda mitad del siglo XX: dos décadas de teatro 1950–70'. [Theatre in Guatemala in the second half of the twentieth century: Two decades of theatre 1950–70]. In *Historia general de Guatemala.* [A general history of Guatemala].

Klein, Maxine. 'A Country of Cruelty and Its Theatre'. *Drama Survey* 7, nos. 1–2 (winter 1968–spring 1969): 164–70.

Peña, Mancilla, and Gabriel Roberto. 'El signo en el teatro'. [Signs in theatre]. PhD dissertation, Facultad de Humanidades, Universidad de San Carlos, 1975.

Solórzano, Carlos. *Teatro guatemalteco contemporáneo.* [Contemporary Guatemalan theatre]. Madrid: Aguilar, 1973.

GUYANA

(see **COMMONWEALTH CARRIBEAN**)

HAÏTI

(Overview)

Sharing the Caribbean island of Hispaniola with the Dominican Republic, Haïti, situated between Jamaica and Puerto Rico, was one of the colonial jewels of France until a general uprising of slaves in 1791, which led to the country's independence in 1804. With both French and Creole (the Caribbean dialect of the French language) speakers, Haïti in 1994 had a population of 6.7 million, who live in an area of just 27,750 square kilometres (10,715 square miles). Over 1.5 million live in the capital, Port-au-Prince.

Haïti is the poorest country in the western hemisphere. The minimum wage is about US$4 per day. Rarely experiencing political stability, the country has long been torn by conflict between a dominant black and Métis (people of mixed aboriginal and French ancestry) economic and political elite and the overwhelming majority of poor and underprivileged people. The years from the 1950s on were typical. Following the dictatorship (1957–71) of François 'Papa Doc' Duvalier (1907–71) and that of his son Jean-Claude Duvalier (b. 1953) from 1971 to 1986, Jean Bertrand Aristide (b. 1953) became the first freely elected president in the history of the country in 1990. But Aristide was overthrown by the army in a bloody coup ten months later. Between 1991 and 1994 the country was isolated by the international community because of the military's refusal to restore democracy. Following United Nations Security Council resolutions, a US-led invasion restored President Aristide to power in October 1994.

Haïtian theatrical expression is rooted in various facets of the indigenous religion, voodoo. A product of African sects and Catholicism, voodoo developed its own techniques of dramatic and musical expression in order to establish a relationship between the gods of the cosmos and the transplanted African slaves. Reaching back to a period before the written text established its supremacy in western

297

theatre, voodoo traces its roots to the very origins of classical theatre, whether African, Greek or Asian. Theatre that is lived and experienced rather than merely performed, voodoo's cultic representations do not attempt to achieve a realistic depiction of life. They are rather attempts at communal participation that break down the traditional barriers between actors and spectators. The climax of the voodoo ceremony – in which a spirit takes possession of the body of an individual – can be seen as a character attempting to obtain the favour of the gods through a faithful enactment of rites and gestures. The voodoo ceremony is therefore itself a performance in which priests and celebrants become at the same time actors and spectators in a kind of ecstatic fusion of the imaginary and the real.

The country also has a very long European theatrical tradition dating back to the period of French colonial rule when plays were performed by and for French settlers. These included, from the eighteenth century, successes from Paris. Because of their popularity, theatre buildings were established in Port-au-Prince, and at Léogâne. Jean Fouchard, in his history of theatre in Saint-Domingue (the colonial name for Haïti), has noted the use of a Creole dialect in certain of these plays and the use of local black actors.

The theatrical life provided by French touring companies to the wealthy colony was considerably diminished during the Haïtian Revolution (1791–1804). A fight for liberation left the island ravaged but plays continued to be staged, particularly in the style referred to in Haïti as the 'historic school'. Following independence, playwrights such as Antoine Dupré (d. 1816), Jules Solime Milscent (1778–1842), Juste Chanlatte (1766–1828) and Jean Jacques Romane (1807–58) glorified the heroes of the struggle in a series of historical melodramas. Strongly influenced by the French writer Alphonse de Lamartine, who wrote *Toussaint Louverture* (1848), a play about the life of the black liberation hero, Haïtian writing turned towards romanticism from the mid-nineteenth century. A national literature began to affirm itself with new works by writers such as Auguste Théodore Eugène Nau, Pierre Faubert (1806–68), Liautaud Ethéart (1826–88) and Alibée Fleury (1819–96), among others.

An economist by training, Nau was the author of *La Fiancée de Léogâne* (*The Fiancée from Léogâne*), a five-act verse drama first performed in 1857. Faubert, director of a secondary school and private secretary to one of Haïti's most savage dictators, Jean-Pierre Boyer (1818–43), staged his *Ogé, ou le préjugé de couleur* (*Ogé, or The Prejudice of Colour*) in 1851. Published in Paris in 1858, the play dramatized the first revolt of freed slaves against the caste system. An educator, minister and secretary of state for foreign affairs, Ethéart was also the author of numerous works, including the historical dramas *La Fille de l'empéreur* (*The Emperor's Daughter*, 1860) and *Un Duel sous Blanchelande* (*The Duel Below Blanchelande*, 1860). His one-act *Génie d'enfer ou la main de Dieu* (*The Spirit From Hell or the Hand of God*, 1855) dramatized the story of a young mulatto (of mixed black and European ancestry) woman coveted by a cruel white settler. Fleury published two comedies, *Les Rimeurs* (*The Rhymers*), a satire of the literary milieu, and *Le Barbon amoureux* (*The Amorous Old Man*), a comedy of morals. Fleury's plays were published in 1876 in *Les Essais littéraires* (*Literary Essays*).

The movement towards an authentic indigenous literature was accelerated by the US occupation of Haïti from 1915 to 1934, which traumatized the country's political and cultural life. Many young writers sought at this time to validate local traditions and their celebration of Haïtian life was often effectively accomplished through the theatre. Dominique Hyppolite (b. 1889), the most important Haïtian playwright in the first half of the twentieth century, wrote a series of plays appealing to the public interest – some historical, some political and some social satire.

Despite the creation of an indigenous theatre, French influence in the post-World War II period continued to be strong. The Institut Français administered the major theatre in Haïti and in 1994 was still the primary training centre for Haïtian theatre artists despite the existence of companies and training institutes such as the Société Nationale d'Art Dramatique (National Society of Dramatic Art, 1948–63), the Conservatoire National d'Art Dramatique (National Conservatory of Dramatic Art) and Gérard Résil's Institut National de Formation Artistique (National Institute for Artistic Training). Only the Théâtre National d'Haïti (National Theatre of Haïti), a state institution, was able to offer regular training programmes year round but even these were limited by the minimal resources provided by the government.

In dramatic terms, Haïtian theatre in the second half of the twentieth century varied between plays influenced by French literary dramatic styles and a popular theatre consisting of political/social dramas and historical plays such as Roger Dorsainville's (b. 1911) *Barrières* (*Barriers*, 1945); Henock Trouillot's (b. 1923) *Le Regard de Christophe* (*Christophe's Glance*) and *Retour en Afrique* (*Return to Africa*), staged at the Institut Français in 1965; and Jean F. Brièrre's (b. 1909) *Les Amours de Loas* (*Loas's Loves*). Popular theatre emerged in the works of Théodore Beaubrun and Alcibiade (Pierre Nicolas Rolin, b. 1938), both of whom wrote for more than thirty years.

Beaubrun mounted over a dozen plays between 1942 (*Languichatte se marie/Languichatte Gets Married*) and 1980 with his company La Troupe Languichatte (Beaubrun's stage name). Alcibiade began his career in 1954 with his Troupe Alcibiade, which continued producing until the end of the 1970s. A painter combining French and Creole themes, Beaubrun was the most popular Haïtian theatrical figure during this time. His *Languichatte à New York* (*Languichatte in New York*, 1980) dramatized the vicissitudes of the lives of Haïtian immigrants in the United States.

Critic Pradel Pompilus has suggested that

one can reproach [Beaubrun] for always rewriting the same play, for giving too much prominence to burlesque, to puns and funny language, and for more or less exploiting the slight texts of the French *théâtre de boulevard*, but it is nevertheless true that he greatly contributed to the creation of a popular theatre and to the theatrical education of the public at large.

With Mona Guérin (b. 1934), the author of *L'Oiseau de ces dames* (*Caged Bird*, 1966), *Les Cinq Chéris* (*Five Darlings*, 1969) and *La Pieuvre* (*The Squid*, 1971), vaudeville yielded its place to more dramatic studies reflecting Haïtian social conditions. In *La Pieuvre*, a tale of a father and his two daughters struggling against an abusive mother, Guérin deals with the theme of the destructive influence of family conflict on children.

Popular theatre productions have been generally critical of the dictatorships in Haïti. This was clear in the extraordinary success of *Pélin Tèt* (*Head Trap*, 1978) by Frankétienne (b. 1936), a free adaptation into Creole of Polish dramatist Sławomir Mrożek's *The Emigrants*. In the play, two Haïtian immigrants in New York from different social classes both attack and sympathize with one another. Their ironic

and critical examination of New York was an obvious and effective way of circumventing censorship during the Duvalier dictatorship.

Pélin Tèt was performed in Haïti in 1984 by François Latour and Roland Dorfeuille in a production directed by Latour. The positive public response and the more than thirty sold-out performances, however, led to the production being closed down by the Duvalier government. Frankétienne staged two further plays after 1986 in his quest to create a Creole aesthetic: *Bobomasouri* (1984) and particularly *Kaselezo* (*Womb Waters Breaking*, 1985), a remarkable denunciation of the condition of women in Haïtian society. This was also the first time that a male writer had so frankly treated this almost taboo theme.

A whole constellation of Haïtian writers, performers and writer-performers began to establish themselves in the 1970s: Max Vallès (b. 1939), Charles Alexandre Abellard, Bob Lemoine and especially Hervé Denis (b. 1939) and Syto Cavé (b. 1944). Cavé's *Kavalye Polka*, a superb metaphor on the theme of domination, was performed by Denis and Cavé at the Rex Theatre in Port-au-Prince in 1987. In the play, a blind man pushes a man in a wheelchair but instead of enjoying a mutually beneficial relationship, each claims to be the indispensable element, a comment on the impossibility of existence in a society that generally turns its back on disabled people.

Cavé subsequently staged *Songe que fait Sarah* (*Sarah's Dream*), while Denis attempted to establish a professional company, La Compagnie Hervé Denis. With the assistance of the Coopération Culturelle Française, this latter company staged Martinique playwright Aimé Césaire's *La Tragédie du roi Christophe* (*The Tragedy of King Christophe*, 1990) and Franck Fouché's (1915–78) *Général Baron-la-Croix* (1990), a large poetic fresco denouncing the Duvalier dictatorship.

Several younger playwrights in the 1980s attempted to follow their example. Evans Paul (b. 1955) became known particularly with *Debafre*, a drama with revolutionary themes performed only once and banned during the Jean-Claude Duvalier dictatorship but remounted after Duvalier's fall. Paul, elected mayor of Port-au-Prince in 1990, is also the author of half a dozen other dramas written between 1980 and 1990: *Debride* (*The Dejected Bride*), *Eksetera*, *Général Lacroix*, *Pou-ki-tan-n* (*Why Wait?*), *Dekore pawòl* (*The Parodied Speech*) and *Li pa mouri* (*He Isn't Dead*).

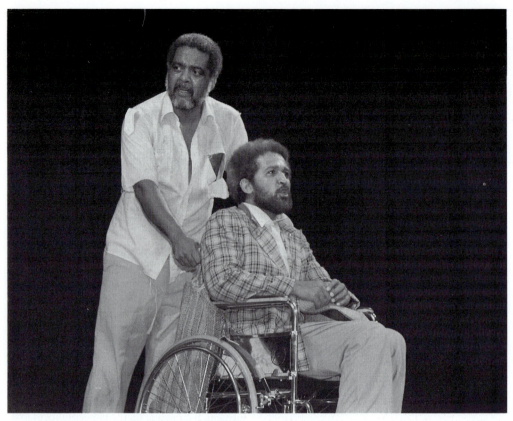

Hervé Denis and Syto Cavé in the 1987 Port-au-Prince production of Cavé's *Kavalye Polka*. Photo: Pierre Michel Lesperance.

Frédéric Surpris, one of the most prolific of the 1980s playwrights, wrote a series of socio-political dramas including *Mèt Kay*, *Lucifer* and *Coup d'état* from 1986 to 1990. Gary Victor (b. 1958) staged his own drama *Zagoyo*, examining the condition of the Haïtian working class, at the Institut Français in 1991.

Jezifra (Fénel Valcourt) is an actor who is following in the footsteps of Languichatte and Alcibiade, playing in numerous productions written for him by Jules Kesner – *Jezifra Candidat* (1987) and *Lanmou pa gen baryè* (*Love Has No Boundary*, 1989) among others. Jezifra and Kesner's *Kraze Lanfè* (1991), about the downfall of a young man entangled in the Duvalier militia, was so successful that it was later turned into a film.

Haïtian ritual dance became known in North America and Europe through the distinguished work of Katherine Dunham (b. 1912), who transposed native traditions into brilliant theatrical presentations. With a solid academic background (a PhD in anthropology from the University of Chicago), she did careful research in Haïti, translating the results of her investigations into vibrant dances for both Broadway and the concert stage.

Despite these successes it must still be said that because of the lack of government and public-sector support there is still relatively little professional theatre in Haïti and almost no infrastructure. As well, the high price of tickets to productions has tended to discourage the general population from attending. Instead, it looks towards carnival and voodoo for self-expression.

One should also note here the large Haïtian community in North America, where important plays have been written and produced by artists such as Gérard Chenet, Anthony Phelps (b. 1928), Toto Bissainthe (b. 1934), Mathilde Beauvoir and particularly Félix Morisseau-Leroy (b. 1912) and Franck Fouché. Morisseau-Leroy is the author of a well-known translation into Creole of Sophocles' *Antigone* (*Antigone In Creole*, 1953), while the prolific Fouché has authored more than twenty stage and radio plays.

Even before his exile from Haïti in 1965, Fouché had written adaptations in Creole of *Oedipus the King* (1953), *Yerma* (1957) and *Bouki nan Paradis* (*Bouki in Paradise*, 1960), dramatizing the folk-tale characters Bouki and Malice and the theme of solidarity, as well as *Feux verts dans la nuit* (*Green Lights in the Night*, 1964), analysing the differences between the bourgeoisie, the peasants and the working class. Fouché became a resident of Québec in 1967. His futuristic absurdist drama *Le Trou de Dieu* (*The Tunnel of God*) was first presented in Montréal that year as was his most important play, *Général Baron-la-Croix ou le silence masqué* (*Général Baron-la-Croix, or The Masked Silence*, 1971). In the drama, a voodoo priest resembling Papa Doc Duvalier uses magic to defeat his adversaries and makes a pact with the god of the dead to keep himself in power but is overthrown during a carnival celebration.

Other important works by Fouché include *Un Fantôme dans un crâne* (*Ghost in a Skull*), the Creole *Ethesin*, and the bilingual *L'École des maris* (*The School for Husbands*), *L'École des politiciens* (*The School for Politicians*) and *Prométhée* (*Prometheus*). Fouché's theories on a popular Haïtian theatre of liberation and indigenous dramatic forms can be found in his *Vodou et théâtre* (*Voodoo and Theatre*, 1976).

The most important Haïtian expatriate theatre company was the collective Kouidor, founded in New York City in 1969 and active until 1977. The nine-person ensemble, which included Hervé Denis, experimented with forms of politically engaged epic theatre, combining the staging theories of Brecht and Erwin Piscator with indigenous theatrical forms based on voodoo folk rituals. Their productions featured a Marxist political perspective and revolutionary topics presented through the oral stories and expression of Haïtian popular culture: the poetry of the Creole language and folklore, music, dance, songs, drumming and the gestures, incantations, trance and transcendence of voodoo rituals and ceremonies.

Kouidor's 1972 *Memoires d'un balai* (*Memorial for a Broom*), for example, dramatized a fictional strike of Haïtian workers. *La Parole des grands fonds* (*Word from the Great*

The 1993 Montréal Theatre Alliance of Young Haïtians' production of Victor Eternel's *The Republic in Chains*.
Photo: Pierre Michel Lesperance.

Estate, 1973) dramatized the relationships between urban and country life and capitalist and semi-feudal modes of economic production. In New York the company performed primarily for Creole audiences at such venues as the Brooklyn Academy of Music and Columbia University. Kouidor also toured to other North American cities of the Haïtian diaspora.

There are, finally, a number of Haïtian community theatres in Montréal though the majority have a religious orientation. One must nevertheless note Fayolle Jean's Théâtre Libre d'Haïti (Haïtian Free Theatre). In 1994, it staged *Twadegout* (the Creole name for a violent poison administered by voodoo sorcerers), a fierce denunciation of Haïtian political practices. Jean also produced other plays such as *Nap Debat* and political theatre analysing popular movements in Haïti and their limitations.

Montréal's Alliance Théâtrale des Jeunes Haïtiens (Theatre Alliance of Young Haïtians), founded by Renord Bain (b. 1963) and Bertry Winder in 1991, produced Victor Eternel's (b. 1950) political drama *La République enchaînée* (*The Republic in Chains*) in 1993. The alliance also produced educational plays such as *Le Sida* (*AIDS*) and *L'Espace interdit* (*The Forbidden Space*). Other artists promoting Haïtian theatre in Montréal include Gladys Démosthène, Mireille Metellus and Dominique Ollivier.

In general in the early 1990s, the Haïtian ruling elite, having seen the potential power of theatre to influence popular taste, seemed no longer willing to allow its existence in the country except as commercial enterprise.

Gary Victor
Translated by Anton Wagner

Further Reading

Alcide, Marie-José. 'Theatrical and Dramatic Elements of Haitian Voodoo'. PhD dissertation, City University of New York, 1988. 272 pp.

Anderson, Michelle. 'Authentic Voodoo is Synthetic'. *The Drama Review* 26, no. 2 (summer 1982): 89–110.

Bauduy, Robert. 'Aux sources du théâtre populaire haïtien'. [Roots of Haïtian popular theatre]. *Revue Conjonction* 24, no. 3 (1969).

——. 'El teatro haitiano contemporáneo'. [Contemporary Haïtian theatre]. *Conjunto* 84 (July–September 1990): 43–8.

Clark, Vèvè A. 'Campesinos-actores en Haití: el peso de la tradición'. [Peasant-actors in Haïti: The weight of tradition]. *Conjunto* 70 (September–December 1986): 14–22.

——. 'Contemporary Forms of Popular Theatre in Haiti'. *Ufahamu* 12, no. 2 (1983): 93–100.

——. 'Fieldhands to Stagehands in Haiti: The Measure of Tradition in Haitian Popular Theatre'. PhD dissertation, University of California, Berkeley, 1983. 585 pp.

——. 'Haiti's Brechtian Playwrights'. *Communications from the International Brecht Society* 13, no. 2 (April 1984): 28–34.

——. 'Haiti's Tragic Overture: (Mis)Representations of the Haitian Revolution in World Drama (1796–1975)'. In *Representing Revolution: Essays on Reflections of the French Revolution in Literature, Historiography and Art*, ed. James Heffernan. Hanover, NH: University Press of New England, 1991.

——. 'When Womb Waters Break: The Emergence of Haitian New Theater (1953–1987)'. *Callaloo* 15, no. 3 (1992): 778–86.

Cornevin, Robert. *Le Théâtre haïtien des origines à nos jours*. [Haïtian theatre from its beginnings to the present]. Collection Caraïbes. Montréal: Leméac, 1973. 301 pp.

Denis, Hervé. 'Introduction à un manifeste pour un théâtre haïtien'. [Introduction to a manifesto for a Haïtian theatre]. *Nouvelle optique* 1, no. 1 (January 1971): 132–41.

Dunham, Katherine. *Dances of Haiti*. Los Angeles: Center for Afro-American Studies, University of California at Los Angeles, 1983.

Étienne, Gérard. 'Sur la Vie et l'oeuvre de Franck Fouché'. [On the life and work of Franck Fouché]. *Présence francophone* 16 (spring 1978): 191–200.

Fouchard, Jean. *Le Théâtre à Saint-Domingue*. [Theatre in Saint-Domingue]. Port-au-Prince: Editions Henri Deschamps, 1988. 294 pp.

Fouché, Franck. *Vodou et théâtre: pour un nouveau théâtre populaire*. [Voodoo and theatre: Towards a new popular theatre]. Montréal: Editions Nouvelle Optique, 1976. 125 pp.

Frankétienne. 'Kaselezo: Frankétienne, écrivain haïtien'. [Womb Waters Breaking: Frankétienne, Haïtian writer]. Edited by Jean Jonassaint. *Dérives* 53/54 (1986/87): 125–63.

Gouraige, Ghislain. *Histoire de la littérature haïtienne de l'indépendance à nos jours*. [History of Haïtian literature from independence to the present]. Port-au-Prince: N.A. Théodore, 1960.

Kouidor. 'La Présentation (Notes pour un travail)'. [Presentation (Notes for a piece of work)]. *Nouvelle optique* 9 (January–March 1973): 121–46.

Lemoine, Michèle. 'Les Chemins de *Kaselezo*'. [The ways of *Womb Waters Breaking*]. *Dérives* 53/54 (1986–87): 165–9.

Louis-Jean, Antonio. *La Crise de possession et la possession dramatique*. [The convulsion of possession and dramatic possession]. Montréal: Leméac, 1970.

Pompilus, Pradel. 'Les Chances du théâtre haïtien contemporain'. [The opportunities for contemporary Haïtian theatre]. *Revue Conjonction* 24, no. 3 (1969): 18.

——, and les Frères de l'Instruction Chrétienne. *Manuel illustré de l'histoire et de la littérature haïtienne*. [Illustrated guide to Haïtian history and literature]. Port-au-Prince: Editions Henri Deschamps, 1961.

Viatte, Auguste. *Histoire littéraire de l'Amérique française, des origines à 1950*. [Literary history of French America from its origins to 1950]. Québec/Paris: PUL/PUF, 1959.

Una familia como hay tantas (*A Family Like So Many Others*).

Claudio Barrera, also a winner of the Premio Nacional de Literatura and a poet with a place of honour in Central American literature, wrote for the theatre as well. His pieces had a higher intellectual level than those of Laínez. Influenced by García Lorca, Barrera experimented with a poetic drama in *María del Carmen*, a two-act play set during the Spanish Civil War. Another well-known play of his is *La niña de Fuenterrosa*.

The year 1945 also marked the beginning of a theatre concerned with social issues. Medardo Mejía (1907–82), a lawyer, essayist and journalist, wrote a short one-act play, *Los chapetones* (the word is slang for a Spaniard newly arrived in the Americas), which was published in the Guatemalan weekly *Mediodía*. An analysis of the problem of landownership in Central America, the play presents the story of two families – one that had worked the land for generations and another, newly arrived from Spain, that was the heir of the colonizers who first exploited the lands.

In the 1950s, the Honduran government extended an invitation to Santiago F. Toffé (1910–83), a Spanish-born Honduran, to establish a chair in speech in the School of Music. Toffé quickly created a theatre company there known as the Cuadro Artístico Teatral Hondureño (Honduran Art Theatre Company), with which he produced plays mostly by Spanish playwrights. A second group was founded in 1956 by residents of the United States' community in Honduras. The group, called Grupo Dramático Tegucigalpa, was bilingual, had its own space and presented plays by Spanish and US dramatists. By 1990, the company had produced more than 200 scripts and still had a small but faithful audience.

Still another company opened at this time in the city of San Pedro Sula, El Círculo Teatral Sampedrano (San Pedran Theatre Circle). Led by actor Francisco Salvador (b. 1934), the group had a similar Spanish and US repertoire, but larger audiences. It is still the most stable theatre in the country.

The Teatro Universitario (University Theatre) also produced plays directed by Salvador, among them Cervantes's *Los entremeses* (*Interludes*), Lope de Rueda's *Los pasos* (*Sketches*), Jean-Paul Sartre's *The Respectful Prostitute* and *No Tomb for the Dead*, Guatemalan Hugo Carrillo's *La calle del sexo verde* (*Green Sex Street*) and León Felipe's *Juglarón* (*The Minstrel*). Salvador eventually left the Teatro Universitario in the hands of the US teacher-director Norma Miller from San Francisco. In her teaching, Miller emphasized body movement. Her major productions included García Lorca's *La zapatera prodigiosa* (*The Shoemaker's Prodigious Wife*) and Leonid Andreev's *He Who Gets Slapped*. The Teatro Universitario was later led by other distinguished directors including Rafael Murillo (b. 1935), the Guatemalan René Figueroa, and the Argentine actress Iris Morenza.

In 1959 Mercedes Agurcia Membreño (1903–79) founded the Teatro Infantil de Honduras (Honduran Children's Theatre), where she often staged plays based on national themes such as *La india triste* (*The Unhappy Indian Maid*), *Historia olvidada* (*Forgotten Story*), *La espera* (*The Waiting*), *Bajo el mismo alero* (*Under the Same Wing*) and *En el teatro como en la vida* (*In Theatre As In Life*). Salvador Lara, a member of the Teatro Infantil, later founded his own company, El Teatro de los 10 (Teen Theatre). With this company, he produced Edgar Neville's *Adelita* and Salvador Novo's *A ocho columnas* (*Eight Columns*), as well as stories of his own creation: *Zompopo* and *La tabla de oro* (*The Golden Board*).

In 1961, the Spanish playwright and literature professor Andrés Morris (b. 1928) came to Honduras. He organized the Teatro de la Escuela Superior de Profesorado (Teachers' College Theatre Company) in Tegucigalpa, whose first productions were Medieval farces, followed by Jean Anouilh's *Antigone* and Cervantes's *El retablo de las maravillas* (*Wonder Show*) and *El viejo celoso* (*The Jealous Old Husband*).

The creation of an official, professional and permanent theatre company was proposed to the Honduran government in 1964 by Salvador and Morris and, in 1965, the military government authorized the creation of the Compañía Nacional de Teatro (National Theatre Company), under the administration of the Ministry of Public Education. The Compañía Nacional operated under the leadership of five directors: Salvador, Morris, Toffé, Argucia Membreño and Laínez. In its first three years, from 1965 to 1967, the Nacional produced Molière's *The Miser*, Fernando de Rojas's *La celestina* (*The Madame*), Patrick Hamilton's *The Rope*, Armand Gatti's *The Buffalo Toad*, Eliseo Pérez Cadalso's *El Máusimo*, Agurcia Membreño's *Historia olvidada*, Morris's *El Guarizama* (1966) and José Reina Valenzuela's *Cañas*, *libertador de esclavos (Cañas, Liberator of Slaves).*

Honduran playwriting also began to follow new impulses in the late 1960s. The actress Lucy Ondina organized the Teatro Popular Universitario (University Popular Theatre), which toured across the country with poetry readings and performances of short, issue-oriented plays. Ondina was also the first to introduce into Honduran theatre the dances of the Garífunas, a black ethnic group from the country's north coast. The late 1960s also saw essayist Medardo Mejía's (1907–82) trilogy on the political history of the country during the nineteenth century: *La ahorcancina, Cinchonero* and *Medinón*. The Teatro Universitario, directed by Armando Valeriano, represented Honduras at the Central American Theatre Festival of 1971 in Costa Rica with a production of the third part of this trilogy.

Andrés Morris also wrote a trilogy, his based on the theme of underdevelopment and its consequences. Written in an absurdist style and performed under the general title *Trilogía istmica (Isthmus Trilogy)*, the three plays are *El Guarizama*, set in a rural environment; *La miel del abejorro (Bumblebee's Honey, 1968)*, dealing with technical development and the struggle for land; and *Oficio de hombres (A Profession for Men, 1967)*, perhaps the most sophisticated of the three, dealing with technical training for workers in urban areas. The Teatro Universitario subsequently toured this piece to other parts of Central America, as well as to London, Madrid and Valencia in a production directed by Salvador. Salvador also began writing plays. His first was *El sueño de Matías Carpio (Matías Carpio's Dream, 1967)*, for which he won the Reyes Prize, awarded by the Escuela Superior de Profesorado.

Another young writer of this time was Roberto Soto Rovelo, who wrote several short *costumbrista* pieces such as *Buenas tardes Señor Ministro (Good Afternoon, Mr Minister), El misionero (The Missionary), El pequeño señor (The Little Sir)* and the satirical comedy *Jardín de Italia (Italian Garden)*.

In 1969, during the war between Honduras and El Salvador, Rafael Murillo created *Los patrulleros (The Patrolmen)* with the Compañía Nacional, a collective creation based on a script by Andrés Morris. This experience led to interest in collective creation as a form, and a second collective was created, *Alta es la noche (High Is the Night)*, based on a script by Saúl Toro (b. 1939) and Toffé about the struggle

among traditional political parties. Another important collective from this period was *Los 400 años (400 Years)*, about the history of Tegucigalpa, by the Compañía Nacional, directed by Mimí Figueroa.

In the 1970s and 1980s, a theatre movement with genuine national characteristics was born. Theatre companies began to look for new ideas and possibilities, new scenic languages and new themes that would depart from the fashion of the day and would deal with Honduran reality.

In 1972, director Rafael Murillo presented a proposal to the Universidad Nacional Autónoma (Autonomous National University) to create its own University Theatre. Thus was founded the Teatro Universitario La Merced, operating out of the university's central hall in La Merced Square, in central Tegucigalpa. During its seven years of life, from 1972 to 1979, the Teatro Universitario La Merced developed both regular seasons and stable audiences. Among the major productions Murillo directed were adaptations of the Guatemalan Manuel José Arce's play *Sebastián sale de compras (Sebastián Goes Shopping, 1975)*, Molière's *Le Bourgeois Gentilhomme (The Bourgeois Gentleman)*, a collective creation – *El Huracán Fifi (Hurricane Fifi)* – and Peter Weiss's *Gesang vom lusitanischen Popanz (Song of the Lusitanian Bogey)*. In 1976, one of the members of the group, Roberto Silva, directed the Chilean Isadora Aguirre's *Los que van quedando afuera (Those Who Are Left Outside)*, while another, Gloria del Carmen Zepala, directed several children's plays.

The year 1977 marked the beginning of an ideological crisis that would eventually divide the company. Out of this division came the Teatro Obrero del Pueblo Unido (United People's Workers' Theatre), directed by Miguel Gutiérrez, which showed its work in parks, streets and working-class neighbourhoods. Some of its best known plays were *La huelga (The Strike)* and *A desalambrar (Taking Down the Wires)*, whose political and social message was well received by working-class audiences. Later, the company continued its artistic and political work under the leadership of Jesús Bertrand Meza, who kept the group operating until 1979.

The Academia Nacional de Arte Dramático (National Theatre School) was created in 1976 as a wing of the Compañía Nacional de Teatro, with the goal of training young actors in order to have a stable cast for the Compañía Nacional. The Academia Nacional was directed by Toffé until it closed in 1978, when the

Compañía Nacional also ceased operation. That same year theatre in Honduras entered a serious crisis, and for many years the only companies operating were those formed by students. The exceptions to this were small companies organized by the actor Isidoro España in workers' unions. España later created the Fundación Camino Real (Royal Path Foundation), a company that was still operating in the 1990s, producing the work of Honduran playwrights.

In 1979 Saúl Toro returned from Colombia, where he had studied directing, and proposed that the government organize a new theatre school, to be called the Escuela de Teatro (Theatre School). The school opened the same year and continues to operate. Under the administration of the Ministry of Culture, the school eventually formed its own producing company – the Teatro Taller Tegucigalpa (Tegucigalpa Theatre Workshop). This new company, influenced by Brecht's ideas of epic theatre as well as by collective creation, produced the work of Brecht and Latin American authors. The company was later directed by Karen Matute and Tito Estrada and has played at theatre festivals in Spain, Costa Rica, Guatemala and México.

From discussions and panels organized at the Escuela de Teatro came an interest in having theatre artists organized at the national level. This led to the creation of the Comunidad Hondureña de Artistas (Honduran Artists' Community), which through the years has represented artists as well as organized numerous national festivals and congresses and has helped to revive theatre across the country.

New theatre companies and regional events continued to get started through the late 1980s and 1990s both in the capital and in the provinces. Among them were Candelario Reyes and his company Yamala, from Santa Bárbara; the group Rascaniguas, directed by Rafael Murillo, which incorporated music and theatre; Fanny Suazo and Moisés Landaverde in San Pedro Sula, and the Escuela de Teatro in Tegucigalpa, which both promoted puppet theatre; there was even a theatre in the north for the Garífuna ethnic group.

Mime theatre appeared in Honduras for the first time in the 1980s as well, promoted by the Honduran mime Leonardo Montes de Oca. His work led to the creation of several companies that offered classes throughout the country.

A National Theatre Festival was held for the first time in 1968, sponsored by the Banco de Ahorro Hondureño (Honduran Savings Bank), but only groups from the capital participated. In 1982, a national theatre congress was held at which plans for subsequent theatre festivals and regional showcases were made. Three more festivals had been held in the city of San Pedro Sula by 1994, and three others in Tegucigalpa. There have also been children's festivals held in the capital, in San Pedro Sula and in El Progreso, while three festivals 'for peace' were held in the city of El Ceiba.

The only journal that specializes in theatre is *Cuadernos de Teatro* (*Theatre Notebook*), which is published by the Academia Nacional de Arte Dramático (National Academy of Dramatic Art). It publishes mainly theoretical material.

Saúl Toro
Translated by Mayte Gómez

Further Reading

Ardón, Víctor F. 'La producción dramática en Honduras'. [Dramatic production in Honduras]. *Humanismo* 6, nos. 48–9 (March–June 1958): 116–26.

Caballero, Alma, and Francisco Salvador. *Teatro en Honduras*. [Theatre in Honduras]. 2 vols. Tegucigalpa: SECTIN, 1977.

Durand, Jorge Fidel. 'Sobre el teatro en Honduras'. [On theatre in Honduras]. *Honduras Rotaria* 17, no. 183 (June 1958): 12–13.

——. 'Teatro en Honduras'. [Theatre in Honduras]. *Boletín de la Academia Hondureña de la Lengua* 10, no. 11 (November 1965): 55–9.

Fernández, Mauro. 'El teatro en Honduras'. [Theatre in Honduras]. *Repertorio Latino Americano* 2, no. 18 (September 1976): 18.

Reyes, Candelario. 'El movimiento teatral hondureño'. [The Honduran theatre movement]. *Conjunto* (March 1991): 85–6.

JAMAICA

(see COMMONWEALTH CARIBBEAN)

MARTINIQUE

(see FRENCH CARIBBEAN)

MÉXICO

The northernmost country of Latin America, México is the third most populous nation in the western hemisphere, with a population in 1992 of 88.1 million (only the United States and Brazil have a larger population). With a land area of some 1.9 million square kilometres (761,600 square miles), México is the fifth largest country in the hemisphere.

More than 1,000 years before Hernándo Cortés landed in what is now called México, great empires had arisen. First the Olmec, then the Maya, followed by the Toltec, Zapotec, Mixtec and once again the Maya, created major cities and established important religious centres. At the time of the Spanish conquest the Aztecs were the most powerful of these indigenous peoples.

The first Spaniards to reach México arrived in 1517. Two years later, Cortés began the country's conquest. By 1522, he had opened for Spain a territory from what is now the southwestern United States to the Isthmus of Panamá. From 1522 to 1821, México, then called New Spain, was a Spanish colony. The church brought Christianity and European-type schools to the country. By the nineteenth century, the church also held 50 per cent of the country's land and capital.

Napoleon's invasion of Spain in 1808 set off a Mexican independence movement led by Miguel Hidalgo y Costilla (1753–1811), a Spaniard born in the colony. After he was defeated by the Spanish, his struggle was continued until Vicente Guerrero (1783–1831) compelled the Spanish to agree to independence for México in 1821. The nineteenth century saw a territorial war with the United States (1846–8), the framing of a constitution (1857) and an invasion by France (1862). Porfirio Díaz (1830–1915) took the presidency by force in

1876 and ruled the country for most of the next thirty years. During that time, railroads were built, harbours improved, agricultural production increased, an oil industry started and foreign investment grew. But workers had no right to strike, the indigenous peoples had less land than ever before and all opposition was suppressed. In 1910, a revolution broke out, led by Pancho Villa (1877–1923) and Emiliano Zapata (c.1877–1919). In 1917 a new constitution was drafted offering free public education and laws to regulate work hours and wages.

Since 1920 no Mexican president has been overthrown by military uprising nor has the nation suffered major civil conflicts. Between 1960 and 1970 industrial production tripled, and a Free Trade Agreement among México, the United States and Canada signed in 1993 promised even further gains in this area. Despite the positive economic picture, poverty was still significant both in rural areas and in and around major cities which, like the capital México City with its 14 million people, remained badly polluted and overcrowded.

As for México's theatrical history, when the Spanish *conquistadores* arrived in the sixteenth century, they found among the indigenous populations a series of well-established religious ceremonies of a theatrical nature, which were normally performed on esplanades in front of the various temples. Early Spanish chroniclers such as Friar Toribio de Benavente (called Motolinía) and Bernardino de Sahagún wrote about the beauty, scenic colour and opulence of these performances, in which participants – dressed as jaguars, birds, butterflies, or other representations of pre-Hispanic gods – would create a kind of theatre strongly influenced by dance, and whose objective was to pay homage to their deities.

310

The descriptions of plays performed in Cholula, in honour of the goddess Xechiquetzali, give testimony to the chroniclers' admiration of this art, which they nevertheless considered primitive: 'it contained little speech, and was performed by skilled actors in houses close to the temples'. The *conquistador* Cortés, in one of his letters to the king of Spain, praises the beauty of this early religious theatre of the Americas, the subject matter of which would later be explored by modern stage directors. In general, these ceremonies were directed by priests, who controlled all movement, rhythm and the arrival and departure of the actors on the stage. The actors were surrounded by other members of the society participating in a ceremony that they felt united them with the great forces of nature.

In spite of the Spaniards' admiration, it was obvious that the native religious beliefs were contrary to Spanish objectives and the ceremonies began to be suppressed in favour of a European evangelical theatre, which was also directed by priests, in this case Franciscan and Dominican monks.

Sadly, no traces of these ceremonies have been found. In the 1970s and 1980s, however, research indicated that the plans for these events were more like modern-day screenplays than dramatic scripts, indicating movements, positions and changes of actors on stage. This focus on movement, bodily expression and the symbolic value of costume was what brought the French actor-theorist Antonin Artaud to México in the 1920s, in search of a genre of theatre that had disappeared four centuries earlier, but whose influence, he believed, still existed in some form.

Though no text of this theatre survives in México, texts written in the Nahuatl language do exist in Guatemala (*Rabinal Achí*) and Nicaragua (*El Güegüence*, a dance-comedy) and these give some sense of its form and structure. This form of theatre was replaced by the European religious theatre that contributed to the diffusion of Catholicism and the latter was imposed by the *conquistadores* 'in the name of God and the king'; the new presentations included *autosacramentales* (one-act religious plays), religious *coloquios* (dialogues) and *loas* (short dramatic panegyrics in verse). Gradually, the memory of the pre-conquest theatre was erased. Both inside and outside the churches, monks performed only the new symbolic plays, in which characters embodied the essential virtues and vices defined by the Catholic religion.

Among these early writers were Juan Pérez Ramírez (1545–?), author of *Desposorios espirituales entre el pastor Pedro y la Iglesia Mexicana* (*The Spiritual Wedding of Peter the Shepherd and the Mexican Church*, 1574); and Fernán González de Eslava (*c.*1534–*c.*1601), the son of *conquistadores*, who dedicated his life to the theatre within the church, but nevertheless adopted words and situations from the pre-conquest Nahuatl culture.

In the seventeenth century, this religious theatre achieved it greatest quality and beauty in the play *El divino Narciso* (*The Divine Narcissus*, *c.*1680), by the nun Sor Juana Inés de la Cruz (1651–95). In this play, the characters embody various meanings; its perfection can be compared only to that of the great Spanish master Pedro Calderón de la Barca.

Juan Ruiz de Alarcón (1581–1639), another major Mexican writer, emigrated to Spain and became a member of the Spanish theatrical elite. Unlike Sor Juana, who had included in her works indigenous characters and symbols reminiscent of the ancient Aztec cultures, Ruiz de Alarcón never even mentioned México in his plays. He achieved great success in Spain with sixteen plays, and returned to México only to die. His most famous play, *La verdad sospechosa* (*The Doubtful Truth*, 1621), was an influence on Corneille, who wrote *The Liar* after having read Ruiz de Alarcón's works.

Also in the seventeenth century, the viceroy and his court fostered the production of the plays of Sor Juana, and several theatres were established in the Mexican capital, in which Spanish plays, as well as some written in México, were presented.

The imitation of Spanish models was the keynote of Mexican theatre during the eighteenth century, but by the nineteenth century, after Mexico declared independence from Spain, a new theatrical form began to affirm itself, trying to define, through its characters, situations and language, the identity of the Mexican people. After the French invasion and the fall of the empire of Maximilian of Habsburg on Mexican soil, a true nationalist impetus in the theatre began to emerge. During this period, in which romanticism governed theatrical creation, several authors appeared, the best known being Fernando Calderón (1809–45), author of *A ninguna de las tres* (*None of the Three*, 1839).

Near the end of the century, Mexican authors began writing works that reflected clear disagreements with the policies of President Porfirio Díaz and challenged the social injustice and misery suffered by the Mexican people. Two authors are especially significant in this period:

Marcelino Dávalos (1871–1923) and Federico Gamboa (1864–1939). Dávalos wrote, among other plays, *Así pasan* (*So They Go By*, 1908), romantic in tone, but of special interest because it covers three periods of national history in its three acts: the empire of Maximilian, the republic of Benito Juárez (1806–72) and the period immediately preceding the 1910 revolution.

Gamboa, a well-known novelist and playwright, wrote *La venganza de la gleba* (*The Revenge of the Soil*, 1904) six years before the revolution. It is a testimony to México's social organization, where the caste system of the colonial period still survived, a system that included *criollos* (people of Spanish ancestry born in the Americas), *mestizos* (people of mixed European and native ancestry) and native Indians.

Though the revolution interrupted theatrical activity, it formed a new consciousness among writers. The goal of defining the national character and national ways of life led to the creation of a nationalist theatre which, from 1910 to 1915, became resolutely dedicated to defining the essence of México and all things Mexican.

If independence was the triumph of the *criollos*, who no longer wanted to be dependent on the Spanish crown, then it was the revolution of 1910 that affirmed the reality of the *mestizos*, who were trying to leave behind the degrading concept by which they had been defined during the 400 years of their history. By 1924, more than 1 million people had died in the struggle. Peace was at last established, and theatrical activity became visible once more, but it was now imbued with a new accent, and new creative pathways began to open up.

Mauricio Magdaleno (1906–86) and Juan Bustillo Oro (1904–89), two writers, founded the Teatro de Ahora (Now Theatre), indicating with this name that their main concern was to create a modern dramatic theatre in the country. As playwrights, they wrote works of social criticism. Magdaleno's major play in this style was *Pánuco 127* (1933), a study of the problems resulting from the expropriation of petroleum. The most important play by Bustillo Oro was *San Miguel de las espinas* (*St Miguel of the Thorns*, 1930), which demonstrated how the revolution had changed the reality of the nation only in part. The story takes place in a town situated in a very dry region – a common problem in México – in which the people try to build a dam to alleviate the drought. The ending is disheartening, for it affirms that even after what was called a popular revolution, the peasants continue to live in the same unprotected state, without any true rights to demand improvement in their way of life.

At the same time, another group of writers called Los Contemporáneos (The Contemporaries) aspired to bring to México the new cultural currents born in Europe after World War I. Some, however, disregarded the social changes within their own country and simply tried to reproduce some of Europe's avant-garde orientations. In general, they created a culturally refined circle, the main tendency of which was to affirm that their reality was the same as all other writers of the world: the search for a dramatic art that disdained the ideologies and mechanisms of power. Well known in this group were Xavier Villaurrutia (1903–50) and Celestino Gorostiza (1904–67), both playwrights and directors. They received official support for their work from José Vasconcelos (1881–1959), the minister of education and also a man of letters. Together they founded the Teatro de Ulises (Ulysses Theatre) and, later, the Teatro Orientación (Orientation Theatre), the only aim of which, as its name indicated, was to guide public taste away from psychological realism, and to show the latest works of European writers such as Cocteau and Pirandello.

Villaurrutia wrote several short theatrical pieces about characters who simply forget about the objective world and the reality that surrounds them. His plays *El ausente* (*The Absent One*, 1934), *En qué piensas?* (*What Are You Thinking About?*, 1934), *Ha llegado el momento* (*The Moment Has Arrived*, 1934) and *Sea usted breve* (*Be Brief*, 1934) are comparable to the short works of García Lorca. Villaurrutia also wrote longer plays such as *La hiedra* (*The Ivy*, 1941), which is reminiscent of Racine's *Phèdre*, but because of their allusions to the beauty of the lifestyle enjoyed by the Mexican aristocracy before the revolution, they retained only minimal interest for audiences. In short, Villaurrutia believed that the country's cultured classes had been trapped by a revolution that had not led to real social progress.

Perhaps the most important theatrical figure in the post-revolutionary period was Rodolfo Usigli (1905–79), a contemporary of Villaurrutia. Like Villaurrutia, Usigli received a scholarship to study dramatic arts at Yale University, but their respective creations had very different conceptual aims. While Villaurrutia insisted on a theatre in which the subconscious would hold the most prominent place, Usigli dedicated his whole existence to the creation of a theatre that would examine the social problems of the Mexican nation. All his works dramatize the problems that arose as a result of México's colonial origins.

To Usigli, the complexes of the Mexican people, their behaviour and lack of confidence, were the result of the subjugation of the indigenous peoples, especially women. This phenomenon, still present in the late twentieth century, remains responsible for many of México's modern problems. Three of Usigli's best plays focus on historical events that have become myths in Mexican life: *Corona de sombra* (*Crown of Shadow*, written in 1937, performed in 1947), about the Maximilian Empire; *Corona de fuego* (*Crown of Fire*, 1960), about the sacrifice of the Aztec Emperor Cuahutemoc (1502–25) at the hands of Cortés; and *Corona de luz* (*Crown of Light*, 1964), about the apparition of the Virgin of Guadalupe and the idolatrous fervour it created. The most important play by Usigli, however, is *El gesticulador* (*The Gesticulator*, 1937), which he called 'a comedy for demagogues'. In this play, fraud and greed are presented with extraordinary theatrical skills. For Usigli, the revolution only awakened México's baser instincts, without helping the country as a whole to evolve.

While Villaurrutia was writing for a small minority, Usigli aspired to create awareness among middle-class audiences about the mediocrity and lack of culture that he saw among the governing military. *El gesticulador* was a great success on its opening, but it was quickly closed down by the government because of its criticism of aspects of the revolution.

The early works of Celestino Gorostiza achieved little success, even though his play *Escombros del sueño* (*Dream Debris*), is an extraordinary re-creation of the world of dreams. Gorostiza eventually turned to writing *comedias de costumbres* (comedies of manners) critical of the upper middle class that had been formed after the revolution. His *El color de nuestra piel* (*The Colour of Our Skin*, 1952) deals with the shame felt by people of indigenous ancestry.

Other playwrights tried to follow in the footsteps of Usigli, some in order to exalt the eternal beliefs of the Mexican people, such as Luis G. Basurto (1921–91), who wrote several plays with this theme. Only his *Los reyes del mundo* (*The Kings of the World*, 1986), however, was of any real literary quality. In these writers' works a commitment to a magical, ceremonial theatre alternated with a continuing commitment to realist theatre rooted in the works of the Spaniard Jacinto Benavente. The former did not have much success until after World War II, when several writers demonstrated that human beings can understand reality by means other than reason.

As well as a traditional literary theatre, there has also been a popular theatre in México since the revolution. In general, it has bitterly criticized the revolutionary government, sometimes denouncing the vices of both the governing system and its members. Another form of popular theatre was to be seen in the work of the Teatro de la Carpa (Tent Theatre), which worked in a large circus-like tent. Its productions were fragmentary, quickly set-up shows in which musicians, singers and dancers performed improvised sketches based on events of the day. Similar to *commedia dell'arte* or to North American vaudeville, but with its own Mexican style, this type of theatre produced stars such as 'Panzón' ('Big-Belly') Soto (1886–1960) and 'Cuatezón' ('Buddy') Beristain (1875–1948), as well as other comedians who became even more famous after working in films. Perhaps the most famous of these was Cantinflas (Mario Moreno, 1911–93), who first began working with his partner, Manuel Medel (1910–63), in the 1930s. Starting in Mexican cinema, he later went to Hollywood and made a number of hit movies. This particular theatrical style ultimately came to be known as *género chico* (short comic pieces) and as far back as the end of the nineteenth century it dared to comment on and ridicule the government.

In the 1990s, the *género chico* moved closer to the Parisian-style *café théâtre*, in which short avant-garde or issue-oriented plays were presented, often for university students.

Just after World War II, a number of outstanding actors who had begun their careers around the beginning of the century began to form their own companies. Virginia Fábregas (1870–1950) performed in her own theatre, while María Teresa Montoya (1898–1974) and Alfredo Gómez de la Vega (1897–1958) usually performed at the Palacio de Bellas Artes (Palace of Fine Arts). Though these companies did not enjoy great stability, they did introduce the works of writers such as Eugene O'Neill, Gabriel D'Annunzio, Jacinto Benavente, Friedrich Hebbel and Friedrich Schiller, among others. Rarely would a play run for more than a month, and only the works of García Lorca managed to catch the real attention of the public. *La casa de Bernarda Alba* (*The House of*

Bernarda Alba), García Lorca's most famous play, actually had its world première, presented by Fábregas, in México in 1944.

Another company of note formed at this time was that of the sisters Anita and Isabel Blanch, originally from Spain, who rented the 500-seat Ideal Theatre, where they presented a different Spanish play each week. Comedies by the Alvarez Quintero brothers alternated with *astracáns* (coarse Spanish farces) and light comedies. The company followed the traditions of the Italian and Spanish theatres of the nineteenth century and major characters tended to remain at centre stage, close to the prompter's box, while secondary actors would move around them; little was done in the way of stage settings.

The state itself funded three or four productions a year in the Palacio de Bellas Artes, which also served as a *de facto* National Theatre. Eventually public taste began to awaken to new theatrical currents. Realist theatre from the United States (plays by Clifford Odets, Maxwell Anderson and Sherwood Anderson particularly) inspired actors to seek a different style of expression far removed from the mannered recitals that had reigned for the first half of the century. The arrival of the Japanese stage director Seki Sano (1905–66) contributed other elements to this evolution in actor expression. A disciple of Stanislavski, Seki Sano cultivated what he called the *vivencia* (experiencing) style, in which actors gave themselves over completely to their characters. His production of Tennessee Williams's *A Streetcar Named Desire* was memorable for the depth of its performances. Seki Sano later founded his own acting school in México City, which produced many fine actors and directors.

Other directors also came to México in the wake of World War II, seeking refuge and favourable circumstances in which to carry out their activities. Among them was Charles Rooner, a disciple of Max Reinhardt who cultivated an expressionist theatre and directed several important plays such as Kafka's *The Trial*

André Moreau's 1969 UNAM production of Albert Camus's *The Just*.

(1958) and Christopher Fry's *The Lady's Not For Burning* (1952). André Moreau, a French actor in the company of Louis Jouvet, decided to stay in México while on tour with Jouvet's group. The US director and teacher Allan Lewis moved to México to avoid McCarthy-era persecution, stayed in México for several years, and produced such plays as Irwin Shaw's *Bury the Dead* (1955) and *Las manos de Dios* (*The Hands of God*, 1956) by Carlos Solórzano (b. 1922).

The arrival of these foreign directors actually heightened the interest of the middle-class public, which had never fully appreciated theatrical activity in México. During the presidency (1946–52) of Miguel Alemán, the Dirección de Bellas Artes (Office of Fine Arts) was elevated to the rank of Instituto Nacional de Bellas Artes (INBA; National Institute of Fine Arts), with various sections, among them a Department of Theatre headed by Salvador Novo (b. 1904). Novo introduced a number of playwrights who would later become major figures in Mexican theatre.

From 1946 onwards, a series of small *salas de bolsillo* (pocket theatres) also emerged in México City, imitations of the *théâtres de poche* found in Paris. In these halls, which held no more than 100 spectators, the works of Jean-Paul Sartre began to be seen, arousing great interest among the minority who remained faithful to theatre. By then, the population of México City had reached 4 million with the influx of large numbers of people from the provinces looking for work and opportunity.

The Universidad Nacional Autónoma de México (UNAM; National Autonomous University of México) too created its own professional theatrical institution at this time, a small company run by professional actors and directors. Some were foreigners, some were young Mexican disciples of the directors who had come to México and had established teaching academies for directors and actors.

In its early years, with construction of the university campus not yet complete, theatrical activity was carried out in small downtown halls where, for the first time in México, audiences could see the plays of Albert Camus, Samuel Beckett, Eugène Ionesco and Michel de Ghelderode, authors who posed questions about human destiny and existence. The objective of this type of theatre was not only to entertain but also to create a consciousness of contemporary issues. The plays of Bertolt Brecht also began to be performed by student groups, who saw in the German playwright's creations the possibility to discuss the differences between the bourgeoisie – who became wealthy almost overnight following the revolution – and the precarious living conditions of the people in general.

Much theatrical activity was also carried out in small theatres such as La Capilla (The Chapel); the Coyoacán, a beautiful theatre built of materials from old colonial buildings; and the Teatro del Seguro Social (Social Security Theatre), which could hold 700 spectators, and in which the Teatro Universitario presented its plays, often to full houses on weekends. Little by little the theatregoing public rose in number and sophistication.

In the Palacio de Bellas Artes, both foreign plays and plays written by young Mexican authors who began working in the *costumbrista* (featuring local manners and customs) style of theatre were presented. Many of these plays told stories of a frustrated middle class in both the capital and in the provinces, a middle class that

Blas Braidot's 1986 Contigo America production of Sergio Magaña's *Los motivos del lobo*.
Photo: Fernando Moguel.

Music Theatre
Dance Theatre

There remained a strong underlying pre-Hispanic influence in much Mexican music, dance and theatre even in the 1990s. Although this early theatre was comprised of dance more than dramatized language, after the conquest these dances were affected by a didactic language that tried to demonstrate the benefits of Spanish civilization over the indigenous cultures.

The most outstanding example of this type of theatre, which includes dance and the accompaniment of musical instruments such as the flute and the *teponaztli* (tambourine), is the *Danza de la pluma* (*Feather Dance*), which still survives in some states, especially Oaxaca. This dance includes long spoken passages, in which the Aztec Emperor Moctezuma is warned of the arrival of Cortés. Moctezuma himself has long speeches that alternate with dance segments. All participants are dressed in the traditional clothing of the ancient inhabitants of México. Cortés's appearance in the piece is portrayed through dance and not by words and we witness the fall of Moctezuma as a piece of choreography. In the Oaxaca version, an especially splendid plume of *quetzal* (a colourful long-tailed bird) feathers is worn by Moctezuma.

Essentially, these dances are derived from the *Danza de Moros y Cristianos* (*Dance of the Moors and Christians*), which was very popular at the time the Spaniards drove the Arabs out of Spain. In the Americas, the place of the Moors was filled by the indigenous peoples and the Spaniards continued to be agents of good and carriers of the insignias of the Christian god.

In the popular *fiestas* (festivals) in small towns, *loas* and *pastorelas* (pastorals) – again involving much music and dance – are presented at Christmas close to the churches. Both celebrate the birth of Christ, and are directed and performed by townspeople. Occasionally, priests are involved in organizing these productions.

Another massive theatrical event is the representations of *La pasión de Cristo* (*The Passion of Christ*), some of which have a profoundly tragic character, such as the one that takes place in Taxco. In this version, penitents cover their bodies with thorns and carry crosses, as was done in Medieval celebrations. The most famous of these passions is the one held in Ixtapalapa, near México City. Thousands of spectators gather to see this surprisingly sumptuous spectacle. Far from being a sober drama like the one performed in Taxco, the passion of Ixtapalapa emerges in a *fiesta* in which all the elements of the early theatre can be seen: music, dance, poetry and mime as well as confusion, promiscuity and a spirit of celebration far removed from traditional Christian religious devotion.

In more modern Mexican tradition, the musical theatre has usually been tied to the *género chico* and variety shows, these being divided into musical numbers, dance numbers and comic sketches with political overtones. The strong tradition of Spanish-style operettas and *zarzuelas* (musical comedies) of the nineteenth century was actually replaced by the *género chico*, which is more authentically Mexican and more elementary in structure. México City's Teatro Lírico (Lyric Theatre) produced several stars who worked almost exclusively in this genre, among them the actress Lupe Vélez (1910–44), who later had a successful career in Hollywood.

One of the few modern Mexican musical comedies is *Rentas congeladas* (*Frozen Rents*, 1959) by Sergio Magaña. Magaña's play has a theatrical structure, as well as modern musical rhythms, songs and dances in the Mexican cabaret style, a popular accent and simple lyrics.

In effect, there are no stage directors who do not use music to give emphasis to their productions. Some choose one melody to accompany all the dramatic development, while others make free use of modern Mexican and foreign music, and even of nineteenth-century waltzes, which have a strong evocative flavour. Some plays, the music of which has become famous, have been given original scores in México. Such is the case with Brecht's *Der gute Mensch von Sezuan* (*The Good Person of Setzuan*, 1964), for which the composer Rocío Sanz (b. 1933) wrote music that is totally different from the original score by Kurt Weill. The new musical structure allowed the Spanish translation of the lyrics to fit completely into the music. Leonardo Velázquez is a musician best known for his understanding of the dramatic text when composing incidental music. His most outstanding creation in this sense is the music for the play *No es cordero que es cordera* (*It's

Not a Ram It's a Ewe, 1953), an adaptation of Shakespeare's *Twelfth Night* written by the Spanish poet León Felipe.

In the 1980s and 1990s, there were also Mexican versions of several US and British musicals. These generally reproduce in detail the original productions of such shows as *My Fair Lady*, *Mame* and *Cats*.

Carlos Jiménez Mabarak (d. 1993) has written a modern opera based on a short play by Carballido entitled *Misa de seis* (*Mass At Six*, 1969).

As for Mexican dance, in 1932 two painters, Carlos Orozco Romero (1898–1984) and Carlos Mérida (1891–1986), founded a National Dance School in México City. Through them, two American modern dancers, Anna Sokolow and Waldeen (von Falkenstein) came to teach and choreograph in México. Sokolow returned on a number of occasions, but Waldeen spent most of her time in México. Both produced works in line with their individual styles.

In 1943, the sisters Nelly (b. 1909) and Gloria (1919–68) Campobello founded the México City Ballet, which featured works based on Mexican themes as well as works in a neo-romantic style. The Academy of Mexican Dance was established in 1947 by Ana Mérida (b. 1924) and Guillermina Bravo (b. 1923) to develop a Mexican genre of classical dance; this led to the founding of the Ballet Nacional de

México in 1948. In the 1940s Mexican choreographers were largely concerned with works containing social and political criticism.

In 1952 the Ballet Folklorico de México was founded by Amalia Hernández (b. 1918), who choreographed the entire repertoire based on what little was known of pre-Hispanic ceremonial rites as well as on surviving folk forms. A new ballet company, the Compañía Nacional de Danza, was formed in the 1970s with assistance from Cuba's Alicia Alonso. In 1991, Bravo moved her company to the town of Querétaro and set up the Centro Nacional de Danza Contemporánea (National Contemporary Dance Centre) there. The emphasis is on expressive dance, based on the technique of the American Martha Graham.

Sadly, the Mexican-born dancer most widely known in the world spent little of his professional life in his native country. In 1950, after thirty-five years in the United States, José Limón (1908–72) was invited back to México by Miguel Covarrubias (1904–57), who was then director of the Academia Nacional de la Danza. Returning again in 1951, Limón created *The Four Seasons* to music by Carlos Chávez (1899–1978), a piece dealing with the Aztec myth of creation. Though invited then to settle permanently in México, Limón chose to remain in the United States.

Theatre for Young Audiences

In general, theatre for young audiences does not play a significant role in Mexican theatre life though there has long been a Department of Children's Theatre at the National Institute of Fine Arts. Run by actress Clementina Otero (b. 1912) from 1943, the department early on sponsored a company called Teatro Infantil, which did adaptations of well-known stories such as *Little Red Riding Hood*, *Sleeping Beauty* and *The Little Prince*. The productions, presented on Sunday mornings, were meticulous. Oscar Ledesma (b. 1932) later ran another group called Teatro Infantil, which put on a similar repertoire at the Teatro del Bosque. This group added new stories into the mix that dealt with such subjects as modern technology, spaceships and space travel.

From 1959, it was obligatory for all secondary schools to have a student theatre group, in which performance skills could be put to work, but this requirement declined in the 1980s.

Few authors of adult plays have paid attention to children's theatre, with the exception of Sergio Magaña, who wrote *El viaje de No Crecida* (*The Journey of Not Grown*, 1953), which tells of the vicissitudes in the life of of a young girl and her problems growing up in an overpopulated city. For the most part, the semiprofessional groups that stage children's shows on weekends offer productions that are usually ill prepared and often ill conceived.

her life to the operetta with great success. The 1,500-seat Iris Theatre, after being acquired by the city government, had its name changed to the Teatro de la Ciudad (City Theatre).

For many years, UNAM's theatre events took place in the 800-seat Anfiteatro Bolívar (Bolívar Amphitheatre), which features a splendid mural by Diego Rivera. Not particularly suitable for dramatic theatre, however, it is now mainly used for university ceremonies. UNAM's University Cultural Centre includes the 420-seat Ruiz de Alarcón Theatre, the 100-seat Sor Juana Inés de la Cruz Hall and the 725-seat Miguel Covarrubias Dance Theatre. There is also a large space called El Espacio Escultórico (The Sculptural Space), a huge asymmetrical room bordered by masses of sculptures by the German Mathias Goeritz, a longtime resident of México.

In México City's Bosque de Chapultepec, the university owns the Casa del Lago (Lake House), a small nineteenth-century mansion where theatrical presentations are given for small audiences. Also in this old area of the city are the small Teatro de la Conchita (Shell Theatre) and the Teatro Coyoacán, both used for more experimental productions.

The forty theatres built by the Institute of Social Security between 1965 and 1970 are similar in style. The seats are arranged in the shape of a fan, with a central aisle and an aisle down either side. The biggest of these is the Teatro Hidalgo (Noble Theatre), with 800 seats. Some of México's most important shows since the 1980s have been presented there. The rest of the theatres, some open air, generally have seating capacities of about 400.

The theatres of the Institute of Social Security were designed and built by the architect

Charles Rooner's 1973 UNAM production of Luigi Pirandello's *Six Characters in Search of an Author*.
Photo: Walter Reuter.

Alejandro Prieto (b. 1919), with his brother, stage designer Julio Prieto, serving as adviser. While not models of beauty or innovation, they are practical, and whatever one thinks of them they are the model most used throughout the country.

There also remain some great courtly theatres that were damaged during the revolution in 1910 but which have been slowly restored, such as the Teatro Juárez in Guanajuato, the Degollado in Guadalajara and the Macedonio Alcalá in Oaxaca.

In the capital, the Teatro Silvia Pinal and the Teatro Diego Rivera follow a democratic plan in which all seats are arranged on one level; the price of the ticket depends on how close to the stage the seat is.

The Sociedad General de Escritores (General Society of Writers) owns the 200-seat Wilberto Cantón Theatre, named for the playwright, who left an endowment to be used to build the theatre. The Asociación Nacional de Actores (National Actors' Association) owns the 800-seat Jorge Negrete Theatre.

There are other smaller theatres such as the 200-seat Teatro Arlequín (Harlequin Theatre), which belongs to the actress Nadia Haro Oliva (b. 1922), and the 400-seat Virginia Fábregas, which belongs to this actress's grandson. The National Institute of Fine Arts, as well as owning the Teatro de Bellas Artes, also owns the 1,100-seat Teatro del Bosque, the 200-seat Teatro del Granero and the 300-seat Galeón, located in the Artistic and Cultural Centre in México City's Bosque Chapultepec.

Occasionally, theatrical works have been performed at the Castle of Chapultepec, which is said to have been the hunting ground of Emperor Moctezuma. The castle that now exists was the headquarters of Emperor Maximilian of Habsburg, and later the residence of Mexican presidents. Currently it is the Museum of History, but its spaciousness allows for lavish theatrical presentations, with portable seats for the audience.

The Teatro Nacional uses several locales in México City ranging from the large Teatro del Bosque to small spaces in historic buildings, such as the Museum of the Viceroyalty, the Cultural Houses of San Miguel and the Palace of the National Museum of Arts.

In Guanajuato is the Teatro Juárez, designed by José Noriega. This beautiful theatre, which seats some 500 spectators, is the main location of the Festival Cervantino.

In Guadalajara, theatrical companies, opera companies and concert artists perform at the Teatro Degollado, while in Jalapa, capital of the State of Veracruz, there is a major university theatre.

Training

The country's most comprehensive training in theatre is offered by the Universidad Nacional Autónoma de México (UNAM). A Bachelor's degree in dramatic arts is offered within its Faculty of Arts. This is a four-year programme, providing training in acting, directing and design. History of theatre and critical analysis are also taught.

The Instituto Politécnico Nacional (National Polytechnic Institute) and the National Actors' Association also have their own schools. The goal of the latter has been primarily to train actors and technicians for cinema and television.

The National Institute of Fine Arts also has a school.

Apart from these institutions, many other universities in the country have begun to create courses, schools and workshops to train actors, directors and designers. The most important of these are the universities of Veracruz, Guadalajara and Guanajuato and the Polytechnical Institute of Monterrey.

Apart from these institutional courses of study, there are also many private schools, usually directed by actors, which train students in voice, movement and scene study.

Criticism, Scholarship and Publishing

Many of the important literary artists in México have written about theatre even if they have not themselves written plays. One such was Alfonso Reyes (1889–1959), who wrote only one play, *Ifigenia cruel* (*Cruel Iphigenia*, 1926), inspired by Euripides' *Iphigenia in Tauris*. Reyes's essays about the theatre are essentially philosophical treatments of the nature of the art. Later, playwrights Rodolfo Usigli and Xavier Villaurrutia wrote regularly for newspapers and magazines, to help the public to understand the transformations that the theatre had undergone in the years before World War II. Usigli also wrote a book of theatrical theory and history entitled *Itinerario del autor dramático* (*The Playwright's Itinerary*, 1940), fundamental for an understanding of the evolution of the theatre in México up until the time when this playwright was writing his own best works.

Villaurrutia wrote several essays and newspaper articles containing his views on poetic theatre, and defended the right of authors not to write about contemporary events.

Emilio Carballido, Sergio Magaña and Luisa Josefina Hernández also wrote as critics, sometimes to defend the realistic theatre that they created, which was regularly challenged by the expressionist, surrealist and Theatre of the Absurd movements in the 1950s. Carlos Solórzano wrote a regular column for the cultural supplement of *Novedades* (*News*) and *Siempre* (*Always*). He continued these weekly columns for ten years. Some of these articles were later collected and published by UNAM in a book entitled *Testimonios teatrales de México* (*Theatrical Testimonies of México*, 1973).

Another writer of note is Juan Miguel de Mora (b. 1921), who published a book called *Panorama del teatro en México* (*Overview of the Theatre in México*, 1970). De Mora is also a playwright, author of *Los héroes no van al frente* (*Heroes Don't Go to the Front*, 1952), an existentialist drama.

Without doubt, the critic with the most experience, objectivity and culture was Armando de María y Campos (1897–1967). He wrote about everything theatrical, from circus and puppets to the philosophical concepts of Theatre of the Absurd. His works have been collected in more than twenty volumes, in themselves a history of theatre in México. His work is equalled only by that of Enrique de Olavarría y Ferrari (1844–1918), who analysed Mexican theatre up to the revolution of 1910. The work of María y Campos could be considered a continuation of that of Olavarría, and the two combine to create an almost complete history of Mexican theatre.

Luis Reyes de la Maza (b. 1932) wrote several books about nineteenth-century Mexican theatre while working with the Instituto de Investigaciones Estéticas (Institute of Aesthetic Research) at UNAM. His works focus on the role of theatre within society.

The Fondo de Cultura Económico (Cultural Economic Fund) has published several play anthologies and individual plays. Aguilar of Madrid, which has a branch office in México, has also produced many important Mexican theatre books. The Joaquín Mortiz publishing house, which deals mainly with novels, has published many of the most successful plays in México.

The country's most important theatrical magazines, unfortunately, have usually been short-lived. Still publishing in the mid-1990s were *Escénica* (*Scene*), published by UNAM since 1983, and *Escenología* (*Scenography*), published privately since 1990.

Carlos Solórzano
Translated by Joanne Rotermundt-De la Parra

Further Reading

Alcaraz, José Antonio. *Suave Teatro, 1984.* [Smooth theatre, 1984]. Azcapotzalco: Universidad Autónoma Metropolitana, 1985. 215 pp.

Argudín, Yolanda. *Historia del teatro en México.* [History of theatre in México]. México City: Editorial Panorama, 1986. 221 pp.

Artaud, Antonin. *México et le voyage à la Tarahumaras.* [México and the trip to the land of the Tarahumaras]. Complete works. Paris: Gallimard, 1956–65.

Azar, Héctor. '¿Qué pasa con el teatro en México?'. [What has happened to theatre in México?]. *Cuadernos de Bellas Artes*, 11 (September–October 1966): 94–100.

Beardsell, Peter. *A Theatre for Cannibals: Rodolfo Usigli and the Mexican Stage.* London/Toronto: Associated University Presses, 1992. 242 pp.

Beloff, Angelina. *Historia técnica y función educativa del teatro de muñecos en México y en el mundo.* [The technical history and educational function of puppet theatre in México and in the world]. México City: Secretaría de Educación Pública, 1945.

Burgess, Ronald Dave. *Mexican Theatre: The Generation of 1969*. Ann Arbor, MI: University Microfilm International, 1985. (PhD dissertation, University of Kansas).

——. *The New Dramatists of México, 1967–85*. Lexington, KY: University Press of Kentucky, 1991. 166 pp.

Cervera, Andrade, and Alejandro Cervera. *El teatro regional de Yucatán*. [Theatre in Yucatán]. Mérida: Imprenta Guerra, 1947. 98 pp.

Díaz Plaja, Guillermo Monterde, and Francisco Monterde. 'Historia de la literatura española e historia de la literatura mexicana'. [History of Spanish literature and history of Mexican literature]. *Enciclopedia del arte escénico*. [Encyclopedia of performing arts], ed. Porrúa. México City: 1966.

Espinosa, Tomás. 'Teatro de la nación'. [Theatre of the Nation]. *Tramoya*, 9 (October–December 1977): 43–59.

Foster, David William. *Estudios sobre teatro mexicano contemporáneo: semiología de la competencia teatral*. [Studies on contemporary Mexican theatre: Semiology of theatre]. Utah Studies in Literature no. 25. New York: Peter Lang, 1984. 149 pp.

Frischmann, Donald Harry. *El nuevo teatro popular en México* [New popular theatre in México]. México City: Instituto Nacional de Bellas Artes, 1990.

Gorostiza, Celestino, ed. 'Introduction'. *Teatro mexicano del siglo XX*. [Mexican theatre of the twentieth century], vol. III, 7–57. México City: Fondo de Cultura Económica.

Horcasitas, Hernándo. *El teatro Nahuatl*. [Nahuatl theatre]. México City: Universidad Nacional Autónoma de México, 1974. 647 pp.

Jiménez, Sergio, and Edgar Ceballos, eds. *Teoría y práctica del teatro en México: compilación de textos de Usigli, Novo, Seki Sano, Wagner, Moreau, Azar, Mendoza, Sarrás, Gurrola, Castillo, Tavira y Sabido*. [Theory and practice of theatre in México: A compilation of texts by Usigli, Novo, Seki Sano, Wagner, Moreau, Azar, Mendoza, Sarrás, Gurrola, Castillo, Tavira and Sabido]. México City: Gaceta, 1982. 396 pp.

Lambs, Ruth. *Mexican Theatre of the Twentieth Century*. Claremont, CA: Ocelot, 1975. 143 pp.

Leñero, Vicente. *Vivir del teatro*. [Living by the theatre]. Colección Contrapuntos. México City: Joaquín Mortiz, 1982. 252 pp.

Magaña-Esquivel, Antonio, ed. *Medio siglo de teatro mexicano*. [Half a century of Mexican theatre]. México City: Instituto Nacional de Bellas Artes, 1964. 173 pp.

——. *El teatro: contrapunto*. [Theatre: Counterpoint]. Colección Presencia de México no. 12. México City: Fondo de Cultura Económica, 1970. 111 pp.

María y Campos, Armando de. *Crónicas de teatro de 'Hoy'*. [Theatre reviews from *Hoy*]. México City: Botas, 1941. 249 pp.

——. *Entre cómicos de ayer*. [Among yesterday's comedians]. México City: Arriba el Telón, 1950. 204 pp.

——. *Informe sobre el teatro social de los siglos XIX y XX: testimonios y comentarios*. [A report on social theatre of the nineteenth and twentieth centuries: Testimonies and commentaries]. México City: Confederación de Trabajadores de México, 1959. 150 pp.

——. *Los payasos, poetas del pueblo: el circo en México*. [Clowns, the poets of the people: The circus in México]. México City: Botas, 1939. 249 pp.

——. *El teatro del aire: notas para periódicos*. [Open-air theatre: Newspaper reviews]. México City: Botas, 1937. 231 pp.

——. *El teatro está siempre en crisis . . . crónicas de 1946 a 1950*. [Theatre is always in crisis . . . reviews from 1946 to 1950]. México City: Arriba el Telón, 1954. 240 pp.

——. *Teatro mexicano de muñecos. Prólogo y notas: antología de 25 piezas de teatro guiñol*. [Mexican puppet theatre. Prologue and notes: An anthology of 25 puppet shows]. México City: El Nacional, 1941. 362 pp.

——. *La Vírgen frente a las candilejas o el teatro Guadalupano*. [The Virgin Mary in the footlights or theatre in Guadaloupe]. México City: Ediciones Populares, 1954. 148 pp.

Mendoza Gutiérrez, Alfredo. *Nuestro teatro campesino*. [Our peasant theatre]. 2nd ed. Colección del Instituto Nacional de Capacitación del Magisterio no. 31. México City: Secretaría de Educación Pública, 1964. 292 pp.

Mendoza López, Margarita. 'Españoles en el teatro mexicano'. [Spaniards in Mexican theatre]. *Primer Acto* 201 (November–December 1983): 15–22.

——. *Primeros renovadores del teatro en México 1928–41: vivencias y documentos*. [Renewers of Mexican theatre 1928–41: Documents and personal experiences]. México City: Instituto Mexicano del Seguro Social, Coordinación de Teatros, 1985. 174 pp.

Monterde, Francisco. *Bibliografía del teatro en México*. [Bibliography of theatre in México]. Introduction by Rodolfo Usigli. New York: Burt Franklin, 1970. 649 pp.

——. *Teatro mexicano del siglo XX*. [Mexican theatre in the twentieth century]. México City: Fondo de Cultural Económica, 1956.

Mora, Juan Miguel de. *Panorama del teatro en México*. [Overview of theatre in México]. México City: Latinoamericana, 1970. 292 pp.

Moreau, Andrade. *Entre bastidores*. [In the wings]. México City: Arana, 1965. 308 pp.

Rabell, Malkah. *Luz y sombra del antiteatro*. [Lights and shadows of the anti-theatre]. México City: Universidad Nacional Autónoma de México, 1970.

Reyes de la Maza, Luis. *Cien años de teatro en México*. [100 years of theatre in México]. Sepsetentas no. 61. México City: Secretaría de Educación Pública, 1972. 161 pp.

——. *En el nombre de Dios hablo de teatro*. [In the name of God I speak of theatre]. México City: Universidad Nacional Autónoma de México, 1984. 200 pp.

Royaards, Rense. *Mexican Drama*. Trans. by Christine Boom. Amsterdam: International Theatre Bookshop, 1992. 109 pp.

Solórzano, Carlos. *Testimonios teatrales de México*. [Theatrical testimonies of México]. México City: Universidad Nacional Autónoma de México, 1973. 240 pp.

Spencer, L. Anne. 'Aztec Elements in Twentieth Century Mexican Drama'. PhD dissertation, University of Kansas, 1974. 203 pp.

Sten, María. *Vida y muerte del teatro Nahuatl*. [The life and death of Nahuatl theatre]. Sepsetentas. México City: Secretaría de Educación Pública, 1974. 208 pp.

Suárez, Luis. 'La aventura del teatro estudiantil'. [The adventure of student theatre]. *La cultura en México* 39 (14 November 1962): viii–xiii.

Usigli, Rodolfo. *Itinerario del autor dramático. ¿Qué pasa con el teatro en México?* [The playwright's itinerary. What is happening to theatre in México?]. México City: Imprenta Mondial, 1940. 217 pp.

——. *Teatro completo*. [Complete theatre]. 3 vols. México City: Fondo de Cultura Económica, 1963–6.

MONTSERRAT

(see **COMMONWEALTH CARIBBEAN**)

NETHERLANDS ANTILLES AND ARUBA

(Overview)

With hundreds of miles of Caribbean Sea in between, the Dutch Windward islands – Saba, St Maarten and St Eustatius – and the Dutch Leeward islands – Aruba, Bonaire and Curaçao – together form the remnants of Dutch expansion in the New World and are still Dutch territories. In total, these islands have a population of some 264,000 (1992) spread across 1,000 square kilometres (386 square miles).

Until its independence in 1975, the territory of Suriname on the South American coast was also Dutch, while continual controversy over internal political and economic power between Curaçao and Aruba fed the desire of the latter to leave the constellation of Dutch Caribbean islands to form a relatively autonomous part within the Kingdom of the Netherlands. This

was granted in 1986, leaving the other five islands to form the Netherlands Antilles.

Being the political, economic and educational centre, Curaçao – the largest of the islands – has been the seat of most cultural activities, with Aruba – with the second largest population – as 'runner up'. In various respects, post-war theatre created a breach with pre-war theatre. Indeed, the tradition of performances in Dutch (the official language), Spanish and English (both widely known) by visiting, professional companies and local, amateur groups was continued – a tradition that dates back deep into the nineteenth century. The growing influence of the Netherlands, however, through industrial exertions and government policy, ultimately resulted in an unparalleled number of performances of well-known Dutch plays from the Netherlands and of Dutch translations, which eventually overwhelmed those in Spanish.

However, to this was added the adaptation of internationally renowned plays into the Creole vernacular spoken by over 90 per cent of the population: Papiamento. Among them were a large number of classic and modern plays by playwrights such as Shakespeare, Molière, Chekhov, Rostand, Brecht, Shaw, Sartre, Paso, Williams, García Lorca and Genet. While they retained their thematic preoccupations, these would be embodied and voiced by locally identifiable characters who moved in a locally recognizable linguistic, social and physical setting.

Particularly successful were adaptations by May Henríquez-Álvarez Correa (b. 1915, Curaçao), Jules Ph. de Palm (b. 1922, Curaçao) and Nydia Ecury (b. 1926, Aruba). These formed a significant break with the dominant tendency in pre-war decades of staging plays solely in Papiamento – translations and some original works – that adhered to strict Roman Catholic principles and that yielded little, if any, artistic satisfaction. This shift exemplifies the society-wide process of secularization that the islands have found themselves in since the late 1930s.

Instrumental in staging these adaptations, more specifically between about 1955 and 1975, were the local branches Cultureel Centrum Curaçao (CCC; Cultural Centre Curaçao) and Cultureel Centrum Aruba (CCA; Cultural Centre Aruba) of the Dutch Stichting voor Culturele Samenwerking (STICUSA; Foundation for Cultural Cooperation), which was funded by the Dutch government. STICUSA/CCC/CCA not only financially supported performances (including rehearsals, stage properties, scenery and makeup) but also, through these years, would pay for professional stage-directors from the Netherlands to direct and guide the local amateurs. Especially important were the Dutch directors Paul Storm, Henk van Ulsen, Piet Kamerman and Elly Ruimschotel, whose work succeeded in raising the level of acting of amateurs to a professional level, of which some – such as Rina Penso of Curaçao – gained regional recognition, and in training some of these amateurs, such as Nydia Ecury, Bunchi Römer (b. 1927, Curaçao) and Burny Every (b. 1939, Aruba), to become self-reliant directors.

To obtain a greater say in future developments and to strengthen their independence vis-à-vis STICUSA/CCC/CCA, groups of amateurs organized themselves into acting companies,

such as Mascaruba in Aruba (since 1961) and Thalia in Curaçao (since 1967). They would also stage adaptations in Papiamento without the support of STICUSA/CCC/CCA, as Sociedad Pro Arte Escenico (Society for Play Acting) had been doing ever since the early 1950s under the direction of Eddie Pieters Heyliger in Curaçao. Companies in Curaçao would generally perform in the Theatre Roxy, which had opened in 1931, while in Aruba the CCA building, which opened in 1958, had its own wide range of stage facilities.

Since 1968 Curaçao has boasted a 700-seat theatre. Besides these buildings, companies have found accommodation in parish churches, community centres, cinemas, the public library and, at times, on tractor-trailers.

By the end of the 1960s, especially in Curaçao, a younger generation expressed discontent with the absence of professional directors of Antillean descent and the lack of production of original plays in Papiamento. As such this formed an integral part of deeply rooted feelings of dissatisfaction and anger among the black and racially mixed people on the island, the socio-economically weakest groups in society. This would result in a relatively violent revolt in May 1969 on Curaçao.

Some original works had been written in Papiamento after World War II but virtually all these texts stayed close to the pre-war Catholic ideological guidelines, for example those by René A. de Rooy (1917–74), born in Suriname but a resident of Curaçao during the 1940s and 1950s, and by Hubert Booi (b. 1919, Bonaire).

The adaptations, which had been considered a major step forward in developing a local theatrical tradition, were denounced as too 'colonial' and too 'high-brow' to be of any use to a people with 'African roots' and on the road to political and socio-cultural independence. Thematically, too, plays would have to centre around the past, present and future of the island's common people. Sharp criticism on forms of exploitation by the colonial mother country and the local white elite, a reassessment of black resistance in the days of slavery and of the traditional Afro-Curaçaoan lifestyle and/or a 'handout' with allegedly revolutionary guidelines for independence, formed essential motifs in the dramatic writing of such young writers as V.H. 'Pacheco' Domacassé (b. 1941, Bonaire), Rhonny Sillé and Stanley Bonifacio.

They gathered around them young actors and musicians such as Diana Lebacs (b. 1947, Curaçao), Laura Quast, Edsel Provence, René

Pacheco Domacassé's *Tula*.
Photo: Collection Domacassé-Lebacs.

V. Rosalia and Angel Salsbach, who would all win their spurs in various artistic fields locally. Two of Domacassé's plays – *Konsenshi di un pueblo* (*A People's Conscience*, 1973) and *Tula* (about the 1795 slave rebellion in Curaçao, 1975) – would even appear in print in Curaçao. Privately published, these were rare examples of original drama writing in Papiamento; they were also meant to be read and thus gain a somewhat wider audience. Not only thematically but also in other respects these plays would try and break away from the adaptations. Traditional folklore (such as forms of storytelling), songs, music and related dances (such as the *tambú*, of African origin) also formed essential elements of the dramatic performances as a whole.

While the demand was there and political pressure increased, STICUSA and its local branches changed tack. Despite criticism against it for being a 'colonial institution', many of the new local experiments were supported by this foundation, while the first professional director with an Antillean background, A. Harcourt Nicholls of Curaçao, arrived in 1972. As well, a number of local people were awarded grants to study abroad to become actors or directors.

In the course of the 1970s and 1980s, however, under pressure of decolonization, funding with potential Dutch interference was resented more and more. From the mid-1980s on, substantial funds were remitted directly to the local government organizations Overlegorgaan Kulturele Samenwerking Nederlandse Antillen (OKSNA; Consultative Committee for Cultural Cooperation in the Netherlands Antilles) and Union di Organisasionnan Cultural Arubano (UNOCA; Union of Cultural Organizations in Aruba). The allocation of money was to be left to expert local civil servants, among whom Domacassé and Salsbach acquired great influence. However, as far as OKSNA is concerned this has not turned out to be very successful: in 1993 administrative and financial chaos led the Netherlands to stop the direct transfer of money to OKSNA. In early 1995 this was still the case.

These experiments also reached Bonaire through Domacassé, who took his plays to his native island. Developments in Aruba were hardly affected, however. This is partly to be attributed to the fact that ethnically Aruban society differs substantially from Curaçao, which has a large Afro-Caribbean population. The Aruban population is predominantly of European, Latin American and Indian descent. This

Indian background is exploited and given mythical proportions in some plays by Ernesto E. Rosenstand (b. 1931, Colombia) of Aruba.

In Curaçao this 'revolutionary' drama, which was to serve the cause of independence, was to step out of theatre buildings and to find squares in the major city, Willemstad, and in small villages in the late 1970s and the first half of the 1980s.

The initiative was taken by Gibi Bacilio (b. 1950, Curaçao), who gathered around him a group of amateur actors, who operated, inspired by Augusto Boal, under the name Teatro Foro (Forum Theatre). They would lay down a rough outline of a play for their audience, invariably focusing on socio-cultural problems of the people such as housing, schooling, medical care and political patronage. Next they would invite members of the audience to participate, to take roles and to change the course of events. Bacilio's *Na boka di pos* (*At the Well's Mouth*, 1985), for example, was sharply critical of the local branch of an international oil refinery, which was represented by actors in rat masks. The various parts of these street performances would be intertwined by rhythmical poetry, Afro-Caribbean drumming – at times by the local expert group Isoco – and various acts of encouragement. Sharply critical of the local government, Bacilio was given little support from that side to continue his dramatic experiments in the streets.

While in the 1980s 'bad government' and economic problems gradually tempered the desire to become independent, the number of migrants from the Dutch Antilles to the Netherlands grew to unprecedented heights (about 80,000 people had migrated by the mid-1990s). In the Netherlands grants from funds for theatre companies, playwrights and actors with a Third World background provided new, though limited, opportunities, from which a number of Antilleans, temporarily or permanently residing in the Netherlands, profited. In the Netherlands the work of Antilleans such as Norman de Palm, Felix de Rooy (b. 1952), Fridi Martina, John Leerdam and Jeroen Heuvel all of Curaçao – who tend to turn to Dutch or English rather than Papiamento – has had to compete with that of other fringe theatre productions, which it does but so far without distinguishing itself extraordinarily.

Gibi Bacilio's 1985 Forum Theatre production of his *At the Well's Mouth*.
Photo: Collection Gibi Bacilio.

The problematic nature of Third World migrants' vicissitudes, the loss of fixed points of identification or the socio-cultural heritage from a former colony, as seen from an Antillean point of view, has not (yet) gained a wide appeal in the Netherlands. If staged in Curaçao or any one of the other islands, the appeal has so far been moderate and has not given any significant impulse to new developments.

These productions as well as the innovations of the 1970s and 1980s mentioned earlier have had to compete more and more with unpretentious popular plays in the vernacular, which at times may have a satirical undertone where local politics are concerned but are generally meant to provide uncomplicated diversion. Especially instrumental in this development has been Eligio Melfor, whose popular productions in the vernacular had the possibility of being financially profitable.

On the Dutch Windward Islands, where writing is primarily in English, this has actually been the one and only trend. In St Eustatius (population 2,100), the St Eustatius Action Theatre has produced one original play a year since its founding in 1983. The company's director, Ellis Lopes (b. 1936, St Eustatius), has contributed three dramas: *Independence ... Our Slow Death?*, *Forsaken Children* (about the disabled) and *Dirty Hands* (about superstition and venereal disease). The company tours to neighbouring islands and has also performed in the United States and Canada.

Partly to counter the tendency of common popularization and in order to raise the level of performances, CCA initiated the Aruba International Theatre Festival in 1976, to be organized every other year. Ever since, the festival has drawn companies from many parts of the world. The ninth festival, organized by a committee headed by Oslin Boekhoudt in 1994, included companies from Aruba, Austria, Canada, Colombia, Curaçao, the Dominican Republic, France, Ireland, Jamaica, Japan, the Netherlands, Perú, Suriname, the United Kingdom and the United States. It is considered to have contributed to the emancipation of Papiamento: as a consequence of the festival the Mascaruba company from Aruba has received reciprocal invitations to perform in Papiamento in South America, the US and Japan. Averaging two productions a year since its creation in 1961, the group – still operating in the 1990s – has performed more than a dozen original works as well as established plays by Tennessee Williams, Noël Coward, Carlo Goldoni, Lorraine Hansberry, Anton Chekhov, Georges Feydeau, Alejandro Casona, Alfonso Paso and Franklin Domínguez, to mention just a few.

Aart G. Broek with Oslin Boekhoudt and Ellis Lopes

Further Reading

Broek, Aart G. 'The rise of a caribbean island's literature: The case of Curaçao and its writing in Papiamentu'. PhD dissertation, Free University of Amsterdam, 1990.

Gordijn, W. *Culturele kroniek '48–'68*. [Cultural chronicle '48–'68]. Amsterdam: Stichting voor Culturele Samenwerking, 1970.

Heuvel, Pim, and Freek van Wel. *Met eigen stem: herkenningspunten in de letterkunde van de Nederlandse Antillen en Aruba*. [A voice of their own: Points of reference in literary writing of the Netherlands Antilles and Aruba]. Assen/Maastricht: Van Gorcum, 1989.

Palm, Jules Ph. de, ed. *Encyclopedie van de Nederlandse Antillen*. [Encyclopedia of the Netherlands Antilles]. 2nd ed. Zutphen: de Walburg Pers, 1985. S.v. 'Literatuur' [Literature] and 'Toneel' [Drama].

Rutgers, G.W. 'Schrijven is zilver, spreken is goud: oratuur, auratuur en literatuur van de Nederlandse Antillen en Aruba'. [Writing is silver, speaking is gold: Oratory, aural experience and literature of the Netherlands Antilles and Aruba]. PhD dissertation, Utrecht University, 1994.

NICARAGUA

(Overview)

A Central American republic with a 1992 population of 4 million, Nicaragua stretches over 148,000 square kilometres (57,000 square miles), from the Atlantic to the Pacific between the republics of Costa Rica to the south and Honduras to the north. It is separated from El Salvador by the Gulf of Fonseca on the Pacific coast.

According to historical legend, the country takes its name from Nicarao, a native chieftain who was defeated in 1522 by Spanish conquerors led by Gil González de Avila. Most of the country was colonized by the Spanish, who ultimately mixed with the native population. The twentieth century's largely peasant, Spanish-speaking society is roughly 70 per cent *mestizo* (of mixed European and native ancestry); about 20 per cent of the population is Caucasian. Native cultures persisted in some areas into the twentieth century, but have for the most part been assimilated, leaving under 10 per cent officially classified as native.

The social composition of the population reflects the country's economic development. The neo-feudal model of the *hacienda* (ranch estate) dominated in various areas, with cash crops emerging as major sources of income by the beginning of the twentieth century, creating a rural proletariat of farm workers. In the north, gold mining and cattle ranching grew, while, by the end of the nineteenth century, the fertile volcanic soil of the southwest had been coopted for the production of cash crops, chiefly cotton, sugar and coffee.

The capital, Managua (established in 1852), holds between 15 and 20 per cent of Nicaragua's population, which remains largely rural. Historically important cities (all with populations of under 100,000) are León and Granada (both founded in 1524), Matagalpa, Estelí and Masaya.

In the southern Atlantic region of the country, the culture is distinctly Caribbean, and it is populated chiefly by people of African origin brought from the West Indies by the British as a labour force. The British influence on the Atlantic coast, particularly around Bluefields (a port established by them in 1678), is seen to this day in the use of English as the main language among the local population and in such cultural manifestations as the Palo de Mayo, derived directly from the English Maypole dance.

El Güegüence (*The Old Man*) is the only traditional performance extant in Nicaragua. Created by an unknown author, the earliest version of it was retrieved and published in 1883. Mainly performed during the feast days of Diriamba, it is also presented in other towns. Composed originally in the Spanish and Nahuatl languages some time between the sixteenth and the early eighteenth centuries, the action takes place in an urban setting with central characters including agents of the Spanish administration, who are the butt of trickery by the hero, an old *mestizo* buffoon. The character, in fact, appears in both early Spanish drama and in the drama of various other native American nations prior to the conquest.

The dialogue relies on comic repetitions and the action on slapstick. The female characters have no speaking parts, another characteristic of early American drama. The characters include anthropomorphized animals, seen also in native dance dramas, who use various devices to evade punishment after mocking the colonial authorities and criticizing their abuse.

El Güegüence is very much an expression of Nicaragua's *mestizo* culture, not only because it synthesizes clearly identifiable European and native American elements, but, more significantly perhaps, because it relies on elements common to the traditions of both Europe and the Americas. These include stock characters, masked protagonists, rudimentary plot, simple dialogue and minimal complication. During the performance, the actors dance among the audience both in church atriums and in the streets. The ending actually includes the audience in the dance. Of pre-conquest origins, this dance drama is probably a remnant of a Medieval pageant theme traceable to the fourteenth-century Corpus Christi processions and used by Catholic missionaries in proselytizing during the conquest.

The Diriamba *fiestas* also traditionally include the dance drama *El gigante* (*The Giant*), also known as the dance drama of David and Goliath; and *El toro-huaco* (*The Guaco Bird-Bull*), which is closer to a ritual dance proper. The latter two have no known texts. *El toro-huaco* is a re-enactment of the myth of the Plumed Serpent, in which the masked and feathered dancers, covered in flowers, are accompanied by drums and tin flutes and bird-song imitations, in a minimally choreographed snaking line. Both bear some similarities to Mexican dance dramas.

Other than these examples, culture has been generally neglected by the central government well into the twentieth century. The history of most of Nicaragua's territory is, in fact, linked by colonial patterns to México and Central America, first by the expansion of Nahuatl influence, then by Spanish administrations based in México and Guatemala. After gaining independence from Spain in 1821, the country was officially part of the Mexican empire for two years, then a member of the Central American Federation from 1823 to 1838.

When the federation broke up, civil conflicts emerged between liberals, whose power base was in León, and conservatives, with their power base in Granada. This was not resolved even after Managua was established as a compromise capital. León remained the centre of intellectual and political activity, and Granada persisted as the stronghold of the aristocracy.

The influence of the United States has also long been significant. As far back as 1855–7, a US soldier of fortune, William Walker, sought to annex Nicaragua to the United States as a state supporting slavery; after a brief period as

president of Nicaragua he was forced to leave the country, but as he retreated he burned the city of Granada.

Under José Santos Zelaya (1853–1919), the liberals enacted reforms between 1893 and 1909, took over the Atlantic region but ran foul of foreign interests. A rebellion supported by the United States forced Zelaya to resign. In 1910, a financial stabilization plan drawn up by the US Congress was rejected by Nicaragua, but in 1912 US-backed President Adolfo Díaz (1877–1964) agreed to allow United States Marines to occupy Nicaragua in order to enforce that plan.

The US occupation lasted until 1933, with some armed resistance by the liberals. From 1926 to 1933 Augusto César Sandino (1895–1934) led an effective guerrilla war against US troops, who retaliated by carrying out the first recorded bombing of civilian populations in the Americas. When they departed, the US-trained replacement for the Marines, the National Guard, effectively took over control of Nicaragua. Its leader, Anastasio Somoza, Sr (1893–1956), assassinated Sandino and later seized the presidency. After a democratic hiatus, he took office again in 1947, shortly after the election of Leonardo Argüello, and succeeded himself through fraudulent elections. After his assassination in 1956, his son Luis (1922–67) assumed the presidency, to be succeeded at his death by his brother, Anastasio Somoza Debayle (1925–80).

The Frente Sandinista de Liberación Nacional (FSLN; Sandinista National Liberation Front) was organized by Carlos Fonseca Amador (1936–76), Tomás Borge (b. 1930) and others in 1961; it was composed initially of students, artisans and self-employed small business people. It is significant that the 1969 manifesto of the FSLN included a section providing for a 'revolution in culture and education', which placed art and culture at the heart of the revolutionary process. The armed struggle began in 1967, but the FSLN did not score its first significant victory until 1979.

The economy continued to suffer despite foreign aid and a massive volunteer reconstruction effort. The Sandinistas won the 1984 elections but, subjected to intense military and economic pressure by the United States, they lost the 1991 elections to a coalition led by Violeta Chamorro (b. 1928), the widow of the slain editor of *La Prensa* (*The Press*), whose goal was to restore harmony to the country.

The Sandinistas nevertheless could claim a

number of achievements, including a successful literacy campaign, land reform, education and health care. Their support for areas of cultural production was rooted in a day-to-day, hands-on involvement that was an organic part of their process of organization and mobilization.

Looking back over its complicated history, one can say that the relatively small size of the country, its economic development, its relative isolation, the late rise of a bourgeoisie and the concentration of literacy, education and the limited production of 'high culture' in urban centres along with the oppressive living conditions of the great majority of the population were all key reasons for the relative absence of a European-style, professional tradition of dramaturgy and performance in the country and for the dominance of amateur groups.

Traditional performance arts, therefore, such as the aforementioned dance dramas and folk drama, still represent the richest continuum of theatrical activity in Nicaragua, one that continues to be enriched to this day by the persistence of religious and 'pagan' traditions of indigenous, Spanish and Afro-Caribbean origin in towns and villages throughout the country. These traditions continue to be kept alive by the involvement of anthropologists, community cultural workers with formal training, and international cultural agencies that provide financial backing for this work.

The country's educational tradition is also of note in the maintenance of a national cultural tradition. Rooted in schools established by European priests and nuns in the colonial period, this tradition probably goes back to the centres run by the Nahuatl cultures (for example, the Aztecs). The first Nicaraguan university was actually established in 1680 in León and theatre was performed there. Other universities in Managua, León and Granada were incorporated in 1879; the National University was established in 1947 with the Central American University begun in Nicaragua in 1961. University-based and -trained youth have played a key role in modern times, in nourishing the limited urban professional theatre, the amateur groups and a national dramaturgy and, since the 1940s, in raising the profile of folk arts and drama and in integrating popular traditions with professional theatre and with social activism.

A synthesis of folk and popular traditions, university and community theatre has emerged in the grassroots theatre movement represented most importantly in the work of the Nicaraguan Alan Bolt. This modern movement is part of the Latin American movement known as *nuevo teatro popular* (new popular theatre), which originated in the 1960s.

The Ministry of Culture and the Asociación Sandinista de Trabajadores de la Cultura (Sandinista Association of Cultural Workers) also actively promotes poetry, theatre and dance, visual arts, museums, libraries, music, arts education and training in the various disciplines through Popular Centres of Culture, unions and even the army. The reduced financial capability of the Chamorro government to maintain such a course in the 1990s under US and International Monetary Fund coercion was reflected in difficulties experienced by cultural workers, who previously had received wages and were provided with outlets for their creations.

Though some literary dramas were penned in the late nineteenth century, the country's principal playhouses until World War I were mainly venues for touring Spanish and Mexican companies: the León Theatre, built in 1885; the Granada Theatre in 1889; the Teatro Castaño in 1896 and the Variedades about 1910. Productions by these touring groups essentially served as models for Nicaraguan writers, who in turn helped to create national groups to stage their own works.

The first popular success was *Ocaso* (*The Decline*) by Santiago Argüello (1871–1940), based on a true story of adultery. The play was staged in León by a Venezuelan company. A second playwright of note was Hernán Robleto (1892–1968), whose *La rosa del paraíso* (*The Rose of Paradise*, 1921) was staged by the first national drama company, a group organized by Robleto.

Robleto, the father of the *costumbrista* (featuring local manners and customs) genre in Nicaragua, also injected comedy and politics into his works. His *Pájaros del norte* (*Birds from the North*, 1936) is a mordant critique of Nicaraguan admirers of the US occupation forces.

José Coronel Urtecho (1906–84), one of Nicaragua's best known poets, and the playwright Joaquín Pasos (1915–47), co-authored the first original work of the literary avant-garde, a social satire in verse, *Chinfonía burguesa* (*Bourgeois Symphony*, written as a poem in 1931 and reworked for the stage in 1939). A short whimsical work with clever verbal pyrotechnics, the play gives equal voice to the members of a model anti-family and to their living-room furniture, exploding social convention in a wild display of nonsense verse, pointed criticism and grotesque fun. Because of its free use of Nicaraguan idiomatic Spanish and its harsh attack on the *nouveaux riches*, it stands out as an important national play. There are also, in *Chinfonía burguesa*, resonances of *El Güegüence*. A radical departure from other Nicaraguan dramatic literature, which has been dominated by realism, historical subjects, comedies of manners and poetic themes, the play also reveals the author's admiration for the early experiments of Spanish poets García Lorca and Alberti.

The Movimiento Literario de Vanguardia (Avant-Garde Literary Movement) was founded in 1931 by Pablo Antonio Cuadra (b. 1912), one of Nicaragua's most distinguished and outstanding poets, journalists and playwrights. In 1935, his group fulfilled its pledge to promote theatre by staging a classic in the Teatrito Lopé (Lopé Little Theatre), located in the alumni house of the Central American College (a Jesuit school). In 1942, Cuadra also published a new edition of *El Güegüence* and in 1961 he established the Güegüence de Oro Prize to stimulate Nicaraguan theatre. He has as well been an important supporter of new talent through the weekly magazine *Prensa Literaria* (*Literary Press*).

Cuadra's social drama *Por los caminos van los campesinos* (*Down the Road the Peasants Go*, 1937) explored the psychological impact of civil war, and his dramaturgy integrates folk elements with naturalism. *Satanás entra en escena* (*Enter Satan*, 1948) presents the struggle for freedom as both a religious and a political theme. Other plays by Cuadra include *Pastorela* (*The Shepherds' Play*, 1940), *El bailete del oso burgués* (*The Dance of the Bourgeois Bear*, 1942) and *El que parpadea pierde* (*The First One to Blink Loses*, 1943). With *Máscaras exige la vida* (*Life Demands Masks*, 1952), Cuadra introduced a Pirandellian style to Nicaraguan dramaturgy.

Alberto Ordóñez Argüello (1914–91) is known for his play *La novia de Tola* (*Tola's Bride*, 1939). Despite analogies that can easily be drawn with García Lorca's *Bodas de sangre* (*Blood Wedding*), this play's own strengths and originality recommend it. Acclaimed for its astute portrayal of national traits and its ambiguous ending, it is especially strong in its presentation of the *hechicera* (sorceress/wise woman).

Octavio Robleto (b. 1935) is probably best known for criticizing social mores in his comic trilogy published between 1974 and 1976: *Doña Ana no está aquí* (*Doña Ana Is Not Here*);

Nueva historia de la Cucarachita Mandinga y del Ratoncito Pérez (*The New Tale of the Little Cockroach Mandinga and the Little Mouse Pérez*), an elaboration of a popular work of children's literature; and *Han robado a Don Evaristo* (*They've Robbed Don Evaristo*). In this trilogy one finds clear resonances of *Chinfonía burguesa*.

But Robleto also belongs to the current of critical playwrights who lent artistic and intellectual support to the political opposition in the 1970s. Another trilogy of his is critical of the abuses of military power: *La autoridad* (*The Authorities*, 1972), *Que las paredes no oigan* (*Careful, the Walls Have Ears*, 1973) and *Por aquí pasó un soldado* (*A Soldier Has Been Here*, 1975). He has also been an important contributor to young people's theatre.

Two other widely anthologized playwrights are Alberto Ycaza (b. 1945) and Rolando Steiner (1936–87), the latter also a film and theatre critic. Ycaza's best known works include the one-act play *Ancestral 66* (1966), *Escaleras para embrujar tiempo* (*Stairs to a Bewitched Time*, 1965) and the more experimental *Nosotros* (*Us*, 1964), which involves actors working on a play in a false intellectual environment dominated by immature artists.

Steiner's work tends to focus on middle-class romance and on political themes. He used classical frames of reference in his best known plays: *Judit* (*Judith*, 1957), *Antígona en el infierno* (*Antigone In Hell*, 1958) and *Pasión de Helena* (*Helen's Passion*, 1963). His best works are considered to be the award-winning *Un drama corriente* (*An Ordinary Drama*, 1963), staged in Madrid in 1964; and *La puerta* (*The Door*, 1966), which represented Nicaragua at the 1968 Olympics in México City. His political themes were developed in *La noche de Wiwilí* (*The Night of Wiwili*, 1982), *Paz en la sombra* (*Peace In the Shade*, 1984) and *La historia de Bruce* (*Bruce's Story*, 1984).

Other playwrights include Jaime Alberdi (b. 1932 in France, raised in Barcelona), author of numerous plays and also director and founder of the Teatro Profesional de Managua (Managua Professional Theatre) and the Teatro de Cámara de Managua (Managua Chamber Theatre); Julio Valle Castillo (b. 1953), a writer mainly of political plays, including a version of the national play called *Coloquio del Güegüence y el Sr Embajador* (*Dialogue of El Güegüence and the Ambassador*, 1981); Jesús Miguel 'Chuno' Blandón (b. 1940), author of satirical radio and television dramas; and Enrique

Bolívar González's 1991 Teatro Experimental de Managua production of Rolando Steiner's *Judith*.
Photo: Uriel Molina.

Fernández Morales (1918–82), author of three historical dramas.

Because of the general enthusiasm for collective creation in the 1970s, few individual playwrights emerged at this time. The best of the popular theatre of that radical period is represented by Alan Bolt's *Banana Republic* (1982), a look at Nicaraguan history using street circus techniques from magic tricks to sword-swallowing, nursery rhymes and folk tales, music and colour.

Amateur student groups at the universities in Managua and León received support in the 1950s and 1960s with the introduction of theatre programmes. The staging of specific plays on these campuses sometimes led to the formation of *ad-hoc* companies, one of the most significant being the small theatre group that performed Pablo Antonio Cuadra's *Máscaras*

exige la vida in 1952 and later that year became the Teatro Experimental de Managua (TEM).

The Escuela Nacional de Bellas Artes (National School of the Fine Arts) formed its theatre arts programme in 1955. The first director of the school was the Italian Lucio Ranucci, who in 1956 was first jailed and then deported for political reasons. He was succeeded by Alfredo Valessi (Manuel Valés Rodríguez, b. 1925), who had just returned from studying in México under the Stanislavskian Japanese director and teacher Seki Sano.

The school was founded at the urging of influential directors of the Teatro Experimental de Managua, Gladys Ramírez de Espinosa (b. 1925) and Gloria Pereira de Belli. The TEM collaborated with the new theatre school, sharing performance space for some time before moving to the Teatro Rubén Darío, a 1,300-seat

Alan Bolt's *Banana Republic*, 1982.
Photo: O. Cantarero, courtesy *Conjunto*.

performance space. Since 1979, the TEM has also performed in a variety of *ad-hoc* spaces, including church auditoriums, hotel conference rooms and cinemas.

The Channel 6 Theatre Company was formed in 1958 for the production of weekly live television drama. Under the direction of Alfredo Valessi, Jaime Alberdi, Ricardo Quinteros and others, it offered an eclectic selection that included works by such internationally known writers as Albert Camus and J.B. Priestley. The plays were performed before live audiences.

Las Máscaras (The Masks) was begun in 1965, touring extensively and setting up another theatre school. Also established during this same period were the Rubén Darío Workshop at the Escuela Nacional de Bellas Artes, directed by Alberto Ycaza; the Teatro Experimental at the National Autonomous University; and an experimental theatre group in Boaco, where theatre festivals were held in 1972 and 1973. As well, the Comedia Nacional de Nicaragua was started by theatre school graduate Socorro Bonilla Castellón (b. 1932), who later became director of the Rubén Darío Popular Theatre, specializing in theatre for young audiences and political drama.

Numerous short-lived groups also emerged, among them the Teatro Profesional de Managua, which presented a record thirty performances of García Lorca's *Yerma* before disappearing due to lack of funds; the Comedia del Arte, directed by Adán Castillo until his death in 1973; the Teatro Arena de Nicaragua, founded by Tacho Sánchez; and the Teatro Experimental Universitario de León, directed in 1962 by Ricardo Quinteros and Jaime Alberdi, who introduced post-performance forums to Nicaragua.

Finally, two groups focusing on children's work are the Teatro Experimental Miguel de Cervantes, directed by Oscar Méndez and mainly using collective creation, and the Guachipilín Puppet Workshop.

The groundwork for a new theatre in Nicaragua was laid in the 1970s and 1980s through the efforts of grassroots groups such as Cantimplora and Los Alpes, both led by former theatre students involved in the FSLN. They saw theatre as a collective expression of commitment designed to involve its practitioners in social transformations that ranged from the psychological empowerment of its largely rural and working-class audiences to the affirmation of cultural tradition. Between 1979 and the mid-1980s numerous other theatre groups were founded, some with government support and some with funding from non-governmental organizations, including foreign foundations.

The establishment of a farmers' cultural organization, the Movimiento de Expresión Campesina Artística y Teatral (MECATE; Movement of Peasant Artistic and Theatrical Expression), encouraged the development of small non-professional companies through exchanges, tours and workshops. At the same time, the work of the Theatre Artists' Union of the Sandinista Association of Cultural Workers, founded in 1980, has included the sponsorship of a number of national and international theatre festivals and conferences. The 1983 international workshop was part of a hemispheric continuum of Latin American popular theatre that every year brings practitioners and researchers together for periods of ten days to several weeks in different venues.

The arts, like other sectors (for example, health and education), attracted a considerable number of foreigners interested in revolutionary projects. One of the strongest theatre groups to emerge after 1979 was the Justo Rufino Garay workshop, founded by Lucero Millán, a Mexican. Oriented mainly towards students and workers, it was recognized for its high artistic and production values. Others have included both professionals and amateurs. Most perform in community centres, churches, plazas and streets.

Gonzalo Cueller's 1993 Guachipilín Puppet Workshop production of Onelio Jorge Cardoso's *Francisca and Death*.

Nixtayolero's production of *Ojo al Cristo (Watch Out For Christ)*.
Photo: courtesy *Conjunto*.

Without doubt, though, the most important of the new theatre groups has been Alan Bolt's Nixtayolero, formed in 1979 during the revolution and continuing into the reconstruction period as a vehicle for consciousness raising, for the retrieval and diffusion of traditional popular forms, and for the artistic education of the people. The leading director of the new theatre in Nicaragua, Bolt combines anthropological research with workshops and performances using collective creation, dance theatre, history, myth, politics, folk genres and community participation both in discussion and in performance. His prime interest is in traditional performance genres.

The grassroots movement, for Bolt, is closely connected to environmental concerns and an interest in learning from the disenfranchised – social and national groups that had formerly been denied access to public institutions. Bolt's operational model involves self-sufficiency in food supplies, ecologically safe production, the community as a social unit, diversified spaces for cultural expression, the preservation of local history through the use of symbols, music, dance, drama and colour, and preventive medicine and herbal remedies. Art for him is to be part of everyday life, and drama should be closely linked to the community. The practice of the new Nicaraguan popular theatre is inextricably tied to this philosophy, as much by circumstance as by intent.

Another grassroots theatre group is Teyocoyani. Co-founded by Gabriel Cossoy, who later returned to educational theatre work in his native Argentina, Teyocoyani evolved as part of the farming and mining communities in which it worked, reflecting the lives and concerns of its people. Like Nixtayolero, the group established an agricultural cooperative and ran leadership training workshops.

Judith A. Weiss

Further Reading

Arellano, Jorge Eduardo. 'Teatro'. ['Theatre']. Chap. in *Panorama de la literatura nicaragüense*. [An overview of Nicaraguan literature]. Managua: Editorial Nueva Nicaragua, 1986.

Bolt, Alan. 'Magic Theater. Political Theater'. *Communications from the International Brecht Society* 15, no. 2 (April 1986): 48–51.

——. 'Teatro en Nicaragua: arquetipos y símbolos'. [Theatre in Nicaragua: Archetypes and symbols]. *Conjunto* 94 (1993): 43–53.

——. 'El teatro estudiantil universitario'. [University student theatre]. *Conjunto* 45 (1980): 5–13.

Brookes, Chris. *Now We Know the Difference*. Vancouver: NC Press, 1983. 140 pp.

——. 'Notes on Nicaragua: Two Theatres'. *Theaterwork* 2, no. 3 (March 1982): 18–20.

Caballero, Attilio. 'Semana Santa en Nicaragua: rito, tradición y contemporaneidad'. [Holy Week in Nicaragua: Ritual, tradition and contemporaneity]. *Conjunto* 77 (1988): 92–6.

Craven, David. 'Art in Contemporary Nicaragua'. *Oxford Art Journal* 11, no. 1 (1988): 51–63.

Cuadra, Pablo Antonio. 'Breve nota sobre el teatro nicaragüense'. [Brief notes on Nicaraguan theatre]. Chap. in *Tres obras de teatro nuevo*. [Three plays from the new theatre]. Ediciones de la Academia Nicaragüense de la Lengua, 1957.

Gómez, Mayte. 'No More Black Sheep: A Women's Theatre Collective in Nicaragua/No Más Ovejas Negras: Colectivo de teatro de mujeres en Nicaragua'. *Aquelarre* 2, no. 4 (winter 1990): 20–4.

Kaiser-Lenoir, Claudia. 'Arte y práctica social: el nuevo teatro en Nicaragua'. [Art and social practice: The new theatre in Nicaragua]. *Conjunto* 78 (January–April 1989): 75–9.

——. 'Nicaragua: Theatre in a New Society'. *Theatre Research International* 14, no. 2 (1989): 122–30.

Kidd, Ross. 'Testimony from Nicaragua: An Interview with Nidia Bustos'. *Theaterwork* 2, no. 6 (September–October 1982): 32–40.

Martin, Randy. 'Country and City: Theatre in Revolution'. *The Drama Review* 31, no. 4 (winter 1987): 58–76.

Morton, Carlos. 'The Nicaraguan Drama: Theatre of Testimony'. *Latin American Theatre Review* 17, no. 2 (spring 1984): 89–93.

Pérez Estrada, Francisco. *Teatro folklore nicaragüense*. [Nicaraguan folklore theatre]. Managua: Editorial Nuevos Horizontes, 1946.

Ruf, Elizabeth. 'Teatro del pueblo, por el pueblo y para el pueblo [Theatre of the people, for the people and by the people]: An Interview with Alan Bolt'. *The Drama Review* 31, no. 4 (winter 1987): 77–90.

Sáenz, Faustino. 'Revalorización de nuestra Comedia Maestra'. [A re-evaluation of our national play]. *Ventana* 23 (January 1988): 7.

Weiss, Judith. 'Teyocoyani and the Nicaraguan Popular Theatre'. *Latin American Theatre Review* 23, no. 1 (fall 1989): 71–9.

Wise, Debra. 'Puppetry in the New Nicaragua'. *Puppetry Journal* 36, no. 2 (winter 1984): 19–20.

PANAMÁ

Panamá has long been the centre of transportation routes between the Caribbean Sea and the Pacific Ocean. Located on a small isthmus of 77,060 square kilometres (29,750 square miles), the Panamá Canal in 1914 further enhanced Panamá's importance as the main hemispheric link between east and west as well as between southern Central America (Costa Rica) and northern South America (Colombia). Panamá also has hundreds of islands scattered along its coast which results in varying versions of its actual land area.

A narrow, tropical country divided by several mountain ranges, Panamá had a 1992 population of 2.4 million people, making it one of the least populated countries in Latin America. Some 70 per cent of the population is of mixed native and European ancestry. Other important racial groups include blacks and mulattos (people of mixed black and European ancestry). Spanish is the country's official language, though English is spoken widely; many Panamanians are fluently bilingual. Panamá City, situated at the Pacific end of the canal, is the country's capital as well as its commercial and cultural centre.

Panamá was part of the Spanish viceroyalty of Perú from the time of its European colonization. In 1717, it became part of the viceroyalty of New Granada (now Colombia, Venezuela and Ecuador) and continued to belong to Colombia after Colombia became independent from Spain in 1821. There were several later attempts at political independence; during 1840 and 1841 the country was, in fact, independent for thirteen months.

In 1903, Colombia refused to sign a treaty giving the United States permission to build a canal in Panamá. On 3 November 1903, Panamanians revolted against this decision and the United States sent warships to the area in support of the revolt, bringing to a head the attempts of Panamanians to secede from Colombia over several years. In the Hay-Bunau-Varilla Treaty (1903), the United States guaranteed the independence of Panamá, granted the new nation US$10 million and began to pay, after 1913, a yearly sum in return for canal rights.

The US has frequently intervened in internal Panamanian political affairs despite Franklin Roosevelt's 'good neighbour policy' towards Latin America, which from 1936 began to change these interventionist policies. After World War II, Panamanians also began to demand revisions to the 1903 treaty. In 1964, riots broke out in the Canal Zone and relations with the United States were briefly severed. In 1968, further political instability led to the overthrow of the government and General Omar Torrijos Herrera (1929–81) became the country's new leader. In 1977, Torrijos signed new treaties with the US granting Panamá control over the canal and the Canal Zone beginning in 1999.

By 1978, the government came under civilian control with Torrijos remaining as its military leader. In 1981, however, Torrijos died in a plane crash and two years later Manuel Noriega (b. 1934) emerged as the country's new head of the military. But Noriega, despite close contacts early in his career with the United States' Central Intelligence Agency, was indicted by the US on charges of drug trafficking in 1988 and calls were issued both in the US and within the Organization of American States for him to step down. In December 1989, the US invaded Panamá, arrested Noriega and jailed him in the United States. Panamanian nationalists, even many of those who disagreed with Noriega's policies and methods, began to question once again the country's real independence.

Panamá's theatre history is likewise divided into several periods. Without looking at the quasi-dramatic rituals of the indigenous peoples of the area, it is clear that the period up to the 1930s can be seen as one in which theatrical art was essentially European in nature. The majority of plays seen were European and European performance styles dominated.

In his *Historia del teatro en Panamá* (*History of Theatre in Panamá*), historian Héctor Rodríguez C. links the growth of European drama in the country to the development of the canal itself. Because of French involvement in its construction, many French theatre troupes performed, among them Sarah Bernhardt's, at the Teatro de Las Monjas (Theatre of the Nuns) in Panamá City. Given that Panamá City at that time had only a few thousand residents, was surrounded by tropical jungle and suffered from regular outbreaks of malaria, Bernhardt's appearance was significant.

By the early part of the twentieth century, however, a movement began towards the creation of a Panamanian National Theatre. Inaugurated in 1908, the company's role in Panamanian theatrical development since that time has been significant. In its first decades, the company continued in the European tradition although it regularly produced Latin American evenings as well, events that came to be known as *Noches tropical* (Tropical Nights).

As a Panamanian middle class began to develop, professional companies from Spain, Argentina and México also began to be invited to the National Theatre, offering more modern styles of production with particular relevance to local audiences. Of special appeal were performances of opera, operetta and the *zarzuela* (Spanish-style musical comedy).

Panamanian plays themselves continued to be rare until after World War II, though there were attempts at creating them as early as 1809, when Víctor de la Guardia y Ayala (1772–1824) wrote *La politica del mundo* (*World Politics*). It is possible, though, to identify only another half dozen or so such attempts from then until the beginning of the twentieth century, when canal activity brought a new effervescence to the theatrical life of the country. The Depression of the 1930s did little to help the situation.

Perhaps the first modern Panamanian play of real importance is the musical farce *La cucarachita mandinga* (*The Impish Little Cockroach*), produced in 1937. Written by Rogelio Sinán (Bernardo Domínquez Alba, b. 1904) with music by Gonzalo Brenes, the production was staged in the country's interior in Penonomé, the largest city in Panamá at that time. The show ran for more than a month. Sinán had spent part of the 1920s in Europe studying theatre and when he returned he became both a producer and promoter and quickly emerged as Panamá's first professional playwright. Among Sinán's other important plays are *Chiquilinga o la gloria de ser hormiga* (*Chiquilinga, or The Glory of Being an Ant*, 1927), *El desquite de Caperucita Roja* (*The Revenge of Little Red Riding Hood*) and *Lobo Go Home* (*Wolf Go Home*, 1978), about US intervention in Panamá.

Along with Anita Villalaz, Sinán dominated the Panamanian theatre over the next three decades performing not only at the National Theatre but also at many other venues in Panamá City, as well as outside the capital. Because of its geographical importance, the country grew in stature during the war years as did the number of theatre professionals in Panamá City, the number of performances and the sizes of audiences.

By the 1950s, for the first time in the country's history, Panamanian theatres were being run by Panamanians. As a result, a whole new generation of playwrights began to emerge: Gumercinda Páez, Renato Ozores (b. 1910), Mario Riera Pinilla (1920–67), Juan Díaz Lewis (b. 1916), Mario A. Rodríguez and Mario J. de Obaldía (1891–1951) among them. At the same time, many new theatres began to emerge in which their plays could be produced. Among these was the Teatro Infantil (Children's Theatre) created by Dora McKay.

So active had the theatrical scene become that in 1952 a theatre union was formed – the Cooperativa Artística Teatral Istmeña (CATI; Isthmus Theatre Artists' Cooperative). Five years later, Panamá's first experimental theatre opened its doors – the Teatro Experimental de Panamá, under the direction of the Spanish priest Ramón María Condomines. Its first production was Sophocles' *Oedipus Rex*. Condomines's influence in Panamá was significant in inspiring many young people to professional careers and it was a loss when his company ceased operation in the early 1960s. The most widely produced playwright during this period was the Spanish dramatist Alejandro Casona.

In 1961, Miguel Moreno founded the Teatro Club and the Teatro Estudiantil Panameño

(Panamanian Student Theatre), both of which were still operating under Moreno's direction into the 1990s. Though neither was intended to become a fully professional theatre, both helped train a generation of young actors and directors through Moreno's skills as a teacher.

Still another group formed at this time was the Teatro en Círculo (Theatre in the Round), which experimented with new staging techniques and which in 1979 built its own 250-seat theatre, only the second to be built in Panamá since the construction of the National Theatre in 1908. It must be said, however, that its architecture and acoustics have always left much to be desired.

The University of Panamá established its own group, Teatro Universitario (University Theatre), in 1959. The university itself was only twenty-four years old at that point but was starting to be recognized as the country's most important cultural centre. The group opened with a production of Thornton Wilder's *The Matchmaker* staged by Yale University Professor Frank McMullan, who remained in Panamá to teach. For all its importance, however, the group was still without a theatre building in 1995.

José Díaz, from Puerto Rico, replaced McMullan at the university and in the early 1960s created some outstanding productions with his students, many of whom later went on to important careers in theatre, including Jarl Babot, Miriam Bethancourt, Gladis Vidal and Isis Tejeira. The work of important European playwrights was also introduced to Panamá at this time by Díaz, and optional theatre courses began to appear in the curriculum.

The military seized power in the country in 1968, an action that affected everyone and had its ramifications in the theatre. For one thing, many writers chose to leave rather than live under what amounted to a constitutional dictatorship. The new constitution, while giving workers a number of rights, effectively

Jarl Babot's 1979 production of Tennessee Williams's *The Glass Menagerie*.
Photo: Héctor Rodríguez C.

killed off small industry and increased unemployment.

As well, anyone involved in what was perceived to be opposition media lost their jobs and such organizations were closed down. The new government did win Panamanian rights over the canal but debates raged well into the 1980s over whether such treaties were advantageous to Panamá or not. Though Panamanians benefited from abundant loans from the World Bank (creating one of the world's largest per capita debts), the theatre was forced to develop without benefit of free speech, and with exiled writers.

This was, in fact, a turning point for Panamanian theatre. On the one hand, there was government-sponsored theatre, and on the other, the independent, non-government groups. The former were represented by the university and the Instituto Nacional de Cultura (National Institute of Culture), and the latter mostly by Broadway-style productions.

In 1970, the University Theatre reopened under the direction of Roberto McKay. During his three years as head of the Departamento de Expresiones Artísticas (DEXA; Department of Artistic Expression) at the university, he managed to stage eighteen productions, including many by Panamanian and other Latin American playwrights.

Opening soon after at the university was still another group – the Teatro Taller Universitario (University Theatre Workshop), which produced plays by Panamanian dramatists such as José de Jesús Martínez, Agustín del Rosario, Enrique Chuez and Manuel de la Rosa, along with plays by Latin American dramatists such as José Triana and Guillermo Gentile. Among European authors produced by the group were Bertolt Brecht and Eugène Ionesco.

Two other state-sponsored groups founded in the 1980s were Teatro de la Dirección General de Desarrollo para la Comunidad (DIGEDECOM), founded and directed by Carlos Van Der Hans, and Teatro Obrero (Workers' Theatre). Neither group had a profound artistic vision; the Teatro Obrero closed after just a few seasons.

It should be noted here that, despite state support, the university-connected groups always operated on very modest budgets while the independent productions and the National Theatre had enormous sums of money to work with.

The Teatro Experimental de Panamá emerged in a new form in 1969 with a stable and talented group of actors and directors, many of whom had studied with Condomines. Among its productions were plays by Edward Albee, Albert Camus and Henrik Ibsen.

Another short-lived but important group was El Topo (The Mole), which operated in 1972 and 1973. Directed by Alejandro Massey and Eduardo Barril, both South Americans, the group staged a number of extraordinary productions including Michel de Ghelderode's *Escorial* and Barril's own *Tarde de reyes* (*King's Afternoon*).

Many small groups continued to emerge during the late 1970s, the 1980s and into the 1990s: the Nuevo Teatro (New Theatre) of Roberto McKay, Iván García and Antonio Jiménez; the Junta Teatral Victoriano (Victoriano Theatre Union) in 1976; the Compañía América and the Teatro La Mosca (The Fly Theatre) in 1977; and the Grupo Galaxia (1978).

The Junta Teatral Victoriano survived until 1981 and during its existence staged a number of important productions, including José de Jesús Martínez's *La guerra del banano* (*The Banana War*, 1976) and Alfredo Arango's *Pepita de marañón* (*Cashew Seed*). Among its directors were the South Americans Domingo Logiudice, Soberón and John Ryan. The Compañía América was directed by Iván García and staged such classics as August Strindberg's *Miss Julie* and Machiavelli's *Mandragola*.

La Mosca operated between 1977 and 1981 under the direction of Jarl Babot and Ricardo Gutiérrez. During the group's existence it staged works by Samuel Beckett, Brecht, Harold Pinter and Albee.

The year 1976 also saw the creation of the first Panamanian International Festival of Theatre. Sponsored by DEXA in association with the National Tobacco Company, this two-week event brought to Panamá companies from Argentina, Brazil, Costa Rica, Puerto Rico, México and Venezuela as well as from West Germany, Iceland, Poland, Yugoslavia and the United States. Never before in Panamá had there been a theatrical event of such scope.

The 1980s also saw the regular production of an even larger number of national writers such as del Rosario, Raúl Leis (b. 1947), Babot, Arango, de la Rosa, Eustorgio Chong Ruíz and Enrique Chuez. Their plays became more Latin American, more political and more national.

In 1980, for the first time in a dozen years, an opposition newspaper openly operated and there were direct elections for the presidency. In

Ricardo Gutiérrez's 1978 La Mosca production of Beckett's *Endgame*.
Photo: Héctor Rodríguez C.

1986, the Catholic Church sponsored an in-depth economic study showing the economic problems of the majority of Panamanians and the great contrast existing between the rich and the poor of the country. Political and economic scandals occurred frequently and in 1987 the so-called 'Panamanian crisis' exploded. As a result, new censorship laws arose and opposition media were again closed down. A clear confrontation took place between state law enforcement agencies and people on the street. Omnipresent was the influence of the United States.

From the 1980s, Panamanian theatre became much more clearly divided into three basic styles of production: the high-budget commercial productions, university theatre productions, and productions by small, independent non-commercial groups.

The high-budget, commercial productions very often featured foreign stars, typically Mexican and Venezuelan television actors. Intended to reach a large, cash-paying audience, these large shows were usually technically superb but aesthetically unchallenging.

The best known producer of these works was Ileana de Krupnik, who often boasted that her actors were as well paid as those in New York. She generally produced two shows each season and each would run for no more than a month in Panamá City. During the early 1980s, her producing career reached its peak.

In 1984, a second university became involved in theatrical work – Universidad Santa María la Antigua. Staging only one play per season, the university's company, El Desván (The Attic, still active in the mid-1990s), has tended to produce the works of only Latin American authors. For most of its history, the group has been run by Eugenio Fernández.

As for the small, independent non-commercial groups, their major problem in the 1990s has continued to be a lack of continuity. Companies appear, stage a number of productions and then fade from view only to emerge some years later in a slightly different form.

As late as 1994, Panamanian theatre was still not a fully professional entity. Though many of its regularly performing artists were paid,

production was still not consistent enough for most people to survive from their theatrical earnings. The result was productions rounded out by semi-professional performers or even sometimes non-professionals.

Structure of the National Theatre Community

For a discussion of the **Structure of the National Theatre Community**, see the opening, historical section.

Artistic Profile

Companies

Many of Panamá's small theatre groups began their lives in some way connected to the University of Panamá. Though many of the groups have benefited from modest state support, few have been able to provide company members with the means to work exclusively in the theatre. It should be noted as well that though there seem to be many groups, the same actors and directors appear over and over again in most of them. This is the Panamanian theatrical reality: a small number of people working in different ways with different companies.

One such group was El Búho (The Owl), formed in 1963 by Jarl Babot. Based at the University of Panamá, it was the first to introduce Brecht to the country. Among its successful productions were *Mutter Courage und ihre Kinder* (*Mother Courage and Her Children*, 1985) and two plays by Sophocles, *Electra* and *Antigone*. Babot later studied at the Lunacharsky State Institute for Theatre Arts in Moscow.

Also based at the university was the Círculo de Arte Dramático de Panamá (Dramatic Arts Circle of Panamá), founded and directed by José Avila. The company operated for more than a decade, specializing in the staging of existentialist plays including many written by Avila himself. In total, the group staged over forty productions.

Teatro Taller Universitario and Los Trashumantes (The Nomads) have been Panamá's two most daring groups and both have represented Panamá at experimental festivals outside the

country. Teatro Taller Universitario attracted many young people, some of whom had been trained outside Panamá, and tended to focus on new dramaturgy.

Los Trashumantes, directed by Manuel de la Rosa, tended more towards collective creation, with de la Rosa serving as the writer when needed. De la Rosa's productions focused on contemporary Panamanian social and political issues. In the early 1970s, the group did much of its work in public plazas, inner city neighbourhoods and peasant communities. In 1976, the group represented Panamá at the First Festival of Popular Latin American Theatre in New York.

In the late 1970s, both these groups began to change their styles. Babot, then recently returned from Europe, staged a strong production with Teatro Taller Universitario of a play by del Rosario, *A veces esa palabra libertad* (*Sometimes That Word Liberty*), and the production toured successfully throughout the country. The script was a commentary on the bloody political events of January 1964 in Panamá. His last productions with the company included plays by Brecht and by the Peruvian writer Alonso Alegría. The company's direction was then taken over by Avila, who produced many Panamanian scripts. In 1979, Héctor Rodríguez became director of the group and staged two productions of note: *Suceden cosas extrañas en tierra del emperador Cristóbal* (*Strange Occurrences in the Land of Emperor Christopher*) by del Rosario and *La Orgía* (*The Orgy*) by the Colombian writer Enrique Buenaventura.

Later, Rodríguez did a production of note

Héctor Rodríguez's 1980 Los Trashumantes production of Jarl Babot's *Where the Lobster Lives*.
Photo: Héctor Rodríguez C.

with Los Trashumantes, a play by Babot called *Donde vive la langosta* (*Where the Lobster Lives*, 1980).

Los Mosqueteros (The Musketeers) was an offshoot of Teatro Taller Universitario. Under the direction of Ricardo Gutiérrez, the group leaned towards the didactic, and to children's theatre.

It was the governmental agency the National Institute of Culture that was responsible for the establishment of a National Theatre School and in 1975 for the establishment of a national theatre company, the Compañía Nacional de Teatro. Directed by Roberto McKay, the National Theatre mounted five productions in 1975 and 1976 and then closed down. Of the five plays, two had been by Panamanian authors: *Celeste por la mañana* (*Heavenly in the Morning*) by Carlos García de Paredes and *Lobo Go Home* by Sinán.

The National Institute of Culture also supported several independent productions, most noted for their large budgets. Among them were *El gran drama* (*The Great Drama*) by Condomines, *Jesus Christ Superstar* by Andrew Lloyd Webber and Tim Rice, and two plays by the French dramatist Jean Anouilh, both directed by José Sarsanedas.

One of the longest continuously operating groups since the early 1980s has been Tablas, under the direction of Norman Duglas. The company tends to be totally focused around Duglas's choice of actors and scripts but has done some useful work especially in the production of Latin American scripts.

Also continuing has been the Teatro en Círculo, which, since the establishment of its own theatre in 1979, has also operated continuously. The group's repertoire, however, has been less than impressive, concentrating almost exclusively on light comedies. Among the most popular have been the works of the Spanish dramatist Alfonso Paso.

Dramaturgy

The 1960s saw a new generation of playwrights emerge – Ernesto Endara, Miguel Moreno, Carlos García de Paredes, José de Jesús Martínez (1929–91) and José Avila. Inspired by Jean-Paul Sartre and Camus, their plays were for the most part existentialist dramas that connected profoundly with younger audiences.

Martínez was born in Nicaragua and educated in México City, Madrid and Heidelberg. He nevertheless spent most of his working life in Panamá, where he taught philosophy and mathematics. A poet, he also became a close friend of General Torrijos. His dedication to the general's cause and to the social progress of Central America were effectively documented in Graham Greene's novel *Getting to Know the General* (1984).

Martínez was the author of fifteen plays, and his best known work, *El juicio final* (*Final Judgement*, 1962) was included in one of the standard anthologies of Hispanic theatre, *El teatro hispanoamericano contemporáneo* (*Contemporary Spanish American Theatre*), edited by Carlos Solórzano and published by Fondo de Cultura Económica in México City in 1964. An existentialist play, the script focuses on a man who, after death, appears before God, who is dressed in normal clothes and seated behind a desk, to argue falsely that his life deserves to be rewarded. Other important works by Martínez include *La mentira* (*The Lie*, 1955), *Caifás* (*Caiphus*, 1961) and *Segundo asalto* (*Second Assault*, 1968).

Unfortunately, the various political crises in the country through the late 1980s and into the mid-1990s made it increasingly difficult for Panamanian playwrights to be effectively produced. Indeed, only one new Panamanian writer emerged during this period – Rosa Britton.

Directors, Directing and Production Styles

For a discussion of directing, see previous material in **Artistic Profile** and the opening, historical section.

Héctor Rodríguez C.

Federico García Lorca, Ovidio Benítez Pereira (b. 1939), Josefina Plá, Néstor Romero Valdovino and Julio Correa. TEL has regularly toured the interior of the country, contributing to the expansion of popular theatre, poetry and art in Guaraní and Spanish. TEL receives some public financial support and pays its members.

The influence of Polish director Jerzy Grotowski was very strong in Paraguay in the late 1960s and the greatest response to it was the formation of the group Tiempoovillo in 1969. Its first members were all students of the Faculty of Architecture, who began their theatre work with a production of *Curriculum vitae*, loosely based on Michel de Ghelderode's *The Strange Rider*. The group later produced plays by Jean Genet, Monnier, Fernando Arrabal and Jorge Díaz as well as their first Paraguayan play, *La tortura como una de las bellas artes* (*Torture as One of the Fine Arts*) by José Antonio Pratt Mayans. In 1973, they produced the collective creation *De lo que se avergüenzan las víboras* (*What the Serpents Are Ashamed Of*), a play about the exploitation of the indigenous people. The group later performed at festivals in Colombia, Venezuela, Honduras, El Salvador, México and Panamá.

In 1967, the Asamblea Nacional Constituyente (National Constituent Assembly) took over the Teatro Municipal for seven months and the growing number of theatre companies in Asunción had to find alternative spaces. It was at this time that film houses such as the Teatro Guaraní and Teatro Victoria began to be used for theatrical productions.

The 1970s, perhaps the greatest decade to that point in the history of Paraguayan theatre, saw the creation of even more new companies, a growth in audiences and the creation of new spaces. Runs became longer, actors were better trained and plays from the international repertoire were seen in greater numbers. Still, there was no official cultural policy or funding and the Teatro Municipal was rented out without any clear guidelines.

Gente de Teatro (Theatre People) was one of the many new groups born at this time. Directed by Gustavo Calderini (b. 1944), this company produced both modern classics and new works, including George Bernard Shaw's *Pygmalion* (1973), Leonard Gershe's *Butterflies Are Free* (1975), *Esquina peligrosa* (*Dangerous Corner*, 1977) and *Réquiem para una mujer* (*Requiem for a Nun*, 1978). The company was also

Gustavo Calderini's 1973 Gente de Teatro production of Shaw's *Pygmalion*.
Photo: Fototecnica Cibils.

responsible for bringing to Paraguay a number of well-known guest directors and teachers from abroad.

La Farándula, another 1970s group, also featured the work of foreign companies, while Ernesto Baéz's company continued producing the work of national authors in Asunción and on tour. Perhaps the most interesting of the new authors was Alcibíades González del Valle (b. 1936).

In 1974, playwrights Antonio Carmona (b. 1940) and González del Valle joined with a group of actors to establish the theatre company Aty Ñeé (Assembly), a group that attempted to foster close relations between the theatre and the country's large peasant population. In their best work, they achieved this – *Yvi reñoi, Pochonto reasái, La fábula de la creación del buey* (*The Fable of the Creation of the Ox*) and *Perú Rimá*. The group also produced *Las veladas* (*Cultural Evenings*), a collection of plays about a group of touring actors. In later years, the company experimented with Brechtian ideas in productions like *La pesca* (*Fishing*), *Kuré Kosé* and *De la guerra al cabaret* (*From War to Cabaret*). Other 1970s companies of note were La Tropa (The Troupe), directed by Humberto Gulino, the Teatro Laboratorio (Lab Theatre), and Pirirí Teatro, a children's theatre company, founded by Erenia López.

In the 1980s, theatre activity began to decline. It was, in fact, a time of contradictions: while some theatres closed down, other companies had great success, especially with stage adaptations of Paraguayan novels: *Yo, el supremo* (*I, the Supreme*, 1917) by Augusto Roa Bastos and *La babosa* (*The Slug*) by Gabriel Cassacia, for example. But once again, a lack of administrative policy at the Teatro Municipal and a general lack of support for maintenance of the building caused its closure for several years in the 1980s. Yet during the early 1980s, the Municipal continued to house Baéz's company and produced the work of the actors Rafael Rojas Doria and César Alvarez Blanco. The Compañía de Comedias del Ateneo ceased operation in 1987 and its disappearance after four decades was a genuine loss. Also closing at this time was Gente de Teatro, a company that had operated with extraordinary energy and enthusiasm.

Nevertheless, the creation of the Centro Paraguayo de Teatro (Paraguayan Theatre Centre) in 1980 served to bring together theatre artists. The centre organized panels, gatherings and workshops, and also acted as a kind of actors' union. In the 1980s as well, the Centro Cultural Juan de Salazar (Juan de Salazar Cultural Centre), especially under the leadership of Francisco Corral, became a strong supporter of independent theatre, offering financial and emotional support to the many companies that used the centre's small theatre space or its gardens. Some of the productions sponsored by the centre were Calderón de la Barca's *El gran teatro del mundo* (*The Great Theatre of the World*), directed by Humberto Gulino; *Punto de partida* (*The Starting Point*), directed by Arturo Fleitas; *Cervantes al aire libre* (*Cervantes Outdoors*) and *Corral de comedias* (*Open-Air Theatre*), directed by Edy Benítez; and *Las viejas difíciles* (*The Difficult Old Ladies*), by Rudi Torga.

Another group emerging in the 1980s was Arte Acción (Art Action), directed by Gardés Gardés, a graduate of the Escuela Municipal. It produced, among other plays, *Waiting for Godot* and *Six Characters in Search of an Author*. In 1987 Alexis González founded a theatre department at the Universidad Católica (Catholic University), a training centre committed to experimental productions. Although this venture worked unevenly, it did some important productions, among them plays by Moncho Azuaga, directed by Miguel Gómez.

Perhaps the most interesting of the 1980s groups was the Arlequín Teatro, founded in 1982 by José Luis Ardissone, a former member of Gente de Teatro. Until it closed down, Arlequín presented an average of six new productions each season plus several children's plays. It also hosted more than a dozen foreign companies and established a theatre school. Its productions ranged from plays by García Lorca to those of Jean Genet and Tennessee Williams. In 1989, Arlequín organized a Festival de Mayo de Teatro Internacional (May Festival of International Theatre) in Asunción, with the participation of twenty-one companies from around the world. Arlequín also had a presence in foreign festivals, especially in Argentina.

In 1989, Lucio Sandoval, Teresita Pesoa and Fermín Martínez, among others, formed the group Actores Asociados, with the goal of producing popular theatre in Guaraní and Spanish. They began their first season with a production of Correa's well-known *Yvy yara* directed by Erenia López, with which they toured the country and travelled to the Londrina Festival. Among later productions were Correa's *Nande mbaé ra'i*, also directed by López, *La babosa* and *Kalai to Pombero* by Antonio Escobar Cantero, based on the novel by Tadeo Zarratea (b. 1947), directed by Tito Chamorro.

Carlos Aguillera's 1982 Arlequín Teatro production of García Lorca's *The House of Bernarda Alba*.

Agustín Núñez's 1991 Centro de Investigación y Divulgación Teatral production of Augusto Roa Bastos's *I, the Supreme*, designed by Ricardo Migliorisi.
Photo: Juan Montes.

The *coup d'état* of 1989 brought a number of Paraguayans home from abroad and new energy to a generally quiet theatre scene: Agustín Núñez, a director, came back after working extensively and successfully in Colombia. He directed important plays such as *Yo, el supremo* (*I, the Supreme*, 1991) by Augusto Roa Bastos. Another, Miguel Gómez, trained in Argentina, taught in the Escuela de Teatro (Theatre School) of the Universidad Católica, where he produced two important shows written by Moncho Azuaga – *Los niños de la calle* (*Street Kids*) and *Salven a Matilde* (*Save Matilde*). He also directed Skarmeta's *Ardiente Paciencia*, Wedekind's *Spring's Awakening*, and María Teresa Encina's *Nuestra María . . . nuestro José* (*Our Mary . . . Our Joseph*).

Among other important national playwrights of the late 1980s and 1990s, Moncho Azuaga stands out for his socially critical works, as does Antonio Escobar Cantero for his concerns with justice and social order. His *Tekojojá* (*Justice*, 1981), produced by the Teresita Pesoa Company and directed by Mario Prono, had a great social and theatrical impact. Escobar Cantero also wrote *Preso Sambukú* (*Prisoner Sambukú*, 1981) and *Norairó opá riré* (1982), about those who fought in the war with Bolivia. Another writer of note is Ovidio Benítez Pereira, author of the award-winning *Como la voz de muchas aguas* (*Like the Voice of Many Waters*), *Morituri* and *Puente sobre el barranco* (*A Bridge Over the Cliff*). Erenia López, an actress and director, is significant for her children's plays – *El pícaro sueño sale de paseo* (*The Naughty Dream Goes for a Walk*), *Por el sendero llega Platero* (*Here Comes Platero*) and *Cuentos de mi pueblo* (*Stories from My Village*). She also wrote plays for adults: *El spray tragalotodo* (*The Spray that Swallows Everything*), *Condenados* (*Condemned*) and *Caretas* (*Masks*).

Polkas and *guaranías* (native music/dances) are musical forms with popular roots in Paraguay. As a result, theatre with this kind of music, as well as the Paraguayan *zarzuela* is very popular. Frutos Pané and Juan Carlos Moreno González collaborated on several musical productions including *La tejedora de*

Mario Prono's 1981 Teresita Pesoa Company production of Antonio Escobar Cantero's *Tekojojá* (*Justice*).

Ñandutí (*The Weaver of Ñandutí*, 1956), *María Pacurí* (1959), *Corochiré* (1961), *Las alegres Kyguá verá* (1961) and *Paloma Pará* (1964). These plays were written following the structure of Spanish *zarzuela* and demanded large teams of musicians, dancers, actors and singers.

Apart from the contributions made by Josefina Plá, winner of the 1984 Ollantay Prize for her theatre history research, there is no professional theatre scholarship to speak of in Paraguay. Neither the government nor the universities provide any financial support for such endeavours. In the 1990s, however, the Ministry of Education and Culture established a Cultural Development Plan, part of whose intent was to provide funds for cultural scholarship.

Mario Prono
Translated by Mayte Gómez

Further Reading

Benítez, Luis G. *El teatro paraguayo*. [Paraguayan theatre]. Lima: Servicio de Publicaciones del Teatro Universitario de San Marcos, 1971.

——. 'Teatro'. [Theatre]. Chap. in *Historia de la cultura del Paraguay*. [History of Paraguayan culture]. Asunción: Comuneros.

Bogado, Víctor. '1980–90: un decenio de teatro en el Paraguay'. [1980–90: A decade of theatre in Paraguay]. *Latin American Theatre Review* 25, no. 2 (spring 1992).

Cardozo, Efraín. 'El teatro'. [The theatre]. Chap. in *Apuntes de historia cultural del Paraguay*. [Notes on Paraguay's cultural history]. Asunción: Biblioteca de Estudios Paraguayos, 1985.

Carmona, Antonio, and Edda de los Ríos. 'Paraguay'. *Diógenes. Anuario crítico del teatro latinoamericano*, vol. II, 107–12. 1986.

Centurión, Carlos. 'Teatro'. [Theatre]. Chap. in *Historia de la cultura paraguaya*. [History of Paraguayan culture]. Asunción: Biblioteca Ortíz Guerrero, 1961.

de los Ríos, Edda. 'El Teatro Municipal de Asunción, Paraguay: historia y reflexion'. [Municipal Theatre of Asunción, Paraguay: History and reflection]. *Latin American Theatre Review* 21, no. 1 (fall 1987): 109–14.

Novoa, Bruce, and C. May Gamboa. 'Tiempoovillo: Paraguayan Experimental Theatre'. *Latin American Theatre Review* 8, no. 2 (spring 1975): 75–83.

Plá, Josefina. *Cuatro siglos de teatro en el Paraguay*. [Four centuries of theatre in Paraguay]. Colección Teatro. Asunción: Universidad Católica, 1990. 225 pp.

Rodríguez Alcalá, Hugo. 'El teatro'. [The theatre]. In *Historia de la literatura paraguaya*. [History of Paraguayan literature], 189–94. México City: Studium, 1970.

Rodríguez Medina, Carlos. 'El teatro en el Paraguay'. [Theatre in Paraguay]. Chap. in *Teatro y cine: aproximaciones*. [Approaches to theatre and film]. 7th ed. Asunción: FVD.

Vallejos, Roque. 'El teatro en el Paraguay'. [Theatre in Paraguay]. Chap. in *La literatura paraguaya como expresión de la realidad nacional*. [Paraguayan literature as an expression of national reality]. Asunción: Don Bosco, 1971.

Velázquez, Rafael Eladio. 'El teatro'. [The theatre]. Chap. in *Breve historia de la cultura en Paraguay*. [A short history of culture in Paraguay]. Asunción: El Gráfico, 1980.

Viola, Alfredo. 'El teatro en las últimas décadas'. [Theatre in recent decades]. Chap. in *Reseña del desarrollo cultural del Paraguay*. [An outline of cultural development in Paraguay]. 2nd ed. Asunción: Comuneros, 1982.

PERÚ

The third largest country in South America at 1.29 million square kilometres (496,200 square miles), Perú's geography follows the Andes Mountains along the continent's Pacific coast from Ecuador and Colombia in the north through Chile and Bolivia in the south. Much of the country's eastern border is with Brazil.

Two groups of indigenous people – the Quechua and the Aymará – make up about half of Perú's population of 22.5 million (1992). Most of them inhabit the mountainous region in the country though some live in the jungle and forest areas. About one-third of the population is *mestizo* (of mixed European and native ancestry) and these people are known as *cholos*. They form the nucleus of Perú's middle class. The *criollos* (people of Spanish ancestry born in the Americas) have long controlled much of the country's power and wealth though they remain a minority in the country. During the early days of Spanish colonization blacks were brought from Africa as slaves. A large number of Germans and Italians immigrated to Perú in the nineteenth century as did some Chinese and Japanese early in the twentieth century.

Peruvian history is usually divided into three periods: the Inca Empire, the Spanish colony and the modern republic, although great cities existed on the coast long before the Incas spread their rule over much of western South America between the twelfth and sixteenth centuries. When the Spanish *conquistadores* came to Perú (1531–3), fine roads connected Cuzco, the Inca capital, with most parts of the empire. After Francisco Pizarro (*c*.1478–1541) and his small army captured the Inca leader Atahualpa (d. 1533), the Inca Empire fell quickly. In 1535, Pizarro moved the capital to what is now Lima. Over most of the next 200 years, Lima was the capital of all Spanish South America.

Perú was finally liberated from Spain in 1821 by the combined efforts of the Argentine José de San Martín, the Venezuelan Simón Bolívar and the Chilean Bernardo O'Higgins. The final victory in this war of independence came in 1824. Over the next half century, the country was run by a series of military dictators. In the War of the Pacific (1879–83) Perú lost its southern provinces to Chile, Lima was occupied and the country was left bankrupt.

After World War I, Perú began to grow economically and in 1924 Víctor Raúl Haya de la Torre founded the progressive American Popular Revolutionary Alliance (APRA). In 1968, the military took power and began reforms dividing up large estates, raising taxes on businesses and nationalizing foreign-owned property. New constitutions were adopted in 1979 and 1993, and in 1980 a civilian government again took control.

Theatrical activity has long been part of Peruvian culture, especially folk-rooted dance and music forms such as could be seen in the ritual *tarquis* festivals dating from the pre-Hispanic period. This remains especially true in the mountain communities where music, dance, costumes and masks are still used to create works that are clearly filled with violent social satire. The aesthetic richness and the variety of forms of this folk theatre continue to represent part of the country's indigenous contribution to the dramatic arts and can still be seen in Cajabamba, Buldibuyo and Huavlillas.

The first great work of pre-Columbian literature in the native Quechua language (an official co-language with Spanish since 1975) was *Ollantay*, an affirmation of independence and a celebration of the spirit of rebellion. Most Peruvian plays, however, have been written in emulation of Spanish styles and Lima itself was long the centre of Spanish culture in South America. Under Spanish influence, Peruvian dramatists into the twentieth century often imitated European romantic and realist plays. When local customs and manners were shown, they were often the object of satire in such works as *La de cuatro mil* (*One of Four Thousand*) and *Domingo siete* (*Sunday the Seventh*), both written by Leonidas Yerovi at the beginning of the twentieth century.

Among the earliest writers were Juan del Valle y Caviedes (1652–94), a satirist and author of numerous *entremeses* (one-act farces); Lorenzo de las Llamosas (1665–1705); and Pedro de Peralta Barnuevo (1664–1743), the author of several historical plays based on classical and neo-classical themes.

The first play written after Perú's independence in 1821 was *Frutos de la educación* (*Fruits of Education*, 1830) by Felipe Pardo y Aliaga (1806–68), a Spanish-trained neo-classicist. Probably the best known work from this period is *Ña Catita* (1856) by Manuel Ascencio Segura (1805–71), a play about a Lima matchmaker.

In 1938, the Asociación de Artistas Aficionados (AAA; Association of Amateur Artists) was founded. Though its roots were in the amateur movement, its founding was a major step in the development of a professional infrastructure in the country. Dedicated to promoting drama, dance and music, AAA's major director was Bernardo Roca Rey (1918–84). In 1945, Carlos Revolledo founded the Sindicato de Actores del Perú (Peruvian Actors' Union), another step towards the professionalization of actors, musicians, singers and dancers. In the years since, each of these disciplines has formed its own separate union. Since 1978, a number of attempts have been made to bring the various groups back together, most notably through the Federación Nacional de Trabajadores Artistas y del Espectáculo (National Federation of Artistic and Stage Workers).

When José Luis Bustamante y Rivero was elected president of the republic in 1945, he named Peruvian historian Jorge Basadre Minister of Education. It was Basadre who placed theatre under the protection of the state, a move that led to the creation of a Department of Theatre within the ministry, to the establishment of an Escuela Nacional de Arte Escénica (ENAE; National School of Theatre Arts) and a Compañía Nacional de Comedias (National Drama Company).

Edmundo Barbero, an actor who first came to Perú with the exiled company of the Spanish actress Margarita Xirgú, was made the first director of both the ENAE and the Compañía Nacional de Comedias. In 1946 Manuel Beltroy, a professor who in 1941 had formed the Teatro Universitario de San Marcos (University Theatre of San Marcos), formed, upon his return from Argentina, the semi-professional Teatro del Pueblo (People's Theatre). The founding of the Compañía Nacional de Comedias and the Teatro del Pueblo marked the real beginning of modern theatre in Perú.

Under the policy of promoting theatre, a series of National Playwriting Competitions was established beginning in 1946. Early winners included Juan Ríos Rey (b. 1914), Percy Gibson Parra (b. 1908), Sebastián Salazar Bondy (1924–65), Raúl Deústua and Ricardo Roca Rey. At the ENAE, the Spaniard Santiago Ontañón began to train the country's first set designers, with Alberto Terry standing out from this group. Among the Compañía Nacional de Comedias's early productions were several non-Spanish works including plays by Eugene O'Neill and Ben Jonson.

The military coup of 1948, although effectively putting an end to a democratic way of life, did not cause the state to lose interest in the theatre. Guillermo Ugarte Chamorro became director of the ENAE and continued the training of new generations of theatre professionals.

Interdisciplinary work became significant in the 1960s. Ricardo Blume at the Teatro de la Universidad Católica (Catholic University Theatre) was deeply committed to such experiments, while Luis Peirano, a sociologist recently returned from Santiago, further explored the nature of collective creation and open stage settings. Another group of note was Yuyachkani, whose early work was politically rooted.

During this period, the country's best known group was Cuatrotablas (Four Stages). In 1972, it represented Perú at the First Latin American Theatre Festival in Ecuador, thus initiating the group's international interests: in 1973 it went to Cuba, and later to the Ninth World Festival of Youth and Students in East Germany. Upon its return it presented *El sol bajo las patas de los caballos* (*The Sun Beneath the Horses' Hooves*) by the Ecuadoran Jorge Enrique Adoum, which it also performed at the Third International Festival in Caracas.

In 1975 the group created *La noche larga* (*The Long Night*), inspired by *La cena* (*The Dinner*) by the Portuguese group A Comuna (The Commune), which they had seen in Caracas. At this point, a period that the critic

Hugo Salazar called 'epic-historic reflection' came to an end, and a new stage of development began, one that delved into the personal life experiences of group members. Influenced by Eugenio Barba's Odin Teatret, works from this stage included *Encuentros* (*Meetings*, 1977), *Equilibrios* (*Equilibrium*, 1979) and *La agonía y la fiesta* (*The Agony and the Party*, 1980). Cuatrotablas gradually separated itself from the Peruvian theatrical movement but one particular product of its work was the Encounter Ayacucho '78 festival, which allowed the group to consolidate its teaching activities.

The Instituto Nacional de Arte Escénico (formerly the Escuela Nacional) reflected these transformations. In 1971, its students performed Euripides' *The Trojan Women*, paralleling the Greek tragedy with the events of the war in Vietnam. After a visit by the Colombian group La Candelaria, which brought the collective creation *Nosotros los comunes* (*We the Common Ones*), the Instituto Nacional presented *Un muchacho llamado Tim* (*A Guy Called Tim*) by César Vega Herrera (b. 1936) and the collective creation *Perú – Problema* (1972), made up of various plays created by the students. One of these works was written in Quechua: *Hatun llacta* (*Big Town*). In 1971 *La huelga* (*The Strike*) by Gregor Díaz (b. 1933) was presented at Teatro La Cabaña, with a stage setting composed of concrete and found objects.

By the 1980s theatrical spectacle came to include celebrations of the lives of the indigenous peoples in open spaces with up to a thousand spectators in attendance. This return to a theatre of celebration, the oldest form of theatre in Perú, could be seen in the work of groups such as Teatro del Sol (Theatre of the Sun), founded in 1979 by Luis Felipe Ormeño and Alberto Montalva. Later in the 1980s, this group was responsible for well-known productions including the first stage version of the Argentine Manuel Puig's novel *The Kiss of the Spider Woman*.

In 1981, Jorge Chiarella Kruger formed the group Alondra (Lark). Its first play was the collective *¿Amén?* created with writer Juan Rivera Saavedra (b. 1930). Without scenery, Chiarella managed to convey the vicissitudes of the lives of numerous victims of repression showing an almost musical conception of the dramatic process and the rhythm of the stage. His earlier work on *Lucía, Manuel, un viejo cuento* (*Lucía, Manuel, an Old Tale*), produced with the group Telba, showed his ability to fill the stage with multiple images of the political history of Perú

Luis Felipe Ormeño's 1995 Salazar Bondy Theatre production of *Frida Kalho*, costume design by César Toledano.
Photo: Germán Ballesteros.

or of the Third World. *Dos mañanas* (*Two Mornings*) dealt with two political periods in the country's history, using the situation of a family as its central image. In $\frac{1}{2}$ *kg de pueblo* ($\frac{1}{2}$ *kg of People*), a chicken coop is used as a stage setting, with a musical group creating the atmosphere. Chiarella also introduced music into many of his other works and even composed music for the production of Uruguayan director Atahualpa del Cioppo's *Ubu Roi* done in Lima. This was taken further with the presentation of *Volver a vernos* (*To See Ourselves Again*), written by Chiarella, Fedor Larco and Max Silva, a play that used myth, dance and ritual to mirror history.

The 1980s saw the stages of Lima full of a variety of high-quality productions. Luis Peirano staged *El día que me quieras* (*The Day You Love Me*) and *Acto cultural* (*Cultural Act*) by the Venezuelan José Ignacio Cabrujas and *Tabla de multiplicaciones* (*Multiplication Table*) by Abelardo Sánchez León. Alberto Isola, winner of the National Award for Directing in 1988, recreated *La salsa roja* (*Red Salsa*) by Leonidas

Yerovi. He directed *Viaje a la tierra de Jauja y otras peregrinaciones del hambre* (*A Trip to Shangri-La and Other Pilgrimages of Hunger*), based on texts by the Spaniards Lope de Rueda and Cervantes, interconnecting the texts with references to the Spanish acting companies that visited Perú in colonial times, as well as Brecht's *Der gute Mensch von Sezuan* (*The Good Person of Setzuan*) and *Bodas que fueron famosas del pingajo y la fandanga* (*The Famous Wedding of Rags and the Fandango Dancer*) by José María Méndez.

There were also productions by director Jorge Guerra such as Brecht's *Herr Puntilla und sein Knecht Matti* (*Herr Puntilla and His Man Matti*), *Class Enemy* by Nigel Williams, adapted to a neighbourhood of Lima, and, in 1987, a free version of Euripides' *The Bacchae*.

In 1983, Peirano, Isola and Guerra helped to create the Asociación de Estudios y Producción Teatral (ENSAYO; Association of Theatrical Studies and Production), an association for directorial research and theatrical studies. Actors from various generations of the Peruvian theatre eagerly participated in the productions of ENSAYO. Among them were Luis Alvarez and Delfina Paredes, the latter a winner of the National Acting Prize in 1988. This well-known actress later played the lead role in the world première of Mario Vargas Llosa's (b. 1936) *La chunga* (*The Jest*). In 1994, Vargas won Spain's Miguel de Cervantes Prize for Literature.

In the late 1980s, Telba became part of the current that became known as 'urban theatre', theatre dealing with the problems of the intellectual, upwardly mobile middle class. This work began with *El que se fue a Barranco* (*He Who Went to Barranco*), an ironic succession of typical characters picking up the neo-costumbrista (featuring local manners and customs) style of Salazar Bondy. *Marite*, the story of a woman journalist of the 1950s, allowed the group to recreate that earlier period, while *Amor de mis amores* (*Love of My Loves*) presented love as a means of examining the weaknesses of various social classes.

Two young writers were part of the collective team involved in these works – Rafael León and Fedor Larco. During this same period, one of Perú's major female directors, Ruth Escudero, staged *Tres Marías y una Rosa* (*Three Marías and a Rose*), by the Chilean dramatist David Benavente, for Telba. Telba also presented *AM/FM* by Roberto Angeles and Rafael Dumett, *Guayasamín en Senegal* (*Guayasamín in Senegal*) by Larco and León and *El terno blanco* (*The White Suit*) by Alonso Alegría (b. 1940), directed by Hernando Cortés (b. 1927). In 1988, Cortés presented *¿Quieres estar conmigo?* (*Do You Want to Be With Me?*) by Roberto Angeles and Augusto Cabada, a self-criticism of the younger generation.

Structure of the National Theatre Community

More than 60 per cent of Perú's national theatre activity takes place in and around Lima, home to some two dozen theatre groups. It is in the rural areas, however, where truly indigenous theatrical presentations can still be seen, especially during agrarian festivals or on saints' days. Beginning in 1986 in the city of Cuzco, annual national festivals of *teatro campesino* (country theatre) began to be held. There are a number of regional theatre festivals along with festivals for mime companies, children's groups, university groups and independent companies.

Peruvian theatre as a whole can be divided into three basic types: the national groups, which receive modest state support; the independent groups, which emerge for specific productions or which operate on an ongoing basis; and the university groups. The national groups are fully professional, the university groups generally non-professional, and the independent groups fall somewhere between the two.

There are commercial theatres or, as they are called, impresario theatres; these tend to present light comedies and charge relatively high ticket prices.

Most groups tour to supplement their income, with the independent and university groups performing in non-traditional venues across the country. In 1987 in the city of Andahuaylas, for example, more than 5,000 people showed up to see a performance by the group Raíces (Roots). Though there is no official structure in place, discussions have long taken place towards establishing a decentralized regional theatre system involving six autonomous areas of the country.

Among the most significant theatre organizations in Perú are the Sindicato de Artistas del

Perú (Union of Peruvian Artists); the Movimiento Teatral Independiente de Lima (Independent Theatrical Movement of Lima), which represents independent groups in the capital; the Asociación de Actores y Directores de Teatro de Loreto (Association of Theatre Actors and Directors of Loreto), with its headquarters in Iquitos; the Centro de Estudios de Teatro Peruano (Centre for Peruvian Theatre Studies); the Centro Peruano de Autores Teatrales (Peruvian Centre for Theatrical Writers); the Consejo de Danza Perú (Dance Council of Perú); and Peruvian branches of organizations such as the Centro Latinoamericano de Creación e Investigación Teatral (CELCIT; Latin American Centre for Theatrical Creation and Research), International Association of Children's and Young People's Theatre (ASSITEJ), the International Puppeteers' Union (UNIMA) and the International Theatre Institute (ITI).

The Movimiento Teatral Independiente de Lima, among other activities, organizes national workshops and publishes the magazine *Colectivo* (*Collective*). The Centro de Estudios de Teatro Peruano organizes round-table discussions and seminars in conjunction with universities. The major national theatre event in Perú is the Muestra de Teatro Peruano (Peruvian Theatre Exposition), which brings plays and theatre artists together for debate and artistic comparisons.

Though most theatre seasons see more than 100 plays presented, total audiences rarely exceed 15,000 since most theatres play to no more than 150 spectators. This small audience base makes it impossible to risk large-scale productions. As a result, most people working in the theatre cannot earn a living by their theatre activity alone. Given this general situation, it is of interest to note that more than 2,700 people declared themselves to be actors in 1992.

Though the government offers subsidies to some theatre groups, this rarely accounts for more than 15 per cent of the total investment in a production. Important and well-known groups often obtain additional funding from corporations or invest heavily in touring. Again because of a lack of finances, joint productions are common; no municipal theatres exist in the country.

A Centro de Documentación e Información de Teatro Peruano (Centre for Documentation and Information Peruvian Theatre), whose major task is the organization of a national register of theatre people and organizations, is now run by the state.

A series of National Theatre Awards from the Instituto Nacional de la Cultura (National Institute of Culture) was initiated in 1946. By the 1990s it included prizes for writing, acting, directing, promotion and research.

The Teatro Universitario de San Marcos has an annual competition for plays, both for school theatre and for adults.

Artistic Profile

Companies

The country's oldest continuing group, the Asociación de Artistas Aficionados, was founded in 1938, while the Club de Teatro of Lima was established by playwright Sebastián Salazar Bondy in 1953. The Club de Teatro, the first of the country's important independent groups, also established Perú's first independent theatre school.

It was these two groups, along with Histrión (1956–77), that introduced the works of major Peruvian dramatists, including Juan Ríos, Salazar Bondy, Enrique Solari Swayne (b. 1915), Julio Ramón Ribeyro (b. 1929), Juan Rivera Saavedra and Gregor Díaz among others.

Yego (Committed), a group founded in 1961, was among the first to turn to collective creation. Director Carlos Clavo and other young artists began staging works such as *Alicia encuentra el amor en el maravilloso mundo de sus quince años* (*Alice Finds Love in Her Fifteen-Year-Old Wonderland*).

Most of these groups were slowly politicized through the influence of foreign writers such as Bertolt Brecht. Into the 1970s, Brechtian and non-Brechtian experiments in political theatre abounded. Some were even done at the Instituto Nacional Superior de Artes Dramáticas (Higher National Institute of Dramatic Arts).

The Cajamarca-based group Algovipasar, focusing on popular stories from its region, uses local handicrafts made there and local issues for

his playwriting career with *La gallina* (*The Hen*). A year later he received first prize in a one-act play competition at the Teatro Universitario de San Marcos for his next play, *El gallo* (*The Rooster*). The figure of the Andean man was presented powerfully and without moralizing in his next five plays: *El collar* (*The Collar*), *El cargador* (*The Loader*), *El turno* (*The Shift*), *El arpista* (*The Harpist*) and *La yunta* (*The Yoke*). Zavala's influence was felt throughout the 1970s and well into the 1980s with *Fiebre del oro* (*Gold Fever*), *La fábula de los ricos* (*The Fable of the Rich*) and *El caso del viejito que caminaba* (*The Case of the Old Man Who Walked*).

When the Histrión group travelled to Chile in 1964, it took *El fabricante de deudas* and *La chicha está fermentando* (*The Chicha Is Fermenting*, 1963) by Rafael del Carpio, and the revival of a play that first appeared in 1960, *Vida y pasión de Santiago el pajarero* (*The Life and Passion of Santiago the Bird Man*) by Julio Ramón Ribeyro, a play that was awarded the National Theatre Prize in 1959. This 1960 version, under the direction of Hernando Cortés, constituted the first epic to be done on a Peruvian stage. The theatrical works of Ribeyro are precise and ordered, an approach evident from his 1959 play *El sótano* (*The Basement*) and throughout his later works of the 1960s: *Fin de semana* (*The Weekend*, 1961), *Los caracoles* (*The Sea Shells*, 1964), *El último cliente* (*The Last Client*, 1965), *El uso de la palabra* (*The Use of Words*, 1965) and *Confusión en la prefectura* (*Confusion in the Prefecture*, 1965). In this last play, Ribeyro paints a grotesque picture of the instability of Perú's governments.

In 1965, Teatro de la Universidad Católica presented *Pasos, voces, alquien* (*Footsteps, Voices, Someone*), a programme made up of four short plays by Julio Ortega (b. 1942): *El intruso* (*The Intruder*), *La campana* (*The Bell*), *Perfecta soledad* (*Perfect Solitude*) and *La ley* (*The Law*). This author's plays work on the level of paradigms and reflections, but with tinges of Peruvian irony that make them more accessible. The majority of these plays are schematic and sometimes have a Kafkaesque tone but one can perceive Ortega's preoccupation with the events and people of Perú. Examples of this include his *El paraíso de los suicidas* (*Suicide Heaven*) and *Invasión de una calle* (*Invasion of a Street*). The guerrilla bands of 1965 inspired him to write *Mesa pelada* (*Bare Table*), while the urban situation in Lima is the theme of *Balada de la dirección correcta* (*Ballad of the Right Direction*) and *Infierno peruano* (*Peruvian Hell*).

The same commitment to a national viewpoint is also found in the works of Gregor Díaz. He first came to attention in 1968 with *Los del cuatro* (*People of the 40s*), which was presented the following year by Histrión. His early plays showed his ability to reproduce artistically the language and manners of the poor. In *La huelga*, he focused on construction workers. Díaz's later plays – *Valsecito del cuarenta* (*Forties Waltz*) and *Sitio al Sitio* (*Make Room for Room*) – show him moving into a symbolic-expressionistic form in which he presents the world of the outcast and of the exploited victims of social abuse. Working in a Genet-like way in the trilogy *Con los pies en el agua* (*With Feet in the Water*), *Cercados y cercadores* (*The Besieged and the Besiegers*) and *Cuento del hombre que vendía globos* (*Tale of the Balloon Seller*), he exposes with acid cruelty the condition of the underprivileged of the world. His drama *Réquiem para siete plagas* (*Requiem for Seven Plagues*) is a mass of sorts synthesizing the miseries of the Peruvian people. Mention should also be made here of his short play *El mudo de la ventana* (*The Mute in the Window*), one of the most moving dramas in the national canon, about the loneliness of abandoned children, and of *El buzón y el aire* (*The Mailbox and the Air*), in which dialogue disappears entirely and is replaced by two fragmented monologues.

Estela Luna López made her reputation as a children's writer. Her works for adults tend to focus on human hypocrisy and irresponsibility towards the protection of life and the environment. *Pecadores a la hora del té* (*Sinners at Tea Time*), *El espacio* (*Space*), *El lobo viste mandil blanco* (*The Wolf is Wearing a White Apron*), *Eva no estuvo aún en el Paraíso* (*Eve Still Hasn't Been to Paradise*), *¿Qué tierra heredarán los mansos?* (*What Kind of Earth Shall the Meek Inherit?*) and *El hueso del horizonte* (*The Bone on the Horizon*) are direct allegations against, respectively, the subhuman living conditions that exist even as the human race is exploring outer space, corruption in the medical profession, the condition of women, pollution of the environment and the lack of support for young people.

Another writer who began her career in children's theatre is Sara Joffré. Also dedicated to exploring national problems, she has written about the abandonment of children in *Una obligación* (*An Obligation*). Her humanistic concerns were corroborated in *Pre-texto*

(Pre-Text), *Los tocadores de tambor* (*The Tambourine Players*), *Se consigue madera* (*Wood Is Found*) and *Al fondo hay sitio* (*There's Room at the Back*).

Alonso Alegría won Cuba's Casa de las Américas Prize for Latin American playwriting in 1969 for *El cruce sobre el Niágara* (*Crossing Niagara*), becoming the first Peruvian playwright to win an international award. Alegría had already won the Teatro Universitario de San Marcos Competition in 1968 for the same play, and was also considered a promising director. Director of the group Alba, which presented the first works of Sara Joffré, Alegría later moved to the United States where he lived until the late 1980s. Back in Perú, he committed most of his time to writing and teaching.

In *El cruce sobre el Niágara*, Alegría tells the story of the French tightrope walker Blondin, who crossed the Niagara Falls carrying a man on his shoulders. The play is essentially a dialectic between the decisions of the spirit and the physical strength necessary to carry them out. This play has been done internationally more than any other Peruvian work. Other significant works by Alegría include *Remigio, el huaquero* (*Remigio, the Huaco Digger*), winner of the National Theatre Award in 1965, and *El terno blanco* (1971), inspired by a story by Ray Bradbury. Both are technically strong, have dramatic depth and are accurate in projecting Perú's socio-political reality.

César Vega Herrera is another internationally distinguished Peruvian playwright. In 1976 he was given the Tirso de Molina Award for *¿Qué sucedió en Pazos?* (*What Happened in Pazos?*). In this play, as well as in *Un muchacho llamado Tim* and *La reina de la primavera* (*The Queen of Spring*), the language of the characters evokes the Third World. For this reason, the attempt by some to reduce his 1969 play *Ipacankure* to a type of Latin American *Waiting for Godot* would seem inappropriate and limited, while his *Arí, arí, guaguamundo* (*Yes, Yes, Son of the World*) borders on historical drama. Vega has also received the National Award for Children's Theatre and on several occasions has been awarded First Prize in the Teatro Universitario de San Marcos Competition.

Hernando Cortés began his theatrical career as an actor and director. In 1967 he wrote *La ciudad de los reyes* (*The City of Kings*), an epic succession of vignettes depicting the multiple faces of urban cruelty. A long monologue from the play – *Abusa usted de las cholas* (*You Are Taking Advantage of the Indian Women*) – is a perennial favourite of Peruvian actresses, who cannot resist the intense drama of this vigorous anatomization of inhumanity and exploitation. In his play *Verdadera crónica de la conquista del Perú* (*The True Account of the Conquest of Perú*, 1976), Cortés takes a look at history, denouncing the savagely adventurous character of the *conquistadores*. The play is written in an Artaudian style – for example, the native women are presented as horses in one scene. In *Tierra o muerte* (*Land or Death*, 1986), a child, a native, a *mestizo* and a traveller share a provincial jail cell. The older ones are witnesses to the torture of the child, as he is believed to be an accomplice to the rebels. The characters do not communicate clearly with each other because each speaks a different language. In the end, the child dies, his cries of agony becoming intertwined with those of a woman in labour.

Among the authors who inspired the Dramatists' Round Table, Aureo Sotelo Huerta (b. 1935) is another who slowly moved from children's theatre to theatre for adults. He was first known for the farce *El derecho de los asesinos* (*The Right of the Assassins*), a play prohibited by municipal authorities when it was first done at the Segura Theatre for posing 'a threat to state security'. Some of his plays, for example *La lluvia güena* (*The Gentle Rain*), which was lengthened into *El Huancapetí está negreando* (*The Huancapetí Is Turning Black*), explore agrarian themes.

Another member of the Round Table, Alberto Mego Márquez (b. 1954), alternates between writing plays for adults and writing plays for children. His social and political concerns are typical of 1970s writers. In 1973 he published *La cordura* (*Wisdom*), *La ceremonia* (*The Ceremony*) and *Patria o muerte* (*Fatherland or Death*), all irate, iconoclastic cries against injustice and abuse. The attitude becomes more radical in his later plays *Inkarri* and *Ushanam Jampi*, the latter an adaptation of a story by Enrique López Albújar. Disillusionment unifies his work: *Identikit* (1975), *Adiós, Señor Pérez* (*Goodbye, Mr Pérez*, 1977), *Adiós, compañeros* (*Goodbye, Friends*, 1978), *La última* (*The Last*, 1978) and *La obra debe continuar* (*The Show Must Go On*, 1979).

José Adolph creates a symbolic theatre, the focal point of which is sharp, scathing dialogue. His works present conceptual conflicts between recognizable Peruvian symbols. *Asedio y liberación del ciego y la parturienta* (*Siege and Liberation of the Blind Man and the Woman in Labour*) won the Teatro Universitario de San

Marcos Competition in 1977. It is a nihilistic and desolate portrait of the unsuccessful revolution of 1968. In *Trotsky debe morir* (*Trotsky Must Die*, winner of the Teatro Universitario de San Marcos Competition in 1979), Adolph displayed verbal pyrotechnics, while his 1985 play *Amigas* (*Friends*) won an Honourable Mention in the Manuel Ramos Competition for theatrical works about women. His indisputable talent and sharp critical vision have made him one of Perú's most respected dramatists.

Other writers who emerged in the 1970s and 1980s include Jorge Díaz Herrera (b. 1941), author of *Tiene miedo el oidor* (*The Judge is Afraid*, 1970), and César de María (b. 1960), who shared First Prize in the 1977 San Marcos Competition with Juan Rivera Saavedra for *Juvenil II* and later wrote *Miedo* (*Fear*), *La celda* (*The Cell*), *Hoy saldremos a las doce* (*Today We'll Go Out at Twelve*) and *Del bolsillo ajeno* (*From Someone Else's Pocket*). De María also worked with puppets with his group Politeatro, and wrote a number of energetic plays for children including *Mamotaro San*. Two younger writers of note are Luis Gómez Sánchez, author of *El gran giro* (*The Big Turn*), and Enrique Ráez Mendiola, author of *La rutina* (*The Routine*) as well as a musical revue of social criticism entitled *El rito del ratón* (*The Ritual of the Rat*) and a play about the revolution of Atusparia called *El canto de los siemprevivos* (*The Song of the Ever-Living*).

Nicolás Yerovi (b. 1951), the grandson of Leonidas Yerovi, is a playwright who moves between making fun of himself and making fun of others. He has edited a humourous magazine that his grandfather had formerly directed: *Monos y monadas* (*Monkeys and Monkey Business*). In 1980, along with Rafael León, Yerovi created *La divina comedia* (*The Divine Comedy*), directed by Fedor Larco, which premièred in 1981 in the Cocolido Theatre in Miraflores. Four characters made popular in *Monos y monadas*, two members of the bourgeoisie and two from the lower classes, show a total inability to understand one another. After the success of this play, the group put on two works based on local memories of the neighbourhood: *Bienvenido amor* (*Welcome Love*) and *Adiós amor* (*Goodbye Love*). Again, a lack of comprehension among various social classes is clear. It is seen again in *Hasta que la vida nos separe* (*Till Life Do Us Part*, 1984), about two couples whose commitments end up being intertwined.

Among other playwrights of note who should be mentioned in this general stocktaking are Julio Ramón Ribeyro, Edgardo Pérez Luna (b. 1928), Víctor Zavala Cataño and Mario Vargas Llosa, the novelist and politician who also wrote two children's plays of note, *La señorita de Tacna* (*The Girl from Tacna*, 1981) and *Kathie y el hipopótamo* (*Kathie and the Hippopotamus*, 1983).

Directors, Directing and Production Styles

Despite the growth of collective theatre, many excellent Peruvian directors emerged in the 1970s and most were still working in the 1990s. Carlos Padilla Pardo, a graduate of the Institutio Nacional Superior de Artes Dramático who later studied in Brazil, emerged as one of the most creative directors in the country. His sensual, Baroque style was unmistakable, as seen in *Eros-Orestiada*, which deals with the eternal battle between the Apollonian and the Dionysian. Padilla has also directed political works including *Mariana Pineda* by García Lorca, and *El tío Mac Pato y la píldora* (*Uncle Mac Duck and the Pill*) by Augusto Boal. Founder of the group Comunidad de Lima (Community of Lima), he produced with them in 1984 a staging of Gabriel García Márquez's *Cándida Eréndira y su abuela desalmada* (*Cándida Eréndira and Her Cruel Grandmother*).

José Carlos Urteaga, an actor with Cuatrotablas, began to direct with the group Magia, which he helped to create in 1983. He trains his own actors and specializes in one-person plays. Among his large-cast plays, his most successful have been *Piantao*, a theatrical dance with the Argentine Astor Piazzola's music, and two works based on Oscar Wilde – *The Party* (a free version of *Lady Windermere's Fan*) and *Salomé*. His production of *El ahogado más hermoso del mundo* (*The Most Beautiful Drowned Person in the World*) by Gabriel García Márquez was also presented in Cuba.

Ruth Escudero is the founding director of Quinta Rueda, not so much a feminist group as a group interested in discussing problems related to the situation of women or couples. Another talented director who worked with the group was Alicia Saco, trained at the Caragiale Institute in Bucharest.

Perhaps Perú's most iconoclastic director is Ricardo Santa Cruz, director of the group Raíces. Beginning his career in collective creations with Cuatrotablas, Santa Cruz's physical and verbal style break with most models of theatre. After mounting Santa Cruz's *Sol y sombra* (*Sun and Shadow*) and *Trozos de vida* (*Slices of Life*), Raíces's efforts crystallized in *Baño de pueblo* (*Town Bath*), an exploration of images of torture and repression that confront spectators with modern tragedy. With minimal text and consciously forced relationships, his actors, using a kind of calculated violence, bear painful witness to issues that are very close to home for audiences.

Alfonso Santistevan, a director, actor and author who also worked for a time with Cuatrotablas, has staged a number of experimental versions of classics, reflecting in the process Perú's contemporary reality. In *El caballo del libertador* (*The Horse of the Liberator*, 1986), death and terror arrive at the house of an old man and a pregnant native woman. Their desperation in this case is an analogy for modern Perú. The same connection is made in his *Pequeños héroes* (*Small Heroes*, 1987).

One of Perú's most spectacular directors is Ricardo Roca Rey, a man of the theatre whose work includes research on the history of Peruvian theatre. His presentations of religious plays in the open air of the atrium of the Cathedral of Lima and the Church of San Francisco are clear examples of the spectacular nature of his productions – movement by masses of people, choruses and individual characters. These plays represent Roca Rey's desire to take culture to the people.

Others have also followed in this style – the group Histrión did when it performed Ibsen's *An Enemy of the People* in the Plaza de Armas in Chincha, and Jorge Chiarella Kruger staged

Maeterlinck's *The Blue Bird* in 1979 in the Plaza de Toros in Acho. The Maeterlinck play involved simultaneous scenes in the vast expanse of a bullring and included an apparition of God among a flight of doves.

Reynaldo D'Amore Black, however, developed a Stanislavskian production style and helped to introduce the method of this Russian director to Perú. His teaching and developmental work, in fact, tended to replace his important work as a director in the late 1980s. He is particularly important for his work on the plays of young authors, presenting such works as *En el cielo no hay petróleo* (*There's No Gas in Heaven*) by Salazar Bondy, and *Pruvonena* by José Miguel Oviedo.

José and Carlos Velásquez both cultivate a very lively, histrionic stage style that also requires large spaces. In each of their productions, these brothers caricature national forms of conduct, even in the case of classical plays such as Ben Jonson's *Volpone*.

The group Histrión has been among the most international and avant-garde in style. Among its many interesting productions have been *Six Characters in Search of an Author* by Luigi Pirandello; *Revolution in South America*, the play that first introduced Augusto Boal to Perú; *The Bullfrog* by Armand Gatti; *Vida y pasión de Santiago el pajarero* by Ribeyro; *El fabricante de deudas* and *La escuela de los chismes* by Salazar Bondy; *La chicha está fermentando* by del Carpio; *Los del cuatro* by Díaz; *López Von Braun* by Schul and especially *Marat/Sade* (1968) by Peter Weiss, directed by Sergio Arau.

Music Theatre
Dance Theatre

One of Perú's few theatre groups working in the area of musical theatre is Yuyachkani, which presented *Los hijos de Sandino* (*The Sons of Sandino*, 1981), about the revolution in Nicaragua, where they also presented the play. Upon their return, they created *Los músicos ambulantes* (*The Strolling Minstrels*, 1983), a light, very sharp and well-acted testimony to the migration of people from the provinces to Lima, pushed by the misery created by a centralist system. Musical rhythms represent the different regions of Perú, united by the same poverty that

is shared by all the country's poor. *Los músicos ambulantes* is popular theatre with a fresh, direct style. Acting as an ambassador for Peruvian theatre, the group has performed this play in sixteen countries.

The musical style of Yuyachkani was also used in the ambitious project *Encuentro de zorros* (*Meeting of Foxes*), created in collaboration with Peter Elmore. In this play, the theme of identity, so important to the group, is dealt with in an even more complex manner than in their earlier work.

Another director whose work is closely connected to that of Yuyachkani is Willy Pinto. Staging works based on the situation of migrants from the provinces, his major productions include *El cuento del botón* (*The Story of the Button*) and *Ande por las calles* (*Walk the Streets*).

Theatre for Young Audiences
Puppet Theatre

The history of children's theatre in Perú began with the efforts of Guillermo Ugarte Chamorro, founder of the Precocidad (Precocious Theatre, 1935), and Ernesto Gassols, founder of the Peruvian Children's Company (1935). Also important was the work of the Asociación de Artistas Aficionados, founded in 1938, which presented plays for children.

In the 1960s, a youth group called Alba (Dawn) was created, and presented, among other works, *En el jardín de Mónica* (*In Monica's Garden*, 1962) by Sara Joffré. In 1964, Estela Luna López presented her science fiction piece *Los monstruos del espacio* (*The Space Monsters*) with the group Histrión. *Pecadores a la hora del té*, by the same author, expresses the indignation of youth when faced with the hypocrisy of adults.

In 1963, Joffré created a new company, Homer – Teatro de Grillos, a group that lasted until 1981 and also published all the works it performed. Yego, a group concerned with the problems of young people, directed by Carlos Clavo, was formed in 1967. It was a successful attempt at creating theatre by, about and for young people.

In 1974, Telba celebrated its fifth anniversary by organizing the First Festival and Seminar of Children's Theatre, an important competition that brought together children's theatre and puppet groups from across the country to discuss technical concepts and make practical proposals for improvements in the field.

Jorge Chiarella Kruger emerged from this festival as a major director in the field and it is he who has been the force behind the most popular show for children on Peruvian television, *La casa de cartón* (*The Cardboard House*), produced by the Instituto Nacional de Teleducación (National Institute of Teleducation). The three subsequent festivals organized by Telba during the 1970s introduced a number of important authors of children's plays: Chiarella himself; Celeste Viale, Ismael Contreras and Ernesto Ráez Mendiola.

Also in the 1970s, Estela Luna López began to create new children's stories for the stage. Verbally fluid and tremendously imaginative, her play *Flor de retama* (*The Broom Flower*) first brought her to national attention. Others of her major plays in this genre include *Las arenas doradas* (*The Golden Sands*), *Viaje a la capital* (*Trip to the Capital*) and *La papa de oro* (*The Golden Potato*).

Among her plays for adolescents have been *El joven príncipe* (*The Young Prince*), while her *Eva no estuvo aún en el Paraíso*, produced by Los Grillos and directed by Sara Joffré, provoked a battle between feminists and antifeminists in the audience.

In 1975 the Centro Cultural Nosotros (Cultural Centre 'Us'), coordinated by Myriam Reátegui, also inaugurated a series of cultural, recreational and creative activities for children. These included musical comedies such as *La casita bonita* (*The Pretty Little House*) and *El rey pomposo* (*The Pompous King*). In *El rey de los animales* (*King of the Animals*), songs and costumes typical of Perú were used and this play became a form of street theatre.

In the area of puppet theatre, leaders include Gastón and Vicky Aramayo from the group Kusi Kusi, and Marcela Marroquín and Felipe Rivas Mendo, from the Peruvian Puppet Institute.

The creations of Jorge Acuna are outstanding in the area of pantomime, as are those of Juan Piqueras. Emilio Vásquez Galli, who worked for several years in Paris, is another important promoter of Peruvian mime.

Design
Theatre Space and Architecture

The first theatre building in Lima dates from the late sixteenth century, among the earliest on the continent. Over the next four centuries, many others were built, most following European styles. In the late twentieth century, the municipality of Lima has three theatre buildings: the Municipal, the Manuel A. Segura, and the Sala Alcedo. The Instituto Nacional de la Cultura (National Institute of Culture) administers the Salazar Bondy Theatre. Independent groups such as Yuyachkani, Cuatrotablas, Histrión, the AAA, and the Club de Teatro, now in the Lima suburb of Miraflores, also have their own facilities. Los Grillos have given their centre in San Joaquín to the group Raíces. Other independent groups, such as Magia and Nosotros, rent spaces in which to work.

Companies run by impresarios tend to have the best permanent facilities. Argentine-born actor Oswaldo Cattone has used the Marsano Theatre while Horacio Paredes presented his shows in the Royal Theatre. The actor Tito Salas worked in the Miraflores Auditorium. The Larco Theatre in Miraflores and the Harlequín in Jesús María are other private establishments rented out by owners.

Foreign cultural associations in Perú also rent out valuable facilities: the Alliance Française in Lima and Miraflores, the Peruvian–North American Cultural Centres in Lima and Miraflores, the Peruvian–Russian Cultural Centre in Jesús María, the Goethe Institute in Jesús María, the Italian Cultural Institute, which has both a small hall and the Antonio Raymondi Theatre, and the British Theatre in Miraflores.

Municipal spaces in the provinces are gener-

César Toledano's costume design for Martín Moscoso's 1995 Salazar Bondy Theatre production of García Lorca's *The Love of Don Perlimplín With Belisa in His Garden.*

ally used as cinemas but touring groups do play in them. They charge high rents, however, and are usually poorly equipped. The best installations in the country are the auditoriums in schools, universities and parish halls.

Given the poor facilities and high costs, it is not surprising that many groups prefer outdoor forms of theatre, including street theatre, which do not require extensive set-ups or rents.

Training
Criticism, Scholarship and Publishing

The training of Peruvian actors is done both by professional companies and in university theatres. Most of the country's major actors have developed in this way.

There are also two national theatre schools: the Instituto Nacional de Arte Escénico

(National Institute of Theatre Arts, founded in 1945 as the Escuela Nacional de Arte Escénico), run for many years by the actor and director Alfredo Ormeño Felice, and the Escuela Regional de Arte Dramático (Regional School of Dramatic Arts) in Trujillo, under the direction of

produced mostly by Spanish-born residents and visitors for a very educated and wealthy class, identified for the most part with the Spanish monarchy. The plays imitated the styles and themes of the Spanish theatre of the time. Although there is a long list of names and titles from this time, none has had significant literary or artistic influence on the contemporary theatre. During this period there is also evidence of church censorship of theatre as well as of segregated theatre practices.

In the mid-nineteenth century, two *criollos* (people of Spanish ancestry born in the Americas) began to produce works with elements of a genuine national sentiment. Alejandro Tapia y Rivera (1826–82) and Salvador Brau (1842–1912) dealt in their work with social problems such as racism and the social inferiority of women as well as with historical issues. To avoid censorship, Tapia located his plays outside Puerto Rico. The peasant theatre of Ramón Méndez Quiñones (1847–89) was also part of the folkloric current of the time. His theatre was created specifically for an educated *criollo* class.

The political change of 1898 – some have called it an occupation – after the US won the Spanish–American War, brought to the theatre new themes as well as an attempt at inculcating US values. The result was an ongoing debate over national identity and crises over cultural values, language and the role of art. This was a socially oriented theatre, attempting to show Puerto Rico's multiple faces from many different perspectives, while at the same time carrying a strong message of national liberation. The great interest in social movements during the 1980s also brought back to life a little-known workers' theatre group that had been operated during the first decades of the century by, among others, Luisa Capetillo (1879–1922), an outstanding figure of the time, known for her contribution to the social struggle and her feminist ideas.

By the beginning of the Spanish Civil War in 1936, direct connections between the Spanish stage and Puerto Rico were severed since Spanish groups could not easily travel. Puerto Rican groups took centre stage.

The year 1938 was of great importance in the development of Puerto Rican theatre for it marked the beginning of a dramaturgy of genuine national character. Three key plays in this regard – winners of a competition organized that year by the Teatro del Ateneo Puertorriqueño (Theatre of the Puerto Rican Cultural Association) – were *El clamor de los surcos* (*The Clamour of the Furrow*) by Manuel Méndez Ballester (b. 1909), *Esta noche juega el jóker* (*The Joker Plays Tonight*) by Fernando Sierra Berdecía (1903–62) and *El desmonte* (*The Felling*) by Gonzalo Arocho del Toro (1898–1954). Another outstanding playwright of this time was Emilio S. Belaval (1909–72), founder of the company Areyto.

All these writers differed from those of previous decades in their nationalistic views of Puerto Rican values following the political change of 1898. Still another writer of note was Luis Rechani Agrait (b. 1902), author of *Mi señoría* (*My Lordship*, 1948), a comedy criticizing corruption and the political system.

After World War II, Puerto Rico had ceased being simply an agrarian economy; because of war needs it had become industrialized. Operation Bootstrap was an economic plan, sponsored by the United States, that allowed for this sudden development, which turned the island into a societal showcase, a model, it was hoped, for the rest of Latin America. This process was both successful and traumatic, causing the displacement of a large agrarian population into slums in the metropolitan area and beginning constant migration to the US. This process can be seen in the play *La carreta* (*The Oxcart*), a Puerto Rican theatre classic written by René Marqués (1919–79) in 1952.

Cultural organizations also felt the impact of this economic development. The Ateneo Puertorriqueño (founded in 1876) intensified its theatre programme and established a short-lived experimental theatre project in 1952; the new Commonwealth of Puerto Rico established its own cultural programme in 1955, which in 1958 began an annual festival. These two projects – together with the founding of the Teatro Universitario (University Theatre) in 1941, and the creation of the department of drama at the University of Puerto Rico in Río Piedras – were the most significant contributors to the growth of theatre during the 1940s and 1950s.

Francisco Arriví (b. 1915) and René Marqués, who became two of the most respected and well-known playwrights in Puerto Rico, also made their débuts during the 1940s. The former explored themes of indigenous identity and racial prejudice in plays such as *Sirena* (*Mermaid*, 1957) and *Vejigantes* (*Masquerade*, 1958). Marqués's play *Los soles truncos* (*The Truncated Suns*, 1957) experimented with flashbacks and dream sequences while accusing the US of attempting to destroy the land and its culture. Both writers used poetic as well as colloquial language, experimented with time and space, and mixed realistic techniques with those of existentialism and the absurd.

Among those writers who followed Arriví and Marqués, Luis Rafael Sánchez (b. 1936) and Myrna Casas (b. 1934) are among the most important. Casas's work relies on absurdist techniques to speak about individual repression. Sánchez's works include dramas such as *La pasión según Antígona Pérez* (*The Passion of Antígona Pérez*, 1968), a Latin American adaptation of the Antigone story, and *Quíntuples* (*Quintuplets*, 1984) a variation on the ideas of Pirandello's *Six Characters in Search of an Author*.

The rebellious energy of the 1960s in Puerto Rico coincided with political turmoil in Latin America, the Vietnam War (meaning conscription on the island) and the emergence of a revitalized Puerto Rican statehood party. This decade of social and political uproar and cultural changes also saw the birth of many new theatre groups, which took on the role previously played by these individual dramatists. The ideological spirit of the times affected social relations in theatre as well as modes of production.

Theatre took to the streets and union halls; it became a mouthpiece for social and political causes; it developed within groups (Anamú, 1969–75; Moriviví, 1971–5), breaking the authority of the text, the author and the director; it attempted collective creation or coauthorship. Many plays were site, situation and audience specific. Others had massive audiences. Since pieces stressed other theatrical languages over text (puppets, songs, masks and mime) many pieces were not scripted. Theatrical activity was significant, urgent and vital.

Major dramatists of the 1970s included Lydia Milagros González (b. 1942), director of El Tajo de Alacrán (The Scorpion's Bite, 1966), whose one-acts were evidence of the strength of the farcical language of this period; Pedro Santaliz (b. 1938), director of El Nuevo Teatro Pobre de América (The New Poor Theatre of America, 1967), who worked with dream sequences and performed in open spaces, and Jaime Carrero (b. 1931), the most conventional of the three. Carrero's *Flag Inside* (1972) is based on the true story of a Puerto Rican soldier

Gilda Navarra's 1980 Taller de Histriones production of her mime drama *The Woman With a Fan*, costumes by Gloria Sáez.

admission), though tickets to some productions at the Teatro de Bellas Artes (Fine Arts Theatre) or the Teatro Tapia went as high as $25.

In the context of theatre activity in Puerto Rico, festivals are quite important. The Festival de Teatro Puertorriqueño, sponsored by the Instituto de Cultura Puertorriqueña, has offered additional production opportunities to playwrights and has helped educate theatre audiences. Other festivals, such as the Festival de Teatro Internacional (International Theatre Festival, founded in 1966) and the Festival de Teatro de Vanguardia (Avant-Garde Theatre Festival, founded in 1967), are also sponsored by the institute. Since 1984 these have been joined by the Temporadas de Teatro Experi-

mental and the Festival de Nuevos Dramaturgos (New Playwrights' Festival), which continue to encourage developing writers. Beside these, universities organize their own festivals, such as the Festival de Teatro Latinoamericano (FESTELAT; Latin American Theatre Festival), organized since 1991 by the drama department and the cultural activities programme at the University of Puerto Rico.

The Sociedad Nacional de Autores (National Writers' Association) represents dramatists in Puerto Rico.

In 1994 there were ten fully equipped theatres on the island, six of them owned by the government and four operating independently; this includes the university theatres.

Artistic Profile

Companies

Areyto, founded in 1939 by Emilio S. Belaval, was the first Puerto Rican company to produce plays that responded to the idea of a national theatre. Its manifesto emphasized the need to create Puerto Rican characters, situations and landscapes for the stage. Although it lasted only until 1941, the spirit of Areyto has inspired many of the most important theatre companies and groups since then.

One company following Areyto's lead was El Tajo de Alacrán, which existed from 1966 to 1975 and was directed by Lydia Milagros González. The company toured the island and created its own plays about specific social and political problems. El Tajo de Alacrán also paved the way for the development of many street theatre groups such as Anamú and Morivivi that followed.

El Nuevo Teatro Pobre de América was begun in 1967 by Pedro Santaliz, a director and writer of alternative political theatre, who was still directing the group in 1994. The group takes its theatre pieces to poor neighbourhoods and disadvantaged areas. The company has also travelled regularly to New York to produce for the Puerto Rican community there.

In 1963 actress Iris Martínez and producer Norberto Kerner opened La Tierruca, a café-theatre dedicated to the production of theatrical experiments, poetry and song. Its success prompted the establishment of similar projects in both San Juan and other cities. The most

prominent of these was La Tea (The Torch), operated by Abelardo Ceide, who provided space for talented and later very well-known performers such as Sunshine Logroño and Antonio Pantojas and even wrote cabaret pieces for them. La Tea closed in the early 1980s.

Among the more stable companies, El Teatro del Sesenta is still the most popular. First connected to the University of Puerto Rico, it later became independent. Under artistic directors José Félix Gómez (b. 1948) and Idalia Pérez Garay (b. 1946), the company has become known for its productions of both Latin American and Puerto Rican scripts. Among its most notable productions have been *Puerto Rico Fua* (1974) and *La verdadera historia de Pedro Navaja* (*The True Story of Pedro Navaja*, 1980), a musical revived in 1994.

The Teatro Experimental del Ateneo has operated since its foundation in 1952 under the direction of José Lacomba (b. 1922). Until the early 1990s, when the company lost its space, it produced two or three plays per season. The Teatro Rodante, founded in 1945, did many open-air stagings and is best known for its productions of Spanish golden age classics directed by Dean Zayas (b. 1939), and for experimental stagings, often directed by José Luis Ramos Escobar.

During the early 1980s a truly experimental theatre group, El corral de la Cruz (The Cruz Corral) staged reinterpretations of classics such as *Macbeth*, Peter Handke's *Kaspar* and J.M. Synge's *Riders to the Sea* in a dilapidated movie

Rosa Luisa Márquez and Antonio Martorell's 1993 production of *Foto-estáticas*.
Photo: M. Villafañe.

the *sainete Bill Jones* (1916), by Cristóbal Real (1873–1966) and Evaristo Rivera Chevremont (1896–1976). It is an irreverent look at the political changes of 1898 and the legal consequences. Just after World War II, an outstanding two-act *zarzuela*, *El misterio del castillo* (*The Castle's Mystery*, 1946), was written by Manuel Méndez Ballester, with music by the well-known composer Arturo Somohano (1910–77). Another was *Cofresí* (1949) by the poet Gustavo Palés Matos (1907–63), with music by the popular composer Rafael Hernández (1891–1965). Both of these *zarzuelas* attempt to make this a nationalist genre.

Two quite popular shows with music were *Puerto Rico Fua* and *La verdadera historia de Pedro Navaja*, both produced by Teatro del Sesenta. The former, written by Carlos Ferrari (b. 1931 in Argentina), attempted to show the

José Félix Gómez's 1994 Teatro del Sesenta production of *La verdadera historia de Pedro Navaja*, designed by Pedro Juan Texidor and Idalia Pérez Garay.
Photo: Joe Colón.

history of Puerto Rico through a diversity of social-satirical situations. The latter, a collective work, was a *criollo* adaptation by Pablo Cabrera of Bertolt Brecht's *Die Dreigroschenoper* (*The Threepenny Opera*, 1980). This production – entertainment with a social message – became a critical and box-office success, with a run of sixteen weeks and revivals in 1984 and 1994.

In the 1980s, the company Nuestro Teatro (Our Theatre) also entered the musical arena, again showing Ferrari to be a master of musical farces with social commentary.

As for dance theatre, Puerto Rico's Ballets de San Juan has been operating since 1958. An academy, it produces two professional programmes each season. The Ballet Folklórico de Puerto Rico regularly tours the island and has been seen abroad as well.

In dance theatre groups, the emphasis is on the actor's body and in this respect the mime work of Gilda Navarra with Taller de Histriones has been important. For fourteen years in the 1970s and 1980s, the group produced a piece per year using a highly codified kind of modern dance. Navarra became well known for her mime dramas *Ocho mujeres* (*Eight Women*, 1974), based on García Lorca, and *Asíntota* (1976), based on Dante's *Inferno*.

During the 1990s the most outstanding work was that of Viveca Vázquez, who staged multimedia experimental work and since 1990 has produced a biennial marathon of new pieces called *Rompeforma* (*Form Breaker*), based on body movement and post-modern dance.

The Ballets de San Juan was founded by Ana García and Gilda Navarra in 1954. Although it began as a company devoted to Spanish dance forms, it has added both classical and neoclassical ballets as well as some modern and experimental work. The repertoire has included works by George Balanchine as well as by native choreographers. Librettos, musical scores, costumes and décor are by native Puerto Ricans.

Two professional ballet companies were formed in the 1970s. Ballet Concierto de Puerto Rico, headed by Lolita San Miguel, focuses on full-length classical ballets. Ballet Teatro Municipal de San Juan, directed by Juan Anduze, tends more towards Latin American choreographers.

There are also small individual groups of experimental choreographers, some of whom deal with social and political issues while others concentrate on improvisation.

Theatre for Young Audiences
Puppet Theatre

The longest-standing theatre company for young audiences has been Arlequín (founded in 1961), directed by Maricusa Ornés (b. 1929 in the Dominican Republic), who as early as 1952 was running the Academia de Artes Escénicas de Santo Domingo (Academy of Performing Arts of Santo Domingo) for children. Arlequín was still operating in 1994.

An even earlier venture – the Teatro Infantil Universitario (University Children's Theatre) – began in 1946 and was later known as the Comedieta Universitaria (University Comedy). Founded by its longtime director Leopoldo Santiago Lavandero (b. 1912), the company ceased operation in 1964. Still another early effort was the Instituto de Cultura Puertorriqueña's own festival of children's theatre, which operated through the 1950s and into the 1960s.

Despite this activity, most theatre for young audiences remains very commercialized. Most playwrights who have written for young people have not developed special plays for children but rather have simply adapted classic stories for the stage. This has been the case with Edwin Pabellón (b. 1963), who, from the mid-1980s, has been very successful with his adaptations of Hans Christian Andersen's *The Ugly Duckling* (1986) and the traditional *La cucarachita Martina* (*Martina, the Little Cockroach*, 1991), based on the original stories of the same names.

In 1960, Santiago Lavandero created children's theatre workshops for the Department of Public Education. This led to the creation of the Compañía Teatral de Maestros (Teachers' Theatre Company) and the Teatro de Títeres (Puppet Theatre, founded in 1957), which was

Rey Pascual's 1992 Teatro del Sesenta T60 on Wheels production of Osvaldo Cintron's AIDS prevention play, *Meta mano … es cuestión de bregar!*, designed by Miguel Vando, puppets by Carmen Romero.
Photo: Willy Echevarria.

exclusively on text, often searching for some manifestation of the national identity. This explains why a text such as René Marqués's *La muerte no entrará en palacio* (*Death Will Not Enter the Palace*, 1957) created such great academic interest even before its first production in the 1980s at the Puerto Rican Travelling Theatre in New York.

The most comprehensive history of Puerto Rican theatre is *Literatura puertorriqueña: su proceso en el tiempo* (*Puerto Rican Literature: Its Development Through Time*, 1983), written by Josefina Rivera de Alvárez (b. *c.*1920). A useful doctoral dissertation on the island's theatre is Angelina Morfi's (1920–89) *Historia crítica de un siglo de teatro puertorriqueño* (*Critical History of a Century of Puerto Rican Theatre*, 1980), in which she discusses and sums up a large selection of plays including Marqués's.

Matías Montes Huidobro's (b. 1930 in Cuba) book *Persona: vida y máscara del teatro puertorriqueño* (*Persona: Life and Image of the Puerto Rican Theatre*, 1986) is a detailed study of the most common themes in the work of the best known playwrights of the twentieth century, including Luis Rafael Sánchez. Nilda González's (b. 1912) *Bibliografía del teatro puertorriqueño* (*Bibliography of Puerto Rican Theatre*, 1979) is useful in identifying nineteenth- and twentieth-century theatre companies, authors, premières, book reviews and research.

Rosalina Perales has published two useful volumes of information on theatre and drama throughout Latin America from 1967 to 1987, *Teatro hispanoamericano contemporáneo* (*Contemporary Spanish-American Theatre*, 1989, 1993). The second volume has a chapter dedicated to contemporary Puerto Rican theatre.

The publication *Intermedio* (*Intermission*) operated in 1985–6 but was discontinued due to lack of funds. Even so, its founding editors – Roberto Ramos Perea, José Luis Ramos Escobar and Edgar Quiles Ferrer (b. 1946) – managed to create new interest in Puerto Rican theatre from the 1970s and the beginning of the 1980s.

The Fundación René Marqués (René Marqués Foundation), created in 1983, has a bibliographic archive as well as a collection of newspaper articles about theatre activity in the country. It is one of the most important theatre research centres on the island.

Grace Dávila-López
Translated by Mayte Gómez

(See also UNITED STATES OF AMERICA)

Further Reading

Arriví, Francisco. *Conciencia puertorriqueña del teatro contemporáneo: 1937–56.* [Puerto Rican conscience in the contemporary theatre: 1937–56]. San Juan: Instituto de Cultura Puertorriqueña, 1967. 207 pp.

——. 'Evolución del autor dramático puertorriqueño a partir de 1938'. [Evolution of the Puerto Rican playwright from 1938]. Chap. in *Areyto Mayor.* San Juan: Instituto de Cultura Puertorriqueña, 1966.

Arroyo de Hernández, Anita. 'Instantáneas del teatro en Puerto Rico'. [Impressions of theatre in Puerto Rico]. *Revista del Instituto de Cultura Puertorriqueña* 9, no. 32 (July–September 1966): 17–22.

Babín, María Teresa. 'Veinte años de teatro puertorriqueño'. [Twenty years of Puerto Rican theatre]. *Asomante* 20, no. 4 (October–December 1964): 7–20.

Braschi, Wilfredo. *Apuntes sobre el teatro puertorriqueño.* [Notes on Puerto Rican theatre]. San Juan: Coqui, 1970. 111 pp.

Collins, J.A. *Contemporary Theatre in Puerto Rico: The Decade of the Seventies.* Río Piedras: Editorial Universitaria, 1982. 178 pp.

Cypess, Sandra Messinger. 'Women Dramatists of Puerto Rico'. *Revista/Review Interamericana* 9, no. 1 (spring 1979): 24–41.

Falcón, Rafael. 'El tema de la emigración a Nueva York en el teatro puertorriqueño'. [Emigration to New York as a theme in Puerto Rican theatre]. *Revista de la Crítica Literaria Latinoamericana* 18 (1983): 97–106.

García del Toro, Antonio. *Mujer y patria en la dramaturgia puertorriqueña: proyecciones del sentimiento patrio en la figura de la mujer como protagonista de la dramaturgia puertorriqueña.* [Women and homeland in Puerto Rican plays: Projections of patriotism and women as protagonists in Puerto Rican theatre]. Madrid: Playor, 1987. 267 pp.

González, Nilda. *Bibliografía del teatro puertorriqueño (siglos XIX y XX).* [Bibliography of Puerto Rican theatre (nineteenth and twentieth centuries)]. Río Piedras: Editorial Universitaria, 1979. 223 pp.

La gran enciclopedia de Puerto Rico. Vol 6: *Teatro/Religión.* San Juan: Ediciones R, 1976. s.v. 'El teatro en Puerto Rico'. [Theatre in Puerto Rico], by Angelina Morfi.

Manrique Cabrera, Francisco. 'De los treinta al presente: el teatro'. [From the 1930s to the present: The theatre]. In *Historia de la literatura puertorriqueña.* [History of Puerto Rican literature], 326–37. Río Piedras: Cultural, 1971.

Márquez, Juan L. 'Crítica y teatro en Puerto Rico: una propuesta para su revitalización'. [Theatre and criticism in Puerto Rico: A proposal for its revitalization]. *Revista del Instituto de Cultura Puertorriqueña* 59 (1973): 9–14.

Márquez, Rosa Luisa. *Brincos y saltos: el juego como disciplina teatral.* [Leaps and bounds: Play as theatrical discipline]. San Juan: Ediciones Cuicaloca, 1992.

Meléndez, Priscilla. 'Teoría teatral y teatro puertorriqueño de los 80'. [Dramatic theory and Puerto Rican theatre in the 1980s]. *Latin American Theatre Review* 25, no. 2 (spring 1992): 151–67.

Montes Huidobro, Matías. *Persona: vida y máscara del teatro puertorriqueño.* [Persona: Life and image of the Puerto Rican theatre]. San Juan: Instituto de Cultura Puertorriqueña, 1986. 631 pp.

Morfi, Angelina. *Historia crítica de un siglo de teatro puertorriqueño.* [Critical history of a century of Puerto Rican theatre]. San Juan: Instituto de Cultura Puertorriqueña, 1980. 569 pp.

Navarra, Gilda. *Polimnia: Taller de Histriones, 1971–1985.* [Polimnia: Players' Workshop, 1971–85]. Barcelona: 1988. 200 pp.

Pasarell, Emilio J. *Orígenes y desarrollo de la pasión teatral en Puerto Rico.* [Origins and development of theatrical passion in Puerto Rico]. 2 vols. Río Piedras: Editorial Universitaria, 1967.

Quiles Ferrer, Edgar H. *Teatro puertorriqueño en acción (dramaturgia y escenificación) 1982–9.* [Puerto Rican theatre in action (dramaturgy and production) 1982–9]. San Juan: Ateneo Puertorriqueño, 1990.

Ramos Perea, Roberto. *Perspectivas de la nueva dramaturgia puertorriqueña: ensayos sobre el nuevo teatro nacional.* [Perspectives on the new Puerto Rican drama: Essays on the new national theatre]. Cuadernos del Ateneo Collection, Theatre Series no. 1. San Juan: Ateneo Puertorriqueño, 1989. 93 pp.

Rivera de Alvárez, Josefina. *Literatura puertorriqueña: su proceso en el tiempo.* [Puerto Rican literature: Its development through time]. Madrid: Ediciones Partenon, 1983. 953 pp.

Saez, Antonia. *El teatro en Puerto Rico: notas para su historia.* [Notes for the history of Puerto Rican theatre]. 2nd ed. San Juan: Editorial Universitaria, 1972. 134 pp.

ST KITTS AND NEVIS

(see **COMMONWEALTH CARIBBEAN**)

ST LUCIA

(see **COMMONWEALTH CARIBBEAN**)

TRINIDAD AND TOBAGO

(see **COMMONWEALTH CARIBBEAN**)

UNITED STATES
OF AMERICA

A federal democratic republic, the United States is comprised of fifty states and the District of Columbia (where the capital, Washington, is located). All states except Hawaii are in the North American land mass although the US has jurisdiction over islands in the Pacific Ocean and West Indies, as well as an association with the free commonwealth of Puerto Rico. The total area of all US states and jurisdiction is more than 9.4 million square kilometres (3.6 million square miles). Although the official language is English, almost every other language and dialect in the world is spoken somewhere in the US; Spanish is the second most commonly spoken language.

Other than the native Americans (also called American Indians), residents of what is now the US since the sixteenth century have been either immigrants or descendants of immigrants from every part of the world (initially primarily from England and Spain), descendants of enslaved Africans, or descendants of intermarriage among these three groups. Although most contemporary US citizens who profess a religious belief are Christian, virtually all other religious beliefs are observed, as is atheism. The American Revolution of 1775–83 separated the original colonies from British rule and began the establishment of a confederation of states under a constitution guaranteeing, among other rights, freedom of religious expression and the separation of church and state. The population of the United States grew from 131.6 million in 1940 to 255.6 million in 1992, with the majority now living in urban areas.

The US theatre has been shaped by individuals and cultural forces more than by governmental institutions or edicts. Other than for several years in the 1930s, the US government has granted funding to theatre only since

1965; no theatres or artists are fully subsidized by the government. It can be said that US society was imprinted from its beginnings by revolutionary and pioneering ethics, individualism and multiculturalism, elements that have also long characterized the US theatre.

US theatre history has seen over 200 years of variations on tensions between regional and/or 'alternative' theatre efforts on the one hand, and a theatrical 'capital' or 'mainstream' on the other. Early on, theatre spread across the country but eventually began to be controlled from New York City by monopolistic Broadway producers. In the post-World War II period, it diversified once again into a mosaic of regional and culturally specific theatres. Non-controversial mainstream fare has therefore always been in a dialectical tension with alternative fare. In colonial days, productions of Shakespeare coexisted with dramatic dialogues read in private drawing rooms to spread revolutionary sentiments. In the 1990s, productions in large regional theatres of critically sanctioned dramas coexist with productions in small theatres of plays that generally challenge political, social and aesthetic norms. Historically, the smaller alternative experiments have stimulated change in the mainstream theatre, while regional theatre creativity has stimulated change in the more commercially oriented Broadway theatres. Conversely, the well-funded mainstream and Broadway theatre regularly challenge alternative theatre by serving as a showcase for the nation's most skilled and well-known artists.

The United States' theatre continually invents, absorbs and discards, bearing in mind market-place pressures. And capitalism awards more status to theatres and artists who make money, especially those who become big 'stars', as opposed to those who work for more aesthetic or socially beneficial ends. In the 1990s, an actor well known from film and/or television is often a greater asset to a theatre production than an actor of greater skill, because the former can attract audiences. Still, contemporary US theatre is more active, more widely spread geographically, and more expressive of a broad range of cultural voices than ever before.

Prior to the establishment of the first English colony in 1607, many native American tribes performed theatrical events, and Spanish drama was presented as early as the late 1500s. There was little other theatrical activity in the generally Puritan English colonies before the mid-eighteenth century, and some colonies actually prohibited theatre on religious grounds. A British company toured beginning in 1737, then splintered into several new companies after the Revolutionary War. As the population spread westward from the Atlantic Ocean, touring circuits operated along major riverways. Theatre then followed the new railroads as well as the populace across the continent; an intercontinental railroad was completed in 1869. There continued to be relatively little theatre activity in the southern states, however, where the population's dispersal across rural farms and plantations inhibited large public gatherings. Some municipalities also forbade theatre productions for fear that fires would start in the wooden buildings that housed them.

By the mid-nineteenth century, though, there were more than fifty professional theatre companies in the US, most based in regional population centres. These companies toured to the many auditoriums constructed across the country. Alongside them, new waves of European and Asian immigrants created their own ethnic theatre in most major cities, and stars regularly visited from abroad. US stars, such as Edwin Forrest (1806–72), Edwin Booth (1833–93) and Charlotte Cushman (1816–76), also emerged. At this time, the 'combination company' was devised, by which a show began in New York with stars and a set, then toured cross-country by rail, hiring local talent in supporting roles, precipitating the ultimate demise of many regional companies.

The Theatrical Syndicate, a coalition of six New York producers, booking agents and theatre owners, was formed in 1898. Owners of almost all the theatre houses in New York as well as those 'on the road', the Syndicate ultimately constituted a virtual monopoly of US theatre. Syndicate producers would usually open shows in their New York houses, then send them on the road in combination companies. By the end of the nineteenth century, New York dominated US theatre with only eight resident companies remaining elsewhere. A few defiant New York producers, however, such as Minnie Maddern Fiske (1864–1932), struggled independently of the Theatrical Syndicate to produce theatre of high artistic quality and to introduce challenging new drama, such as Shaw and Ibsen, to the US public. The Shubert brothers (Sam, 1877–1905; Lee, 1875–1953; and Jacob, 1879–1963) finally broke the Syndicate's hold in New York in 1912–13, then bought several road houses, beginning their own eventual control of much US commercial theatre.

Countering New York control was the emergence across the country of 'little theatres', especially following World War I; these produced new European plays and classics alongside Broadway hits. Like Fiske's Manhattan Theatre Company in New York, Hull-House Theatre and Maurice Browne's (1881–1955) Little Theatre in Chicago, the Toy Theatre in Boston, the Cleveland Playhouse (Ohio) and the Pasadena Playhouse (California) all aspired to emphasize theatre artistry over commercialism. Soon after these little theatres took root nationwide, college and university theatre departments began developing and expanding. In little theatres and university theatres, the fare was usually a combination of Shakespeare, Renaissance classics, eighteenth-century British comedies and the works of modern 'masters' such as Shaw.

The stock market crash in 1929 severely depressed the entire US theatre. In the 1930s, the government's Works Progress Administration (WPA) created jobs that put people to work in ways that benefited the country, on new highways and dams as well as on arts and crafts projects. In 1935, WPA hired Hallie Flanagan (1890–1969) to direct the Federal Theatre Project, which paid artists to create productions all over the country at accessible prices; it eventually staged over 1,200 productions to over 30 million people. The Federal Theatre Project's many units – living newspapers, Negro groups, new plays, experimental production techniques, vaudeville, children's plays and others – employed thousands of people and generated plays about most aspects of US life. Although the overwhelming majority of its fare was not controversial, some living newspaper productions, such as *Triple-A Plowed Under* (1936), a leftist commentary on US agriculture, brought the project under attack. Public outcry followed the 1936 dramatization of Sinclair Lewis's (1885–1951) novel *It Can't Happen Here*, about fascism in the US, which was premièred simultaneously in seventeen cities. The US Congress also forbade production of Marc Blitzstein's (1905–64) call to revolution, *The Cradle Will Rock* (1937). Because it was perceived that the Federal Theatre Project was promoting communist propaganda, Congress terminated the project in 1939. Nevertheless, the Federal Theatre Project laid the cornerstone for the government arts funding that began in the 1960s, as well as for regionally based, non-profit theatre.

In the war years of the 1940s, most US theatre activity was once again centred in New York. The US musical theatre came of age at this time with the first show that integrated story and song, Richard Rodgers (1902–79) and Oscar Hammerstein II's (1895–1960) *Oklahoma!* (1943). In 1946, the Tony Awards, named after wartime theatre leader Antoinette Perry (1888–1946) were established for the season's top production in New York. Outside Broadway, only a few theatres attempted non-commercial approaches. One of Tennessee Williams's (1911–83) early poetic plays was nourished first in the 1940s in Dallas, Texas, by Margo Jones (1913–55) and her Theatre-in-the-Round and only then brought to Broadway, prefiguring the practice common at the end of the twentieth century of developing a play in a regional theatre, then taking it to New York.

As Broadway claimed the centre of US commercial theatre after World War II, more alternatives to Broadway developed in small theatres in other parts of Manhattan. Called 'Off' Broadway for both their geographical distance from the Broadway theatre district and their more experimental dramatic fare and production techniques, many of these groups pioneered new approaches to US drama, acting and scenography. Also in the post-war era the Actors Studio, begun in 1947 in Manhattan, developed a distinctively US realistic performance style. The group's artistic heritage dated back to the Washington Square Players (1914–18), one of Manhattan's most influential little theatres. Some of Washington Square's founders, led by Lawrence Langner (1890–1962), formed the Theatre Guild in 1918, which produced significant new US drama for decades, premièring Eugene O'Neill (1888–1953), Elmer Rice (1892–1967), Sherwood Anderson (1876–1941) and Robert E. Sherwood (1869–1955), among others, and introduced the notion of audience subscriptions to seasons of plays. The Guild's influence lasted until after World War II.

In 1931, the Group Theatre formed as an experimental offshoot of the Theatre Guild, aiming to create a theatre with a political voice, as opposed to the apolitical Guild, and a permanent acting company. The Group Theatre's members included directors Harold Clurman (1901–80), Lee Strasberg (1901–82) and Elia Kazan (b. 1909), with actors Stella Adler (1903–92) and Morris Carnovsky (1897–1992), playwright Clifford Odets (1906–63), producer Cheryl Crawford (1902–86), and others. Strasberg and Adler in particular were eager to introduce acting techniques based on the teachings of Konstantin Stanislavski, whose Moscow Art Theatre made a powerful impression with its naturalistic stagings when it toured the US in 1923–4. The Group Theatre was dissolved in 1939.

In 1949, a number of small groups began to form a League of Off-Broadway Theatres. By 1950, the average cost of a non-musical Broadway production had risen to $80,000, compared to a mere $5,000 required Off-Broadway. In New York, the Circle in the Square Theatre, begun by José Quintero (b. 1924), Theodore Mann (b. 1924) and others in 1950, staged an acclaimed revival of Williams's *Summer and Smoke* in 1952 (the play had failed on Broadway); the production made Off-Broadway a serious artistic and box-office venture. Joseph Papp (1921–91) began the New York Shakespeare Festival in 1954, and it quickly developed into another major multifaceted Off-Broadway production company. By the mid-1950s, more than ninety Off-Broadway groups were operating.

Also beginning in the early 1950s, people could obtain inexpensive entertainment easily through television or movies. As the population expanded and more people pursued college educations, the economy expanded and theatre came out of the dark tunnel of the Depression and the war years. Professional theatre development outside New York also began in earnest. Among the major pioneers were the Alley Theatre (Houston, Texas, 1947), founded by Nina Vance (1915–80); the Arena Stage (Washington, DC), founded by Edward Mangum (b. 1913) and Zelda (b. 1924) and Thomas C. (b. 1915) Fichandler; the Milwaukee (Wisconsin) Repertory Theater, founded in 1954 by Mary John; and the Academy Theatre (Atlanta, Georgia), founded in 1956 by Frank Wittow (b. 1930).

Just after the war, as US theatre tried honestly to address contemporary issues, the House of Representatives Un-American Activities Committee began to hold hearings into possible communist infiltration of the entertainment industry. These hearings led to the blacklisting of artists suspected of communist sympathies, intimidated theatre pioneers and ruined a number of careers. The height of these investigations was in 1953–4, when Wisconsin Senator Joseph McCarthy (1908–57) pursued US citizens with leftist leanings to unprecedented lengths, before being censured himself by the Senate. This scare also discouraged debate in the theatre. Yet this congressional avenue for unofficially censoring theatre was similar to the one used in the 1930s to end the Federal Theatre Project, and it continues into the 1990s with regular attacks by legislators on the annual budget of the National Endowment for the Arts (NEA).

There were as well several groups and individuals in the 1950s who developed theatres that supported European avant-garde dramatists such as Eugène Ionesco, Samuel Beckett, Jean-Paul Sartre, Luigi Pirandello and Bertolt Brecht, along with jazz events, happenings, 'beat' poetry and non-representational art. Jules Irving's (1924–79) and Herbert Blau's (b. 1926) Actors' Theatre in San Francisco (1952) brought poets, dancers, philosophers and musicians together. Café Cino (New York, 1958) was the beginning of Off-Off-Broadway theatre, which welcomed a blending of happenings, music, poetry and politics.

Julian Beck's (1925–85) and Judith Malina's (b. 1926) Living Theatre introduced the ideas of Antonin Artaud and was among the first of Off-Off-Broadway's political theatres. The San Francisco Mime Troupe began in 1959 and mixed traditional *commedia dell'arte* with US cartoon sensibility to create a liberal agitprop theatre.

Many US theatre artists at this time preferred regional theatres to Broadway. As well, the country shifted from paradigms established by the early Anglo-American hegemony into the diverse values and aesthetics of a multiracial and multicultural nation. Together with this regionalization emerged new voices from the feminist, gay, Chicano, Amer-Asian, native American, deaf, regional/folk, and other communities.

In 1959, W. McNeil Lowry (1913–93) led the Ford Foundation in funding these regional professional theatres, inspiring philanthropy from other private foundations. These efforts paved the way for the creation of the National Endowment for the Arts in 1965, which began with a total of $5 million for all the arts but by 1994 was giving out $78 million annually.

Changes in training, rehearsal, production style and scenography also marked the experiments of the 1960s. Collectives and ensembles dedicated to 'alternative' theatre, rather than traditionally scripted drama, explored techniques imported by devotees of Artaud, Jerzy Grotowski, Peter Brook and others. US theatre experimented as never before with audience–performer relationships, often setting theatrical events in public spaces and non-theatrical environments, surrounding audiences or interspersing performers among audience members. Directors also became more influential, sculpting the theatrical event with actors, environments and/or scenography. The 'performance text' often dominated the traditionally scripted text. Theatre began to emphasize a dense aural and visual design, combining poetic language, music and soundscapes with visual effects, utilizing new technologies and de-emphasizing linear cause and effect.

Edward Albee's (b. 1928) *Zoo Story*, produced in New York in 1959, is considered the first US 'absurdist' drama. Inspired by the new European theatre, in the 1990s it was also recognized as a pioneering work in gay theatre. Peter Schumann (b. 1934) began his Bread and Puppet Theatre in New York in 1961; in the 1990s it continued to combine mask, music and celebration with spiritual and political messages. Ellen Stewart (b. 1920) began Café La MaMa in New York in 1962, which continued to nurture experiments in the 1990s.

Joseph Chaikin (b. 1935), Roberta Sklar (b. 1940) and others created the Open Theatre in New York in 1963, combining political views with 'transformational' acting that broke with Stanislavskian character-based performance. Many Open Theatre members had studied with Nola Chilton, who developed sound and movement exercises divorced from emotional expression for actors to use in performing absurdist theatre. The Open Theatre enabled actors' bodies to transform elastically from character to object to metaphor, and it enabled actors to play roles outside their character 'type'. What began as a laboratory developed into a collective producing theatre. Its production of Jean-Claude Van Itallie's (b. 1936) *America Hurrah!* in 1966 successfully combined its unusual performance style with social commentary.

Richard Schechner (b. 1934) and his Performance Group (New York, 1968) experimented with theatrical environments, disruptions of conventional character–audience relationships, theatre that verges on ritual ecstatic experience, and cross-gender casting, all of which were incorporated into the US theatre vocabulary by the mid-1990s. Richard Foreman (b. 1937) began his Ontological-Hysteric Theatre in New York in 1968, which playfully altered perceptions of space and language. Influenced by the poet Gertrude Stein (1874–1946), his early plays, such as *Total Recall (Sophia=Wisdom): Part 2* (1970) and *Hotel China* (1971), introduced his highly formalistic uses of displacement, ritual, fragmentation and repetition, all of which have joined the currency of postmodernism. Mabou Mines was begun in 1969 by Lee Breuer (b. 1937), JoAnne Akalaitis (b. 1937), Ruth Maleczech (b. 1939), David Warrilow (b. 1934) and composer Philip Glass (b. 1937). Their highly original triptych of 'animations' (comic fables featuring animals as central characters) – *The Red Horse Animation* (1970), *The B-Beaver Animation* (1974) and *The Shaggy Dog Animation* (1978) – were also pioneers in post-modern theatre sensibility.

In 1968, Robert Wilson (b. 1941) created in New York his epic 'theatre of images', which manipulated images and time in startling new ways. Combining his training in visual arts with his personal experiences in speech therapy, Wilson's early collage *The King of Spain* (1969) slowed action so that the audience could 'enter' his visual images.

The 1960s were not just a time of upheaval. There was significant continuity in some US styles that might now be seen as 'classical'. Neil Simon (b. 1927) began writing comedy in 1961, and continues to contribute new work to Broadway that sells out in theatres all over the country. Edward Albee's *Who's Afraid of Virginia Woolf?* (1962) and Arthur Miller's (b. 1915) *After the Fall* (1964) continued the genre of powerful US social realism. The Tyrone Guthrie Theatre was established in Minneapolis in 1963 to build a repertory theatre of classically trained actors to perform the best of the world's dramatic literature.

In the 1970s and 1980s, US theatre gave greater attention than ever before to new plays, and to the expansion and development of theatre in locales outside New York. One of the leaders in this movement was the Eugene O'Neill Memorial Theatre Center in Waterford, Connecticut, a new play development centre founded in 1963 by George C. White (b. 1935) and Lloyd Richards (b. 1923). Regional theatres also found success with new work from the Long Wharf Theatre under Arvin Brown (b. 1940) in New Haven, the Actors Theatre of Louisville under Jon Jory (b. 1938), Theatre Atlanta, and the Mark Taper Forum in Los Angeles. By the 1990s, Pulitzer Prizes had, in fact, been given more often to plays originating in the regional theatres than to those originating on Broadway, beginning with Arena Stage's production *The Great White Hope*, starring James Earl Jones (b. 1931). The institution of televised production through the television

The Mark Taper Forum in Los Angeles, designed by Welton Beckett.
Photo: Courtesy Mark Taper Forum.

station WNET's 'Theatre in America' series, begun in 1973, also helped spur appreciation for contemporary US theatre.

Some producers merged conventional practices with new ones to buffer the financial risks of new plays. Joe Papp successfully opened the ensemble-created musical *A Chorus Line* (1975) in his Off-Broadway Public Theater (founded in 1966), then took it to Broadway where it scored financially, which helped finance the Public Theater's other new projects. This pattern of beginning a show in a non-profit theatre and moving it into the profitable realm of Broadway had become common by the 1990s.

Regional theatres also began developing their own programming and audience bases, creating plays not intended for New York. Theatre in Chicago, for example, became more local and topical with the creation of the popular Second City improvisation comedy troupe. Chicago theatre came into its own in the late 1970s with the emergence of a major regional institution, the Goodman Theatre (founded in 1925;

revitalized in 1969); and playwright-director David Mamet's (b. 1947) work, which captured Chicago's aggressively visceral and athletic style, often associated with the Steppenwolf Theatre Company, founded in 1976. Other groups such as Victory Gardens, founded in 1974, also nurture Chicago-area writers.

Ethnic theatre developments in the 1970s and 1980s included a Native American Theatre Ensemble (NATE), spearheaded by writer-director Hanay Geiogamah (b. 1945) and sponsored by La MaMa, which toured the US and Europe before splintering into some regionally and tribally based troupes in the late 1970s. The first National Hispanic Theatre Conference (San Antonio, 1986) drew more than 150 US and Puerto Rican groups. Mixed Blood Theatre Company was founded by Jack Reuler (b. 1953) in Minneapolis in 1976 as a multiracial theatre while Tisa Chang (b. 1945) founded the Pan Asian Repertory Theatre in New York in 1977, adding a resident ensemble in 1987, to produce the work of Asian-American playwrights as well as to translate Asian masterpieces into English and innovatively adapt western classics.

In addition to these assertions of ethnic cultural diversity, over 100 women's theatres, many of them collectives, explored the implications of creating a vocabulary from the new feminist consciousness. Women active in the experimental theatres of the 1960s were often most instrumental in beginning these feminist theatres, such as Martha Boesing (b. 1936), who co-created At the Foot of the Mountain in Minneapolis; the Open Theatre's Roberta Sklar, who directed and developed scripts with performer Sondra Segal for Womanrite Theatre Ensemble in New York; and Muriel Miguel, who co-founded the Spiderwoman Theatre Workshop.

Other feminist groups of note include Maxine Klein's (b. 1934) Little Flags Theatre Collective in Boston, which created political musicals, and Karen Malpede's (b. 1945) New Cycle Theatre in Brooklyn, which delved into women's history. Susan Ogden Malouf's Role Over Theatre in Minneapolis explored stereotypes in gender, race, class and physical disability. The work of several feminist companies affected the gender referents of US drama generally and supported greater participation for female theatre artists, some of whom now direct large theatres.

Paralleling women's liberation was the gay theatre movement, giving voice to the gay and lesbian experience and combating homophobia. Some feminist theatres were lesbian in their orientation, such as Lavender Cellar in Minneapolis, Red Dyke in Atlanta and Rites of Women in Philadelphia. Split Britches, a lesbian collective in New York's East Village, introduced a witty blend of lesbian feminist politics and post-modern textual deconstruction.

One of the first gay theatres, the Other Side of Silence (1972–7), was formed by Doric Wilson (b. 1939), who had been a member of the earlier Café Cino. The Glines Company premièred gay plays in all genres, including Jane Chambers's (1937–83) Last Summer at Bluefish Cove (1980). Enough gay theatres organized in major cities to form a Gay Theatre Alliance in 1978, their missions usually being like that of Los Angeles' Celebration Theatre (1982): 'to entertain and enlighten and to combat homophobia, not only in the straight world but also amongst homosexuals.'

What had been a marginalized subject entered the mainstream when in 1982 Harvey Fierstein's (b. 1954) autobiographical Torch Song Trilogy (1981), in which the author also performed, won a Tony and several other drama awards, after having been nurtured at La MaMa in previous years. The gay political movement and theatres were challenged by the rise to epidemic proportions in the 1980s of acquired immune deficiency syndrome (AIDS), which claimed many gay theatre artists' lives. By the 1990s, AIDS had become the most persistent and significant subject for gay theatre. Tony Kushner's (b. 1956) AIDS-themed 1993 and 1994 Tony Award-winning play Angels in America: Millennium Approaches and Perestroika emerged from the gay theatre movement, regional theatres (it was developed at the Eureka Theatre in San Francisco, then staged at the Mark Taper Forum in Los Angeles, and in England, before being produced in New York), and the staging experiments of past decades.

Truly new directions in US theatre were few after the explosive 1960s, but Bill Irwin's (b. 1950) 'new vaudeville' (Regard of Flight, 1977) integrated mime and physical humour with an intellectual, post-modern attitude and content. Where once theatre aesthetics drew firm boundaries between drama and other performance forms, experimental work since the 1960s has not only blurred those boundaries but also embraced the commonalities among all performance forms, from parades and rodeos to vaudeville and circuses. One of the most popular theatrical entertainments in the United States in the 1990s was a circus without animals, Le Cirque du Soleil (Circus of the Sun, originally from Montréal), which combined circus gymnastics and clowning with elements of story and character.

Cornerstone Theatre, begun in 1986, committed itself to communities, and stages productions that bring people together across race, age, class and other invisible boundaries; its 1989 production in a small Mississippi town of Romeo and Juliet brought together black and white teenagers in a dynamic revelation of that play's social core.

Although US theatre at the end of the twentieth century is no longer the cultural force it once was, having been eclipsed by film, television and popular music (recorded and in concert), it is still an integral part of the formation and reflection of the vast country's psyche.

African-American Theatre

When fifty African slaves disembarked from French ships in Florida in 1564, African culture, ritual, music and dance disembarked with them, and while it has changed over 400 years, it has continually enriched both the white and the black United States. Topsy, when asked in the novel *Uncle Tom's Cabin* (1852) who her parents were, replied that she had none, that she had 'jes grew'. This is also so with black folk culture: its musicians, street performers, church singers and riverboat roustabouts will remain forever unknown, but their songs, dances and verbal play remain a seminal force in US theatre.

A second branch – the literary 'race' drama that African Americans created in order to 'advance', as well as entertain themselves – left a traceable lineage. In 1821, William Henry Brown established the African Grove Theatre in New York City, where he produced not only Shakespeare, but also *The Drama of King Shotaway* (1823), the first play written by an African American. Following the theatre's demise in 1823, the literary tradition remained more or less dormant, with the exception of an ex-slave, William Wells Brown (1819–84), who wrote an abolitionist melodrama, *The Escape; or A Leap for Freedom* (1858). The literary tradition blossomed again in the 'Harlem renaissance' of the 1920s, when African-American writers published their plays and criticism, and received recognition from the white world. The intellectuals, particularly W.E.B. Du Bois (1868–1963), Alain Locke (1886–1954) and James Weldon Johnson (1871–1938), consciously and forcefully nourished literary 'race' drama, insisting that Negro drama be by, about, for and near Negroes. Performed in art and community theatres by amateur thespians such as the Krigwa Players, this genre embraced plays about lynchings, birth control and patriotism.

A third genre – commercial theatre – drew on both the 'jes grew' of the folk culture and the literary 'race' drama of the intellectuals. Its career began with speciality acts like that of William Henry Lane (*c.*1825–52), who danced as 'Juba' in the Georgia Champion Minstrels (1845). After the Civil War (1861–5), speciality acts evolved into African-American minstrel troupes, which developed into the ragtime musicals of the 1890s. Finally, in the 1920s, came the 'black' musicals, beginning with *Shuffle Along* (1921) and ending with *Blackbirds of 1928*. During the same jazz decade, black playwrights Willis Richardson (1889–1977), author of *The Chipwoman's Fortune* (1923), Garland Anderson (1887–1939), author of *Appearances* (1925), and Wallace Thurman (1902–34), author of *Harlem* (1929), appeared on Broadway. However, long runs for Negro playwrights waited another decade for Langston Hughes's (1902–67) *Mulatto* (1935) and Richard Wright's (1908–60) *Native Son* (1941).

In the United States during the decades prior to World War II racial segregation enjoyed legal status. Negro theatre, as it was called in the 1930s, suffered from segregation; white authors wrote plays with all-Negro casts – Marc Connelly's (1890–1980) *The Green Pastures* (1930) and *Porgy and Bess* (1935), by Du Bose (1885–1940) and Dorothy (1890–1961) Heyward with music by George Gershwin (1898–1937) – and in commercial houses, audiences remained segregated; on stage, Negroes played servants or slaves, and Negro playwrights were relegated to community theatre and college productions. Ironically, the Depression gave African Americans an opportunity to earn a living while learning stage

The comic Dewey 'Pigmeat' Markham at the Apollo Theatre, Harlem, in the 1930s.
Photo: Courtesy Hatch-Billops Collection.

crafts. The Federal Theatre Project established sixteen segregated Negro Units for the production of plays by or about African Americans. When Congress closed the project, many blacks had been trained in backstage technology and theatre management as well as in acting, writing and directing.

In 1940, Frederick O'Neal (1905–92) and Abram Hill (1910–86) founded the most renowned African-American theatre group of the 1940s, the American Negro Theatre (ANT). Its constitution stated that Negroes brought a special gift to US theatre. Their small stage in the basement of a library in Harlem accommodated the blacks who made up the majority of its audiences; many of the plays authored by African Americans concerned black life – Theodore Browne's (1910–79) *Natural Man* (1941), Hill's *Walk Hard* (1944) and Owen Dodson's (1914–83) *Garden of Time* (1945). An impressive list of distinguished actors trained and taught at the ANT: Harry Belafonte (b. 1927), Sidney Poitier (b. 1924), Alice (1920–94) and Alvin (1908–86) Childress, Osceola Archer (*c.*1890–1983), Ruby Dee (b. 1923), Earle Hyman (b. 1926), Hilda Simms (b. 1920) and many others. The ANT's greatest success contributed to the group's demise – *Anna Lucasta* (1944), a drama originally about an immigrant Polish family written by Philip Yordan (b. 1914). Adapted for the ANT's black actors, the play was seen by director Harry Gribble (1896–1981), who saw its merits and took it to Broadway. The result: its best actors left the ANT for commercial work, and the spirit of community commitment to an art theatre changed to one of seeking personal, professional advancement.

The 1950s began auspiciously at the Club Baron in Harlem. Alice Childress, a director-actor trained at the American Negro Theatre, wrote a double bill, adapting Langston Hughes's *Just a Little Simple* and her own one-act, *Florence*, in 1950. In 1955, Childress's play *Trouble in Mind* won an Obie Award as the best Off-Broadway play produced that year. Author of nearly twenty plays, Childress wrote in the well-structured tradition of Lillian Hellman (1906–84), composing the most professionally crafted plays in black theatre. The best example is her one-act comedy-drama *Wine in the Wilderness* (1969), which adroitly weaves the issues of class, race and sexism into an intricate tapestry.

In African-American drama, the family play has also been a major genre, and the 1950s produced two of exceptional merit: Louis Peterson's (b. 1922) *Take a Giant Step* (1953) and Lorraine Hansberry's (1930–65) *A Raisin in the Sun* (1959), which became the first African-American play by a woman to reach Broadway. The director, Lloyd Richards, the first black to direct on Broadway, would return in the 1980s with three August Wilson (b. 1945) dramas. *A Raisin in the Sun* remains the most widely recognized African-American play, perhaps because it endorsed the aspiration for a middle-class life, a dream that white audiences shared. Although Hansberry wrote several other dramas – an integrationist work, *The Sign in Sidney Brustein's Window* (1964); a dramatic examination of neo-colonialism in Africa, *Les Blancs* (1970); and an autobiographical play, *To Be Young, Gifted and Black* (1971) – none achieved the success of her first effort, which in 1973 was adapted by her husband, Robert Nemiroff (d. 1991), into the musical *Raisin*.

The change that presaged the Hansberry triumph had been the US Supreme Court's 1954 ruling that school segregation was illegal. The Greenwich Mews staged Loften Mitchell's (b. 1919) *Land Beyond the River* (1957), a successful dramatization of the court's decision. Other civil rights plays appeared: Ossie Davis's (b. 1917) *Montgomery Footprints* (1956), C. Bernard Jackson's (b. 1915) and James Hatch's (b. 1928) *Fly Blackbird* (1962) and James Baldwin's (1924–87) *Blues for Mister Charlie* (1964). *Purlie Victorious* (1961), virtually the only comedy on a civil rights theme, starred its author, Ossie Davis, and his wife, Ruby Dee. This successful play later became the basis of the musical *Purlie* (1970).

Obie Award-winning playwright Imamu Amiri Baraka (LeRoi Jones, b. 1934), with his one-act *Dutchman* (1964), followed by his furious plays *The Toilet* (1964), *The Slave* (1964) and *The Baptism* (1964), initiated a militant black theatre in the late 1960s and 1970s. With increasing political and racial consciousness, Baraka moved to Harlem in 1965 to found the Black Arts Repertory Theatre/School, which excluded from its classes and productions all people except blacks, a policy that angered those white organizations that funded the school. In 1966, Baraka moved to New Jersey to start his own community theatre, Spirit House; there he produced his own plays and poetry.

For his episodic *No Place to Be Somebody* (1970), Charles Gordone (b. 1925) became the first African-American dramatist to win the Pulitzer Prize. His play dramatized the dilemma facing many blacks in the 1960s: to choose Malcolm X's (Malcolm Little, 1925–65) racial solidarity and separation, or to join Martin Luther King's (1929–68) struggle for an integrated society. Gordone's commercial success, coupled with that of Hansberry and Baraka, inspired literally hundreds of activists to write plays. Between 1964 and 1974, over 600 African-American theatre companies across the United States sprang into existence. The majority were housed in universities and community theatres; some survived the next decade, but most lasted only a year or two.

An exception was the Inner City Cultural Center of Los Angeles, founded in 1965. In the mid-1990s, the organization was still pursuing its original mission: to train minority youth in the theatre arts and to present plays that have relevance to their lives. Their best known 'graduate' is George C. Wolfe (b. 1955), who would later head New York's Public Theater.

Another early regional theatre grew out of the Tougaloo Drama Workshop in Mississippi. Gilbert Moses (b. 1942), Doris Derby and John O'Neal (b. 1940) christened themselves the Free Southern Theatre (1963–80) and toured Mississippi and Louisiana. Most of their short didactic skits shaped messages of self-pride for rural audiences, many of whom in seeing the Free Southern Theatre witnessed a live stage performance for the first time.

Producing groups sprang up in every major city. In 1968, Val and Francis Ward founded Kuumba in Chicago. They celebrated their twenty-fifth anniversary in 1993. Kuumba, meaning 'to celebrate', has served the black community much as the South Side Community Center did in the 1930s and 1940s, providing a space for the creative arts.

On the east coast in 1965, Robert Hooks (b. 1937) produced Douglas Turner Ward's (b. 1930) Day of Absence and Happy Ending. Two years later Ward, as artistic director, and Hooks, as executive director, joined with Gerald Krone (b. 1933), as administrative director, to charter the Negro Ensemble Company. They assembled a group of experienced actors at the St Marks Playhouse and conducted actors' workshops, held readings of new scripts and mounted four or five major shows a year.

Except for its first production, Song of the Lusitanian Bogey (1967) by Peter Weiss, all of the scripts staged by the group over the next twenty years were by blacks – American, Caribbean and African. Some became critical successes: The River Niger (1972) by Joseph

Walker (b. 1935) won a Tony Award for the best play on Broadway; The First Breeze of Summer (1975) by Leslie Lee (b. 1935) won an Obie as the best Off-Broadway drama; and A Soldier's Play (1981) by Charles H. Fuller, Jr (b. 1939), won the Pulitzer Prize. Phillip Hayes Dean's (b. 1939) Sty of the Blind Pig (1971) won a Drama Desk Award. Realism dominated the Negro Ensemble Company's style in acting, writing and production; audiences greeted the company's more experimental efforts with less enthusiasm.

The New Lafayette Theatre (1966–72) initially opened in a church that had been the site of the old Lafayette Theatre in Harlem. Its prime mover, Robert Macbeth (b. 1934), while working in a Kennedy-era poverty programme, had directed Ron Milner's (b. 1938) Who's Got His Own (1967) and Athol Fugard's Blood Knot (1967). A year later, Macbeth brought together a new company, including several playwrights: Richard Wesley (b. 1945), who would edit their publication Black Theatre Magazine (1968–72); Sonny Jim Gaines (b. 1928) – What If It Had Turned Up Heads (1972); Martha Charles – Jamimma (1971); and Ed Bullins (b. 1935), who wrote nearly fifty plays, winning an Obie Award for The Fabulous Miss Marie (1971) and a Critics Circle Award for The Taking of Miss Janie (1975). In his plays Bullins brought to the stage a gallery of 'street' people who spoke with diction not previously heard in the US theatre. For a decade, Bullins was the most produced and discussed playwright in black theatre.

Macbeth also created a series of 'rituals' including A Black Time for Black Folk (1970), The Devil Catchers (1970) and The Psychic Pretenders (1971). Embracing music, improvisation, poetry and dance, the rituals invited their audiences to enter the spiritual realm of their African ancestors. The company closed in 1972, but it had been a leader in setting a militant mood for African-American theatre across the nation.

National Black Theatre was founded in 1968 in Harlem by actress Barbara Ann Teer (b. 1937). Its primary mission was to 'raise the level of consciousness through liberating the spirits and strengthening the minds of its people'.

One of the country's most interesting black directors, Vinnette Carroll (b. 1922), head of the Urban Arts Corps, nurtured performer-writer Micki Grant (b. 1941) and took her revue Don't Bother Me, I Can't Cope (1970) to Broadway. Carroll, Grant and Alex Bradford (1926–78)

then conceived *Your Arm's Too Short to Box with God* (1975), a gospel musical. This form of African-American theatre derived from the black church. Whites had long admired gospel performance, beginning with the concert tours of the Fisk Jubilee Singers in 1871. In the 1920s, the concert tours of Marian Anderson (1902–93) and Roland Hayes (1887–1977), who always concluded their performances with spirituals, had further popularized the form. The transition from black church to the commercial stage of Broadway occurred when white audiences flocked to hear Hall Johnson's (1888–1970) choir in *The Green Pastures*. The gospel-musical form was enlarged by Langston Hughes's *Black Nativity* (1961), *Tambourines to Glory* (1963) and *The Prodigal Son* (1965). Lee Breuer and Bob Telson's (b. 1949) *The Gospel at Colonus* (1983), an adaptation of Sophocles' *Oedipus at Colonus*, may be the most unusual example of the genre. It toured Europe and returned to play on Broadway in 1988. One of the most frequently performed gospel plays has been an adaptation of James Weldon Johnson's *God's Trombones*, written in 1927. Vy Higginsen's *Mama I Want to Sing* (1980) holds the record for the single longest running gospel show – eight years.

Hazel Bryant (1939–83) came to New York in 1963 to establish the Afro American Total Theatre. Later renamed the Richard Allen Center, her theatre produced an eclectic variety of works from gospel to a highly acclaimed all-black *Long Day's Journey into Night* (1981). Bryant served as secretary of the Black Theatre Alliance (1969–82), a not-for-profit umbrella group for struggling black theatres. The alliance developed new programmes and funds, held an annual theatre festival, published a quarterly newsletter and provided workshops in management and technical theatre. At one time, seventy-five theatre and dance companies belonged, fifty-two of them in New York.

In 1963, Woody King, Jr (b. 1937) left Detroit to make his career in New York. He persuaded the Henry Street Settlement House to give the New Federal Theatre a home; for nearly thirty years it served the community of the lower east side. His production of J.E. Franklin's (b. 1937) *Black Girl* (1969) toured eighty-five universities and colleges. King developed Ron Milner's *What the Wine Sellers Buy* (1973), which later played at Lincoln Center. Among King's Broadway successes are *Checkmates* (1988) by Milner, and Ntozake Shange's (Paulette Williams, b. 1948) *For Colored Girls*

Who Have Considered Suicide/When the Rainbow is Enuf (1976).

The actress Rosetta Le Noire (b. 1911) celebrated 'the unification of all peoples' by creating the AMAS Musical Theatre (1969–92). Emphasizing its multicultural workshops for children, adults and senior citizens, AMAS (Latin for 'you love') produced a number of in-house as well as professional shows, including musicals based on African-American theatre history. *Bubbling Brown Sugar* (1975), written by Loften Mitchell and Le Noire, played on Broadway and in London, bringing to the stage impressions of the famous black musical entertainers from the first half of the twentieth century.

The movement of the 1960s and 1970s generated its own drama critics. The leading theorists were Larry Neal (b. 1937), whose essays, collected in *Visions of a Liberated Future* (1989), were widely read, and Addison Gayle (1932–91), an academic at City University of New York, whose books *The Black Situation* (1969) and *The Black Aesthetic* (1971) were influential among artists, as were essays published in the journal *Home* by poet-playwright Amiri Baraka.

Adrienne Kennedy's (b. 1931) *Funnyhouse of a Negro* (1963), directed by Edward Albee, won an Obie Award and established her as a poet of the theatre. Three other surrealistic one-acts followed in 1965: *The Owl Answers*, *The Rat's Mass* and *Cities in Bezique*, written in a style of visual and aural metaphors that invited the viewer to weave her images together into dramatic meaning.

The newer playwrights of the 1980s reflected diverse styles, addressing race, gender and class through deconstruction of incident and event. Suzan-Lori Parks (b. 1963) seized upon the assassination of Abraham Lincoln (1809–65) for *The American Play* (1993). She used a traditional music structure of theme and variation in lieu of plot development, much as she had done in her previous play, *The Death of the Last Black Man in the Whole Entire World* (1990). Robbie McCauley (b. 1942) and Anna Deavere Smith (b. 1950) both performed in their own plays. McCauley's *Sally's Rape* (1989) received an Obie Award in 1992.

August Wilson's plays, *Ma Rainey's Black Bottom* (1984), *Fences* (1987), *Joe Turner's Come and Gone* (1988), *The Piano Lesson* (1990) and *Two Trains Running* (1992) were all workshopped by director Lloyd Richards at the Eugene O'Neill National Playwrights'

Marcus Stern's 1994 American Repertory Theatre production of Suzan-Lori Parks's *The American Play*, set design by Allison Koturbash, costume design by Gail Buckley. Photo: T. Charles Erickson, courtesy ART.

Conference before travelling to several regional theatres and then on to Broadway. Once on Broadway, they won two Pulitzer Prizes and two Tony Awards. Wilson hoped to create a series of dramas that traced urban working-class life from the 1920s to the 1960s.

Wilson came to the public's attention at Lou Bellamy's Penumbra Theatre in St Paul, Minnesota, one of several vital regional African-American theatres. Others in the 1990s include Jomandi Productions in Atlanta, Black Repertory in St Louis, Freedom Theatre in Philadelphia, and Crossroads Theatre in New Jersey (1976), which premièred George C. Wolfe's *The Colored Museum* (1986).

Wolfe's career rose rapidly with his Broadway musical *Jelly's Last Jam* (1992), which broke new ground by presenting a central character, a black ragtime-jazz musician, Jelly Roll Morton (1885–1941), as an egotistic, racist, unsympathetic hero. Wolfe later directed Tony Kushner's

Tony Award and Pulitzer Prize plays *Angels in America*.

James V. Hatch

Chicano Theatre

Mexican Americans, also known as Chicanos, form the largest group of Hispanics in the United States. Historians have posited that the Chicano was 'born' when the land encompassing what are now the states of Arizona, California, Colorado, Nevada, New Mexico and Texas was ceded by México at the conclusion of the Mexican–American War in 1848. These people, who had previously considered themselves Spanish, Mexicans or Californios, were suddenly foreigners in their own land: they did not come to the United States, the United States came to them. Instantly marginalized, the newly created foreigners relied on their religious beliefs, their cultural production and their language to hold on to their transforming identities. Dramatic expression helped these people maintain a viable connection with their roots, for the Spanish religious theatre was a continuous presence in their churches and communities. Dramatizations of stories from the Bible and the lives of the saints were very popular and some of these plays still continue to be performed, such as *Las cuatro apariciones de la Virgen de Guadalupe a Juan Diego* (*The Four Appearances of the Virgin of Guadalupe to Juan Diego*) and the ever-popular *Los pastores* (*The Shepherds*).

Spanish-language theatre actually began in what is now the United States in 1598, when a group of colonizers on their way to Santa Fe, New Mexico, presented a play about their journey near El Paso, Texas. Although this lost play was not spiritual in nature, it continued the Spanish missionaries' long tradition of proselytizing through theatre. While this theatrical activity was being promoted by priests as a part of the colonization process, by the nineteenth century professional, secular theatre was also being developed in the larger centres of Spanish-language populations of the southwest.

Between the mid-nineteenth and mid-twentieth centuries a considerable amount of professional Spanish-language theatre was being produced in the Spanish-speaking communities of the southwest. Many important companies from México toured to centres of Mexican-American population, performing classics from Spain as well as Mexican melodramas, pageants and plays with political themes relevant to the homeland. There were also *carpas* (popular entertainments performed in tents), in which companies from México would present political sketches, satirizing both the Mexicans from México and the recent arrivals in the United States.

A common theme of the *carpas* was the transculturation the Chicanos could not escape, losing their language, their customs and their Mexican identity in the process. By 1935–40, the professional theatre had diminished.

In 1965, Luis Valdéz (b. 1940) founded El Teatro Campesino, initiating the contemporary Chicano theatre movement. The original Teatro Campesino was a troupe of striking farm workers, who attempted to educate and entertain fellow strikers and potential union members. This theatre had its roots in the *commedia dell'arte*, the *carpas*, and in Brechtian political theory and praxis. Improvising with his farm workers-cum-actors, Valdéz guided the troupe in the creation of bilingual *actos* (sketches), which satirized the wealthy growers and their henchmen while presenting the incipient union as a viable tool in their common struggle for better wages and improved living and working conditions. The sketches were performed mostly in English with Spanish added for humour and political commentary.

When the Teatro Campesino began performing at colleges and community centres throughout the United States, the troupe inspired other, mostly urban, Chicanos to form their own theatres. These groups created sketches about issues such as unequal educational opportunities, drug abuse, police brutality and other social ills. This theatrical activity, produced mainly by students and community activists, marked the beginning of a network of theatre groups that extended throughout the western and midwestern United States. By 1971, the theatres formed a national coalition of Chicano theatres, the Teatro Nacional de Aztlan (a Nahuatl term referring to the mythical homeland of the Aztecs). Originally, this coalition was dedicated to the artistic and political evolution of Chicano theatre troupes and individual artists; it now encompasses all US Latino theatre groups and individuals.

Initially, Chicano theatre could be described as collective in nature, composed of non-theatre personnel more interested in politics than aesthetics. The message outweighed the medium as these political activists continued in the tradition of agitprop theatre. Valdéz began to explore themes beyond the farm worker issues when he and his troupe left the labour union in 1967 to work independently.

As the 1970s approached, Valdéz began to investigate indigenous Aztec and Maya thought and culture. He created plays he termed myths, which differed from the sketches in their mixture of politics and spirituality, a uniquely Valdézian fusion of Meso-American and Christian philosophies. During this period, the Vietnam War was also raging, as were demonstrations against it. Many theatres created sketches about the war in an effort to get Chicanos not to fight in what they considered an unjust and corrupt cause. Valdéz contrasted his sketch *Soldado razo* (*Private Soldier*, 1969) with his myth *Dark Root of a Scream* (1971), both of which are about the death of a Chicano in Vietnam. The myth focuses on a mother's loss; the title is taken from the mother's lament at the conclusion of García Lorca's *Bodas de sangre* (*Blood Wedding*). Valdéz juxtaposed Aztec gods with Mexican revolutionary icons to dramatize the fact that a disproportionate number of Chicanos were dying in Vietnam.

In 1971, Valdéz began to develop another genre, the *corrido* (ballad), as a way of dramatizing popular Mexican ballads. In the *corrido*, a singer-narrator offers up the lyrics while actor-dancers move in stylized fashion to the text, bringing legendary folk heroes, heroines and villains to life. Other groups also explored the *corrido* form, adapting it to dramatize current issues by singing the original music to new lyrics. Under the direction of Adrian Vargas, Teatro de la Gente of San Jose, California, adapted the *corrido* style to an Argentine play, *El hombre que se convirtió en perro* (*The Man Who Turned Into a Dog*) in 1977. This script, written in story theatre style by the Argentine writer Osvaldo Dragún, tells of a man who literally turns into a dog when he can find employment only as a watchdog for a company. The adaptation by Vargas and his troupe gave this play a distinctly Chicano sensibility by adding familiar *corridos*. This production also exemplified the Chicanos' growing interest in Latin American plays, playwrights and theatre companies.

By 1974 there were over 100 Chicano theatres throughout the country. Annual festivals organized by the Teatro Nacional de Aztlan brought together the leading troupes of the time, including El Teatro de la Esperanza, founded in Santa Barbara in 1971. This troupe can be credited with bringing Brechtian docu-drama to Chicano theatre with *Guadalupe*, collectively created under the direction of the troupe's founder, Jorge Huerta (b. 1942), in 1974. This piece exposed the rural California town of Guadalupe as a microcosm of any Mexican-Chicano community, including police corruption, poor working and living conditions, anti-union control by the growers, drugs, and an insensitive school system.

In 1976 Teatro de la Esperanza collectively created *La víctima* (*The Victim*), a docu-drama that mingled historical fact with fiction to relate the story of a young Mexican girl who immigrates to the United States during the Mexican Revolution. Teatro de la Esperanza moved to San Francisco in 1986 under the artistic leadership of Rodrigo Duarte-Clark and Ruben Castro-Ilizaliturri. This company is second only to the Teatro Campesino in longevity and importance within the Chicano theatre community.

Two other highlights of the 1970s were Luis Valdéz's *Gran carpa de los rasquachis* (*Great Tent of the Underdogs*, 1974) and his most notable play, *Zoot Suit* (1978). The *Gran carpa de los rasquachis* was the Teatro Campesino's first full-length collective creation and also the culmination of Valdéz's work with the sketch, myth and *corrido* forms. It wove the tale of the trials and tribulations of a Chaplinesque figure who immigrated to the United States but found nothing but misery there. A mimetic piece, it is a truly Valdézian expression in movement and song, like a *commedia dell'arte* scenario. This production toured widely between 1973 and 1978, keeping the Teatro Campesino at the forefront of the Chicano theatre movement.

Zoot Suit was co-produced by the Teatro Campesino and the Center Theatre Group of Los Angeles in 1978–9. This play dramatized the events surrounding a murder trial of the 1940s in Los Angeles, revealing the historical fact that a group of Chicano youths was unjustly accused, tried and convicted in a shamelessly biased trial. *Zoot Suit* ran for eleven months, an achievement unheard of at the time. It also became the first play by a Chicano to be produced on Broadway. *Zoot Suit* remains the most successful Chicano play to date in terms of audience exposure and critical response.

Valdéz's success with *Zoot Suit* marked a turning point for this director-playwright and for Chicano theatre in general, beginning an era of professional Chicano theatre. The evolving Chicano theatre movement also inspired individual playwrights to begin adding their voices to the few who had developed in the 1970s. Most notable of these early playwrights were Estela Portillo Trambley (b. 1936), the first Chicana to publish a play, *Day of the Swallows* (1971); and Carlos Morton (b. 1947), whose docu-drama *The Many Deaths of Danny Rosales* has been produced throughout the United States.

During the 1980s a few non-Latino theatre companies began to court prospective Latino patrons by offering Chicano or Latino/Hispanic 'projects'. One of the most notable of these was the Los Angeles Theatre Center's Latino Lab, under the direction of José Luis Valenzuela (b. 1951) from 1985 to 1990. Under Valenzuela's direction the Latino Lab commissioned and produced some of the most notable Chicano playwrights, including Cherrie Moraga (b. 1952), Milcha Sánchez-Scott (b. 1955) and Octavio Solis (b. 1958). Sánchez-Scott's most important play was *Roosters* (1987), which explored relationships in a rural Chicano household through poetic realism.

The two professional companies, the Teatro Campesino and Teatro de la Esperanza, developed and produced the plays of writers such as Lalo Cervantes, Roy Conboy, Rodrigo Duarte-Clark and Josefina López (b. 1969). López's comedy *Real Women Have Curves* (1990) was first produced by the Teatro de la Esperanza and subsequently by many other groups, both Latino and non-Latino, making it the most produced Chicano play. Set in a Los Angeles garment factory, it argues that women must stop trying to please a diet-conscious society.

The 1990s began auspiciously with another docu-drama, a collective creation directed by Valenzuela with the Latino Lab entitled *August 29th*. This play was created to honour the memory of Ruben Salazar (1928–70), a *Los Angeles Times* columnist killed during the Chicano Moratorium of 1970, a massive demonstration against the Vietnam War that ended in police violence. Salazar became an instant martyr for the Chicano movement when he was killed by a Los Angeles sheriff's tear gas canister.

Twenty years later the Latino Lab created a moving drama about a fictitious Chicana history professor writing a book about Salazar. Mingling fact with fantasy, the play revealed historical references while it examined an impossible love affair between the historian and Salazar's ghost. As in many other Chicano plays, the central character must choose between her community and the establishment, between tokenism and oppression.

Another significant play was Cherrie Moraga's *Heroes and Saints* (1989), first produced in San Francisco in 1992. Also mingling fact with fantasy, the play exposes the severe illnesses, birth defects and even deaths of farm workers due to pesticides. Luis Valdéz's first play, *The Shrunken Head of Pancho Villa*, written in 1964, was also about a farm worker family in crisis. Valdéz's surreal play revolved around a character who is only a head, a metaphor for the stunted Mexican and Chicano revolutions. Moraga's central character is a metaphor for all Mexican and Chicana women who have little or no control over their bodies. Of interest here is the fact that Chicana playwrights came to the

The 1990 Teatro de la Esperanza production of Josefina López's *Real Women Have Curves*.
Photo: Francisco García, courtesy Teatro de la Esperanza.

fore for the first time in the 1980s, the same period that homosexuality first emerged as a thematic concern in the community.

Moraga was the first Chicana to write about homosexuality. Her first play, *Giving Up the Ghost* (1986), boldly discussed what it was like to be three times marginalized: as a Chicana, as a woman and as a lesbian. Moraga wrote from personal experience in her first play, inferred both male and female homosexuality in her second play, *Shadow of a Man* (1988), and created an openly gay man in her next play, *Heroes and Saints*.

Jorge Huerta

Cuban-American Theatre

Given the proximity of Cuba to the United States, it is not surprising that so many aspects of Cuban culture have been felt in the US, among them theatre. The most compelling reasons for this transcultural phenomenon are political and economic. Cuban nationalist themes in the nineteenth century were subjected to censorship by Spanish authorities. Thus, for political reasons, many Cuban plays were first published in New York by important and controversial authors such as José María Heredia (1803–39) and José Jacinto Milanés (1814–63).

Spanish censorship also had the effect of relegating Cuban themes to comedy and farce. This tradition was reinforced by its folkloric appeal and survived in Cuba after that country's independence from Spain in 1898. It also became evident in Tampa, Florida, later in New York, and was still thriving in Miami in the 1990s.

The most important centre of Cuban theatre outside Cuba in the late nineteenth century was Tampa. A great influx of Cubans and Spaniards settled there for economic reasons, developing the cigar industry. Several Spanish regional centres or mutual aid societies staged theatre as part of their cultural offerings, giving rise to non-commercial theatre. The first professional Cuban resident company in New York was the Compañía de Teatro Español, established in 1921 and aimed at middle-class Spaniards and Cubans, who constituted over half the Hispanic population of New York City. Soon, many other theatres emerged.

The Depression devastated Hispanic theatre in general. Only in Tampa was there a Hispanic company supported by the WPA's Federal Theatre Project; known as the Cuban Company, it presented *zarzuelas* (Spanish-style musical comedies) and melodramas in Spanish. In 1958, the Spanish Repertory Theatre was founded in Tampa, presenting both Spanish and Cuban *zarzuelas*, along with serious plays from the Hispanic world and Broadway musicals translated into Spanish.

This theatre activity, aimed at a Spanish-speaking public and with no intention of expanding its influence to the general US public, can be termed Cuban immigrant theatre. While this kind of theatre had relatively little development in the 1940s and 1950s, back in Cuba changes were taking place. In order to understand Cuban-American theatre, therefore, one must first understand the theatrical traditions that Cubans brought with them to the United States. Only the *zarzuela* had flourished from the late 1920s onwards. Only one author had distinguished himself writing for the stage: José Antonio Ramos (1885–1946), who penned incisive social drama. In his masterpiece, *Tembladera* (*Tremor*, 1918), he warned about North American economic expansion into the Cuban fields.

There were important playwrights during this period in Cuba: Virgilio Piñera (1912–79), Carlos Felipe (1914–75) and Rolando Ferrer (1925–76). Piñera wrote *Electra Garrigó* (1948), directed by Francisco Morín, in the same year. In it the classical myth is parodied with *choteo* (a form of Cuban humour that takes nothing seriously), while a sense of national identity emerges reflected in the generational strife within the family. Felipe depicted a world of prostitutes, sailors and pimps, transcending through poetry a facile folklorism in *El Chino* (*The Chinaman*, 1947). Ferrer's *La hija de Nacho* (*Nacho's Daughter*, 1951) and *Lila la mariposa* (*Lila the Butterfly*, 1954) reflect the language and viewpoints of the middle-class family, infused with a mythical poetic force. In the mid-1950s Fermín Borges (1931–87) premièred three short plays in the neo-realistic vein: *Gente desconocida* (*Unknown People*), *Pan viejo* (*Old Bread*) and *Doble juego* (*Double Game*).

Just prior to the revolution in 1959, Havana had about ten small theatres seating some 1,900 spectators and three large theatres – one in the Palacio de Bellas Artes, built in 1956; one in the Comedia Theatre, which presented traditional dramatic fare; and the Teatro Martí, which specialized in Cuban farces. The emergence of television in 1949 brought high-quality plays and *zarzuelas* to the population at large.

In 1959, dictator Fulgencio Batista fled the country, signalling a victory for Fidel Castro.

The first year of the revolution witnessed the staging of forty-eight plays by Cuban authors, as well as the beginning of full official backing for the theatre.

Abelardo Estorino's first play, *El robo del cochino* (*The Theft of a Pig*, 1961), portrays realistically daily life in the provinces during the last days of the Batista regime. These years also witnessed the appearance of the work of Manuel Reguera Samuell (b. 1928), who recorded the existence of the provincial middle class with *Sara en el traspatio* (*Sara in the Backyard*, 1960). *Recuerdos de Tulipa* (*Remembrances of Tulipa*, 1962) depicts the struggle of a strip-tease artist.

Thus the theatre in Havana in the 1950s presented a wide spectrum of plays including the European repertoire – classics as well as the avant-garde – and recent plays from the United States. In addition, a new generation of Cuban playwrights had started writing serious and sophisticated theatre. This theatrical activity on the island provides an insight into the artistic milieu from which the exiled playwrights and their public sprang.

The first large wave of Cuban exiles started in 1960, even before Castro's famous address 'Palabras a los intelectuales' ('Words to Intellectuals') outlined the aesthetic and intellectual constraints to be imposed. Thus Fermín Borges went to the United States, José Triana to France and Reguera Samuell to Spain. The works of these authors, as well as those by Piñera, Estorino and Carlos Felipe, have since been included regularly in the repertoires of theatrical companies directed by Cubans in New York and Miami.

It is estimated that since 1960 over 1 million Cubans have left the island. The upper, middle and professional classes did so first during the early 1960s, followed by members of the working classes. This exodus continued on a lesser scale in the 1970s and peaked in 1980, when over 100,000 Cubans entered the United States. Again, in 1994, over 20,000 Cubans left the island on rafts.

Whereas it is relatively easy to consider the dramatic output of Cuban authors in the US prior to 1959 as immigrant theatre, it is far more complicated to classify these works thereafter. The generational approach by date of birth, useful as it might seem, poses problems. Thus María Irene Fornés (b. 1930), who arrived in the US in 1945, writes in English, whereas Iván Acosta (b. 1948) writes in Spanish. Obviously, for each author the key factor is the length of time spent in Cuba and whether their

environment in the United States is English or Spanish. For the former, the term 'exile theatre' seems the most appropriate; for the latter, Cuban-American theatre. These groups could be further subdivided, according to whether the exiled playwrights had started their careers in Cuba and, in the case of the Cuban Americans, whether they are preoccupied with Cuban themes. Some playwrights, such as Fornés, elude this classification altogether.

Leopoldo Hernández (b. 1921) began his literary career in Cuba. In 1961 he moved to the United States, where he wrote *Guáimaro* (1960), *940 S.W. Segunda calle* (*940 S.W. Second Street*, 1969), *Hollywood* (1970), *Ana* (1971), *Martínez* (1981) and *Siempre tuvimos miedo* (*We Were Always Afraid*, 1987). *Martínez* deals with the assertion of the self, pitting the Latino identity of the protagonist against the absurdities of his US environment. In *Siempre tuvimos miedo*, an exiled brother returns to Cuba and confronts his sister, who has remained on the island. There is no rational or political resolution to this dilemma, only an emotional one.

Matías Montes Huidobro (b. 1930) has distinguished himself as both a critic and playwright. *Sobre las mismas rocas* (*On the Same Rocks*) was staged by Prometeo in Havana in 1951; this was followed by *Los acosados* (*The Accosted*, 1959), published in the literary supplement *Lunes de Revolución*. *Gas en los poros* (*Gas Through the Pores*) was staged by Morín at Prometeo in 1961, the year the author went into exile in the United States. Also in 1961, he wrote *La madre y la guillotina* (*The Mother and the Guillotine*) and *La sal de los muertos* (*The Salt of the Dead*). He has authored some twenty plays. Among those written in exile are *La navaja de Olofé* (*Olofé's Razor*, 1981), *Exilio* (*Exile*, 1986) and *Su cara mitad* (*Your Better Half*). *La navaja de Olofé* is rooted in African mythology: Olofé, the god of virility, descends upon a young mulatto (of mixed black and European ancestry) man and a middle-aged mulatto woman, who move between acting as lovers and as child and mother. In *Exile* and *Su cara mitad*, Montes Huidobro resorts to the meta-theatrical technique. In *Exile* two Cuban couples – a playwright and his actress wife, a poet and his political activist wife – and their mutual friend, a homosexual theatre director, meet at three different moments as exiles: during the years of the Batista regime in 1957, in Havana in 1963 and in New York in 1983.

Raúl de Cárdenas (b. 1938) premièred his *Cuando los hombres lloran* (*When Men Cry*) in 1959 in Havana, followed by *Los ánimos están cansados* (*Courage Is Tired*, 1960) and his greatest success *La palangana* (*The Basin*, 1961). He resumed his theatrical career in Los Angeles during the 1980s with *La muerte de Rosendo* (*Rosendo's Death*, 1986), *Al ayer no se le dice adiós* (*You Never Say Goodbye to Yesterday*, 1986), the popular *Las Carbonell de la calle Obispo* (*The Carbonell Woman from Obispo Street*, 1986), *Recuerdos de familia* (*Family Remembrances*, 1989) and *Así en Miami como en el cielo* (*In Miami as It Is in Heaven*, 1990). He writes in a realistic style, casting a nostalgic glance at Cuban traditions that no longer exist. In the last play mentioned, however, which takes place in the United States, a son is killed in the Vietnam War and the remaining son confesses his homosexuality to a disgruntled Cuban *paterfamilias*.

René Ariza (1940–93) was an actor and director in Havana; in 1967 his play *La vuelta a la manzana* (*The Stroll Around the Block*) earned him the Unión de Escritores y Artistas de Cuba (Union of Cuban Writers and Artists) Prize. Four years later, though, he was dismissed from his job, and in 1977 was sentenced to eight years in prison for writing 'counter-revolutionary propaganda'. He continued to write in prison and was freed in 1979 as part of an amnesty programme for political prisoners as a result of pressure from the international community. He arrived in Miami in 1980. His short plays include *The Meeting* (1971), an absurdist satire about a political leader unable to speak in public, and *A Flower Vendor for These Times* (1980), in which the main character learns to derive aesthetic enjoyment from decay in order to cope with her miserable life.

Julio Matas (b. 1931) interrupted his graduate studies in the United States in order to return to Cuba after the triumph of the revolution. He held the directorship of the National Theatre in Havana for a short period of time. His play *La crónica y el suceso* (*The Chronicle and the Event*) was published in 1964. Disenchanted with the revolution, he returned to the United States. In 1990 three of his plays were published in Miami: *El extravío* (*The Loss*), *La crónica y el suceso* and *Aquí cruza el ciervo* (*Here Crosses the Deer*). In *Dialogue of the Poet and the Supreme Leader*, a jailed poet is offered freedom if he recants his revisionistic attitude towards the revolution; the poet, however, refuses to compromise his ideals.

In contrast to these playwrights, who had all established careers before leaving Cuba, there are several authors whose theatrical careers started only after they arrived in the United States. These authors also deal with the theme of exile, the revolution, identity in a new country, Latino survival in an alien environment – themes shared by the playwrights who had started their literary careers in Havana. But these playwrights who started writing in the US add a new concern: the crisis of the traditional Cuban family when it confronts new social structures. In addition, homosexuality, which had been a taboo topic in Cuba, now emerged as a major theme.

José Sánchez Boudy (b. 1927) belongs to this group. Although concerned with the destructive forces of revolutions, he avoids direct allusions to the Cuban situation. Thus *La rebelión de los negros* (*The Revolt of the Blacks*, 1980) takes place in imperial Rome. Mario Martín (b. 1934) alludes directly to contacts between Cubans on both sides of the Strait of Florida in *La libertad prestada* (*Freedom on Loan*, 1980), in which an exile visits the island; he has also written *Mamá cumple ochenta años* (1982) about life as an exile in the United States. José Corrales (b. 1937) was a drama critic in Cuba for *Bohemia* and *La gaceta de Cuba* (*Cuban Gazette*). His career as a playwright started in New York, however, with *Faramalla* (*Blarney*, 1971); followed by *Spics, Spices, Gringos y Gracejo* (1976), a bilingual farce in commemoration of the bicentennial of the United States; *Nocturno de cañas bravas* (*Bamboo Nocturne*, 1994); and *De cuerpo presente* (*Lying in State*, 1991), which centre on homoerotic and bisexual themes. In collaboration with Manuel Pereiras he has written *Las hetairas habaneras* (1977). Based on Euripides' *The Trojan Women*, the action takes place in Havana at the start of the Castro regime, in a brothel overseen by Diosdada. In the emerging intertextuality, Menelaus-Fidel becomes a destructive force of a pre-revolutionary carnivalesque Cuba. Its demise, however, is not viewed as progress.

Miguel González-Pando (b. 1941) is a well-known political activist. Exiled during the final year of the Batista regime, he returned to Cuba, only to leave again for the United States when Castro took over. He has written five plays. Among them are *La familia Pilón* (*The Pilón Family*, 1982), a title inspired by a famous television situation comedy from the 1950s in Cuba, and *Había una vez un sueño* (1987), rewritten in English as *Once Upon a Dream*

(1990), which pits a mother who lives in a fantasy world of the past against her blind son, unable to avoid the dangers of growing up in New York's Spanish Harlem.

Reinaldo Arenas (1943–90) wrote exclusively in Spanish. This famous novelist arrived in the United States in 1980, settled in New York and tried his hand at dramatic writing. In *Traitor* (1986), an old woman in front of a television recreates in a monologue the life of her lover, a man who hated the revolution so much that he decided to participate in it as a party member. Having lived a lie, he is executed after the fall of Castro. The fear instilled by the communist revolution was greater than his hatred of it.

Pedro Monge Rafuls (b. 1943), director of the Ollantay Center of the Arts in New York, has written several plays with a wide thematic range. In *Solidarios* (*United*, 1990), a group of Hispanics set aside their differences to protect a Dominican woman from the immigration officers. *Noche de ronda* (*Party Night*), about a group of gay Latino men who discuss the dangers of AIDS and the impact that it has had in their lives, was staged in three separate productions in 1990–1. Of particular interest is *Nadie se va del todo* (*Nobody Leaves Completely*), where Lula and her son Tony return to Cuba to visit. Lula forgives the woman responsible for the execution of her husband and Tony discovers his Cuban identity.

Héctor Santiago (b. 1944) wrote six children's plays in his native Havana. There he was imprisoned for five years for political reasons. He was able to leave Cuba in 1979, first going to Madrid for a year, then settling in New York. In *Balada para un verano en La Habana* (*Ballad for a Havana Summer*, 1992), Santiago, a homosexual living in exile, returns to Cuba to visit his sister. Despite the tensions arising from the prejudices and revolutionary fervour of the latter, an affectionate understanding ensues. In *Madame Camille: Escuela de danza* (*Madame Camille: School of Dance*) Camille teaches two couples how to dance, but the dance steps resemble military drills, with sado-masochistic overtones, and the ultimate goal of mastering the skill is to learn how to please an all-powerful leader.

Iván Acosta studied film at New York University. His first play, *Grito 71* (*Scream 71*) was a multimedia happening in which six actors mingled with the audience, while psychedelic images were projected on a screen and a live band played. His most famous play, *El super* (1977), was written to be staged at the Centro Cultural Cubano, an organization he headed. It centred on the difficulties of the superintendent of a building and his family coping with the hardships of daily life in New York. A film version has enjoyed critical acclaim. *Recojan las serpentinas que se acabó el carnaval* (*Pick Up the Streamers For Mardi Gras Is Over*) is a satire of a dictatorship in an unspecified Latin American country.

René R. Alomá (1947–86) left Cuba in 1947 and settled in Canada. After working for two years on his first play *The Exile*, he changed its title to *A Little Something to Ease the Pain*; it was produced by Toronto's CentreStage Company in 1980. In it a visiting exiled Cuban returns to the island and establishes a tense relationship with his revolutionary cousin. Underneath the tumultuous dialogue lies the desire to exchange the circumstances of their lives.

The first play by Luis Santeiro (b. 1947) was *Our Lady of the Tortilla* (1987), centring on the problems of assimilation of a Cuban family. The play takes an unexpected turn when a spinster aunt, while pondering the sexual freedom of the younger generation, sees an apparition of the Virgin on a tortilla. *Mixed Blessings* (1989) is an adaptation of *Tartuffe* set in a Cuban-American family embroiled in politics, while his *The Lady from Havana* (1990) traces the process of assimilation into the Miami exile community.

Eduardo Machado (b. 1953) is among the best known Cuban-American playwrights. Born in Havana, he was sent to the United States when he was 8. In the early 1980s he started to write a series called *The Floating Island Plays*, which includes *The Modern Ladies of Guanabacoa* (1984), *Broken Eggs* (1984), *Fabiola* (1985) and *In the Eye of the Hurricane* (1989). In 1994, the tetralogy was staged in two segments at the Mark Taper Forum in Los Angeles. It dramatizes the saga of a Cuban family, beginning in the 1920s in Cuba and ending in Los Angeles in 1979, where the family ended up in exile. The general tone of this tetralogy is bittersweet, with humorous touches, ranging from the grotesque to the absurd, tempering the inner conflicts of each character. Machado has also written *Rosario and the Gypsies*, *Once Removed*, *Wishing You Well* and *Why to Refuse*. In the latter, the protagonist is imprisoned because of his opposition to a totalitarian regime.

Another group of Cuban-American playwrights are first- or second-generation Americans of Cuban descent. Among these writers there is less of an identity problem, as

Oskar Eustis's 1994 Mark Taper Forum production of Eduardo Machado's four-play saga, *The Floating Island Plays.*
Photo: Jay Thompson, courtesy Mark Taper Forum.

compared to those who came young to the United States, and their vision of Cuba is the fruit of imagination rather than experience. Still they all share Cuban themes within the wider thematic range of their works. This group includes Ramón Delgado (b. 1937), Charles Gómez-Sanz (b. 1954) and Al Septién (b. 1962).

Delgado is a second-generation Cuban American born in Tampa. His play *A Little Holy Water* revolves around an experience lived by his grandparents during a cigar workers' strike in Tampa during the 1930s.

Gómez-Sanz, born in Miami of Cuban parents who had immigrated to the United States in the 1940s, writes in English. His *Bang Bang Blues* (1988) deals with the distortion of the news on television, while *Adiós, Tropicana* (1989) centres on the separation of a family because of the revolutionary process.

Septién is a first-generation American of Cuban parents. In *Birthday Present* (1987), a Cuban refugee in his 60s initiates into manhood his US-born grandson by taking him to a prostitute whom he used to frequent himself. Here traditional Cuban sexual mores prevail over US ones.

Renaldo Ferradas (b. 1932), Manuel Martín, Jr (b. 1934) and María Irene Fornés form a group apart. They arrived in the United States prior to the Cuban revolution and write in English, but all have maintained close contact with the successive waves of exiled Cubans.

Although Ferradas arrived in New York in 1948, he did not start writing for the stage until the 1970s, with *A Crock of Daisies* (1975) and *Love Is Not For Sale*. In 1984 his play *La visionaria* (*The Visionary*) was produced at the Public Theater's Festival Latino. *Birds Without Wings* (1987) focuses on two Latino adolescents from New York who are placed in foster care with a middle-aged woman, who forces them to sell drugs.

Martín arrived in the United States in 1953. He studied with Lee Strasberg at the Actors Studio and co-founded and directed Duo Theatre in New York. His initial interest in historical dramas – *Francesco: The Life and Times of the Cenci* (1973) and *Rasputin* (1976) – soon gave way to Hispanic and Cuban themes: *Carmencita* (1980), a musical based on Bizet's opera set among Puerto Ricans in New York, and *Swallows* (1986), a musical about the bonds of fraternity between Cubans on both sides of the Strait of Florida. In 1988 Duo staged *Rita and Bessie*, an imaginary meeting at the gates of heaven of two black singers, the Cuban Rita Montaner and the American Bessie Smith. In *Union City Thanksgiving* (1983), an exiled family constantly reminisces about Cuba during a Thanksgiving dinner. The observance of this US tradition underscores the distance from the island, as well as the hardships that the family experiences in the United States.

Fornés's prolific career has included over twenty plays, among them *Fefu and Her Friends* (1977), a milestone in the development of feminist theatre in the United States; *Mud* (1983); and *The Danube* (1982). In *Sarita* (1984), a musical, and in *The Conduct of Life* (1985), Fornés focuses on Hispanic themes. In the former, a young Latino girl's life is dramatized from age 13 to 24; she is left pregnant by her Latino boyfriend, who later reappears to extort money. Not being able to withstand his advances, she kills him and ends up in an insane asylum. In *The Conduct of Life*, a torturer for the regime rapes a 12-year-old girl repeatedly as he confesses his pleasure in destroying people.

As director of New York's International Arts Relations (INTAR) Playwrights-in-Residence

Laboratory, Fornés has trained and inspired several of the playwrights mentioned: Eduardo Machado, Manuel Martín, René Alomá, José Peláez, Manuel Pereiras and Charles Gómez-Sanz. This workshop also signalled the appearance of Cuban-American feminist theatre, starting with Fornés herself. Ana María Simo, Caridad Svich and Dolores Prida (b. 1943) have all been in residence at the workshop, producing a dramatic opus with a clear feminist vision. In Prida's first play, *The Beautiful Señoritas* (1977), she focuses on a beauty contest in which traditional feminine Hispanic roles and the implicit macho attitude associated with them are satirized. She has also written *Coser y cantar* (*Sewing and Singing*, 1981), *Savings* (1985), *Pantallas* (*Screens*, 1986) and *Botánica* (*Botany*, 1990). In *Coser y cantar*, a one-act bilingual fantasy of two women, there is an exchange between two aspects of the self, which is split.

Alina Troyano, under the name Carmelita Tropicana – evoking both the famous Havana nightclub and an orange juice brand name – is responsible for several post-modern musical plays: *Memories of the Revolution* (1986), *Candela y azúcar* (*Candle and Sugar*, 1989) and *Milk of Amnesia* (1994). The first has an all-female cast, who also impersonate the male roles, and the title refers to feminism, not Castro. In her world, a cultural syncretism operates at several levels: Cuban roots, Catholicism, Europe and exile in New York. All coexist in a post-modern tapestry, depicting a carnivalization of life.

The majority of these playwrights focus on the plight of other Hispanic minorities, directly or indirectly. At times, a composite Hispanic figure emerges with some Cuban touches, evident in González Pando's *Once Upon a Dream* and in Fornés's *Sarita*. Generally, this is not so in the case of the other two distinct Hispanic dramaturgies in the United States.

Although Miami has become the Cuban capital in exile, the metropolitan New York/New Jersey area also has a large Cuban population, and it is here that a number of small companies have sprung up, producing quality theatre despite the limited economic means at their disposal. Thus in the early 1960s Andrés Castro, who in Cuba had headed the groups Las Máscaras and Yesistas, became the director of the West Repertory Theatre.

In 1968 Gilberto Zaldívar, exiled from Cuba in 1961, and René Buch founded the Repertorio Español, which presents plays only in Spanish. At first it was devoted to staging mainly Spanish

incarnates a totally different cultural point of view. In *Ariano*, racial prejudice is carried to such an extent that the Puerto Rican protagonist pays a blonde woman to carry his child because he wants to father a white baby. Only later does he accept his Puerto Rican identity.

Three Puerto Rican playwrights have also managed to become known to mainstream audiences: Miguel Piñero (1947–88), John Jesurun (b. 1951) and José Rivera (b. 1955). *Short Eyes* (1974) is the best known of Piñero's works. It takes a tough, cruel look at a house of detention where Puerto Rican, black and white prisoners jockey for power in a tense, unstable hierarchy. With astonishing verbal brilliance – the prisoners speak both English and Spanish – Piñero sketches in the despair that settles over the prison. And since the cell block is a microcosm of the world outside, the fate that awaits the prisoners when they pass through the bars is to die in the street 'like a dog'. Based on Piñero's experience in a federal prison, *Short Eyes* won both the New York Drama Critics' Circle Award for Best American Play of 1973–4 and an Obie Award.

Piñero's later *Outrageous* (1986) and *La Bodega Sold Dreams*, a collection of poems, also draw bitter portraits of the United States.

If Piñero's stagecraft is rooted in his ability to transmute street language into poetry, the theatre of John Jesurun – some critics classify it as performance art – juxtaposes language with images in a post-modern collage. Trained in the visual arts, Jesurun started out as a sculptor and film-maker before turning to theatre. In *White*

Water (1986) much of the dialogue comes from television monitors. *Deep Sleep*, another of his imaginative dramas, won an Obie Award for best play in 1986.

José Rivera's *The House of Ramón Iglesia* was staged in 1983 and aired on public television in 1986. In it a hard-working Puerto Rican father with little self-esteem is pitted against his assimilated, college-educated son. In *Marisol* (1992), an allegory, the protagonist moves from the Bronx to the emptiness of Manhattan to a vaster cosmogony in which a dying god is being replaced by angels bringing humanity hope. Here ethnicity finds no solace in a mainstream society headed towards apocalypse.

Two distinct currents emerge in plays written by female Puerto Rican playwrights. Yolanda Rodríguez's *Rising Sun, Falling Star* (1991) is a gripping play delving deep into the psychology of its mostly male characters. An older brother, afflicted with AIDS from drug abuse, reluctantly goes back to dealing drugs to save his younger brother from a similar fate. In Migdalia Cruz's play *Miriam's Flowers*, the protagonist is traumatized by the accidental death of her younger brother. A poetic allegory, in this play religious beliefs are ethnically interiorized as her only possible relief.

Although Puerto Rican theatre in the United States has now become distinct from that of the island and in many ways exerts an influence on it, communication between the two communities helps to ensure the general health of both.

Antonio Cao

(See also PUERTO RICO)

Structure of the National Theatre Community

Professional theatre in the United States can be divided generally into either not-for-profit or commercial groups. The former are eligible for government funding; the latter hope to make a financial profit on a successful show. Ticket prices in the not-for-profit theatres are usually lower than in the commercial sector, with not-for-profit prices often beginning at between $10 and $20, while some commercial shows cost around $70 a ticket (ten times a film ticket price). There is sometimes crossover between the two; for example, the Shubert Foundation (whose income is derived from the commercial Broadway theatre) makes grants to not-for-profit theatres.

All not-for-profit theatres must follow strict legal and tax procedures to maintain their status. For example, while staff and contract workers may earn salaries, no individual can 'profit' from a theatre's production, and the company itself cannot earn a profit for its investors. If a company makes more money than anticipated, the excess must be added to the company's operating budget.

There are also tax benefits in being a not-for-profit arts organization. Such a group is allowed to give a tax receipt for any donation it receives and a not-for-profit group can also receive grants from government agencies and foundations. As a result, groups working in this sector

Robert Falls's 1985 Wisdom Bridge Theatre production of *Hamlet*.
Photo: Jennifer Girard, courtesy Wisdom Bridge Theatre.

tend to have ongoing stability. Typically, such a theatre is begun by one or more entrepreneurs who stage shows without benefit of grants, then apply for grants based on their artistic achievement and audience base. At that point, the founders might leave, while the institution continues to evolve with other leadership, selected by the staff and a board of directors. For example, David Beaird (b. 1945) founded Wisdom Bridge Theatre in Chicago in 1974; it later developed into a theatre noted for artistic innovation by Robert Falls (b. 1954) and Jeffrey Ortmann (b. 1954).

Not-for-profit theatres are required to have unpaid boards of directors – people drawn from the community – that advise management and participate in fundraising. Box-office receipts usually account for about 50 per cent of the budget. Public grants usually spur additional private funding, giving the imprimatur of worthiness to a theatre.

Most US federal funding comes through the National Endowment for the Arts, which gave grants to 231 not-for-profit theatres in 1994, most in the form of matching grants. Most theatres have one or more series of shows to

which audiences subscribe at various discounts. Other funds are raised through benefits, auctions and the sale of gift items, books and even videos and audio cassettes. Other monies can come through theatre classes and refreshment vending. Theatres often commit significant monies to marketing and fundraising.

Some not-for-profit companies own their performance spaces; others rent. Some establish endowments that provide continuous operating funds. The not-for-profit theatres usually do not pay their workers as well as the commercial theatres, but they can usually offer longer-term commitments.

Most not-for-profit theatres, regardless of size, provide various ancillary services for the communities in which they are situated. These include performances for school children, educational materials to amplify a production's impact (such as lobby displays or newsletters with historical and critical information about the play), discussions after performances with the artists, lectures, classes, special performances offered free or for little cost, festivals and concerts. The more heavily funded an institution, such as New York's Lincoln Center, the more it is expected to be such a cultural centre for its city.

The Theatre Communications Group (TCG), an organization for not-for-profit theatres, regularly publishes data supplied by its professional member companies. In 1993, TCG represented theatres in 131 communities, thirty-nine states and the District of Columbia.

Founded in New York in 1961 with Ford Foundation support as a service organization for not-for-profit theatres, TCG held its first nationwide conference in 1976. In the mid-1990s, TCG was offering grants, fellowships, awards, conferences, workshops, government liaison services, surveys, research, a national arts employment bulletin and many publications. Most not-for-profit regional theatres were founded in the 1970s and 1980s, and while some do not belong to TCG, 186 theatres in 1992 reported revenues of more than $366 million for the year, with more than 16 million admissions. These theatres employed nearly 28,000 actors, directors, designers, playwrights, administrators and technicians. This was in spite of a recession that forced some closures (the Los Angeles Theatre Center, for example) and deficits as well as downscaling by many companies.

The annual budgets of the most heavily subsidized not-for-profit regional theatres range from The Group, a Seattle-based multicultural theatre at just over $1 million, to the Oregon Shakespeare Festival at $11.6 million and Lincoln Center Theatre at $19.5 million.

The oldest not-for-profit regional theatre is the Cleveland Play House, founded in 1915, with a $6.7 million annual budget in 1994. Pioneer Theatre Company of Salt Lake City ($2.2 million), another resident professional theatre, draws audiences from four states, while Steppenwolf Theatre Company of Chicago ($4 million) is an ensemble of actors and directors, many of them active in television and film, who make collective artistic decisions; the company produces on its two stages and sometimes takes productions to New York. The Mark Taper Forum in Los Angeles, still another not-for-profit regional theatre ($10.5 million), has theatres seating 760 and 99, for its six productions a year, while the not-for-profit O'Neill Theatre Center in Connecticut fosters new plays through its internationally known Playwrights' Conference each summer.

Theatres with much smaller budgets often produce work focused on more specific audiences but, like the larger institutions, they offer workshops, touring and various outreach programmes.

Ellen Stewart's long-serving La MaMa Experimental Theatre Club produces dozens of shows a year on its four stages in New York City and offers free rehearsal space, a cabaret and an art gallery, all on a budget of some $945,000. The Perseverance Theatre of Douglas, Alaska, in contrast, inaccessible by road from outside Juneau, offers productions on three stages ($982,000). Playhouse on the Square, in Memphis, Tennessee ($789,000; fifteen productions a year), with a core acting company, is one of the few professional companies serving the mid-south.

Theatres with the smallest budgets are often the laboratory theatres of individual artists or artistic families. Chris Hardman's (b. 1950) experimental Antenna Theatre offers three productions a year in Sausalito, California ($260,000), while Ping Chong (b. 1946) and Company in New York produces this artist's distinctive collaborative performance art ($275,000). Germinal Stage Denver is another actors' theatre that presents five shows annually in an eight-table restaurant on a budget of $93,000.

Many theatres also serve more specific constituencies. Theatres for children often tour to schools and rural communities as well as to youth detention facilities. Academy Theatre in Georgia ($220,000) offers issue-oriented, original work, while the Children's Theatre Company of Minneapolis ($5.6 million) specializes in adaptations of children's literature on its two stages, with eighty full-time staff and a school.

Theatres formed to provide development and production opportunities for playwrights run the gamut from the Playwrights' Center in Minneapolis, which sponsors workshops, readings, conferences and fellowships; through Victory Gardens, Chicago, which is committed to Chicago and midwestern playwrights; to Playwrights' Horizons in New York with a 1992 budget of $4.5 million, which also hosts Young Playwrights Inc., with its own $607,000 budget for writers 18 and under.

Other theatres create productions based on regional, racial or ethnic cultures. Regionally specific theatre is especially strong in the southern states. Horse Cave Theatre, for example, serves Kentucky writers and audiences; the Road Company investigates and expresses its upper-east Tennessee community; Kentucky's Roadside Theater performs work about Appalachia with an ensemble drawn mostly from Appalachia; and Virginia's Lime Kiln performs indigenous stories and music on its two stages and with its touring tent. Mad River Theater Works is a tent theatre that created plays for the rural mid-United States while Cornerstone Theatre Company, a consensus-run ensemble, collaborates with a variety of communities.

Some theatres, such as Seattle's The Group, consciously strive to place multicultural theatre at the centre. A Travelling Jewish Theatre, for instance, tours extensively from its base in San Francisco, where it plays on two small stages. Most US cities have theatres devoted to the African-American experience, with Crossroads Theatre Company in New Jersey ($2.6 million budget) providing a haven for major black artists in its season of four or five plays and an annual festival. The Puerto Rican Travelling Theatre in Manhattan presents mainly Puerto Rican playwrights while Repertorio Español in New York ($1.5 million; 140 seats) produces *zarzuelas* and a wide range of Hispanic plays, with a simulcast system that provides English translation for the audience. Pan Asian Repertory ($500,000) in New York houses a resident ensemble that articulates the experiences of Asian peoples.

Still under the general rubric of not-for-profit theatre are groups such as LA Theatre Works, which produces live radio broadcasts of plays featuring some of the nation's most skilled actors in a ballroom that seats 400. The Wooster Group in New York is a collective that owns the 200-seat Performance Garage, a flexible space that was once the home of Richard Schechner's Performance Group. The company, founded in 1975, develops one or two original theatre and media pieces annually. Julia Miles (b. 1930) founded the Women's Project & Productions in New York to provide women across the country with a place to experiment and develop skills; the company also publishes anthologies of plays produced there.

Illusion Theater in Minneapolis is a not-for-profit group that develops new plays that address social problems and change, such as sexual abuse, interpersonal violence and AIDS. Free Street Programs in Chicago creates original performances in various city neighbourhoods.

On the commercial side, the several dozen theatre buildings that house the plays commonly referred to as Broadway are clustered primarily in Manhattan near the intersection of Broadway and Forty-Second Street, where a thriving entertainment mecca was created early in the twentieth century. The area has declined greatly since World War II as theatre dispersed into Off-Broadway, Off-Off-Broadway and the regional theatres, and audience attendance dropped rapidly. At the same time, other parts of Manhattan developed alternative entertainment districts. However, in the 1980s and 1990s, a number of organizations have formed to redevelop the Broadway district, with major investors such as the Walt Disney Company buying real estate and refurbishing the stately, gracious and commodious old auditoriums. In 1992, Broadway theatres generated approximately $2.3 billion in revenues for Manhattan businesses (hotels, restaurants, taxis and so on).

Most Broadway theatres are owned and/or operated by the Shubert Organization, owner of sixteen theatres, in 1994 run by Gerald Schoenfeld (b. 1924) and Bernard Jacobs (b. 1916); the Nederlander Organization, owner or operator of ten, run by brothers James (b. 1922) and Robert (b. 1933) Nederlander; and Jujamcyn Theaters, which has five houses owned by James H. Binger (b. 1916) and Virginia McKnight Binger (b. 1916), who named the organization from an amalgam of their children's names; it has been run since 1987 by Rocco Landesman (b. 1947). Landesman's innovative approaches are turning Jujamcyn into a producing organization that in some ways resembles a not-for-profit company, while the other organizations primarily serve as landlords or sponsoring venues. The Shuberts and Nederlanders own theatres 'on the road' as well, while Jujamcyn also runs theatres in Boston, Philadelphia and Chicago.

Commercial theatres across the country often imitate Broadway production models. Broadway shows themselves are financed by many investors, large and small, and only one in four earns back its investment. Sometimes even an award-winning show cannot make a profit because it is so expensive to produce and market. The traditional approach to producing on Broadway had been to cast and rehearse a show for a month, try it out in Boston or Philadelphia, then in less than another month revise it and open on Broadway. But some Broadway successes have more recently come directly from regional theatres, where time permits rewriting, restaging and recasting as needed. Jujamcyn is now into its own development process, employing a resident creative director and artistic director, commissioning plays by young writers, and investing development money in its shows.

Collaborations between Broadway producers and the regional theatres had become commonplace by the 1990s. A Tony Award-winning drama, *Angels in America: Part I Millennium Approaches*, in 1993 was backed and produced by Jujamcyn, put on by the Mark Taper Forum, and funded as well by individuals and an investment group; *Passion* (1993), a musical, was produced by the Shubert Organization, Capitol Cities/ABC (television), Lincoln Center Theatre and various individuals; and a revival of *Carousel* was produced by Lincoln Center, the Royal National Theatre (United Kingdom), the Rodgers and Hammerstein organization and various individuals.

Broadway productions generally take the greatest financial risks but can also earn the greatest financial rewards. Because musicals draw the largest attendance, they are a staple on Broadway, which is able to pay for the most skilled artists and craftspeople. Many other plays, however, are produced around the country on a commercial basis. Individual investors and producers underwrite production costs, rent a theatre and mount a show, hoping to reap a profit from its success. A show that begins as an independent commercial venture might eventually move to New York and there be produced again, either independently or in conjunction with one of several regularly active Broadway producers.

Theatre in the US is still a business even when it is not operated for profit, and most theatre artists and technicians have unionized to provide collective bargaining opportunities for salaries, benefits, pensions and other rights. Actors' Equity Association, founded just before World War I, approves contracts between management and actors and stage managers though contractual agreements vary depending on the city, the size of theatre and budget, and the requirements of the production. Equity has a range of contract types, which are re-examined and negotiated every few years.

Other major theatrical unions include the Society of Stage Directors and Choreographers, United Scenic Artists, Musicians' Union, Songwriters' Guild, International Alliance of Theatrical Stage Employees, Theatrical Wardrobe Attendants and the Dramatist Guild. Individual writers, actors, directors, musicians and designers are often represented by talent agencies and/or managers, who take a percentage of the client's pay (typically 10–15 per cent) to promote the client and to negotiate contracts.

Linda Walsh Jenkins

Artistic Profile

Companies

US theatre tends to be a localized activity, except for touring companies of big commercial shows, usually musicals. Despite the commercial dominance of Broadway, therefore, there is no national theatre in the United States and no single centre; rather, there are numerous epicentres located all across the country from New York and Chicago to Los Angeles and San Francisco.

As a movement, regional theatres sprang up as an alternative to the commercial theatre that was dominant well into the 1960s. A sense of the vastness of the movement can be gained by identifying just a few of the leading regional theatre companies in the 1990s: the American Repertory Theatre (ART; Cambridge, Massachusetts); the Hartford Stage Company (Connecticut); the Long Wharf Theatre and the Yale Repertory Theatre (New Haven, Connecticut); the Studio Arena Theatre (Buffalo); Lincoln Center Theater (at the Vivian Beaumont Theatre), the Manhattan Theatre Club, the Public Theater and the Roundabout (New York City); the Arena Stage and the Shakespeare Theatre (Washington, DC); the Goodman Theatre and Steppenwolf (Chicago); the Guthrie Theatre (Minneapolis); the Alley Theatre (Houston); the Actors Theatre of Louisville (Kentucky); the Mark Taper Forum (Los Angeles); American Conservatory Theater and the Berkeley Repertory Theatre (San Francisco); La Jolla Playhouse (San Diego), and the Intiman, the Seattle Repertory Theatre and A Contemporary Theatre (Seattle). The Theatre Communications Group publishes a directory each year with the names, addresses, phone numbers, artistic directors and other important personnel of these regional companies.

The majority of the regional theatres do not have permanent acting companies *per se*, nor are they dominated by one directorial vision. Since their work tends to be eclectic, it becomes difficult to define a house style. Nevertheless, some of these theatres have distinguished themselves in special areas. Each spring, for example, the Actors Theatre of Louisville puts on an important festival of new US plays while Steppenwolf has developed an ensemble of actors whose work is characterized by intense physicality, known as the Chicago style. The Guthrie tends to produce lavish revivals from the classic repertoire, while the Oregon Shakespeare Festival (1935) has earned a reputation for stylish and literate productions of Shakespeare and other seventeenth-century drama.

The Roundabout presents an eclectic mix of modern classics with high-profile movie stars. The theatre revived Eugene O'Neill's *Anna Christie* with British actors Natasha Richardson and Liam Neeson in 1993 and Harold Pinter's *No Man's Land* with Canadian Christopher Plummer and Jason Robards, Jr (b. 1922) in 1994. The Vivian Beaumont at Lincoln Center mounts elegant productions of modern US plays such as John Guare's (b. 1938) *Six Degrees of Separation* (1990).

Since these companies vary greatly, it may be useful to look at one in some detail – the American Repertory Theatre, based at Harvard University. Not so much typical of all US companies, it is rather one of the more distinguished such groups in the 1990s and its range of activities is not atypical.

Founded by critic-scholar-director Robert Brustein (b. 1927), the ART produces innovative reinterpretations of classics as well as new works by contemporary playwrights. One of the few companies in the country with a resident acting ensemble performing in rotating repertory, it has garnered numerous awards, including a 1983 Pulitzer Prize, the first one ever awarded to a play produced outside New York – Marsha Norman's (b. 1947) *'night, Mother*. In 1985 the Pulitzer Prize was awarded for the ART's production of Robert Wilson's *the CIVILwarS*. In 1985, the ART won the Jujamcyn Award for outstanding contributions to the development of creative talent and in 1986 a Tony Award for continued excellence in resident theatre. In 1986, French drama critics lauded it with the Best Foreign Work Award for Wilson's production of Euripides' *Alcestis*.

The ART has presented world premières of

JoAnne Akalaitis's 1985 American Repertory Theatre production of Samuel Beckett's *Endgame*, designed by Douglas Stein.
Photo: Richard M. Feldman, courtesy ART.

surprisingly, in two important plays by African Americans: *A Raisin in the Sun* by Lorraine Hansberry and *Dutchman* by Amiri Baraka (LeRoi Jones). In *A Raisin in the Sun*, Hansberry, who claimed her play was 'actively a protest', introduces a character new to the US stage: an African intellectual, Asagai. Beneatha, a young African American, is confused about many issues, including her identity. To dramatize this issue, Hansberry presents her with two suitors – George, a member of the black bourgeoisie who despises Africa, and Asagai, a Nigerian who helps Beneatha discover her roots. Choosing one man over the other represents more than a love-object choice. It represents a system of values, a way of life and an identity. 'Assimilationism is so popular in your country,' Asagai tells her. 'We have a great deal to talk about. I mean about identity'.

A Raisin in the Sun dramatizes not only the prejudices African Americans face – the plot turns on whether or not Beneatha's family will move into a white neighbourhood – but also that African Americans come out of a complex history. In *Les Blancs*, her last play, unfinished at her untimely death at age 34 from cancer, Hansberry returned to the theme of identity in a more overtly political way. In the soul of Tshembe Matoseh, a self-divided character, his African heritage and his links with Europe set off a complex, dynamic, evolving relationship.

As in Hansberry, questions of race and identity come up in the work of Amiri Baraka. Anxiety over assimilation and the loss of identity run throughout his plays, which he calls a revolutionary theatre. In *Dutchman*, Lula, a white, apple-crunching *agent provocateur*, waltzes around Clay, a young black man she bumps into in a subway. By turns seductive and caustic, she castrates him symbolically and murders him literally – an allegory of the conspiracy of white society to deprive blacks of their heritage, identity, dignity and, ultimately, lives.

Besides economic, educational and social oppression, *Dutchman* dramatizes an even more insidious form, the repression of a self that mirrors the interior world. These concerns are also crucial in the plays of Adrienne Kennedy – *Funnyhouse of a Negro* and *A Movie Star Has to Star in Black and White* (1976), and Suzan-Lori Parks – *The Death of the Last Black Man in the Whole Entire World* and *The America Play* (1993). In the first act of *The America Play* a black imitates Abraham Lincoln so that other blacks can assassinate him in a shooting gallery;

in the second act, two blacks dig desperately in the abyss of history, trying to recuperate a past that has been denied them. History is an important part of one's self-fashioning.

All these plays fall broadly under the aesthetic of realism, except *Dutchman*, which moves towards allegory, and the works of Kennedy and Parks, which chronologically come later and show the influence of the avant-garde.

In the 1960s several social movements – civil rights, feminism, the sexual revolution, ecology, consumer advocacy, health food, hippies, the protest against the war in Vietnam – radically questioned US values and the US way of life. Dedicated to social and political change, many of these movements attempted to create a new society and a counter-culture. 'Tune in, turn on, drop out,' preached Timothy Leary (b. 1920), the prophet of LSD, expressing the hostility that the youth of the United States felt towards the military-industrial complex and the myths of suburbia. Love beads, marijuana, communes – disenchanted youth tried many avenues of escape from the repressive mechanisms of a dehumanized society whose major concern was competition and the efficient production of material goods.

Hair (1967), the tribal love rock musical, celebrated sex, drugs, and rock and roll while protesting against Vietnam. The 1960s saw a general malaise settle over the country; however, a sense of exhilaration and hope sprang up, especially among the young, about the possibilities of change and renewal.

To understand the alternative dramaturgy that emerged in the United States at this time, one must place it back into the social and historical context of the counter-culture. Realism, linked to Broadway, and a middle-class worldview, began to appear more and more obsolete. Under the influence of Artaud, Brecht and Grotowski, talented and innovative theatre artists wanted to create a new theatre. They did. The US avant-garde brought poetry back to the stage, but it was a poetry of the theatre – to use Cocteau's phrase – not verbal poetry. They turned their backs on the literary traditions of theatre.

In the bubbling cauldron of artistic experimentation that was downtown Manhattan in the 1960s, new forms and visions took hold. Inspired by choreographer Merce Cunningham (b. 1919) and musician John Cage (1912–92) and by the phenomenon of the 'happening' (a semi-structured event in which the audience participated), much of the new dramatic work cut across traditional boundaries, incorporating elements from theatre, dance, the visual arts, film, opera, agitprop and ritual. Multi became the most commonly used prefix for the new theatre: multimedia, multi-channelled, multilayered. Unlike Broadway, the goal of the alternative theatre was not to make handsome profits by churning out entertainment, but, using ritual as the model, to restructure consciousness and change the world.

In many ways, the Living Theatre, which began in the 1950s, paved the way for much of the experimentation. Using the commune as its model, scripts were often fashioned collectively, often from found texts (the concept of private property had even become suspect); spectators were no longer left alone to watch passively, but were confronted and forced to participate; performances often took place in makeshift spaces without décor – actors and audience together created the environment; performers did not assume characters but accomplished simple, physical tasks wearing ordinary street clothes or

in the nude; the visual gained ascendancy over the verbal; and a written text was replaced by the performance as text. The realistic theatre's sense of self and identity – anchored in the bourgeoisie's overemphasis on the individual – was dismissed. Most importantly, the Living Theatre wanted to break down the dichotomy between art and life.

Paradise Now (1968), its most famous work began, 'I'm not allowed to take my clothes off. I'm not allowed to smoke hashish. When you criticize radically, you construct.' The audience was then invited to violate social taboos by taking off its clothes and smoking pot. *Paradise Now* ended with the war cry: 'You are the leader of your revolution. The theatre is in your life. Free the theatre. Free your life. The theatre is in the street. Free the theatre. Free the street.' The company's production of *Frankenstein* (1965) demonstrated how capitalism creates monsters, while the group's *Antigone* (1967) was a significant anti-war protest.

The major theatrical figure to arise from this

The 1986 American Repertory Theatre production of *Alcestis*, conceived, directed and designed by Robert Wilson.
Photo: Richard M. Feldman, courtesy ART.

Harvey Keitel and William Hurt in Mike Nichols's 1984 Goodman Theatre production of David Rabe's *Hurlburly*.
Photo: Tom Lascher, courtesy Goodman Theatre.

David Wheeler's 1981 American Repertory Theatre production of Sam Shepard's *True West*, set design by Kate Edmunds, costume design by Nancy Thun.
Photo: Richard M. Feldman, courtesy ART.

Gerald Gutierrez's 1983 Playwrights Horizons production of Wendy Wasserstein's *Isn't It Romantic*.
Photo: Peter Cunningham, courtesy Playwrights Horizons.

Like the other plays written by women discussed here, *Isn't It Romantic* demonstrates that forging a self, especially if the identity one wants to create goes against society's grain, is difficult but possible. For the female protagonist to move towards a self that better mirrors her own interior world and needs, she must, lucidly and aggressively, reject the identity imposed on her by men, gain self-assurance and self-reliance, and learn how to support herself economically and emotionally.

Since the 1980s one of the most exuberant and popular dramatic genres has been the monologue. A sub-genre of performance art, the monologue enables the actor-author to represent and project an identity – usually to an intimate audience – by weaving autobiographical tales: self becomes the performed text. Spalding Gray's (b. 1941) *Sex and Death to the Age of 14* (1986), and *Swimming to Cambodia* (1985), about filming *The Killing Fields*, are two of the finest examples.

One of the artists who set off a hurricane in Congress about the NEA's alleged funding of 'obscene art' in 1990 was monologist Holly Hughes (b. 1951). The chair of the NEA said, 'Holly Hughes is a lesbian and her work is very heavily of that genre'. Hughes uses this quotation to introduce herself in a performance piece called *Clit Notes* (1993). Like many monologists, Hughes excavates her past and ponders her present to dramatize the mystery of an identity that keeps changing, an identity that discards old roles and experiments with new ones yet still recognizes itself as 'the same, only different'. Ruminating on her father's impending death, she explores her difficult relationship with him and her unresolved Oedipal complex. Her attitude towards her father is a delicate minuet of anger, contempt and shy affection.

In her monologue, Hughes discusses the normative sexual patterns of US society against which she defines her sexuality and identity. Dancing a tarantella on her chair, half guerrilla warrior, half Lucille Ball, Hughes thrusts and parries with her rapier wit to reduce her enemy – the coercive self-righteousness of the not-so-silent majority – to the absurd. But underneath the mirth, streaks of anger and pain flash through. 'I have been the subject', she confesses, 'of lies, tears, and congressional investigations'. For Hughes, wit is not only a weapon to defeat the enemy, but also therapy to detoxify bitterness, fear and shame.

In *Imagine Being More Afraid of Freedom than Slavery* (1993), Pamela Sneed, an African-American performance artist, draws parallels between her racial and sexual marginalization as a black lesbian. Like it does for Hughes, the act of performing becomes a therapeutic psychodrama. And like Hughes, she uses the monologue to fashion a persona that mirrors not what society expects but what she feels. But in contrast to Hughes, who uses wit as a defensive and offensive weapon, Sneed finds strength and solace in communion with her race and in her attempt to establish and maintain contact between her race, her sexuality and her yearning for the sacramental, something beyond the ordinary, something transcendent.

One often hears that every country has the theatre it deserves. If this is true, then the United States has a much greater theatre than it deserves. In the period since World War II, theatre has been one of the most vital and creative aspects of US culture. Its dramatists have persistently examined, questioned and challenged the prevailing myths of US society, and the quantity, quality and diversity of US plays written during this period is indeed staggering. Why and how this occurred in a country where the government is generally opposed to the arts and the majority of the citizens are not only ignorant of but also indifferent to them is little less than a miracle.

Arthur Holmberg

(See also culturally specific discussions relating to playwriting in subsections on **Native-American Theatre**, **African-American Theatre**, **Chicano Theatre**, **Cuban-American Theatre** and **Puerto Rican-American Theatre**, in the opening, historical section.)

Directors, Directing and Production Styles

Like playwriting, US styles of directing can be divided roughly into three periods: realism (1945–60, dominated by a balance among important actors, directors and playwrights – Broadway defines success); the triumph of the avant-garde (1960–80, dominated by auteur-directors – Off-Broadway, Off-Off and the developing importance of regional theatres); and diversity, eclecticism and a return to kinetic realism (1980 to the present, dominated by playwrights).

The strongest influence on US realism among directors and actors was Konstantin Stanislavski, the Russian actor-director whose system profoundly affected the Group Theatre, a company that played a pivotal role in the creation of US realism. But Stanislavski's system was reinterpreted – some say misinterpreted – into a distinctly US style, often called 'the method' and associated most closely with Lee Strasberg and the Actors Studio, founded in 1947 by Elia Kazan, Cheryl Crawford and Robert Lewis; Strasberg joined two years later. The Studio gave actors a place to work seriously on their art, and it left a legacy of unforgettable performances.

Important US directors working in this style included Kazan – *All My Sons* (1947) by Arthur Miller, *A Streetcar Named Desire*, *Death of a Salesman* and *Cat on a Hot Tin Roof*; Harold Clurman – *Golden Boy*, *The Member of the Wedding* (1949) and Inge's *Bus Stop* (1955); and José Quintero – *Summer and Smoke*, O'Neill's *The Iceman Cometh* (1956) and *Long Day's Journey into Night*.

In the 1960s many forces converged to pull US theatre away from the method and realism. While realism continued in a box set behind the invisible fourth wall in the commercial theatre, the avant-garde asserted itself with a vitality that could not be ignored. The influence of the Theatre of the Absurd, especially director Alan Schneider (1917–84) and his work on the plays of Albee and Beckett, the examples of Peter Brook and Jerzy Grotowski, the impact of Brecht and Artaud, and the radical social climate – all pulled the most inspired US directors in a new direction in an attempt to renew US theatre.

Whereas the method stressed introspection, psychology, and the actor's connection to the role in order to project the illusion of realistic character, the avant-garde turned its back on character. Influenced by post-modern dance, the emphasis shifted to the physical presence of the performer, often doing simple, physical tasks, not the illusion of a make-believe character. Whereas the method had been psychological, interior and emotionally intense, the new rehearsal techniques that emerged, drawing on Grotowski, Artaud, and the improvisational games of Spolin, led to a performance style more physicalized, more external.

The importance of these theatre games and of improvisation cannot be overemphasized. They changed the way actors rehearsed and the way productions looked. In the Living Theatre's *Mysteries and Smaller Pieces* (1964), for example, these improvisational games formed a large part of the production itself. In addition, especially in the case of Robert Wilson, much more emphasis was given to the formal aspects of staging, especially to line, spatial relationships and movement patterns, rather than to plot or character. Moving theatre away from literature and towards the visual arts and dance, Wilson demonstrated how much and how quickly the eye understands. Unlike other directors who emerged in the 1960s, however, Wilson from the beginning was set apart by his insistence on precision, virtuosity and classical balance in his visual compositions. Other directors purposely created productions that looked rough and improvised.

Wilson's unique rehearsal methods resulted in productions that privileged the visual. For actors trained in realism, the method and psychology, it is difficult to adjust to Wilson, who insists that actors act with a total awareness of their body's movement through space. In a Wilson rehearsal, actors do not sit and analyse motivation. They learn and practise complex movement sequences much like a tap dancer. *DEAFman GLANCE* is Wilson's signature piece. In the prologue, a mother in a black Victorian dress first gives milk to her children and then murders them. The older brother witnesses the murder, and in the trauma loses his power of speech. He wanders into a magical dreamland where a series of surrealistic marvels unfold. *DEAFman GLANCE* sums up an era in US theatre during which language was marginalized and auteur-directors created a new visual poetry to force the audience to see the world with new eyes.

According to Robert Brustein,

American theatre was virtually revolutionized from the sixties on by the influence of Peter Brook and the immigration of European stage directors, particularly such Romanians as Liviu Ciulei, Andrei Şerban, Lucian Pintilie and Andrei Belgrader. These artists, coming from non-English speaking countries, brought a bright insouciance to the staging of English classics, as well as a natural affinity for non-representational plays and production techniques in stark contrast to the traditional American realism of, say, Kazan, and the English-influenced Shakespeare of the American Shakespeare Festival at Stratford, Connecticut. In addition to these auteurs, there was the monumental influence of Robert Wilson ... who, along with his own scenarios, began to stage the work of Euripides, Ibsen, Büchner, and other classic writers as if they were episodes in a continuing dream. And there was the influence of such performing groups as Mabou Mines and the Ontological-Hysterical Theatre, whose various directors were engaged in deconstructing the classics (in the case of the Wooster Group such American classics as *The Crucible* and *Our Town*) and transforming them into auteur exercises. The result of these various influences was the formation of some of the most adventurous directors of the day: Richard Foreman, JoAnne Akalaitis, Lee Breuer, Elizabeth LaComte, Anne Bogart, Robert Woodruff and many others, all devoted to wholly experimental probes into the classics and new plays, while mainstream American drama remained connected to realistic plays and realistic production techniques.

In Brustein's view, therefore, the major thrust of the avant-garde was the visionary director. Actors and playwrights in the avant-garde had a much less central role.

These new tendencies were brilliantly realized in the Performance Group's production of *Dionysus in 69* (1968), staged by Richard Schechner. Using a Brazilian birth ritual as one of his models, Schechner powerfully transformed Euripides' *The Bacchae* into an intense confrontation with the mystery of life and the mystery of death.

Another major 1970s production was Andrei Şerban's *Fragments of a Greek Trilogy*: *Medea* (1972), *Electra* (1973) and *The Trojan Women* (1974). By stitching together a stage language of ancient Greek and Latin pierced by human cries, Şerban created a sensuous sound spectrum that explored not so much the meanings of words but their music. His reinterpretation of Euripides' great anti-war play *The Trojan Women*, situated in an environment created by the audience's milling closely around the actors, remains one of the most memorable nights in modern US theatre.

Andrei Şerban's 1984 American Repertory Theatre production of Carlo Gozzi's *King Stag*, designed by Julie Taymor.
Photo: Richard M. Feldman, courtesy ART.

After this period of experimentation, US theatre settled down again to a basically realistic style, but there is more diversity in US theatre in the mid-1990s than ever before and the avant-garde changed forever the way that US actors act, US directors direct, and US designers design. Many of the avant-garde directors continue to work, especially in the regional theatres.

And even in present-day realism, the style is more physical, more extroverted. The emphasis is no longer on introspective emotion but on the physical act itself. One fine example of this new breed of realistic directors is Frank Galati (b. 1943), who often directs at Steppenwolf in Chicago.

Another major influence in US theatre in the 1980s and 1990s comes from Asia, especially Japan. Tadashi Suzuki, who devised a series of intense physical exercises that change the way an actor moves, has, through his productions and workshops, touched many US directors and actors. In 1988 he staged a memorable all-male *King Lear* in a co-production among three resident theatres: Berkeley Repertory Theatre, the

Arena Stage, and Stagewest in Springfield, Massachusetts. Eric Hill (b. 1953), the artistic director of Stagewest, is one of Suzuki's leading disciples, teaching the Suzuki method and staging productions using this technique. Like Wilson's, Suzuki's theatre is formal, stylized and anti-realistic.

After the great age of avant-garde auteur-directors, few new directors have been able to establish a reputation for themselves; more significant in the mid-1990s is the large crop of interesting and diverse playwrights. Few young directors stand out with a distinctive style. The two notable exceptions are Peter Sellars (b. 1957) – known for his radical revisions of classic texts such as Mozart's *Don Giovanni* (1989) – which he set in New York's Spanish Harlem among dope-pushers – and Anne Bogart (b. 1951), who carries on many of the experiments launched in the 1960s, especially in her attention to physical movement in plays such as Calderón's *Life Is a Dream* (ART, 1988). In his production of Sophocles' *Ajax* (1986), Sellars used African-American music. He built the choral odes on spirituals, Mississippi moans and

Frank Galati's 1988 Steppenwolf Theatre Company production of *The Grapes of Wrath*, adapted by Galati.
Photo: Courtesy Steppenwolf Theatre.

chain-gang chants. Other directors, such as California-based George Coates (b. 1952), work with projections and other electronic media, but these experiments have yet to culminate in a major achievement.

Arthur Holmberg

Music Theatre

Popular US musical theatre in the post-World War II period has been essentially a commercial entertainment centred on Broadway. Available to a broad middle-class audience, it was structured according to a post-war vision of 'the American dream'. By the 1990s it had developed into a neo-romantic, escapist spectacle available, for the most part, only to upper-income audiences.

The opening in 1943 of *Oklahoma!*, by composer Richard Rodgers and lyricist Oscar Hammerstein II, saw the form develop a new structure, which came to be called the 'integrated musical' or 'book show', in which dialogue, song and dance were consciously tied to the development of a story. It has been argued, however, that Hammerstein's collaboration with Jerome Kern (1885–1945) in *Show Boat* (1927) was the prototype of such book musicals.

The most common form of popular musical theatre in the United States prior to 1943 had followed the revue format in which the structure was a device on which to hang popular songs and dances. Like radio, the Broadway musical of the first part of the century was a showcase for new 'tunes'. The change that *Oklahoma!* represented occurred not so much in the structure of the musical as in the nature of the plots and social forces that shaped the stories being told, as well as the types of characters inhabiting these 'musical plays', as Hammerstein preferred to call the genre.

One factor facilitating this reformation of the

The 1994 Live Entertainment Corporation's Broadway production of Jerome Kern and Oscar Hammerstein's *Show Boat*, directed by Harold Prince, at the Gershwin Theatre. Photo: Catherine Ashmore.

musical was the dominance in film and drama of realist acting methods re-enforced in the United States by the Actors Studio. By the 1950s the method was virtually the only training curriculum offered to US actors. This created in librettists, actors and audiences the expectation of 'rounded' characters with complex psychologies.

One of the primary effects of these new musical plays was the way dance was used. The vision of classically-trained choreographer Agnes de Mille (1909–93) – the creator of the dance sequences for *Oklahoma!* – signalled the inclusion of dance as a fundamental part of the storytelling rather than the more common practice of creating a chorus line to give tired businessmen a chance to look at pretty showgirls.

During the 1950s, the integrated musical developed a variety of styles. With works such as *Carousel* (1945) and *The Sound of Music* (1959), Rodgers and Hammerstein harked back to the sentimental romantic forms of the operettas of Victor Herbert and Sigmund Romberg, popular on Broadway in the 1920s. Composer Frederick Loewe (1904–88) and lyricist Allan Jay Lerner (1918–86) continued this tradition in their lushly melodic scores and their

penchant for the British Isles with works such as *Brigadoon* (1947) and *My Fair Lady* (1956), a musical version of Shaw's *Pygmalion*.

Another type of book show was the 'city show'. These musicals concentrated on life in New York. Their dialogue and music reflected the fast-paced challenges of urban living. The form was best exemplified in works such as *Wonderful Town* (1953), with book and lyrics by Betty Comden (b. 1915) and Adolf Green (b. 1915) and music by Leonard Bernstein (1918–90), and Frank Loesser's (1910–69) *Guys and Dolls* (1950), with book by Abe Burrows (1910–85) and Jo Swerling (b. 1897).

Not all Broadway musicals of the period were completely transformed by the structures of the integrated musical. Artists such as Cole Porter (1891–1964), with his facility for witty and sophisticated lyrics, continued the tradition from the 1920s and 1930s of the revue format. Porter's most successful work, *Kiss Me, Kate* (1948), entwined Shakespeare's *Taming of the Shrew* with a backstage tale of stormy romance and an abundance of popular songs.

The integrated musicals between 1943 and 1964, though written by a wide variety of creative artists, all had a common formula and unconscious social message. Their stories

439

supported the post-war necessity of re-establishing the mythology of the American dream as defined by the dominant white middle class. The artists themselves believed in American mythologies. They were easterners, mostly privileged, upper-middle class, Caucasian males (with the notable exception of Betty Comden), well educated and often of Jewish immigrant origins.

They used source materials from other media, mostly novels, to fashion stories that reinforced the ideals and secular creeds created about the United States in the nineteenth century. This American dream was made precious by the real threats to democracy from the fascist powers that caused the reluctant entry of an historically isolationist United States into World War II.

These book musicals contained four inter-dependent myths.

The Romance. This is the belief that one's stability and worth comes from a love relationship sanctioned and restricted by Protestant ideals of marriage. A typical story is the plot of *Guys and Dolls*, in which Sarah Brown, the virginal Salvation Army crusader, falls in love with the gambler Sky Masterson, reforms him by the power of her love and marries him at the mission. In a comic subplot, Adelaide, a nightclub dancer, schemes to marry Nathan Detroit, Sky's henchman. By their entering into these romantic relationships, which they understand must be permanent and monogamous, the men are seen to give themselves over to the Puritan ethic of their intended wives.

The Hometown. A married couple should create a moral home for raising children by settling in a suburb or small town, free from the corruptions of business and city life. Meredith Willson's (1902–84) nostalgic look at a late-nineteenth-century small US town, *The Music Man* (1957), exemplifies the myth through the female lead Marian, the town librarian, who stands up for the misguided salesman Harold Hill. Hill proves his ability to become a moral father through his relationship with her young brother. Marion falls in love with the 'real' man behind the salesman, and by the play's end we know they will be married and settle down in River City, Iowa, a quintessential US hometown.

The Woman as Homemaker. To heal a perceived breach in the social contract caused by World War II, women were seen as needing to return from the workforce to become homemakers and the prime supporters of their husbands' careers. This is essential to the genre.

Almost every plotline in the integrated musical between 1945 and 1964 deals with a working woman who, by the end of the story, leaves her work or puts it in a secondary place behind her intention to marry and support the man with whom she falls in love. If the female lead fails to do this, she is punished. There are two prime examples of this punishment ritual. The first was Rodgers and Hammerstein's *The King and I* (1951), in which Anna refuses to marry Edward and return home and quite literally causes the king to die. The other was *Gypsy* (1959), with music by Jule Styne (1905–94), book by Arthur Laurents (b. 1918) and lyrics by Stephen Sondheim (b. 1930). In this plot, Mama Rose refuses to marry Herbie and set up a home and thereby nearly succumbs to a nervous breakdown in the final song. In the end she comes to a tenuous reconciliation with her daughter, Louise. Both women are portrayed as unfulfilled. The mother had pushed her daughter into becoming a stripper. Louise became the star Gypsy Rose Lee and thus was denied the possibility of a happy home and family. Significantly, this work has had a continuous history of successful Broadway revivals and reveals the continuing dilemma of the place of women in US society.

The Pioneer. US men must seek out a territory to conquer; career success is the key to personal identity. The integrated musical taught men that they must fall in love, become monogamous and allow their wives to nurture their husbands' search for success; success will not come if the man does not allow this process of domestication to occur. Jeff in *Bells Are Ringing* (1956), by Jule Styne with book and lyrics by Comden and Green, is typical of the male lead. Having lost his partner, he must now try to become a successful playwright on his own merit. He falls in love with Ella, who proves to him that (with her help) he can do it all alone.

Such musicals were New York-based phenomena and depended on the image of being a 'hit' on Broadway in order to gain acceptance in the larger popular culture. Few musicals could enter into mainstream culture if they were not 'on Broadway', an icon of the US ideal of success. One notable exception was Tom Jones (b. 1928) and Harvey Schmidt's (b. 1929) *The Fantasticks*, which opened at a 110-seat theatre Off-Broadway in 1960 and was still running in 1994.

Hit shows often entered the mainstream of popular culture. Many Broadway musicals were made into films. Show tunes became a major medium through which the messages of the

American dream were celebrated throughout society. Songs from hit musicals readily entered common currency via recordings and variety shows on television. One could not escape show tunes even at work since a company called Muzak piped orchestral versions of such scores into office buildings, department stores and any elevator that could be wired up.

In the 1960s, the structure of the musical changed as quickly and radically as did the historical events that changed US society. A multitude of counter-culture movements both challenged and changed the common cultural definition of the United States imposed on post-World War II society by the heretofore dominant white middle class. New musical structures were created that expressed these changes.

The integrated musical could no longer function as a ritual of the American dream. A consensus as to its efficacy no longer existed within the dominant white culture. The destruction of that common belief system forced the musical comedy to change its ritual structure as well.

New technologies (amplified sound, video and cassette tape, and computers) that better suited the new society created performance environments and symbologies that were more powerful than those of the musical comedy. The middle class turned away from the theatre as a common form of popular entertainment to newer forms of popular music, including rock and roll, which revolutionized live performances by the introduction of amplification and non-acoustic instruments. Movies also provided mass entertainment that was readily available and affordable while television refined its equivalent of the integrated musical, the situation comedy.

Hello, Dolly! (1964), with music and lyrics by Jerry Herman (b. 1932) and book by Michael Stewart (1929–87), opened less than two months after the Kennedy assassination and proved to be the final recapitulation of the mythology of the American dream. Dolly, the ageing female lead, is a widow trying to marry a successful businessman who can provide her with a home in the late-nineteenth-century New York suburb of Yonkers.

The next hit on Broadway, which opened only nine months later, was *Fiddler on the Roof* (1964). With music by Jerry Bock (b. 1925), book by Joseph Stein (b. 1912) and lyrics by Sheldon Harnick (b. 1924), the work dramatizes a journey story in which the lead is not a romantic female but Tevye, a poor, ageing Jewish dairyman whose traditional family disintegrates amidst a background of social chaos. The piece was written in the form of a serio-comic melodrama, in which Tevye heads for the United States at play's end in an attempt to claim the American dream for an audience that was, in fact, no longer sure where it had gone.

One of the more obvious changes in the structure of the musical was the gradual abandonment of a defined melody and the use of individual songs as the structural basis for the score. The arrival of the Beatles in the US in 1964 and the consequent turning of the music industry to a youth market created a musical sound in popular entertainment that no longer coincided with the sound of the integrated musical. Beat replaced melody as the foundation for pop music. Instruments were not used as mere accompaniment but for their own particular sound. Commonly this new song structure included no specific ending or 'button' as in the songs from a musical. Because the melody no longer had precedence, the common 'AABA' form of songwriting was abandoned.

This new sound lessened the dependence of the music on the lyric. The voice no longer provided the focal point of the structure. It became just another instrument among many. In this new stage sound, the voice no longer served as a vehicle for the lyric; on the contrary, it was blended into a larger compositional structure. Lyrics were used as vehicles for a sound quality.

Amplified sound created a new wall between actor and audience by separating the performers from their own voices. The audience had to respond to a voice coming from a place different from the position of the actor. Further, the voice was synthesized so as to eliminate its natural resonance and overtones. Performers could no longer create a dynamic focus and stage presence because they had lost control over their performance. The sound technician now controlled the performance.

One of the first musicals on Broadway to use rock orchestrations and instrumentation was *Hair* (1968), with a score by Canadian-born Galt MacDermot (b. 1928) and book and lyrics by Gerome Ragni (1942–91) and James Rado (b. 1932). Billed as '*the* rock musical' it used rock sound to protest against the Vietnam War. It glorified the counter-culture, which encouraged dropping out of a corrupt US society run by the military-industrial complex and expanding social and individual consciousness through drugs.

By the late 1960s, popular music represented

the 'youth culture'. Previously, the adult world had set the social agenda, and the music of the adults, who sought to maintain the status quo, had constituted pop music. With the coming of the youth market in the music business, in the mid-1960s, pop music became the symbol of the counter-culture, which saw the American dream as a bankrupt myth. The two forms were incompatible cultural forces, and the stronger won out: rock music. The US musical began a swift decline as an entertainment for mass audiences. Quickly it became the province of only an upper-middle class that could afford the rising ticket prices and who would not object to the more liberal content of the work of the new generation of theatre artists.

Though the change in the ritual structure of musical comedy seemed almost instantaneous, the precedents for such a change had been set as far back as 1957 in Leonard Bernstein's landmark work *West Side Story*, with book by Arthur Laurents and lyrics by Stephen Sondheim. After its controversial première, theatre critics hailed it as the dawn of a new age of musical theatre. Some years later, many theatre historians called it the last true US musical comedy and the final perfection of the genre.

West Side Story contained within it all the signs of the death of the integrated musical. The most prominent sign was the ritual story, which revealed the failure of the romantic myth within the context of the American dream. Set in the ghettos of New York City, the US that it portrayed was a demoralized, urban society incapable of solving the crises that threatened the American dream. For the first and perhaps only time in a Broadway musical, the audience was forced into a conscious confrontation with the inability of the white middle class to deal honestly with racism.

The civil rights movement of the 1960s coupled with the new rock sound provided an entrée in the 1970s for the 'black musical'. Works such as *Purlie* (1970) and *The Wiz* (1975) at last openly acknowledged forms of African-American music, which had given birth to much of US popular music in the twentieth century, from blues to jazz to rock. *Purlie* was the first of this type. With book by Ossie Davis, Phillip Rose (b. 1921) and Peter Udell (b. 1934) and a score based on gospel music by Gary Geld (b. 1935), it showed the challenges of a young black preacher returning to his home in Georgia to improve the living conditions of southern African Americans.

These musicals were not authentic stories out of the black experience. On the contrary, they reverted to the revue format and were crafted for white audiences who came primarily to be entertained. *The Wiz*, with a score by Charlie Smalls (b. 1943), was an all-black version of the classic US children's story *The Wizard of Oz* (1903). This reverted to a common form of musical current in the 1930s (such as Michael Todd's (1907–58) production of *The Hot Mikado* in 1939) in which material familiar in white culture was reworked to a score with a contemporary swing sound and performed by an all-black cast, which played to an all-white audience. The social and cultural realities of the black community that created these musical forms were not honestly addressed but caricatured. At bottom the 'black musical' could not genuinely celebrate the black or the white United States. The plotlines sustained the white middle-class version of the romantic myth, but the real issues of the various crises in civil rights were sidestepped.

With the rise of a larger black middle class by the 1980s, Broadway could more confidently invest in musicals that spoke more clearly to the African-American experience and targeted more specifically black audiences. *Jelly's Last Jam* (1991) exemplifies the trend in its attempt to create 'crossover' entertainment that could be marketed to both black and white audiences. Within the black community itself, gospel-based musicals were being performed that were direct reflections of the African-American experience. Created by black artists for black audiences, shows such as David Payton's *A Good Man is Hard to Find* (1988) were mounted as touring shows, not as vehicles for Broadway. This was the first effort to create musicals for a mass audience that bypassed the seeming cultural and commercial necessity of the Broadway hit.

Another form of musical score to rise from the disintegration of the integrated musical was the return to a type of operetta, as exemplified in the later works of Stephen Sondheim. Beginning with *A Little Night Music* (1973), the score required a more complex pit orchestra with its own independent texture and the dropping of the conventional 'musical comedy' voice, which had a range and resonance of an average person. The score required the trained sound familiar in traditional opera and operetta. The musical comedy voice, which was crafted to present lyrics clearly and melody simply, was no longer needed because the score was no longer based on a song structure but on a musical structure perfected by Wagner and Verdi, by which a score is 'through composed'.

Songs tended not to have a definite beginning or end but were connected by complex recitative structures. These are sophisticated pieces with complex ideas woven into intricate lyrics. From *Night Music* on, Sondheim's works had trouble commercially. They rarely appealed to a broad middle-class audience but found a hearing in the urban, educated classes. Sondheim created a new structure for the musical, which gave currency to the name 'musical theatre' and the currently preferred 'music theatre'. The term dispensed with the necessity of defining pieces as genres such as 'opera', 'operetta' or 'musical play'.

Concurrent with Sondheim's work, another form of the musical took on the dimensions of grand opera. English composer Andrew Lloyd Webber was the primary force in this development. In his work, the libretti and scores returned to the sentimentality of Puccini and the leitmotif structure of Wagner. These musicals were staged spectacles built around stories often based on late-nineteenth-century European neo-romanticism. Lloyd Webber's *Phantom of the Opera* (1985) typifies this development.

In fact, the economics of the theatre has removed such large-scale musicals from the realm of mass entertainment. The rapid escalation of ticket prices made it increasingly elitist. From a stable top ticket price of $6 in the late 1940s prices jumped to $15 within the space of three years between 1965 and 1968. By the 1990s the same ticket cost an average of $65 with prices going as high as $125.

Economics also forced the restructuring of the libretto and score. The number of scenes had to be reduced to lower design costs. The number of union stagehands required to operate a show had to take account of 'featherbedding' practices in union regulations. The cast had to be cut to offset higher union and star salaries. The orchestra had to be reduced, and the length of the score had to be cut to accommodate no more than a three-hour call for union musicians.

By the late 1970s the US musical was no longer created primarily through collaborative effort but rather under the single vision of one person. Such 'superdirection' was a trend whereby the director, who was often also the choreographer, controlled every aspect of the production and generally employed a unifying principle, other than the plot, to create the sense of a whole piece. This marked the structural alteration of the 'integrated musical' to the 'concept musical'.

The most significant example of this development was *A Chorus Line* (1975). The show had no plot but was a series of personal stories held together by the concept of a director holding an audition. It was performed without stars, there was no intermission and the scenery was minimal. This idea originated with the director-choreographer Michael Bennett (1943–87). Late in the process, the composer Marvin Hamlisch (b. 1944) was engaged to create a score. It was an immediate success and ran on Broadway for over ten years. The score provided a vehicle for a variety of dancers to present their life stories in rapid succession. Though unrelated, each story revolved around the urgency of attaining success through a job in a Broadway show. The audience found itself engaged in these dancers' search for personal identity and self-actualization.

The 1980s saw an increase in revivals of integrated musicals. Whether driven by nostalgia or an attempt to reassert its values or the sheer entertainment value of the older musical comedies, Broadway consistently staged and toured large-scale revivals. The integrated musical had always survived in suburbs and small towns through revivals. Dinner theatres and high schools regularly produced these shows.

Rock concerts have become the newest mass medium of music theatre. They originated in the counter-cultural movements of the 1960s, and their form is based both on the use of spectacle and the desire to create a communal audience response. The music is felt as much as heard. The performance creates a total environment in which there is a direct audience–actor exchange. This interactive experience depends on the electronic reproduction of the sound in a large space, generally a sports stadium, which creates the binding force between performer and audience.

There is an enormous variety of 'sounds' and bands, each with its own type of culture and audience. An intergenerational group such as the Grateful Dead appeals to the older myths of world peace, expanded consciousness through drugs, and the communal ideal of human solidarity. Heavy metal bands such as Guns 'n' Roses draw on the need to express protest through violence and project a working-class ideal that strongly rejects what it sees as radical elements such as feminists and homosexuals. More serious social protest bands such as U-2

dreams in composing *Street Scene*: writing a US opera, and creating 'a special brand of musical theatre which would completely integrate drama and music, spoken word, song and movement'. *Street Scene* was well received and ran for 146 performances.

Weill's subsequent works included the one-act opera *Down in the Valley* (1948), written with folk-like simplicity for school performances, and his next work for Broadway, *Lost in the Stars*, with a book and lyrics by Maxwell Anderson (1888–1959). Based on Alan Paton's South African novel *Cry the Beloved Country*, this was a musically ambitious and politically passionate theatre piece, which opened in 1949.

Marc Blitzstein, only five years younger than Weill but cast in the role of disciple, captured in his musical play *The Cradle Will Rock* (1937) the liberal spirit of the 'new deal' United States that emerged in the years following the Depression. There was a turning away from the idealization of wealth and privilege. The crash of the stock market had destroyed the United States' faith in the benevolence of capitalism, and much of the work of this era dealt with the common people and their relationship to corrupt plutocrats. But it was the latter group that caught Blitzstein's attention in his single full-length opera, *Regina* (1949), based on the play *The Little Foxes* (1939) by Lillian Hellman. The play showed the spectacle of an avaricious southern family disintegrating into a morass of hatred; in short, the plutocrats getting their due. Blitzstein's musical language was heavily influenced by Weill, though *Regina* was even more ambitiously operatic than *Street Scene*. Also opening on Broadway in 1949, it survived for only fifty-six performances. Nevertheless, it was later brought into the repertoire of the New York City Opera and has been frequently and successfully revived.

While the theatre critics of the 1940s and 1950s had been receptive to operatic endeavours on Broadway, the music critics of the 1960s had little patience for works that seemed tainted by the commercial theatre. The chasm between popular and serious, which these composers had tried so hard to close, was reopening.

The most promising talent to heal this breach was Leonard Bernstein, a glamorous figure in the early 1940s, both as composer and conductor. His two most significantly operatic works were *Trouble in Tahiti* (1952) and *Candide* (1956). The one-act *Trouble in Tahiti* used pop music techniques juxtaposed with more traditionally operatic scenes and arias. The opera portrayed the emptiness and boredom of conventional suburban life. It was first performed at Brandeis University in Massachusetts, where Bernstein was a faculty member.

Candide opened on Broadway and was an extravagant financial failure. Nevertheless, an original cast recording kept the score alive, and eventually, in 1973, with a reworking of the book and the addition of music that had been cut from the Broadway production, it was accepted as a valuable US operetta and is now widely performed. The buoyant and lively score uses conventional operatic forms – duets, ensembles, and even a coloratura aria. When Bernstein became the musical director of the New York Philharmonic in 1958, his composing activity diminished. Bernstein did not return to operatic form in any significant way. His later stage works, *Mass* (1971) and *A Quiet Place* (1983), an expansion of the earlier *Trouble in Tahiti*, seemed forced and ineffective compared with the earlier work.

The final composer who must be considered during the Broadway era of US opera is Gian Carlo Menotti (b. 1911). Though Menotti was born in Italy, he came to the US as a teenager and studied at the Curtis Institute in Philadelphia, as did Bernstein and Samuel Barber (1910–81), who will be considered later. Menotti's first opera was a tuneful comic work, *Amelia Goes to the Ball* (1937), first performed at Curtis. Its great success and Menotti's charm and excellent connections in the music world led to three performances at the Metropolitan Opera in 1938.

Amelia Goes to the Ball hardly represented a difficulty for the Met audience as Menotti's music was in the mainstream of conservative Italian operatic composition. *The Medium* (1947) ran for seven months on Broadway, on a double bill with *The Telephone* (1947). It established Menotti, who wrote his own libretti, as the most successful practitioner of contemporary *verismo*. The skilful melodrama, enriched with appealing melodies, and the presence of an effective central role, were very much in the tradition of Puccini, whose works had by this time established a near stranglehold on the repertoire of conservative opera houses.

Later seen on Broadway were Menotti's *The Consul* (1950) and *The Saint of Bleecker Street* (1954), both tremendously successful, both winners of the Pulitzer Prize. A commission from the National Broadcasting Company brought forth *Amahl and the Night Visitors*

(1951), intended for television during the Christmas season. It has had hundreds of productions since. The success of these four works, in addition to those of Blitzstein, Thomson, Gershwin and Weill, made for an era in which a US opera tradition seemed not just possible, but present.

In 1927 the second act of Gounod's *Faust* was broadcast via radio live from the Chicago Opera. The Metropolitan initially regarded opera broadcasts as a stunt, beneath the dignity of the institution. In the face of the promise of considerable income, however, they soon surrendered to the inevitable, and the first broadcast from the stage of the Met was Humperdinck's *Hansel and Gretel* during Christmas 1931; the first Saturday matinée broadcast occurred during the 1933–4 season, and by the end of the decade these broadcasts were an established feature of each opera season.

'Saturday Afternoon at the Met' brought opera to a vast new nationwide audience. This popularization, compounded by the introduction of the long-playing record in the early 1950s and widespread television broadcasts of opera two decades later, led to the proliferation of new opera companies in smaller cities and towns throughout the country. One of these organizations was founded right under the nose of the Metropolitan: the New York City Opera.

The founding of the City Center, of which the City Opera was but one component, was a complex and convoluted affair, but it was essentially the creation of two men: Morton Baum (1905–68), an attorney with political connections to the mayor of New York, and the socially well-connected Newbold Morris (1902–66). These men shared a vision of a producing organization that would bring theatre, ballet and particularly opera to a large New York audience who could not afford the ticket prices at the Metropolitan or on Broadway. In February 1944, the New York City Opera opened with a performance of the ever-present *Tosca*.

Although the company initially seemed like a poor person's version of the Metropolitan, in 1949 it gave the world première of African-American composer William Grant Still's (1895–1978) *Troubled Island* (1941). This was not considered a success at the time, though Still's many operas, including *Bayou Legend* (written in 1941, premièred in 1974), *Minette Fontaine* (composed in 1958, first produced in 1985) and *Highway 1, USA* (1962), have

proven effective and continue to be performed occasionally. He was the first African-American composer to have an opera performed by a major US company. Works by Menotti later came into the repertoire: *The Telephone* and *Amelia Goes to the Ball* in 1948, *Amahl and the Night Visitors* and *The Consul* in 1952 and *The Medium* in 1953. Also in 1953 the company staged Blitzstein's *Regina*. It was taking into its repertoire US works that had proven their audience appeal in long Broadway runs.

The next wholly new work was Aaron Copland's (1900–91) *The Tender Land* (1954). Copland was writing appealing music using US folk and traditional themes set into a rather spiky and urbane orchestral context. The combination, pioneered by Virgil Thomson, led to Copland's being considered the leading US composer of the era. His opera was eagerly awaited, but it failed to please. It seemed inert, in spite of attractive music.

The City Opera lived a precarious existence, and financial crises were constant. Baum sought assistance from the Ford Foundation. W. McNeil Lowry, director of the foundation, was not interested in simple deficit financing, however; he and Baum came up with a project that would be the most serious and far-ranging attempt at promoting US opera to that time, and in fact nothing since has matched it. The plan, initially opposed by company director Julius Rudel (b. 1921), was to use the spring seasons to produce a full season of contemporary US operas, drawing principally on works that had been previously produced with some success. Rudel acquiesced on the condition that the season also include at least one première of a new work. These men understood that while US works were frequently produced, they almost never got a second chance, the chance to prove themselves as viable repertoire pieces that a company could bring back in future seasons and that might thereby develop a committed, rather than merely curious, audience. The autumn seasons would continue to be composed of repertoire standards.

The first such season was 1958. Works performed were *The Ballad of Baby Doe* by Douglas Moore (1893–1969), a double bill of Bernstein's *Trouble in Tahiti* and Mark Bucci's (b. 1924) *Tale for a Deaf Ear*, Weill's *Lost in the Stars*, *The Taming of the Shrew* by Vittorio Giannini, Blitzstein's *Regina*, Menotti's *The Old Maid and the Thief* (1939) and *The Medium*, the world première of Robert Kurka's (1921–57) *The Good Soldier Schweik*, and

composed for the performing forces of a conventional opera house. The third of his 'portrait' operas, *Akhnaten* (1984), was then commissioned by the Stuttgart Opera and a subsequent production was seen at the Houston Opera, the New York City Opera and the English National Opera. The text was sung in ancient Egyptian, Akkadian (the ancient Babylonian language), and ancient Hebrew, with a spoken narration and final scene in the language of the audience. Subsequent works have included *The Fall of the House of Usher* (American Repertory Theatre and the Kentucky Opera, 1987), *The Making of the Representative for Planet 8* (a 1987 Houston Opera commission), and in 1992 *The Voyage* was commissioned and performed by the Metropolitan Opera itself.

These works, and the extent to which they have brought a new audience into the opera house, have helped develop an audience receptive to unfamiliar work. Among these have been John Adams's (b. 1947) popular operas *Nixon*

in China (1987) and *The Death of Klinghoffer* (1991), which also derive from a minimalist base but Adams has enriched the harmonic vocabulary and orchestrated with a lushness not previously heard in this kind of music. The Metropolitan also had a success with its commissioned work from John Corigliano (b. 1938), *The Ghosts of Versailles* (1991), which, with its libretto based on Beaumarchais and its highly eclectic score with musical references to a multitude of past styles, particularly those of Mozart and Rossini, represents a musical version of post-modernism.

All of these works have depended to a great degree on elaborate visual presentation. Whether they prove to have lasting musical value remains to be seen, but in the mean time opera houses seem in some sense revitalized; for the first time in the history of opera the work of US composers is being seen on opera stages in other parts of the world.

Fred Kolo

Dance Theatre

In the early 1940s, theatrical dance in the United States seemed to be comprised of three distinct categories: ballet, modern dance, and dance in musical theatre. Over the next five decades, each of these categories diversified and the borders between them became less distinct.

In the 1930s, the New Dance Group was founded to spread the idea of 'theatre as a weapon in the class struggle'. The group's programmes depicted the plight of workers impoverished by the Depression, and later raged against the Nazis. Larger audiences, however, were diverted from the reality of the economy by popular tours of groups such as the Ballets Russes, which offered European fairytales and graceful, virtuosic divertissements, along with elaborate costumes and designs. Until nearly the end of the decade, US dancers were rarely seen on the professional ballet stage; US subjects were not appealing and US culture, apparently, was inferior to that of Europe.

That attitude, however, was soon challenged. Supported by the vision and devotion of Lincoln Kirstein (b. 1907), Soviet choreographer George Balanchine (1904–83) moved to the United States in 1933. His works used modest scenery and costumes and were often abstract, depending heavily on the beauty of classical

ballet technique. Early in his US career, only small audiences were attracted to the work. His *Serenade* (1935, music by Tchaikovsky) set the tone; he described it as telling a 'story' musically and choreographically, with no need to resort to extraneous narrative. The Balanchine-Kirstein company was called the American Ballet (it became the New York City Ballet in 1948).

Kirstein also helped to create a touring offspring, the Ballet Caravan (1936–40), which produced Eugene Loring's (1914–82) US saga *Billy the Kid* (Aaron Copland, 1938). In this work, a story about cowboys and a notorious outlaw was told not only through ballet vocabulary but also by original movements, motivated primarily by character and emotion.

In 1939, another new company, the Ballet Theatre (from 1956 the American Ballet Theatre) began as a home for dancers using foreign, often Russian, choreographers. The Russians were soon joined by Antony Tudor (1908–87), a British choreographer, whose *Pillar of Fire* (music by Arnold Schönberg, 1942) revealed a Freudian theme of sexual frustration, a considerable shift in balletic subject matter.

Americans themselves began to appear more frequently as ballet characters. Agnes de Mille's

Rodeo (music by Copland, 1942) featured ranchers and a cowgirl doing square dances. Jerome Robbins's (b. 1918) *Fancy Free* in 1944 (music by Leonard Bernstein) portrayed three sailors who shuffled under a streetlamp while looking for dates.

By this time, however, the US had also seen the emergence of new choreographers who believed dance could deal with more serious issues. For them, the flowing elegance of ballet classicism would no longer do; a new vocabulary had to be invented. Martha Graham (1894–1991) had asserted that 'life today is nervous, sharp, and zigzag. This is what I aim for in my dances'. Doris Humphrey (1895–1958) defined the basis of modern dance as 'moving from the inside out'. No longer content with elaborating a technique that dated from the eighteenth century, these choreographers began with a feeling that they wanted to communicate and then sought the movement that would best convey that feeling to an audience. Rejecting ballet's traditionally rigid torso and brilliant legwork, they concentrated on movements stemming from the centre of the body.

The new modern dance produced powerful dramas, tense even in lyrical passages, admitting that harsh reality threatened even the most idyllic moments. Humphrey's *Day on Earth* (Copland, 1947) told the life of Everyman – his work, the departure of his first sweetheart, marriage and family, loss of loved ones, refuge in work. In 1953 she created two major contrasting works. In *Ritmo Jondo* (music by Carlos Surinach) four men courted four women with sweeping abandon, then casually left them to pursue other interests. *Ruins and Visions* (music by Benjamin Britten) showed a possessive mother learning to face reality when her son is killed in war.

Graham's *Night Journey* (music by William Schuman, 1947) retold the Greek story of Oedipus and Jocasta as a universal tragedy of misguided love. The climax of her rendition of Greek tragedies came with *Clytemnestra* (music by Halim El-Dabh, 1958), a full-evening work that showed the Greek queen re-enacting the tragic story of her life. For many of Graham's works, the designer Isamu Noguchi (1904–88) provided symbolic sculptures that enhanced the drama.

Comedy was seldom presented by the modern dance choreographers. There were exceptions, such as Graham's joyous *Diversion of Angels* (music by Norman Dello Joio, 1948) and

Acrobats of God (music by Surinach, 1960), a celebration of dancers. Humphrey's *Story of Mankind* (music by Lionel Nowack, 1946) traced a woman pushing her sluggish mate towards her idea of refinement from the caveman to a modern penthouse. Charles Weidman's *Flickers* (music by Nowack, 1942) played with the clichés of silent movies.

Both Graham and Humphrey encouraged their students and company members to experiment with choreography. A number of them produced significant works. José Limón (1908–72) created *The Moor's Pavane* (music by Henry Purcell, 1949) using just four dancers to tell the story of *Othello*, with elegant court dances framing the violent emotions. In *There Is a Time* (music by Dello Joio, 1956) verses from Ecclesiastes led the performers through enactments of the phases of human life.

A student of Graham, Anna Sokolow (b. 1912), created *Lyric Suite* (music by Alban Berg, 1953), in which she revealed a range of feelings motivated by the music, from *allegreto joviale* to *adagio apassionato*. Primarily serious and emotionally intense, Sokolow developed her own form of comment on contemporary life. *Rooms* (music by K. Hopkins, 1955) was a series of desperate solos by lonely people: unable to cope with reality, they imagined themselves as the people they longed to be.

Meanwhile, the US musical had been developing a style of its own. Fred Astaire (1899–1987) had set the debonair manner in dance routines only loosely connected to the story. Astaire's popularity continued while other approaches appeared. Ballet choreographer de Mille created dances for *Oklahoma!* (Richard Rodgers and Oscar Hammerstein II, 1943). Here movement was always related to dramatic action, especially in the 'dream ballet' danced by the heroine.

Helen Tamiris (1905–66), established as a social activist modern dancer with the Federal Theatre Project in the 1930s, turned to Broadway, scoring a special success with her dances for *Up In Central Park* (music by Sigmund Romberg, 1945), in which her 'skating ballet' was performed under falling snowflakes. Another modern dance choreographer, Hanya Holm (1893–1992), supplied *Kiss Me, Kate* (music by Cole Porter, 1948) with not only formal court dances but also witty jitterbug sessions, according to the characters involved. Jack Cole (1913–74), known in nightclubs and films as well as in theatre, combined modern dance with jazz and movements drawn from dances of the Middle East in *Kismet* (music adapted from Alexander Borodin, 1953).

As the country recovered from World War II, experiments flourished. In the early 1950s, a young dancer named Merce Cunningham, working with a young composer named John Cage, broke all the rules by making dances with no explicit subject matter. Further, Cunningham devised movements that bore no apparent relation to the sounds accompanying them and followed no perceivable sequence, as in *Suite by Chance* (1952). They proved that dance movement could be interesting in itself; adding plot, characterization or emotion only distracted from the movement. Cunningham continued to extend his inventiveness. In 1964, he devised 'events', made up of segments of earlier pieces. In the 1990s he was choreographing with computers.

Also initially perplexing to many viewers were the works of Alwin Nikolais (1910–93). For the many multimedia pieces that he created from the early 1950s, Nikolais composed his own electronic scores, designed his own costumes, and experimented with new kinds of lighting devices. The dancer was only one of a number of moving objects on his stage, as in *Masks, Props and Mobiles* (1953).

The next requisite to be discarded was established forms of technical skill. In line with the youthful, rebellious temper of the 1960s, the group known as the Judson Dance Theatre performed ordinary movements with slouching nonchalance, claiming to reduce dance to its essentials. Some choreographers set up external structuring devices: charts, tasks to be fulfilled, objects that restricted the space. They followed trends set by contemporary visual artists: collage and radical juxtaposition. Yvonne Rainer (b. 1934) said she was searching for the incongruous. Her *Trio A* (1966) used three dancers, each performing his own series of seemingly unrelated steps at his own speed. What were actually complex phrases were made to look commonplace.

An alumna of the Judson, Trisha Brown (b. 1936) created 'equipment pieces' that forced her dancers to adjust their movements to a situation, for example where they moved along ropes attached to a wall. Later 'accumulation

Merce Cunningham's 1968 *RainForest*, music by David Tudor, designed by Andy Warhol. Photo: Oscar Bailey, courtesy Cunningham Dance Foundation.

pieces' employed collections of movements, which might begin with a single gesture repeated, then joined by a new phrase, then another and another.

New streams of ingenuity continued to appear. Led by Steve Paxton (b. 1939), the approach of contact improvisation required intense sensitivity to the moves of a partner when no particular actions had been set. Key words were 'harmony' and 'spontaneity'. Lucinda Childs worked with cool formality on variations of geometric shapes and rhythmic structures. Laura Dean (b. 1945) chose repetition of unchanging movements to produce a hypnotic effect on the audience. For Molissa Fenley (b. 1954) it was driving motions set to a percussive, rhythmic accompaniment. David Gordon (b. 1936) and Valda Setterfield (b. 1939) linked movements with words to tell ambiguous bits of unfinished stories.

Thus, modern dance, stripped of linear content and dexterity, concentrated on a variety of ways of analytically conceiving movement in time and space and earned the title 'post-modern'.

Some choreographers, however, were difficult to pinpoint. Paul Taylor's (b. 1930) early solo *Epic* (1957) consisted of his standing still while a taped voice announced the time every twenty seconds; *Aureole* (1962) was lyrically danced by his company to music by Handel; *Big Bertha* (1971), to music of St Louis band machines, portrayed a 'typical American family' visiting a fair but lured to violence by a huge amusement park automaton. Then, in 1981, there was a return to lyricism in *Arden Court* (music by William Boyce), full of bravura solos and tender duets.

In 1965 Twyla Tharp (b. 1941) formed her own group to experiment with jazz-accompanied dancing that could look frantic but was always rigidly structured. In *Deuce Coupe* (music by the Beach Boys, 1973) Tharp happily combined classical and vernacular movements; in *Push Comes to Shove* (1976) for the American Ballet Theatre, she used classical music by Hayden and ragtime music by Joseph Lamb (1887–1960) to accompany dancers performing a segment of balletic leaps and turns, then a set of jazzy wiggles. Stylistic barriers were breaking down.

Other barriers were weakening as well. In the 1960s minority groups became prominent. The black company of Alvin Ailey (1931–89) infused the spirit of its African-American heritage in works such as *Revelations* (1960),

powerfully danced to stirring, traditional spirituals. He also drew on black jazz composer Duke Ellington (1899–1974) for *The River* (1970). Donald McKayle's (b. 1930) *Rainbow 'round My Shoulder* (1959), using prison songs of the old south, dealt with the suffering and the dreams of men in a chain gang. Moving in another direction, Arthur Mitchell (b. 1934), already a principal with the New York City Ballet, founded the Dance Theatre of Harlem in 1971, which gave black dancers an opportunity to perform the most demanding of ballets, full of graceful, ornate passages, as well as modern dance works that required percussive movements.

The revived interest in ethnic origins led to the formation of a number of companies that used folk idioms as a base for inventive choreography. Urban Bush Women, founded by Jawole Willa Jo Zollar (b. 1950) in 1984, drew on African traditions of chants, folk tales and movements. The American Indian Dance Theatre, founded in 1987, chose to present native ceremonial and seasonal dances from many regions of North America in their original form, adjusted only to the time and space made available by the theatre.

Meanwhile, ballet was thriving. For the New York City Ballet, Balanchine developed dancers of extraordinary speed and clarity of line. He was seldom concerned with narrative; his creations were rooted in the shapes of the music. His musical tastes were broad. Balanchine's repertoire for the company ranged from the gentle romanticism of Brahms (*Liebeslieder Waltzer*, 1960) to the lyrical classicism of Gluck (*Chaconne*, 1976) and the sharp modernism of Stravinsky (*Agon*, 1957).

Robbins joined the New York City Ballet in 1949 and, the following year, created *Age of Anxiety* to music by Bernstein. In contrast to Balanchine's plotless ballets, this was a dramatic portrait of contemporary insecurity seen through the meeting of four strangers at a bar and their attempt to establish meaningful relationships. In time, however, Robbins turned from his original dramatic orientation to give the company *Dancers at a Gathering* (1969), which followed the episodic moods of Chopin's music – in turn pensive, sad, contented, ecstatic. The direction of the company was taken over in 1983 by Peter Martins (b. 1946), who initiated a programme to give opportunities to young choreographers.

The American Ballet Theatre managed for long periods without a single resident choreographer. The repertoire was strengthened with revivals of nineteenth-century classics, and star dancers were brought from England, France and Russia to perform them.

One company member emerged as a choreographer. Eliot Feld (b. 1942) created the poetic *At Midnight* (music by Gustav Mahler, 1967). Two years later he established his own company and began to choreograph his own repertoire in diverse styles. While not neglecting classically based lyricism, he ventured into diverse styles. *Footstep of Air* (Irish and Scottish folk songs, 1977) drew on folk-style movements. For *Aurora 11* (music by Steve Reich, 1985), Feld had his performers jumping over, rolling down and dancing around a set of slanting boards that both restricted and stimulated their movements.

During the same time period, the Joffrey Ballet, founded by Robert Joffrey (1930–88) in 1954, was establishing a repertoire of wide-ranging styles. In 1967 Joffrey had arranged for Kurt Jooss to revive his *The Green Table* (music by Frederic Cohen), a landmark of German modern dance that juxtaposed scenes of statesmen going through the motions of peace-making while war devastated the lives of their people. Also in 1967, Joffrey created *Astarte* to music by Crome Syrcus, which featured images of the hippie culture; live scenes were interspersed with films of dancers in a rock club. Later, works were commissioned from post-modern choreographers, such as Tharp and Dean. Then, with 1987, came a reversal of direction. The company took on the reconstruction of Vaslav Nijinsky's experimental *Le Sacre du printemps* (*The Rite of Spring*, music by Stravinsky, 1913), meticulously researched by Millicent Hodson and Kenneth Archer. It was an unprecedented historical venture.

Meanwhile, the ideas of modern dance were attracting more young, creative talents. Now, they avoided simple, chronological sequence in favour of more adventurous, sometimes stream-of-consciousness structures. Reluctant to rely on movement alone, the new choreographers added other media – words or symbolic properties – to convey their ideas. The proscenium stage was often deserted for spaces that allowed the audience to feel closer to the performers; sometimes both audience and performers moved from one place to another – from a room to a park to a garage – to participate together in an event. The choreography itself was sometimes a collaborative venture, with dancers developing their own roles within the basic structures.

Meredith Monk (b. 1942) used many of these devices. She not only choreographed but also composed her own music, often playing and singing as well. Live sequences were often interspersed with films, dancing with song and speech; episodes replaced chronological narrative, and reality was juxtaposed with fantasy. In *Quarry* (1976), Monk played a sick child lying on a bed, surrounded by apparently unrelated figures: an elderly couple, men who look like biblical ancestors, three drab young women. In time, they are revealed as victims of the Holocaust.

In 1993 three Americans collaborated on *Necessary Weather*. Choreographers Dana Reitz (b. 1948) and Sara Rudner (b. 1944) worked with lighting designer Jennifer Tipton (b. 1937) to explore the interrelationship of movement and light; as rays traversed the stage in various shapes and spaces and tempos, the dancers responded with actions motivated by the actions of the beams.

Reflecting the rebellious nature and eclectic tastes of his time, Mark Morris (b. 1956) was a maverick. His dancers formed the lines and circles of his folk dance heritage, yet their movements were drawn from any style and combined in bizarre ways. *The Hard Nut* (music by Tchaikovsky, 1991) was an update of Lev Ivanov's 1892 *Nutcracker*, with its originally decorous, aristocratic children replaced by naughty teenagers, and with a Christmas tree visible only on a television screen. But there were also works such as the lyrical *L'Allegro, Il Penseroso, Ed Il Moderato* (1988), based on the poems of John Milton and accompanied by the music of Handel.

Meanwhile, the theatre generally had become more conscious of dance and of the potentially effective role that designed body movement could play on the dramatic stage. There was increasing concern with the use of non-verbal techniques. Courses in 'movement for actors' proliferated. The need was recognized, and choreographers had already started to take over as directors of newly integrated productions.

The first landmark was *West Side Story* (Bernstein, 1957), to which Robbins's choreography gave dynamic coherence. The gang wars of young hoodlums were shown in conflicting movement styles – the Latin rhythms of the Hispanics played against the US jazz steps of their adversaries. The lives of dancers constituted the subject of *A Chorus Line* (music by Marvin Hamlisch, 1975), in which Michael Bennett had young dancers who were applying for jobs in a show dance out their personal fears or fantasies. Kinetic flow distinguished all of Stephen Sondheim's *Sunday in the Park with George* (1983), as characters moved through an impressionistic landscape. Significantly, choreographer Randolyn Zinn was credited with the play's 'movement'.

What became known as the 'dance explosion' of the 1970s was due to a number of causes, but a primary factor was the appearance of dance programmes on television, especially the 'Dance in America' series, which enabled thousands to become acquainted with the art at home and encouraged them to follow it into the theatre.

While most of these developments came from New York City, the rest of the country was not idle. Spurred by the courage of Dorothy Alexander (1904–86), who determined to establish ballet in her native Atlanta, teachers in other cities began to form companies based on their own schools. Feeling isolated from the mainstream and sensing what they could learn from one another, they established annual festivals that encouraged higher quality dancing and choreography.

Interest in dance developed in universities as well. Although modern dance had been taught on campuses since the 1930s, it had existed primarily in departments of physical education. In the 1960s it began to move into theatre departments, and eventually became independent. Although the original goal was to train teachers, the curriculum broadened as larger numbers of talented students enrolled and stimulated concert performances. Academic interests developed, too, as courses in dance history and criticism entered curriculums.

Dance writing acquired new stature as critics concentrated on careful description and analysis of what they saw rather than on flippant statements of personal opinion. In the 1990s, new publications, such as *Dance Ink*, joined the veteran *DanceMagazine* and *Ballet Review*. An important purpose was to serve the growing number of dance readers with observant, thoughtful reviews of performances and provocative essays on timely topics. A primary goal was stimulating new audiences to attend and appreciate the latest directions in avant-garde choreography.

While some looked to the future, others were concerned with dance's past. Dance scholars who were attracted to Renaissance and eighteenth century dances collaborated with music-ologists to stage performances of masques and early operas. Dance notaters recorded the results of their endeavours for use in the future. Tap dancing lured researchers into seeking out veteran black performers, such as Honi Coles (1911–92), encouraging them to revive their most popular numbers and also to teach a new generation.

Summer educational programmes were also being offered in rural areas where related performances were planned to give both the student and the weekend visitor a taste of new developments. The first, the Jacob's Pillow Dance Festival, was initiated by Ted Shawn (1891–1972) in 1932. Two years later Martha Hill founded a similar programme that eventually assumed the name American Dance Festival. Originally devoted exclusively to modern dance, both programmes gradually broadened their agendas, including not only classical but also ethnic dance classes and performances by artists drawn from many countries. In the 1990s, American Dance Festival director Charles Reinhart (b. 1930) was sending Americans around the world to teach their own idioms, while urging each country to develop its own style in the spirit of modern dance.

As new styles proliferated, some choreographers looked back to the social and political approaches of the New Dance Group of the 1930s. In 1994 Bill T. Jones (b. 1954) made *Still/Here*, a lament for those who died and were dying of AIDS and a plea for action to stop the spread of the disease. Through the 1990s, the Liz Lerman (b. 1947) Dance Exchange was performing works that combined speech and movement in seniors' centres, churches, synagogues, schools and prisons as well as in theatres. Her aim was to address 'private visions and public realities'.

In 1945 US theatrical dance was divided. By the mid-1990s the diversity of styles on view made categories difficult to define. A case in point was the founding in 1990 of Russian-born Mikhail Baryshnikov's White Oak Dance Project. With a repertoire that included works by Hanya Holm, Jerome Robbins, Merce Cunningham and Mark Morris along with premières by just-emerging choreographers, this very successful company defied classification.

By the mid-1990s, the one constant for US dance was change.

Selma Jeanne Cohen

Theatre for Young Audiences

A turning point in the development of US theatre for young audiences took place in 1944, when Winifred Ward (1884–1975) called together eighty-three practitioners, mostly directors, producers and educators from colleges and universities, where the study of children's theatre already was established as part of the curriculum, to discuss the future of their field. Through workshops, lectures and books, notably *Creative Dramatics* (1930), Ward had gained national attention for her work in both classroom drama and children's theatre, and thereby spearheaded two movements at once: the use of informal dramatics in education and the production of well-acted plays with casts of children and adults in formal theatrical presentations. These two areas have dominated theatre in the lives of US children throughout the second half of the twentieth century – the first by involving participants directly in an artistic experience, the second by offering dramatizations of classics and new plays written especially for young audiences.

The organization that Ward and her colleagues formed evolved into the American Alliance for Theatre and Education, still the most powerful advocate for theatre for children and adolescents in the US. Moreover, the goals determined in 1944 remain just as essential in the 1990s: to improve standards of writing and directing, to encourage new talent, and to recognize the work of important producing groups.

From 1945 onwards, theatre for young audiences has continued to develop from three basic sources: universities and colleges, regional and community theatres, and professional companies. In the mid-1990s, most university theatre departments offer courses that prepare

Coleman Jennings's 1975 University of Texas at Austin production of Aurand Harris's *Steal Away Home*.
Photo: Courtesy Department of Drama, University of Texas at Austin.

specialists in the field; several give advanced degrees, most notably Emerson College (Boston), the University of Texas at Austin, Arizona State University and New York University. As part of their training, these college programmes produce plays acted by students before local school children. New plays are often tested here. In the 1980s and 1990s, university productions still provide the field with a stability of service that small companies and independent groups cannot guarantee.

Even so, a number of outstanding regional theatres have earned both local support and national recognition for their artistic accomplishments. Founded in 1961, the Children's Theatre Company of Minneapolis moved in 1975 into its modern building next to the city's museum and art gallery, where its large-scale productions of original scripts (*The Dream Fisher*, 1977) and adaptations (*The 500 Hats of Bartholomew Cubbins*, 1980) attract audiences of all ages. Other important regional theatres performing both classics and new works may be found in Atlanta, Nashville, Phoenix, St Louis,

and Honolulu. One of the most adept at developing new plays, the Children's Theatre of Seattle, opened its splendidly equipped theatre in 1993 with a perceptive study of a girl's loneliness, *Afternoon of the Elves*, an adaptation of the novel by Janet Taylor Lisle (b. 1947). For years, this company, like so many in the US, performed in a variety of local playhouses and on tour before gaining a permanent home.

By far the most enduring and original professional company, the Obie Award-winning Paper Bag Players, founded in New York in 1958 by Judith Martin (b. 1918), specializes in a distinctive performance style of short skits, often developed by Martin, Irving Burton and Betty Osgood, that combine mime, music and settings made largely of discarded cardboard boxes. Travelling widely in the United States and abroad, the 'Bags' have experimented with ideas and forms on a variety of subjects, ranging from Darwin's theory of evolution to the importance of taking a bath, but always set in a musical revue format, with original music by Donald Ashwander (b. 1929), and bearing titles

Judith Martin's 1988 Paper Bag Players production of her *No Problem*.
Photo: Gerry Goodstein, courtesy Paper Bag Players.

such as *Ma and the Kids* (1960), *Group Soup* (1961) and *Dandelion* (1968).

Another successful company, Theatreworks/USA, operating since 1962 in New York under the artistic direction of Jay Harnick (b. 1928), also tours widely, giving more than 850 performances a year of original musicals and plays drawn from literature and from the biographies of famous Americans such as Abraham Lincoln, Eleanor Roosevelt (1884–1962), Jim Thorpe (1887–1953) and Martin Luther King, Jr.

When Broadway witnessed the commercial success of the musical *Annie* (1977), based on a famous comic-strip character, producers recognized the eagerness of parents to bring their children to appropriate shows. Later the musicals *Big River* (1985), derived from Mark Twain's (Samuel Langhorne Clemens, 1835–1910) *Tom Sawyer*, and *The Secret Garden* (1991), inspired by the novel by Frances Hodgson Burnett (1849–1924), also attracted young audiences. But it was not until 1994, when Walt Disney produced an extravagant stage version of its animated film *Beauty and the Beast* and announced a plan to revitalize the New York theatre district with other Disney musical productions, that New York producers began to realize the full potential of such family shows. The Broadway box-office record for single-day ticket sales was established on 13 June 1994, when *Beauty and the Beast* took in $1.3 million, passing the previous single-day sales of $920,000 recorded by *The Phantom of the Opera* in 1987. Clearly, children are seen in the 1990s as big business.

The need for playwrights remains a continual cry from those working in the field. Before 1945 only Charlotte Chorpenning (1873–1955) had emerged, with works based mostly on traditional sources, such as *The Emperor's New Clothes* (1938). But in the 1950s and 1960s, Aurand Harris (b. 1915) established a national reputation for a series of adaptations and original plays. The success of his *Androcles and the Lion* (1963), set in a *commedia dell'arte* style, established him as the most produced US playwright for young people, both in the US and abroad. After publishing more than forty plays, Harris continues to offer a new script every season. His work ranges from serious themes, such as death in *The Arkansaw Bear* (1980), to suspenseful adventure in *The Prince and the Pauper* (1994). In the 1970s and 1980s, Suzan Zeder (b. 1948) composed a number of award-winning plays, some dealing with contemporary problems such as divorce (*Step on a Crack*,

1976) and the right to be different (*Mother Hicks*, 1986).

In the mid-1990s, a new generation of dramatists includes Joanna Halpert Kraus (b. 1937), author of *The Ice Wolf* (1963), a tragedy about nonconformity and prejudice against a fair-haired child born in an Inuit village; Flora Atkins (b. 1919), author of *Golliwoppers* (1973), a comedy containing four tall tales drawn from US folklore; Brian Kral (b. 1955), who wrote *Special Class* (1981), a serious exploration of handicapped children, and *Apologies* (1988), a play about teenage suicide; Virginia Glasgow Koste (b. 1924), author of *The Chicago Gypsies* (1991), a look at life in a US theatrical family in the 1930s; and James Still (b. 1906), author of *Amber Waves* (1991), an examination of generational relationships in a Kansas farm family.

Since the 1980s, some plays have also dealt with cultural pluralism, notably Laurence Yep's (b. 1948) *Dragonwings* (1991), depicting the difficulties of Chinese immigrants in San Francisco; Lowell Swortzell's (b. 1930) *Cinderella: The World's Favorite Fairy Tale* (1992), offering three versions of the Cinderella story as it is known in China, Russia and to native Americans; and Kraus's *Kimchi Kid* (1987), probing questions of individualism when Korean and US cultures meet, mix and clash.

A number of dramatists from the adult theatre have also written plays for young audiences. David Mamet has written *The Revenge of the Space Pandas* (1978), a science-fiction satire; *The Poet and the Rent* (1981), a cops-and-robbers farce; and *The Frog Prince* (1982), a burlesque of the fairytale genre. These works reflect Mamet's enormous talent for stimulating dialogue. William Gibson's (b. 1914) *The Miracle Worker* (1959), an account of how a teacher finally communicates with a deaf, blind and undisciplined young child, has become a modern standard. The most compelling voice belongs to Wendy Kesselman (b. 1940), whose *Maggie/Magalita* (1981) looks at three generations of women living in a bilingual household. Young Maggie and her mother speak Spanish to her grandmother and English to everyone else as they find themselves caught between two cultures. Kesselman has also written the psychological fantasy *Becca* (1988) and the tender *I Love You; I Love You Not* (1990), a two-character play in which she explores the relationship between a young girl and her grandmother, a victim of the Nazi Holocaust.

With an avalanche of interest in audience-participation plays in the 1960s and 1970s, productions often encouraged playgoers to engage in games and other activities. Such work reflected the tendency of the adult theatre at this time to substitute improvisatory techniques for texts. By the 1980s, however, the fad for audience participation largely was exhausted.

A Young Playwrights' Festival, based on a British model, has been held in New York City every year since 1981. It attracts over 1,000 original submissions from dramatists between 8 and 19. Four or five scripts are selected for professional productions at Off-Broadway theatres; most have been published in anthologies, which constitute a vivid commentary on the major social and political concerns of their teenage authors. The New York festival has inspired similar regional projects, although none with its close ties to the professional theatre.

In contrast to the Young Playwrights' Festival, two bilingual programmes encourage adults to write for young audiences. The Kennedy Center in Washington, DC, hosts a forum of rehearsed readings of plays in progress called New Visions/New Voices. Indiana University-Purdue University at Indianapolis sponsors the National Children's Theatre Playwriting Competition, which selects four new plays to receive rehearsed readings and critical discussion. Both attract publishers, producers, directors and educators, as well as dramatists ranging in experience from beginners to fully established professionals.

Opera for Youth, an organization of composers, librettists and educators founded in 1978, fosters the development of musicals and operas for performance by both children and adults through its publications and annual conferences. Gian-Carlo Menotti, the best known US composer for young audiences (*Amahl and the Night Visitors* is the most frequently performed US opera), has written numerous short works presented in schools and by community groups. His *Help, Help the Globolinks!* (1968) is a science-fiction parable in which the world is saved from invaders by the power of music; other operas include *Chip and His Dog* (1979) for very young audiences and *Martin's Lie* (1964) for adolescents.

Operas by Kurt Weill (*Der Jasager/He Who Says Yes*) and Benjamin Britten (*Noye's Fludde/Noah's Flood*) also are widely produced for students. As well, professional companies, such as the Metropolitan Opera and the New York City Opera, operate educational programmes and tour to schools.

Theatre-in-Education (TIE), which began as a movement in the United Kingdom in the 1960s to make education more absorbing by incorporating performance into classroom presentations and workshops, has been widely introduced and adapted in the United States in the 1980s and 1990s. Teams of five to eight actors devise plays aimed at provoking discussion about issues such as the environment and racial prejudice; representing differing viewpoints, they actually engage audiences in debate. The Creative Arts Team of New York University, founded in 1973, has become the leading exponent of TIE in the United States, acclaimed for its work on the subjects of child abuse, drug addiction and AIDS.

Lowell Swortzell

Puppet Theatre

In the 1930s and 1940s, puppet theatre in the United States was dominated by variety entertainment and children's theatre, the latter usually consisting of adaptations of children's literary classics or European fairytales. During the late 1940s and the 1950s, puppets were also used increasingly for advertising, education and therapy, with most puppeteers favouring the mimetic capabilities of the string-marionette (in the United States, in fact, the term 'marionette' refers exclusively to string-operated figures with the generic term for the medium being 'puppet').

Most puppet companies ran touring shows, although by the early 1960s a few important groups had established fixed theatres. The Yale Puppeteers presented musical comedies and revues at their Turnabout Theatre in Hollywood from 1941 until 1966. In a renovated dentist's office in New York, a group called the Little Players performed hand-puppet parodies of stage classics from 1960 to 1982. Both theatres were remarkable in attracting major portions of their audiences from the performing arts communities of those cities.

From 1967 to 1977, the Bil Baird Marionettes maintained a permanent puppet theatre in New

York's Greenwich Village. Although chiefly known for its marionette musicals for children, one of the original goals of the theatre was the promotion of a serious puppet theatre for adults, a theme that became a rallying cry for puppeteers over the next three decades. In night-clubs and touring shows, on Broadway, in film and on television, the extraordinarily prolific work of Bil Baird (1904–87) had spanned all the major trends of the 1950s and early 1960s. While continuing practices inherited from the previous decades (marionette variety and children's touring shows), his flair for abstraction and caricature in puppet design made him a pioneer in the development of new commercial, industrial and educational uses of puppetry, both in live performance and on television.

Traditional marionette and hand-puppet prosceniums lent themselves readily to adaptation by television, and the early bond between television and puppetry has had enduring consequences. While television puppets of the 1940s and 1950s such as Burr Tillstrom's (1917–85) Kukla (a hand-puppet) and Rufus Rose's Howdy Doody (a marionette) have become US icons, the most extensive development in puppetry since 1960 is attributable to the enormous popular television success of Jim Henson's (1936–90) Muppets. Specifically designed to accommodate the television medium, the flexible foam-rubber mouth-puppet has rapidly supplanted the marionette as the dominant puppet genre in US.

In the theatre, the 1960s saw a proliferation of new approaches to puppetry, all informed by a spirit of reaction against the string-marionette and its structural parallels with the European tradition of proscenium-bound, illusionistic stage realism. Prominent among alternative methods, Asian-inspired rod-puppets came increasingly into fashion, both in the productions of major companies such as the Bil Baird Marionettes and in the work of solo artists such as Dick Myers, whose idiosyncratic rod-puppet fairytales parodied the generic expectations of the medium.

But the first important group totally to disregard the familiar conventions and applications of puppetry was Peter Schumann's Bread and Puppet Theatre. Nurtured within the alternative theatre community of the 1960s, Schumann's highly innovative productions fused political messages with abstract, animistic imagery, drawing upon the wider symbolic resources of the puppet. Opposed to the commercial theatre's slick technology, Schumann espoused a deliberately naive aesthetic rooted in folk art for his ritualistic plays on political topics, and his giant masks and puppets were regular components of political demonstrations, parades and peace marches, a utilization of carnival motifs that has since been widely imitated.

Schumann's metaphysical use of the puppet demonstrated its high artistic potential, and established a place for puppetry within the theatrical avant-garde after the 1960s. In this context, puppets have occasionally supported human actors as supplementary non-naturalistic devices in productions by experimental directors such as Lee Breuer, Charles Ludlam (1943–87), Andrei Şerban, Elizabeth Swados (b. 1951) and Robert Wilson. On the periphery of the avant-garde, and specifically known for their work with puppets, puppet designer-directors such as Ralph Lee, Eric Bass and Julie Taymor have also explored the puppet's relationship with traditions of mask and myth, frequently recycling themes and techniques from non-European puppet traditions.

The mid-1970s saw an awakening of interest in the formal aspects of puppetry as a performance-based visual art form, a tendency first evident in the work of performance artist Winston Tong, and puppeteers Robert Anton and Bruce D. Schwartz. In contrast to the sometimes huge, communal celebrations of the Bread and Puppet Theatre, the intimate, intense little rituals of solo puppeteer Anton had the character of secret alchemical ceremonies. Similar in his rarefied aestheticism, the performances of Schwartz in the late 1970s featured skilfully manipulated rod-puppet vignettes on themes of personal nostalgia and regret. Both performers exploited the visible presence of the puppeteer in performance, a typical convention of experimental puppetry consistent with the use of puppet theatre as a vehicle for individual artistry.

In the 1980s, practitioners of performance art continued to discover common ground with puppet theatre. Some, such as Theodora Skipitares, have been sufficiently drawn into the practice of traditional puppetry arts to be considered puppeteers. At the same time, postmodern puppeteers have developed presentational structures similar to those of performance. Juxtaposing traditional and experimental devices, the work of Roman Paska, for example, creates theatrical poetry consistently subverted by self-parody. At another extreme, in his substitution of unmodified found objects for sculpted or articulated

Ralph Lee's puppets for Nancy Swortzell's 1984 New York University production of *Gulliver's Travels*, dramatized by Lowell Swortzell.
Photo: L. Pellettieri, courtesy NYU Program in Educational Theatre.

figures, the topical skits of Paul Zaloom (b. 1951) represent the ultimate reduction of the puppet to a simple performance object, a tendency that has affinities with the contemporary European Object Theatre movement.

In the late 1980s, all of the trends of the previous half-century continued to find adherents within the puppetry community. Successful performers of marionette variety such as David Syrotiak coexist with television puppeteers and exponents of experimental alternatives, resulting in a greater contemporaneous range of styles and techniques than ever before. Together with increasing diversification, the puppet theatre is also achieving a modicum of critical recognition as a serious theatre form, a common goal to which US puppet artists of all inclinations aspire.

Roman Paska

Design

Though realism has been the dominant style of US theatre through the twentieth century, a distinctive US design style did not emerge until the decades between the two world wars, a style that contrasted sharply in many ways with the naturalistic and psychological drama it was intended to support. Strongly influenced by European designers Adolphe Appia, Edward Gordon Craig, Oskar Strnad and Joseph Urban (who brought bold colour and pointillist tech- nique to both opera and the Ziegfeld Follies), and to some extent by the productions of Max Reinhardt and Jacques Copeau, US designers, led by Robert Edmond Jones (1887–1954), Lee Simonson (1888–1967) and Norman Bel Geddes (1893–1958), created a style known as the 'new stagecraft', a style typified by abstraction, fragmentary realism, symbolism, expressionistic motifs and open-space stages. This new stagecraft and its practitioners formed the aesthetic bedrock of all that would follow in twentieth-century US design.

By the end of World War II this first generation of modern US designers had been supplanted by those who had trained under them. The new generation was dominated by Jo Mielziner (1901–76) and a style known as poetic realism. As US drama, especially in plays by Tennessee Williams and William Saroyan (1908–81), began to use a cinematic structure and to explore dreamscapes, literal realism in design seemed no longer a viable solution. Scenography had to depict inner states of mind and the fluid movement of an emotional rather than a physical landscape.

Similarly, the US musical was reaching maturity, and the design for the works of Rodgers and Hammerstein and Lerner and Loewe, for instance, needed to suggest a heightened world of fantasy and ebullience while somehow remaining rooted in a plausible, if theatrical, reality. This quality was achieved by designers such as Howard Bay (1913–86) in shows including *The Little Foxes*, *Come Back, Little Sheba*, *Up in Central Park* (1945) and *The Music Man*, and Lemuel Ayers (1915–55) with *Oklahoma!*, *Kiss Me, Kate* and *Camino Real*, but it was Mielziner's lyrical, painterly style that captured just the right qualities of heightened reality, elegance and theatrical magic in plays such as *The Glass Menagerie*, *A Streetcar Named Desire*, *Death of a Salesman* and *Look Homeward, Angel* (1957) and musicals including *South Pacific* (1949), *Carousel*, *Guys and Dolls* and *Gypsy*.

There was often an ethereal quality to many of these designs that informed the spectator that this was a world of fantasy, heightened emotion and theatricalism. One of Mielziner's trademarks was a reliance on scrims, which added to the incorporeal quality of many productions. This device, together with fragmentary scenic units, allowed a cinematic movement from scene to scene through the manipulation of light rather than depending on more cumbersome and illusion-shattering shifts of scenery. As mid-century drama took on the rhythms and vocabulary of film, the scrim and the fluid movement of scenery became essential.

Another dominant designer of the post-war era was Oliver Smith (1918–94). Smith began his career designing for dance, working with the choreographers Agnes de Mille and Jerome Robbins. Despite the lyric and painterly quality of much of his work, his designs were often conceived as choreographic pieces. Typically, he combined sculptural and painterly elements that moved unobtrusively across the stage or from scene to scene. If Mielziner obtained fluidity through shifting perspectives and vistas, Smith achieved an equivalent effect through graceful, choreographed movement of scenery. Though all his work was marked by a characteristic elegance, he was eclectic enough to design such diverse musicals as *My Fair Lady*, *West Side Story* and *Hello, Dolly!*

Of equal significance during this period, though less commercially successful, was Boris Aronson (1898–1980). This Russian-born designer had studied with Aleksandra Ekster in Russia and brought to his work constructivist influences, as well as the cubist-fantastic style of the painter Marc Chagall. Though highly regarded by his peers, Aronson had difficulty finding a consistent outlet for his scenography. None the less, during the 1950s he helped shape the look of US theatre through designs for *The Rose Tattoo* (1951), *The Crucible*, *Bus Stop*, *The Diary of Anne Frank* and *J.B.* (1958). In all these, an underlying realism was offset by essentially cubo-futurist or constructivist motifs that placed the locale of the action in a more universal, more theatrical context. Audiences could be led towards far-reaching understandings of the plays while still being grounded in specific, identifiable environments.

Aronson, however, became an 'overnight sensation' after forty years in the US theatre when he created the designs for *Fiddler on the Roof* (1964). Here, the Chagall motifs were the perfect complement to Jerome Robbins's staging. This production led to a decade-long collaboration with the innovative producer-director Harold Prince (b. 1928) and a reworking of the musical form.

Through the 1960s the US musical moved away from its simple narrative structure to so-called concept musicals, structured around thematic devices. During this period Aronson designed *Cabaret* (1966), *Zorba* (1968), *Company* (1970), *Follies* (1971), *A Little Night Music* (1973) and *Pacific Overtures* (1976). Many of these were typified by abstract scenic pieces, moving screens, steps and platforms, and fantastic imagery. These were not clear-cut examples of one style or another, but an amalgamation of myriad twentieth-century avant-garde styles that had been Aronson's forte for half a century, now brought to bear on a uniquely US theatrical form.

A fourth significant figure in the post-war era was the Armenian American Rouben Ter-

Arutunian (1920–92). Though his Broadway output, which included *Redhead* (1959) and *The Milk Train Doesn't Stop Here Anymore* (1963), was relatively modest, he designed several notable productions at the American Shakespeare Festival in Connecticut, including *King John* (1956), *Measure for Measure* and *Much Ado about Nothing*, plus a permanent setting used for six plays during 1960–2. Ter-Arutunian exerted an important influence on the development of US design through his sculptural style, often evident in his work for ballet, which included designs for the New York City Ballet, American Ballet Company, Martha Graham, the Joffrey, Glen Tetley, Paul Taylor and Alvin Ailey companies. His textured, three-dimensional scenic units allowed a strong definition of space on an otherwise sparsely decorated stage.

During the 1950s the course of US design and theatre began to be influenced by the avant-garde, primarily in the work of the Living Theatre. Julian Beck, its co-director, brought the aesthetic of abstract expressionist painting to the sets he created. In *The Life of the Theatre* (1972), Beck decried 'the terrible false dirt of Broadway'. The Living Theatre abandoned the slickness of commercial theatre for the raw energy of urban streets. Beck's sets for productions, including *Doctor Faustus Lights the Lights* (1951), *The Connection* (1959), *The Brig* (1963), *Mysteries and Smaller Pieces* and *Frankenstein*, created at first in Off-Broadway theatres and lofts and eventually in makeshift spaces and converted non-theatrical structures in the US, Europe and South America, had a home-made quality and even an ugliness that challenged the perfection and order of the commercial theatre that led, Beck believed, to sentiment and false emotion. This approach would have a far-reaching effect on a wide range of experimental theatre artists and ultimately on commercial theatre as well.

A significant shift in mainstream scenographic style occurred in the early 1960s with the work of Ming Cho Lee (b. 1930), who had been an assistant to Mielziner, Aronson and Ter-Arutunian. Lee virtually changed the US approach to design overnight with his 1964 production of *Electra* for the New York Shakespeare Festival's outdoor theatre in Central Park. The set was a multilevelled thrust stage backed by three highly textured emblematic scenic pieces hanging from a pipe-batten gridwork. The set appeared to be carved out of stone. Lee extended his influence with the first

production of *Hair*, which employed collage and scaffolding; *Two Gentlemen of Verona* (1971); *Much Ado about Nothing* (1972), and *K2* (1983).

Lee has acknowledged that he set out to counteract the pictorialism of Mielziner and others working at the time, including George Jenkins (b. 1909), David Hays (b. 1930) and Peter Larkin (b. 1926). One aspect of Lee's style came from Chinese watercolour landscape painting. But he absorbed the sculptural style of Aronson and Isamu Noguchi, the sculptor and scenic artist who worked with choreographer Martha Graham; from Ter-Arutunian came the idea of textured surfaces. Perhaps even more important were the influences of Brechtian design from the Berliner Ensemble and German opera design of the 1950s, both of which Lee absorbed through German theatre and opera journals.

Lee considers the style he forged in the 1960s an American Brechtianism, although his approach owes more to the visual aesthetics of Brecht's chief designer Caspar Neher than to any reflection of Brechtian theories. In place of poetic realism Lee and his contemporaries created sculptural settings of natural materials such as wood and metal; painterly fantasy was replaced by texture; colour and ornament were replaced by formality and spatial relationships. Lee brought this same aesthetic to opera with similar results in numerous productions including *Don Rodrigo* (1966), *Roberto Devereux* (1970), *Boris Godunov* (1974) and *Khovanshchina* (1985).

Lee's work in the 1960s and 1970s was most closely associated with pipe-work scaffolding, which created a practical, flexible and theatrical environment that emphasized stage space over pictorial illusion while creating the possibility of multilevel playing areas. Lee brought a sense of verticality to US design. But he also pioneered the use of collage, soft-fabric design, architectural design, ultra-realism and new materials including mylar and urethane foam. Partly because of the high visibility of Lee's work at the New York Shakespeare Festival for some ten years and at the New York City Opera and Metropolitan Opera as well as at various regional theatres, and largely because of his work as a teacher, Lee exerted an enormous influence on the development of US design.

Well into the 1980s much US theatre was typified by highly textured, emblematic and sculptural scenery. Wood-plank flooring, erosion cloth, pipe scaffolding and collage seemed to be the basic vocabulary of US design. A

United States emerged primarily in opera in the 1970s and 1980s, particularly in the work of designers John Conklin (b. 1937), George Tsypin (b. 1954), Robert Israel (b. 1939) and Adrianne Lobel (b. 1955), and to some extent in the work of Michael Yeargan (b. 1946) and Douglas Stein, though it is also characteristic of the work of James Clayburgh with the avant-garde Wooster Group.

The new approach is typified by a multiplicity of incongruous, competing and conflicting images within a single work, thereby creating a fragmented, pan-historical, omni-stylistic view. Post-modern designs, such as Conklin's 1983 'Ring Cycle' at the San Francisco Opera, or Tsypin's *Don Giovanni* (1987) directed by Peter Sellars and *Henry IV, Parts 1 and 2* (1991) directed by JoAnne Akalaitis at the New York Shakespeare Festival, make wide-ranging references to disparate periods of art and architecture, to other productions, and to themselves as a production. The Wooster Group's work may be considered more deconstructionist than post-modern. In works such as *Brace Up*, the theatrical world is deconstructed by merging off-stage and on-stage space, often through the use of video and sound, simultaneously creating disjuncture through the separation of the performer, the voice and the image, and by incorporating high- and low-tech elements and objects in an almost random and unfocused way within the performing space.

Post-modernism has also fostered a return to the proscenium arch. The initial impetus may have come from opera, since it was the first form to encourage post-modern design on a large scale and since most opera stages are prosceniums. However, the proscenium harks back to the Renaissance stage in which a single frame often sequentially unified a multiplicity of divergent, even discordant, images and this works well in the contemporary aesthetic environment. Furthermore, much post-modern design embodies a kind of irony that requires the distance of a proscenium arch – not the intimacy of a thrust or environmental stage. The proscenium is inherently theatrical and thus

provides the best forum for what Foreman calls the 'dialectical examination of the problematics of seeing'.

While a post-modern style dominates critical attention in the 1990s, no single style dominates contemporary US theatre and, in fact, a typical Broadway or regional theatre season may incorporate virtually all twentieth-century styles from naturalism and symbolism through post-modernism and photo-realism. Broadway has become increasingly dominated by glitter, spectacle and technological wizardry, especially in British imports such as *Cats*, *Miss Saigon* and *Phantom of the Opera*.

The technical splendour of rock concerts and even electronic advertising displays in such venues as Times Square or sports stadiums has also had an effect on audience perceptions. Not only have audiences come to expect spectacle, but also they have become deadened to subtlety in lighting and scenic effects. Since Tharon Musser (b. 1925) first used a computerized lighting control system for *A Chorus Line* in 1975, lighting designers have had to use increasing quantities and movement of light in order to be 'visible'.

Regardless of style, in the 1990s design has often come to dominate the stage and take precedence over the text. This is not only evident in the aforementioned spectacle plays, but also true in productions ranging from operas such as Philip Glass's *The Voyage* designed by Robert Israel to dramas such as *An Inspector Calls* (1994, a British import designed by American Ian MacNeil) in which the production and the set become inextricable. There is no single explanation for the trend. It has happened many times in theatre history and tends to coincide with periods in which visual communication is stronger than the verbal, and periods in which there is a fascination with technology. While de-emphasizing language has been bemoaned, the trend may also be seen as a re-privileging of the inherent theatricality of the dramatic form that requires a different sort of sophistication on the part of the viewer.

Arnold Aronson

Theatre Space and Architecture

Prior to World War II, commercial theatre – driven by an insatiable profit motive – dominated the United States. As a result, theatre

spaces were usually large – 900 to 1,800-seat proscenium spaces, laid out in the nineteenth-century tradition with an orchestra seating section, a mezzanine, a balcony, and boxes flanking either side of the stage. Copies of this style of theatre spread from Broadway across the nation. Most, in fact, were owned by the Shubert brothers, or the Klaw and Erlanger Syndicate, who saw theatre as a money-making proposition. In an age of monopoly capitalism, it was essential that theatres from one city to another had similar-sized prosceniums, similar sightlines and similar backstage conditions and equipment so that they could be used for either touring companies or pre-Broadway try-outs.

The Colonial Theatre in Boston, designed by architect Clarence Blackall (1857–1942), typifies this type of commercial house. Built in 1900 and shimmering with gold and ivory, dappled with murals that recall Boucher, the lobby imitates a rococo *château* – flamboyant, opulent, giddy. Waving garlands of roses, butterball cupids hover over the doors, twinkling. On every available surface, gilded seashells and arabesques glow. The allegorical figures in the dome of the auditorium represent Tradition, Truth and Inspiration. In the adjoining circles the spirits of Epic Poetry, History, Tragedy and Pastoral Verse smile benevolently down on the evening's entertainment, which usually has little to do with epic, history, tragedy or pastoral. The Colonial, the oldest theatre in Boston still operating under its original name, seats 1,600 and has premièred works by Irving Berlin (1888–1989), Sigmund Romberg (1887–1951) and Rodgers and Hammerstein – productions that were tried out in Boston before moving on to New York.

Because of the Depression and World War II, few new commercial theatres went up during the 1930s, 1940s and 1950s, and the architects who had designed the theatres of the 1920s were no longer active when a boom in the US economy in the 1960s and 1970s led to a boom in theatre construction. The new demand, however, was not for commercial theatres but for the rapidly expanding not-for-profit regional theatres, university theatres, Off-Off-Broadway houses and performing arts centres. Recognizing that most US architects had little or no experience in theatre design, the Ford Foundation in 1961 initiated a project aimed at raising awareness among architects, theatre directors, producers and designers to the infinite possibilities in design as well as to a recognition that theatre design, like stage design, must be a collaborative effort. Forty scenic designers were invited by the Ford Foundation to submit theatre design proposals. Eight widely different proposals were selected and the designers were asked to invite architects to collaborate on the projects, which varied from a semi-open-air festival theatre in a public park to an all-purpose, womb-shaped performance space of reinforced concrete.

'The Ideal Theatre: Eight Concepts' became the project title. Complete plans and elevations were drawn, and models were built as though the theatres were actually going to be constructed. These drawings and models formed an exhibition that toured the United States from 1962 to 1964. The project proved highly influential. It opened up new possibilities in design. In addition, it defined the role of the theatre consultant in creating a viable theatre, and it brought consultants, stage designers and architects together for the first time in the United States.

When the building boom began in the 1960s, the style of architecture that ruled imperiously was the international modern style, which reached elegant perfection in the pristine monuments of glass and steel that Mies van der Rohe erected in Chicago in the 1950s. Rational, logical and unrelentingly geometric, the international modern style emphasized primal squares and rectangles and eschewed decoration.

At this time, a swing occurred away from the proscenium towards various prototypes of the open stage: arenas, thrusts and end-stages (a raised platform at one end of the auditorium, no proscenium). These configurations, which recapitulate the performance spaces that antedated the Italian proscenium, dominated theatre design through the 1950s, 1960s and 1970s. The goal of all these open stages was to involve the audience more directly and intimately in the performance. In the most radical experiments, the spectators became part of the event. The move into more open spaces paralleled a rejection of realistic illusionism. The stage would no longer pretend to be anything but what it was: a playing space.

There were also practical reasons for this swing away from the proscenium. Both the young regional theatres and the new Off-Off-Broadway companies were strapped for funds and personnel to mount elaborate scenic productions; the open stages required less scenery. Also, new lighting equipment allowed for compact remote control systems and for presetting light levels for several scenes in advance. Thus lighting, in addition to creating time and place, was playing a more important role in expressing mood.

As early as the 1950s, regional theatres began

filling the void created by the collapse of the commercial touring companies and the decline of the amateur community theatres. The Arena Stage in Washington, the Tyrone Guthrie Theatre in Minneapolis and the American Place Theatre in New York City offer early examples of the three open configurations most often used by regional theatres, in addition to the proscenium.

Founded in 1950, Arena Stage adapted an abandoned brewery as its first home. When it moved to its own sleek, modern theatre in 1961, it retained the arena configuration (Harry Weese (b. 1915), architect). This theatre, with an 827-seat capacity, has steep banks of seats on all four sides of the flat floor stage. Actors enter and scenic pieces are delivered to the playing arena through a vomitorium placed at each of the four corners; trapdoors in the stage floor and a system of catwalks over the stage can also be used. Arena Stage hedged its choices by making it possible to remove the block of seats from one end of the theatre, thus converting the space into a thrust. The thrust configuration, however, is seldom used.

As early as 1914 Norman Bel Geddes had designed a circular theatre, and other early examples of arena stages include the Penthouse Theatre at the University of Washington, Seattle (1935; remodelled 1940); Margo Jones's Theatre '47, Dallas (1947); the Playhouse Theatre in Houston (1950); and the Casa Mañana Theatre, Fort Worth (1958). The Penthouse, the first permanent theatre built in the round, has an elliptical stage surrounded by three rows of seats that can accommodate 140 spectators. It was designed by Carl F. Gould (1877–1939) in consultation with theatre historian Glenn Hughes (1894–1965). Theatres-in-the-round present special problems with the entrances, exits and the movement of performers as well as with the use of scenery and props.

The 1,441-seat Tyrone Guthrie Theatre is an early prototype of the thrust stage. Designed by Guthrie and Tanya Moiseiwitsch, with Ralph Rapson (b. 1915) acting as architect, to recapture aspects of Elizabethan staging, the theatre opened in 1963. Subsequently renovated, the Guthrie now seats 1,309 with an asymmetrical thrust and steeply banked seating; it is an excellent stage for Shakespeare. Unlike Guthrie's theatre in Stratford, Ontario, an earlier thrust,

The Tyrone Guthrie Theatre in Minneapolis, designed by Guthrie, Tanya Moiseiwitsch and Ralph Rapson.
Photo: Courtesy Guthrie Theatre.

no permanent acting levels were built in back; the rear wall can be removed, allowing props and scenic elements to be moved into the playing space. Despite its large seating capacity, audiences feel very much a part of the action. In addition to using the vomitoria at the forward corners of the thrust, actors sometimes make entrances and exits through the aisles. Since the stage is a deep thrust, some sightline problems do exist. This is a common flaw found in other deep three-sided thrust stages such as the Hartford Stage Company.

In New York City, the American Place Theatre (founded 1964) is an end-stage with a seating capacity of 350. The stage is wide and, unfortunately, too low. Off-stage space is cramped, and there is no fly space over the stage. Although seats are comfortable, seat risers are not quite high enough to provide a totally unobstructed view of the stage.

Frank Lloyd Wright (1869–1959), perhaps the greatest US architect, had long wanted to free the stage of its 'peep-show character', his derisive term for the proscenium stage. In 1932 Wright worked on a project called 'A New Theatre', intended to liberate the stage from the proscenium. 'The idea of a proscenium is a thing of the past – old stuff,' he declared. 'It used to be that you saw the show through a hole in the wall. Audience in one room, performance in the other.' Wright wanted to bring both 'together under one ceiling'. In 1959, for the Dallas Theater Center, he designed the Kalita Humphreys Theatre (404 seats in eleven rows). While still forging an intimate bond between performers and audience, Wright tried to preserve some of the scenic possibilities that thrust and arenas had thrown overboard. Wedge-shaped rows face a circular stage (40 feet in diameter) with a 32-foot turntable. The stage rises a mere 15 inches from the floor. The walls of the auditorium continue on past the stage and serve as a cyclorama, creating a feeling of unity between the playing space for performers and the seating space for spectators.

As in his 1932 project, Wright's overriding concern was to make audience and performers feel at one. Built of concrete in cantilever construction, a circular tower tops the building, providing fly space and housing a front curtain, should one be needed. The circular tower contrasts with the low, spreading rectangles of the main building. The exterior has since been remodelled to provide studio space, destroying the subtle harmonies of shape Wright originally intended.

Like the Guggenheim Museum in New York (completed 1960), the Humphreys Theatre typifies the final stages of Wright's organic style of architecture, radically different from the international modern style, which, ironically, his early work had inspired. To the end, Wright displayed a freshness of approach that always surprised. In 1959 he built the Grady Gammage Memorial Auditorium at Arizona State University in Tempe, his last non-residential design (3,000 seats). Fifty graceful columns spring 55 feet into the air to support the circular-domed roof that looks like a turban. Inside the desert-rose coloured building, a 145-foot steel beam suspended from the rear auditorium wall supports the grand tier, an ingenious solution to the acoustic problems created by placing a seating space between orchestra and balcony.

Universities gave architects and theatre consultants another arena to experiment in, especially in the 1950s, 1960s and 1970s, when drama departments expanded rapidly. The theatre at Sarah Lawrence College, Bronxville, New York, for instance, has a trapeze-shaped stage projecting 18 feet in front of a proscenium stage (1952, 500 seats).

One of the most innovative and influential of the university theatres is the Loeb Drama Center (built in 1960) at Harvard, currently the home of the American Repertory Theatre. Architect Hugh Stubbins (b. 1912) and theatre consultant George Izenour (b. 1912) designed a space with both flexible stage and flexible seating configurations. With the use of analogue computers, motorized sections of seating in the main auditorium can be repositioned, and hydraulic lifts can raise or lower sections of the floor, creating a four-sided arena, a three-sided thrust or arena, an end-stage or a proscenium. Although the ART uses the space most often as a proscenium with a seat count of 556, it changes the configuration on average once each season, usually to a three-sided thrust or arena.

One of the most successful aspects of the Loeb is the Experimental Theatre, a neutral black-box space. As early as 1950 Norman Bel Geddes had asserted that 'the proper theatre for an educational institution is one where the auditorium and the stage are in one large, empty room'. In the Loeb Experimental Theatre sections of stepped seats make possible any number of combinations of stage and seating. An overhead grid enables lights to play a major role in modelling environments. By permitting maximum flexibility, this studio encourages experimentation, and it has been widely imitated.

Another successful university complex is the Spingold Theatre Arts Center at Brandeis University (1965), designed by Max Abramovitz (b. 1908). The most striking aspect of the Spingold is its shape: a circular red-brick drum topped by a row of graceful white arches of poured concrete. Thrusting boldly skyward from centre is a round tower, providing a large fly area over the stage. Since the stage is the central core of the building and since the three theatres and the rehearsal rooms all open on to it, a variety of arrangements are possible that enable one playing space to expand into the other.

Abramovitz also designed Avery Fisher Hall in Lincoln Center. Built in the mid-1960s on Manhattan's upper west side, Lincoln Center became the touchstone for performing arts complexes built since. Avery Fisher Hall (formerly Philharmonic Hall) itself opened in 1962 and seats 2,738. Across from Avery Fisher is the 2,737-seat New York State Theatre, designed by Philip Johnson (b. 1906) and completed in 1964. A proscenium theatre conceived for the New York City Ballet, the building also houses the New York City Opera, although its acoustics are less than optimal.

The impressively scaled Metropolitan Opera House (1966), with five arches that soar 96 feet above the ground, commands the central position of the Lincoln Center Plaza. Glass arches open the lobby to the plaza, and a double curving staircase sweeps up to a grand tier lobby, flanked on either side by a large Chagall painting.

The auditorium – 72 feet high from floor to ceiling with a 54-foot wide proscenium – seats 3,800 in a traditional Italian horseshoe. Despite the extraordinary size of the auditorium (873,000 cubic feet), the acoustics are excellent, and the sightlines from the majority of seats are unobstructed.

The enormous backstage is equipped to handle repertory programming, with spaces to preset five full-stage settings at one time. The full front and backstage area measures 16,960 square feet. Ten storeys high (three below stage level), the Opera sits atop anti-vibration pads constructed of lead to soundproof the building. Wallace Harrison (1895–1981), who also played a major role in building Rockefeller Center and the United Nations Headquarters, was the chief architect.

The Lincoln Center for the Performing Arts in New York.
Photo: Susanne Faulkner Stevens, courtesy Lincoln Center.

The other spaces for the performing arts at Lincoln Center are also impressive. They include the 1,100-seat Vivian Beaumont Theatre and the 299-seat Mitzi Newhouse Theatre, both for drama. Both have circular thrust stages surrounded by steeply banked tiers of seats. Eero Saarinen (1910–61) was the architect; Jo Mielziner was the theatre designer and consultant.

Lincoln Center's Alice Tully Hall is a 1,096-seat concert hall designed with excellent acoustics for chamber music. Also at Lincoln Center is the Juilliard School (Pietro Belluschi, architect) for music and drama; it has several performing spaces: the Juilliard Theatre, a 933-seat facility designed for concerts, dance, theatre, chamber music and opera productions (the space is flexible, the ceiling moves and the orchestra pit can be covered); a 206-seat Drama Theatre; Paul Hall, a 278-seat formal recital hall with an organ; and Morse Recital Hall, a 200-seat flexible space designed as a multipurpose hall that can be partitioned into two separate performing spaces at once.

The Walter Reade Film Theatre is a 268-seat theatre run by the Film Society of Lincoln Center for screening rare films while Damrosch Park is an open-air band shell.

The New York Public Library for the Performing Arts, also at Lincoln Center, includes the Billy Rose Theatre Collection.

Following the positive responses to the creation of Lincoln Center, a proliferation of performing arts centres sprang up across the country. A partial list of centres that owe a debt to Lincoln Center includes the Krannert Center for the Performing Arts in Urbana, Illinois (1969); the John F. Kennedy Center for the Performing Arts, Washington, DC (1971); Portland (Oregon) Center for the Performing Arts (1987); the Tampa Bay (Florida) Performing Arts Center (1987); the Wortham Center, Dallas, Texas (1987); and the Kravis Center for the Performing Arts, West Palm Beach, Florida (1992).

An earlier complex – though also inspired by Lincoln Center – is the Los Angeles Performing Arts Center. Its principal facilities are the Dorothy Chandler Pavilion for music and opera (3,131 seats); the Ahmanson Theatre for musical theatre and touring attractions (2,071 seats); and the smaller Mark Taper Forum for more intimate plays (752 seats).

During the 1960s and 1970s, while many cities were building these performing arts centres, the avant-garde was rejecting traditional ways of staging plays, including the proscenium arch and, finally, the concept of the theatre building itself. The desire to erase the distinction between art and life propelled the avant-garde out of theatres and into warehouses, garages and streets.

The Living Theatre created new environments for each production, often with the action in the middle of the audience. Richard Schechner's *Dionysus in 69* created an environment in a garage by seating the audience on wooden scaffolding arranged along the walls. The performance spread throughout the entire space, rippling through the audience and, at the end, flowing out into the night. The Bread and Puppet Theatre took to the streets with its gigantic puppets to protest against the war in Vietnam.

The economics of real estate as well as aesthetics played a part in shaping these new theatre movements. Many of the new Off-Off-Broadway companies and regional theatres commenced operations on shoestring budgets. Consequently, they had to choose inexpensive, non-traditional spaces frequently located in marginal neighbourhoods. They created imaginative, non-traditional theatres by transforming warehouses, old movie houses, libraries, schools, storefronts, houses, restaurants, clubhouses, fire stations, banks and even mortuaries. The result was theatres in a wide spectrum of sizes, styles and configurations.

Playwrights Horizons, started in 1971 in New York City, found itself unexpectedly without a theatre space in 1975. As a temporary venue, it took over a small West 42nd Street movie theatre surrounded by sex shops, peep shows and massage parlours. Instead of moving to a better location, Playwrights Horizons decided to stay. The company was instrumental, along with the 42nd Street Local Development Corporation, in creating what was to be called Theatre Row: five derelict tenements that were cleaned out and converted into a block of Off-Off-Broadway theatres.

The designs for each theatre vary slightly, but the concept is the same: street level and the floor above, or street level and basement, were gutted and opened up vertically to give sufficient height for a theatre, thus creating auditoriums with approximately 99 seats (Playwrights Horizon has 141) and end-stage playing spaces approximately 20 feet high, 22 feet wide and 90 feet deep. Light and sound control booths were installed at the rear, usually above the small

Single-handedly, he brought the Jacobean playwrights back into fashion. In his celebrated essay on 'Hamlet and His Problems', he judged *Hamlet* an artistic failure and coined the phrase 'objective correlative' to explain why

> the only way of expressing emotion in the form of art is by finding an 'objective correlative'; in other words, a set of objects, a situation, a chain of events which shall be the formula of that *particular* emotion; such that when the external facts, which must terminate in sensory experience, are given, the emotion is immediately evoked. (1919)

Theatre for Eliot is an art of objective correlatives. The inner world must be externalized.

Although Eliot's plays failed to usher in a new golden age of poetic drama, his essay 'Poetry and Drama' remains the best exploration in English of the function of poetry in the theatre. In works such as *The Sacred Wood* and *The Use of Poetry and the Use of Criticism*, Eliot examined the varied uses of criticism and forced critics to reflect on what they thought they were doing.

More by preaching than by example, Eliot helped assure the triumph of the New Criticism, which started in the 1940s and dominated US criticism for three decades. Eliot called for a spirit of objectivity in criticism and urged critics to study literature as literature, not as something else.

The New Critics – led by John Crowe Ransom (1888–1974), Cleanth Brooks (b. 1906) and R.P. Blackmur (1904–65) – rejected the biographical-historical approach to focus on verbal textures and image patterns. Banishing all considerations of the author's intent or the historical circumstances of production, the New Criticism believed that the proper object of study was the work of art as an autonomous, autotelic artefact. The New Criticism fostered a careful scrutiny of texts that resulted in detailed and often brilliant interpretations of individual works.

The widely read *Understanding Drama* (1945) by Brooks and Robert Heilman (b. 1906), however, demonstrates the blindness of New Critics to theatrical values. Only the literary qualities of drama are discussed. By obsessing over the linguistic components of a text, the New Critics flattened out generic differences.

Eric Auerbach, a German philologist of Romance languages, broadened the prevailing formalistic approach. A sworn enemy of the New Critics, Auerbach inserted his close explications of texts into a cultural and historical matrix. In 'The Weary Prince' – Auerbach's reading of *Hamlet* in *Mimesis* (1953) – he analyses Shakespeare against the increasing sense of historical perspective in the sixteenth century. Auerbach still read texts closely, but he decried the New Criticism's ostracism of history.

In *The Anatomy of Criticism* (1957), Canadian Northrop Frye – strongly influenced by Jung and by Frazer's *The Golden Bough* – elaborated a taxonomy of literature. Throughout his work, Frye stressed the central role of the imagination in trying to understand the world. Consequently, he approached literature through myths and archetypes. Frye linked literary genres to a ritualized seasonal pattern of birth, death and rebirth. In *A Natural Perspective* (1965), he associated the energy of Shakespearian comedy with spring and the rebirth of society.

Like Frye, Francis Fergusson (1904–86) – under the influence of anthropologists such as Francis Cornford (1874–1943) (*The Origins of Attic Comedy*, 1914) and literary scholars like Gilbert Murray (1866–1957) – used myth and ritual as a framework for understanding the drama. In *The Idea of Theatre*, Fergusson saw the tragic hero as scapegoat and related the histrionic sensibility to ritual.

Many US critics argued that the conditions of the modern world precluded tragedy, among them Joseph Wood Krutch (1893–1970) in *The Modern Temper* (1929), Elder Olson (b. 1909) in *Tragedy and the Theory of Drama* (1961) and George Steiner (b. 1929) in *The Death of Tragedy* (1961). Arthur Miller contended that not only was it possible to write tragedies in the twentieth century, but also he had written some ('The Nature of Tragedy' and 'Tragedy and the Common Man', both 1949).

Other genres seduced other critics. For some, farce and tragi-comedy reflected better the modern sensibility. Influential critics who explored this grotesque fusion included Albert Bermel (b. 1927) in *Farce* (1982) and *Comic Agony* (1993), Martin Esslin (b. 1918) in *The Theatre of the Absurd* (1961), Rosette Lamont in *Two Faces of Ionesco* (1978), Karl Guthke (b. 1933) in *Modern Tragicomedy* (1966) and J.L. Styan (b. 1923) in *The Dark Comedy* (1962). In his essay 'The Psychology of Farce', critic Eric Bentley (b. 1916) got to the heart of the matter:

> the marriage joke could be abolished if the

family were the unmixed blessing that many of our contemporaries take it for. ... Farce ... begins by accepting the bland, placid, imposing façade of life, proceeds to become farcical by knocking the façade down. The farceur, like the lunatic and the unruly child, flies in the face of decorum. Harpo Marx is the supreme case in point. ... Many other comedians destroy things. Few manage so impressively as Harpo to convey the idea of human nature as in itself destructive. (1958)

Lionel Abel (b. 1910) gave currency to the word 'meta-theatre', which he defined as drama that represents life as already theatricalized. The key metaphors of this genre are the world as stage and life as dream. In the twentieth century this self-reflexive genre culminates in Pirandello, Genet and Beckett.

Some critics tried to define the genre-specific qualities of drama, albeit from perspectives circumscribed by literary concerns: Bentley in *The Life of the Drama* (1964), Esslin in *An Anatomy of Drama* (1977), Ronald Peacock (b. 1907) in *The Art of Drama* (1957) and Styan in *The Elements of Drama* (1960). Whereas all these critics assumed that definite parameters existed in a Platonic realm of ideal genres, Una Ellis-Fermor (1894–1958) took a more innovative approach. While not explicitly denying genres, by exploring a conflict between form and content in dramatists pushing against boundaries – Strindberg, O'Neill, Pirandello and T.S. Eliot – Ellis-Fermor by implication throws the concept of genre into doubt in *The Frontiers of Drama* (1945).

The books of three major theatre critics helped establish and illuminate the canon of modern drama: Bentley – *The Playwright as Thinker* (1946); Richard Gilman (b. 1925) – *The Making of Modern Drama* (1974); and Robert Brustein – *The Theatre of Revolt* (1964). Using Nietzsche, Camus and Frye as his intellectual framework, Brustein dubbed the modern dramatists 'apostate priests' and pointed to the conflict between idea and actions as 'the central dialectic of the modern drama'.

Almost all of the works cited above followed models drawn from literature or intellectual history which negate the theatricality of drama. The New Criticism had reduced theatre to words on a page; by the mid-1960s, however, several factors converged to bring about stage-centred criticism: the triumph of non-literary theatre; the increasing attention paid to the history of plays in production, especially Shakespeare; and the influence of semiotics.

By the late 1960s it was clear that the vitality of US theatre had migrated from Broadway to Off-Broadway and beyond and that the creative energy of the best theatre artists was finding expression in non-traditional forms that rebelled against the tyranny of words. Happenings; performance art; street theatre; avant-garde companies; the silent visions of Robert Wilson; the breaking down of boundaries among drama, dance, opera and the visual arts; mixed media – this bubbling cauldron of artistic experimentation sent critics scrambling to find new vocabularies and new concepts to confront new forms. The impotence of literary analysis in dealing with non-verbal performance, visual communication and the theatricality of theatre became axiomatic.

One of the most provocative essays inspired by this ferment was Susan Sontag's (b. 1933) 'Against Interpretation':

What is important now is to recover our senses. We must learn to *see* more, to *hear* more, to *feel* more. Our task is not to find the maximum amount of content in a work of art, much less to squeeze more content out of the work than is already there. Our task is to cut back content so that we can see the thing at all. ... In place of a hermeneutics we need an erotics of art. (1964)

Under the inspired editorship of Richard Schechner, *TDR* (*Tulane Drama Review* through the fall of 1967; afterwards, *The Drama Review*) – herald and chronicle of the new aesthetics – leaped into the hermeneutico-erotic breach. *TDR*, based at New York University, not only championed the new modes of performance but also described and analysed them, going beyond literary models, borrowing insights from the social sciences. Anyone interested in US drama from 1960 to 1980 must begin with *TDR*. Schechner's article 'Drama, Script, Theatre, and Performance' (1973) stands not only as an exemplar of interdisciplinary scholarship but also as one of the most stimulating essays written on theatre by an American.

TDR's publication of Andrei Șerban's 'The Life in a Sound' (1976) demonstrates its sensitivity to the non-verbal aspects of theatre and its awareness of the rise to power of the auteur-director. Critics soon began to give as much attention to directors as to playwrights. The text to be read was the performance; the author was

criticism brought theatre and post-structuralist theory together: Gayle Austin's (b. 1949) *Feminist Theories for Dramatic Criticism* (1990), Sue-Ellen Case's (b. 1942) *Feminism and Theatre* (1988), Jill Dolan's (b. 1957) *The Feminist Spectator as Critic* (1988), and Lynda Hart's (b. 1953) *Making a Spectacle: Feminist Essays on Contemporary Women's Theatre*. Generally speaking, these critics adopt an anti-essentialist stance, showing through theatre how gender is socially constructed. By decentring the self and radically questioning the binary oppositions between male and female, post-structuralist theory has given feminists weapons to deconstruct the patriarchal order. Male feminists include Joseph Boone (b. 1951) and Michael Cadden (b. 1949), editors of *Engendering Men* (1990); and David Savran (b. 1950), author of *Communists, Cowboys, and Queers* (1992).

Gay and lesbian concerns have also been addressed, and some critics have questioned to what degree sexuality is socially constructed: Alan Bray in *Homosexuality in Renaissance England* (1982), John Clum (b. 1941) in *Acting Gay: Male Homosexuality in Modern Drama* (1992), Jill Dolan in *Presence and Desire: Essays on Gender, Sexuality, Performance* (1993), and Jonathan Goldberg (b. 1943) in 'Sodomy and Society: The Case of Christopher Marlowe' in *Staging the Renaissance* (1991), edited by David Kastan (b. 1946).

Catherine Belsey's essay on Shakespeare, 'Disrupting Sexual Difference: Meaning and Gender in the Comedies', shows how a critic can bring together historical erudition, a sophisticated theoretical apparatus, feminist questions and literary and theatrical sensitivity.

The theatricality of transvestitism has attracted the attention of other critics interested in exploring the interrelations between gender and performance: Marjorie Garber (b. 1944) in 'The Logic of the Transvestite' in *Staging the Renaissance*, edited by Kastan (1991), and *Vested Interests: Cross-Dressing and Cultural Anxiety* (1992). Gender as role playing leads inevitably to the question of gender as masquerade, a question raised as early as 1929 by Joan Riviere (1883–?) in 'Womanliness as a Masquerade'. One of the best studies informed by feminism is historian Faye Dudden's (b. 1948) *Women in the American Theatre: Actresses and Audiences 1790–1870* (1994). Combining history, sociology and literature, Dudden digs into the past to uncover possibilities for the future.

Much of the best work currently being written comes from historians. A revalorization of history across disciplines can be traced directly to the French critic Michel Foucault, who since about 1970 has loomed as the dominant influence over the intellectual life of the United States.

The third movement that has transformed academia and furthered theatre studies during the 1980s and 1990s is cultural studies and performance studies. Their rapid ascendancy has augmented the significance of performance as a paradigm for studying many different aspects of society. Although the two fields are distinct, cultural studies and performance studies share many features in common. Both are adamantly cross-disciplinary and both have broadened the terrain of what is studied in universities. Both have scrutinized popular culture and cultural practices formerly considered unworthy of serious academic attention – Mickey Mouse and other Disney characters, for instance, or pornography.

The methodology and practice of each field could be called *bricolage* (poaching) and both are in the process of transforming what can be studied and how it can be studied. Both manifest a desire to connect with reality, which deconstruction had placed under erasure. The waxing of these two fields parallels a waning of formalistic theory and a return to broader material concerns.

Performance studies sees life as meta-theatre and ordinary human activity as already theatricalized. It studies performance in everyday life and in relation to other cultural practices. Theatre scholars have frequently turned to anthropology, and Victor Turner's (1920–83) *From Ritual to Theatre: The Human Seriousness of Play* (1982) explains the spirit animating performance studies. According to Turner, society is drama and the systemic contradictions within any group frequently bubble over into what Turner dubs 'social drama', which follows the 'Aristotelian description of tragedy', or rather, Greek drama imitates the structure of social drama: breach, crisis and reconciliation or rupture.

The leading proponent of performance studies is Richard Schechner of New York University, whose many books define the field: *Between Theater and Anthropology* (1985), *By Means of Performance* (1990) and *Performance Theory* (1988). In Illinois, Northwestern University's department, led by Canadian anthropologist Dwight Conquergood, is another major centre.

Many forces, as we have seen, have conspired to decentre the dominance of the written text as the sole basis of a serious study of the drama. But the written text has not disappeared; some books have analysed texts closely, reflecting the importance of language in the work of playwrights such as David Mamet, David Rabe and Sam Shepard. Anne Dean's (b. 1950) *David Mamet: Language as Dramatic Action* (1990) paid close attention to Mamet's linguistic strategies.

As for criticism in the media, it tends to lean towards pulp journalism. Openings of plays are treated as news items and are usually reviewed the following day. Reviewers in many parts of the country often have minimal background in theatre. Consequently, the quality of writing and thinking is rather low and reviews tend to be consumer guides.

A typical newspaper review consists of a brief plot summary, a few comments on actors and a blanket command: 'Don't miss this show!' or 'Stay home and watch TV'. This thumbs-up, thumbs-down approach leaves little room for analysis or thoughtful commentary. Unfor-

tunately, reviews have an enormous impact not only at the box office, but also in the corridors of power where funds from foundations, corporations and the government are divided up among starving theatres.

One should also note that most US cities have only one major newspaper; consequently, there is not a plurality of voices expressing a range of views and the opinion of one person often determines the fate of a production or an entire company. Another problem is that newspapers are a local enterprise, closely tied to the city in which they appear; this means that standards of judgement are local and narrow and that anyone trying to keep abreast of theatre from coast to coast will find it an arduous task.

In their Sunday editions, many large newspapers have special cultural sections that include more reflective pieces, interviews with artists and articles that analyse broad trends. Over the years, for instance, such articles in the arts and leisure section of the *Sunday New York Times* have acquired enormous historical importance.

American Theatre is worth noting here – a monthly magazine put out by the Theatre

The 1982 Goodman Theatre production of David Mamet's *Edmond*.
Photo: Courtesy Goodman Theatre.

479

——. *The Dance in Mind: Profiles and Reviews, 1976–83.* Boston, MA. 307 pp.

Kanellos, Nicolás. *Mexican American Theatre: Legacy and Reality.* Houston, TX: Arte Público, 1987. 120 pp.

——, ed. *Hispanic Theatre in the United States.* Houston, TX: Arte Público, 1984.

——, ed. *Mexican American Theatre: Then and Now.* Houston, TX: Arte Público, 1983. 120 pp.

Kintz, Linda. *The Subject's Tragedy: Political Poetics, Feminist Theory, and Drama.* Ann Arbor, MI: University of Michigan Press, 1992. 329 pp.

Kirby, Michael. *Happenings.* New York: Dutton, 1965. 288 pp.

Kornick, Rebecca H. *Recent American Opera: A Production Guide.* New York: Columbia University Press, 1991. 352 pp.

Kreemer, Connie. *Further Steps: Fifteen Choreographers on Modern Dance.* New York: Harper & Row, 1987. 270 pp.

Larson, Gary. *The Reluctant Patron: The United States Government and the Arts, 1943–1965.* Philadelphia, PA: University of Pennsylvannia Press, 1983. 314 pp.

Larson, Orville K. *Scene Design in the American Theatre from 1915 to 1960.* Fayetteville, AR: University of Arkansas Press, 1989. 385 pp.

Leavitt, Dinah. *Feminist Theatre Groups.* Jefferson, SC: McFarland, 1980. 153 pp.

Malpede, Karen. *Women in Theatre: Compassion and Hope.* New York: Drama Book Publishers, 1983. 281 pp.

McCarthy, Mary. *Mary McCarthy's Theatre Chronicles, 1937–1962.* New York: Noonday, 1963. 248 pp.

McCaslin, Nellie. *Historical Guide to Children's Theatre in America.* New York: Greenwood Press, 1987. 348 pp.

——, ed. *Children and Drama.* 2nd edn. Lanham, MD: University Press of America, 1987. 348 pp.

McFerran, Virginia Derus. *Chicana Voices in American Drama: Silviana Wood, Estela Portillo Trambley, Cherrie Moraga, Milcha Sánchez-Scott, Josefina López.* PhD dissertation. Ann Arbor, MI: University of Michigan Press, 1991. 239 pp.

McPharlin, Paul, and Marjorie Batchelder. *The Puppet Theatre in America.* Boston, MA: Plays, Inc., 1969. 734 pp.

Marranca, Bonnie. *Theatre Writings.* New York: Performing Arts Journal Publications, 1984.

——, and Gautam Dasgupta. *American Playwrights: A Critical Survey.* New York: Drama Book Specialists, 1981.

Mendenhall, Christian. *American Musical Comedy 1943–64: A Theoretical Investigation of Its Ritual Function.* Ann Arbor, MI: University of Michigan, 1989. 284 pp.

Mielziner, Jo. *The Shapes of Our Theatre.* New York: Clarkson Potter, 1970. 160 pp.

Mitchell, Loften. *Black Drama.* New York: Hawthorne Press, 1967. 248 pp.

Molette, Carlton W., and Barbara J. Carlton. *Black Theatre: Premise and Presentation.* Bristol, IN: Wyndham Hall Press, 1986. 166 pp.

Mordden, Ethan. *The American Theatre.* New York: Oxford University Press, 1981. 365 pp.

Novack, Cynthia J. *Sharing the Dance: Contact Improvisation and American Culture.* Madison, WI: University of Wisconsin Press, 1990. 258 pp.

Novick, Julius. *Beyond Broadway.* New York: Hill & Wang, 1968. 393 pp.

Owen, Bobbi. *Lighting Design on Broadway.* Westport, CT: Greenwood Press, 1991. 159 pp.

——. *Scenic Design on Broadway.* New York: Greenwood Press, 1991. 286 pp.

Pecktal, Lynn. *Designing and Painting for the Theatre.* New York: McGraw-Hill, 1995.

Perkins, Kathy. *Female Black Playwrights.* Bloomington, IN: University of Indiana, 1989. 288 pp.

Peterson Jr, Bernard L., ed. *A Century of Musical in Black and White: An Encyclopedia of Musical Stage Works By, About, or Involving African Americans.* Westport, CT: Greenwood Press, 1993. 529 pp.

Pottlitzer, Joanne. *Hispanic Theatre in the United States and Puerto Rico.* New York: Ford Foundation, 1988. 85 pp.

Sanders, Leslie Catherine. *The Development of Black Theatre in America: From Shadow to Substance.* Baton Rouge, LA/London: Louisiana State University Press, 1988. 252 pp.

Schechner, Richard. *Between Theater and Anthropology.* Philadelphia, PA: University of Pennsylvania Press, 1985. 342 pp.

——. *Environmental Theatre.* New York: Hawthorn, 1973. 339 pp.

——. *Performance Theory.* London: Routledge, 1988. 304 pp.

Schlueter, June, ed. *Modern American Drama: The Female Canon.* Rutherford, CA: Fairleigh Dickinson Press, 1990. 308 pp.

Seller, Maxine Schwartz, ed. *Ethnic Theatre in the United States.* Westport, CT: Greenwood Press, 1983. 606 pp.

Shank, Theodore. *American Alternative Theatre.* New York: St Martin's Press, 1988. 202 pp.

Siegel, Marcia B. *The Shapes of Change: Images of American Dance.* Boston, MA: Houghton Mifflin, 1979. 386 pp.

Smith, Ronn. *American Set Design 2*. New York: Theatre Communications Group, 1991. 210 pp.

Sokol, Martin L. *The New York City Opera: An American Adventure*. New York: Macmillan, 1981. 562 pp.

Speck, Frank G., Leonard Broom, and Will W. Long. *Cherokee Dance and Drama*. Norman, OK: University of Oklahoma Press, 1983. 112 pp.

Spolin, Viola. *Improvisation for the Theater*. Evanston, IL: Northwestern University Press, 1963. 397 pp.

Swain, Joseph P., *The Broadway Musical: A Critical and Musical Survey*. New York: Oxford University Press, 1990. 384 pp.

Swortzell, Lowell, ed. *All the World's a Stage: Modern Plays for Young People*. New York: Delacorte Press, 1972. 610 pp.

Turner, Victor. *From Ritual to Theatre: The Human Seriousness of Play*. New York: Performing Arts Journal, 1982. 127 pp.

Weales, Gerald. *American Drama Since World War II*. New York: Harcourt, Brace & World, 1962. 246 pp.

Williams, Mance. *Black Theatre in the 1960s and 1970s*. Westport, CT: Greenwood Press, 1985. 188 pp.

Wilmeth, Don B., and Tice L. Miller. *The Cambridge Guide to American Theatre*. Cambridge: Cambridge University Press, 1993. 547 pp.

Woll, Allen L. *Dictionary of the Black Theatre: Broadway, Off-Broadway and Selected Harlem Theatres*. Westport, CT: Greenwood Press, 1983. 359 pp.

Young, Edgar. *Lincoln Center: The Building of an Institution*. New York: New York University Press, 1980. 334 pp.

Young, William, ed. *Famous American Playhouses, 1716–1971*. 2 vols. Chicago: American Library Association, 1973.

Zalacaín, Daniel. 'Introduction'. *New Beats: Hispanic American Plays*, 5–10. New Brunswick, NJ: Slusa, 1990.

Ziegler, Joseph. *Regional Theatre: The Revolutionary Stage*. New York: Da Capo, 1977. 283 pp.

presentation of national plays was essential to the early success of the new theatre. It became apparent quickly, though, that the number of high-quality Uruguayan works was not sufficient to maintain the repertoire and the company soon added in the classics.

By the end of the 1950s, some twenty-one independent groups – six in the provinces – existed, half owning their own performance spaces. FUTI itself – as an umbrella group – had its own totally equipped portable tent that could hold more than 600; it was used by many of the independent groups to take theatre to other areas.

Even the Comedia Nacional had a strong audience base by 1956, drawing more than 60,000 spectators to see a new Uruguayan play, *Procesado 1040 (Accused No. 1040)* by Juan Carlos Patrón (1905–79). Some other companies – for example the Teatro Circular – were able to perform several times a week, for months at a time, such plays as Shelley's *The Case of Isabel Collins* (1956). Around this time as well, El Galpón, Teatro Circular, Teatro Libre and Teatro del Pueblo all began to add dramatic training to their operations.

By 1959, more than 700,000 people were going to the theatre annually in Montevideo alone, a city whose population at that time was only about 1 million. In this same period, those who would ultimately be the founders of a thriving theatrical profession all began to appear: actors, directors, writers and designers.

In 1973, however, a *coup d'état* led Uruguay once again into a military dictatorship. It was during this period that independent theatres were investigated and many of their members imprisoned and/or exiled. In 1976, the government took away all legal rights of the Teatro El Galpón and confiscated its holdings. Later, the Sala Mercedes, the group's smaller venue, was demolished and its Sala 18 taken over by the state.

El Galpón fled to exile in México, not returning to Uruguay for almost ten years. Its opening performance on its return in 1984 was *Artigas general del pueblo (Artigas, the People's General)* by Ruben Yáñez (b. 1929) and Milton Schinca (b. 1923). Premièred in México by the company in 1981, its opening in Montevideo created an extraordinary public response but a much less enthusiastic one from the critics. Focusing on the life of a Uruguayan major, the play was done in a Brechtian style; the audience reaction, however, was clearly an emotional one.

In 1980, an historic referendum marked the beginning of the end of the dictatorship. From then until 1984, the level of repression continued to diminish and the theatre community began to recover other spaces that had been lost. As these companies reopened, still newer groups were formed: Teatro de la Ciudad (Theatre of the City), Teatro de la Gaviota (Seagull Theatre), Teatro Sincueva (Theatre Without a Cave) and Grupo Café-Teatro de la Asociación Cristiana de Jóvenes (Café Theatre Group of the Young Men's Christian Association).

Local theatre groups had appeared in the provinces during the first decades of the century but they were not consistent in their programmes, and many disappeared rather quickly. In the second half of the century, the situation changed somewhat, as companies managed to have longer lives. The best example was the Pequeño Teatro de Durazno (Durazno Little Theatre), which was still operating in 1995. As the interior opened, there were also a number of national festivals and showcases, isolated events, but important nevertheless. In 1983, for example, theatre companies from Paysandú, a city 400 kilometres northwest of Montevideo, organized a festival with other theatres from the interior. This Primer Encuentro de Teatros del Interior (First Encounter of Theatres from the Interior) took place in Paysandú and even attracted companies from the capital. Other such festivals followed: in Paysandú again in 1984; in Maldonado in the south of the country in 1985; and then Paysandú permanently from 1987 on a biannual basis. In 1988 and 1990, between festivals, there were regional competitions to select participants for the festival the following year. At first, the festival gave priority to national plays; later, it included all Latin American plays. Since 1991, it has accepted plays from anywhere.

Formalized in 1985 with the creation of the Asociación de Teatros del Interior (ATI; Association of Theatres from the Interior), this association from its inception made it clear that it did not intend to be in opposition to theatre companies from the capital but rather to work with them. As a result, ATI has always had its own space in the head offices of the Sociedad Uruguaya de Actores (Uruguayan Actors' Association) as did FUTI or the national branch of the International Theatre Institute, all based in Montevideo.

ATI members also participated in the organization of the Primer Congreso Nacional de

Teatro (First National Theatre Congress) in 1987. By 1990, ATI included more than thirty groups as members and it was recognized by the Ministry of Culture. The Ministry of Culture also began outreach work in the 1980s and 1990s, sending theatre artists from the capital as teachers to the provinces.

In the mid-1980s, many dramatists who had been silent or exiled returned to work in the theatre – Mauricio Rosencof (b. 1935), Híber Conteris (b. 1933), Milton Schinca, Carlos Maggi (b. 1922) and others. Two historical plays of note were performed in 1985: *Salsipuedes* (*Leave-If-You-Can*) by Alberto Restuccia (b. 1942), dealing with the extermination of Uruguay's indigenous people; and Maggi's *Don Frutos*, a revisionist version of the life of President Fructuoso Rivera. More subjective and metaphysical plays were also staged at this time, the most successful being *All That Tango* (1988) by Alvaro Ahuncháin (b. 1962) and *Los girasoles de van Gogh* (*The Sunflowers of van Gogh*, 1989) by Luis Vidal (b. 1955).

Also frequently seen were adaptations of novels such as *El coronel no tiene quién le escriba* (*The Colonel Has No One to Write to Him*), by the well-known Colombian writer García Márquez. It was produced by Teatro Circular in 1988. Literary works by other international figures such as Kafka and Tolstoi were also adapted for the stage in the late 1980s and early 1990s.

These years also saw the rise of director Nelly Goitiño with such productions as Peter Handke's *Kaspar*, *El castillo* (*The Castle*, 1988), based on the Kafka novel, and Brecht's *Der gute Mensch von Sezuan* (*The Good Person of Setzuan*, 1992). Another director, María Azambuya (b. 1944), had begun her career in children's theatre, but in 1990 started to explore with a group of young actors a series of productions based on their personal stories.

Jorge Curi (b. 1931) has regularly shown both Brechtian and Stanislavskian traits in productions such as *Los caballos* (*The Horses*, 1992) by Mauricio Rosencof. Rooted in the classic texts of Florencio Sánchez (1875–1910), he finds images of the Uruguayan as prisoner of the land. His work has been influenced as well by the scenography of Osvaldo Reyno (b. 1941).

Among younger artists emerging in the 1990s, the best known was Roberto Suárez (b. 1970), whose major productions – *Las fuentes del abismo* (*The Fountains of the Abyss*, 1992) and *Kapelusz* (1994) – were mounted in nontraditional spaces. Both opened the theatre to

fantasy and expressionism. Tabaré Rivero's *La ópera de la mala leche* (*The Foul Milk Opera*, 1991) and *Qué te comics – te?* (*What Did You Swallow?*, 1992) took politics into an anarchic sphere, typical of this author-director. Still another working in this style was Leo Masliah, a musician, composer and writer, who explored life in an absurd, delirious way, sarcastically commenting on human relations in plays such as *El ama de llaves* (*The Housekeeper*, 1991), *No juegues con fuega que lo podés apagar* (*Don't Play With Fire You Might Put It Out*, 1993) and *Puedo escribir las más atroces barbaridades esta noche* (*I Can Write the Most Awful Things Tonight*).

César Campodónico

A few words here about the Uruguayan carnival and its influence on the development of popular theatrical forms. Dating from the nineteenth century, the Uruguayan carnival is a significant cultural manifestation that attracts tens of thousands who both attend and participate in it. A kind of competition, in carnival one sees hundreds of groups moving around performing at various locations creating a true art of, for and by the people.

Perhaps the most important forms of carnival are the *candombe* and the *murga*, musical forms that transcend their music. Linked to masked dances, the *candombe* have evolved over generations with each new generation adding its own music and dances. This combination, rooted in African ritual, particularly the coronation rites of African kings, has slowly fused with local cultural traditions.

The *candombe* is especially popular during the Montevidean carnival period, especially during the carnival's major parade through the city centre where people dance to the rhythm of the drums.

Of the two, the *murga* is less folk rooted but equally Uruguayan. A part of carnival since the late nineteenth century, with origins in Cádiz, Spain, this music/dance form contains typically Montevidean rhythms and rituals. Rooted in grotesque gestures that connect to *commedia dell'arte* but appear as *kitsch* to foreign eyes, the *murga* begins in a vision of white and evolves through the *candombe* through various musical manifestations involving the loud beating of drums and an even louder clashing of cymbals.

Nothing is as unique to the *murga* as the sound of its chorus involving nasal cries projected over long distances. A blending of various sounds and voices, the *murga* creates a

many directors from the independent theatre movement, helping to expand its repertoire.

In the 1990s El Galpón remains Uruguay's major independent company, the quintessential Uruguayan theatre. Built around the personality and theatrical ideas of its director, Atahualpa del Cioppo, the group – like del Cioppo – began with its roots in Stanislavski but evolved over several decades into a Brechtian style. At its best it blended these styles – the former more emotional, the latter more cerebral – into an effective stage reality with clear ideological content while retaining the coherence and validity of each character.

Among other theatres of note, the Teatro Circular stands out for its many excellent directors. These have included the Argentine Omar Grasso (1940–90), Héctor Manuel Vidal (b. 1943), Antonio Larretta and especially Jorge Curi. The group's style has been influenced by its unusual space, a space that has led to a unique type of representational intimacy. During the military dictatorship the theatre created a repertoire of resistance, taking it from a traditional type of playwriting to a dramaturgy that spoke in code of daily realities. One of the most popular works in this style was Curi's and Mercedes Rein's *El herrero y la muerte* (*Death and the Blacksmith*, 1981). The production ran for over five years.

Dramaturgy

Among the early major national dramatists were Florencio Sánchez, Ernesto Herrera, Yamandú Rodríguez (1891–1957), José Pedro Bellán (1889–1930), Zavala Muniz (1898–1968), Carlos Princivalle (1887–1959) and Angel Curotto (1902–90).

Most of these playwrights have written in a variety of styles from the Spanish *costumbrista* (featuring local manners and customs) to more modern experiments in absurdist comedy. This said, realistic genres focusing on plays of genuine social criticism have dominated.

Since few have been able to survive by writing for the theatre alone, most Uruguayan dramatists have made careers in other fields. Some have earned livings as novelists and journalists while others have taught, been lawyers or worked as actors or directors. One playwright of note whose work was produced in the 1950s and 1960s – Híber Conteris – was a Protestant minister who was imprisoned in the 1970s for several years by the military dictatorship. His

dramatic works include *Enterrar a los muertos* (*Bury the Dead*, 1959), *Este otro lado del telón* (*This Other Side of the Curtain*, 1960), *El socavón* (*The Hole*, 1963) and *El desvío* (*The Detour*, 1963). As could be expected, ideological concerns dominated his theatre.

Among the few playwrights who have survived almost exclusively on their dramatic writing is Carlos Maggi. Both a popular writer and an experimenter with form, Maggi's works have included both social dramas and absurdist comedies. During the 1970s, he too was persecuted by the military regime.

His works include *La trastienda* (*The Back Room*, 1958), *La biblioteca* (*The Library*, 1959), *Las llamadas* (*The Calls*, 1960), *Cosentino, Un motivo* (*A Motive*), *La noche de los ángeles inciertos* (*The Night of the Uncertain Angels*, 1960), *Esperando a Rodó* (*Waiting for Rodo*, 1967), *El apuntador* (*The Prompter*, 1962), *Un cuervo en la madrugada* (*A Raven at Dawn*, 1962), *La gran viuda* (*The Great Widow*, 1961), *El pianista y el amor* (*Love and the Pianist*, 1965), *El patio de la torcaza* (*The Dove's Patio*, 1967) and *Don Frutos* (1985).

Among the first of the important modern dramatists was Carlos Denis Molina (b. 1918), who established his reputation earlier as a novelist and poet and worked as an actor, director and administrator mostly at the Teatro Solís in Montevideo. Working in a variety of styles, Molina's most significant plays included *Golpe de amanecer* (*Dawn Hit*, 1935), *Por el pulmón del retrato respiran los ángeles* (*The Angels Breathe Through the Lung of the Painting*, 1939), *La niña y el espantapájaros* (*The Little Girl and the Scarecrow*, 1944), *El otro lado de la medalla* (*The Other Side of the Medal*, 1946), *El regreso de Ulises* (*The Return of Ulysses*, 1948), *Orfeo* (*Orpheus*, 1950), *Morir, tal vez soñar* (*To Die, Perchance to Dream*, 1953), *Si el asesino fuera inocente* (*If the Killer Were Innocent*, 1956), *En las mejores familias* (*In the Best of Families*, 1958), *Un domingo extraordinario* (*An Extraordinary Sunday*, 1958), *La boa* (*The Boa*, 1973) and *Soñar con Ceci trae cola* (*Dreaming of Ceci Has Its Consequences*, 1983).

In the decades that followed, realistic theatre came to dominate in the works of such dramatists as Andrés Castillo (b. 1920) and Juan Carlos Legido (b. 1924). Castillo is the author of *Llegada* (*Arrival*, 1950), *La cantera* (*The Quarry*, 1957), *Parrillada* (*Barbecue*, 1958), *La noche* (*The Night*, 1959), *La bahía* (*The Bay*, 1960), *La jaula* (*The Cage*, 1961) and *Cinco* goles (*Five Goals*, 1963). Contributing to the theatre in more ways than just his writing, Castillo was also a co-founder of the Teatro Universitario, an initiator of the Federación de Teatros Independientes and, being a lawyer, the legal consultant for many theatre groups. His works observe the life and customs of Uruguay in a realistic way. On occasion, they lean towards the grotesque and farcical.

Legido's theatre also moves between a kind of poetic naturalism and gentle farce. A critic and scholar as well, his works for the stage include *La lámpara* (*The Lamp*, 1952), *Dos en el tejado* (*Two on the Roof*, 1957), *La piel de los otros* (*The Skin of the Others*, 1958), *Veraneo* (*Summer Holidays*, 1961), *Los cuatro perros* (*The Four Dogs*, 1963), *El tranvía* (*The Streetcar*, 1965) and *Historia de judíos* (*Story of Jews*, 1968).

Other writers working in a realistic and/or socially critical style emerging in the 1950s and 1960s included Mario Benedetti (b. 1920), Rubén Deugenio (b. 1925), Antonio Larreta (b. 1912), Héctor Plaza Noblia (1923–90) and Jacobo Langsner (b. 1927).

Benedetti is a storyteller, poet, essayist and well-known journalist. Among his important dramatic works are *El reportaje* (*The Interview*, 1958); *Ida y vuelta* (*The Return Trip*, 1958), a monologue of humorous and characteristically critical sketches directed by Emilio Acevedo Solano; and *Pedro y el Capitán* (*Pedro and the Captain*, 1978), first performed by Teatro El Galpón while the group was in exile in México, directed by Atahualpa del Cioppo, and later made into a film. The latter piece is an ardent testimonial against torture, in keeping with the author's passionate attitude of resistance toward the military dictatorship in Uruguay between 1973 and 1985.

Deugenio began his career as a radio dramatist, often writing about famous authors, a theme he continued in the theatre with *La tregua* (*The Truce*, 1963), about Mario Benedetti, and *Ana en blanco y negro* (*Ana in Black and White*, 1965), based on *Una virgen* (*A Virgin*) by Juan José Morosoli (1899–1957). Deugenio's other works include *Quiniela* (*Bookmaking*, 1958), *El ascenso* (*The Promotion*, 1958), *Dieciséis años y una noche* (*Sixteen Years and a Night*) and *El peregrino con taparrabo de arpillera* (*The Pilgrim with a Loincloth of Sacking*, 1961).

Larreta, in addition to being a playwright, is also an actor, director and critic. He contributed a penetrating analysis of the evolution of Uruguayan theatre as a reflection of the intellectual and socio-political evolution of the country. When the military dictatorship came to power, he went to Spain where he continued his career with a critically acclaimed novel, *Volaverunt*, and numerous works for television. A co-founder of Montevideo's Club de Teatro in 1949 and later of the Teatro de la Ciudad de Montevideo, Larreta's dramatic works include *Una familia feliz* (*A Happy Family*, 1948), *La sonrisa* (*The Smile*, 1950), *Oficio de tinieblas* (*Dark Occupation*, 1955), *Un enredo y un marqués* (*A Mix-Up and a Marquis*, 1963) and *Juan Palmieri* (1973).

Plaza Noblia's dramatic works are in varying realistic styles and are usually controversial in content. His major plays include *El puente* (*The Bridge*, 1950), *La clave perdida* (*The Lost Key*, 1950), *El cono de luz* (*Cone of Light*, 1951), *La cajita de música* (*The Music Box*, 1954), *Los puros* (*The Pure Ones*, 1953), *Los jugadores* (*The Players*, 1957), *Los ojos en el espejo* (*The Eyes in the Mirror*, 1960), *La enfermedad de Arlequín* (*The Illness of Harlequin*, 1959), *La última madrugada* (*The Last Morning*, 1982) and *Ensayo Nro. 4* (*Essay No. 4*).

Langsner's prolific *oeuvre* includes *El hombre incompleto* (*The Incomplete Man*, 1951), *Los ridículos* (*The Ridiculous Ones*, 1951), *El juego de Ifigenia* (*The Game of Iphigenia*, 1952), *La rebelión de Galatea* (*The Rebellion of Galatea*, 1956), *Llegaron los artistas* (*The Artists Have Arrived*, 1956), *Los elegidos* (*The Chosen Ones*, 1957) and *Esperando la carroza* (*Waiting for the Carriage*, 1962), perhaps his most famous piece, which was later adapted for film. Among his later plays are *Un inocente adulterio* (*An Innocent Act of Adultery*, 1962), *El tobogán* (*The Toboggan*, 1970), *La gotera* (*The Drip*, 1971), *El terremoto* (*The Earthquake*, 1973), *Una corona para Benito* (*A Crown for Benito*, 1973), *Pater noster* (1976) and *La planta* (*The Plant*, 1982).

Other essentially realistic writers who emerged in the 1970s include Victor Manuel Leites (b. 1933), Mauricio Rosencof and Milton Schinca.

Leites began his career as a television writer and later did theatrical criticism. His dramatic works include *Informe para distraídos* (*Report for the Absent Minded*, 1968), later called *Cantata popular de Montevideo* (*People's Cantata for Montevideo*, 1970); *Crónicas de bien nacidos* (*Chronicles of the High-Born*, 1973); *Quiroga* (1975), a biographical drama; *Doña Ramona* (1982), inspired by a story by

Between these two directors came Rubén Castillo (b. 1925), co-founder of the Teatro Libre in 1955. Under Castillo, the group produced the works of a number of important Latin American dramatists such as Sastre and Gorostiza, as well as European and American dramatists such as Arthur Miller. Miller's *Death of a Salesman* was one of Castillo's major successes. In addition to his stage work, he was also a critic, journalist and media personality.

Other directors of note include Federico Wolff (1926–88), founder of the Teatro Universal and director of works by writers such as Peter Weiss and Friedrich Dürrenmatt; Antonio Larreta, a playwright, actor and director whose many productions included a version of *Fuenteovejuna* (*The Sheep Well*) that played to over 100,000 spectators; Juver Salcedo (b. 1934), trained at El Galpón, an actor and director whose career included periods as director of the only regularly producing radio theatre company on the continent; Jorge Curi, also trained at El Galpón; Eduardo Schinca (b. 1929), trained under Margarita Xirgú; Nelly Goitiño, a director with a very personal vision of performance space and the actor's body; César Campodónico, a co-founder of El Galpón and one of the major heirs of the del Cioppo style; and Carlos Aguilera (b. 1945), whose work was mostly in the regional and provincial theatres.

Victor Manuel Leites

Music Theatre

Between about 1850 and 1945, Uruguay had one of the oldest and best musical theatre traditions in South America because of the ease with which touring European opera companies visiting Buenos Aires could also stop over in Montevideo. Entire seasons of European opera were arranged this way by private impresarios. During this time there were occasional attempts by Uruguayan composers to create new operas. Among those whose works were done were Luis Sambucetti, León Ribeiro, César Cortinas and Alfonso Broqua (1876–1946). Though some were actually staged, only two managed to remain in the repertoire.

After World War II, however, the situation changed substantially. The main responsibility for musical theatre and musical life generally was taken over by the Servicio Oficial de Difusión Radio Eléctrica (SODRE, the state radio and television network), which had been established in 1929. Those in charge assigned opera only secondary importance, a policy maintained for years. The result was the disappearance of a generation familiar with operatic genres. Though amateur associations tried to remedy the situation, they had only partial and sporadic success.

Despite this, a number of musical theatre events did take place that deserve to be noted here, including the première of *El regreso* (*The Return*) by Ricardo Storm (b. 1930), in 1958. The book, also written by Storm, was based on Esquilo's tragedy *Las coéforas* but transferred the action to the Uruguayan countryside. Though the work is not specifically folkloric, it does include a musical piece taken from the rural area near the town of Minas and maintained virtually in its original form. *El regreso* is a dramatic opera based on tense melodic lines. The author later revised it twice for performances in 1972 and 1980 but the modifications did not alter the basic characteristics of this fascinating piece.

The third Uruguayan opera, premièred in 1967, was *Marta Gruni*. Written by Jaures Lamarque Pons (1917–82) and based on a play by Florencio Sánchez, the opera is set in a rooming house and describes people and situations typical of Montevideo at the beginning of the century. Lamarque Pons underscores the urban theme by incorporating an accordion and two small drums into the traditional orchestra, these instruments being typical of popular urban music in Uruguay.

La cruz del sud (*The Southern Cross*) by Alfonso Broqua was composed between 1917 and 1921 and was intended to be presented at the Teatro Colón in Buenos Aires but the performances never took place. Finally premièred in Montevideo in 1979, its theme was inspired by *The Captive*, a story by the English writer Robert Graham. Set in the land of the Calchaquí Indians, it tells the tale of the son of Chief Yurú, who dies while saving his mother, a captive white woman. Broqua's music evokes Hispanic America and is consistently inspired by native rhythms with an orchestra made up of thirty-eight traditional instruments including a *carambasú*, a Bolivian percussion instrument made from the hollow trunk of two types of trees, each one producing a different sound.

In 1980 the première of still another Uruguayan opera, *Nobleza campera (Country Nobility)* by Mario Belardi (b. 1905), took place in Montevideo. Based on a story by Italo Raffi, the action is set on a small farm on the banks of the Uruguay River at the beginning of the twentieth century. Belardi uses traditional instrumentation, adding to it several guitars, the most typical instrument of the countryside. That same year, César Cortinas's 1916 opera *La última gaviota (The Last Seagull)* was also staged.

In addition to these Uruguayan operas, *La zapatera prodigiosa (The Prodigious Shoemaker's Wife)*, by the Argentine composer Juan José Castro, based on a text by García Lorca, also had its world première in Uruguay in 1949. The composer conducted this work, which was staged by Margarita Xirgú. The work was modern without breaking tradition, while also staying in harmony with the poetic essence of García Lorca's play.

Other Uruguayan premières of foreign works include *Euridice* (1949) by Peri y Rinuccini, directed by Lamberto Baldi; Menotti's *El cónsul* (1950) in Italian, and Britten's *Peter Grimes* (1962), also in Italian.

Opera seasons in Montevideo during these years were short, with works from the international repertoire alternating with more modern pieces. Among the latter were works by Menotti, Poulenc, Ravel and Debussy.

In 1985 the Sociedad Uruguaya de Amigos de la Opera (Uruguayan Society of Friends of the Opera) was founded, through the efforts of the Minister for Foreign Affairs, Enrique Iglesias (b. 1929), who was the society's first president. This group aims to work in collaboration with SODRE and the municipal government of Montevideo to return the country to its nearly forgotten musical traditions.

Barrett Puig, César Campodónico

Dance Theatre

The history of European-style dance theatre is almost entirely a post-World War II phenomenon. Prior to the creation of SODRE dance was seen only in the occasional visits of foreign companies. Since its inception, SODRE has been the major source of live dance performance – mostly ballet – in the country.

That said, SODRE has been broad in its stylistic orientation and, though its dancers and choreographers have all been classically trained, the company has included modernist directions in its work. Nevertheless, the general lines of this national dance company have alternated between French and Russian styles and only occasionally have strayed into more modern areas.

The first important Uruguayan choreographer was Alberto Pouyanne, who came to national attention in 1935 with the première of SODRE's ballet *Nocturno nativo (Native Nocturne)* to a score by Vicente Ascone. From this beginning, major artists from Europe and the Americas regularly committed themselves to periods of time in Uruguay, each leaving influences on local dancers and choreographers. During this time as well, an enthusiastic and discriminating public was developed for ballet, especially Pouyanne's work.

During the 1940s, his fame rested on his many staged oratorios and several other unusual works: *Joan of Arc in Flames* by Honegger and *The Martyrdom of St Sebastian* by Debussy. Other significant choreography of his includes *Istar*, based on music by D'Indy, *Festival of the Spider* by Roussel, *La Peri* by Dukas and works based on Satie's *Gymnopédies* and Poulenc's *Rapsodia negra (Black Rhapsody)*.

Pouyanne had built an audience by the end of the 1940s and the public responded enthusiastically to new works by foreign choreographers just as his dancers responded to foreign teachers. One of the first to commit himself to an extended period in Uruguay was Roger Fenonjois, première dancer of the Paris Opera ballet company. His innovative influence was felt through the 1950s and he found a close collaborator in Juan José Castro, who had replaced the congenial Lamberto Baldi as SODRE's conductor at this time.

Together, Fenonjois and Castro introduced to Montevideo audiences works based on the music of Stravinsky (*Romeo and Juliet* and *Orpheus*) and Ravel (*Daphnis et Chloë*). *Coppélia* was also seen for the first time in Uruguay under Fenonjois, who brought to Montevideo Lolita Parent, who later became the prima ballerina of the company.

But the modernity of the Parisian style imposed by Fenonjois left many longing for a more classical repertoire, closer to the kinds of works they had seen earlier. As a result, Tamara Grigorieva, formerly of Russia's Basil troupe, was hired as the company's director. The SODRE company soon became a major exponent of the Diaghilev tradition not only in Montevideo but also in Buenos Aires. She quickly recreated a great number of Russian ballets, especially those of Massine, Lichine and Fokine. As a dancer, Grigorieva continued to attract large audiences in the Río de la Plata region and for many years her work was a paradigm of the best traditions of character dance.

In 1954, following Grigorieva's tenure in Uruguay, came Vaslav Veltchek, a Czech choreographer and dancer who had been working in Brazil, where he had created a children's ballet company. Equally innovative as teacher and choreographer, his major works with the company included *Prague Symphony* by Mozart, *Dance of the Dead* by Honegger, Stravinsky's *Persephone* and three ballets with Uruguayan music: *Mburucuyá* by Fabini, *La isla de los Ceibos* (*Ceibos Island*) and *Suite Segun Figari,* the latter two by Lamarque Pons.

After Veltchek, a refined neo-classicist, came more of the Russian repertoire created by the Polish choreographer and teacher Yurek Shabelewsky, who had worked with Grigorieva in Russia. He presented SODRE with personal visions of the major classics including *The Nutcracker* and *Sleeping Beauty*. During Shabelewsky's stay in Montevideo, the company added several dancers who had been working in Buenos Aires – Margaret Graham, Eduardo Ramírez and Tito Barbon – who would later occupy important positions with the company. Barbon became the company's leading choreographer, staging ballet versions of *La Beri* (Dukas), *Opus 2* (Menotti), *Medea* (Barber) and *The Messenger* (Bartok).

Other fruitful contacts were with the Argentine dancer Maria Ruanova and the Russian dancer Tatiana Leskova, who had been dancing in Rio de Janeiro. Both directed the company in the 1960s. A strong and dominant figure both on stage and off, Ruanova imposed an important discipline on the SODRE dancers while Leskova extended the repertoire to include music by Cesar Franck and Kabalevsky.

The North American tradition came to Uruguay through the work of William Dollar, one of George Balanchine's leading dancers in New York. Dollar brought a new energy to the company in such Balanchine works as *Concierto* (Mendelssohn) and *El combate* (*Combat*). Concluding the 1960s was a brief period under the English choreographer Norman Dixon, who helped the dancers refine their technique along the lines of London's Royal Ballet.

The 1970s saw a period of official indifference to the company and significant funding problems. Special support at this time was given by Margaret Graham, Tito Barbon and Eduardo Ramírez, who all became Uruguayan citizens and assumed various administrative duties. Prokofiev's *Romeo and Juliet* and Stravinsky's *The Rite of Spring* were highlights of this period, which showed both Soviet influence and, later, the influence of the Belgian Maurice Béjart. Also of import at this time was the work of Domingo Vera, who brought the influence of modern dance to such works as *El retrato* (*The Picture*) to music by Edith Piaf.

The 1980s saw directors of SODRE in their posts for even briefer periods. The modern dancer Adriana Coll came for three seasons and staged such works as *Carmina Burana*, while Grigorieva returned from time to time from Buenos Aires to restage works of the Russian repertoire. Graham returned in *Giselle*, a work that she dominated stylistically.

The pattern of short-lived artistic directors continued into the 1990s. Among those who have run SODRE's dance programme for brief periods of time have been the Soviet dancer Vilen Kalstian, the Cubans Lydia Diaz, Alberto Alonso and Gustavo Herrera, and the French dancers Françoise Adret and Gigi Cacciuleanu. Perhaps the finest of the Uruguayan-born dancers turned out by the company has been Sara Nieto, for several years a leading dancer in Santiago.

As for dance training, this has long been in the hands of private schools though SODRE did have its own school for a short time. Only in the 1970s did an Escuela Nacional de Danza (National School of Dance) emerge, funded by the Ministry of Culture and run by Margaret Graham, a graduate of the Royal Ballet School in London. Not surprisingly, Graham chose to establish a curriculum based closely on that of the Royal Ballet. The school has since turned out many strong dancers, some of whom have remained in Uruguay; many others have chosen to dance in other countries, notably Argentina, Chile and Brazil.

Theatre for Young Audiences

Professional children's theatre in Uruguay is a form that dates back to the 1930s. It was then that two groups came into being: the Carlos Brussa Company and La Isla de los Niños. Brussa, an outstanding actor and director, founded his group in 1938 and this first professional company for children worked out of the SODRE Hall. Its repertoire was based on stage adaptations of such classic stories as *Tom Thumb* (1938), *Little Red Riding Hood* (1939) and *Puss 'n Boots* (1940).

Working in a more innovative way was the group La Isla de los Niños, created in 1940 by Ofelia Naveira (b. 1907) and later run by director Atahualpa del Cioppo. Working with Montiel Ballesteros (1888–1971), Ramón Otero (1897–1968) and Juan Severino (b. 1893), this same group of people would later evolve into Teatro El Galpón.

When del Cioppo took over La Isla de los Niños' artistic direction, he began to develop a specific pedagogical style focused on young actors. The majority of these young people would later join El Galpón. The group continued for several seasons staging mostly original works and adaptations of classic stories, many combining live actors with puppets.

Following del Cioppo's exile to México with El Galpón and his return to Uruguay in 1984, he resumed doing children's work as well. Among the company's major productions were *El pozo de las monedas* (*The Wishing Well*); *Las medias de los flamencos* (*The Flamingo's Stockings*), staged by Bernardo Galli; *Buscabichos* (*Searching for Bugs*) and *Tabaré* both staged by María Azambuya; and *Ruperto de terror* (*Ruperto the Terrible*) and *Ruperto contraataca* (*Rupert Strikes Back*), both written by Roy Berocay in 1955 and staged by Dervy Vilas (b. 1933).

During the 1960s a theatre movement for children began to crystallize in Uruguay, with the creation of several groups dedicated exclusively to this activity. After graduating from the Municipal School of Dramatic Arts in 1962, the actress España Andrade (b. 1939) founded, along with Roberto Rius (1932–88), the Children's Theatre of Montevideo, putting on *El pirata* (*The Pirate*, 1962) by the Brazilian author Jurandir Pereira, and *Pluft el fantasmita* (*Pluft the Little Ghost*, 1964) by Maria Clara Machado, also from Brazil. The group later performed a wide variety of classic children's stories in stage adaptations. Through the years, several other small groups merged with the Children's Theatre, such as Teatro Circular, Nuevo Teatro Circular and Os Mambembes. Once again the repertoire returned to original plays by Brazilian authors, such as *La brujita que era buena* (*The Good Little Witch*, 1965), *O boi e o burro no caminho de Belem* (*The Ox and the Donkey on the Way to Bethlehem*, 1968) and *Little Red Riding Hood* (1972) by Machado, directed by Andrade.

In 1963, Teatro de Cámara (Chamber Theatre) appeared, directed by Luis Cerminara (b. 1936), who later founded the Teatro Uno (Theatre One) along with Alberto Restuccia (b. 1942). Among the original productions put on by this group were *Esperando a Todot* (*Waiting for Todot*, 1964) and *Doña Disparate y Bambuco* (*Miss Nonsense and Bambuco*, 1977), both by the Argentine María Elena Walsh, and *El humor en la escuela* (*Fun at School*, 1979). The company was still active into the 1990s with such plays as *Cóntame un cuento* (*Tell Me a Tale*, 1980), based on Ionesco, *Cuando llegue el cumpleaños* (*When the Birthday Arrives*, 1982), *Gogó y Didí* (1984), *El Prinsokito* (1990), *Frankensteinsito* (*Little Frankenstein*, 1992) and *Aladino* (1994).

Dervy Vilas, an actor and director with both Teatro El Galpón and Teatro Circular, began writing and directing for children's theatre in 1968. His plays *Sin ton ni son* (*Without Rhyme or Reason*, 1968), *La ronda Gironda* (*The Gironde Round*, 1969) and *El niño de las luciérnagas* (*The Glow-Worm Boy*, 1970) are characterized by their commitment to helping children understand who they are.

In 1967, Angelita Parodi (b. 1924), director of the Teatro Moderno, began staging plays for children, such as *El raterillo* (*The Pickpocket*), *La rebelión de los juguetes* (*The Rebellion of the Toys*, 1970), *La niña y el burrito* (*The Little Girl and the Donkey*, 1973), *El circo de Rataplán* (*Rataplán's Circus*, 1977) and *The Wizard of Oz* (1979), all in her own versions. Her work is characterized by its freshness of language and charming storylines.

Walter Rey (b. 1940) and Susana Mazzuchelli (b. 1940) both wrote and directed for the Teatro del Niño from the 1970s, staging even more contemporary versions of classics such as *Las bodas de Caperucita* (*Little Red Riding Hood's Wedding*, 1970), *Rongo el gato que* queria ser niño (*Rongo, the Cat Who Wanted to Be a Boy*, 1971), *La abuelita espacial* (*The Space-Travelling Grandma*, 1973) and *América niña* (*Little America*, 1978).

A number of directors in the years since have turned to the form with enthusiasm, including Elena Zuasti (b. 1938), Werther Gluck (b. 1920), Jorge Cifré (b. 1944), Raquel Azar (b. 1930) and Estela Mieres (b. 1951).

Since 1980, several more groups have emerged in Montevideo, which remains the national focal point of the theatre for children movement.

España Andrade

Puppet Theatre

Puppets have long been part of the popular imagination in Uruguay. During the colonial period, a puppet style was created known as *Misericordia Campana* (Mercy Bell). Its most popular figure – a black slave named Ambrosio, a church bell-ringer – would challenge authority by butting powerful people with his head, a type of fighting called *capoeira*. This fighting slave-puppet was clearly committed to the needs of the exploited.

In 1945, a group of law students began a series of 'socio-pedagogic missions', inspired by the Spanish Civil War and the literacy campaigns in México. Puppets played a part here as well and their tours to rural towns often resulted in the formation of small theatres. In this way, groups of independent puppeteers were formed led by people such as Rosita Baffico (1909–94), Juan M. Tenuta (b. 1923) and Bruno Musittelli (b. 1924).

The Spanish dramatist García Lorca visited the region in 1933 with his Teatro La Tarumba. Among those who came under his influence then were Baffico and the teacher Irma Abirad (b. 1914) from the School of Dramatic Arts. Abirad left the school soon after to create her Retablillode Maese Pedro on a professional basis, while Baffico moved her puppets into the independent theatre movement. In 1954 she was invited to create a national puppet workshop, which ultimately led to the establishment of an independent school of puppetry within the Teatro El Galpón.

At the popular level, puppets also took many forms including giant-headed puppets that appeared in parades or on small carnival stages, a style whose main exponent was Jaime Urrutia (1919–85).

In 1954, Grupo Ensayo (Rehearsal Group) was formed in Piriápolis, a city in the province of Maldonado. This group would later be transformed into Títeres de Potichín (Puppets of Potichín), a company with a wide variety of company members, among them nurses, sailors, hotel-keepers, teachers, construction workers and carpenters. The group was active until 1976 under the direction of Gustavo Sosa Zerpa (b. 1928). Other groups of note are the Marionetas Vilas and Marionetas Pulgarcito (Little Thumb Marionettes), the latter connected with the family of the well-known musician, Federico García Vigil.

Uruguayan support of the republic during the Spanish Civil War lasted long after the conflict in Spain had ended; supporters included a group of graduates from the Escuela de Bellas Artes (School of Fine Arts). A number from this group were invited by César Campodónico to participate in the creation of stage sets for Teatro El Galpón. Over time, the work of Nicolás Loureiro (b. 1924) began to stand out and he later became the director of the puppet school at El Galpón.

Among the more interesting groups are those of the Di Mauro brothers and Javier Villafañe, who perform and teach in schools, in the countryside, and even on boats, using the sails as a stage curtain.

The 1960s was a decade of transformation in which the national puppet movement reached new heights. Influential in this was the creation of the Convención Nacional de Trabajadores (National Workers' Centre). Social developments were also significant, particularly a visit by the Cuban revolutionary Che Guevara, and the music of the Beatles. This led to a sense of social activism. Puppet shows began to be performed in the streets, in union halls, at meetings and in the independent theatres. Several more groups began to appear: Angel Alonso, La Farándula, Vilas Marionettes, Hernán Rodríguez, Rius Marionettes, Gallo

Pinto (Spotted Rooster) and El Duende (The Goblin).

Books began to be published about puppets, including ¿*Cómo son los títeres?* (*What Are Puppets?*), written by the puppeteers Nicolás Loureiro and Aída Rodríguez, with a prologue by Rolando Speranza.

By the 1970s, the number of puppet groups began to diminish as the national political situation worsened. When the government moved to the right, national culture – including puppetry – suffered enormously. When the dictatorship decreed that Teatro El Galpón be closed in 1976 and all its property confiscated, the situation reached its nadir. Only months before, the puppeteer and teacher Gustavo Sosa Zerpa had been arrested and imprisoned.

Puppets once again joined the resistance, performing in bunkers, concentration camps, private homes and housing cooperatives. In 1978, a puppet play called *El mono ciclista* (*The Biker Monkey*) was performed at Teatro del Notariado, under the direction of Loureiro and Speranza. Although it was not advertised and there were no programmes, it had large audiences. The majority of participants were from El Galpón, the group that led the cultural resistance even when its members were living in exile.

Due to the extent of the repression, very little of the work of the puppeteers during this period was documented, since most of their shows were performed secretly. In 1984, a second meeting of independent puppeteers took place and called for a National Convention of puppeteers. Among the initiatives springing from this was the Galpón school of puppetry, opened in 1985 and still Uruguay's only school of puppetry.

Gustavo Martínez Barbosa

Design

Uruguay is a country that tends to receive rather than create trends and this is certainly so in the area of theatre design, which began to take on contemporary qualities only in the post-war years of the late 1940s. Until that time, until the creation of the Comedia Nacional and even later with the development of independent groups, Uruguayan design tended to focus on descriptive scenic space.

But new developments in the visual arts after World War II began to be reflected in Uruguay at the Comedia Nacional as new developments in scenography, especially sculptural solutions, began to be felt in the country. Attractive both for their imaginative qualities and for their transforming powers on stage, the new approaches began to be seen first in the work of Hugo Mazza (b. 1928), Mario Galup (1924–82), Carrozzino-Prieto (b. 1939) and Osvaldo Reyno, who brought to stage design sometimes new and revolutionary ideas that broke with tradition to create this new visual language.

Later generations continued this effervescence which could be seen clearly in the developing aesthetic of Carlos Pirelli (b. 1952), Claudio Goeckler (b. 1935) and Carlos Musso (b. 1956). Considering that there has never been a lot of interchange in this area with the international community (especially among working visual artists) such developments in the design field are impressive and have made a real contribution to the development of Uruguayan theatre.

Jorge Abbondanza

Theatre Space and Architecture

The earliest theatre building in Uruguay was the Casa de Comedias (Comedy House), built by private initiative in 1792 in what is modern-day Montevideo. This modest wooden building followed the eighteenth-century Spanish theatre style – a pit close to a stage with balconies separating the different social classes. Most of the audience stood through the performances. Important renovations took place after 1855 but by 1879 the Casa de Comedias had been

Rúben Yáñez's 1992 Teatro Circular
production of Carlos Gorostiza's
Aeroplanos, designed by Osvaldo Reyno.
Photo: Mario Persichetti.

demolished in order to create a new theatre on
the same site.

The new theatre was called Teatro de San
Felipe y Santiago (designed by Uruguayan
architect José Claret and opened in 1880) and
ended up being one of the most significant
buildings in Montevideo. Reflecting the move
away from Spanish architectural principles and
towards those of Italy and France, this theatre
was one of several built at this time. Another
was Teatro Solís, designed in 1844 by the Italian
architect Carlos Zucchi. Not only was Teatro
Solís built to function as a social and cultural
centre but also it was the first Uruguayan
theatre in which architecture was conceived as
an integral part of the urban whole and in which
French neo-classic principles were used.

Though the Solís basically followed the horseshoe design of La Scala in Milan, its façade
followed other models, such as the Teatro Carlo
Felice in Genoa. The original had a Doric six-
sided peristyle across one level, proper for
romantic classicism, but the Solís followed the

Corinthian style, with eight components instead
of six and with two levels instead of one.

Inaugurated in 1856, the Solís underwent
several subsequent transformations including
one directed by the French architect Rabú.
Many publications of the period considered the
Solís one of the most important buildings in
Montevideo, a symbol of the new culture in the
country.

Later came the Teatro Cibils (1871–1912)
and the Alcázar Lírico (1869–71), both located
in old Montevideo, the most culturally and
socially active part of the city at that time. These
also had the same internal organization and
were built with similar materials. The first one
searched for a language close to classicism, with
an obvious preference for the Corinthian style.

Two other theatres also built in eclectic styles,
but associated with classic and Baroque components, were the Larrañaga and Stella D'Italia.
Both of them were designed at the end of the
nineteenth century by the Italian L. Andreoni.
The Larrañaga was built in the city of Salto,
following the horseshoe shape and with three
levels in the interior. A 620-seat space, the Stella
was inaugurated in 1895 and boasted electricity.
It managed to bring cultural and social activities
beyond Montevideo.

At the turn of the twentieth century, a number
of new spaces were renovated to accommodate
theatre. Some of these were able to function as
theatres for many years and featured consistent
programmes and important performances.
Among these were the Casino Oriental, later
known as Teatro Nacional, the Teatro de
Verano (Summer Theatre) and the Politeama.

The Urquiza was inaugurated in 1905 and
was designed by G. West, although the façade
was designed by the architect Horacio Acosta y
Lara (1875–1966). Though it still had some
classical elements, this theatre was the first
expression of modernism in Uruguay. Its glass
porch was built on a metal frame. The Urquiza
was well equipped and decorated inside. Its
curtain was regarded by professionals and critics
as the best of the time.

The Teatro 18 de Julio also showed signs of
modernity on its façade. Situated on Montevideo's main street, it was opened in 1910. Its
structure had two levels and was divided into
three vertical spaces. The second level was twice
as high as the lower. In the centre there was a
rose window, flanked by large parts of the
façade ornamentation, in the *art nouveau* style.
The use of iron and glass for the lower roofs
made obvious the ties with modernist art. In its

The Teatro Solís, designed by Carlos Zucchi, in Montevideo.
Photo: Matilde C. Texeira.

interior, this theatre, like so many others, maintained the elliptic shape and the four traditional levels for balconies. The stage also had an orchestra pit. Its seating capacity was 1,630.

Other theatres built in the same era and with the same spirit were the Teatro Artigas (1908–71), Teatro Colón (1910–65) and Teatro Albéniz (1918–39). All three have since been razed.

Of unusual importance was the Teatro Zabala. Built in 1922, this theatre operated until the 1980s, when it was destroyed by fire. A creation of French architect C. Gardelle, the Zabala was part of a larger, still-existing complex, considered the greatest building on Montevideo's main street.

In the 1950s, a number of old music conservatories were converted into theatres. This was the case with the Carlos Brussa, the Odeón, the Sala Verdi and the Teatro Victoria. The Brussa building was inaugurated in 1885, but was later partially demolished and was finally rebuilt in the 1950s. Its façade was strongly classical.

The Sala Verdi, also converted to a theatre in the 1950s, was created originally in 1894 by the English architect John Adams.

Finally, it is important to mention the circuses, temporary theatres built in tents supported on wooden structures. This nomadic type of construction was part of the urban landscape of Montevideo for several decades, and often housed theatre performances. The Circo Criollo (Criollo Circus) was home to the production of many plays by national authors who later became famous. Some of the productions presented at the Solís were first produced at such neighbourhood circuses.

In the 1930s, the government assumed an important role in the purchase and sale of the country's theatre spaces. In 1937 La Comuna (the city council) purchased the Teatro Solís. Nine years later, it bought the Sala Verdi and in 1962 the Teatro Apolo, later known as the Florencio Sánchez. In the 1970s the Ministry of Culture declared Teatro Victoria an historical monument and part of the national heritage; this was part of a strategy to prevent the disappearance of these important buildings.

In the 1960s, many independent groups tried to make their dreams of having their own space come true by renovating buildings that existed for other purposes. This was the case at Teatro Circular, El Tinglado and Teatro del Centro.

Others attempted to build their own theatres, such as El Galpón, which began its construction in 1949. In a very small space, the group built a theatre that had a very down-to-earth image and personality. Built with metal plates, it differentiated the theatre from other urban constructions, although the theatre was of a more modest nature than other buildings, since it represented a storehouse, symbol of the suburban and rural areas of the country. This building survived for more than twenty years until it was demolished in the 1970s.

Prior to its closure, the group had managed to build a second space, purchasing a movie theatre known as the Grand Palace, on Montevideo's main street. A renovation was led by architects Mariano Arana (b. 1933) and Mario Spallanzani (b. 1938), who in their designs combined the needs of a traditional theatre with those of an experimental one. The space was designed with a uniform orchestra pit, situated where the seats of the old cinema had been. The stage was originally conceived as asymmetrical, with one of its sides expanding into the pit, bringing it closer to the audience.

In 1975 the Teatro del Notariado was created in the basement of a shopping mall, a symbol, as with El Galpón, of democratic theatre.

Most theatre spaces in Uruguay are owned by private organizations such as the Alianza Francesa (Alliance Française), the Sociedad Uruguaya de Actores and the Notaries' Guild.

There are two other kinds of spaces for theatre in Uruguay – summer theatres and theatre in public spaces such as squares or parks. Almost all cities have summer theatres, and often these spaces are associated with parks, thus forming part of the landscape. The summer theatres are an important part of the cultural life in many cities. For example, in Montevideo the Teatro de Verano Ramón Collazo (Ramón Collazo Summer Theatre) is an active centre for popular art. The Collazo is built in a natural valley, thus being incorporated into the landscape.

Some other performances are also created outdoors at fairs and exhibits, on streets, squares and parks and give rise to the notion of a 'theatre without architecture'.

William Rey Ashfield

Rúben Yáñez's 1994 Comedia Nacional production of Justino Zavala Muniz's *Crónica de un crimen*, adapted by Walter González.

Training

A number of important theatre schools have developed during the twentieth century in Uruguay. The oldest of them is the Escuela del Arte Dramático founded in Montevideo in 1913 by the Italian actress Giacinta Pezzana. This school was the main training centre in the country until the creation of the SODRE school in 1941. A third school was founded in 1949 by the actress Margarita Xirgú, the Escuela Municipal de Arte Dramático.

It was the graduates of Xirgú's school who eventually came together to form the Comedia Nacional and the school still supplies the company with most of its members. In addition to breaking down the old declamatory style of acting and transforming training to the newer Stanislavski system, the school has also provided its graduates with an ethical base for their work.

El Galpón began a school for its company in 1952. Also influenced by the Stanislavski system, it has nevertheless provided training in a range of styles generally built around the needs of realizing various styles of writing. Galpón grants a certificate to its graduates, mostly actors and some puppeteers. The school takes in new students based on the needs of the company rather than on traditional academic years.

Another company working in a similar way on training is the Teatro Circular. Other schools have also appeared in the 1980s and 1990s including the school of Luis Cerminara, which has tended to explore the ideas of Antonin Artaud, and Alambique, a school founded by Mario Aguerre (b. 1944), which is based on the training of the French mime Jacques LeCoq.

Criticism, Scholarship and Publishing

Angel Rama (1926–83) was an essayist, critic, narrator and playwright who wrote several studies on the evolution of Uruguayan and Latin American literature. Walter Rela (b. 1922) is another researcher on the history of the theatre in Uruguay and in other Latin American countries. His investigations are obligatory reading for all specialists in this area.

There is a small theatre museum in the Teatro Solís and also in the Asociación General de Autores de Uruguay (Authors' Association of Uruguay) as well as some small theatre bookstores. The Sociedad Uruguaya de Actores (Uruguayan Actors' Association) has a theatre library of some 1,300 volumes. El Galpón has its own library of about 1,700 volumes, while at the Teatro Solís there is the Florencio Sánchez Municipal Library with some 3,500 volumes. The library has published forty titles since 1948.

The Uruguayan Centre of the International Theatre Institute, with the support of UNESCO, began in the early 1990s a Latin American theatre databank.

Article coordinated by César Campodónico
Further Reading *section by Roger Mirza*
Translated by Joanne Rotermundt-De la Parra,
Mayte Gómez and Erminio Neglia

Further Reading

Ayestarán, Lauro. *El centenario del Teatro Solís.* [Centenary of the Solís Theatre]. Montevideo: Comisión de Teatros Municipales, 1956.

Castillo, Andrés, and A. Queirolo de la Sovera. *Il teatro indipendente.* [Independent theatre]. Italy: Centro Di Azione Latina, 1964.

Dibarboure, José Alberto. *Proceso del teatro uruguayo.* [The evolution of Uruguayan theatre]. Montevideo: Editorial Claudio García, 1940.

Diverzo, G., and E. Filgueiras. *Montevideo en Carnaval.* [Montevideo in carnival]. Montevideo: Editorial Monte Sexto, 1990.

El Galpón: un teatro independiente uruguayo y su función en el exilio. [El Galpón: An independent Uruguayan theatre and its role in exile]. México City: Cuadernos de Difusión Cultural de la Institución Teatral El Galpón, 1983. 55 pp.

Landó, Cristina. *Cuarenta años: Comedia Nacional.* [Forty years: Comedia Nacional]. Montevideo: Departamento de Cultura de la Intendencia Municipal de Montevideo, 1987. 28 pp.

Legido, Juan Carlos. *El teatro uruguayo.* [Uruguayan theatre]. Montevideo: Ediciones Tauro, 1968. 160 pp.

Literatura uruguaya del medio siglo. [Uruguayan literature of the mid-century]. Montevideo: Alfa, 1966.

Mibelli, Américo, and Wilson Armas. *Las dependencias del teatro independiente, 1937–52.* [Dependencies of the independent theatre, 1937–52]. La Paz/Canelones: Talleres Gráficos Vanguardia, 1960.

Mirza, Roger, ed. *Teatro uruguayo contemporáneo: antología.* [Contemporary Uruguayan theatre: An anthology]. Madrid: Ministerio de Cultura/Fondo de Cultura Económica, 1992. 1,112 pp.

Montero Zorrilla, Pablo. *Montevideo y sus teatros.* [Montevideo and its theatres]. Montevideo: Monte Sexto, 1988.

Ostuni, Omar. *Por los teatros del interior.* [Around the provincial theatres]. Montevideo: Asociación de Teatros del Interior, 1993.

Pignataro, Jorge. *Directores teatrales uruguayos. 50 retratos.* [Uruguayan theatre directors: Fifty portraits]. Montevideo: Proyección, 1994.

——. *El teatro independiente uruguayo.* [Uruguayan independent theatre]. Montevideo: Editorial Arca, 1968. 134 pp.

Rela, Walter. *Historia del teatro uruguayo, 1808–1979.* [History of Uruguayan theatre, 1808–1979]. Montevideo: Editorial Alianza Cultural Uruguay-EEUU, 1980.

——. *Repertorio bibliográfico del teatro uruguayo.* [A bibliography of Uruguayan theatre]. Montevideo: Editorial Síntesis, 1965.

——. *El teatro uruguayo.* [Uruguayan theatre]. Montevideo: Ediciones de la Alianza, 1980.

Scoseria, Cyro. *Un panorama del teatro uruguayo.* [Overview of theatre in Uruguay]. Montevideo: Publicaciones AGADU, 1963.

Silva Valdés, Fernán, ed. *Teatro uruguayo.* [Uruguayan theatre]. Madrid: Aguilar, 1966.

Vanrell Delgado, Juan María. *La historia de la Comedia Nacional.* [History of the Comedia Nacional]. Montevideo: Intendencia Municipal de Montevideo, 1987. 249 pp.

VENEZUELA

One of the northernmost countries in South America, Venezuela is a land of physical diversity, with the Andes Mountains in the west, tropical forests in the east and south, and vast lowlands (*llanos*) in the centre. Covering 912,100 square kilometres (352,100 square miles), it is bordered by Colombia, Brazil and Guyana. Venezuela's 1992 population was 18.9 million.

In the mid-1990s, oil still accounted for more than 90 per cent of the country's exports. In 1976, the government had nationalized the oil industry and had begun to develop the Orinoco tar belt, believed to contain one of the world's largest oil reserves.

Christopher Columbus landed in Venezuela on his third voyage to the western hemisphere in 1498. A year later, another Spanish expedition reached Lake Maracaibo and found an Indian village with huts built on stilts over the lake. Because it reminded them of Venice, they named the place Venezuela (Little Venice). The first Spanish settlement was established soon after on Cubagua Island.

The Royal Guipuzcoana Company, founded in 1728, brought Venezuela trade with other parts of the world and the colony was extended to its present borders in 1777. The late eighteenth and early nineteenth centuries were marked by struggles in which Venezuelans tried to win their independence from Spain. The first attempt, in 1797, failed. So did the efforts of Francisco de Miranda (1750–1816) in 1811 and 1812. Miranda's efforts were taken up by his disciple Simón Bolívar (1783–1830), who was born in the country's largest city, Caracas, and sought to unite Venezuela, Colombia and Ecuador into a single nation called Gran Colombia. Bolívar achieved victory in 1821; in 1830, the federation collapsed, however, and Venezuela became an independent state.

Between 1830 and 1900, there were a number of rebellions, some violent, with the central government overthrown thirteen times. In 1908, Juan Vicente Gómez (1859–1935), known as the 'tyrant of the Andes', took over. Gómez favoured family and friends and kept his opponents in jail or exile. His rule lasted until his death.

In 1945, the Democratic Action Party, led by Rómulo Betancourt (1908–81) and the novelist Rómulo Gallegos (1884–1969), ousted the successors of Gómez. Betancourt was selected to serve as president. In 1947, Gallegos, who had immortalized the inhabitants and the folklore of the main regions of Venezuela in his novels *Doña Bárbara* (1929), *Cantaclaro* (1934) and *Canaima* (1935), won the first direct popular vote in the country's history, but he remained in office for only nine months. A military *coup d'état* brought about a period of dictatorship under Marcos Pérez Jiménez (b. 1914) that lasted ten years until it was overthrown by the 'Patriotic Junta'. Betancourt was elected president in 1958, beginning a long period of democratic rule.

During the Gómez dictatorship as well as in the decade leading up to 1945, it was difficult to present political or social issues in any of the arts. The prevailing style was a very visual one, the *costumbrista*, a nineteenth-century Spanish style with an emphasis on local colour and folk customs. Utilized as well were Spanish staging techniques from the previous century including *morcillas* (improvised dialogue), painted flats and prompters. Because of this emphasis on colour and customs, the theatre was extremely provincial and of little social relevance.

Despite this, there was a group of authors who did have wider concerns and expectations and who focused on national issues, although still within the accepted approaches. Among them were Rafael Guinand (1881–1957) and Leoncio (Leo) Martínez (1888–1941), whose work was of paramount importance in modernizing the theatre of the time.

The first companies both to create a more modern directorial style and to present national authors were the Compañía Venezolana de Dramas y Comedias (Venezuelan Drama and Comedy Company) and the Sociedad de Amigos del Teatro (Friends of the Theatre Society). Among the writers whose work they produced were Guillermo Meneses (1911–78), Andrés Eloy Blanco (1899–1955), Víctor Manuel Rivas (1909–65), Aquiles Certad (b. 1914) and Angel Fuenmayor, all precursors of modern Venezuelan playwriting.

It was César Rengifo (1915–80) who wrote the play that is considered the point of transition between the *costumbrista* style and the modern period in Venezuelan theatre. The play *Por qué canta el pueblo?* (*Why Are the People Singing?*, 1938) was neither published nor produced in its time but has long been considered a key part of Venezuelan literature. To all intents and purposes, Rengifo is the father of modern Venezuelan theatre and is the country's most widely translated and produced author as well as one of the most widely anthologized Venezuelan playwrights in the Americas and Europe.

For purposes of understanding, the years since 1945 can basically be divided into three periods. The first, from 1945 to 1960, was one in which new ideas and styles were attempted. The second, from 1960 to 1973, was one of experimentation and the search for new theatrical methods. The last, beginning in 1973, is when the Venezuelan theatre achieved maturity and began to be recognized internationally.

To look in detail at these periods is to understand the extreme importance of the late 1940s in Venezuelan theatre. In 1945, Alberto de Paz y Mateos (d. 1967), a young Spanish producer-director, arrived in the country as a refugee from the Franco regime. Paz y Mateos tended to emphasize the visual in his productions, focusing his experiments on costume and lighting. He also brought the works of classic writers such as García Lorca to the Venezuelan public. Two years later, the Venezuelan government invited Jesús Gómez Obregón, a Mexican actor and director, to visit the country. Gómez Obregón opened the country's first centre for actor training in 1947 – the Taller de Capacitación Teatral (Workshop for Theatrical Training) – based on the Stanislavski system.

The Argentine actress and teacher Juana Sujo (d. 1961) and Chilean director Horacio Peterson arrived in 1949. Sujo emphasized the importance of the actor in theatrical production as well as the professional responsibilities of the theatre artist. In 1952, Sujo founded the Escuela Nacional de Arte Escénico (National School of Dramatic Art), which offered serious training to young artists in theatre, film and television. Also in the early 1950s, the Argentine actor Francisco Petrone began to tour the country. A populist, he worked in many styles of theatre making them all available to a large general public.

These five, each with a particular style and area of expertise, were jointly responsible for the modern renewal of theatre in Venezuela.

For the most part, Venezuelan theatre activity (including ballet and opera) has traditionally taken place in Caracas. In 1945 it was, in fact, centred in only two locations in Caracas, one owned by the municipal government and the other by the federal government. In the rest of the country, major performances were seen only occasionally, most often in Maracaibo, Valencia and Barquisimeto. Audiences, early on, were generally drawn from the upper classes, for whom theatre was mainly a social event. Most significant productions before 1945 were from outside Venezuela and not easily affordable for the general public.

Direct government subsidy for the arts began in 1958 with the creation of the Instituto Nacional de Cultura y Bellas Artes (National Institute of Culture and Fine Arts), which in 1975 changed its name to Consejo Nacional de Cultura (CONAC; National Cultural Council). This organization established a structure for subsidies in the arts and set up a series of drama, puppet and children's theatre festivals at both the regional and national levels. Decentralization of cultural resources became a hallmark of the new government policy.

At the same time, theatre began to be recognized as a contributing social form, with universities and other educational bodies incorporating theatre studies into their curriculums and public festivals further widening the audience base.

In 1984, the government itself created the Compañía Nacional de Teatro (National Theatre Company) under the direction of the playwright Isaac Chocrón (b. 1933). Its members were hired for year-round seasons and it received 75 per cent of its budget directly from the government. The company performs at the Teatro Nacional (National Theatre) in Caracas.

Structure of the National Theatre Community

Government support of the arts in Venezuela is fairly evenly spread across the twenty states and two federal dependencies that comprise the country. In Caracas alone, there are more than twenty theatres.

At some of Venezuela's theatres, such as the Teresa Carreño Cultural Centre in Caracas, high prices and society audiences are still the norm. Most, however, are committed to attracting a wide range of audiences.

Among the most influential of the modern cultural agencies has been the Ateneo de Caracas, founded in 1931 to promote Venezuelan culture. Well funded, the Ateneo has supported a wide range of theatre companies, helped to build a major theatre in Caracas and in 1971 helped to create one of Venezuela's most important companies, Rajatabla. The Ateneo was also behind the Caracas International Theatre Festival – the largest in Latin America – and the establishment in 1975 of Latin America's most important regional theatre research centre, the Centro Latinoamericano de Creación y Investigación Teatral (CELCIT; Centre for Theatrical Creation and Research), located in Caracas. The Ateneo has funded theatre training through the years and has even acted as a cultural publishing house.

Despite such support, few people are able to make a living simply from theatre and most do additional work in film, television or teaching. Nevertheless, theatre artists are widely respected and admired. The Premio Nacional de Teatro (National Theatre Award) is given annually for career achievement in the theatre.

There are two organizations in Venezuela dealing with theatre for social action – the Asociación Venezolana de Teatro Popular (Venezuelan Association of Popular Theatre) and the Teatro para Obreros (Workers' Theatre). Both have member groups across the country.

Critics for the daily press have their own professional organization – the Círculo de Críticos de Teatro de Venezuela (Venezuelan Theatre Critics' Circle), which has as one of its goals the training and education of its members. Known as CRITVEN, it also organizes regional and national conferences and presents a series of annual awards.

As in many countries, television has had an enormous impact on live theatre in Venezuela. In 1952, when television became available, theatre life was just beginning to become significant in the country. Many young actors began their careers in television, while others, already established in theatre, moved to the new medium. As a result, even in the 1990s, the life and continuity of theatre production is more or less dependent on fluctuations in television activity. Most actors do not want to be tied to lengthy theatre seasons if they have the possibility of working for shorter and better paid periods on television, especially in *telenovelas* (soap operas). Thus long theatre runs are all but non-existent in Venezuela.

Artistic Profile

Companies

Historically, theatre companies in Venezuela were created for specific productions and then disbanded. The decision of the Ateneo de Caracas to create a permanent company – Rajatabla – in 1971 influenced the creation of other permanent groups although the tradition goes back as far as 1951, when Máscaras (Masks) was founded. Other important permanent groups have been Yare and Proa.

Rajatabla, under the direction of the Argentine-born Carlos Giménez (1945–93),

now has its own theatre school, the Taller Nacional de Teatro (National Theatre Workshop), founded in 1985. The company began its work with a particular focus on theatre for young people and an emphasis on music. By the 1980s, it had shifted more towards experimentation, using both classic and modern texts by Venezuelan writers from the past and present. Under Giménez its shows tended to be visually spectacular, trying to incorporate the public into the theatrical event. As such, the text was often an excuse for spectacle.

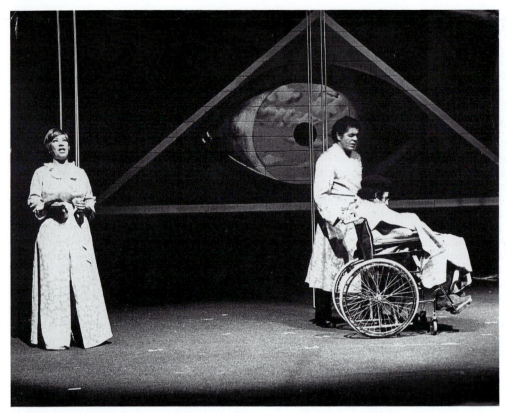

El Nuevo Grupo's production of *Los 7 pecados capitales* (*The 7 Deadly Sins*).
Photo: Miguel Gracia, courtesy *Conjunto*.

The group's ideological interest has been in the political structure of Latin American countries, their problems of dependency, submission, rebellion and despotism. Its stylistic basis is dazzling spectacle, the plastic elements of theatre, lights, colours, striking visual images, exaggerated gestures and sonorous enunciation by the actors. It appeals to the senses of the public, which does not have to be Spanish speaking to understand the basic message of the plays.

Among Rajatabla's major productions have been *Señor Presidente* (*Mr President*, 1977), *El candidato* (*The Candidate*, 1978), *La muerte de García Lorca* (*The Death of García Lorca*, 1979) and *Bolívar* (1982, 1988). Based in Caracas, Rajatabla performs regularly across the country and has toured abroad on many occasions.

Another company of particular importance is El Nuevo Grupo (The New Group). Established in 1967 by Isaac Chocrón and two other playwrights – Román Chalbaud (b. 1931) and

José Ignacio Cabrujas (b. 1937) – El Nuevo Grupo, by the beginning of the 1990s, had two spaces of its own and was producing seasons of plays by classic and modern authors in both traditional and experimental styles. Eventually emphasizing plays by Venezuelan authors, the company has produced more than a dozen plays by the three founding playwrights and has also established its own national playwriting award and published several scholarly works on Venezuelan theatre as well as a journal that has appeared occasionally through the years.

The Grupo Actoral 80 (Acting Group 80) was formed in 1980 following a workshop offered by the Argentine actor, director, playwright and teacher Juan Carlos Gené (b. 1928) under the auspices of CELCIT. Still a part of CELCIT, Grupo Actoral 80 has its own small theatre space and focuses its energies on the work of the actor in its productions of plays by both Latin American and Spanish writers. The group has long been committed to the idea of Latin American cultural and political integration.

Ricardo Lombardi's 1988 Grupo Actoral 80/CELCIT production of Roberto Cossa's *Yepeto*.
Photo: Samuel Dembo, courtesy *Conjunto*.

Two other significant experimental groups are Theja (founded in 1974) and Autoteatro (1985). Many of Autoteatro's members have joined Theja through the years and at the beginning of the 1990s Theja was still the dominant group in the experimental field. Both companies work freely with text, movement and space, play with images and often bring controversial issues to the stage. Theja also does work with children. Its first production was *Fulgor y muerte de Joaquín Murieta* (*Splendour and Death of Joaquín Murieta*) by the Chilean Pablo Neruda. Like many of the other groups, it has its own theatre school.

Another Caracas group of note is the Centro Prisma, again with its own theatre school. The group produces mostly avant-garde style plays.

The Compañía Nacional de Teatro has presented a series of diverse seasons since its founding under the direction of Isaac Chocrón in 1984. Productions have ranged from classics (Ruiz de Alarcón, Shakespeare and Goldoni), to modern writers such as Arthur Miller, to national playwrights such as Chocrón, Rengifo, Chalbaud and Cabrujas. The Compañía Nacional has also developed a steady and faithful audience by presenting its low-priced productions at unconventional times – mainly early evenings and weekend afternoons.

In 1985 a Programe de Formación Teatral (Programme of Theatrical Training) was established. It offers scholarships for study in different areas of theatre. The Compañía Nacional de Teatro received financial assistance from CONAC and from the Federal District Foundation for Culture and Arts (FUNDARTE). Its performances are generally sponsored by private companies and public institutions.

Another company with a significant following is the Grupo Compás, which works as a kind of binational institution, mounting realistic plays from France.

As the 1990s began, there were five commercial companies in Caracas presenting, for the most part, light comedies. Some of them regularly tour to other cities in the country.

Outside of Caracas, most theatre activity is either semi-professional or amateur; there are more than 100 such groups in existence. Maracaibo, the second largest city in the country, has its Sociedad Dramática (Drama Society), which is supported by the state and has its own space. In Ciudad Guayana, the company La Barraca (The Shed) produces regular seasons; in Maracay, the major company is La Misere; and in Valencia, Arlequín.

The oldest amateur company in the country is the Teatro Universitario at the Universidad Central de Venezuela (Central University of Venezuela), founded in 1946. Other universities also have their own companies.

Most of the groups mentioned, both professional and amateur, are supported by the state and also receive private funding. The commercial groups, however, depend solely on private funds. The importance of all these groups lies in their continuity and their particular working styles. All have annual seasons and reasonably faithful audiences. For the most part, each also has its own space.

Dramaturgy

The most widely produced playwright in Venezuela is, without doubt, César Rengifo, who has nearly fifty plays to his credit. Rengifo's plays, which present new interpretations of the country's past and a hopeful vision of the future, are popular not only with professional companies but also with university and amateur groups. His play *Lo que dejó la tempestad* (*What the Tempest Left Behind*, 1957) was, in fact, the first hit of the first season of the Compañía Nacional.

Prior to that, a number of writers who had shown promise as dramatists seemed to be turning away from the theatre. Among them were Ida Gramko (b. 1924), author of the plays *María Lionza* (1943), *Belén Silvera* (1943) and *La Rubiera* (1956); Elizabeth Schon (b. 1921), author of *Melissa y yo* (*Melissa and I*, 1960) and *La aldea* (*The Village*, 1959); and Arturo Uslar Pietri (b. 1906), a novelist and essayist as well as the author of such plays as *Chuo Gil* (1959) and *El día de Antero Albán* (*Antero Albán's Day*, 1944).

Some writers, however, continued to work in the theatre throughout their careers; for example Isaac Chocrón, whose plays border on the absurd but remain rooted nevertheless in a realistic world. His plays often deal with loneliness, the doubts and frustrations of the individual in society, and the non-biological family. Chocrón's most profound plays are *Mónica y el Florentino* (*Monica and the Florentine*, 1955), *Simón* (1985) and *Clipper* (1987).

Román Chalbaud, both a theatre artist and a film-maker, deals in his work with social

marginality, particularly as it has been created since the 1940s in major cities such as Caracas. *Los ángeles terribles* (*The Terrible Angels*, 1967), *Caín adolescente* (*Adolescent Cain*, 1955) and *La quema de Judas* (*Judas Burning*, 1964) are among his most widely regarded plays. Halfway between realism and expressionism, his dramas play with the language, philosophy and poetry of daily life and create an irrational, half-real, cruel and hostile environment. Chalbaud's work in theatre was particularly important between the 1950s and 1970s, after which he left the theatre almost entirely for cinema.

José Ignacio Cabrujas tends to cross between dramatic comedies and *costumbrista*-style sketches in his work, which effectively reflects the idiosyncrasies of contemporary Venezuelan life. The plays *Profundo* (*Deep*, 1971), *Acto cultural* (*Cultural Act*, 1976) and *El día que me quieras* (*The Day You Will Love Me*, 1979) are typical of Cabrujas's work. Early in his career, he dealt with historical themes in a Brechtian style in plays such as *Juan Francisco de León* (1959), *En nombre del Rey* (*In the Name of the King*, 1963) and *El extraño viaje de Simón el malo* (*The Strange Journey of Simon the Bad*, 1961). In time, his works became a social reflection of the thoughts and actions of the people of contemporary Venezuela.

Rodolfo Santana (b. 1944), one of the most prolific authors in the country, looks at the reality of Venezuela through a variety of genres including farce, traditional comedy and dramatic modes and through styles ranging from expressionism, to the absurd and realism. In his more than sixty plays, he has attacked many of the contradictions inherent in contemporary society both in the middle classes and in marginal social groups. He uses classical and historical mythology (Oedipus, Joan of Arc) and figures from Venezuelan folklore such as the Coromoto Virgin and José Gregorio Hernández, a well-known religious figure. He presents his characters in contemporary situations, thus contrasting past and present to analyse the modern world. *Historias de cerro arriba* (*Stories from the Mountain*, 1977), *Fin de round* (*End of Round*) and *Gracias por los favores recibidos* (*Thanks for the Favours*, 1977) are among his best known works.

José Gabriel Nuñez (b. 1937) uses realism and surrealism with great doses of both humour and sarcasm. His works attack social conventions and prejudices. *Quedó igualito* (*It Remains the Same*, 1975), *Tú quieres que me come el tigre*

(*You Want the Tiger to Eat Me Up*, 1970), *Madame Pompinette* (1980) and *Los peces del acuario* (*The Fish From the Aquarium*, 1966) are typical of his vision and his generally confrontational attitude. He is also one of the few national writers who has created strong female protagonists in his works.

Edilio Peña (b. 1951), a novelist, playwright and all-round man of the theatre, is a writer whose work stands halfway between the absurd and Artaud's Theatre of Cruelty. His works are rooted in contemporary human relationships and often deal with repression, torture and superstition. His most representative plays are *Resistencia* (*Resistance*, 1975), *El círculo* (*The Circle*, 1975) and *Los hermanos* (*The Brothers*).

Other significant contemporary writers are Alejandro Lasser (b. 1916), Elisa Lerner (b. 1932), Gilberto Pinto (b. 1930), Ricardo Acosta (b. 1934), Paul Williams (b. 1942), Andrés Martínez, Mariela Romero, José Antonio Rial Gonzáles (b. 1911) and Néstor Caballero (b. 1953). All reflect both the past and present of Venezuelan society in their work and the vast social, economic and political changes taking place in the country.

Directors, Directing and Production Styles

Prior to 1945, directing in Venezuela was primarily the responsibility of each production's leading actors. Between 1945 and 1960, however, the role of the director *per se* began to develop. In the 1940s, it was people such as Alberto Paz y Mateos, Jesús Gómez Obregón, Juana Sujo and Horacio Peterson who led the way; in the 1950s, the leaders were two Argentine expatriates – Carlos Gorostiza (b. 1920) and Juan Carlos Gené.

During the 1950s many playwrights turned to directing their own works. Nicolás Curiel, for example, staged many of his plays at the Teatro Universitario at the Central University and his emphasis on the visual and the experimental influenced the later directorial styles of Herman Lejter, Eduardo Gil, Alberto Sánchez and Eduardo Mancera.

In 1960, Gil staged an immensely successful production of Peter Weiss's *Song of the Lusitanian Bogey* and was later influenced by the work with actors of the Polish director Jerzy Grotowski. Still later, he began to work

with the Taller de Experimentación Teatral (Experimental Theatre Workshop) in Caracas.

As the director became a more powerful figure in Venezuelan theatre, a number of formal experiments began. In the late 1960s, text became secondary to movement, light and colour and the name of Edward Gordon Craig began to be heard in the more avant-garde theatres. There were also sporadic attempts at this time to create a Venezuelan musical theatre. These, however, did not bear fruit. Through the 1980s and into the 1990s, Venezuelan directors returned to an emphasis on text while managing to retain their interest in experimental styles.

Perhaps the best known director in Venezuela during the 1970s and 1980s was Carlos Giménez. Founder and director of the group Rajatabla, his work was spectacular in style and the company's productions were seen at festivals in Caracas, across the Americas and in Europe. Among Giménez's major productions were *Señor Presidente*, a theatrical version of the novel by Miguel Angel Asturias; *La muerte de García Lorca* and *Bolívar* by José Antonio Rial Gonzáles; and *Historia de un caballo* (*Story of a Horse*), based on the novel by Leo Tolstoi.

Another director working in a 'spectacular' style is the Italian-born Antonio Constante. Combining an interest in both staging and text, Constante's work, with its heavy emphasis on music, clearly shows the influence of his opera background. His most important productions include *Ardiente paciencia* (*Burning Patience*, 1983), by the Chilean Antonio Skarmeta, and *Una viuda para cuatro* (*One Widow for Four*, 1987), based on Carlo Goldoni's *La vedova scaltra* (*The Cunning Widow*).

A small number of directors are both actor- and text-oriented. In this category are Uruguayan-born Ugo Ulive, Juan Carlos Gené, Armendo Gota and Luis Márquez Páez. Ulive is equally at home in a variety of styles. Seeing theatre as a total art and placing special emphasis on the surroundings of the central action, Ulive has staged successful productions of Jean Genet's *The Balcony*, Argentine playwright Osvaldo Dragún's *Historias para ser contadas* (*Stories to Be Told*), Eugene O'Neill's *Long Day's Journey Into Night*, *Beckett hoy* (*Beckett Today*), based on several Beckett plays, and Heiner Müller's *Hamletmachine* (1969).

Elia Schneider is one of the few female directors in the Venezuelan theatre. Her work tends towards experimentation in its use of space and actors and has been consistently

Theatre for Young Audiences
Puppet Theatre

Despite the fact that the majority of Venezuela's population is under 30 years of age, theatre for young audiences has not been significantly developed in the country and has had little impact on professional theatre activities. Two notable exceptions have been commercial productions of the musicals *Jesus Christ Superstar* and *Godspell*.

What professional children's theatre there is, is centred in Caracas. Notable are the groups Ocho Tablas (Eight Tables) at the Central University, later renamed El Chichón (The Bump); Los Carricitos; and Taller de Arte Infantil y Juvenil (Studio for Child and Youth Art).

As with other aspects of Venezuelan theatre, influences and individuals from abroad were instrumental in bringing puppet theatre into the country's theatrical life. It was in 1939 that the Italian puppet troupe Piccolo de Podrecca first visited Venezuela. Lola Cueto and the Mexican Roberto Lago in 1947 gave a series of workshops at the invitation of Federico Reyna and Pérez De Vega, who had the previous year founded their own puppet troupe, El Tamborón, the country's first modern puppet company. Through the years, El Tamborón organized workshops and classes and their efforts were instrumental in developing puppetry as a viable theatrical form in Venezuela.

El Tamborón rooted its work in the popular but somewhat idiosyncratic national puppetry tradition, the *títere de guante* (glove-puppet). Reyna's creations – 'Juan Bimba', 'Juan Barrigón' and 'Cantalicio' – achieved immense popularity. Reyna subsequently took his puppets to France where, according to Enrique and Hugo Cerda's 1965 Ministry of Education-sponsored study, *Teatro de Guiñol* (*Puppet Theatre*), he became 'a master of the art'. He returned home to create and direct the Escuela de Marionetas (School of Puppetry) in 1950. The school, however, closed after just two years of operation.

During the 1950s, a number of hand-puppet companies came into being, most of them involved in education. The primary force behind this movement was a Bolivian-born poet and novelist, Luis Luksic.

Both the Ministry of Education and the Venezuelan Council for Child Welfare actively supported the creation and development of puppet theatre groups, and of workshops and conferences on the subject. The Ministry of Labour through its Cultural Division, and various universities through their art programmes, also helped to expand the general interest in puppetry. The Ministry of Labour was particularly involved with founding the groups El Guácharo (The Nightingale) and Juan Camejo.

Other key figures in the field have been José León, who started his career as a hand-puppeteer in the 1950s and whose influence was especially strong between 1960 and 1980; and Eduardo Calcaño, a director and teacher as well as a prolific author of puppet plays.

During the 1970s, many of the existing puppet groups in the country began organizing local, regional and national events and, in fact, created a national puppet organization. Leading the way at this time were two universities – Universidad Central de Venezuela, with its puppet group Cantalicio, and the Universidad de Oriente, through the work of the artist Hugo Arneodo.

Only one professional theatre group, Tilingo, (Fool) founded by Clara Rosa Otero Silva, has been heavily involved in the production of puppet plays. Often involving both puppets and actors and producing both classical and original pieces, the company organized an International Puppet Play Competition in 1981 that attracted more than 100 productions from all across Latin America.

In schools, children often take courses on how to make puppets and how to put on their own shows. Puppet plays are performed regularly on weekends in Caracas and other cities. Eduardo Di Mauro, an Argentine-born puppeteer, has established permanent puppet theatres in such cities as Barinas and Guabare with the cooperation of municipal governments. He has also toured the country with his groups and has been involved in exchanges with foreign companies. This is the first time in Venezuela's cultural history that a particular artistic activity has been more profoundly developed outside the capital than in it.

Design

The work of Alberto de Paz y Mateos opened the way for other directors working in Venezuela to include design as an integral element in their productions and for other designers to think about directing. As part of this development, a number of visual artists became involved in theatre, among them Carlos Cruz Diez, also known as a film-maker. Even composers became involved, with Cuban-born Alejo Carpentier (b. 1904) among the earliest.

Carlos Salas and Guillermo Zabaleta were other early designers but the evolving tradition led to many people working simultaneously as both directors and designers, for example Herman Lejter and Eduardo Mancera.

Stage designer José Luis Gómez Fra and costume designer Elías Martinello were leaders in the field through the 1970s and 1980s and both have worked in a variety of styles. Gómez Fra's major designs include Genet's *The Balcony*, Kroetz's *Solitary Heart* and Müller's *Hamletmachine*.

Continuing the tradition of both directing and designing was Carlos Giménez with the Rajatabla company. The most successful of his avant-garde works from a visual standpoint were *Señor Presidente*, *La muerte de García Lorca* and Andrés Eloy Blanco's *Abigail*. In each, the design created a central metaphor against which the play was juxtaposed.

Theatre Space and Architecture

From the nineteenth century and through the beginning of the twentieth, Venezuelan theatres were generally built in the Italian style in order best to fit operatic spectacle, the form that dominated theatrical production in both Caracas and the rest of the country. Among the best known of these buildings were the Teatro Municipal and the Teatro Nacional in Caracas, the municipal theatres in Valencia and Puerto Cabello, Teatro Juáres in Barquisimeto, Teatro Baralt in Maracaibo, Teatro Cajigal in Barcelona, and the Ateneo in Maracay.

When Caracas' University City was built for the Universidad Central in the 1950s, Carlos Raúl Villanueva – considered the master of modern Venezuelan architecture – was chosen to design the 3,500-seat Aula Magna (Great Hall) with a thrust stage, and the 450-seat Concert Hall. Both these facilities have nearly perfect sightlines and acoustics and both have been regularly used for theatre, music and ballet as well as the traditional academic activities of the university.

Tomás Lugo was the architect responsible for the design of the Teresa Carreño Cultural Centre in central Caracas. Surrounded by a magnificent park, the Cultural Centre was a 1983 bicentennial project celebrating the birth of Simón Bolívar. It boasts two performance spaces – the 450-seat José Felix Ribas and the 2,500-seat Ríos Reyna. The Ribas was designed as a concert hall but has been pressed into service as a theatre space during national and international festivals. The Reyna, an adjustable thrust stage (at its largest it is 30 metres wide and 40 metres deep), has been used for many types of productions.

During the 1970s and 1980s, a number of new theatre spaces were built ranging in size from 250 to 400 seats. Among the most useful of these was an auditorium in the headquarters of the Ateneo de Caracas; the Teatro Cadafe, a space owned by the national electricity company that was redesigned and modernized by Héctor Del Campo, a Chilean designer resident in Venezuela; the Teatro Rafael Guinand, owned by the national telephone company; and the Teatro de Las Palmas. The stages of these theatres range from 10 to 15 metres both in width and depth. Another ten or so flexible spaces with smaller capacities – but which are important in design terms – now also exist in the capital.

Outside of Caracas, a number of old and/or abandoned spaces – many of them former movie houses – have been renovated and are now regularly used by theatre groups. At the beginning of the 1990s, there were in total twenty operable theatres in the capital and another twenty or so in the rest of the country.

Training

From the 1940s on, the development of effective theatre training programmes was a key part of the work of those artists trying to bring about change in the Venezuelan theatre. Especially important in this regard was the work of Paz y Mateos with the Fermín Toro School; Gómez Obregón, with his Studio and later his Taller de Capacitación Teatral (Workshop for Theatrical Training); Juana Sujo with her Estudio Dramático (Drama Studio), founded in 1940 and subsequently called the Escuela Superior de Arte Escénico (Higher School of Theatre Art) and later the Escuela Juana Sujo (Juana Sujo School), and Horacio Peterson, who led the theatre school of the Ateneo de Caracas between the 1950s and the 1970s, and who was later the director of the Laboratorio Teatral Ana Julia Rojas (Rojas Theatre Laboratory).

In 1975, an irregularly working National Theatre School existed. Thanks to government support, a more regularly functioning school was created under the name Instituto de Formacion para el Arte Dramático (Training Institute for the Dramatic Arts). Six years later, the Escuela Superior de Artes Escénicas César Rengifo (César Rengifo Higher School of Theatre Arts), considered the most comprehensive of all the schools, was established. Most schools have two-year programmes based on four hours of classes per day. The Rengifo school has a four-year programme based on eight hours of classes per day. Also, while other schools train only actors, the Rengifo also trains set, costume and lighting designers as well as cultural animators – people who will develop amateur theatre programmes in factories, rural areas, prisons, hospitals and unions. The Rengifo is also the only theatre school in the country that gives an official diploma and whose curriculum is recognized and supported by the Ministry of Education.

In total, there are usually about 1,000 students studying theatre in one form or another across the country, either in one of the aforementioned schools or in one of the twenty or so private theatre schools and studios that exist both in and outside of Caracas.

Most theatre schools base their actors' training on the Stanislavski system although that system is interpreted in many ways. Some of the private schools – as well as groups such as the Laboratorio Teatral Ana Julia Rojas, the Taller de Experimentación Teatral and Theja – focus their work on newer developments in the field of actors' training and their methods can be considered more experimental.

At the university level, a Faculty of Arts was established in 1978 at the Universidad Central. The faculty's theatre department offers a five-year *Licenciatura* (equivalent to a Bachelor's degree) and trains people as researchers, historians and critics. In 1986, the Instituto Pedagógico de Caracas (Caracas Pedagogical Institute) was established to train teachers in these same areas for other schools and theatrical institutions.

The Venezuelan-based CELCIT is a theatrical research unit for all of Latin America. A studio for already-established theatre professionals, based on Stanislavski models, CELCIT is a place where actors can return to school for a time to renew studies in their craft as well as a place where young actors can receive training. CELCIT's research work extends to many other areas of theatre and has played an important role in both the Latin American and Venezuelan theatre communities.

Criticism, Scholarship and Publishing

Theatre criticism has developed in Venezuela mainly as an adjunct to journalism; most of those writing on theatre for newspapers, magazines, radio stations and television channels have little real training in the art.

As far back as 1975, the Consejo Nacional de la Cultura attempted to correct this situation by creating a theatre journal, *Escena* (*Stage*), but the experiment lasted only a short time. Other publications that have similarly started and then closed down include *Imagen* (also published by the Consejo Nacional de la Cultura) and *Criticarte*, published by FUNDARTE, the cultural branch of the Caracas municipal government.

On the scholarly side, there is a developing interest in the study of theatre history at universities in Caracas, Merida (the Universidad de los Andes) and Maracaibo (the Universidad del Zulia). Performance research, however, is done by theatre groups themselves. Particularly important in this regard has been the work of Rajatabla, Theja and the Taller de Experimentación Teatral.

Theatre publishing has always been a scattered and scarce activity in the country. The state-owned publishing company, Monte Avila, began a theatre collection that allowed many new playwrights to become more widely known. Although it still publishes theatre materials from time to time – including studies of Venezuelan and international theatre – its overall interest in theatre has gradually decreased over the years.

FUNDARTE regularly publishes plays by Venezuelan writers that have already been produced, while some of the universities occasionally publish plays. Given this situation, playwrights have, more often than not, chosen to publish new works themselves.

In 1983, as part of the Sixth National Theatre Festival, thirty plays were published in nine volumes by the Asociación Venezolana de Profesionales del Teatro (Association of Professional Theatre Artists of Venezuela). Unfortunately, this singular publishing event was not repeated.

Orlando Rodríguez B.
Translated by Mayte Gómez

Further Reading

Antillano, Sergio. 'Ideas actuales en el teatro venezolano'. [Current ideas in Venezuelan theatre]. *El Farol* 23, no. 196 (September–October 1961): 3–11.

Arrom, José Juan. 'En torno al teatro venezolano'. [On Venezuelan theatre]. *Revista Nacional de Cultura* 7, no. 48 (January–February 1945): 3–10.

Azparren Giménez, Leonard. *Teatro en crisis*. [Theatre in crisis]. Caracas: FUNDARTE, 1987. 104 pp.

——. *El teatro venezolano*. [Venezuelan theatre]. Caracas: Departamento de Literatura del Instituto Nacional de Cultura y Bellas Artes, 1967.

——. 'El teatro venezolano en una encrucijada'. [Venezuelan theatre at the crossroads]. *Latin American Theatre Review* 20, no. 1 (fall 1986): 79–84.

——. *El teatro venezolano y otros teatros*. [Venezuelan theatre and other theatres]. Caracas: Monte Avila Editores, 1979.

——, ed. 'A Special Issue on Contemporary Venezuelan Theatre'. *Latin American Theatre Review* 21, no. 2 (spring 1988).

Castillo, Susana. *El dessarraigo en el teatro venezolano: marco histórico y manifestaciones modernas*. [Uprooting in the Venezuelan theatre: Historical background and modern examples]. Caracas: Ateneo de Caracas, 1980.

Chocrón, Isaac. 'Los cinco años de "El Nuevo Grupo"'. [Five years of El Nuevo Grupo]. *Tramoya* 7 (April–June 1977): 114–17.

——. *Nueva crítica del teatro venezolano*. [A new analysis of Venezuelan theatre]. Colección Cuadernos de Difusión, no. 67. Caracas: FUNDARTE, 1981.

——. *El nuevo teatro venezolano*. [New Venezuelan theatre]. Caracas: Oficina Central de Información.

Feo Calcano, Guillermo. *Teatro municipal, 1881–1981*. [Municipal theatre, 1881–1981]. Caracas: FUNDARTE/CROMOTIP, 1981.

Fernández Salomón, Eduardo, Alfonso López, and Pedro Marthan. 'Los teatros universitarios en Venezuela'. [University theatres in Venezuela]. *Tramoya* 7 (April–June 1977): 101–3.

Guerrero Matheus, Fernando. *Teatro y gente de teatro en el Zulia*. [Theatre and theatre artists at the Zulia]. Maracaibo: Universidad de Zulia, 1962.

Hernández, Gleider. *Tres dramaturgos venezolanos de hoy: Chalbaud, Cabrujas y Chocrón*. [Three contemporary Venezuelan playwrights: Chalbaud, Cabrujas and Chocrón]. Caracas: Ediciones El Nuevo Grupo, 1979.

Korn, Guillermo. 'Un teatro campesino en Venezuela'. [Peasant theatre in Venezuela]. *Latin American Theatre Review* 10, no. 1 (fall 1976): 102–5.

——. *Unos pasos por el teatro*. [A few steps in the theatre]. Caracas: Ediciones Casuz/Italgráfica, 1979.

Monasterios, Rubén. *Un enfoque crítico del teatro venezolano*. [A critical look at Venezuelan theatre]. Caracas: Monte Avila Editores, 1975.

——. *Un estudio crítico y longitudinal del teatro venezolano*. [A critical study of Venezuelan theatre]. Caracas: Universidad Central de Venezuela, 1974.

——. *La miel y el veneno*. [Honey and poison]. Valencia: Universidad de Carabobo, 1971.

——, and Herman Lejter. *Formación para un teatro del tercer mundo*. [Education for theatre in the Third World]. Caracas: Consejo Nacional de la Cultura/Imprenta Saman, 1978.

Palenzuela, Juan Carlos. 'El teatro venezolano de los años cincuenta'. [Venezuelan theatre in the 1950s]. *Escena* 10 (September 1976): 33–48.

Peraza, Luis. 'El indio y el negro en nuestro teatro'. [Indian and black characters in our theatre]. *El Farol* 7 (May 1946): 2–30.

Ramón y Rivera, Luis Felipe. *Teatro popular venezolano.* [Venezuelan popular theatre]. Quito: Instituto de Artes Populares, 1981.

Rojas Uzcategui, José, and Lubio Cardozo. *Bibliografía del teatro venezolano.* [Bibliography of Venezuelan theatre]. Mérida: Universidad de los Andes, Facultad de Humanidades y Educación, 1980.

Salas, Carlos. *Cien años de teatro municipal.* [100 years of Municipal Theatre]. Caracas: Consejo Municipal del Distrito Federal, 1980.

——. *Historia del teatro en Caracas.* [History of theatre in Caracas]. Caracas: Secretaría General de la Gobernación del Distrito Federal, 1967.

Suárez Radillo, Carlos. 'Un medio a ensayar para la creación de un teatro auténtico popular en Hispanoamérica: el teatro de los barrios de Venezuela'. [A way to create true popular theatre in Spanish America: Community theatre in Venezuela]. *Anales* (1972): 127–41.

——. *Trece autores del nuevo teatro venezolano.* [Thirteen authors from the new Venezuelan theatre.] Caracas: Monte Avila Editores, 1971.

Various. *Imagen del teatro venezolano.* [Images of the Venezuelan theatre]. Caracas: Venezuelan Centre of the International Theatre Institute, 1978.

Various. *Valores teatrales.* [Theatrical values]. Caracas: Círculo Musical, 1967.

Villasana, Angel Raúl. *Ensayo de un repertorio bibliográfico venezolano: años 1808–1950.* [A bibliography on Venezuela: 1808–1950]. 6 vols. Caracas: Banco Central de Venezuela, Talleres de Artegráfica, 1969–79.

VIRGIN ISLANDS

(see **COMMONWEALTH CARIBBEAN**)

WEST INDIES

For an overview of the predominantly English-language theatre in Antigua and Barbuda, Barbados, Dominica, Grenada, Guyana, Jamaica, Montserrat, St Kitts and Nevis, St Lucia, and Trinidad and Tobago, see COMMON-WEALTH CARIBBEAN. For an overview of the predominantly French-language theatre of French Guyana, Guadeloupe and Martinique, see FRENCH CARIBBEAN. For an overview of the predominantly Dutch-language theatre of Aruba and the Netherlands Antilles (Bonaire, Curaçao, Saba, St Eustatius and St Maarten), see NETHERLANDS ANTILLES AND ARUBA. See also CUBA, DOMINICAN REPUBLIC, HAÏTI and PUERTO RICO.

FURTHER READING

THE AMERICAS

Reference Works/Dictionaries/ Encyclopedias/Bibliographies

Acuña, René. *El teatro popular en Hispanoamérica: una bibliografía anotada.* [Popular theatre in Spanish America: An annotated bibliography]. México City: Universidad Nacional Autónoma de México, Instituto de Investigaciones Filológicas, Centro de Estudios Literarios, 1979. 114 pp.

Allen, Richard. *Teatro hispanoamericano: una bibliografía anotada.* [Spanish-American theatre: An annotated bibliography]. Boston, MA: G.K. Hall & Co., 1987.

Carpenter, Charles A. 'Latin American Theatre Criticism 1966–74: Some Addenda to Lyday and Woodyard'. *Revista Interamericana de Bibliografía* 3 (1980): 246–53.

Finch, Mark Steven. *An Annotated Bibliography of Recent Sources on Latin American Theatre.* Ann Arbor, MI: University Microfilms International, 1986.

Hebblethwaite, Frank P. *A Bibliographical Guide to the Spanish American Theatre.* Washington, DC: Pan American Union, General Secretariat, Organization of American States, 1969.

Hoffman, Herbert H. *Latin American Play Index.* 2 vols. Metuchen, NJ: Scarecrow Press, 1983–4. 131 pp.

Lyday, Leon, and George Woodyard. *A Bibliography of Latin American Theatre Criticism 1940–74.* Austin, TX: Institute of Latin American Studies, University of Texas, 1976.

Pérez Coterillo, Moisés, ed. *Escenarios de dos mundos: inventario teatral de Iberoamérica.* [Stages of two worlds: A theatre inventory of Iberoamerica]. 4 vols. Madrid: Centro de Documentación Teatral, Ministerio de Cultura, 1989.

Quién es quién en el teatro y el cine español e hispanoamericano. [Who's who in the Spanish and Spanish-American theatre and cinema]. 2 vols. Barcelona: Centro de Investigaciones Literarieas Españolas e Hispanoamericanas, 1991.

Roster, Peter, and Fernando de Toro. *Bibliografía del teatro hispanoamericano contemporáneo, 1900–80.* [A bibliography of contemporary Spanish-American theatre, 1900–80]. 2 vols. Frankfurt am Main: Vervuert, 1985.

Waters, Harold A. *Théâtre noir: encyclopédie des pièces écrites en français par des auteurs noirs.* [Black theatre: Encyclopedia of plays written in French by black authors]. Washington, DC: Three Continents Press, 1988. 214 pp.

Theatre History

Adams, Mildred. 'The Drama of Spanish America'. In *A History of Modern Drama*, eds. Barrett H. Clark and George Freedley, 576–92. New York: Appleton Century, 1947.

Amate Blanco, Juan José, and Marina Gálvez Acero. *Poesía y teatro de Hispanoamérica en el siglo XX.* [Spanish-American poetry and theatre of the twentieth century]. Cuadernos de Estudio,

Serie Literatura, no. 34. Madrid: Cincel, 1981. 88 pp.

Baralt, Luis Alejandro. 'The Theatre in Latin America'. In *Lectures Delivered at the Hispanic American Institute*, ed. J. Fiis Owre, 9–26. Hispanic American Studies Collection no. 5. Coral Gables, FL: University of Miami, 1948.

Boal, Augusto. 'Caminos del teatro latinoamericano'. [Paths of Latin American theatre]. *Conjunto* 16 (April–June 1973): 77–8.

Boorman, Joan R. 'Contemporary Latin American Woman Dramatists'. *Rice University Studies* 64 (1978): 69–80.

Brownell, Virginia. *Views of Religion in Contemporary Spanish American and Brazilian Drama*. Ann Arbor, MI: University Microfilm International, 1975.

Buenaventura, Enrique. 'Situación actual del teatro en Latino América'. [The current situation of theatre in Latin America]. *Poligramas* 7 (1981): 120–32.

Cea, José Roberto. *Teatro en y de una comarca centroamericana*. [Theatre in and of the Central American region]. San Salvador: Canoa Editores, 1993.

Cypess, Sandra M. 'Overview of an Oversight: Latin American Women Dramatists'. Chap. in *Studies in Romance Languages and Literatures*. Lawrence, KS: Coronado, 1979. 195 pp.

Dauster, Frank. *Ensayos sobre teatro hispanoamericano* [Essays on Spanish-American theatre]. México City: Secretaría de Educación Pública, Dirección General de Divulgación, 1975. 196 pp.

——. *Historia crítica del teatro hispanoamericano contemporáneo: siglos XIX y XX*. [History of Spanish-American contemporary theatre: The nineteenth and twentieth centuries]. 2nd ed. México City: De Andrea, 1973.

——. 'Recent Research in Spanish American Theatre'. *Latin American Research Review* 1, no. 2 (spring 1966): 65–76.

Eidelberg, Nora. *Teatro experimental hispanoamericano 1960–80: la realidad social como manipulación*. [Latin American experimental theatre 1960–80: Social reality as manipulation]. Series Towards a Social History of Spanish and Luso-Brazilian Literatures. Minneapolis, MN: Institute for the Study of Ideologies and Literature, 1985. 221 pp.

——. *El teatro en Iberoamérica: memoria del 12°. Congreso del Instituto Internacional de Literatura Iberoamericana*. [Theatre in Latin America: Proceedings of the twelfth congress of the International Institute of Ibero-American Literature]. México City: Instituto Internacional de Literatura Iberoamericana, 1975. 192 pp.

Elliot, Norma Jean. *Spanish American Contemporary Theatre 1959–70*. Ann Arbor, MI: University Microfilm International, 1986.

Espener, Maida Watson, ed. 'Proceedings of Symposium on Latin American Theatre, Florida International University, April 1979'. *Latin American Theatre Review* 13, no. 2, supplement (summer 1980): 1–117.

Foster, David William. *The Argentine 'Teatro Independiente', 1930–55*. York, SC: Spanish Literature Publishing, 1986.

Franco, Adolfo, ed. *National Symposium on Hispanic Theatre, 1982*. Cedar Falls, IA: University of Northern Iowa, 1985. 275 pp.

Gálvez Acero, Marina. *El teatro hispanoamericano*. [Spanish-American theatre]. Madrid: Taurus, 1988. 176 pp.

Guerrero Zamora, Juan. 'Hispanoamérica'. [Spanish America]. Chap. in *Historia del teatro contemporáneo*. [History of contemporary theatre], vol. 4. Barcelona: Juan Flors, 1967.

Instituto Internacional de Teoría y Crítica de Teatro Latinoamericano. *Reflexiones sobre el teatro latinoamericano del siglo XX*. [Reflections on Latin American theatre of the twentieth century]. Buenos Aires: Galerna, 1989; Frankfurt am Main: Lemcke Verlag, 1989.

Jones, Willis Knapp. *Behind Spanish American Footlights*. Austin, TX: University of Texas, 1966. 609 pp.

——. *Breve historia del teatro latino americano*. [A short history of Latin American theatre]. México City: De Andrea, 1956. 239 pp.

Kaiser-Lenoir, Claudia. 'The New Theatre of Latin America'. *Theatre Research International* 14, no. 2 (1989): 109–85.

Lyday, Leon, and George Woodyard. 'Studies on Latin American Theatre 1966–9'. *Theatre Documentation* 2, nos. 1–2 (fall 1969–spring 1970): 49–84.

Monleón, José. 'España y el teatro latinoamericano'. [Spain and Latin American Theatre]. *Cuadernos de Investigación Teatral* 5 (1979): 1–13.

Moretta, Eugene L. 'Spanish American Theatre of the 50s and 60s: Critical Perspective on Role Playing'. *Latin American Theatre Review* 13, no. 2 (spring 1980): 5–30.

Perales, Rosalina. *Teatro hispanoamericano contemporáneo, 1967–87*. [Contemporary Spanish-American theatre, 1967–87]. Series Escenología, no. 9. México City: Grupo Editorial Gaceta, 1993.

Pianca, Marina. 'The Latin American Theatre of Exile'. *Theatre Research International* 14 (1989): 174–85.

——. 'Post-colonial Discourse in Latin American Theatre'. *Theatre Journal* 41 (1989): 515–23.

——. *El teatro de nuestra América: un proyecto continental, 1959–89.* [Theatre of our America: A continental project, 1959–89]. Minneapolis, MN: Institute for the Study of Ideologies and Literature, 1990.

——. *El teatro latinoamericano frente a la historia 1959–80.* [Latin American theatre facing history 1959–80]. Ann Arbor, MI: University Microfilms International, 1987.

Pottlitzer, Joanne, ed. *The Drama Review* 14 (winter 1970). Special section.

Rizk, Beatriz. *El nuevo teatro latinoamericano: una lectura histórica.* [The new Latin American theatre: A historical reading]. Series Towards a Social History of Hispanic and Luso-Brazilian Literatures. Minneapolis, MN: Institute for the Study of Ideologies and Literature/Prisma Institute, 1987. 143 pp.

Rojo, Grínor. 'Estado actual de las investigaciones sobre teatro hispanoamericano contemporáneo'. [Present state of research on contemporary Spanish-American theatre]. *Revista Chilena de Literatura* 2, no. 3 (spring 1970): 133–62.

——. *Los orígenes del teatro hispanoamericano contemporáneo: la generación de dramaturgos de 1927. Dos direcciones.* [The beginnings of contemporary Spanish-American theatre: The playwrights' generation of 1927. Two directions]. Colección Universidad, Serie Investigación. Santiago: Universitarias de Valparaíso/Universidad Católica de Valparaíso, 1972. 227 pp.

Saz Sánchez, Agustín del. *Teatro hispanoamericano.* [Spanish-American theatre]. Nueva Colección Labor, no. 57. Barcelona: Labor, 1967. 176 pp.

——. *Teatro social hispanoamericano.* [Spanish-American social theatre]. Barcelona: Editorial Labor, 1967. 177 pp.

Solórzano, Carlos. *El teatro latinoamericano en el siglo XX.* [Latin American theatre in the twentieth century]. México City: Editorial Pormaca S.A., 1964. 200 pp.

Ugarte Chamorro, Guillermo. *Las más antiguas vinculaciones de los teatros peruano y chileno.* [The most ancient connections between the Chilean and Peruvian theatres]. Series IV: Estudios de Teatro Peruano, no. 41. Lima: Servicio de Publicaciones del Teatro Universitario San Marcos, 1965.

Velasco, María M. de. 'La creación colectiva y la colonización cultural en América Latina'. [Collective creation and cultural colonization in Latin America]. *Gestos* 7 (1989): 75–91.

Weiss, Judith, ed. 'Latin American Theater Today: An Introduction'. *Theater* 12, 1 (fall/winter 1980): 5.

Criticism and Aesthetics

Adler, Heidrun. *Politisches Theater in Lateinamerika: von der Mythologie über die Mission zur kollektiven Identität.* [Political theatre in Latin America: From the mission mythology to a collective identity]. Beiträge zur Kulturanthropologie. Berlin: Dietrich Reimer, 1982. 171 pp.

Albuquerque, Severino Loão. *Violent Acts: A Study of Contemporary Latin American Theatre.* Detroit, MI: Wayne State University Press, 1991. 298 pp.

Apstein, Theodore. 'New Aspects of the Theater in Latin America'. In *Proceedings of the Conference on Latin American Fine Arts: June 14–17, 1951,* 27–41. Austin, TX: University of Texas Press, 1952.

Arrom, José Juan. 'Perfil del teatro contemporáneo en Hispanoamérica'. [A profile of contemporary Spanish-American theatre]. In *Certidumbre de América.* [America's certainty], 2nd ed., 172–83. Madrid: Gredos, 1971.

Arrufat, Antón, *et al.* 'Charla sobre teatro'. [Discussion about theatre]. *Casa de las Américas* 2 (1961): 88–102.

Azor, Ileana. *Origen y presencia del teatro en nuestra América.* [Origin and presence of theatre in our America]. Havana: Letras Cubanas, 1988. 304 pp.

——. *Variaciones sobre el teatro latinoamericano.* [Variations in Latin American theatre]. Havana: Editorial Pueblo y Educación, 1987. 117 pp.

Bagby, Beth. 'El teatro campesino: Interviews with Luis Valdez'. In *The Drama Review: Thirty Years of Commentary on the Avant-Garde,* eds. Brooks McNamara and Jill Dolan, 127–39. Theatre and Dramatic Studies no. 35. Ann Arbor, MI: University Microfilms International Research, 1986.

Baycroff, Bernardo. 'Brecht in Latin America: The Ideology and Aesthetics of the New Theatre'. *Communications from the International Brecht Society* 15, no. 2 (April 1986): 43–7.

Bissett, Judith Ismael. 'Consciousness-Raising Dramatic Structures in Latin America's Theatre of Commitment'. PhD dissertation, Arizona State University, 1976. 305 pp.

Boal, Augusto. *Categorías del teatro popular.* [Categories of popular theatre]. Buenos Aires: CEPE, 1972. 90 pp.

——. *Stop: c'est magique.* [Stop: It's magic]. Rio de Janeiro: Editora Civilização Brasileira, 1980.

——. *Teatro do Oprimido e outras poéticas politicas.* [Theatre of the Oppressed and other political poetics]. Rio de Janeiro: Editora Civilização Brasileira, 1979.

——. *Técnicas latinoamericanas de teatro popular: una revolución copérnica al revés.* [Latin American techniques of popular theatre: A Copernican revolution the other way around]. Buenos Aires: Corregidor, 1975. 212 pp.

——. *Theatre of the Oppressed.* Translated by Charles McBride and María-Odilia Leal. New York: Theatre Communications Group, 1985. 208 pp.

Bolet Rodríguez, Teresa. *Modalidades del caso y del proceso jurídico en el drama hispano-americano.* [Models of indictments and judicial process in Spanish-American drama]. Miami, FL: Ediciones Universales, 1990.

Bonilla, María, and Vladich Stoyan. *Teatro latino-americano en busca de su identidad cultural.* [Latin American theatre in search of its cultural identity]. San José: Culturart, 1988. 327 pp.

Bravo-Elizondo, Pedro J. 'Constantes dramáticas en el nuevo teatro hispanoamericano de crítica social, 1950–70'. [Dramatic constants in the Spanish-American theatre of social criticism 1950–70]. PhD dissertation, University of Iowa, 1974. 267 pp.

——. 'La realidad latinoamericana y el teatro documental'. [Latin American reality and documentary theatre]. *Teatro Crítico* 5, no. 14 (July–September 1979): 200–10.

——. *El teatro hispanoamericano de crítica social.* [Spanish-American theatre of social criticism]. Madrid: Playor, 1975. 175 pp.

Castagnino, Raúl. *Semiótica, ideología y teatro hispano-americano contemporáneo.* [Semiotics and ideology in contemporary Spanish-American theatre]. Biblioteca Arte y Ciencia de la Expresión. Buenos Aires: Nova, 1974. 267 pp.

Dauster, Frank. 'Social Awareness in the Contemporary Spanish American Theater'. *Kentucky Romance Quarterly* 14, no. 2 (1967): 120–5.

Davis, R.G. 'El teatro de guerrilla'. [Guerrilla theatre]. *Conjunto* 5 (October–December 1967): 10–14.

de Toro, Fernando. *Brecht en el teatro hispanoamericano contemporáneo.* [Brecht in contemporary Spanish-American theatre]. Ottawa: Girol Books, 1984.

——, ed. *Semiótica y teatro latinoamericano.* [Semiotics and Latin American theatre]. Buenos Aires: Editorial Galerna; Ottawa: IITCTL.

Flores, Arturo. *El teatro campesino de Luis Valdez.* [Luis Valdez's peasant theatre]. Colección Pliegos de Ensayo. Madrid: Pliegos, 1990. 130 pp.

Galich, Manuel, and Federico García Céspedes. 'Defender el horizonte de todos: la investigación de la historia del teatro latinoamericano y caribeño en Cuba revolucionaria'. [In defence of our horizon: Research on Latin American and Caribbean theatre history in revolutionary Cuba]. *Cuadernos de Investigación Teatral* 4 (1979).

García, Santiago. *Teoría y práctica del teatro.* [Theory and practice of theatre]. Bogotá: CEIS, 1983.

Garzón Céspedes, Francisco, ed. *Recopilación de textos sobre el teatro latinoame-ricano de creación colectiva.* [Essays on collective creation in the Latin American theatre]. Serie Valoración Múltiple. Centro de Investigación Literaria. Havana: Casa de las Américas, 1978. 564 pp.

Green, Joan Rea. 'Character and Conflict in the Contemporary Central American Theatre'. In *Contemporary Latin American Literature*, eds. Harvey L. Johnson and Philip B. Taylor, Jr, 93–102. Houston, TX: Latin American Studies Committee, University of Houston, 1973.

Gutiérrez, Sonia, ed. *Teatro popular y cambio social en América Latina: panorama de una experiencia.* [Popular theatre and social change in Latin America: Overview of an experience]. Colección DEI. San José, CR: Editorial Universitaria Centro Americana, 1979. 487 pp.

Huerta, Jorge A. *Chicano Theater: Themes and Forms.* Ypsilanti, MI: Bilingual Press, 1982. 274 pp.

Kaiser-Lenoir, Claudia. 'The New Theatre of Latin America'. *Theatre Research International* 14, no. 2 (1989): 109–85.

Lena Paz, Marta. 'La crítica teatral y América Latina'. [Theatre criticism in Latin America]. In *Hacia una crítica literaria latinoamericana.* [Towards a Latin American literary criticism], ed. Graciela Maturo, 213–25. Buenos Aires: García Cambeiro, 1976.

Luzuriaga, Gerardo. *Introducción a las teorías latino-americanas de teatro.* [Introduction to Latin American theatre theories]. Puebla: Universidad Autónoma de Puebla, 1990.

——. 'Rumbos del nuevo teatro latinoamericano'. [Paths of the new Latin American theatre]. *Alero* 16, 3rd epoch (January–February 1976): 22–7.

——, ed. *Popular Theater for Social Change in Latin America: Essays in Spanish and English.* Los Angeles: University of California at Los Angeles, Latin American Center, 1978.

Lyday, Leon, and George Woodyard. *Dramatists in Revolt: The New Latin American Theatre*. Austin, TX: University of Texas Press, 1976. 275 pp.

Menéndez Quiroga, Leonel, ed. *Hacia un nuevo teatro latinoamericano: teoría y metodología del arte escénico*. [Towards a new Latin American theatre: Theatre theory and methodology]. San Salvador: Universidad Centroamericana, 1977. 767 pp.

Monleón, José. *América Latina: teatro y revolución*. [Latin America: theatre and revolution]. Caracas: Editorial Ateneo de Caracas/CELCIT, 1978.

Neglia, Erminio. *El hecho teatral en Latino America*. [The theatre event in Latin America]. Rome: Bulzoni, 1985. 216 pp.

Ochsenius, Carlos, *et al. Práctica teatral y expresión popular en América Latina: Argentina, Chile, Perú, Uruguay*. [Theatre practice and popular expression in Latin America: Argentina, Chile, Perú, Uruguay]. Buenos Aires: Paulinas, 1988.

Petrucelli, María Rosa, ed. *El III encuentro regional de teatro: Latinoamérica y el Caribe. Las nuevas tendencias del teatro de Latinoamérica y el Caribe en el contexto mundial*. [The third regional theatre meeting: Latin America and the Caribbean. New trends in Latin American and Caribbean theatre in a global context]. Buenos Aires: Argentine Centre of the International Theatre Institute, 1992. 167 pp.

Pianca, Marina. *Testimonios de teatro latinoamericano*. [Testimonies from the Latin American theatre]. Buenos Aires: Grupo Editor de América Latina, 1991.

——, ed. *Diógenes: anuario crítico del teatro Latinoamericano*. [Diógenes: Critical yearbook of the Latin American theatre]. 3 vols. Ottawa: Asociación de Trabajadores e Investigadores del Nuevo Teatro/Girol Books, 1987–9.

——, ed. *Diógenes: anuario crítico del teatro Latinoamericano*, vol. 4. Buenos Aires: Grupo Editor Latinoamericano, 1990.

Quackenbush, Howard L. 'Variations on the Theme of Cruelty in Spanish-American Theatre'. In *Myths and Realities of Contemporary French Theater: Comparative Views*, eds. Patricia Hopkins and Wendell Aycock, 99–113. Lubbock, TX: Texas Technical Press, 1985. 195 pp.

Quiles Ferrer, Edgar. 'The Theatre of Augusto Boal'. PhD dissertation, Michigan State University, 1981. 348 pp.

Rizk, Beatriz. *Buenaventura: la dramaturgia de la creación colectiva*. [Buenaventura: The dramaturgy of the collective creation]. México City: Grupo Editorial Gaceta, 1991.

Royaards, Rense. *De quien vienen ustedes: de Dios o del Diablo; experimentos de teatro en América Latina*. [From whom do you come: God or the Devil; theatrical experiments in Latin America]. The Hague: Centre for the Study of Education in Developing Countries, 1989.

Suárez Radillo, Carlos Miguel. *Lo social en el teatro hispanoamericano contemporáneo*. [Social issues in contemporary Spanish-American theatre]. Caracas: Equinoccio, Editorial de la Universidad Simón Bolívar, 1976. 394 pp.

Taylor, Diana. *Theatre of Crisis: Drama and Politics in Latin America*. Lexington, KY: University Press of Kentucky, 1991. 277 pp.

Villegas, Juan. 'El discurso dramático-teatral latinoamericano y el discurso crítico: algunas reflexiones estratégicas'. [Dramatic discourse in Latin American theatre: Reflections on strategies]. *Latin American Theatre Review* 18, no. 1 (fall 1984): 5–12.

——. *Ideología y discurso crítico sobre el teatro de España y América Latina*. [Ideology and critical discourse in the theatre of Spain and Latin America]. Minneapolis, MN: Prisma Institute, 1988.

Weisman, John. *Guerrilla Theater: Scenarios for Revolution*. New York: Anchor Press, 1973.

Woodyard, George. 'The Search for Identity: A Comparative Study in Contemporary Latin American Drama'. PhD dissertation, University of Illinois, 1966. 272 pp.

Zalacán, Daniel. *Teatro absurdista hispano-americano*. [Spanish-American Theatre of the Absurd]. Valencia, Spain: Albatros Hispanofilia, 1985.

Theatre Arts

Javier, Francisco. *Notas para la historia científica de la puesta en escena*. [Notes on the scientific history of theatre production]. Buenos Aires: Editorial Leviatán, 1985. 121 pp.

Pereira, Teresinha. *La actual dramaturgia latinoamericana*. [Playwriting in Latin America today]. Bogotá: Tercer Mundo, 1979. 87 pp.

Saz Sánchez, Agustín del. *Seminario regional sobre teatro Latinoamericano y Caribeño contemporáneo. Dramaturgia y puesta en escena en el teatro latino americano y caribeño contemporáneo.* [Regional seminar on contemporary Latin American and Caribbean theatre. Playwriting and production in Latin American and Caribbean theatre]. Paris: UNESCO, 1988. 128 pp.

Anthologies

Alpern, Hymen, ed. *Teatro hispanoamericano.* [Spanish-American theatre]. New York: Odyssey Press, 1956.

Andrade, Elba, and Hilde F. Cramsie, eds. *Dramaturgas latinoamericanas contemporáneas (antología crítica).* [Contemporary Latin American female dramatists (a critical anthology)]. Madrid: Editorial Verbum, 1991.

Casas, Myrna, ed. *Teatro de la vanguardia.* [Avant-garde theatre]. Lexington, KY: D.C. Heath, 1975.

Colecchia, Francesca, and Julio Matas, eds. *Selected Latin American One-Act Plays.* Pittsburgh, PA: University of Pittsburgh Press, 1973.

Dauster, Frank, ed. *Teatro hispanoamericano: tres piezas.* [Spanish-American theatre: Three plays]. New York: Harcourt, Brace & World, 1965.

——, and Leon F. Lyday, eds. *En un acto.* [In one act]. New York: Van Nostrand, 1974.

——, and George Woodyard, eds. *Nueve dramaturgos hispanoamericanos.* [Nine Spanish-American playwrights]. 3 vols. Ottawa: Girol Books, 1979.

Eidelberg, Nora, and María Mercedes Jaramillo. *Voces en escena: antología de dramaturgas latinoamericanas.* [Voices on stage: An anthology of Latin American women playwrights]. Medellín, Colombia: Universidad de Antioquía, 1991.

Jones, Willis Knapp, ed. *Antología del teatro hispanoamericano.* [Anthology of Spanish-American theatre]. México City: Ediciones de Andrea, 1958.

Lamb, Ruth, ed. *Three Contemporary Latin American Plays.* Waltham, MA: Xerox College, 1971. 203 pp.

Luzuriaga, Gerardo, and Richard Reeve, eds. *Los clásicos del teatro hispanoamericano.* [The classics of the Spanish-American theatre]. México City: Fondo de Cultura Económica, 1975. 905 pp.

Luzuriaga, Gerardo, and Robert Rudder, eds. *The Orgy: Modern One-Act Plays from Latin America.* Los Angeles: UCLA Latin American Center, 1974.

Neglia, Erminio, and Luis Ordaz. *Repertorio selecto del teatro hispanoamericano contemporáneo.* [A selection of contemporary Spanish-American drama]. 2nd ed. Tempe, AZ: Arizona State University, Center for Latin American Studies, 1980.

Oliver, William I., ed. *Voices of Change in Spanish American Theatre: An Anthology.* Austin, TX: University of Texas Press, 1971.

Pas, Elena, and Gloria F. Waldman, eds. *Teatro contemporáneo.* [Contemporary theatre]. Boston, MA: Heinle & Heinle, 1983. 297 pp.

Quackenbush, Howard L. *Teatro del absurdo hispanoamericano: antología anotada.* [Theatre of the Absurd in Spanish America: Annotated anthology]. México City: Editorial Patria, 1987. 270 pp.

Ripoll, Carlos, and Andrés Valdespino, eds. *Teatro hispanoamericano: antología crítica.* [Spanish-American theatre: Annotated anthology]. 2 vols. Madrid: Anaya Books, 1973.

Rodríguez-Sardiñas, Orlando, and Carlos Miguel Suárez Radillo, eds. *Teatro selecto contemporáneo hispanoamericano.* [Selection of contemporary Spanish-American theatre]. Madrid: Escelicer, 1971.

Solórzano, Carlos, ed. *El teatro actual latinoamericano.* [The present theatre of Latin America]. México City: Ediciones de Andrea, 1972.

——. *Teatro breve hispanoamericano contemporáneo.* [Contemporary short theatre of Spanish America]. Madrid: Aguilar, 1970.

——, ed. *El teatro hispanoamericano contemporáneo.* [Contemporary Spanish-American theatre]. 2 vols. México City: Fondo de Cultura Económica, 1964.

Woodyard, George, ed. *The Modern Stage in Latin America: Six Plays.* New York: E.P. Dutton, 1971.

INTERNATIONAL REFERENCE

SELECTED BIBLIOGRAPHY

The following is a list of significant theatre books that have been published since the early 1950s. For a complete listing of world theatre publications, see volume 6 of this encyclopedia, *World Theatre Bibliography/Cumulative Index*. This section was prepared with the collaboration of the Belgian scholar René Hainaux and the Centre de Recherches et de Formation Théâtrales en Wallonie with the assistance of collaborators from Europe, North and South America, Africa, the Arab World and Asia.

Reference Works/Dictionaries/ Encyclopedias/Bibliographies

Attisani, Antonio. *Enciclopedia del teatro del '900.* [Theatre encyclopedia of the twentieth century]. Milan: Feltrinelli, 1980. 598 pp.

Bailey, Claudia Jean. *A Guide to Reference and Bibliography for Theatre Research.* 2nd ed. Columbus, OH: Ohio State University Libraries, 1983.

Banham, Martin, ed. *The Cambridge Guide to World Theatre.* Cambridge: Cambridge University Press, 1988. 1,104 pp.

Brauneck, Manfred, and Gérard Schneilin, eds. *Theaterlexikon: Begriffe und Epoche. Bühnen und Ensembles.* [Theatre lexicon: Terms and periods. Stages and ensembles]. Hamburg: Rowohlt, 1986. 1,120 pp.

Cao, Yu, and Wang, Zuo Ling, eds. *China's Great Encyclopedia of World Theatre and Drama.* Beijing/Shanghai: China's Great Encyclopedia Press, 1989. 583 pp.

Cohen, Selma Jeanne, ed. *International Encyclopedia of Dance.* Oxford: Oxford University Press, 1996.

Corvin, Michel. *Dictionnaire encyclopédique du théâtre.* [Encyclopedic dictionary of theatre]. Paris: Borduas, 1991.

Couty, Daniel, and Alan Rey, eds. *Le Théâtre.* [Theatre]. Paris: Borduas, 1980.

D'Amico, Silvio, ed. *Enciclopedia dello spettacolo.* [Encyclopedia of the performing arts]. 11 vols. Rome: Le Maschere, 1954–66.

Dahlhaus, Carl. *Pipers Enzyklopädia des Musiktheaters.* [Piper's encyclopedia of music theatre]. 5 vols. Munich: Piper, 1986– .

Esslin, Martin, ed. *The Encyclopedia of World Theater.* New York: Scribner, 1977.

Fielding, Eric, gen. ed. *Theatre Words: An International Vocabulary in Nine Languages.* Prague: Publication and Information Exchange Commission of OISTAT, 1993.

Gassner, John, and Edward Quinn, eds. *The Readers' Encyclopedia of World Drama.* New York: Thomas Y. Crowell, 1969. 1,030 pp.

Giteau, Cécile. *Dictionnaire des arts du spectacle: Théâtre-Cinéma-Cirque-Danse-Radio-*

Marionettes-Télévision-Documentologie.
[Dictionary of the performing arts: Theatre-
Film-Circus-Dance-Radio-Puppetry-Television-
Documentation]. Paris: Dunod, 1970. 430 pp.
In French, English and German.

Gregor, Josef, and Margret Dietrich. *Der
Schauspielführer: der Inhalt der wichtigsten
Theaterstücke aus aller Welt.* [The play guide:
Synopses of the most important plays from the
whole world]. 15 vols. Stuttgart: Anton Hier-
seman, 1953–93.

Hainaux, René, ed. *Stage Design Throughout the
World.* 4 vols. London: Harrap; New York:
Theatre Arts Books, 1956–75.

Hartnoll, Phyllis, and Peter Found, eds. *The
Concise Oxford Companion to the Theatre.* 2nd
ed. New York: Oxford University Press, 1992.
586 pp.

——. *The Oxford Companion to the Theatre.* 4th
ed. London: Oxford University Press, 1983.
934 pp.

Hawkins-Day, Mark, ed. *International Dictionary
of Theatre.* Vol. 2: *Playwrights.* Detroit/
London/Washington, DC: Gale Research
International/St James Press, 1994. 1,218 pp.

Hochman, Stanley, ed. *McGraw-Hill Encyclopedia of World Drama.* 2nd ed. 5 vols. New
York: McGraw-Hill, 1984.

Hoffmann, Christel, ed. *Kinder- und Jugend-
theater der Welt.* [Children's and youth theatre
of the world]. 2nd ed. Berlin: Henschelverlag,
1984. 276 pp.

Kienzle, Siegfried. *Schauspielführer der Gegen-
wart: Interpretation zum Schauspiel ab 1945.* [A
guide to contemporary plays: An interpretation
of plays since 1945]. Stuttgart: Alfred Kröner
Verlag, 1978. 659 pp.

Koegler, Horst, ed. *The Concise Oxford Dictionary of Ballet.* Oxford: Oxford University
Press, 1987. 458 pp.

Kullman, Colby H, and William C. Young.
Theatre Companies of the World. 2 vols. New
York/London: Greenwood Press, 1986.

Leleu-Rouvray, Geneviève, and Gladys Langevin,
eds. *International Bibliography on Puppetry:
English Books 1945–1990.* Paris: Institut
International de la Marionnette/Associations
Marionnette et Thérapie, 1993. 281 pp.

Matlaw, Myron. *Modern World Drama: An
Encyclopedia.* London: Secker & Warburg,
1972. 960 pp.

Mikotowicz, Thomas J., ed. *Theatrical Designers:
An International Biographical Dictionary.*
Westport, CT: Greenwood Press, 1992. 365 pp.

Mokulski, S.S., and P.A. Markov, eds. *Teatralnaia
Entsiklopedia.* [Theatre encyclopedia]. 6 vols.
Moscow: Sovetskaia Entsiklopedia, 1961–7.

Ortolani, Benito, ed. *International Bibliography of
Theatre.* 7 vols. New York: Theatre Research
Data Center, 1985–93.

Pavis, Patrice. *Dictionnaire du théâtre: termes et
concepts de l'analyse théâtrale.* [Dictionary of
the theatre: Terms and concepts of theatrical
analysis]. 2nd ed. Paris: Editions Sociales, 1987.
477 pp.

Philpott, A.R. *Dictionary of Puppetry.* London:
MacDonald, 1969. 291 pp.

Queant, G., ed. *Encyclopédie du théâtre contemporain.* [Encyclopedia of contemporary theatre].
Paris: Olivier Perrin, 1959. 211 pp.

Rischbieter, Henning. *Theater-Lexikon.* [Theatre
lexicon]. Revised edn, Zurich-Schwäbisch Hall:
Orell Füssli, 1983. 484 pp.

Sadie, Stanley, ed. *The New Grove Dictionary of
Opera.* 4 vols. London: Macmillan, 1992.

Schindler, Otto G. *Theaterliteratur. Ein bib-
liographischer Behelf für das Studium der
Theaterwissenschaft.* [Theatre literature. A bibliographic guide for theatre studies]. 3 vols.
Vienna: Institut für Theaterwissenschaft, 1973.

Shigetoshi, Kawatake, ed. *Engeki Hyakka
Daijiten.* [Encyclopedia of world theatre]. 6
vols. Tokyo: Heibonsha, 1960–2.

Swortzell, Lowell, ed. *International Guide to Children's Theatre and Educational Theatre. A Historical and Geographical Source Book.*
Westport, CT: Greenwood Press, 1990. 360 pp.

Trapido, Joel, ed. *An International Dictionary of
Theatre Language.* Westport, CT: Greenwood
Press, 1985. 1,032 pp.

Veinstein, André, and Alfred Golding, eds. *Performing Arts Libraries and Museums of the
World/Bibliothèques et musées des arts du spectacle dans le monde.* 4th ed. Paris: Centre
National de la Recherche Scientifique, 1992.
773 pp.

Wilcox, R. Turner. *The Dictionary of Costume.*
New York: Scribner, 1969. 406 pp.

Theatre History

Anderson, Jack. *Ballet and Modern Dance: A Concise History.* 2nd ed. Princeton, NJ: Princeton
Book Company, 1992. 287 pp.

Arnott, Peter. *The Theatre in its Time.* Boston,
MA: Little, Brown, 1981. 566 pp.

Aslan, Odette. *L'Art du théâtre*. [The art of theatre]. Verviers: Marabout, 1963. 672 pp.

Awad, Louis. *Al masrah al âlami*. [World theatre]. Egypt, 1964.

Brockett, Oscar G. *History of the Theatre*. 6th ed. Boston, MA: Allyn & Bacon, 1990. 680 pp.

Calendoli, Giovanni. *Storia universale della danza*. [General history of dance]. Milan: Mondadori, 1985. 288 pp.

Dumur, Guy, ed. *Histoire des spectacles*. [History of the performing arts]. Encyclopédie de la Pléiade Collection. Paris: Gallimard, 1965. 2,010 pp.

Jurkowski, Henryk. *Dzieje teatru lalek: Od wielkiej reformy do współczesności*. [History of the puppet theatre: From theatre's reform to today]. Warsaw, 1984.

——. *Ecrivains et marionnettes: quatre siècles de littérature dramatique*. [Writers and puppets: Four centuries of dramatic literature]. Charleville-Mézières: Institut National de la Marionnette, 1991.

Kuritz, Paul. *The Making of Theatre History*. Englewood Cliffs, NJ: Prentice-Hall, 1988. 468 pp.

Kybalova, Ludmila, Olga Herbenova, and Milena Lamarova. *The Pictorial Encyclopedia of Fashion*. New York: Crown, 1968. 604 pp.

Londré, Felicia Hardison. *The History of World Theater*. 2 vols. New York: Continuum, 1991.

Molinari, Cesare. *Teatro*. [Theatre]. Milan: Mondadori, 1972.

——. *Theatre Through the Ages*. New York: McGraw-Hill, 1975. 324 pp.

Mordden, Ethan. *The Fireside Companion to the Theatre*. New York: Simon & Schuster, 1988. 313 pp.

Nagler, A.M. *A Sourcebook in Theatrical History*. New York: Dover, 1952. 611 pp.

Nicoll, Allardyce. *The Development of the Theatre: A Study of Theatrical Art from the Beginnings to the Present Day*. 5th ed. London: George G. Harrap, 1966. 318 pp.

Niculescu, Margareta. *Teatrul de păpuşi în lume*. [Puppet theatre in the world]. Berlin: Henschelverlag; Bucharest: Meridiane, 1966. 230 pp.

Nutku, Özdemir. *Dünya Tiyatrosu Tarihi*. [A history of world theatre]. 2 vols. Ankara: Ankara Universitesi dil ve Tarih Coğrafya Fakültesi Yayıonları, 1973.

Ottai, Antonella, ed. *Teatro oriente/occidente*. [Oriental/occidental theatre]. Biblioteca Teatrale no. 47. Rome: Bulzoni, 1986. 565 pp.

Pandolfi, Vito. *Storia universale del teatro drammatico*. [World history of dramatic art]. 2 vols. Turin: Unione Typografico-Editrice, 1964. 1,626 pp.

Pronko, Leonard C. *Theater East and West: Perspectives Toward a Total Theater*. Berkeley, CA: University of California Press, 1967. 280 pp.

Roose-Evans, James. *Experimental Theatre: From Stanislavksi to Peter Brook*. 2nd ed. London: Routledge, 1989. 224 pp.

Sallé, Bernard. *Histoire du théâtre*. [History of the theatre]. Paris: Librairie Théâtrale, 1990. 320 pp.

Zamora Guerrero, Juan. *Historia del teatro contemporáneo*. [History of contemporary theatre]. 4 vols. Barcelona: Juan Flors, 1961–2.

Criticism and Aesthetics

Appia, Adolphe. *Oeuvres complètes*. [Complete works]. 3 vols. Marie L. Bablet-Hahn, ed. Lausanne: L'Age d'Homme, 1983–8.

Artaud, Antonin. *Oeuvres complètes*. [Complete works]. 25 vols. Paris: Gallimard, 1961–90.

Barba, Eugenio. *Beyond the Floating Islands*. New York: PAJ Publications, 1986. 282 pp.

——. *The Floating Islands*. Holstebro, Denmark: Thomsens Bogtrykkeri, 1979. 224 pp.

——, and Nicola Savarese. *The Secret Art of the Performer. A Dictionary of Theatre Anthropology*. Edited and compiled by Richard Gough. London: Routledge, 1991. 272 pp.

Bawtree, Michael. *The New Singing Theatre*. Bristol UK: Bristol Classical Press; New York: Oxford University Press, 1991. 232 pp.

Beckerman, Bernard. *Dynamics of Drama*. New York: Drama Book Specialists, 1979. 272 pp.

Bentley, Eric. *The Dramatic Event*. Boston, MA: Beaucou Press, 1956. 278 pp.

——. *The Life of the Drama*. New York: Atheneum, 1964. 371 pp.

——. *The Playwright as Thinker*. New York: Reynal & Hitchcock, 1946. 382 pp.

Bharucha, Rustom. *Theatre and the World: Performance and the Politics of Culture*. London/New York: Routledge, 1993. 254 pp.

Birringer, Johannes. *Theatre, History and Post-Modernism*. Bloomington, IN: Indiana University Press, 1991. 240 pp.

Boal, Augusto. *Theatre of the Oppressed*. New York: Theatre Communications Group, 1985. 197 pp.

Brecht, Bertolt. *Kleines Organon für das Theater.* [A little organum for the theatre]. Frankfurt: Suhrkamp Verlag, 1958.

——. *Schriften zum Theater.* [Writings on the theatre]. 7 vols. ed. Werner Hecht. Berlin: Aufbau Verlag, 1963–4.

Brook, Peter. *The Empty Space.* London: MacGibbon & Kee, 1969. 141 pp.

Brustein, Robert. *The Theatre of Revolt.* Boston, MA: Little, Brown, 1964. 435 pp.

Carlson, Marvin. *Theories of the Theatre: A Historical and Critical Survey, from the Greeks to the Present.* Ithaca, NY/London: Cornell University Press, 1984. 530 pp.

Clark, Barrett H. *European Theories of the Drama.* New York: Crown, 1965. 628 pp.

Craig, Edward Gordon. *On the Art of Theatre.* London: Heinemann, 1911, 1968. 295 pp.

——. *Towards a New Theatre.* London: J.M. Dent, 1913.

Dort, Bernard. *Théâtre en jeu.* [Drama in performance]. Paris: Seuil, 1979. 334 pp.

——. *Théâtre réel.* [Real theatre]. Paris: Seuil, 1971. 300 pp.

Epskamp, Kees P. *Theatre in Search for Social Change: The Relative Significance of Different Theatrical Approaches.* The Hague: Centre for the Study of Education in Developing Countries, 1989.

Esslin, Martin. *The Field of Drama.* London: Methuen, 1987. 190 pp.

——. *The Theatre of the Absurd.* Garden City, NY: Doubleday, 1961. 364 pp.

Frye, Northrop. *Anatomy of Criticism.* Princeton, NJ: Princeton University Press, 1957. 383 pp.

Goodman, Lizbeth. *Contemporary Feminist Theatres.* London: Routledge, 1992. 272 pp.

Grotowski, Jerzy. *Towards a Poor Theatre.* New York: Simon & Schuster, 1968. 262 pp.

Innes, Christopher. *Avant-Garde Theatre, 1892–1992.* London/New York: Routledge, 1993. 262 pp.

Ionesco, Eugène. *Notes et contrenotes.* [Notes and counternotes]. Paris: Gallimard, 1962. 248 pp.

Kidd, Ross. *The Performing Arts, Non-Formal Education and Social Change in the Third World: A Bibliography and Review Essay.* The Hague: Centre for the Study of Education in Developing Countries, 1981.

Kott, Jan. *Shakespeare Our Contemporary.* Garden City, NY: Doubleday, 1964. 241 pp.

Mackintosh, Iain. *Architecture, Actor and Audience.* London/New York: Routledge, 1993. 184 pp.

Mitchell, Arnold. *The Professional Performing Arts: Attendance Patterns, Preferences and Motives.* 2 vols. Madison, WI: Association of College, University and Community Arts Administrators, 1984.

Pavis, Patrice. *Theatre at the Crossroads of Culture.* London: Routledge, 1991. 256 pp.

River, Julie, and Germaine Dellis. *L'Enfant et le théâtre.* [The child and the theatre]. Brussels: Labor, 1992. 155 pp.

Schechner, Richard. *Between Theatre and Anthropology.* Philadelphia, PA: University of Pennsylvania Press, 1985. 342 pp.

——. *Environmental Theatre.* New York: Hawthorne, 1973. 339 pp.

——. *Performance Theory.* London: Routledge, 1988. 320 pp.

Schutzman, Mady, and Jan Cohen-Cruz, eds. *Playing Boal: Theatre, Therapy, Activism.* London/New York: Routledge, 1994. 246 pp.

Seltzer, Daniel. *The Modern Theatre: Readings and Documents.* Boston, MA: Little, Brown, 1967. 495 pp.

Stanislavski, Konstantin. *The Collected Works of Konstantin Stanislavsky.* Sharon Marie Carnicke, gen. ed. 10 vols. London: Routledge, 1993– .

——. *Sobraniye Sochinenii.* [Collected works]. 7 vols. Moscow: Iskusstvo, 1954–60.

Strehler, Giorgio. *Per un teatro umano: pensieri scritti parlati e attuali.* [Towards a humanized theatre: contemporary written thoughts and discussions]. Milan: Feltrinelli, 1974. 363 pp.

Turner, Victor. *From Ritual to Theatre: The Human Seriousness of Play.* New York: PAJ Publications, 1982. 127 pp.

Ubersfeld, Anne. *L'École du spectateur.* [The school for theatregoers]. Paris: Editions Sociales, 1981. 352 pp.

——. *Lire le théâtre.* [Reading performance]. Paris: Editions Sociales, 1977. 280 pp.

Wandor, Michelene. *Carry On, Understudies: Theatre and Sexual Politics.* London: Routledge, 1986. 224 pp.

Theatre Arts

Bablet, Denis. *Les Révolutions scéniques du XXième siècle*. [Scenic revolutions of the twentieth century]. Paris: Société Internationale d'art XXième siècle, 1975. 388 pp.

Barton, Lucy. *Historic Costume for the Stage*. London: A. & C. Black, 1961. 609 pp.

Bellman, Williard F. *Scenography and Stage Technology*. New York: Thomas Crowell, 1977. 639 pp.

Braun, Edward. *The Director and the Stage: From Naturalism to Grotowski*. London: Methuen, 1982. 218 pp.

Cole, Toby, and Helen K. Chinoy. *Actors on Acting: The Theories, Techniques and Practices of the Great Actors of all Times as Told in Their Own Words*. New York: Crown, 1970. 715 pp.

Duerr, Edwin, ed. *The Length and Depth of Acting*. New York: Holt-Rinehart & Winston, 1962. 590 pp.

Gaulme, Jacques. *Architectures scénographiques et décors de théâtre*. [Scenographic architecture and theatre design]. Paris: E. Magnard, 1985. 144 pp.

Gillibert, Jean. *L'Acteur en création*. [The actor in creation]. Toulouse: Presses Universitaires du Mirail, 1993. 206 pp.

Gorelik, Mordecai. *New Theatres for Old*. New York: Dutton, 1962. 553 pp.

Grebanier, Bernard. *Playwriting*. New York: Thomas Y. Crowell, 1961. 386 pp.

Izenour, George C. *Theater Design*. New York: McGraw-Hill, 1977. 631 pp.

Jones, David Richard. *Great Directors at Work: Stanislavsky, Brecht, Kazan, Brook*. Berkeley, CA: University of California Press, 1986. 290 pp.

Machlin, Evangeline. *Speech for the Stage*. New York/London: Routledge/Theatre Arts Books, 1992. 254 pp.

Malkin, Michael R. *Traditional and Folk Puppets of the World*. New York: A.S. Barnes, 1977. 194 pp.

Mello, Bruno. *Trattato di scenotecnica*. [A treatise on scene design]. Novara: G.G. Gorlich, Istituto Geografico de Agostini, 1979.

Niccoli, A. *Lo spazio scenico: storia dell'arte teatrale*. [Scenic space: A history of theatre art]. Rome: Bulzoni, 1971.

Pilbrow, Richard. *Stage Lighting*. New York: Drama Book Specialists, 1979. 176 pp.

Saint-Denis, Michel. *Theatre: The Rediscovery of Style*. London: Heinemann, 1960. 110 pp.

——. *Training for the Theatre*. New York: Theatre Arts Books, 1982. 242 pp.

Spolin, Viola. *Improvisation for the Theatre: A Handbook of Teaching and Directing Techniques*. Evanston, IL: Northwestern University Press, 1963. 397 pp.

Tidworth, Simon. *Theatres: An Architectural and Cultural History.*. New York: Praeger, 1973. 224 pp.

Watson, Lee. *Lighting Design Handbook*. New York: McGraw-Hill, 1990. 458 pp.

WRITERS
AND NATIONAL
EDITORIAL COMMITTEES

ARGENTINA

Readers: David William Foster (Director, Spanish Graduate Studies, Arizona State University), Priscilla Meléndez (Associate Professor, Department of Spanish, Italian and Portuguese, Pennsylvania State University), Manuel Prestamo (Lecturer, Marquette University, Milwaukee)

BOLIVIA

Writer: Mario T. Soria (Drake University, Des Moines)
Reader: Willy O. Muñoz (Kent State University, Ohio)

BRAZIL

Writers: Yan Michalski (deceased), Fernando Peixoto (Co-Director, EITALC; Técnico em Artes Cenicas do Instituto Brasileiro de Arte e Cultura), Humberto Braga (former Director, Associação Brasileira de Teatro de Benecos; Co-Director, Instituto Brasileiro de Arte e Cultura), Susana Macedo (Actress; Director), Eduardo Sandroni (Actor; Director; Author of *Maturando: Aspectos de Desenvolvimento do Teatro Infantil no Brasil*)
Reader: Sebastião Milaré (Critic; Researcher; Author of *Antunes Filho e a Dimensã Utópica* and *A Batalha da Quimera – Renato Vianna e o Modernismo Cênico Brasileiro*)

CANADA

Writers: *English Canada*: Alan Filewod (Professor, Drama Department, University of Guelph, Ontario; Editor, *Canadian Theatre Review*), Phillip Silver (Designer; Professor of Design, Theatre Department, York University, Toronto), Anton Wagner (Adjunct Professor, Departments of Theatre and Dance, York University, Toronto), Max Wyman (Dance and Theatre Critic, Vancouver), Andrew M. Zinck (PhD Candidate, Faculty of Music, University of Totonto). *Québec*: Gilbert David (Professor, Theatre Department, University of Montréal; Founding Editor, *Cahiers de Théâtre Jeu*), Hélène Beauchamp (Theatre Department, Université du Québec à Montréal)
Editorial Committees: *English Canada*: Anton Wagner. *Québec*: Gilbert David, Hélène Beauchamp, Paul Lefebvre (École National du Théâtre, Montréal), Lucie Robert (Département d'études littéraires, Université du Québec à Montréal)
Readers: Lawrence Adams and Miriam Adams (Dance Collection Danse, Toronto), Diane Bessai (Department of English, University of Alberta, Edmonton), Andre-G. Bourassa (Département de théâtre, Université du Québec à Montréal; Éditeur, *L'Annuaire théâtral*), David Gardner (Actor; Historian), Denis Johnston (Theatre Historian, Shaw Festival, Niagara-on-the-Lake), Selma Odom (Director, Graduate Programme in Dance, York University, Toronto),

Patrick O'Neill (Department of Speech and Drama, Mount Saint Vincent University, Nova Scotia), Malcolm Page (Department of English, Simon Fraser University, Vancouver), Denis Salter (Department of English, McGill University, Montréal), E. Ross Stuart (Professor of Theatre History, Theatre Department, York University, Toronto), Iro Valaskakis Tembeck (Directrice, Programme de maîtrise en dance, Département de danse, Université du Québec à Montréal), Michel Vaïs (Critic; Director, *Jeu*; Translator)

CHILE

Writer: María de la Luz Hurtado (Professor, Escuela de Teatro, Universidad Católica de Chile, Santiago)

COLOMBIA

Writer: Carlos José Reyes Posada (Playwright; Director, National Library of Colombia)
Reader: Leon F. Lyday (Head, Department of Spanish, Italian and Portuguese, Pennsylvania State University, University Park)

COMMONWEALTH CARIBBEAN

Writer: Errol Hill (Professor Emeritus, Dartmouth College, Hanover)
Readers: Joan Dummett Jason (Author; Broadcaster; Theatre Producer; Critic), Bridget H. Jones (Centre for Research in Modern French and Spanish Studies, Roehampton Institute, London)

COSTA RICA

Writer: Samuel Rovinski (Playwright; Critic)
Reader: Andrés Sáenz (Theatre Critic, *La Nación*, San José)

CUBA

Writers: Rine Leal (Critic; Researcher; Professor of Theatre, Instituto Superior de Arte, Havana), Roberto Gacio (Critic; Researcher, Centro de Investigación de las Artes Escénicas, Havana), Derubín Jácome (Set and Costume Designer, Instituto Politecnico, Madrid), Rogelio Martínez Furé (Ethnologist; Librettist; Adviser, Conjunto Folklorico Nacional), Vivian Martínez Tabares (Critic; Researcher; Editor-in-Chief, *Conjunto*), Magaly Muguercia (Critic; Researcher, Centro de Investigación de las Artes Escénicas), Gilda Santana (Critic; Researcher; Theatre Adviser, Teatro Estudio).
Reader: Judith Rudakoff (Professor of Theatre, York University, Toronto)

DOMINICAN REPUBLIC

Writer: Franklin Domínguez (Playwright; Director)

ECUADOR

Writer: Eduardo Almeida Naveda (Director; President, Ecuador ITI Centre)
Readers: Gerardo Luzuriaga (Department of Spanish and Portuguese, University of California, Los Angeles), Manuel Prestamo (Lecturer, Marquette University, Milwaukee)

EL SALVADOR

Writer: José Roberto Cea (Playwright; Theatre Researcher)

FRENCH CARIBBEAN

Writer: Bridget H. Jones (Centre for Research in Modern French and Spanish Studies, Roehampton Institute, London)
Readers: Maximilien Laroche (Département des littératures, Université Laval, Saint-Foy), Anthea Morrison (Professor, Department of French and Spanish, University of the West Indies, Bridgetown)

GUATEMALA

Writer: Hugo Carrillo (deceased)

HAÏTI

Writer: Gary Victor (Playwright; former Haïtian Minister of Culture)
Readers: Maximilien Laroche (Département des littératures, Université Laval, Saint-Foy), Bridget H. Jones (Centre for Research in Modern French and Spanish Studies, Roehampton Institute, London)

HONDURAS

Writer: Saúl Toro (Director; Actor)

MÉXICO

Writer: Carlos Solórzano (Playwright; Professor Emeritus of Latin American Literature, National Autonomous University of México)
Reader: Isabel Quintanar (Secretary-General, Mexican Centre of the ITI)

NETHERLANDS ANTILLES AND ARUBA

Writers: Aart G. Broek (Director), Oslin Boekhoudt (Director, Aruba International Theatre Festival), Ellis Lopes (Director, St Eustatius Action Theatre)

NICARAGUA

Writer: Judith A. Weiss (Professor, Department of French and Spanish, Mount Allison University, Sackville)
Readers: Jorge Eduardo Arellano (Nicaraguan UNESCO Commission), Diana Taylor (Professor, Spanish and Comparative Literature, Dartmouth College, Hanover)

PANAMÁ

Writers: Héctor Rodríguez C. (Playwright; Professor, Theatre Department, University of Panamá), Teresa Mann (Founder, Teresa Mann School of Dance)

PARAGUAY

Writer: Mario Prono (Historian)
Editorial Committee: Antonio Carmona (Director; Critic; Playwright; Historian)

PERÚ

Readers: David William Foster (Director, Spanish Graduate Studies, Arizona State University), Robert J. Morris (Division of Humanities, Lander University, Greenwood)

PUERTO RICO

Writer: Grace Dávila-López (Pomona College, Irvine)
Readers: José Luis Ramos Escobar (Director; Professor and Chair, Department of Drama,

University of Puerto Rico, Rio Piedras), Rosa Luisa Márquez (Director; Professor, University of Puerto Rico)

UNITED STATES OF AMERICA

Writers: Arthur Holmberg, Editor (Head, Graduate Program in Playwriting and Professor of Dramatic Literature and Theory, Brandeis University, Boston; former Literary Director, American Repertory Theatre), Arnold Aronson (Chair, Theatre Department, Columbia University), Betty Bernhard (Professor of Theatre, Pomona College, Claremont), Antonio Cao (Professor of Spanish Languages and Literatures, Hofstra University), Selma Jeanne Cohen (Editor, *International Encyclopedia of Dance*), James V. Hatch (Co-Director, Hatch-Billops Collection of African American Cultural History), Jorge Huerta (Chancellor's Professor of Theatre, University of California, San Diego), Linda Walsh Jenkins (Producer, Native American Dance Theatre; former Professor of Theatre, Northwestern University), Fred Kolo (Designer), Christian Mendenhall (Professor, Department of Performing Arts, American University Washington), Roman Paska (former Professor of Theatre, Cornell University), Lowell Swortzell (Director, Program in Educational Theatre, New York University)
Readers: Milly S. Barranger (Chair and Professor, Dramatic Art, University of North Carolina, Chapel Hill), Christopher W.E. Bigsby (School of English and American Studies, University of East Anglia, Norwich), Don B. Wilmeth (Professor, Department of Theatre Speech and Dance, Brown University, Providence)

URUGUAY

Writers: César Campodónico (Director; Actor; Secretary-General, Uruguay ITI Centre), Jorge Abbondanza, Milita Alfaro, España Andrade, William Rey Ashfield, Andrés Castillo, Victor Manuel Leites, Gustavo Martínez Barbosa, Roger Mirza, Omar Ostuni, Barrett Puig
Reader: César T. Herrer (Secretary-General, Uruguayan Centre of the ITI)

VENEZUELA

Writer: Orlando Rodríguez B. (Theatre Historian; Critic; Professor, Universidad Central de Venezuela; Director of Research, CELCIT)

INDEX